# THE ART OF HEARING

This ground-breaking study of early modern English preaching is the
first to take full account of the sermon as heard by the listener as well as
uttered by the preacher. It draws on a wide range of printed and
manuscuript sources, but also seeks to read behind the texts in order to
reconstruct what was actually delivered from the pulpit, with due
attention to the differences between oral, written and printed versions.
In showing how sermons were interpeted and appropriated by their
hearers, often in ways that their authors never intended, it poses wider
questions about the transmission of religious and political ideas in the
post-Reformation period. Offering a richer understanding of sermons
as complex and ambiguous texts, and opening up new avenues for
their interpretation, it will be essential reading for all students of the
religious and cultural history of early modern England.

ARNOLD HUNT is a Curator of Manuscripts at the British Library, and
a Senior Research Fellow at King's College, London.

*Cambridge Studies in Early Modern British History*

Series editors

JOHN MORRILL
*Professor of British and Irish History, University of Cambridge, and Fellow, Selwyn College*

ETHAN SHAGAN
*Associate Professor of History, University of California, Berkeley*

ALEXANDRA WALSHAM
*Professor of Reformation History, University of Exeter*

This is a series of monographs and studies covering many aspects of the history of the British Isles between the late fifteenth century and the early eighteenth century. It includes the work of established scholars and pioneering work by a new generation of scholars. It includes both reviews and revisions of major topics, and books which open up new historical terrain or which reveal startling new perspectives on familiar subjects. All the volumes set detailed research into our broader perspectives, and the books are intended for the use of students as well as of their teachers.

*For a list of titles in the series go to* www.cambridge.org/earlymodernbritishhistory

**University of Plymouth Library**
Subject to status this item may be renewed
via your Voyager account
**http://voyager.plymouth.ac.uk**
Tel: (01752) 232323

# THE ART OF HEARING

*English Preachers and Their Audiences, 1590–1640*

ARNOLD HUNT

CAMBRIDGE UNIVERSITY PRESS
Cambridge, New York, Melbourne, Madrid, Cape Town, Singapore,
São Paulo, Delhi, Dubai, Tokyo, Mexico City

Cambridge University Press
The Edinburgh Building, Cambridge CB2 8RU, UK

Published in the United States of America by Cambridge University Press, New York

www.cambridge.org
Information on this title: www.cambridge.org/9780521896764

First published 2010

Printed in the United Kingdom at the University Press, Cambridge

*A catalogue record for this publication is available from the British Library*

ISBN-13: 978-0-521-89676-4 Hardback

# Contents

# Illustrations

# *Acknowledgements*

This project has occasionally felt like Christopher Haigh's *Reformation*, 'a premature birth, a difficult labour and a sickly child', and in the course of turning it into a publishable book I have accumulated a prodigious number of intellectual debts, not all of which can be adequately discharged here. First to be thanked must be the British Academy, for supporting my postgraduate research (more years ago than I care to count), Patrick Collinson, for supervising it with such abundant generosity, patience and good humour, and the Master and Fellows of Trinity College, Cambridge, for electing me to a research fellowship and later extending the term of the fellowship for a year. I count myself extremely fortunate to have been working in Cambridge at what was surely a golden age for early modern studies, alongside some exceptionally talented contemporaries from whom I learned much: among them, Lynn Botelho, Patrick Carter, John Craig, Alan Cromartie, Adam Fox, Seán Hughes, Caroline Litzenberger, Anthony Milton, Richard Serjeantson, Susan Wabuda and Alexandra Walsham. Among older colleagues I particularly want to remember the late Jeremy Maule, whose boundless intellectual curiosity was an inspiring example of how the academic life should be lived. At a late stage in revising this book I came across an early draft of Chapter 2 generously annotated by Jeremy – 'he being dead yet speaketh' – with comments and suggestions which I have gratefully incorporated here. I wish he had lived to read the whole book, which would have benefited enormously from his criticisms.

On leaving Cambridge I began a more itinerant academic existence supported by a series of temporary teaching posts. I am grateful to Christopher Brooks at Durham, Jeremy Boulton at Newcastle, and Simon Ditchfield, Jeremy Goldberg and Bill Sheils at York for their kindness and support. I would also like to thank my circle of friends in Durham, whose support sustained me during some uncertain months, especially James Austen, Michael Brydon, Mandy Griffin, Ann Loades, Richard Maber, Ann Moss, John Munns, Michael O'Neill, Richard Pickett, Sean

Power, Andrew Rudd, Andrew Sanders and David Sudron. In 2001 I was appointed to a post in the Department of Theology at the University of Nottingham, a piece of extraordinary and quite undeserved good fortune without which I doubt whether this book would ever have been finished. I am deeply grateful to Ed Ball, Richard Bell, Hugh Goddard, Philip Goodchild and Karen Kilby, but most of all to Alan Ford, who was a friend, mentor and almost a second supervisor to me as I started the long process of turning my thesis into a book. In 2005 I moved on again, this time to a post in the Department of Manuscripts at the British Library. Here again I have been extremely fortunate in my colleagues, especially Peter Barber, Frances Harris, Giles Mandelbrote and Christopher Wright.

My thanks go to my PhD examiners, Diarmaid MacCulloch and Sir Keith Thomas, for seeing past the flaws of the thesis and encouraging me to think of future publication; to John Morrill for suggesting I offer it to Cambridge University Press, and for much support thereafter; and to my editors at CUP, Michael Watson and Liz Friend-Smith, for bearing with me through so many delays. Andrew Cambers, Elizabeth Clarke, David Como, Nicholas Cranfield, Peter Davidson, the late Robin Dix (sadly missed), Ian Green, Steve Hindle, Juliet Ingram, Peter Lake, Judith Maltby, Michael Questier, Nigel Ramsay, John Spurr and Jane Stevenson supplied notes, references and suggestions. My friends in the antiquarian book trade, including Christopher Edwards, Alex Fotheringham, Arthur and Janet Freeman, Robert Harding and John O'Mara, supplied some of the raw material on which the book is based. I also want to thank David Crankshaw, Liz Evenden, Ken Fincham, Tom Freeman, Susan Hardman Moore, Nicholas Tyacke and Brett Usher, co-convenors of the Religious History of Britain seminar at the Institute of Historical Research, and Hugh Adlington, David Colclough, Karin Ettinhuber, Peter McCullough, Mary Morrissey and Emma Rhatigan, co-editors of the Oxford Edition of the Sermons of John Donne. In the final stages of completing the book I was greatly helped and supported by the counsel of Rory Elliott, the pastoral guidance of Philip Goff and the friendship of Rachel Boulding, Sasha Garwood, Liza Graham, Anthony Ossa-Richardson and Rupert Shortt.

Alison Shell has lived with this project from the very beginning to the very end; her faith in it never wavered, and I could never have finished it without her. I dedicate this book, with love and gratitude, to her and to my parents, Bryan and Fiona Hunt.

# Introduction

'His work in Bodley consisted in reading all the sermons that were ever published.'
'And have a lot been published? I don't think I've ever seen any.'
Jane laughed a little desperately. 'Far more of them than of anything else in the whole world.'

Michael Innes, Operation Pax (1951)

When I first began work on this book, the history of early modern preaching was a neglected and unpopular field of study, around which there hung an air of dusty antiquarianism. The standard textbooks on the subject, including W.F. Mitchell's *English Pulpit Oratory from Andrewes to Tillotson* (1932) and J.W. Blench's *Preaching in England in the Late Fifteenth and Sixteenth Centuries* (1964), though still useful, now seemed decidedly out of date. Nor did their authors show much enthusiasm for the history of preaching; indeed, far from seeking to attract other scholars into the field, they seemed more anxious to turn them away. G. R. Owst, whose *Preaching in Medieval England* (1926) was for many years the standard treatment of its subject, wrote disparagingly of the 'stagnation' of pulpit rhetoric in the later Middle Ages: 'The landscape is barren and monotonous to a degree. He who boldly sets out to follow the dust-laden tracks of the ancient preachers will pass by these dry bones, that whiten the road still further with their testimony to a decaying art, not without some sign of relief.'[1] Mitchell's *English Pulpit Oratory* was advertised as the 'last word' on its subject, 'for it is unlikely that such a study will ever be made again'.[2] And Millar MacLure's monograph, *The Paul's Cross Sermons 1534–1642* (1958), made scarcely any greater effort to render the subject inviting: 'Indeed if the student reads much in the sermon-literature of the period . . . he faces a great mass of repetitious bad rhetoric and must

---

[1]  G. R. Owst, *Preaching in Medieval England* (Cambridge, 1926), pp. 238–9.
[2]  These words appear in the publisher's catalogue (SPCK, January 1932), though not in the book itself.

grow inured to a singularly dull humourless pedestrian thought and expression.'[3]

With friends like these, who needs enemies? It is hardly surprising that scholars attempting to rehabilitate the history of preaching as an academically worthwhile subject have tended to adopt a somewhat defensive tone. The editors of a recent essay collection entitled *The English Sermon Revised* (2000) begin their introduction by remarking that sermons have 'suffered an indulgent, even condescending neglect', widely regarded 'as one of the most lifeless, ancillary aspects of Renaissance literary culture'.[4] Another recent essay collection, *Irish Preaching 700–1700* (2001), opens with a similar complaint. 'Students of history and of literature have seldom been drawn to sermons or been known to take them seriously. For historians, sermons have often been regarded as stock expressions, and tedious ones, of the piety of their age, short on the kind of historically pertinent detail that otherwise might justify their study and make them interesting . . . For historians and literary critics alike, as measured by the lack of secondary analytical work on the subject, the study of sermons has tended to remain with Cinderella in the ashes.'[5] If sermons are a Cinderella subject, then poetry and drama are presumably the ugly sisters, forever hogging the limelight – or so it might appear from another study of pulpit oratory, which modestly suggests that 'the genre can demand (potentially at least) a critical consideration of the same order as poetry and drama . . . although that notion rings strangely in twentieth-century ears'.[6] Or if we are looking for fairy-tale analogies, perhaps a better one would be Sleeping Beauty, still awaiting her scholar-prince to rouse her from the long sleep of critical obscurity.

The last few years, however, have seen a remarkable flowering of new scholarship devoted to preaching, making it more and more difficult to sustain the claim that sermons are languishing in critical disfavour. The study of late medieval preaching has begun to open up, and it has recently been argued that a sympathetic reading of fourteenth- and fifteenth-century sermons reveals 'an astonishing degree of variety and individuality', a far cry from Owst's landscape of barren monotony.[7] In the early

---

[3]  Millar MacLure, *The Paul's Cross Sermons 1534–1642* (Toronto, 1958), p. 143.
[4]  Lori Anne Ferrell and Peter McCullough, eds., *The English Sermon Revised: Religion, Literature and History 1600–1750* (Manchester, 2000), p. 3.
[5]  Alan J. Fletcher and Raymond Gillespie, eds., *Irish Preaching 700–1700* (Dublin, 2001), p. 11.
[6]  Peter Bayley, *French Pulpit Oratory 1598–1650: A Study in Themes and Styles* (Cambridge, 1980), p. 3.
[7]  Siegfried Wenzel, *Latin Sermon Collections from Later Medieval England: Orthodox Preaching in the Age of Wyclif* (Cambridge, 2005), pp. 354, 400. Other recent work on medieval preaching includes Helen Leith Spencer, *English Preaching in the Late Middle Ages* (Oxford, 1993); Anne Hudson, '"Springing

modern period, one critical hotspot has been the study of John Donne's sermons, once studied chiefly for the light they could shed on the poems, but now increasingly coming to be the focus of interest in their own right, and regarded as crucial for an understanding of Donne's politics.[8] Another has been the study of the 'public sphere', with preaching now seen as having played an important part in the transmission of news and the formation of public opinion in the early modern period.[9] More generally, there has been a new wave of interest in the role of religion in early seventeenth-century England, and also in the role of rhetoric in early modern culture, both of which have served to draw attention towards the sermon, now perceived not as a static literary artefact but as a dynamic exercise in religious controversy and rhetorical persuasion.[10] One of the pleasures of pursuing my own research over the last ten years or so has been to watch this new generation of scholarship take shape around me, and to feel myself part of it.[11] It has been an exciting time to be studying

cockel in our clene corn": Lollard preaching in England around 1400', in Scott L. Waugh and Peter D. Diehl, eds., *Christendom and Its Discontents: Exclusion, Persecution and Rebellion 1000–1500* (Cambridge, 1996), pp. 132–47; David D'Avray, *Medieval Marriage Sermons: Mass Communication in a Culture Without Print* (Oxford, 2001); and Carolyn Muessig, ed., *Preacher, Sermon and Audience in the Middle Ages* (Leiden, 2002).

8  The work of Jeanne Shami has been particularly important in fostering a more historicised reading of Donne's sermons: see her 'Introduction: Reading Donne's Sermons', *John Donne Journal*, 11 (Raleigh, NC, 1992), pp. 1–20, and *John Donne and Conformity in Crisis in the Late Jacobean Pulpit* (Woodbridge, 2003). In Peter McCullough's edition of Lancelot Andrewes, *Selected Sermons and Lectures* (Oxford, 2005), we now have a model edition of sermons by one of Donne's most important contemporaries, and the forthcoming Oxford Edition of the Sermons of John Donne, under McCullough's general editorship, promises to bring Donne's sermons further into the critical mainstream.

9  For a stimulating and provocative study of preaching and the public sphere, see Peter Lake and Michael Questier, *The Antichrist's Lewd Hat: Protestants, Papists and Players in Post-Reformation England* (New Haven and London, 2002), esp. pp. 335–76, 'Protestant appropriation: from pamphlet to pulpit and back again'. See also Tony Claydon, 'The sermon, the "public sphere" and the political culture of late seventeenth-century England', in Ferrell and McCullough, eds., *The English Sermon Revised*, pp. 208–34, and, more generally, Peter Lake and Steven Pincus, eds., *The Politics of the Public Sphere in Early Modern England* (Manchester, 2007).

10  See, among others, Mary Morrissey, 'Scripture, style and persuasion in seventeenth-century English theories of preaching', *Journal of Ecclesiastical History*, 53: 4 (2002), pp. 686–706; Peter Mack, *Elizabethan Rhetoric: Theory and Practice* (Cambridge, 2002), esp. ch. 8, 'Religious discourse' (pp. 253–92); and Andrew Pettegree, *Reformation and the Culture of Persuasion* (Cambridge, 2005), esp. ch. 2, 'Preaching' (pp. 10–39).

11  Other important studies of early modern English preaching, besides those already mentioned, include Peter McCullough, *Sermons at Court: Politics and Religion in Elizabethan and Jacobean Preaching* (Cambridge, 1998); Lori Anne Ferrell, *Government by Polemic: James I, the King's Preachers, and the Rhetorics of Conformity 1603–1625* (Stanford, 1998); Mary Morrissey, 'Interdisciplinarity and the study of early modern sermons', *Historical Journal*, 42 (1999), pp. 1111–23; Eric Josef Carlson, 'The boring of the ear: shaping the pastoral vision of preaching in England, 1540–1640', in Larissa Taylor, ed., *Preachers and People in the Reformations and Early Modern Period* (Leiden, 2001), pp. 249–96; Margo Todd, *The Culture of Protestantism in Early Modern Scotland* (New Haven and London, 2002), esp. chapter 2, 'The Word and the people' (pp. 24–83); Susan Wabuda, *Preaching during the English*

early modern preaching, and there is, thankfully, no longer any need to begin with an apology for working on such an unfashionable topic.

Most important of all, the last few years have seen the rise and general acceptance of the new historiographical movement described by Olwen Hufton in a recent article, 'What is religious history now?' – a 'new kind of religious history' in which the focus of attention has shifted from the producer to the consumer. Hufton makes the bold but convincing claim that this precipitated an entirely new understanding of the role of religion in Western culture:

This widening of the framework of reference, if not the only change, I would suggest was the dominant one, transforming the writing of the religious history of Western civilization in the twentieth century. It moved the writing of religious history away from the subject of the establishment, clerical, lay and male, down-market. It also interfaced with other historical concerns which marked the period and from which it became indistinguishable in some cases. Religion by the 1980s was interpreted as an intrinsic part of culture and a producer of culture. Women and men were seen as made, not born, and in that shaping process in the West, religious belief lay at the centre of this process of manufacture.[12]

Preaching – as one of the crucial means by which religious ideas were transmitted from the clerical producer to the lay consumer – clearly has an important part to play here. For a long time, historians of the German Reformation tended to assume that the rapid spread of Reformation ideas was largely the result of printing; and as R. W. Scribner noted in 1989, the role of oral transmission, including preaching, had been 'relatively ignored till recently'. But as Scribner went on to argue, preaching actually had significant advantages over printing in terms of its popularity, its ability to reach the illiterate and its scope for active audience participation and rapid dissemination of the preacher's message.[13]

Yet the chief problem with the earlier generation of religious history, I would suggest, is not that it neglected preaching but that it made some

---

*Reformation* (Cambridge, 2002); Juliet Ingram, 'The conscience of the community: the character and development of clerical complaint in early modern England', (PhD diss., University of Warwick 2004); David J. Appleby, *Black Bartholomew's Day: Preaching, Polemic and Restoration Nonconformity* (Manchester, 2007); and Ian Green, *Continuity and Change in Protestant Preaching in Early Modern England* (Friends of Dr Williams's Library, 2009).

[12] Olwen Hufton, 'What is religious history now?', in David Cannadine, ed., *What Is History Now?* (Basingstoke, 2002), p. 59.

[13] R. W. Scribner, 'Oral culture and the transmission of Reformation ideas', in Helga Robinson-Hammerstein, ed., *The Transmission of Ideas in the Lutheran Reformation* (Dublin, 1989), pp. 83–104. For other recent work on preaching and oral culture, see Adam Fox, *Oral and Literate Culture in England 1500–1700* (Oxford, 2000), and Donald Meek, 'The pulpit and the pen: clergy, orality and print in the Scottish Gaelic world', in Adam Fox and Daniel Woolf, ed., *The Spoken Word: Oral Culture in Britain, 1500–1800* (Manchester, 2002), pp. 84–118.

large and untested assumptions about its effect. For example, historians have often sought to measure the impact and success of the English Reformation in terms of the provision of educated preaching ministers. In part, this is simply a matter of convenience; as Patrick Collinson has pointed out, 'while preaching was not the only or even necessarily the most effective means by which the new religion was disseminated, it is the only one whose progress [the historian] can hope to map and tabulate'.[14] Yet it also reflects an assumption that the laity were wholly passive in their response to sermons – so that, just as a Protestant preacher must inevitably have created a Protestant parish, so a Protestant preaching ministry must inevitably have created a Protestant nation. This assumption now seems highly questionable, and it is for this reason that we need to look again at early modern preaching, focusing this time on the problem of audience response. As Jim Sharpe has astutely remarked, it is natural to assume that popular awareness of topics such as witchcraft or anti-Catholicism must have been sharpened by the experience of listening to sermons in which those topics featured prominently; yet 'the degree to which sermons were attended, how much attention to their content was given by those who did attend, and how much of that content was internalised and affected subsequent behaviour or subsequent patterns of belief, remains unclear'.[15] We know all too little about the ways in which sermons may have influenced popular action and opinion.

So what does this book aim to contribute to the existing literature? As the title suggests, it is essentially a study of *hearing* rather than preaching, focused not on the lone figure of the preacher but on the two-way relationship between the preacher and his audience. Preaching, it has been well said, is 'commonly assumed to be a non-interactive performance in which one dominant speaker's discourse is passively attended to by a silent congregation'.[16] But we should beware of reading this assumption back into the early modern period, for there is ample evidence to suggest that seventeenth-century preachers were very sensitive to the reactions of their audiences, and that audiences in their turn were very far from passive. There is a well-known passage in one of Richard Bancroft's anti-puritan tracts, describing

---

[14] Patrick Collinson, 'The Elizabethan Church and the new religion', in C. Haigh, ed., *The Reign of Elizabeth I* (London, 1984), pp. 169–94 (quotation p. 183).

[15] Jim Sharpe, 'The Devil in East Anglia: the Matthew Hopkins trials reconsidered', in Jonathan Barry, Marianne Hester and Gareth Roberts, eds., *Witchcraft in Early Modern Europe: Studies in Culture and Belief* (Cambridge, 1996), pp. 237–54 (quotation p. 250).

[16] Christine Callender and Deborah Cameron, 'Responsive listening as part of religious rhetoric: the case of Black Pentecostal preaching', in Graham McGregor and R. S. White, eds., *Reception and Response: Hearer Creativity and the Analysis of Spoken and Written Texts* (London, 1990), pp. 160–78.

the audience response at a 'precisian' sermon: the opening prayer, writes
Bancroft, is followed by an *'applaudite'* from the congregation, and whenever the preacher includes a prayer in his sermon, 'the cheif gentleman in
the place begynnynge with a gronynge, but yet with a lowde voyce crieth
most religiously, *Amen*. And then the whole companye of that sect followe.
*Amen. Amen.*'[17] Margo Todd quotes a Scottish sermon which ends in
precisely this way, with a rapid sequence of 'amens' clearly designed to elicit
an answering response from the congregation:

> Let all the congregation say amen
> Let all the saints in heaven and earth praise him,
>      And let all the congregation say amen . . .
> Let men and women praise him,
>      And let all the congregation say amen.

As Todd remarks, 'it is impossible to read these notes without hearing the
parishioners calling out their amens', very much in the manner of modern
Pentecostal preaching, where it is common for members of the audience to
interrupt with cries of 'Amen', 'Hallelujah', 'Praise the Lord', in response to
verbal cues from the preacher.[18]

Nor should we assume that these forms of audience response were
limited to approving cries of 'Amen'. In a sermon at Paul's Cross, John
Donne made some interesting remarks on the audience reaction that a
preacher at the Cross might expect, observing that 'when the Preacher
concludeth any point', he would commonly be interrupted by a buzz of
conversation, taking up as much as 'one quarter of his houre'. Donne was
not wholly opposed to this, as he felt it resembled the custom of the early
Church, where 'the manner was, that when the people were satisfied in any
point which the Preacher handled, they would almost tell him so, by an
acclamation, and give him leave to passe to another point'. However, he
feared that modern audiences were not merely indicating their approval of
the sermon, as the early Christians had done, but were taking the opportunity to criticise it as well – and as if that were not enough, 'many that were
not within distance of hearing the Sermon, will give a censure upon it,
according to the frequencie, or paucitie of these acclamations'.[19] There is a

---

[17] *Tracts Ascribed to Richard Bancroft*, ed. Albert Peel (Cambridge, 1953), pp. 72–3. Patrick Collinson
draws attention to this passage in *The Religion of Protestants: The Church in English Society 1559–1625*
(Oxford, 1982), p. 157. For further examples of 'amen' as an audience response, see my 'Preaching the
Elizabethan settlement' in Hugh Adlington, Peter McCullough and Emma Rhatigan, eds., *The
Oxford Handbook of the Early Modern Sermon* (Oxford, forthcoming 2010).

[18] Todd, *The Culture of Protestantism in Early Modern Scotland*, p. 53.

[19] John Donne, *Sermons*, ed. G. R. Potter and E. M. Simpson (Berkeley, 1953–62), vol. x, pp. 132–3.

documented example of this, also from Paul's Cross, in September 1579, when the preacher was deputed to justify the punishment inflicted on John Stubbes for his tract attacking the Anjou marriage, *The Discoverie of a Gaping Gulf*. Bishop John Aylmer sent a report of the sermon to Sir Christopher Hatton, noting with satisfaction that when the preacher praised the Queen's devotion to true religion, 'the people seemed, even as it were with a shout to give God thanks'. When the preacher turned his attention to Stubbes, however, the audience response was not so favourable, and according to Aylmer, 'they utterly bent their brows at the sharp and bitter speeches which he gave against the author of the book'.[20]

This level of audience interaction remained the norm until relatively recent times. Lawrence W. Levine, writing of theatre and concert performance in nineteenth-century America, has commented that they attracted 'a knowledgeable, participatory audience exerting important degrees of control' and argued that it was only in the late nineteenth century, with the imposition of new standards of public decorum, that audiences began to be transformed from active participants into passive spectators.[21] And in the case of African-American sermons, the interaction between preacher and audience can still be observed today. Bruce Rosenberg, in studying the genre he labels 'folk preaching' or 'spiritual preaching', has shown that the audience plays a crucial role and, to borrow Levine's phrase, exerts an important degree of control, not just by responding to the preacher's cues but by encouraging the preacher if he appears to be flagging or even, through its muted response, signalling its disappointment with a poor sermon. He argues that no judgement of whether a sermon is good or bad can be made without reference to the audience: 'The congregation will intuitively judge; they will know infallibly because in a sense they are the ultimate arbiters. If the congregation is not moved, the sermon has failed. It is almost as simple as that.'[22] Studying preaching as a form of ritual or performance thus requires us to shift our focus from the preacher to the audience and, in the words of another scholar of African-American preaching, to 'the performed sermon as event'.[23]

---

[20] Aylmer to Hatton, 28 September 1579: *Memoirs of the Life and Times of Sir Christopher Hatton*, ed. Sir Harris Nicolas (London, 1847), pp. 132–4. My thanks to Peter Lake for drawing my attention to this reference.

[21] Lawrence W. Levine, *Highbrow/Lowbrow: The Emergence of Cultural Hierarchy in America* (Cambridge, MA, and London, 1988), p. 30.

[22] Bruce A. Rosenberg, *Can These Bones Live? The Art of the American Folk Preacher* (Oxford, 1970; revised edition, Urbana and Chicago, 1988), p. 151.

[23] Gerald L. Davis, *I Got the Word in Me and I Can Sing It, You Know: A Study of the Performed African-American Sermon* (Philadelphia, 1985), p. 34. On preaching considered as a form of ritual, see also Leigh Eric Schmidt, *Holy Fairs: Scotland and the Making of American Revivalism* (Princeton, 1989, repr. Grand Rapids, Michigan, 2001), esp. p. 74.

Some pioneering work on audience response has already been done in the field of Renaissance music, where research has been driven by an interest in the practical aspects of performance and a desire to reconstruct historical performance styles as accurately as possible. The current direction of research is well illustrated by the following list of questions, mentioned at a recent seminar on 'Music as heard' as topics in need of further investigation:

How was music thought to act upon the sense of hearing, the mind, the heart, the body and the soul?

Were music's powers and effects thought to depend on conscious acts of listening and understanding?

What concepts and metaphors did contemporaries use to evaluate and account for their musical experiences?

Were there 'correct' and 'incorrect' modes of listening?

What role and status were accorded to the listener or the audience in theoretical writings on music, and to what extent were their abilities, needs and demands recognised in technical discussion?

What was the perceived relationship between the written and sounding dimensions of music?

In what respects was music listening thought to be a private, communal and/or public activity? Did it involve response, interaction, participation and gesturing, or, conversely, privacy, silence and concentration?

What historical evidence do we possess concerning actual listeners or groups of listeners and their musical 'horizons of expectation'?[24]

For 'music' read 'preaching', and these questions could serve, with only minor alteration, as an agenda for the book you are now holding in your hands.

But how can these questions be answered? As early modern preachers liked to point out, *vox audita perit, litera scripta manet* – the spoken voice perishes, and only the written word remains. It is a relatively straightforward matter to use written and printed sermons as a quarry of primary source-material – and indeed, many of the most influential historical works of the last forty years have done precisely that, as a glance at the footnotes to Christopher Hill's *Society and Puritanism in Pre-Revolutionary England* (1964) or Keith Thomas's *Religion and the Decline of Magic* (1971) will show. It is far less easy to see how the interactive and performative aspects of preaching can be reconstructed. We have no sound recordings of early modern sermons, no archive films of preachers in their pulpits and no time-machines in which to travel back to the early seventeenth century and mingle unobtrusively with the crowd assembled to hear the sermon at Paul's Cross. The speech and gesture of the preacher, the reaction of the audience, and in some cases even

---

[24] 'Music as heard', *Musical Quarterly*, 82: 3/4 (1998), p. 432.

the very words of the sermon, which are not always accurately reported in printed editions, remain largely or wholly irrecoverable.

It is hardly surprising, then, that some scholars have simply rejected the whole exercise as next to impossible. Peter Bayley, for example, comments in his study of French pulpit oratory that 'it is difficult and hazardous to attempt a reconstruction of the living sermon, and I am not convinced that the effort is worth making'.[25] More recently, Colin Haydon – commenting, as it happens, on an article of mine – has pinpointed the reception history of preaching as a methodological problem in need of further investigation. 'What can be said about congregations' reception of, and responses to, sermons?', he asks. 'The sources present many difficulties . . . Probably no methodology can satisfactorily overcome this problem, so, usually, one must be content with the view from the pulpit rather than the pews.'[26] I would be the last person to dismiss these concerns as unimportant. The present book is written out of the conviction that the source-mining of printed sermons is not enough – that, in order to reconstruct the way that sermons were heard and understood by their audiences, one must be prepared to engage with a wide range of material, including manuscript and archival as well as printed sources, and to interrogate it in some imaginative and methodologically sophisticated ways. How well it succeeds in these aims must be left for the reader to judge.

In studying the religious writings of this period, it is hard not to be struck by the enormous importance that early modern Protestants attached to preaching, almost to the exclusion of other pastoral activities. 'This is our worke', declared the Devonshire preacher Richard Carpenter in a sermon before the Bishop of Exeter in 1616, 'as conduit pipes of grace to convey to the thirsty soules of our hearers, the living water of Gods word, and to be as the mesaraicall veynes in the body naturall, through which the spirituall foode must passe, whereby the members of Christs body mystically are to be nourished up unto everlasting life. This is our worke.'[27] The work that Carpenter had in mind was, of course, preaching – and the implication of his metaphor was that a regular supply of preaching was as basic and necessary, and as essential to the good health of the Christian community, as the supply of food and drink to the body. In attaching such critical importance to it, he and other preachers seemed to make it, if not

---

[25] Bayley, *French Pulpit Oratory*, p. 16.
[26] Colin Haydon, reviewing Ferrell and McCullough, *The English Sermon Revised*, in *Literature and History*, 3rd ser. 11: 1 (2001), p. 104.
[27] Richard Carpenter, *A Pastoral Charge, Faithfully Given and Discharged at the Triennial Visitation of the Lord Bishop of Exon* (1616), D5v.

their sole duty, certainly far superior to other clerical duties such as public prayer and the administration of the sacraments. Why was this? In Chapter 1, 'The theory of preaching', I argue that it rested on a distinction which may seem profoundly counter-intuitive to us, between the word read and the word preached, the one seen as passively resting on the page, the other as actively communicated in speech. This distinction not only explains why many English Protestants were so desperately anxious to get educated preaching ministers, as opposed to 'mere readers', into the parishes; it also underlines the extent to which preaching was felt to be a fundamentally oral activity. A sermon on the printed page was arguably not a sermon at all: it could not save souls, because it lacked the converting power of the spoken voice.

What made the sermon special, however, was not simply its orality but its unique and unrepeatable nature, as a discourse addressed and applied to a particular congregation at a particular time and place. In Chapter 2, 'The art of hearing', I try to reconstruct some aspects of the audience response to preaching, by looking at the contemporary handbooks which offered guidance on the best way to listen to sermons, and also at surviving sermon notebooks which tell us something about the way that preaching was filtered through the expectations of individual hearers. This is a subject of wider application than may at first appear. Frank Kermode has recently made the intriguing suggestion that, by studying the ways that early modern congregations listened to sermons, we may be able to learn something about the ways that theatre audiences listened to plays. Shakespeare's language seems difficult and complex to us, and must surely have seemed difficult and complex to many people in the seventeenth century, because of his extraordinary skill and originality in the use of words; but, as Kermode points out, it might have made fewer demands on audiences who were already practised at listening to sermons. They 'were trained, as we are not, to listen to long, structured discourses, and must have been rather good at it, with better memories and more patience than we can boast. If you could follow a sermon by John Donne, which might mean standing in St Paul's Churchyard and concentrating intensely for at least a couple of hours, you might not consider even *Coriolanus* impossibly strenuous. And although Donne wasn't talking down to them, much of his language was familiar to his congregation.'[28]

---

[28] Frank Kermode, *Shakespeare's Language* (New York, NY, 2000), p. 4. Kermode is picking up a suggestion first made by Andrew Gurr: 'If we were habituated to hearing sermons, if we were used to standing in a muddy yard or even sitting on wooden benches by candlelight, we might perhaps be more alert to many features that Elizabethans would have taken for granted.' Gurr, *Playgoing in Shakespeare's London* (3rd edn, 2004), p. 13.

One of the main findings of this chapter is that sermons were addressed to the emotions as well as to the intellect, and were designed not merely to impart doctrinal information but to elicit an affective response from the audience, with the help of voice, gesture and all the other rhetorical skills at the preacher's command. Audiences were encouraged to develop techniques of listening that enabled them to form an emotional rapport with the preacher, even to put themselves in the preacher's place by appropriating the sermon for their own use and preaching it back to themselves and others. And as Patrick Collinson has pointed out, this has far-reaching implications. If early modern preaching was addressed primarily to the emotions, then there is no reason to suppose that there was an intellectual threshold below which the preacher's message could not have penetrated:

Any attempt to decipher and characterise puritanism as a culture must begin, and probably end, with the sermon and its various concomitants. But the sermon must be properly appreciated, not as some kind of text read to an audience, all content and no style or delivery, but as performance, a performance which necessarily eludes us when we encounter, as we must, that same sermon, or rather something like it, in written and, as often as not, printed form. Recent historians of the Reformation have been sadly mistaken in considering the sermon as nothing more than a means of communicating certain religious information, technically demanding and unwelcome information at that, and they have been over-pessimistic in their assumptions about the difficulty, even the impossibility, of instilling that information into hearts and minds not well disposed to receive it.[29]

– to which, in the manner of a seventeenth-century congregation, the present writer can only say 'Amen'. Collinson is referring specifically to puritan preaching; and it is perfectly true that the art of hearing was practised most extensively in puritan circles, where great emphasis was placed on regular sermon attendance as an essential part of the godly life. However, I suggest at the end of Chapter 2 that it also helped to encourage a more internalised form of spirituality which was by no means exclusively puritan in its appeal.

Even a book such as this one, which stresses the orality of early modern preaching, must necessarily rely to a great extent on evidence drawn from printed sermons. This begs obvious questions. How far can we trust printed sermons? How far do they give us an accurate record of the words that were actually spoken in the pulpit? I confront this problem in Chapter 3, where I discuss the process of transmission from pulpit to print, and the revisions

---

[29] Patrick Collinson, 'Elizabethan and Jacobean Puritanism as forms of popular religious culture', in Christopher Durston and Jacqueline Eales, eds, *The Culture of English Puritanism 1560–1700* (New York, NY, 1996), pp. 32–57.

that preachers made when editing their sermons for publication. What emerges clearly from this discussion is that there were often significant differences between the sermon as preached and the sermon as printed. Print was regarded as an inherently 'colder' medium, lacking the personal warmth of the spoken voice, and preachers therefore regarded it as more suited to the purposes of doctrinal instruction than moral exhortation. It was also more open to detailed scrutiny and potentially more vulnerable to hostile criticism, which meant that preachers were likely to exercise more caution in their doctrinal statements, or to retreat behind a defensive barrier of citations and quotations to support their arguments – as well as revising their sermons to remove idiomatic words and phrases that were felt to be unsuited to the dignity of print. If we fail to allow for these factors, we run the risk of underestimating the popular accessibility of preaching. Another, slightly paradoxical conclusion is that if we want to get back to the oral sermon, we need to look at unauthorised editions of sermons taken from shorthand transcriptions, which were bitterly attacked by preachers for their inaccuracy but may, nevertheless, preserve elements of oral preaching in a raw, unaltered state.

The final section of Chapter 3 carries this discussion a stage further, by examining the ownership, readership and use of printed sermons, and showing that the early seventeenth century saw a profound shift in attitudes to printed sermons among the English clergy. In the 1590s, when printed sermons first began to be published in quantity, many preachers were highly suspicious of this new medium – partly because they subscribed to the preaching/reading distinction which, as explained in Chapter 1, implied that printed sermons did not have the power to call the unconverted to repentance – but by the 1620s, as they began to appreciate the evangelical uses of print, they gradually came round to a more favourable view of print publication, with the result that the preaching/reading distinction began to break down. However, the expectations of the clergy who put their sermons into print did not always match the expectations of the laity who bought and read them. The clergy tended to assume that the experience of reading a sermon on the printed page would be similar to that of hearing a sermon delivered from the pulpit, with the reader beginning at the beginning and following the train of argument through to the end. By contrast, many members of the laity seem to have engaged with the printed text in non-linear ways. Very often, they seem to have treated printed sermons as a quarry of proverbial expressions and elegant or striking similes, which could be lifted out of their original context. And by the end of the seventeenth century, the relationship between speech and print had turned back on itself, as preachers increasingly began to use printed sermons as a model for oral delivery.

Students of early modern preaching need to pay attention to these problems of textual transmission. In doing so, they must be prepared to draw not only on printed sources but also on what G. M. Story describes as 'that large body of material, familiar to everyone who has worked with manuscripts of the [early modern] period – the vast corpus of sermon reports, abridgements, epitomes, etc. under whose formidable weight the shelves of the great research libraries groan'.[30] Here again, an analogy with another academic discipline may be helpful. In recent years, legal historians have begun to appreciate the value of manuscript law reports, which not only provide additional details of cases previously known only from abbreviated printed reports, but also shed light on internal court procedures and occasional disagreements among the judges. As James Oldham has remarked: 'We know that the law that has governed us for centuries has been the law reflected in the printed word. Yet, not infrequently, unprinted sources can give us a clearer understanding of facts, context, legal interpretation or behavioural dynamics. This is an obvious fact to the social historian; perhaps it should be more so to the legal historian' – and, one might add, to the religious historian as well.[31] There are, in fact, close similarities between law reports and sermon notes, since many of the students who attended the courts regularly to learn law by reporting cases, such as the young Simonds D'Ewes, were also taking notes on the sermons they heard in church.[32] In other words, law reports and sermon notes are both products of the same habits of participatory listening and note-taking that were such an ingrained part of early modern pedagogy.

The first half of the book, then, is focused on the transmission of sermons – in speech, in print and in manuscript. The second half is focused more directly on the reception of sermons – beginning, in Chapter 4, with an attempt to reconstruct the social composition of the audience and some of the likely patterns of sermon attendance, particularly in early modern London. This requires us to look beyond the confines of the parish, which has until now been the principal focus of most studies of popular religion in

[30] G. M. Story, 'The text of Lancelot Andrewes's sermons', in D. I. B. Smith, ed., *Editing Seventeenth-Century Prose* (Toronto, 1972), pp. 11–23 (quotation pp. 17–18).

[31] James Oldham, 'Detecting non-fiction: sleuthing among manuscript case reports for what was *really* said', in Chantal Stebbings, ed., *Law Reporting in England* (London and Rio Grande, 1995), pp. 133–68 (quotation pp. 154–5).

[32] On D'Ewes, see David Ibbetson, 'Law reporting in the 1590s', in Stebbings, ed., *Law Reporting in England*, pp. 74–88 (esp. p. 79), and *College Life in the Time of James the First, as Illustrated by an Unpublished Diary of Sir Simonds D'Ewes* (1851), p. 76.

England. The focus on the parish is hardly surprising, given that attendance at the parish church – both at the weekly service of Sunday morning prayer and the annual service of Easter communion – was the principal measure of religious conformity. However, it can be misleading when we look at sermon attendance, for two reasons: first, because many sermons were delivered outside the context of the Sunday morning service, and attracted a self-selected audience that was not necessarily representative of the parish as a whole; secondly, because many laypeople regularly crossed parish boundaries to hear sermons by their favourite preachers, a practice known as 'sermon-gadding'. Studying sermon attendance therefore takes us beyond the realm of parochial religion, into the rather more shadowy realm of 'voluntary religion' explored by Patrick Collinson in the final chapter of *The Religion of Protestants*. And this is particularly true of London, where, as Peter Lake has written, 'the day-to-day lives of even ordinary Christians, let alone the godly', were constantly spilling, as though by a process of osmosis, through the permeable boundaries of parish and diocese.[33]

Chapter 4 begins by looking at the contemporary debate on the ethics of sermon-gadding. This is generally regarded as a characteristically puritan practice, but in fact many puritan clergy were strongly opposed to it, since it seemed to them to compromise the faithful relationship that ought to exist between minister and people, as between husband and wife. Despite the opposition of the clergy, however, sermon-gadding was widespread in London and resulted in an unusually stratified pattern of church attendance in which different sermons tended to attract different types of audience. Sunday morning sermons would have been delivered to a largely parochial congregation, but the audience on Sunday afternoons seems to have been more eclectic. Early morning and evening sermons attracted servants and apprentices who could not attend during working hours, while some week-day lectures seem to have attracted a large audience of women. The really interesting question, of course, is how far preachers responded to this by varying the tone and content of their sermons according to the audience. Here again manuscript sources can be very useful, both in reminding us that the sermons that got into print are not necessarily a typical cross-section of the sermons that were preached, and also in giving us a basis for comparison in the form of parallel sermons or courses of sermons delivered by the same preacher on different occasions. What this suggests, perhaps unsurprisingly, is that preachers tended to follow the maxim 'milk for babes, meat for strong

---

[33] Peter Lake, *The Boxmaker's Revenge: 'Orthodoxy', 'Heterodoxy' and the Politics of the Parish in Early Stuart London* (Manchester, 2001), p. 395.

men' in pitching their sermons at different levels of theological sophistication. It is not difficult to find examples, both in print and manuscript, of theologically demanding sermons on the doctrine of predestination, but it would be rash to assume that these were typical of the common run of parochial preaching.

This raises further questions about the effectiveness of Protestant preaching. There is no doubt that the Elizabethan clergy faced a daunting task in planting and establishing the key doctrines of the Protestant faith in a population deeply imbued with Catholic beliefs and stubbornly resistant to change. How far did they succeed? Indeed, how far *could* they have succeeded, given that certain elements of the Reformed faith required a level of familiarity with the Bible, and an ability to grapple with abstract theological ideas, that many ordinary people simply did not possess? I attempt to answer these questions in Chapter 5, where I shift the focus of attention away from London and other large cities and look, instead, at the reception of preaching in the countryside, which was arguably the real testing ground of the Protestant Reformation. There is a strong case to be made that Protestant preaching failed in significant ways to reach the majority of the population; and I argue that the strength of this case – as it were, the case for the prosecution – has not always been fully appreciated by historians anxious to stress the overall success of the Reformation. At the same time, I am not wholly convinced by the arguments of Christopher Haigh and others that the English Reformation was a popular failure. In his recent work, Haigh has rightly stressed the need to move beyond the polarities of 'success' and 'failure' – and one way to do this is, yet again, to look at surviving manuscript sermons, which give us a valuable insight into the specifics of what was actually being preached in particular parishes. In the final section of Chapter 5, I look at several sets of manuscript sermons from Oxfordshire, Derbyshire and Cornwall, from which it appears that Protestant preachers succeeded remarkably well in appropriating the 'moral tradition' of reconciliation that John Bossy has identified as one of the crucial prerequisites of pastoral effectiveness.[34]

The last two chapters carry the argument into less well-charted territory, by exploring the effects that a fully contextualised reading – a 'thick description', fully attentive to all the considerations of textual transmission and reception that I have discussed in this book – might have on the interpretation of early modern sermons. There has, I think, been a tendency for historians to treat the corpus of early modern sermon literature as one

---

[34] John Bossy, *Peace in the Post-Reformation* (Cambridge, 1998).

vast amorphous mass, a gigantic miscellany of statements on religious doctrine, political theory and social behaviour, which can be extracted from their original context and seamlessly interwoven with other types of evidence. For the purposes of this kind of source-mining, it does not greatly matter whether a particular sermon was preached in London in 1590, Lincoln in 1610 or Lowestoft in 1630, as long as it can be treated as broadly representative of contemporary opinion. All is grist that comes to the mill. At its best, this method has produced some impressively detailed and finely textured accounts of early modern culture; but even when it is done well, it is plainly incompatible with the sort of contextualised reading that I have advocated here and elsewhere, in which the 'meaning' of a sermon is not something that can simply be read off from the written text, but emerges from an act of interpretative collaboration between preacher and audience, specific to the moment of spoken delivery. How does this affect the use of sermons as historical evidence? And how far is it possible to construct general interpretations of early modern preaching that will not immediately fracture into a thousand tiny micro-histories of individual sermons? These are the questions addressed in Chapters 6 and 7, which deal, respectively, with political and theological interpretations of early modern preaching.

Preaching has attracted some very diverse political readings. It has sometimes been seen as politically centrifugal, with a constant tendency to fly out of control; and the history of early modern preaching has thus been written in terms of a series of control measures designed to 'tune the pulpits' and keep this subversive potential in check.[35] Yet it has also been seen as politically centripetal, with a constant tendency to gravitate towards established models of order and obedience; and the familiar stereotype of radical puritan preachers scattering the seeds of revolution from their pulpits has come to seem less and less plausible in the light of recent revisionist scholarship showing that the vast majority of early modern sermons operated with a set of utterly traditional assumptions about the necessity of government and the divine origin of political authority.[36] In Chapter 6, I look at what early modern preachers themselves had to say about the pulpit as a platform for political criticism, and find that while they insisted on their freedom to criticise the magistrate when necessary, they were also careful to protect themselves by wrapping up their criticisms in an indirect

---

[35] For a fuller discussion of this, see my 'Tuning the pulpits: the religious context of the Essex Revolt', in Ferrell and McCullough, eds., *The English Sermon Revised*, pp. 86–114.

[36] For a particularly powerful statement of this argument, see Kevin Sharpe, *Politics and Ideas in Early Stuart England: Essays and Studies* (London, 1989), ch. 1, 'A commonwealth of meanings: languages, analogues, ideas and politics' (pp. 3–71).

manner. I illustrate this with reference to two particular genres of sermon: the sermons preached at the opening of the assizes, which often served as an opportunity for disquisitions on political theory, and the sermons preached at Paul's Cross, the best-known and best-attended preaching place in London. In both cases, political criticism was mediated through a set of rhetorical conventions, organised, in the case of assize sermons, around the metaphor of the political body, and in the case of Paul's Cross sermons, around the metaphor of the city as a little commonwealth. By working within these conventions, it was possible for preachers to express some remarkably hard-hitting criticisms of higher authority – criticisms which have not always been apparent to modern scholars unaware of the rhetorical context.

In the final chapter, I look at theological readings of sermons, with particular reference to the doctrine of predestination. The theology of grace and predestination has already generated a substantial secondary literature, much of it arising from Nicholas Tyacke's argument in *Anti-Calvinists* (1987) that a shared belief in predestination was, so to speak, the theological cement that held the Elizabethan and early Stuart Church together.[37] Recent scholarship, however, has tended to assume that the debates on predestination belonged to the realm of academic theology and rarely filtered down into popular preaching. This assumption is, I believe, fundamentally mistaken. In his recent book on the literary culture of Reformation England, Brian Cummings has argued that while 'the history of theology defines predestination in doctrinal terms ... it is just as important to understand the techniques of writing' (and, by extension, preaching) 'needed to define it'. As Cummings observes, the history of predestination is not merely a history of doctrine, but also 'a history of silence', in which theologians came up against the limits of what could be known about the secret counsels of God – and, increasingly in the early seventeenth century, the limits of what the ecclesiastical authorities permitted them to say.[38] Nowhere is this more apparent than in sermons, where preachers took the doctrine of predestination beyond the confines of the study and packaged it in a suitably edifying form for general public

---

[37] Nicholas Tyacke, *Anti-Calvinists: The Rise of English Arminianism, c. 1590–1640* (Oxford, 1987). Tyacke's broader understanding of the late sixteenth- and early seventeenth-century Church of England as theologically Calvinist (or, more accurately, Reformed) achieves magisterial expression in Anthony Milton, *Catholic and Reformed: The Roman and Protestant Churches in English Protestant Thought, 1600–1640* (Cambridge, 1995).

[38] Brian Cummings, *The Literary Culture of the Reformation: Grammar and Grace* (Oxford, 2002), p. 285.

consumption. Preachers were well aware that there were some things that could not or should not be uttered in the pulpit; and this chapter will show how some of them observed, and occasionally overstepped, the limits on acceptable pulpit discourse.

Finally, in the conclusion, I wish to place all this in a wider context. The central story to be told here is a narrative of the decline of preaching in the Church of England, as in other mainstream Christian denominations, from a central to a peripheral activity. Yet there is an alternative story to be told as well, one of religious revivalism in which preaching has played, and still continues to play, a central role. The history of preaching over the last four centuries is not simply a history of decline, but a history of competing forces in which the charisma of the preacher is never quite absorbed into the routine of religious practice. This book has been written in the belief that the most fruitful way to understand preaching is as an encounter between the spoken voice of the preacher and the participatory response of the hearer. In doing so I hope that it may help to explain not only the decline of preaching in the churches of the modern West but also its remarkable powers of persistence.

CHAPTER I

# The theory of preaching

Many clergy in early modern England saw themselves, first and foremost, as preachers. In the portrait frontispieces to their books, they were often shown in the pulpit, their left hand raised in exhortation and their right hand resting on the Bible in front of them (Figure 1). Their funeral monuments, too, often depicted them in the act of preaching, standing over the pulpit cushion with one hand held against their chest as a sign that they were, literally, speaking from the heart.[1] The same image of the godly minister, soberly dressed in a black Geneva gown with a book open in front of him, continued to be used for many years as the standard frontispiece to religious chapbooks, suggesting, as Margaret Spufford has argued, that 'such a picture immediately gave the publication an air of credibility and authority to the reader'.[2] This was the normative model of clerical ministry, and it had the effect of reducing that ministry to little more than a pulpit function. We know from other sources that the clergy had many responsibilities besides preaching: they catechised the young, visited the sick and buried the dead, they administered the sacraments of baptism and the Eucharist, and they acted as mediators and peacemakers between members of their flock. Yet in their writings they frequently gave the impression that preaching was their only function, or the only one that really counted. 'The proper and the principall office of a Pastor', declared Thomas Morton in 1609, 'is the preaching of the word'.[3]

This sermon-centred model of ministry is generally thought of as reflecting the word-centred nature of early modern Protestantism. The

---

[1] See, e.g., the portrait frontispieces to Arthur Hildersham, *The Doctrine of Fasting and Praier* (1633) and Hugh Latimer, *Fruitfull Sermons* (1635). On funeral monuments, see Nigel Llewellyn, *Funeral Monuments in Post-Reformation England* (Cambridge, 2000), p. 370 and Peter Sherlock, *Monuments and Memory in Early Modern England* (Aldershot, 2008), p. 150.
[2] Margaret Spufford, *Small Books and Pleasant Histories* (London, 1981), p. 198.
[3] Patrick Collinson, *The Religion of Protestants: The Church in English Society 1559–1625* (Oxford, 1982), p. 96; Thomas Morton, *A Catholike Appeale for Protestants* (1609), 3A4r.

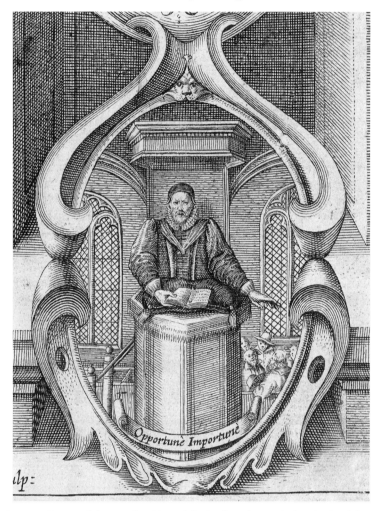

Figure 1 Images of the preacher (1). Rightly dividing the word of truth: detail from the frontispiece to John Boys, *Workes* (1622). Reproduced by permission of Cambridge University Library.

devout layman heard the Word preached by the minister, looked up the proof-texts in a printed edition of the Bible, copied them into a notebook for private reading or group discussion and committed them to memory for use in private prayer or meditation. At the same time, Protestants banished visual images and symbolic ceremonies from their churches, and tried to purge mental images and visual memory-systems from their imagination.

This emphasis on the verbal, as opposed to the visual, was an integral part of Protestant self-definition and a deliberate break with the pre-Reformation Catholic past. It also has suggestive parallels within our own culture: for just as many early modern Protestants feared that the true religion of the Word was being threatened by the seductive temptations of idolatry, so many modern commentators have expressed fears that literacy skills are being undermined by the ubiquity of visual images on film and television.[4] Perhaps this is one reason why the verbal/visual dichotomy has found such ready acceptance, and seems so intuitively right, as an explanation of the difference between Protestant preaching and Catholic sacramentalism.

Yet the importance attached to preaching is indicative of a religious culture centred not just on the word but on the spoken word in particular. Tom Webster has characterised early modern Protestant (and especially puritan) culture as 'intensely phonologocentric' in its privileging of speech over writing. In this culture, he writes, 'voice is associated with self-presence, truth, authenticity and an immediate and transparent movement of meaning, writing with absence and confusion as a secondary, lifeless emanation of speech'.[5] Oral metaphors were used to describe the process ('vocation', 'calling') by which God communicated with men; and one English Protestant author advised his readers to think of the Bible not as a written document but 'as if God himselfe stood by and spake these words unto thee'.[6] This had some paradoxical results which cut across the conventional understanding of Protestantism as a word-centred religion: it led to an emphasis on preaching over and above the written word of scripture; a distrust of printed books; and a belief that 'bare reading', even the reading of the Bible, could not suffice for salvation. Patrick Collinson has remarked that for Protestants, the word was 'primarily the word of the printed page, on which depended the spoken words of sermon and catechism'.[7] In fact it is possible to turn this on its head, and to argue that for many Protestants, the spoken word of the sermon actually took precedence over the printed word of the Bible.

---

[4] The parallel is noticed by Raphael Samuel, commenting on the reluctance of historians to use photographs as documentary evidence: 'Like other social historians of my generation I was completely pre-televisual ... I suspect that, as a committed atheist, I would have thought any indulgence in imagery a throwback to magic and superstition.' *Theatres of Memory*, vol. 1, *Past and Present in Contemporary Culture* (London, 1994), p. 317.

[5] Tom Webster, 'Writing to redundancy: approaches to spiritual journals and early modern spirituality', *Historical Journal*, 39: 1 (1996), pp. 33–56 (quotation p. 41).

[6] Samuel Hieron, *Six Sermons* (1608), B1r.

[7] Patrick Collinson, *The Birthpangs of Protestant England* (New York, NY, 1988), p. 99.

### READING AND PREACHING

At the heart of the Protestant theory of preaching lay one particular New Testament text. That text was Romans 10: 14–17, Paul's account of the inseparable link between preaching, hearing and faith:

> How then shall they call on him in whom they have not believed? and how shall they believe in him of whom they have not heard? and how shall they hear without a preacher? And how shall they preach, except they be sent? as it is written, How beautiful are the feet of them that preach the gospel of peace, and bring glad tidings of good things! But they have not all obeyed the gospel. For Esaias saith, Lord, who hath believed our report? So then faith cometh by hearing, and hearing by the word of God.

Even before the Reformation, this text was being used to emphasise the importance of preaching. John Geiler, preaching in Strasburg in the late fifteenth century, declared that while there was no formal obligation to hear sermons, one should not neglect the opportunity to do so, because of its many spiritual benefits, including faith, hope, charity, contrition for sins and the grace of the Holy Spirit.[8] But it was in the sixteenth century that this text really came into its own, thanks to the Protestant doctrine of justification by faith. Hugh Latimer described Paul's progression of terms (no salvation without calling on God, no calling on God without believing, no believing without hearing, no hearing without preaching) as '*Scala Coeli* ... the true ladder that bringeth a man to Heaven'. Preaching was not merely beneficial; it was indispensable. 'Take away preaching, take away salvation.'[9]

*Fides ex auditu*, 'faith is by hearing', was a precept that Protestant commentators took very literally, believing that saving grace was mediated through the ear and not through the eye. Again and again, they pointed out, God had chosen to reveal himself to his people through the spoken word. At the giving of the Law on Mount Sinai, 'Moses spoke, and God answered him by a voice' (Exod. 19: 20), while at Jesus' baptism, 'a voice came from heaven' (Luke 3: 22), and again at his transfiguration, 'there came a voice out of the cloud, saying, This is my beloved Son: hear him' (Luke 9: 35). According to Calvin, God had 'proclaimed his name' on Mount Sinai (Exod. 34: 5) because 'true knowledge of God is obtained more by the ears than by the eyes', and the sight of God's glory would have been meaningless to Moses without the sound of God's voice. This belief in

---

[8]  E. Jane Dempsey Douglass, *Justification in Late Medieval Preaching: A Study of John Geiler of Keiserberg* (Leiden, 1966), p. 91.
[9]  Hugh Latimer, *Fruitfull Sermons* (1635), E6r, H6r.

the superiority of hearing over sight also informed Calvin's doctrine of the sacraments. If the sacraments were merely presented to the eye, then, Calvin argued, they would be nothing more than dead images; but because they were presented both to the eye and the ear, they had a special status as 'visible words', which set them apart from other signs and symbols. 'Figures are illusory without an explanation. If the vision only had been offered to the eye of the prophet, and no voice of God had followed, what would have been the advantage? But when God confirmed the vision by his word, the prophet can truly say, "I have seen the glory of God". And the same is true of the sacraments. If the bare signs were presented to our eyes, they would be nothing more than ghostly apparitions [*mortua spectra*]. But the word of God breathes life into them.'[10]

In arguing for the superiority of the spoken word, Protestant writers were also indebted to Aristotelian theories of perception, which held that although sight was the highest of the five senses, hearing contributed most to the acquisition of knowledge. When seventeenth-century writers referred to hearing as 'the sense of knowledge' or 'the sense of learning' they were drawing on an Aristotelian commonplace. Indeed, some authors went further than Aristotle and argued that hearing actually took precedence over sight. 'Wee have two Rationall Senses', remarked Arthur Lake, 'and contentions have beene made about their precedencie . . . [but] whatsoever Philosophie thinkes, Divinitie must hold that wee are beholding much more to our Eare, than to our Eye for saving wisedome.'[11] In a treatise bluntly entitled *The Vanitie of the Eie*, George Hakewill argued that hearing was inherently superior to sight, because the ear could perceive the depth of objects ('the soundnesse of timber, the emptinesse of vessels' and so forth) whereas the eye perceived only their 'crust and surface'.[12] As Stuart Clark has recently shown, Hakewill's attack on the superficiality of visual perception was drawing on a long tradition of epistemological doubt about the reliability of the eyesight, which pointed to dreams, delusions, hallucinations and optical illusions as evidence that the eye was not a trustworthy guide to the external world.[13]

---

[10] Ronald S. Wallace, *Calvin's Doctrine of the Word and Sacrament* (Edinburgh, 1953), pp. 72–3.

[11] Arthur Lake, *Sermons* (1629), M5v.

[12] George Hakewill, *The Vanitie of the Eie* (Oxford, 1608), E4r; Aristotle, *De Sensu*, chapter 1 (in *Parva Naturalia*, trans. J. I. Beare and G. R. T. Ross (Oxford, 1908)); for a contemporary citation, see Helkiah Crooke, *Microcosmographia* (2nd edn, 1631), 3G1v (p. 612), 'speech being an audible thing is the verie *Cause* of Learning'. See also Penelope Gouk, 'Some English theories of hearing in the seventeenth century', in Charles Burnett, Michael Fend and Penelope Gouk, eds., *The Second Sense: Studies in Hearing and Musical Judgement from Antiquity to the Seventeenth Century* (London, 1991), pp. 95–113.

[13] Stuart Clark, *Vanities of the Eye: Vision in Early Modern European Culture* (Oxford, 2007), pp. 25–31.

A distinction between true 'ear-worship' and false 'eye-worship' was also a crucial part of Protestant self-definition, and a key weapon in their polemical armoury. On one side of the religious divide, Catholic apologists commonly defended the use of religious images by arguing that most human knowledge was communicated visually. God 'hath so made us', wrote Nicholas Sander in his *Treatise of the Images of Christ*, 'that we can not learne, know, or understand any thing, without conceiving the same in some corporal Image or likenes. Our knowledge commeth by our senses, of the which our eies are the chefe.'[14] Protestants, for their part, responded by condemning Catholic worship for precisely this reliance on the visual. Samuel Hieron believed that a reliance upon cheap visual gratification was the hallmark of all false religion, for 'the nature of man is very enclinable to affect rather that which with some outward shew offereth it selfe unto the eie, than to content it selfe with the bare and naked instruction of the eare: And therefore we see . . . how full all false religions devised by men, have ever beene of outward beauty, of Images, and signes, and bodily representments.'[15]

In his valuable study of the 'oral aspects of scripture', *Beyond the Written Word*, William A. Graham argues that the Protestant insistence on the primacy of hearing should not be taken literally. It should not be taken to imply 'a literal, rationalistic choice of the ear over the eye and hearing over seeing as the preferable organ and sense to be employed by the Christian'. Rather, it should be understood figuratively, as an emphasis on the living, breathing Word of God – even if that word was communicated visually, by means of the written or printed page.[16] Graham is quite right to stress the interdependence of writing and speech – a point to which we shall return in a moment. But whatever he may say, it is quite clear that when Protestant writers declared that hearing was preferable to sight, they meant it quite literally. This comes out clearly in their attitude towards the deaf. If saving knowledge was communicated primarily through the ear, then it followed that the deaf were in a damnable condition – and, sure enough, this is precisely what many Protestant writers believed. 'Deafe men are barred from Faith and Salvation, to be attained by hearing', one English preacher told his audience. 'How miserable then wert thou, if thou wert deafe! for deafe men must needs be miserable, being deprived of the ordinarie meanes

---

[14]  Nicholas Sander, *A Treatise of the Images of Christ* (Louvain, 1567), G3r.
[15]  Hieron, *Six Sermons*, B1v. See also John Brinsley, *The Glorie of the Latter Temple Greater Then of the Former* (1631), C3v.
[16]  William A. Graham, *Beyond the Written Word: Oral Aspects of Scripture in the History of Religion* (Cambridge, 1987), pp. 149–54.

of faith'. The loss of a man's hearing, declared another, 'is worse than if he lost his limbes, or his eye-sight. For wanting them, hee might bee carried to the Church . . . but when the sense of Hearing is gone, then farewell the sound of the word Preached.'[17]

And this uncompromising insistence on the ear, rather than the eye, also explains why many Protestants attached such immense importance to preaching. They were, of course, aware that the Word could take more than one form. It could be read silently, and thus communicated through the eye; it could be read aloud to an audience, and thus communicated through both the eye and the ear; or it could be preached, without the aid of a written text, and thus communicated through the ear alone. To us, there may seem little to choose between these alternatives. Yet many early modern Protestants were adamant that only the Word preached – not the Word read – could suffice for salvation. No one made the point more crisply than the Suffolk preacher Elnathan Parr, in his commentary on Romans:

QUEST.   Shall none be saved, but those which heare Sermons?
ANSW.   No, ordinarily.[18]

When pressed, Protestants were prepared to admit exceptions to this rule. They conceded, for example, that their ancestors living before the Reformation might have been saved by reading the Bible, or hearing it read, even in the absence of a preaching ministry – for when the Church was in a 'ruinous estate', then, as William Perkins explained, 'this word read or repeated, yea, the very sound thereof being once heard, is by the assistance of Gods spirit, extraordinarily effectuall, to them whom God will have called out of that great darknesse into his exceeding light'.[19] But no such exception could be made for those living in the light of the Gospel. 'We cannot ordinarily have faith, till first it be wrought in us by the preaching of the Word', declared John Downame. 'Neither are we to thinke that the Word read, either by our selves or others, is ordinarily sufficient to worke in us grace and godlinesse'.[20] In short, no one who had access to preaching could expect to be saved merely by reading the Bible.

This had some paradoxical implications. It meant that hearing a sermon was guaranteed to be more effectual than reading a sermon, even though,

---

[17] Elnathan Parr, *Workes* (3rd edn, 1632), L1r, N2v (ii. 109, 136); William Worship, *The Pattern of an Invincible Faith* (1616), A4r.
[18] Parr, *Workes*, N3r (ii. 137), commenting on Romans 10: 14–17.
[19] William Perkins, *A Golden Chaine, or the Description of Theologie* (Cambridge, 1591), K2v.
[20] John Downame, *A Guide to Godlynesse, or a Treatise of a Christian Life* (1629), 2T2r.

Figure 2  Images of the preacher (2). Sowing the seed of the Word: frontispiece to Thomas
Taylor, *The Parable of the Sower and of the Seed* (1634). Reproduced by permission of
Cambridge University Library.

as Downame admitted, 'the Sermon which wee reade, may be as good or
better than that which wee should heare'.[21] Better a bad preacher than no
preacher at all – and better a bad sermon heard from the pulpit than a good

<hr />

[21] Downame, *Guide to Godlynesse*, 204r.

sermon read on the page. Protestant writers did not try to evade these paradoxes; indeed, they seemed almost to revel in them. Alexander Cooke posed the question, 'Whether it be soe profitable to read good bookes as to heare indifferent sermons?' and replied, unhesitatingly, that it was not. 'Hearing hath greater promise of blessinge than redinge, for we read that by hearing, faith is wrought, whereas we read of noe such grace that comes by reding. Wherfore hearing must needs be much more profitable than reading.' Cooke dealt briskly with the potential objection that when St Paul had said 'faith cometh by hearing' he meant 'faith cometh by hearing learned sermons'. This, he declared, was a totally unwarranted gloss on St Paul's words – for 'where the scripture distinguisheth not, there neither must we distinguish. And therfore seeing it saith that faith cometh by hearing, and not by hearing of learned sermons, we are soe to understand it, as spoken of hearing any sermon, even a silly sermon.'[22]

What was it that made reading and preaching so different? Protestant writers were not suggesting that there was anything lacking in the written word of scripture which had to be supplied by preaching. But they regarded the written word as a latent force, which had to be activated or 'applied' by the living voice of the preacher in order to strike home to the heart of the listener. 'Doctrine indeed is profitable to perswade the judgement', observed the London preacher Charles Richardson, 'but it is the application of the doctrine, that must worke upon the heart and affections to winne them. So that application is the very life and edge of doctrine; without which it is dull, cold, barren, and as good as dead, and doth little good unto the hearers ... Now the bare reading of the Word cannot doe this; it is the powerfull preaching of it that worketh this effect.'[23] Other writers compared the scriptures to a plaster that was of no practical value until it was applied to the patient's wound, or to seed that could not germinate or take root until it was sown in the ground.[24] Elnathan Parr went so far as to describe the written word as a 'sealed booke' that could do no good until it was opened by the preacher.[25]

The Word of God was thus defined primarily in terms of speech. 'God hath now seen fit', wrote William Whitaker in his influential treatise *De*

[22] Notebook of Alexander Cooke: British Library, London, Harl. MS 5247, f. 47r (hereafter, British Library, London, is abbreviated as BL).
[23] Charles Richardson, *A Workeman, that Needeth not to be Ashamed: or the Faithfull Steward of Gods House* (1616), K3r.
[24] Robert Cawdrey, *A Treasurie or Store-House of Similies* (1600), F2r; R. R., *The House-holders Helpe, for Domesticall Discipline* (1615), C7r.
[25] John Boys, *Workes* (1622), 3O3r; Parr, *Workes*, Y6v.

*Sacra Scriptura*, 'that all that teaching which he delivered of old orally to the fathers should be committed to books and writing'. This not only gave priority to the spoken word as the original form in which the scriptures had been transmitted; it also lent it an authority, as the immediate source of divine revelation, which the written word possessed only at second hand. It was right, Whitaker went on, that God's teaching should have been written down, since this protected it from being corrupted by oral tradition. But it also entailed an element of loss, since 'the living voice of the apostles, when they preached, had more force in it to move the passions of men'. Moreover, if the apostles and prophets had still been alive and living amongst us, 'we might repair to them, and entreat them to disclose to us the meaning of what they had written', whereas now we have to fall back on prayer and study to help us discover their meaning, since 'scripture hath no audible voice'.[26] This was very far removed from a modern fundamentalist conception of biblical authority. In effect, it was a concept of authority focused not on the canon of scripture but on the wider and more elastic category of the 'Word of God', which included both the teaching of the apostles and the preaching of their modern successors. This was made explicit in Bullinger's definition of the Word of God as 'the language of God, the revelation of the will of God', and in the second Helvetic Confession, which states plainly: 'the preaching of the word of God is the word of God'.[27]

This emphasis on the spoken word was taken to extremes by John Smyth, one of the leaders of the English separatist church at Amsterdam. Smyth argued that only spoken language could be admitted into worship, and that written language was excluded. In his view, it was unlawful to read from a book in church, or even 'to have the booke as a helpe before the eye' when preaching or singing psalms. His rejection of the written word was based on the belief that it was a form of pictorial image, and therefore no different in kind from the idolatrous images used by the Papists. 'Bookes or writings are signes or pictures of things signified therby ... Hence it followeth that bookes or writinges are in the nature of pictures or Images and therefore in the nature of

---

[26] William Whitaker, *Disputatio de Sacra Scriptura* (1588), translated as *A Disputation on Holy Scripture, against the Papists* (Cambridge, Parker Society, 1849), pp. 466, 517.

[27] Jaroslav Pelikan and Valerie Hotchkiss, eds., *Creeds and Confessions of Faith in the Christian Tradition: vol. II, Creeds and Confessions of the Reformation Era* (New Haven and London, 2003), p. 460. The assertion that 'the preaching of the word of God is the word of God' is not in the body of the text but appears as a marginal note; see also Edward A. Dowey, Jr, 'The word of God as scripture and preaching', in W. Fred Graham, ed., *Later Calvinism: International Perspectives (Sixteenth Century Essays & Studies, XXII)* (Kirksville, MO, 1994), pp. 5–18.

ceremonies.'[28] As such, they were part of the ceremonial law, and had been formally abolished by Christ when he closed the book in the synagogue at the beginning of his ministry (Luke 4: 20), 'to signifie that that ceremony of bookworship, or the ministerie of the lettre was now exspired, and finished'. This was confirmed by Paul's injunction that 'the letter killeth, but the spirit giveth life' (2 Cor. 3: 6), which Smyth interpreted as a further rejection of the use of written language in worship.

Robert Parker, another of the English separatists, may have had Smyth and his followers in mind when he wrote that '*dicere* and *pingere*' (speech and painting) were so different 'as that the words themselves of Scripture (in some mens judgement) must not be painted on the Church walles, because that place serveth for the preaching and not for the painting of them'.[29] Parker's ostensible source for this distinction was the commentary on Exodus by the Swiss Reformed minister Josias Simler. However, Simler's distinction was between '*scribere*' and '*pingere*' (writing and painting), which implied that written words were acceptable even though painted images were not. Simler had tentatively suggested that it might be more convenient ('*forsan utilius esset*') if the Commandments were not painted on church walls, since the Word of God should be heard rather than read in church ('*audiendum, et meditandum, non in parietibus legendum*'), but stopped well short of condemning the practice.[30] It was left to Smyth to take the further step of rejecting all forms of written language – whether printed, carved or painted – as incompatible with true Christian worship. This directly contradicted the position of the Dutch Reformed Church, which had encouraged the painting of scriptural texts in churches as a new form of religious art, replacing the images that had been destroyed in the iconoclastic attacks of the 1560s.[31]

Smyth's arguments found little acceptance, even among his fellow separatists. As Henry Ainsworth pointed out, his view of words as equivalent to images bore an unexpected similarity to the Roman Catholic view of images as equivalent to words:

---

[28] John Smyth, *The Differences of the Churches of the Seperation* (1608), reprinted in *Works*, ed. W. T. Whitley (Cambridge, 1915), vol. I, p. 273. Smyth's views are briefly discussed in William G. Madsen, *From Shadowy Types to Truth: Studies in Milton's Symbolism* (1968), p. 172.

[29] Robert Parker, *A Scholasticall Discourse against Symbolizing with Antichrist in Ceremonies* (Middelburg, 1607), O2v.

[30] Josias Simler, *In Exodum* (Zurich, 1584), O5v, P2v. For an example of iconoclastic attack on painted texts, see Nigel Yates, *Buildings, Faith, and Worship* (Oxford, 1991), p. 17.

[31] Mia Mochizuki, 'Supplanting the devotional image after Netherlandish iconoclasm', in A. McClanan and J. Johnson, eds., *Negating the Image: Case Studies of Past Iconoclasms* (Aldershot, 2004), pp. 137–62.

If M. Smyth can prove *books* and *images* to be both of a nature, and both alike ceremonies: he may be a Proctour for the Pope, who hath brought *images* into the Church, for *laie mens books*. And if the book be to him that readeth, of the nature that an image is to him that gazeth: who would not plead for them both alike, to be used or rejected?[32]

It would be easy to regard Smyth merely as an eccentric. Yet his position interestingly foreshadows that of modern philosophers and semioticians like W. J. T. Mitchell, who – challenging the intuitive feeling that pictures are images in a 'real' sense, whereas words are images only in a metaphorical sense – argue that mental, verbal and pictorial images all belong in the same category.[33] (Mitchell suggests that we should think of the distinction between words and images as similar to that between algebra and geometry – two equally arbitrary forms of representation, neither one more natural or necessary than the other.) There is nothing naïve or unsophisticated about Smyth's theory of language; and it could be argued that he was simply expressing, in a peculiarly rigorous form, the widespread Protestant belief that speech was superior to writing.

## PURITANS AND CONFORMISTS

Having shown that some Protestants placed greater emphasis on the spoken word of the preacher than on the printed word of scripture, I now wish to argue that this preference for the spoken word was a distinctive feature of puritan culture. At first sight, this may seem a surprising suggestion, given that the culture of Puritanism was, to a large extent, the culture of English Protestantism in general. The traditional opposition between 'radical' Puritanism and 'moderate' Anglicanism has now been decisively discredited; historians have learned to define Puritanism more loosely, in terms of a cluster of attitudes and priorities rather than a set of core principles; and from this perspective, it may seem a retrograde step to suggest that there was anything peculiarly puritan about the distinction between reading and preaching. But it is worth indulging, for a moment, in a little speculation. Could it be that the difficulty in defining Puritanism arises, in part, from the fact that historians have been looking in the wrong place? What would happen if, instead of thinking of puritans as committed above all to the written word of scripture, we thought of them as united by a radical

---

[32] Henry Ainsworth, *A Defence of the Holy Scriptures, Worship, and Ministerie, Used in the Christian Churches Separated from Antichrist* (Amsterdam, 1609), C3v.
[33] W. J. T. Mitchell, *Iconology: Image, Text, Ideology* (Chicago, 1986), esp. chapter 1.

anti-scripturalism? Would this work any better as a definition of Puritanism? Some contemporaries certainly thought so. 'In proving that faith comes by hearing the word preached', declares one of the characters in Edward Vaughan's dialogue on the nature of faith, 'you goe also about to prove, that the word being read privately at home, or publikely in Churches, availes nothing: and therein I hold you a *Puritane.*'[34]

The distinction between reading and preaching was one of the points at issue in the Admonition Controversy, the polemical exchange between Thomas Cartwright and John Whitgift, which effectively defined the terms of the debate between puritans and their opponents. The disagreement revolved around the meaning of the key Pauline proof-text, 'faith cometh by hearing', which was universally regarded as central to the whole debate. Cartwright argued that when St Paul spoke of preaching, he meant the exposition and application of scripture, as opposed to the mere reading of it.[35] Whitgift disagreed. He was prepared to concede that preaching, understood in Cartwright's sense, was 'the most ordinary and usual means that God useth to work by in the hearts of the hearers' – a significant concession, which reminds us that there was a good deal of common ground between the two sides in the debate. However, he insisted that St Paul's famous question, 'how shall they hear without a preacher?', was referring to preaching in a much wider sense. 'I say that St Paul, in that chapter to the Romans, by preaching doth generally understand all kinds of publishing the gospel by the external voice, which comprehendeth reading as well as it doth that which you call preaching.'[36]

This was not merely an academic dispute about the meaning of words. On the contrary, it had drastic implications for the religious life of the Church of England, particularly for the many parishes lacking a regular supply of sermons. A minister might lead a blameless moral life; he might read prayers, lessons and homilies, administer the sacraments, teach his people the basic principles of faith and morality and admonish them when they sinned; but if he did not expound scripture to them from the pulpit, then, by Cartwright's definition, he was no preacher, and his ministry was a sham, 'as evil as playing upon a stage'. And what of his parishioners? Cartwright imagined their cry: 'Surely our sins are grown ripe, our ignorance is equal with the ignorance of our leaders: we are lost; they cannot find

---

[34] Edward Vaughan, *A Plaine and Perfect Method, for the Easie Understanding of the Whole Bible* (1617), B1ov.

[35] John Whitgift, *Works*, ed. John Ayre (Parker Society, 1851–3), vol. III, p. 30.

[36] Whitgift, *Works*, III.30. For another statement of this position, see Inner Temple Library, Petyt MS 538/38, ff. 75–8, 'Whether all ministers of the church should be preachers'.

us: we are sick; they cannot heal us: we are hungry; they cannot feed us, except they lead us by other men's lights, and heal us by saying a prescript form of service, or else feed us with homilies that are too homely to be set in the place of God's scriptures.' Such people were not utterly without hope, for 'it may be that God doth sometimes work faith by reading only', but on the whole, Cartwright was pessimistic. 'There is no salvation without preaching', and where preaching fails, 'the people perish'.

But replace Cartwright's narrow definition of preaching with Whitgift's more inclusive one, and the whole picture changes. 'God worketh by reading the scriptures as well as he doth by preaching, and useth that also as a means to call men to salvation.' By reading the scriptures, or hearing them read, 'many have come to the knowledge of the word', and 'more are converted' every day, 'even such as very seldom or never hear the word preached'. Cartwright had argued, dismissively, that if reading was a form of preaching, then even a child of four or five years old might be able to preach as well as the most learned minister. Yes indeed, retorted Whitgift, and what was wrong with that? 'God, by his word read of a child, may, and doth oftentimes teach us. And hereof we have (God be thanked) many examples in England, of those which, not being able to read themselves, by the means of their children reading to them at home, receive instruction and edifying.' This led Whitgift to take a more optimistic view of the present state of the Church of England, and hence a more pragmatic view of the state of its clergy. One day it might be possible to put an educated preaching minister into every parish; but as things now stood, it was acceptable to ordain men who were not sufficiently learned to compose their own sermons, just as long as they were sufficiently literate to be able to read the scriptures.

The reading/preaching distinction can thus be mapped on to two very different ideological positions. To some extent, as Peter Lake has shown, the Admonition Controversy was about the 'polemical manipulation' of a 'set of essentially shared assumptions' – the common assumption in this case being the centrality of the Word of God (as opposed to the Popish reliance on human tradition) and hence the need for godly preaching and teaching.[37] But the existence of this common ground should not distract us from the differences between the two sides, which amounted to a confrontation between two opposing views of clerical ministry. On the one hand, there was the prophetic model of ministry favoured by Cartwright, in which the preacher wielded the full force of his authority over his flock, first casting

---

[37] Peter Lake, *Anglicans and Puritans? Presbyterianism and English Conformist Thought from Whitgift to Hooker* (London, 1988), p. 24.

them down by the preaching of the law, then raising them up by the preaching of the Gospel. On the other hand, there was the more routine model of ministry favoured by Whitgift, in which the preacher patiently reiterated the words of scripture, week after week, in order to bring his flock to a better understanding of true doctrine. The fact that this disagreement took place within a broad theological consensus – with both parties belonging to the mainstream Reformed tradition and holding similar views on a variety of doctrinal issues, including predestination – did not make the clash of opposing views any less sharp.

This was a practical disagreement as well as an ideological one, for many puritan writers believed that the reading/preaching distinction could be empirically demonstrated by comparing the spiritual condition of parishioners who lived under a preaching ministry with the spiritual condition of those who did not. In the course of a twenty-year ministry in late Elizabethan Kent, Josias Nichols examined all 'strangers' who came to live in his parish, and claimed that whereas 'some that have come from parishes, where there hath bene diligent teaching' could give a good account of their faith, no one who had 'continued under a Non resident and unpreaching ministerie' had any religious knowledge whatever. 'One would not thinke it so: seeinge they have the holy scriptures read in a knowen tongue . . . yet surely it is true in verie many places.'[38] This confirmed Nichols and other puritan ministers in their view that only preaching could suffice for salvation, which had disturbing implications for anyone unfortunate enough to live in a parish without a resident preaching minister. Edward Vaughan put it bluntly: 'If that were true (which *God* forbid) many hundred Congregations were damned, whereof some I know that have not heard a Sermon this twelvemoneth, some others not this seaven yeares, and some people not at all.'[39] And this, in turn, fed directly into the debate over puritan nonconformity – for it implied that preaching was far more important than any other clerical activity, and hence that a minister who preached diligently and well should not be penalised for failing to wear a surplice or use the sign of the Cross.

This debate over the nature and purpose of preaching, begun by Whitgift and Cartwright at a national level, was continued, over the next fifty or sixty years, by many other writers and preachers at a local level. In Devon, the publication of Samuel Hieron's tract *The Preachers Plea* in 1605 sparked off a debate which went on, intermittently, for another twenty years, drawing

---

[38] Josias Nichols, *The Plea of the Innocent* (1602), Q3v. In the Cambridge University Library copy this passage is annotated in a contemporary hand: 'A notorious Lye.'
[39] Vaughan, *Plaine and Perfect Method*, B1ov.

out some of the practical, pastoral implications of the Admonition
Controversy and also providing an insight into some of the problems
encountered by puritan clergy in their day-to-day ministry.[40] Hieron, rector
of the small country parish of Modbury, near Plymouth, wrote his tract to
counter two objections which, he claimed, were 'common in the mouthes
of many, either ignorant or ill disposed persons . . . the one is, *What need al
this preaching?* the other is, *Who knoweth whom to beleeve among these
Preachers?*'[41] These questions, he believed, were major obstacles to the
success of the preaching ministry, and in answering them he touched on
many of the themes we have already encountered in this chapter.

*The Preachers Plea* is written in the form of a dialogue – 'a very good way
(in my seeming) to help the understanding of common men' – between
Epaphras, a godly minister, and Nymphas, a friendly parishioner seeking
advice on how to answer some of the criticisms of the preaching ministry
voiced by his less religiously committed neighbours. ('They will not perhaps
say much to your faces that are Preachers', he tells Epaphras, 'but such as
I am shall often heare them talke at liberty.') What, for example, can be
done about 'ignorant men' who see no need to attend sermons? 'They have
lived (they saie) some thirtie, some fortie, some more years without a setled
ministerie, having onelie (unlesse it were now or then at times) the ordinarie
service read amonge them', and having never felt any need of a preaching
minister 'they can see no reason why there shoulde be more use of preaching
now, then there hath bene in former times'.[42] Epaphras is disgusted by their
ignorance ('it is so grosse') but suggests that a few homely similitudes may
help to break down their complacency. A man in a fainting fit may not wish
to be awakened, but when he has come to his senses he will be grateful that
his friends helped him. A man climbing a steep hill at night may walk
confidently, but when the daylight comes he will be horrified to see the
danger he was in. Just so, a man may say to his minister, 'Oh Mr Preacher,
trouble me not I pray you . . . I am well enough, my soule is in no such
danger', but when God has opened his eyes, 'then he will blesse God for him
that called him, because he will then perceive, that otherwise he had even
runned on to his own destruction.'

---

[40] For Hieron's ministry at Modbury, see Mark Stoyle, *Loyalty and Locality: Popular Allegiance in Devon during the English Civil War* (Exeter, 1994), pp. 196–203; and for his protection by local gentry patrons, see Kenneth Fincham, *Prelate as Pastor: The Episcopate of James I* (Oxford, 1990), p. 215. Both these accounts draw on the biography of Hieron in John Quick's *'Icones Sacrae Anglicanae'*, Dr Williams's Library, MS 38.34.

[41] Samuel Hieron, *The Preachers Plea: or, a Treatise in Forme of a Plaine Dialogue, Making Known the Worth and Necessity of that which We Call Preaching* (1605), A3v.

[42] Hieron, *Preachers Plea*, C4v.

So far, so straightforward. But then Nymphas mentions another objection, not made by ignorant men but, more worryingly, by men who should know better, men who are 'by education learned, and by profession (some of them) Ministers and preachers'. They acknowledge that preaching is the ordinary means of salvation, 'and yet for al that in their ordinarie discourses they make knowne their opinion thus, that the word of God is as effectuall when it is reade, as when it is preached, and that reading is preaching'. Epaphras replies that the superiority of preaching over mere reading is shown by experience. Parishes 'where there hath beene only reading' are full of ignorance and superstition, whereas 'those which have beene furnished with a setled preaching Minister' are well grounded in the scriptures.[43] Moreover, the opposition that preaching arouses is further proof of its power:

Take mee therefore a common man whom you meet by chance and question with him touching the place where he dwelleth, and about his minister: if he be but a Reader, you shall have him say straite, Truely we have a good honest quiet man, mary indeed he cannot preach, but he liveth peaceably, and medleth with no man, and is very well beloved amongst us: for why, he is a fellowlike man, &c: but put case the minister be a painfull preacher, one that seeketh to draw the people from their godlesse and superstitious courses, to the knowledge of God, then you shall heare him in another tune; he wil say then, there we have a man, some say he is learned, but sure I am he hath troubled us all, a good many of us wish he had never come amongst us, we were all quiet before, but now all is out of frame, there is such reproving and finding of fault, and bringing up of new fashions and orders, that we know not what to do, some of the best of our parish will doe what they can to remove him . . .[44]

Epaphras's final, clinching argument is drawn from the style of the scriptures themselves. The Bible is so deep and complex that it requires preaching, rather than mere reading, to open it up and draw out its full meaning: 'for indeede it cannot be, that a briefe clause of holy scripture, wherein in a shorte tenor of wordes (such is the riches of the sacred text) many particulars are comprised, being only reade, shoulde profit so much, as if by preaching it were expounded, and by occasions applied unto Gods people'. Nymphas agrees, and adds that he has found this to be true 'out of my own experience'. He has benefited a great deal from reading the scriptures, or hearing them read by others, yet he has 'often beene altogether mistaken' in his understanding of them, which has taught him to distrust his own judgement until he hears it confirmed by the preacher.[45]

---

[43] Hieron, *Preachers Plea*, H7r.   [44] Hieron, *Preachers Plea*, I2r.   [45] Hieron, *Preachers Plea*, I2v.

Hieron's treatise had a lasting impact – so much so that in 1624, twenty years after its first publication, Bishop Carey of Exeter commissioned another Devonshire minister, John Downe, to preach a visitation sermon responding to it. Downe was respectful towards Hieron (who had died in 1617), and refrained from any personal criticism of him – '*De mortuis nil nisi bene:* he was while hee lived a grave and reverend preacher' – but maintained 'that reading is an ordinary means to beget Faith', a position directly opposed to that of Hieron in *The Preachers Plea*. Oliver Naylor, vicar of Tawstock in Devon, wrote to his friend John Cosin in May 1624 warmly recommending Downe's sermon, which he described as a response to 'the tenents of a Puritan heere amongst us' – almost certainly a reference to Hieron – 'who, amongst other things, defended that there was no ordinarie meanes of salvation in that congregation that had only the publique prayers, the reading of Scriptures and the reading of homilies, the administration of the Sacraments, &c., concluding nothing to be avaylable that way, but only the hearing of sermons'.[46] As this letter suggests, Downe's sermon was not only a replay of the Admonition Controversy, with Downe playing Whitgift to Hieron's Cartwright, but also anticipated what would soon become a central feature of Laudian apologetic, with an emphasis on prayer and the sacraments as a counterweight to the puritan emphasis on preaching. The sermon 'gave so great satisfaction', Naylor told Cosin, 'that his fellow ministers have persuaded him to publish the same, thinking he will doe much good both heere and in other places by it', though it did not in fact appear in print until 1633, in a posthumous edition of Downe's collected works.[47]

Downe argued, as Whitgift had done, that preaching should be defined in broad terms as 'the publishing, or notifying, or making knowne of Gods word', an activity which could include reading the Bible as well as expounding it in a sermon. While he acknowledged that the preaching of sermons was generally more effective than the reading of scripture lessons, he argued that the difference was merely one of degree rather than one of kind – that is, the laity could learn the basic doctrines of Christianity 'more speedily and easily' by listening to a preacher than by reading the Bible for themselves, just as an apprentice could learn his trade more quickly by watching his master than by teaching himself. Thus, in an ideal world, every parish

---

[46] Oliver Naylor to John Cosin, 11 May 1624, in *Correspondence of John Cosin*, ed. G. Ornsby, vol. 1 (London, 1869), pp. 19–20.

[47] 'Concerning the force and efficacy of reading', in John Downe, *Certaine Treatises* (Oxford, 1633), H4v.

would have its own preaching minister, but in places where 'sufficient Ministers, or . . . sufficient maintenance cannot be had', it was acceptable to appoint clergy who could read but not preach. 'In such a case better a Reader than none.' Downe supported this with a more theoretical argument about the relative merits of hearing and sight. The two senses, he declared, were not inherently different, so that reading the Word of God was 'analogicall and proportionable' to hearing it preached. 'In scripture, the heavens and the firmament are said to have a speech . . . The word written hath in like manner *a mouth, a voice, a speech* given unto it, whereby it speaketh, it cryeth, it testifieth: and when we looke upon it or read it for our instruction we are said to heare.'[48] If the written word could 'speak', then how could it be said to differ from the voice of the preacher?

Downe also took issue with Hieron on the question of biblical style. Hieron, as we have seen, argued that scripture was too complex to be fully understood by unaided reading. Downe challenged this, insisting that scripture, on its own, was sufficient to bring people to faith and repentance, even without the added support of the preaching ministry. 'For it presenteth unto us a store of strong motives to perswade, sweet promises to allure, terrible threatnings to affright, notable examples to imitate, and the like: than which there cannot be a better outward meanes, and there needs no more but the inward concurrence of Gods spirit to worke a perfect conversion.' To be sure, there were some difficult passages in scripture, but in the words of St Gregory (in his *Morals on Job*), 'as there are deepe places where the Elephant may swim, so there are shallow where the Lamb may wade', or in the words of St Paul himself (1 Cor. 3: 2), if there is meat for strong men, there is also milk for babes. 'And I boldly affirme that all fundamentall points and duties necessary to salvation are in Scripture so clearly delivered, that if they were written with a sunbeame they could not bee more cleare.'[49] This difference of emphasis – with puritans stressing the depth and complexity of scripture, while conformists stressed its essential simplicity – is one we shall encounter again later.

Similar exchanges were going on in many other parts of the country. In Essex: where two ministers, Thomas Rogers and Miles Mosse, engaged in a fierce debate over the efficacy of the written word. Some deprecatory remarks by Mosse about the superfluity of printed books, in which he declared that 'books are but dead letters', led Rogers to publish a treatise in defence of reading. 'Doth it convert? I thinke it no error to hold that

---

[48] Downe, *Certaine Treatises*, B1r, c3v.  [49] Downe, *Certaine Treatises*, D2r.

writings may convert.'[50] In Kent: where Martin Fotherby preached a
sermon before Archbishop Bancroft in 1607, arguing that 'all the bookes
of the Scriptures are Preachers unto us ... not onely when they bee
expounded, but also when they are humbly and faithfully read'. This
sermon, we are told, was bitterly criticised by 'certaine seduced, and seduc-
ing spirits' who 'make no end of traducing it to the world, as tending
directly unto the disgrace of preaching'.[51] In Lincolnshire: where John
Cotton declared at a visitation sermon in 1614 that 'reading was not preaching', a doctrine which Bishop Neile's commissioners singled out as one of
his principal errors. 'If he had said it had not been interpretation, none
would have gaynsayd or opposed him; but his meaning was as we did gather
it, as if reading were not one of the meanes that God hath appointed for
mans salvation.'[52] In all these cases, the reading/preaching distinction
formed the crucial dividing line between puritans (such as Mosse and
Cotton) on the one hand, and conformists (such as Rogers and Fotherby)
on the other.

   This is a point of considerable significance: for one of the gaps in the
current historiography of the early Stuart Church is a clear analysis of what
divided puritans from conformists. It is clear that they could, and did,
disagree over certain issues of Church discipline (subscription to the
Articles, acceptance of episcopacy) and ceremonial practice (kneeling at
Communion, wearing the surplice, using the Cross in baptism), but it is not
at all clear how these specific issues might relate to more general disagreements over religion and doctrine. Yet here we have a dispute between
puritans and conformists which seems to relate not only to specific issues
of Church discipline, but also to much wider questions about the role of the
ministry, the nature and significance of preaching and even the interpretation of the scriptures. The position I am outlining here is broadly similar to
that of Peter Lake, who has argued strongly that Puritanism had its own
distinctive identity and cannot simply be subsumed into a wider Protestant
consensus.[53] But whereas Lake prefers to speak of a 'puritan style or

---

[50]  Thomas Rogers, *Miles Christianus, or a Iust Apologie of All Necessarie Writings and Writers* (1590), D2v.
     Rogers's annotated copy is in the British Library (shelfmark C. 124. c. 7) and is mentioned and
     discussed in Patrick Collinson, *Godly People: Essays on English Protestantism and Puritanism* (1983),
     p. 478, and Collinson, John Craig and Brett Usher, eds., *Conferences and Combination Lectures in the
     Elizabethan Church, 1582–1590* (Church of England Record Society, 2003), pp. cx–cxi.
[51]  Martin Fotherby, *Foure Sermons, Lately Preached* (1608), A2r.
[52]  'Bishop Neile's primary visitation, AD 1614', *Associated Architectural Societies' Reports and Papers*, 16: 1
     (1881), p. 51.
[53]  Peter Lake, *The Boxmaker's Revenge: 'Orthodoxy', 'Heterodoxy' and the Politics of the Parish in Early
     Stuart London* (Manchester, 2001), p. 12.

attitude', I would go further and argue for the existence of a distinctive puritan ideology. I am not suggesting that the disagreements between puritans and conformists can be boiled down to a difference in theology (Calvinist vs. Anglican) or in philosophical method (Ramist vs. Aristotelian); indeed, it is hard to see how this could possibly be the case, given that puritan and conformist clergy received the same intellectual training at the same academic institutions. Rather, I would describe it as a difference in ecclesiology, with a host of practical implications for the social and cultural life of the Church.

This does not mean that puritans and conformists were locked into fixed ideological positions, endlessly reiterating the same old arguments. For a start, there was a good deal of common ground between the two sides. Hieron, for example, was able to bolster his case for the necessity of preaching by citing the works of Bishop Jewel, one of the books officially ordered to be placed in churches, in which non-preaching clergy were denounced as 'idle and slothfull Ministers' who were failing in their duty to their parishioners. This enabled Hieron to argue, not implausibly, that it was 'the judgement of our Church' – not just the judgement of a few puritan dissidents – that all ministers should be able to preach.[54] In the same way, Downe was able to bolster his case for the sufficiency of reading by citing William Ames's *Medulla Theologiae*, one of the standard puritan textbooks of divinity, in which the hearing of the Word was defined as 'any perceiving of the will of God', not necessarily involving the hearing of an audible voice. This enabled Downe to argue, again not implausibly, that even puritans saw no inherent difference between hearing and reading.[55] To be sure, both Hieron and Downe were keenly aware of the polemical advantage to be gained from turning their opponents' authorities against them. But this was only possible because there genuinely was some common ground here – both sides *did* believe that all ministers should be able to preach; both sides *did* believe that God's will was communicated through the written as well as the spoken word – and this gave writers such as Hieron and Downe a measure of flexibility in the way they chose to frame the debate.

Moreover, both sides drew freely on the same stock of commonplaces. For an example, we can turn to the passage from St Gregory's *Morals on Job*, mentioned above, where the scriptures are compared to a river 'both shallow

---

[54] Samuel Hieron, *The Dignitie of Preaching* (1615), B3r, D1v.
[55] Downe, *Certaine Treatises*, F2v, citing William Ames, *Medulla Theologiae*, 2.8.5–6. See William Ames, *The Marrow of Sacred Divinity* (1642), Hh2v, for this passage in English translation.

and deep, in which the lamb may paddle and the elephant swim'.[56] This was one of the most familiar patristic commonplaces of the early modern period, quoted or cited in almost every discussion of biblical style and interpretation.[57] But it could be used in a variety of different and often contradictory ways. In disputes between Protestants and Catholics it could be used by one side to demonstrate the benefit of reading the Bible (since even the humblest reader might learn something from studying the simpler passages) and by the other to demonstrate the danger of reading the Bible (since unlearned readers might easily find themselves out of their depth). In disputes between conformists and puritans, it could be used by one side to demonstrate the sufficiency of reading (since anyone could understand the fundamental points of scripture without the need for a preacher to interpret them) and by the other to demonstrate the necessity of preaching (since some passages were too difficult to be understood without the help of a skilled interpreter). This use of a shared set of commonplaces is one of the most distinctive aspects of early modern religious controversy, and perhaps one of the hardest for the modern reader to grasp.

We can see how this worked in practice if we look at the way that puritan writers adapted their arguments to different polemical contexts. The basic puritan position, as we have seen, was that reading was insufficient without preaching. As William Perkins put it, the scriptures were 'most perfect in themselves, yet are they not so profitable unto us, till they be explained and applied to our consciences in the ministerie of the word: as a loafe of the finest bread is unfit for nourishment till it be quartered and shived out unto us'.[58] The trouble with this argument was that it came dangerously close to the Roman Catholic position that scripture was insufficient without tradition. Bellarmine, for example, had argued that the clergy had to expound and interpret the scriptures before giving them to the laity, just as a mother would crumble a loaf of bread before giving it to her child. Naturally, conformist writers were quick to seize on this parallel in order to embarrass their puritan opponents. In his *Conference with Fisher*, Laud remarked on the paradoxical fact that 'the Jesuit in the Church of Rome, and the precise

---

[56] Migne, *Patrologia Latina*, first series, vol. LXXV, p. 515: '*quasi quidam quippe est fluvius, ut ita dixerim, planus et altus, in quo et agnus ambulet, et elephas natet*'.

[57] For some typical examples, see Whitaker, *Disputation on Holy Scripture*, p. 374; Downame, *A Guide to Godlynesse*; 3H5v; John Northbrooke, *Spiritus est Vicarius Christi in Terra, The Poore Mans Garden* (1575), G8v; Lake, *Sermons*, 2K4r; Morton, *A Catholike Appeale for Protestants*, H2r; and Griffith Williams, *The Best Religion* (1636), 4X2v.

[58] William Perkins, *A Warning against the Idolatrie of the Last Times* (Cambridge, 1601), O1v. Thomas Taylor declared that doctrine without application was 'as a loafe of bread set among the children, but none can they get cut and given them': *Works* (1653), (E)1r.

party in the reformed Churches' were in agreement on many things, even in those points where 'they would seem most to differ'. Thus, even though they appeared to disagree over tradition – the Jesuit exalting it and the puritan denigrating it – they 'both agree in this consequent, that the sermons and preachings by word of mouth of the lawfully sent pastors and doctors of the Church, are able to breed in us divine and infallible faith: nay, are the very word of God'. 'Howsoever these men may differ from Papists in other opinions', agreed John Downe, 'yet I see not how they can cleare themselves from Popery in this.'[59]

A further problem for many puritans was that they found their own arguments being turned against them by radical separatists. If the reading of a homily was no substitute for the preaching of a sermon, then how – as John Greenwood demanded in 1590 – could the reading of the Book of Common Prayer be justified as a substitute for extempore prayer? If reading was insufficient in the one case, why not in the other? This analogy was developed in more detail by the separatist Sabine Staresmore in a pamphlet uncompromisingly entitled *The Unlawfulnes of Reading in Prayer* (1619). 'If you should take another mans penned sermon, and either read it or repeat it by heart to your auditorie, and would make them beleeve it is your owne Sermon uttered by the Spirit, men of understanding would think you did but mock them.' In the same way, Staresmore argued, 'the bare reading of another mans praier' made a mockery of true prayer, which should arise spontaneously from the heart. And Staresmore concluded by appropriating the very argument that Cartwright had used against Whitgift. Reading 'thrusteth out the ministeriall gift of the spirit', for even 'a child . . . though utterlie voyd of all pastorall gift', could read a prayer as well as any lawfully qualified minister.[60]

Puritans responded to these challenges by shifting their ground. In dispute with conformists, they tended to argue that reading and preaching were fundamentally different in kind: one could convert, the other could not. In dispute with Papists and separatists, they tended to argue that reading and preaching were fundamentally the same, sharing a 'true sense and meaning' that made them interchangeable. Thus Richard Bernard, replying to his separatist opponents, argued that there was no practical difference between written and extempore prayer. 'The Minister reads upon

[59] William Laud, *Works*, ed. W. Scott and J. Bliss (Oxford, 1847–60), vol. II, p. 113. Downe, *Certaine Treatises*, E2v.
[60] John Greenwood, *An Answere to George Gifford's Pretended Defence of Read Prayers and Devised Litourgies* (1590), reprinted in *The Writings of John Greenwood 1587–1590*, ed. Leland H. Carlson (1962), p. 60; Sabine Staresmore, *The Unlawfulnes of Reading in Prayer* (Amsterdam, 1619), C5r.

a Booke, but the people receive his words by voice into their mindes . . . To the people it is all one to heare their Minister pray from the Booke, as from his brayne. For it is the matter agreeing to the words rightly conceaved, and in heart affected, which maketh the thing to be approved of God.'[61] (Why the same argument should not apply to the reading of a homily was a question that Bernard did not address.) Even Henry Ainsworth, in dispute with John Smyth, was prepared to collapse the distinction between reading and preaching, by arguing that 'writing and reading the law is a part of preaching the law': the two are 'one joynt action . . . as one and the same word is used in the holy tongue both for *to read* and *to preach*', and reading the Bible was therefore a lawful part of Christian worship, no less than preaching a sermon. Smyth had used the familiar argument against reading, that even a child could do it. Ainsworth replied that reading and preaching were 'joyned togither', so that 'he that condemns the one outward action because a child can doe it, condemneth also the other by the like reason'.[62]

It is striking to find puritans such as Bernard and Ainsworth adopting what, in other contexts, would be typical conformist arguments about the basic similarity of reading and preaching. It illustrates the fluidity and instability of ideas about spoken and written language – which, it could be argued, is typical of a mixed oral/literate culture such as that of early modern England. But what is also striking is how little the character of the debate changed between 1573, when Cartwright argued in his reply to Whitgift that 'if it be true that reading is preaching, then . . . a child of four or five years old is able to preach because he is able to read', and 1643, when William Dowsing used the same knockdown argument to silence the fellows of Pembroke Hall: 'I told them, if reading was preaching, my child preaches as well as they, and they stared one on another without answere.'[63] This binary opposition between Puritanism and conformism – given its definitive expression in the Admonition Controversy – was certainly not the whole truth, but it was a highly effective way of distinguishing between two alternative (and genuinely different) positions. And at the very heart of the puritan position was a conviction that the spoken word could not be subsumed into the written word, or (to put it in Weberian terms) that the charismatic power of preaching could not be subsumed into the routine act of reading a written text.

---

[61] Richard Bernard, *Plaine Evidences: the Church of England is Apostolicall, the Seperation Schismaticall* (1610), I3r.
[62] Ainsworth, *Defence of the Holy Scriptures*, I2v.
[63] Whitgift, *Works*, vol. III, p. 39; *The Journal of William Dowsing*, ed. Trevor Cooper (Woodbridge, 2001), p. 161. Cf. Francis Rogers, *A Visitation Sermon* (1633), C2r: 'a child of ten, or twelve yeares old may read distinctly, to the edification of the hearer'.

### THE LAUDIAN CHALLENGE

The emergence of Laudianism in the 1620s and 1630s led to a reappraisal of the whole debate on reading and preaching. In this, as in other respects, Laudianism can be seen as an outgrowth of the existing conformist position, characterised, in Anthony Milton's words, by 'the manipulation of inconsistencies' within the Jacobean consensus, rather than by 'the importation of totally new doctrines'.[64] More specifically, it can be seen as a development of some lines of thought begun by Richard Hooker in his classic defence of the Elizabethan settlement, *Of the Laws of Ecclesiastical Polity*. But while its origins were perfectly conventional, its implications were extremely far reaching, for it amounted to a radical downgrading of the role of preaching which went far beyond anything previously seen in the Elizabethan or Jacobean Church.

Hooker's discussion of the issue, in the fifth book of the *Laws*, begins disarmingly by stressing that he does not mean to deny the importance of preaching, but merely to strike the right balance between preaching and reading. Sermons are 'keyes to the kingdome of heaven', 'winges to the soule' and 'spurres to the good affection of man', supplying food to the healthy and medicine to the sick. 'Wherefore how highlie soever it may please them with wordes of truth to extoll sermons, they shall not offend us.'[65] But he argues that by 'overvaluinge their sermons', his puritan opponents have mistakenly undervalued the public reading of the scriptures. Why, he asks, should 'a Christian mans beliefe . . . so naturallie grow from sermons, and not possiblie from any other kinde of teachinge'? While it is true that preaching has 'sundrie peculiar and proper vertues, such as no other waie of teachinge besides hath', it is not the only ordinary means of faith. Reading, too, has the power 'to convert, to edifie, to save soules'. 'In this therefore preachinge and readinge are equall, that both are approved as [God's] ordinances, both assisted with his grace.' And although we may regret the fact that not all parishes in England are supplied with a preaching minister, we may take comfort from the fact that they are 'not left in so extreeme destitution, that justlie any man should thinke the ordinarie meanes of eternall life taken from them, because theire teachinge is in publique for the most parte but by readinge'.[66]

---

[64] Anthony Milton, 'The Church of England, Rome, and the True Church: the demise of a Jacobean consensus', in Kenneth Fincham, ed., *The Early Stuart Church, 1603–1642* (Stanford, CA, 1993), pp. 187–210 (quotation p. 210).

[65] Richard Hooker, *Of the Laws of Ecclesiastical Polity*, Book V, ed. W. Speed Hill (Folger Library Edition of the Works of Richard Hooker, vol. II) (Cambridge, MA, 1977) p. 87 (V.22.1).

[66] Hooker, *Laws*, pp. 104–5 (V.22.17).

Thus far, Hooker's argument does not greatly differ from Whitgift's. It is only when he starts to weigh up the relative merits of reading and preaching that the originality of his position starts to become apparent. Whitgift had argued that while reading was useful, preaching was clearly preferable. 'Both reading and preaching be necessary in the church and most profitable: the commendation of the one doth not take anything from the other. But preaching doth profit more than reading doth, because it is more apt for the ignorant and unlearned ... it doth more commonly profit, and serveth more to the instruction of those which are ignorant ... it more plainly expresseth the meaning of the scripture and applieth the same.' In this he was followed by other conformist writers such as Gervase Babington, who summarised the point pithily: 'reading profiteth, but preaching more: and reading therefore is good, but preaching is better.'[67] Yet Hooker argued that in some respects, reading was actually preferable to preaching. 'For there is nothinge which is not somewaye exceld even by that which it doth excell. Sermons therefore and lessons may ech excell other in some respectes, without any prejudice to either, as touchinge that vitall force which they both have in the worke of our salvation.'[68] This is a startling departure from the standard conformist line.

What, then, does Hooker see as the particular virtues of preaching and reading which cause them 'each to excel the other in some respects'? On the one hand, he argues that the virtue of preaching is derived from its rhetorical power, its 'aptnes to followe particular occasions presentlie growinge, to put life into wordes by countenance voice and gesture, to prevaile mightilie in the suddaine affections of men'. On the other, he argues that the virtue of reading is derived from its direct access to the Word of God, unsullied by human interpretations. 'Readinge dothe convey to the minde that truth without addition or diminution, which scripture hath derived from the holie Ghost.' Preaching, he suggests, does not have the same claim to divine authority:

For touchinge our sermons, that which giveth them their verie beinge is the witt of man, and therefore they oftentimes accordinglie tast too much of that over corrupt fountaine from which they come ... Wherefore when we reade or recite the scripture, we then deliver to the people *properlie* the word of God. As for our sermons, be they never so sound and perfect, his worde they are not as the sermons of the prophetes were, no they are but ambiguouslie termed his worde, because his worde is commonlie the subject whereof they treat, and must be the rule whereby they are framed.

---

[67] Gervase Babington, *A Profitable Exposition of the Lords Prayer* (1588), N7v; Downe, *Certaine Treatises*, E4r.
[68] Hooker, *Laws*, pp. 100–1 (V.22.12).

Sermons are, properly speaking, only commentaries on the Word of God – 'the expositions which our discorse of witt doth gather and minister out of the worde of God' – not the Word of God itself. 'We therefore have no word of God but the Scripture.'[69]

At first sight, this may not seem a particularly remarkable conclusion. After all, everyone – puritans and conformists alike – accepted that scripture had greater authority than preaching. As Arthur Hildersham observed, the Word read was 'of farre greater excellency, authority, and certainety than the Sermon of any Preacher in the world' because it came more immediately from God, 'and though it be translated by men, yet is there in it farre lesse mixture of humane ignorance, and infirmity, than in preaching'. (This led Hildersham to argue that we should take our hats off when hearing the Word read, but not when listening to a sermon, because 'some further gesture and outward signification of reverence is to be used, than is required at the hearing of the Sermon'.) But Hildersham then proceeded to qualify this almost out of existence, by arguing, first, that 'the people of God doe (out of doubt) receive more profit and comfort by the Word preached, than by the Word read', and secondly, that 'God workes more mightily by the preaching of the Word, than by the Word read'.[70] This was an awkward compromise. Scripture, it seemed, was more authoritative than preaching, yet at the same time less profitable, less comfortable and less powerful in its operation. Hooker fastened on the paradox at once, drawing attention to his opponents' very half-hearted justifications of the value of hearing the Word read, and remarking sardonically that it would be strange indeed if 'the verie cheifest cause of committinge the sacred worde of God unto bookes' should have been to provide texts for sermons'.[71]

Hooker's influence can clearly be seen in some of the conformist writings of the early seventeenth century. Martin Fotherby, for example, asserted in 1607 that preaching was 'not alwaies more effectual than reading'. In fact, he went on, reading could be said to be 'the most divine and authenticall kind of Preaching, because it delivereth the word of God, most simply and sincerely in his owne proper forme', without any mixture of human inventions. Thus 'sermons ought to have no greater credit with us, than they can gaine unto themselves by their agreement with the Scriptures', and while they might be

---

[69] Hooker, *Laws*, p. 99 (v.22.10), p. 84 (v.21.2).
[70] Arthur Hildersham, *CVIII Lectures upon the Fourth of Iohn* (2nd edn., 1632), M2v (p. 126), based on sermons preached in 1610. For a similar passage, see Robert Bolton, *A Three-fold Treatise* (1634), P2r, where it is argued that while reading 'is to have place, and due respect in the Congregation . . . wee will not equall it to Preaching', as the latter is 'more excellent, and of greater force to convert'.
[71] Hooker, *Laws*, p. 93 (v.22.7).

called 'the truth of God' or 'the doctrine of God' if their teachings were in accord with the scriptures, they could not be termed 'the word of God', except 'by some Metonymie, or Synecdoche, or some other such unproper and figurative speech'. In short: 'a Sermon is not so the word of God as the text itselfe is, but a discourse framed upon it by the wit of man'.[72] This was taken up by a number of Laudian writers, including Christopher Dow, who declared in 1637 – borrowing Hooker's own words – that 'we have no Word of God but the Scripture', and that sermons were merely 'the expositions which our discourse of wit doth gather and minister out of the Word of God'.[73] Laud himself, in his *Conference with Fisher*, praised sermons as 'most necessary expositions and applications of Holy Scripture, and a great ordinary means of saving knowledge', but stressed that they should not be regarded as divinely infallible, for 'no less than so, have some accounted of their own factious words, to say no more, than as the word of God'.[74]

This forces us to reconsider some of our assumptions about the role of scripture in early modern religious controversy. One tends to assume that it was the puritans who placed most emphasis on scripture, and Hooker who placed most emphasis on tradition, yet here we have precisely the opposite situation, with Hooker and his followers stressing the unique authority of scripture in far stronger terms than their puritan opponents. This anomaly has not gone wholly unnoticed, but the historians who have noticed it have not always grasped the implications. For example, Patrick Collinson's magisterial survey, *The Religion of Protestants*, takes its title from William Chillingworth's famous dictum, 'the Bible, the Bible only I say, is the religion of Protestants', but uses this as the starting point for a discussion of the early modern Church of England in which Puritanism is central and Chillingworth himself (as Collinson frankly admits) 'largely peripheral'.[75] Similarly, Peter Lake has drawn attention to the Laudians' use of arguments from scripture – which, as he rightly points out, is indicative of a more complex and subtle attitude to biblical authority than has generally been assumed – but sees this as largely opportunistic, with the Laudians deploying scriptural arguments chiefly for polemical purposes and only where it suited them to do so.[76] Yet none of this should really surprise us. Just as it was natural for puritans to stress the power of the spoken word, so it was

---

[72]  Fotherby, *Foure Sermons*, H1r.
[73]  Christopher Dow, *Innovations Unjustly Charged upon the Present Church and State* (1637), Y1r.
[74]  Laud, *Works*, vols. II, p. 113, and VII, p. 661.    [75] Collinson, *Religion of Protestants*, p. viii.
[76]  Peter Lake, 'The Laudians and the argument from authority', in B. Y. Kunze and D. D. Brautigan, eds., *Court, Country and Culture: Essays on Early Modern British History in Honor of Perez Zagorin* (Rochester, NY, 1992), pp. 149–76.

natural for Laudians to stress the authority of the written word – and once we have grasped this contrast, it comes as no surprise to find Laudians using scriptural arguments, or the freethinking Chillingworth (no puritan he) writing in defence of a Bible-centred Protestantism.

To return to Hooker for a moment: one of the points which Hooker took particular pains to stress, in his discussion of reading and preaching, was the plainness of scripture. Many things in the scriptures are 'so plaine, that everie common person may therein be unto him selfe a sufficient expounder', and can therefore be understood by reading alone, without the help of preaching. Moreover, these plain doctrines include everything necessary for salvation. 'The force of readinge how smale soever they would have it, must of necessitie be graunted sufficient to notifie that which is plaine or easie to be understood. And of thinges necessarie to all mens salvation . . . they are in scripture plaine and easie to be understood.' Hooker's argument emerges more clearly if we express it in the form of a syllogism:

1. Anything plain or easy to be understood, can be apprehended by reading.
2. But all things necessary to salvation are plain and easy to be understood.
3. Therefore all things necessary to salvation can be apprehended by reading.

'Scripture therefore is not so harde but that the onlie reading thereof may give life unto willinge hearers.' And Hooker goes on to praise the goodness of God in making these things so accessible to us. Is it not a sign of God's wonderful providence that this 'foode of eternall life' is placed within our reach? 'Surely if wee perish it is not the lacke of Scribes and learned expounders that can be our just excuse. The worde which saveth our soules is neere us, we need for knowledge but to read and live.'[77]

Again, this may not seem a particularly surprising conclusion. Everyone – puritan and conformist alike – agreed that all the articles of faith were plainly set down in the scriptures. One of the central arguments of William Whitaker's *Disputation on Holy Scripture* was that 'all things necessary to salvation are propounded in plain words [*apertis verbis*] in the scriptures' so that the Papists had no justification for withholding the Bible from the people. But on close examination, Whitaker's argument proves to be hedged with qualifications. He admits that the plainness of the scriptures enables them to be read by the unlearned with 'some fruit and utility' ('*cum fructu aliquo ac utilitate legi possint*'), but immediately adds that 'there are

---

[77] Hooker, *Laws*, pp. 102–3 (v.22.14–15).

many obscure places; that the scriptures need explication; and that, on this account, God's ministers are to be listened to when they expound the word of God'. In short, the benefits of reading are strictly limited and do not take away the need for preaching.[78] Hooker makes no such qualifications. Instead, he argues that the plainness of the scriptures makes them ideally suited for instructing the unlearned. One of their most important functions is 'to furnish the verie simplest and rudest sorte with such infallible axiomes and preceptes of sacred truth, delivered even in the verie letter of the law of God, as may serve them for rules whereby to judge the better all other doctrines and instructions which they heare'. Thus reading is not only preferable to preaching, but sets the standard against which preaching is to be judged.

This distinctively Hookerian emphasis on the plainness of scripture was enthusiastically adopted by the conformist writers of the next generation – though rather than attributing it to Hooker, they chose to present it as an established part of Protestant orthodoxy. Martin Fotherby, for example, expressed it in terms of a contrast between Popish obscurity and Protestant clarity. The Papists, on the one hand, say that the scriptures 'are darke and obscure, and such as cannot teach us, much lesse preach unto us, because they lacke a voyce'. We, on the other hand, say that the scriptures are like a light shining in the darkness, 'they being in themselves so facile and evident, that they are able to instruct even the simple and idiot, in all doctrine necessarie unto their salvation'. John Downe, too, sought to camouflage the originality of his position by reaching for St Gregory's well-worn simile of elephants and lambs. 'It cannot be denied but that some things [in the scriptures] are difficult: yet as there are deepe places where the Elephant may swim, so there are shallow where the lamb may wade ... And I boldly affirme that all fundamentall points and duties necessary to salvation are in Scripture so clearly delivered, that if they were written with a sunbeame they could not bee more cleare.'[79]

The scriptures were not, of course, uniformly plain and clear. Indeed, certain passages were highly obscure. (This was recognised by one contemporary reader of Fotherby's sermons, who responded to Fotherby's confident assertion of the plainness of scripture with a short but sharp marginal annotation: 'Tell me, Mr Dr, doe you speake of the whole scripture or of part?'[80]) Some conformist writers, however, were ready to counter this objection by arguing that the plain texts of scripture were the only ones

---

[78] Whitaker, *Disputatio de Sacra Scriptura*, p. 364.     [79] Downe, *Certaine Treatises*, D2r.
[80] Fotherby, *Foure Sermons*, E3v; Cambridge University Library, Syn. 7. 63. 56.

that really mattered to ordinary Christians. In a sermon preached at Oxford in 1617, John Hales advised his audience to ground their faith on 'the plaine uncontroversible text of Scripture' rather than struggling to interpret the more difficult passages. Even his fellow preachers, he suggested, would be better advised to concentrate on the 'plaine texts of Scripture', as being of 'sufficient strength' to refute the arguments of their Popish adversaries. As for 'places of ambiguous and doubtfull, or darke and intricate meaning', it would be better to 'suspend our beleefe, and confesse our ignorance' rather than trying to wrest an interpretation out of obscurity.[81] There are clear affinities here with the religious minimalism of the Great Tew circle which, taken to its logical extreme, would eventually lead to the position of Chillingworth (and later Hobbes), that the whole of Christianity was deducible from the single axiom that Jesus was the Christ – all else being both unnecessary and liable to provoke harmful disagreement.[82]

These were strikingly innovative arguments, but, as before, could be camouflaged as harmlessly orthodox by appealing to the traditional Protestant commonplace of the single literal sense of scripture. Emphasis on the literal sense was a standard part of Protestant hermeneutics, most famously expressed by William Perkins in his treatise on preaching, *The Art of Prophecying* (1592) – 'there is one onely sense, and the same is the literall' – in opposition to the medieval theory of the fourfold sense of scripture (literal, analogical, tropological and anagogical).[83] This was echoed by Hales, who declared that 'the litterall, plaine, and uncontroversable meaning of Scripture without any addition or supply by way of interpretation, is that alone which for ground of faith we are necessarily bound to accept'. Edward Boughen, preaching at a visitation sermon in Canterbury in 1635, argued in similar terms that all rules of faith must be interpreted according to their 'common' and 'plaine' meaning, without any metaphors or figures of speech. 'Take the words as they lye, take them *according to the plaine and common sense and understanding of the same words*, and then controversies and contradictions will take their wings, and fly to unsetled and untutor'd Churches. It is a rule in judicious Hooker, *In Scripture, where a literall construction will stand, the furthest from the letter is commonly the worst* . . . I would to God, we were all of Master Hookers minde, and then we should have no divisions among us.'[84]

[81] John Hales, *A Sermon . . . Concerning the Abuses of Obscure and Difficult Places of Holy Scripture* (Oxford, 1617).
[82] For Chillingworth, see Lambeth Palace Library, London, MS 943, p. 876; for Hobbes, see Richard Tuck, *Hobbes* (Oxford, 1989), p. 84.
[83] William Perkins, *The Art of Prophecying*, in *Works* (1613), vol. II, 3I2r (p. 651).
[84] Edward Boughen, *Two Sermons* (1635), D1v, citing Hooker's *Laws*, v.59.

This high view of scripture, and exaltation of the literal sense, were not simply adopted for polemical purposes. Writers in the Hookerian tradition saw the scriptures as safeguarding the stability of Christian doctrine and thus protecting the Church from any contamination by false teaching or preaching. It followed that they could not accept the possibililty of any ambiguity in the written text, for, as Hales pointed out, 'if the words admit a double sense, and I follow one, who can assure mee that that which I followe is the truth?' The logic of their position therefore required them to adopt a highly conservative stance on the textual criticism of the Bible. Edward Kellet was deeply suspicious of Beza's edition of the Greek New Testament because of its alterations to the received text, such as its emendation of Luke 22: 20 to bring it into line with the other Synoptic Gospels. 'To put into the Text, or to take from it', he declared, 'as some Philologizing Neotericks endeavour in their super-nice criticisme', was 'to tear up the very foundation of religion.' It was all right to correct obvious scribal errors by referring to earlier, more authoritative manuscripts, for 'who ever denyed, but that some Copies have been corrupted, and in some of them, some words foisted in?' But to say that all the extant copies were corrupt, and to use one's own judgement in making emendations to the text, was extremely dangerous, for then 'how will you prove any part or word of the New Testament to be uncorrupt? Which razeth up the very Corner-stone of our Faith.'[85]

These arguments were brought to a head in Robert Shelford's *Five Pious and Learned Discourses*, published in Cambridge in 1635. Shelford is a fascinating figure, who had been a pupil of Andrew Perne at Peterhouse in the 1580s and whose churchmanship, while closely aligned with Laudianism in many respects, had been developed in isolation and seems almost to represent a throwback to early Elizabethan styles of divinity predating the ascendancy of Calvinism. The *Discourses* caused consternation in Calvinist circles; from Ireland, Archbishop Ussher wrote to Samuel Ward demanding to know how such a book could have been licensed and printed at Cambridge. 'While we strive here to maintain the purity of our ancient truth, how cometh it to passe that you in Cambridge do cast such stumbling blocks in our way? by publishing unto the world such rotten stuff as Shelford hath vented in his five discourses . . .'[86] Ussher's dismay centred on the fifth of the five discourses, 'A Treatise shewing the Antichrist not to

---

[85] Edward Kellet, *Miscellanies of Divinitie* (Cambridge, 1635), x6v (ii. 36); R. R. Orr, *Reason and Authority: The Thought of William Chillingworth* (Oxford, 1967), pp. 83, 91, 105.

[86] Ussher to Ward, 15 September 1635, printed in Ussher's *Works*, ed. C. R. Elrington and J. H. Todd (1847–64), vol. XVI, p. 9.

be yet come', in which Shelford not only rejected the theory of the Pope as Antichrist but declared that Protestants and Papists were essentially in agreement and that the attitude of Protestants to their Catholic 'brethren' should be one of 'light and oblique dissent' rather than open confrontation. But this was by no means the only controversial section of the book. More significant, for our present purposes, are Shelford's views on the reading/ preaching debate, which develop the Hookerian arguments discussed above and carry them to a new extreme.

To begin with, Shelford argued that reading was preaching – 'and not onely preaching, but lively and working preaching, working upon mens souls to grace and goodnesse'. This was not merely a reiteration of the standard conformist position. Shelford was not arguing, as Whitgift had done, that reading was a part of preaching; nor even, as Hooker had done, that reading was more effectual than preaching in some respects. Instead, he was arguing that reading should take precedence over preaching, because reading was an ordinary part of the minister's duty whereas preaching was only required on certain extraordinary occasions. Preaching had been necessary when idolatry was rife in Judah (2 Chr. 17), when the scribes and pharisees had corrupted the Jewish law (Matt. 5–7) and in the early years of the Protestant Reformation, when the Church was troubled with 'much needlesse, and some unsound teaching'. Now, however, 'the corruptions are removed, and the ancient and true doctrine of the primitive Church by settled articles is restored: therefore this extraordinarie kinde is not now so necessarie, except it be upon some notorious crimes breaking in upon our people'. In normal circumstances, religious instruction should be carried out by the reading of the scripture lessons, the homilies and the Prayer Book services, rather than by the preaching of sermons. Not every minister was qualified to be a preacher; and even those learned and discreet ministers who were capable of preaching would be better advised to do so, at most, once a month rather than once or twice a week.[87]

This went along with a strong assertion of the plainness of scripture. Citing Psalm 19: 7 ('The testimony of the Lord giveth wisdom to the simple'), Shelford declared that the light of the Gospel shone 'so bright' in the scriptures 'that the very blear-eied may see it'. After all, he pointed out, it would be absurd to suppose 'that when God gave his scriptures to the Church, he gave them so darkly, that men might not understand them'. What would be the point of that? If he had made the scriptures too hard for ordinary people to understand, 'then he might as well not have given them'

---

[87] Robert Shelford, *Five Pious and Learned Discourses* (Cambridge, 1635), N2r–N3r.

at all. No: God spoke simply to simple men, 'such men as we our selves are, and used too our own words and dialects. If thou objectest the deep revelations of S. John, or the hard things of S. Paul; then I will tell thee of our Church tenet against Papist and Puritane, that all things necessarie to salvation are so plainely written, and so easie of digestion, that, as Fulgentius writes, *there is abundantly both for men to eat, and for children to suck.*' This left very little for the preacher to do, since the plainness of scripture left little need for interpretation or exposition. Indeed, Shelford went so far as to suggest that everything necessary for salvation was available in the Prayer Book – faith in the creeds, good life in the commandments, prayer in the Lord's Prayer and grace in the sacraments – so clearly expressed that there was no need for any further teaching. 'You will say, We plain people cannot understand these without some to explain them. I answer, Canst thou tell me of one man that can make them more plain to thee by his words, than God himself and his blessed Apostles have done by their words?'[88]

I have argued elsewhere that it is misleading to see preaching and the sacraments as existing in a kind of seesaw relationship, as if a stronger emphasis on the one necessarily led to a weaker emphasis on the other.[89] Many early modern Protestants held a high view of preaching as the means of conversion together with a high view of the sacraments as seals of assurance, and adopted the practice of frequent Communion, with prayers and meditations focused on the presence of Christ in the sacrament, as a central part of their religious life. We therefore need to be very careful in speaking of 'sermon-centred' or 'sacrament-centred' piety, to avoid giving the impression that these were mutually exclusive. Yet Shelford, unusually, was prepared to set up a contrast between preaching and the sacraments, arguing that the preacher's words 'can but onely teach us, and enlighten our understanding' whereas the sacraments 'infuse . . . grace into our souls, and make us acceptable before God'. Like other Laudian divines, he felt that preaching had been over-valued in relation to other religious ordinances, and that it was now time to redress the balance, even at the cost of using harsh and aggressive language to dethrone preaching from its position of pre-eminence.

The distance between the Laudians and their opponents can be measured by their remarks on the relationship between preaching and prayer. (Since 'prayer', in this context, meant the reading of public prayers, this was

---

[88] Shelford, *Discourses*, L3r.
[89] Arnold Hunt, 'The Lord's supper in early modern England', *Past & Present*, 161 (1998), pp. 39–83 (esp. pp. 39, 75).

effectively a replay of the preaching/reading debate.) There were some eminent puritan ministers who argued that preaching was the more important of the two. Samuel Hieron, for example, declared that 'it is more of worth than prayer: for what but preaching shall direct to pray? . . . If then the worship of God is worthie of respect, the exercise of preaching most of all, as being indeed the best of all.'[90] Arthur Dent, in his classic manual of practical divinity, *The Plaine Mans Path-way to Heaven*, also ranked preaching above prayer: 'Prayer is most needfull . . . But yet wee preferre preaching above it.'[91] By contrast, some Laudian divines reversed this order of priorities and argued in equally forceful terms that prayer ranked above preaching. '*Preaching* is a holy institution', declared Peter Hausted in 1636, 'but there be *degrees* in Holinesse. *Prayer* is a *more* holy institution.'[92]

This is a striking contrast. Equally striking, however, is the hesitant response of many moderate puritan preachers. They were clearly worried by the Laudian attempt to demote preaching to a lesser position, and one might have expected them to respond by reasserting the primacy of preaching as the essential duty of the godly minister. But what one finds instead is a search for compromise, and an increasingly agonised attempt to mediate between the two opposing positions by avoiding any comparison between preaching and prayer. 'Indeede there are extremes', declared Francis Rogers in 1633, 'for some would have all praying, no preaching: others would have all preaching, no praying . . . But I wish from mine heart, that preaching and praying might bee like *Hypocrates* two twinnes, live arme in arme together.'[93] The London preacher Josias Shute, expounding St Paul's injunction to 'pray continually' (I Thess. 5: 17), observed that there were some men who misunderstood this as an instruction to 'waive preaching . . . meerely for that dutie of prayer'. But surely, Shute pleaded, 'God never intended that one of his ordinances should justle out another. There must be a time for hearing, and for praying . . . God never intended his ordinances should enterfere, or exclude each other; but they must be sorted out in due time and in fit opportunitie.'[94]

---

[90] Hieron, *The Preachers Plea* (2nd edn., 1605), I5r; *Aarons Bells A-sounding* (1623), B2v; *The Dignitie of Preaching*, C1v.

[91] Arthur Dent, *The Plaine Mans Path-way to Heaven* (14th impr., 1612), S8r.

[92] Peter Hausted, *Ten Sermons* (1636), 2E2r. See also the remarks of Walter Balcanquall, in *The Honour of Christian Churches* (1633), on the superiority of prayer over preaching (C4r–D1r).

[93] Francis Rogers, *A Visitation Sermon, Preached at the Lord Archbishops Triennial and Ordinary Visitation* (1633), C1v. See also John Prideaux, *A Sermon Preached on the Fifth of October 1624* (Oxford, 1625), C4v; John Rogers, *The Doctrine of Faith* (5th edn., 1633), D5r; Roger Matthew, *Peters Net Let Downe . . . Delivered at a Synod at Chipping-Norton in Oxfordshire* (1634), E1r.

[94] Josias Shute, *Judgement and Mercy . . . Delivered in Nine Sermons* (1645), 2B3r (p. 191).

This is a sign of growing dissatisfaction with the reading/preaching distinction. At the beginning of the seventeenth century there were still many divines who held, as Cartwright had done, that only preaching could suffice for salvation. But by the 1630s there seems to have been a general drift away from this view; and even those divines who were broadly sympathetic to the puritan ideal of a godly preaching ministry had now come round to a more Whitgiftian view of reading and preaching as complementary methods of teaching. It was not only Laudians who felt that Puritanism had placed too much emphasis on preaching to the exclusion of other religious ordinances. The moderate puritan Nehemiah Rogers complained in 1632 of 'the laying of our people so much to one Breast [i.e. preaching] without an orderly giving of the other [i.e. prayer]', which, he suggested, was the reason why 'God in many Congregations dryeth up that Breast that was so (in a manner) altogether drawne at, that the other may not grow dry'. Thomas Bedford, another moderate puritan, argued in 1639 that while the Papists 'built all upon the Sacraments, nothing upon the Word', some ministers in the Church of England had gone to the opposite extreme: 'We take from the Sacrament, and give it all to the Word.'[95] In asserting the importance of prayer and the sacraments the Laudians were thus, to some extent, pushing at an open door – for even among their opponents there was relatively little desire to insist on the necessity of preaching as the sole means to salvation.

Moreover, the popularity and availability of printed sermons made it increasingly difficult to maintain the distinction beween reading and preaching, or to argue that the experience of reading a sermon on the page was necessarily inferior to that of hearing a sermon delivered from the pulpit. 'Printed sermons are thy preachers', declared Robert Shelford in 1635. 'For as soon as there is any rare sermon preached, by and by, it is put to print, and from the presse it is disperst all the land over. There is scarce a house in any town, but one or other in it by reading can repeat it to thee.' Shelford, of course, was hardly a disinterested witness; his point was that there was no need for the clergy to preach every week, or for the laity to complain of the lack of preaching, since printed sermons could do the job just as well, if not better. 'Then how shouldest thou starve for want of preaching, when the best preachers in the land, such as thou never sawest, nor they thee, yet by this means continually preach unto thee?'[96] But his observation was a sound one, for with the wider circulation of printed sermons, puritan ministers were obliged to reconsider the relationship between the word preached and the word printed. We will see in

---

[95] Thomas Bedford, *A Treatise of the Sacraments* (1639), 2Z1r.     [96] Shelford, *Discourses*, K2r.

Chapter 3 how they gradually overcame their distrust of print and began to take advantage of its evangelistic possibilities.

The decline of the preaching/reading distinction also helped to precipitate a change in attitudes towards the deaf. As we saw earlier in this chapter, it was widely believed that the deaf were barred from salvation because of their inability to hear the preacher's words. But in the late sixteenth century it was discovered that deaf-mutes could be taught to lip-read, and with this came the realisation that hearing was not necessarily a prerequisite for religious instruction. In his *Survey of Cornwall*, Richard Carew reported the case of one Edward Bone, servant to Peter Courtney of Ladock, who had been deaf from birth but who

> would yet bee one of the first, to learne, and expresse to his master, any newes that was sturring in the Countrie: especially, if there went speech of a Sermon, within some myles distance, hee would repaire to the place, with the soonest, and setting himselfe directly against the Preacher, looke him stedfastly in the face, while his Sermon lasted . . . And to make his minde knowne, in this and all other matters, hee used verie effectuall signes, being able therethrough, to receive, and performe any enioyned errand.[97]

The Gloucestershire minister Tobias Higgins dedicated his sermon *The Deafe Man Cured* (1641) to one of his parishioners, Mrs Elizabeth Spert, who had lost her hearing and was 'heavily afflicted in mind' as a result. Higgins advised her to read the Bible and other godly books, to seek the assistance of a friend in looking up biblical citations during the sermon, and to receive the sacrament, 'a most lively Sermon to the eye'. 'It may be objected: *Faith commeth by hearing*.' This was true, Higgins admitted, yet 'when God denieth one way, he can worke powerfully another. And I doubt not, but many that have wanted the preaching of the word, have bin converted by reading.' Deafness was not a barrier to salvation, for God in his mercy 'hath given a double passage to the soule: Eares, and Eyes; and a double manner: words, and writing.'[98]

### CONCLUSION

Most of this chapter has focused on the writings of a handful of individuals – notably Cartwright, Whitgift and Hooker – where the distinctions between

---

[97] Richard Carew, *The Survey of Cornwall* (1602), 2N3v.
[98] Tobias Higgins, *The Deafe Man Cured* (1641). On the discovery of lip-reading, see James R. Knowlson, 'The idea of gesture as a universal language', *Journal of the History of Ideas*, 26 (1965), pp. 495–508 (esp. p. 499).

reading and preaching were hammered out in the context of the polemical exchanges over the nature of the Elizabethan settlement. But it would be a mistake to see this merely as a conversation taking place among a few theologians. The debate over reading and preaching was not just a debate about the role of the minister or the right way to salvation; it was also a debate about the function of speech and writing, reflecting the changing relationship between orality and literacy in the early modern period. A number of historians have argued that this period marks the crucial shift from an 'age of the ear' to an 'age of the eye', continuing a process that had begun in the medieval period but was greatly assisted and accelerated by the invention of printing.[99] If we accept this thesis, then the reading/preaching debate can be seen as a symptom of the decline of oral culture and the rise of literate culture, with Hooker and his Laudian followers representing not a nostalgic turn back to Catholic sacramentalism but a progressive move forward into the era of the printed book.

The classic account of the transition from oral to literate culture is to be found in the work of Walter Ong. In *Ramus, Method and the Decay of Dialogue* (1958), Ong argues that the Renaissance saw 'a struggle between hearing and seeing' and that, in the end, 'seeing won'. This was symbolised, for Ong, by the decline of Aristotelian logic, with its theory of knowledge as a series of statements (*categoriae*) or spoken utterances on particular subjects, and its replacement by the Ramist system of place logic, with its theory of knowledge as a series of places (*loci*) or pigeonholes to which relevant facts could be assigned. This rearrangement of the mental furniture had far-reaching effects:

We ... think of books as 'containing' chapters and paragraphs, paragraphs as 'containing' sentences, sentences as 'containing' words, words as 'containing' ideas, and finally ideas as 'containing' truth. Here the whole mental world has gone hollow. The pre-Agricolan mind had preferred to think of books as saying something, of sentences as expressing something, and of words and ideas as 'containing' nothing at all but rather as signifying or making signs for something.

Ramism thus rendered the spoken word unnecessary by representing all knowledge in visual form. And Ong sees a clear link between Ramism and Protestantism, arguing that because Protestants were committed to the

---

[99] Notably Lucien Febvre in *The Problem of Unbelief in the Sixteenth Century* (Cambridge, MA, 1982), quoted by D. R. Woolf in 'Speech, text, and time: the sense of hearing and the sense of the past in Renaissance England', *Albion*, 18: 2 (1986), pp. 159–93 (quotation p. 162). For an anthropological perspective, see also Edmund Carpenter, *Oh, What a Blow That Phantom Gave Me!* (New York, 1973), p. 37: 'Synchronizing the senses means one sense dominates all others. Under literacy, that sense is sight. Other senses are muted or used with the bias of the eye.'

written word of the Bible, they were peculiarly receptive to Ramist method when it was codified in the form of diagrams on the printed page. In the long term the spoken word would gradually lose its importance, becoming superseded by the printed word and, as Ong puts it, 'suspect of failing to "let through" the meaning of the Scripture intended by God as well as method and diagrams could'.[100]

Ong was aware that the Protestant emphasis on preaching challenged this model, and in his textbook *Orality and Literacy* (1982) he attempts, not altogether successfully, to repair this hole in his argument. He concedes that 'the emphasis on oral presentation of the word of God in preaching' tended to counterbalance 'the strong stress on the written or printed word', but argues that the emphasis on oral preaching was itself a side effect of the rise of print technology. 'In making the text of the Bible more physically accessible by sheer multiplication of copies, print heightened the attention accorded to words' (as opposed to images or liturgical actions) and hence encouraged a strong reliance on the spoken word. At this point his argument takes an unexpected side-swerve into psychology, maintaining that Protestants 'subconsciously sensed' the power of print to weaken the power of the spoken word, and therefore compensated for this by stressing the importance of preaching.[101] Arguably, Ong's crucial mistake is to associate Protestantism with modernity and to assume that it must therefore have promoted, and been promoted by, the emergence of a modern literate and print-centred culture – whereas in fact, as we have seen in this chapter, early modern Protestants remained deeply and stubbornly attached to oral forms of communication. Inasmuch as the exposition of scripture was perceived, in Ong's phrase, as a process of 'letting through', it was an attempt to let the immediacy of the spoken word emerge through the written text. And insofar as we accept the dichotomy between oral and literate culture, it is fairly clear that early modern Protestantism belongs on the oral rather than the literate side of the divide.

Ong's thesis interestingly anticipates the work of French structuralist and post-structuralist critics for whom the relationship between speech and writing assumed major importance. In *Les Mots et les choses* (1966), Foucault argues that the primacy of writing over speech had been decisively established in the Renaissance, largely because of the invention of printing – pointing out that for sixteenth- and seventeenth-century linguists such as Vigenère and Duret, the written actually preceded the spoken part of

---

[100]  Walter J. Ong, *Ramus, Method and the Decay of Dialogue* (Cambridge, MA, 1958), p. 284.
[101]  Walter J. Ong, *Orality and Literacy: The Technologizing of the Word* (London, 1982), pp. 273, 282.

language. 'Henceforth, it is the primal nature of language to be written. The sounds made by voices provide no more than a transitory and precarious translation of it.' This passage may have been in the mind of Derrida when, in *De la Grammatologie* (1967), he criticised the common assumption that (in Rousseau's words) 'writing is nothing but the representation of speech' and that speech, in turn, is the representation of an objective reality outside the domain of language. For Derrida, the written word is primary and all-pervasive (hence his celebrated dictum, '*il n'y a pas de hors-texte*'), and the writings of Rousseau and others obliquely attest to this fact even while they protest otherwise.[102] The work of Foucault, Derrida and their followers has had the very beneficial effect of forcing all scholars concerned with literary texts to think more carefully about the distinction between writing and speech, yet it can be argued that Foucault falls into the same trap as Ong, in failing to give sufficient attention to the oral features of early modern culture. Ann Kibbey has pointed out that 'Foucault declines to discuss sermon literature even though he emphasises questions about the relative values of writing and speaking, and it is just this kind of literature that offers the most counter-evidence to his thesis.'[103]

At the very least, Ong's thesis is valuable as a reminder that (in the words of Martin Elsky) 'a culture is profoundly affected by the medium it uses to organise, store and communicate its experience'.[104] But a new generation of scholars has now begun to question the whole idea of a 'great divide' between oral and literate culture. Joyce Coleman, in a thoughtful and searching critique of Ong's work, argues that in late medieval England, orality and literacy coexisted in a state of 'acute mixedness'. She posits a middle state between orality and literacy which she calls 'aurality', that is, the oral delivery of a written text, which was dependent on the written word but still had the public and performative attributes of oral culture. This is strongly supported by Adam Fox's work on oral culture in early modern England, which stresses the survival of orality but also the extent to which it was penetrated by written and printed texts. It finds further support in Daniel Woolf's wide-ranging survey of 'the sense of hearing and the sense of the past', which argues that the whole idea of a transition from a sound-orientated (oral) culture to a sight-orientated (visual or literate) culture is

[102] Michel Foucault, *The Order of Things: An Archaeology of the Human Sciences* (New York, 1970; repr. 1977), p. 38; Jacques Derrida, *Of Grammatology*, trans. Gayatri Chakravorty Spivak (Baltimore, 1976).
[103] Anne Ferry, *The Art of Naming* (Chicago, 1988), pp. 15–16; Ann Kibbey, *The Interpretation of Material Shapes in Puritanism* (Cambridge, 1986), p. 163 n. 3.
[104] Martin Elsky, *Authorizing Words: Speech, Writing and Print in the English Renaissance* (Cornell, 1989), p. 5.

fundamentally mistaken; what was going on in the early modern period was not a shift from one mode of perception to another, but rather 'the maintenance of something like a balance between sight and sound'.[105] This invites us to consider the early modern sermon less as an oral phenomenon (with all that this implies about the distinction between orality and literacy) than as an aural one – and to explore it, as we shall be doing in the following chapter, not as an act of speaking but as an act of hearing, with due attention to the audience response.

Nevertheless, the evidence presented in this chapter strongly suggests that a change was occurring in attitudes to speech and writing – not the clear-cut shift from an oral to a literate culture posited by Ong, but a more intricate and long-drawn-out process in which orality became assimilated into a mixed oral/literate culture. It was becoming increasingly difficult to maintain the distinction between reading and preaching – or, to put it another way, increasingly difficult to think of preaching as a pure act of speech, a purely oral activity unrelated to the production and consumption of written and printed texts. W. H. Auden aptly refers to speech and writing as 'two tributary streams, rising at different sources, flowing apart for a time until they unite to form a large river'.[106] In seventeenth-century England, these two streams were on the point of convergence. In due course, the written word and the spoken word, the word read by the eye and the word heard by the ear, would all be assimilated into a single category of verbal expression, and the fine distinctions between them would be lost; but in the early modern period, as D. F. McKenzie has remarked, 'that dual pressure to listen *and* to read created problems of choice and adjustment'.[107] The paradoxical nature of early modern sermons – as oral performances whose virtue was deemed to lie precisely in their oral nature, but existing for us today only in written and printed form – makes that process of adjustment peculiarly visible.

---

[105] Joyce Coleman, *Public Reading and the Reading Public in Late Medieval England and France* (Cambridge, 1996), pp. 1–33; Adam Fox, *Oral and Literate Culture in England 1500–1700* (Oxford, 2000); Woolf, 'Speech, text, and time', pp. 159–93.

[106] W. H. Auden, *Complete Works: Prose, 1926–38*, ed. Edward Mendelson (Princeton, NJ, 1996), p. 16.

[107] D. F. McKenzie, 'Speech–manuscript–print', *Library Chronicle of the University of Texas at Austin*, 20: 1/2 (1990), pp. 86–109 (quotation p. 91), reprinted in McKenzie, *Making Meaning: 'Printers of the Mind' and Other Essays* (Amherst, 2002), pp. 237–58.

CHAPTER 2

# *The art of hearing*

Virginia Woolf's ambition to 'fill in the spaces between the great books with the voices of people talking' presents the historian with a formidable challenge.[1] If we want to know what the past looked like, then we can refer to paintings, drawings and engravings; but if we want to know what the past *sounded* like, then – at least for the era before sound recordings – we have to fall back on our own imagination. Of course we have songs, plays and sermons, all designed to be sung or spoken; we have personal letters, which can give us the sense (or the illusion) of eavesdropping on a conversation; and we have the transcripts of oral testimony in the law courts; but all these have come down to us in written form, and it requires an effort of imagination or interpretation to 'hear' them spoken aloud. As for the auditory texture of everyday life – memorably compared by Woolf to 'the whispering and the pattering of nimble, inquisitive animals going about their affairs in the undergrowth' – this may seem wholly irrecoverable. However detailed our knowledge and however vivid our mental picture of the past, it will always have something of the quality of a still photograph or a silent movie.

But a number of historians have recently attempted this seemingly impossible task. Bruce Smith, in *The Acoustic World of Early Modern England* (1999), seeks to reconstruct the 'acoustic communities' of the past through the 'soundscapes' in which they lived and moved – the soundscape of early modern London, for example, with the pealing of church bells, the rumble of cartwheels, the clip-clop of horses' hooves, the permanent background noise of running water in the conduits, the cries of itinerant pedlars, the buzz of voices in St Paul's or the Royal Exchange, music from taverns, applause from the theatres, the boom of cannons from the Tower. For the most part, he argues, the soundscape of early modern

---

[1] Virginia Woolf, 'Dorothy Osborne's letters', in *The Common Reader, Second Series* (London, 1932; repr. 1935), p. 59.

London was chaotic and cacophonous, but occasionally – in the sermons at Paul's Cross, for example – there was an attempt to 'hear the city whole' by giving it a single, unified voice.[2] Emily Cockayne has extended this analysis in her book *Hubbub* (2007) by looking at the point where 'sound' became 'noise': where the ambient sounds of late seventeenth-century London – street cries, passing traffic, noisy workmen, drunken revellers – began to be perceived by many Londoners as an annoying nuisance. The post-Fire rebuilding of London, she argues, made it easier for people to shield themselves from noise indoors, and therefore made them more sensitive to noise outdoors.[3] Smith and Cockayne adopt very different approaches – one highly theorised, the other highly empirical – but both are surprisingly optimistic about the possibility of reconstructing the sound-worlds of the past.

One of the most interesting products of this new school of acoustic history is Alain Corbin's study of church bells, *Village Bells: Sound and Meaning in the Nineteenth-Century French Countryside* (1998). Corbin is fascinated not only by the rhythms and rituals of bell-ringing – the dawn bell, the midday Angelus – but by the ways the bells were heard: the way the range of their sound defined the limits of the village community; the way they created a sense of 'qualitative time', marking a few key moments in the year, the week and the day, as opposed to the continuous flow of time that comes from access to a clock or watch. He argues that 'the rural peals of the nineteenth century, which have become for us the sound of another time, were listened to and evaluated according to a system of affects that is now lost to us'. The 'heyday of the bell', he suggests, was the first half of the nineteenth century, when there was a growing demand for accurate time-keeping which could not yet be satisfied by clocks or railways. But from the 1860s onwards, 'an entire section of the culture of the senses was impoverished ... with a whole web of sound gradually fading away', not because the bells themselves fell silent but because 'their meaning seemed to fall away, modes of attention collapsed, the usages and rhetoric of the bells grew narrower so that, in short, a whole range of auditory messages were increasingly disqualified'.[4] Corbin's argument is an ambitious one, perhaps over-ambitious in seeking to connect the decline of bell-ringing to the

[2] Bruce R. Smith, *The Acoustic World of Early Modern England: Attending to the O-Factor* (Chicago and London, 1999), p. 70.
[3] Emily Cockayne, *Hubbub: Filth, Noise and Stench in England 1600–1770* (New Haven and London, 2007), p. 130.
[4] Alain Corbin, *Village Bells: Sound and Meaning in the Nineteenth-Century French Countryside* (Columbia, NY, 1998; repr. London, 1999), pp. xix, 189, 307.

Figure 3 Preacher and congregation (1): detail from the frontispiece to Benjamin Spencer, *Chrysomeson, a Golden Meane: or a Middle Way for Christians to Walk By* (1659). Reproduced by permission of St John's College, Cambridge.

'disenchantment of the world' (a process that was already well under way by the mid-nineteenth century), but it is not necessary to accept every point of his thesis in order to agree with his basic contention that what matters is not just the sounds themselves but the way they were heard. As he sums up (with heavy italicisation for emphasis): '*The sense that bell ringing was a necessity* engendered habits of *intense listening.*'

This chapter seeks to reconstruct those 'habits of intense listening' as they might have applied to the early modern sermon. For this purpose Smith and Cockayne are perhaps less helpful guides than Corbin. It would be an interesting exercise to piece together the soundscape of the early modern sermon: the preacher raising his voice in exhortation or even, at outdoor preaching venues such as Paul's Cross, having to shout to make himself heard; the low murmur of voices in the congregation; the cries of 'Amen'; the scratch of pen on paper as some listeners scribbled notes; or perhaps the occasional muffled snore as others nodded off.[5] A good deal of evidence survives to document this, and some of it will be found in the following pages. But like Corbin, I am interested not just in the sound of the sermon but in the way it was heard – and to reconstruct this, I shall be looking at the contemporary literature on the 'art of hearing' that gives this book its title. The art of hearing was essentially an art of memory, designed to help listeners remember what they heard – but it was more than that. It was also a way for them to appropriate what they heard: to take a lengthy and complex body of religious teaching and to make it their own through a process of mental sorting and filtering. It is therefore of the utmost importance to any study of the reception of Protestant doctrine in early modern England, and one of the questions which I shall be pursuing in this chapter is how far it succeeded in making the message of the Protestant preaching ministry more accessible to the laity.

### HOW TO HEAR AN EARLY MODERN SERMON

As Protestant preachers stood in their pulpits and surveyed their congregations, what they saw gave them little cause for optimism. Only a tiny proportion of their hearers – one in a hundred, or even one in a thousand – seemed to be genuinely responsive to their message. Richard Rogers, minister of Wethersfield in Essex, believed that the vast majority of people, 'in number an hundred for one of the other', totally failed to benefit from the sermons they heard. They 'were never troubled in conscience for their sinne, or the woe that it hath purchased them; neither doe once dreame that such a thing is needfull for them'. John Smith, another Essex minister, lamented that 'not one of a thousand of us' had ever been moved to tears by hearing a sermon. 'Many of you', he told his congregation, 'be twenty, thirty, and forty yeares old'; they had grown up with the preaching ministry, they could look back on years of regular church attendance, but had they ever shed a single tear for sin? 'Alas, what shall I say?'[6] Remarks such as these have led many modern scholars to conclude that the Protestant preaching ministry was not a popular success. In Christopher Haigh's words, 'it was clear to the ministers, as it must surely be to historians, that the preaching

---

[5] John Craig has attempted something of this sort in 'Psalms, groans, and dogwhippers: the soundscape of worship in the English parish church, 1547–1642', in Will Coster and Andrew Spicer, eds., *Sacred Space in Early Modern Europe* (Cambridge, 2005), pp. 104–23. See also Laura Feitzinger Brown, 'Brawling in church: noise and the rhetoric of lay behavior in early modern England', *Sixteenth Century Journal*, 34: 4 (2003), pp. 955–72.

[6] Richard Rogers, *Seven Treatises* (1603), C6r; John Smith, *Essex Dove* (1633), V7r.

campaign had produced only a small minority of godly Protestants, leaving the rest in ignorance, indifference or downright antipathy'.[7]

Yet some clerical observers perceived a paradox here. Most laypeople might have been fairly passive in their response to preaching, but this passivity did not appear to arise from any hostility to the preaching ministry. Indeed, George Gifford remarked that many people seemed to think very favourably of their preachers. 'They will say peradventure, after this maner, it was a good Sermon, I woulde wee coulde follow it, hee saide very well: hee is a perfecte readie man in the Pulpet. But aske, what doctrine did he handle? Then are they at a pause, and set at a dead lift.' Even in the stony ground of Popish Lancashire, William Harrison observed the same phenomenon. 'When the people have heard the preacher speake a whole houre together, and deliver many profitable points of doctrine, and that very plainely, yet few can repeate any thing at all: many will say they like him well, he is a good man, and made a very good sermon, yet cannot tell one word that he spake.'[8] The problem, it seemed, was not that people failed to pay attention to the preacher, but that they failed to understand or remember what they heard. Robert Wilkinson compared them to the sick man by the pool at Bethesda (John 5: 5) who was unable to cure himself because he could not step into the water. 'This is the reason why we have so many unfruitfull hearers at this day . . . because when the Angell of Gods will doth preach the word and stirre up the water of life, they know not how to move theyr eares toward it.'[9]

Some clergy sought to meet this need by publishing simple instructional treatises on the right way to hear sermons. The first and most influential of these was Henry Smith's pair of sermons on 'The art of hearing', first published in 1592. Smith's text was Luke 8: 18, 'Take heed how you hear' – a short and simple text, he admitted, yet 'a text which should bee preached before all texts; which because it was not taught and learned at the first, a thousand Sermons have beene lost and forgotten, as though they had never beene preached at all'. The art of hearing was 'the fore-runner, which prepareth the way to the Preacher: like the Plough, which cutteth up the ground, that it may receive the seed'. It was 'the ABC of a Christian', though it was not as simple as it seemed: 'There is nothing so easie as to

[7] Christopher Haigh, 'The Church, the Catholics and the people', in Haigh, ed., *The Reign of Elizabeth I* (1984), pp. 195–219 (quotation p. 209).
[8] George Gifford, *A Sermon on the Parable of the Sower* (1584), A6v; William Harrison, *The Difference of Hearers, or an Exposition of the Parable of the Sower* (1614), D4r.
[9] Robert Wilkinson, *A Iewell for the Eare* (1605), A2r.

*heare*, and yet there is nothing so hard as to *heare well*.'[10] Smith's sermons were quickly followed by others on the same subject, including Robert Wilkinson's *A Jewell for the Eare* (1593), Thomas Wilcox's translation of Wilhelm Zepper's *Ars Habendi et Audiendi Conciones Sacras* (1598), published in English as *The Art or Skil, Well and Fruitfullie to Heare the Holy Sermons of the Church* (1599), and Stephen Egerton's treatise delightfully entitled *The Boring of the Eare* (1623). These were published alongside countless other manuals of practical divinity, such as Lewis Bayly's *The Practice of Pietie*, which gave advice on hearing sermons in the context of more general directions on the day-to-day conduct of the Christian life.

The art-of-hearing literature is an essential starting point for reconstructing the reception of sermons in early modern England. To be sure, it was a puritan genre, reflecting the characteristically puritan concern with the live sermon that we encountered in the last chapter, but it was also an attempt to export this distinctive form of piety beyond the godly community – beyond Rogers's one in a hundred, or Smith's one in a thousand – and into the wider Church. One way in which it did so was by presenting the art of hearing as a useful tool of household government. For most people in early modern England, sermon attendance would not have been a private or individual activity, but a group activity in which they participated with fellow household members. Edward Vaughan regarded the householder as a crucial intermediary between preacher and people. 'Why doth God so charge the Pastor for the publike publication of his will, is it not because the masters of households should with the like charge receive it from them, and deliver it unto their people? Truely, nothing is more plaine.'[11] Much of the art-of-hearing literature was thus addressed to heads of households, who were rightly perceived as having a pivotal role in supporting, reinforcing and (quite literally) bringing home the preacher's message. Of course they were expected to bring their families to the sermon, but – perhaps more importantly – they were also expected to bring the sermon to their families by setting up a regime of regular household worship and religious instruction.

To begin with, it was the householder's responsibility to enforce church attendance, and to ensure that no one stayed away from church without good cause. Zepper acknowledged that 'mothers, wives, or other of the household' might not always be able to attend church 'by reason of their

[10] Henry Smith, 'The art of hearing', in *Thirteene Sermons* (1592), reprinted in *The Sermons of Mr Henry Smith* (1631), T6r–T8r (pp. 299–303).
[11] Edward Vaughan, *A Plaine and Perfect Method, for the Easie Understanding of the Whole Bible* (1617), C12r.

houshold businesses, and attendance of infants upon the Lords daies', but warned that if this were so, they must come 'turne by turne, as it were, upon the next Lords day'.[12] Stephen Egerton also recognised that 'the aged, sicke, and such as have young children' might be hindered from attending church, but laid down four conditions to be observed. First, they must take care 'that they make not a necessitie where none is'; secondly, 'they must endevour though they cannot goe all at once, nor everie Lords Day, yet that they goe as oft as they can by turnes, every one in his course'; thirdly, 'they must be more carefull to aske questions, and to desire repetition of the Sermons, of them that were there'; and finally, 'they must keepe no more at home with them, than of necessitie they need, and such they may lawfully keepe to attend upon themselves'.[13]

It was the householder's duty not only to summon the family to church, but to assemble them as a family group. Nicholas Bownde complained that many families 'come not together, but scattered, and one dragging after another in a confused manner', first the master of the house, then his wife, then the servants, so that 'if the minister tarrie till there be a sufficient congregation, the first commers may bee wearie, and sometimes cold with tarrying' before the latecomers arrive. Rather than tolerate such insubordination, the godly householder should ensure that the whole family went to church together, 'with one consent (as it were one man)'.[14] William Hinde, in his life of the godly gentleman John Bruen, described how Bruen would set off to church 'calling all his family about him, leaving neither Cooke nor Butler behind him, not any of his servants, but two or three to make the doores, and tend the house, untill their returne. And then taking his Tenants and neighbours, as they lay in the way, along with him, hee marched on with a joyfull and cheerefull heart, as a leader of the Lords host, towards the house of God', inviting his family to gather round him and 'joyne together with one heart and voice, to sing Psalmes as they went along'.[15] This was an exemplary model of household unity, which Hinde clearly hoped his readers would imitate.

The church was a public arena in which the hearer was put on show before the community, 'as it were upon the Theater'.[16] The risk that these very public surroundings might draw the mind away from thoughts of

---

[12]  William Zepper, *The Art or Skil, Well and Fruitfullie to Heare the Holy Sermons of the Church* (1599), D3r.
[13]  Stephen Egerton, *The Boring of the Eare* (1623), C6r.
[14]  Nicholas Bownde, *The Doctrine of the Sabbath* (1595), P1r, Mm2v; reprinted in John Dod and Robert Cleaver, *A Godlie Forme of Householde Government*, C2r (p. 35).
[15]  William Hinde, *A Faithfull Remonstrance of the Holy Life and Happy Death of John Bruen* (1641), P1v.
[16]  Zepper, *Art or Skil*, I5v.

religion, towards more mundane matters, prompted some writers to lay down very precise rules for the management of physical behaviour in church. Bownde criticised those who, having said a few prayers on entering the church, were then 'ready to talke of any worldly matter, with any that will give them the hearing'. The godly hearer should refrain from idle conversation with his neighbours, and occupy his mind with 'religious and holy Meditations' until the beginning of the service.[17] Once the service had begun, churchgoers were cautioned against talking, laughing or coughing, 'needelesse shiftinge and stirringe of the bodie', allowing their eyes to wander, or 'standing up to gaze about'. Henry Mason approvingly quoted 'some of the Learned, who prescribe rules of decency in the time of divine service . . . [and] will not permit men, when they are hearing of Gods word, to *smile* in secret, or to *looke about*, or to *laie one legg over another*, or to *whisper in their fellows eare*, or to *look sowre*, as if somewhat displeased them, or to *leane and lie on one side*, &c.' Mason was particularly exasperated by some hearers 'who by clapping their Pew-doores, and sometimes by redoubling the knock, do so disturb the Assembly, that neither the Minister can be heard, nor the people proceed in their devotion'.[18]

There was a tension here between the communal and individual aspects of public worship. Churchgoers were exhorted to 'ioyne themselves in mind and action' with the whole congregation, yet at the same time they were urged to 'make a covenant with their eyes' (Job 31: 1) and avoid eye contact with others. They were advised to fix their attention on the preacher, in order to 'settle the mind where the eies are fixed', or else to 'look downward, or cover the eies; that the minde having no distraction from without, may be the more intent on his present businesse'.[19] In his treatise *The Vanitie of the Eie*, George Hakewill described a church he had seen in Germany, 'the fashion of which is so contrived that neither the men see the women, nor the women the men, and yet both heare the minister sufficiently alike'. This, he suggested, could serve as a model for 'our English churches' where 'the promiscuous sitting of men and women together' tended to distract people from their religious devotions, 'especially our women wearing no manner of vaile which in other countries is usuall not only in their Churches, but in their streetes too'.[20] As Ephraim Udall noted in 1641, it

---

[17] Bownde, *Doctrine of the Sabbath*, Cc2v; Egerton, *Boring of the Eare*, C8r.
[18] Henry Mason, *Hearing and Doing the Ready Way to Blessednesse* (1635), 2F5v, 2F10r.
[19] Mason, *Hearing and Doing*, 2D11v.
[20] George Hakewill, *The Vanitie of the Eie* (Oxford, 1608), F1v. On segregated seating, see Kevin Dillow, 'The social and ecclesiastical significance of church seating arrangements' (unpublished DPhil thesis, University of Oxford, 1990).

was at about this time that box pews began to be introduced in many English churches, 'fitter it may be, for greater attention, than the ancient Pewes, which were not above the middle of the body, and exposed mens eyes to more roving and wandring, than these high Pewes, which are more private'.[21]

And this individualistic tendency – screening out the rest of the congregation and focusing on the one-to-one relationship with the minister – was at its strongest during the sermon itself. Hearers were instructed to fasten their eyes on the preacher and apply the doctrines spoken by him 'unto our selves for our owne particular use, as if they were spoken to none but us'.[22] They were to 'goe along with the Preacher from point to point, applying the Word in particular to the part affected, as the stomacke conveieth nourishment to each member', saying to themselves at each point, 'This is for me; This promise; This comfort; This threatning.'[23] They were to take every point they heard, and turn it to its appropriate use – 'if it be a promise, by beleeving and embracing it', 'if a threatning, by beleeving and fearing it', 'if a precept or dutie laid forth, by beleeving and endeavouring to practise it' – paying special attention to the duties that applied to them in their own particular calling. 'If the Preacher tell Householders of their dutie to their sonnes and servants, he that is a master of a family, presently should say with himselfe, *This commandement is for mee*. And if the Preacher speake of the duty of servants to their masters, hee that is a servant, should say, *This commandement is for me*.' If he commended a duty, they were to pray for grace to perform it; if he reproved a sin, they were to pray for strength to avoid it; if he fell upon some 'hard point', they were to pray for wisdom to understand it; and all this 'without hindering or diverting away our attention from any part of the Sermon'.[24]

This technique of sustained self-application was central to the art of hearing, and the godly clergy were extremely wary of anything that might get in its way. Even the custom of bringing a Bible to church was not universally welcomed. Some writers praised it as a sign of 'excellent zeale towards the word of God' and a great help to the memory, but others saw it as a troublesome distraction, noting that if a preacher cited scripture in his sermon, many members of his audience would 'tosse the leaves of their

---

[21] Ephraim Udall, *Communion Comlinesse* (1641), B3v. This would reach its logical conclusion in the seating arrangements found in some nineteenth-century prison chapels, where the inmates were placed in separate high-walled pews, reminding one observer of 'rows of upright coffins', constructed so that they could see the preacher but not each other: see Michel Foucault, *Discipline and Punish* (1977), plate 8, and Philip Priestley, *Victorian Prison Lives* (London, 1985), pp. 92–3.

[22] John Downame, *A Guide to Godlynesse, or a Treatise of a Christian Life* (1629), 2L5v.

[23] *The Drousie Disease; or, An Alarme to Awake Church-Sleepers* (1638), G11v.

[24] Egerton, *Boring of the Eare*, E2r; Mason, *Hearing and Doing*, 2G8v, 2K7r.

*Bibles* to and fro (to seeke the place hee nominates)' and very often 'close the *Booke* without finding of the same'.[25] Part of the trouble, as Nicholas Bownde remarked, was that many people did not know their way around the Bible, so that preachers were 'driven to name the book, the chapter, the verse, and all too little, to helpe men to finde it out'. But even for those who were familiar with the Bible, Bownde felt that it was counter-productive to look up 'every place that shall be alleaged' in a sermon, 'least in the meane season some other most necessarie doctrine overslip us, and we not marking what went before, and followed after, cannot tel to what ende the place was alleaged, and so we lose the profit of it'. Far better, as another writer suggested, merely to 'fold down a leafe in your Bible from whence the place is recited, that so at your leisure, after you returne from the Church you may examine it'.[26]

The same objections applied to note-taking at sermons, which one might have expected preachers to support unreservedly. Again, some saw it as a useful aid to memory, but others feared that it would actually have the opposite effect, by encouraging hearers to rely on their notes as a kind of artificial crutch instead of applying the sermon to their hearts and memories. Robert Bolton approved of note-taking on the grounds that it 'holds the minde close to all that is said', but went on to discuss some of the objections to it in interestingly measured terms which almost certainly reflect internal disagreements among the puritan clergy. 'Some object indeed, that it hinders affection in hearing: but though it may doe so in some, for the present; yet afterwards it will worke more lasting affections upon the Word. Onely they that use this helpe-meanes, must be carefull that they doe not presume upon their Notes so, as to neglect the recalling of what they have heard (as many use to doe) and so lose all holy affections, and that impression that the Word would make upon their hearts.'[27] Bolton's concerns were echoed by other writers, who warned those hearers who had 'good memories and wits, as we call them, to apprehend and to carry away a Sermon', or who were 'expert in taking notes with the pen', not to pride themselves on their ability. As Nicholas Byfield remarked, it was more important to make good use of a few well-chosen doctrines than to 'repeate all the Sermon *verbatim*'.[28]

[25] Zepper, *Art or Skil*, E6r; James Warre, *The Touch-stone of Truth, wherein Veritie, by Scripture is Plainely Confirmed, and Error Confuted* (1630), G7r.
[26] Bownde, *Doctrine of the Sabbath*, 2D1v; George Webbe, 'A short direction for the daily exercise of a Christian', in Richard Rogers, William Perkins *et al.*, *A Garden of Spirituall Flowers* (1625), G6r.
[27] Robert Bolton, *A Three-Fold Treatise* (1634), (m)8r.
[28] John Mayer, *Praxis Theologica* (1629), R2r; Nicholas Byfield, *The Marrow of the Oracles of God* (6th edn., 1628), 2A1r.

Figure 4  Preacher and congregation (2): illustration from Thomas Williamson, *The Sword of the Spirit* (1613), showing hearers with their Bibles open on their laps. Reproduced by permission of the British Library.

We can now understand more clearly what Henry Smith meant by saying that there was 'nothing so hard as to hear well'. The art of hearing demanded close and sustained attention to a sermon, and intellectual and emotional engagement with its content, for perhaps an hour or more. As William Sclater remarked, it might seem 'most easie' but actually required 'skill more than ordinary', not only 'to tye our minds to attention, that they may be free from wandering' but also 'to apply our affections to the quality of what is taught'.[29] Not surprisingly, even well-intentioned hearers often found it challenging. Some of those who dozed quietly during the sermon were doubtless indifferent to the preacher's message, but the art-of-hearing manuals also recognised that even 'good and godly' hearers might be unable to stop themselves falling asleep. Mason admitted that it was 'harder to forbeare sleepe in the Church, where wee sit still without moving, than it will bee in our shops, or in places abroad, where we are stirring and moving about our occasions'. A tract disarmingly entitled *The Drousie Disease* observed that 'the very sight of others sleeping, may make a man sleepie that were otherwise wakefull', just as 'the very sight of those that yawne, is wont to set others on yawning'. Among the causes of drowsiness, Robert Hill listed 'over-much labouring in our callings the day and night before', 'the heat of the aire, when many are together', which 'may occasion the best to fall asleepe', and (with refreshing honesty) 'too long Sermons'.[30]

Even such a committed sermongoer as the London artisan Nehemiah Wallington sometimes found it impossible to stay awake in church. In his autobiographical writings, Wallington poignantly lamented his inability to concentrate on the word preached: 'I have wished many times when will the Sabbath bee gone: and I have thought longe till the Sarment was done: and looking on the houre glasse wishing it were rune out . . . and I have many times slept at Church hearing of Gods word.' The art-of-hearing manuals offered various hints and tips to overcome this problem. Hearers were advised to go to bed early on Saturday night in order to be ready for church on Sunday. If they started to feel sleepy during the sermon, they were advised to stand up, move about, or utter 'short and sudden ejaculations' in response to the preacher's words. If this failed, they were to remind themselves that the church was a public place and that 'such as see me, will suspect my religion'; and if their neighbours fell asleep, they were to

---

[29] William Sclater, *An Exposition with Notes upon the First and Second Epistles to the Thessalonians* (1627), S6r (i.267).

[30] *The Drousie Disease*, E1v; Robert Hill, *The Path-way to Prayer and Pietie* (1629), T5r. On sleeping in church, see also Bernd Krysmanski, 'Lust in Hogarth's *Sleeping Congregation*, or, how to waste time in post-puritan England', *Art History*, 21: 3 (1998), pp. 393–408.

wake them discreetly by 'privily pulling them, and thrusting them'.[31] Wallington had his own coping strategies. When he felt himself becoming drowsy, he would 'prick my selfe with a pin, some time I would bite my tongue, some time I would pinch my selfe; but because nature wil favour it selfe in these things, therefore I tooke another meanes . . . I would take with me to Church some peper or ginger or some cloves and when I found my selfe sleeppie I would bite some of them and so I have by the goodnesse of God got some victorie over this sinne'.[32]

But even when the sermon was over, the hearer's duty had only just begun. Preachers were well aware that without some follow-up to the sermon, people were all too likely to forget what they had heard; it was, as George Gifford drily remarked, very often a case of 'in at the one eare, and out at the other'.[33] The art-of-hearing literature thus laid great stress on the need for 'repetition' to ensure that the hearers went back over the sermon, stored it in their memories and incorporated it into their private prayers and meditations. 'Record everie note in thy minde as the Preacher goeth', advised Henry Smith, 'and after . . . repeate all to thy selfe'. This should be done immediately on returning home, even before sitting down at table. 'The onely cause why you forget so fast as you heare, and of all the Sermons which you have heard, have scarce the substance of one in your hearts . . . is because you went from Sermon to dinner, and never thought any more of the matter.' According to Smith's account, this technique of repetition had originated in the universities, as a way for novice preachers to train their memories. 'I doo knowe some in the Universitie, which did never heare good sermon, but as soone as they were gone, they rehearsed it thus, and learned more by this (as they said) than by their reading and studie: for recording that which they had heard when it was fresh, they could remember all, and hereby got a better facilitie in preaching, than they could learne in bookes.'[34] From the universities it spread to the parishes; and by the beginning of the seventeenth century it had become firmly established as a key part of the art of hearing.

'Repetition' has been described by Patrick Collinson as one of 'the more neglected words in the religious glossary of the seventeenth century'.[35]

---

[31] Mason, *Hearing and Doing*, 2A12r; *The Drousie Disease*, G10r–11r.

[32] Nehemiah Wallington, 'A record of the mercies of God', Guildhall Library, MS 204, ff. 21–3.

[33] Gifford, *Sermon on the Parable of the Sower*, A6v.

[34] Smith, 'Art of hearing', in *Sermons*, V7r (p. 317).

[35] Patrick Collinson, 'The English conventicle', in W. J. Sheils and D. Wood, eds., *Voluntary Religion* (Studies in Church History, vol. XXIII, 1986), pp. 223–59 (quotation p. 240), reprinted in Collinson, *From Cranmer to Sancroft* (2006), pp. 145–72. See also the discussion of repetition in Collinson, *The Religion of Protestants: The Church in English Society 1559–1625* (Oxford, 1982), pp. 264–8.

Thanks to his work it is now a good deal less neglected, but it is still worth stressing just how crucially important it is for any study of sermon reception. Despite its name, repetition was far from being a derivative activity. In effect, it enabled the hearer to encounter the sermon all over again, or even to preach it over again to themselves; and in many cases this second encounter, or second preaching, may have been more important than the first in determining how the sermon would be used and understood. It could take many forms, but the most commonly cited scriptural precedent was that of the men of Berea (Acts 17: 11), who 'received the word with all readiness of mind, and searched the scriptures daily, whether these things were so'. Following this example, repetition was most often presented as a collaborative activity in which a group of hearers came together to compare notes on the sermon they had just heard, 'one remembring what another hath forgotten, and he againe supplying that wherein the other is defective', with a copy of the Bible ready at hand to check the scripture proofs. Anyone could join in, for, as Bownde declared, 'none that is desirous to learne can bee so ignorant, but hee may aske a question concerning some thing that hath been taught, and say what is the meaning of this? or how doe you understand that? or how was such a thing proved? and so begin the conference'. Even if the participants 'cannot speake so fruitfully of the word as they desire', they may still 'listen diligently unto that which is spoken' and 'give their consent unto it, and seeme to like of it, saying, I, or no'.[36]

Repetition was especially recommended to heads of households as a way of fostering the religious education of their children and servants. The advice in Bayly's *Practice of Pietie* is typical. On returning home from the sermon, the householder was advised to 'meditate a little while upon those things which thou hast heard'. Then, after dinner, 'call thy Family together, examine what they have learned in the Sermon ... Turne to the Proofes which the Preacher alleadged, and rubbe those good things over their memories againe. Then sing a Psalme or more'. Another popular manual of religious instruction, *A Garden of Spirituall Flowers*, prescribed an almost identical sabbath-day routine. After church, the householder was to make 'a briefe repetition in thy minde ... before thy sitting downe to dinner'. Then, before the afternoon service, 'assemble thy Family together ... conferre with them what they have learned at the Sermon; instruct and Catechize them; read, or cause to be read somewhat of the Bible, or some other godly Booke unto them'. The whole exercise could then be repeated

---

[36] Bownde, *Doctrine of the Sabbath*, 2F1v, 2F3r.

on returning from church in the evening.[37] All this, it was confidently expected, would lead to dramatic improvements in social and familial obedience as well as religious observance. 'Which exercise if it were used with us in our housholdes after Sermons, it were to bee hoped that our children and servants which nowe are rude and ignorant, would then become more duetiful and also more religious.'[38]

Another treatise, *The House-holders Helpe* (1615), proposed a stricter regime in which sermon repetition took place as soon as the household returned from church, before sitting down to dinner, and involved a detailed examination of the sermon's content and structure. 'Many men', the author complained, 'are exceeding carelesse herein', never questioning their servants about the sermon except occasionally to ask them 'the Chapter, and the Verse of the Text, which (betwixt the Church doore and home) even a Parrot would be taught to pronounce'. As a result, most servants can only quote 'certain words, and sentences, or similitudes, not understanding the purpose whereto any thing was spoken by the Preacher', instead of being able, as they ought, to 'shew the summe and division of the Text . . . what doctrines were drawne from it . . . how they were confirmed and in the use applied'. Sermon repetition would only be effective if the householder lined up his servants and examined them, one by one, to see what they could remember. 'Where any one faileth, let the next that standeth in order by him, shew and teach him'; and when they have all had their turn, the householder is 'to helpe them therein, by a diligent repetition, confirming and applying to your whole Familie (and to your owne heart and affections) all the doctrines that were delivered'.[39]

This sounds very like the routine adopted by Elizabeth Hoyle, wife of the York alderman Thomas Hoyle, who called in her servants after dinner on Sunday and questioned them on the sermon they had heard that morning. She returned to church in the afternoon, and then held a second session of sermon repetition before supper. 'Oftentimes . . . when a seasonable Truth was delivered', she would say to them: 'Oh! remember this.' After supper the servants were called in again for a further session of repetition, and 'an account was still given of the Word that they had heard, what this or that servant could say, so as they were able to answer in some method, for

---

[37] Lewis Bayly, *The Practice of Pietie* (30th edn., 1632), X10v. Webbe, 'A short direction', in Rogers *et al.*, *Garden of Spirituall Flowers*, G6v.

[38] Robert Cawdrey, *A Shorte and Fruitefull Treatise, of the Profite and Necessitie of Catechising* (1580), preface.

[39] R. R., *The House-holders Helpe, for Domesticall Discipline* (1615), C4r–C5r.

method helpes both judgment and memory'.[40] Repetition reinforced the householder's moral authority, but it could also, on occasion, subvert it. The author of *The House-holders Helpe* suggested that it could serve as an opportunity for self-correction, and gave several examples. In one case, 'a verie religious man' confessed before his whole family that he had 'forgotten one maine and most principle doctrine, this Sabbath day delivered'. In another, a husband and wife 'heard a Sermon on the Sabboth, and . . . received a good monition from the Minister their Preacher: namely, that Masters and Mistresses must not bee like Nabal, froward and angrie'. On returning home they repeated the sermon to their household, humbly confessing their fault in continually 'correcting, chiding and threatning' their servants, and promising to amend their behaviour in future.[41]

Repetition could also take place in church under the supervision of the minister. This enabled preachers to set an example to householders, and also to exercise much tighter control over the reception and interpretation of their sermons. One of the best-documented examples comes from the parish of Batcombe, in Somerset, where Richard Bernard, the author of several influential treatises on preaching and catechising, instituted a regular routine of public repetition, which he described in a letter to James Ussher:

I have a verie gentlemanlike Assembly, & a rich people, and yet, blessed be God, verie tractable, sanctifieing the Saboath with reverence; betweene morning & evening prayer many come to my house to have the sermon repeated, which diverse write, & haveing their notes corrected, do repeate them after publickely before the Congregation, by way of question and answer, I askeing the doctrine & ground, then the proofes, with reasons, & after the uses with motives, & they answer accordingly, which they do very willingly, besids the catechisme questions, & sometyme questions out of a Chapter, and all before the second Servis in the afternoone . . .[42]

Fifteen years later, in 1634, a feud between Bernard and one of his parishioners, James Aishe, spilled over into the ecclesiastical court and resulted in a long court case in which every aspect of Bernard's teaching regime was minutely examined. From this it appears that Bernard had conformed to the 1622 Directions to Preachers to the extent of moving his catechising sessions into the middle of the afternoon service to take the place of the sermon. At the same time, it was alleged 'that hee maketh private repetitions with some

---

[40] John Birchall, *The Non-Pareil, or, the Vertuous Daughter . . . in a Funerall Sermon upon the Death of that Vertuous Lady, Elizabeth Hoyle* (York, 1644), B4r.
[41] R. R., *House-holders Helpe*, B7r.
[42] Bernard to Ussher, 26 May 1619: Bodleian Library, Oxford, MS Rawl. lett. 89, ff. 28–9, printed (slightly modernised) in Ussher's *Works*, ed. C. R. Elrington and J. H. Todd (1847–64), vol. XVI, pp. 360–3.

of his parishioners in the church betweene dinner & evening prayer, by questions & answers before the Catachiseinge', which suggests that the routine of sermon repetition, as described in the letter to Ussher, had continued virtually unchanged.[43]

For fifteen years, therefore, Bernard had exercised an exceptional degree of control over the religious culture of his parish, not just by preaching weekly sermons but by coaching his parishioners, testing their memories and explaining to them exactly how he wished his sermons to be understood. Nor was he unique in this. William Gouge of Blackfriars followed a similar routine, and Samuel Clarke's life of Gouge reports, very revealingly, that many of his parishioners felt they gained more from the repetition of his sermons than from their original delivery. 'On the *Sabbaths*, after his publick labours were ended, divers Neighbours (wanting helps in their own Families) came to his house, where he repeated his Sermons after so familiar a manner, that many have professed that they were much more benefited by them in that repetition, than they were in the first hearing of them; for he did not use word by word to read out of Notes what he had preached, but would by Question and Answer draw from those of his own houshold such points as were delivered.'[44] This helps to make sense of the phenomenon to which Peter Lake has recently drawn attention, of the extraordinarily close correlation between the ideal of the godly man as found in the sermons of the puritan clergy, and the reality of the godly man as found in the writings of Nehemiah Wallington and other devout laypeople.[45] Sermon repetition gave the clergy a highly effective means of reinforcing their pulpit ministry. It meant that in model parishes such as Bernard's Batcombe or Gouge's Blackfriars, there would have been groups of godly hearers who internalised sermons precisely as the preacher expected and intended them to do.

Repetition was important, then, as a bridge between public and private religious exercises, or in Collinson's words, as 'the link, the umbilical cord as it were . . . between the trained and qualified professional, the minister, and his people'.[46] But the point of an umbilical cord, of course, is that sooner or later it will be severed. The paradox of repetition was that while it might join

---

[43]  Bath and Wells diocesan act book, 1634–9: Somerset Record Office, Taunton, D/D/Ca 299, pp. 112–15. Bernard was ordered to use the Prayer Book catechism rather than his own version, but was allowed to continue with the sermon repetition.

[44]  Samuel Clarke, *A Collection of the Lives of Ten Eminent Divines* (1662), O3v (p. 102), reprinted (with some revisions) from the life of Gouge prefixed to his *Learned and Very Useful Commentary on the Whole Epistle to the Hebrewes* (1655), A2v.

[45]  Peter Lake, *The Boxmaker's Revenge: 'Orthodoxy', 'Heterodoxy' and the Politics of the Parish in Early Stuart London* (Manchester, 2001), pp. 76, 390.

[46]  Collinson, 'The English conventicle', p. 243.

the godly laity closer to their preachers, it might also have the effect of emancipating them from parish ministry and giving them the freedom and confidence to expound scripture on their own. The classic example of this is William Kiffin's account of his youthful experiences as one of a group of apprentices who agreed to meet together each week before the morning lecture at St Peter's Cornhill in London. To begin with, Kiffin writes, they met only to pray, to share spiritual testimonies and 'to repeat some sermon which we had heard before', but then 'after a little time', as they gained in confidence, 'we also read some portion of Scripture, and spake from it what it pleased God to enable us'.[47] As long as repetition was confined to 'the derivative exercise of repeating what had been uttered authoritatively from the pulpit', then, Collinson argues, it had no separatist implications. But in casting aside their sermon notes and starting to expound directly from the biblical text, Kiffin and his friends were crossing a decisive line, 'a very thin line . . . a tiny ditch, but a Rubicon nevertheless'.

Yet this line is not quite so easy to draw as Kiffin's account might suggest, for (*pace* Collinson) repetition was never just a derivative activity. John Dod and Robert Cleaver, in their sermons on the Commandments, took it for granted that repetition would be accompanied by a process of 'enlargement' going some way beyond the original sermon. Godly Christians were instructed to confer with their neighbours 'and to talke of the things taught, calling them to minde and how they were prooved unto us, and then further to enlarge them according to our owne particular necessity, and as it were to spread the medicine upon one anothers hearts'.[48] And even the simple exercise of repeating the sermon and looking up the biblical citations was a potential challenge to the preacher's authority. The men of Berea, it was pointed out, had tested the reliability of St Paul's sermons by 'comparing them with the veritie of the word written' and giving them 'no further credite . . . than they were consonant to the written word'. Hearers were enjoined to follow this example, and to exercise their own critical judgement by checking the preacher's proof-texts 'to see whether they be truly alleaged or no'. Stephen Egerton added that for this reason it was important for preachers not to 'swarve from the words of the common Translation' (meaning the Authorized Version), or else their hearers might suppose that the Bible was being carelessly or deliberately misquoted.[49]

[47] William Orme, *Remarkable Passages in the Life of William Kiffin* (1823), pp. 11–12.
[48] John Dod and Robert Cleaver, *A Plaine and Familiar Exposition of the Ten Commandements* (1604), O8r. A sermon by Samuel Hieron gives a brief description of the joys of heaven, 'leaving it to be enlarged in your private thoughts': *The Spirituall Sonne-ship* (1611), B4v.
[49] Edward Philips, *Certaine Godly and Learned Sermons* (1605), N8v; Egerton, *Boring of the Eare*, D3v.

Sermon repetition was thus part of the push–pull relationship between ministers and people which has been well described by Peter Lake as 'a lay/ clerical dialogue with plenty of room for dissent and agreement, as the doctrines of the clergy were by turns internalised, misconstrued or pushed back at the ministers by their . . . lay clientele'.[50] In seeking to broaden the appeal of repetition, the godly clergy were naturally at pains to stress its more conservative aspects. Far from being 'puritanical' it was, they argued, an instrument of order and obedience, and a 'necessary duty' on all householders. In the father–son dialogue in *The House-holders Helpe*, the son remarks to his father: 'Where that course is continued, men are commonly accounted Puritans, and we that have used it, have beene much derided, scorned, and mocked for it, and many men (you know) in the Countrey, doe call it and terme it a *private Preaching*, and do not cease to say, that therein wee shew our selves to bee more precise than wise: what say you of such scorners?' The father replies that although 'such men account this course to be a novelty', it is no such thing. Sermon repetition is commanded in scripture ('Thou shalt whet these words on thy children', Deut. 6: 6–7) and has always been practised among Christians, for St Augustine taught 'that every Householder should bee the same in his owne house, as the Preacher is in the Pulpit'.[51]

Yet, at the same time, the clergy were very much aware of the subversive potential of sermon repetition. This is apparent not so much in the practical handbooks at the more elementary end of the art-of-hearing literature, as in the larger volumes of collected sermons and biblical commentaries intended for a more advanced godly readership. Edward Elton argued that household exercises were, or ought to be, wholly dependent on the public ministry. 'The teaching of Ministers of the Word depends onely on the teaching of Gods Spirit by his Word. But the teaching of Governors in a family depends on publike teaching, and must be ordered by it; and they must teach nothing but that they have learned and received from the publike Ministery, and is agreeable to it.'[52] Similarly, William Sclater argued that although the laity were granted 'power of examination', the main principles of Christianity were beyond dispute: 'God hath not made the people Umpiers of our doctrine . . . their *faith comes by hearing*, and what ever knowledge they have, they have by the Ministerie.'[53] This was, of course, precisely why clergy such as Bernard and Gouge were so anxious to keep

---

[50] Lake, *The Boxmaker's Revenge*, p. 410.   [51] R. R., *The House-holders Helpe*, C5v.
[52] Edward Elton, *Gods Holy Mind* (1625), S3v.   [53] Sclater, *Exposition*, 2K7v (i.540).

repetition under their control, even to the point of holding it in their own houses. And it can be argued that the 'thin line' that Collinson perceives between the repetition of sermons and the unaided exposition of scripture was, in fact, a line drawn by the godly clergy themselves in order to keep these 'right' and 'wrong' forms of repetition strictly apart.

Sclater's remarks are particularly interesting in this context, as he was one of two Somerset clergy, along with Edward Kellet, commissioned by their diocesan bishop, Arthur Lake, to examine an Anabaptist woman accused of preaching to private conventicles. The episode seems to have left a deep impression on all three men, and convinced them all of the need for severe measures to keep radical Protestantism in check.[54] Sclater and Kellet, however, responded in very different ways, Sclater by taking refuge in a conservative presbyterian position, Kellet by moving further in a Laudian direction. In his *Miscellanies of Divinitie*, Kellet offered a radical reinterpretation of the story of the men of Berea and argued that it provided no warrant whatsoever for the practice of sermon repetition. 'These Bereans were learned and eminent men. But every unlearned skullion now, that hath skill onely in the English originall, will contest with the profoundest Clerke. Secondly, these Bereans were unbeleevers ... Art thou an unbeleever? Do thou then as those unbeleevers did. If thou beleevest, shew me one passage of Scripture, where ever the unlearned people did call the doctrine of their learned Pastours into triall.'[55] This is not untypical of the Laudian polemic of the 1630s, where sermon repetition was treated as an inherently subversive and puritanical activity, and the distinction between 'right' and 'wrong' forms of repetition – which the godly clergy had struggled so hard to maintain – was casually dismantled. A preacher at Paul's Cross in 1637 complained that the words uttered from the pulpit 'shall anon become the subject of vaine talke', for 'with many of us our Religion is placed in the Tongue' and 'with the Purest of us a Sermon ends in a Repetition'.[56]

It could be argued that the Laudians had created the enemy they were seeking to combat by taking a huge swathe of perfectly innocuous lay activity and stigmatising it as schismatical. But they were not entirely mistaken in seeing repetition as a potential threat to the public services of the Church. With hindsight we can see that the art-of-hearing literature had a paradoxical effect: it encouraged the laity to pay more attention to the sermons they heard in church, but it also encouraged them to develop richer and more fulfilling

[54] Arthur Lake, *Sermons* (1629), 4F4r.
[55] Edward Kellet, *Miscellanies of Divinitie* (Cambridge, 1633), P1r.
[56] Sermon at Paul's Cross, 2 February 1636/7: Folger Shakespeare Library, Washington, DC, V.a.1, f. 64v.

routines of private devotion which, as Richard Rogers explained, could be used even 'when publike helpes by sermons cannot evermore be enjoyed'.[57] By the 1630s it was not only Laudian divines who were exercised by the possibility that these forms of private devotion might be used as a substitute for the public hearing of the Word. Thomas Gataker complained that some people 'content themselves with their owne private devotions; supposing that they may as well, and as effectually sanctifie a Sabbath by reading and meditating, and praying apart by themselves, as by being present at, and adjoyning themselves to the publike assemblies of Gods Saints'. Sclater, too, was afraid that some of 'our People' (by which he meant Protestants, as opposed to 'recusant Papists') might forsake public worship, 'thinking private devotions are better services'.[58] The art of hearing thus had the double effect of drawing attention towards preaching and drawing attention away from it.

By the early seventeenth century it was a commonplace among puritan divines that private devotions would be more deeply felt than public. 'The true Christian', declared William Whately, 'is rather more vehement in privat than in publike prayers, and can much rather omit the calling upon God with others, than those secret and inward communications with God, wherein he may freely powre his whole soule forth unto the Lord: and he satisfieth not himselfe, in having heard the Sermon, unlesse hee have chewed the cud, and considered if those things were so, and examined himselfe by that rule.'[59] This emphasis on private religious activities inevitably compromised the traditional puritan insistence on the centrality of public preaching. A handbook on private devotion published in the 1650s declared that 'every Sermon is but a preparation for meditation'. Where the divines of an earlier generation had spoken of 'bare reading' needing to be supplemented by preaching, this work spoke of 'bare hearing' needing to be supplemented by private meditation. 'Thus to meditate, one houre spent thus is more worth than a thousand sermons . . . Preaching is but reading of a lecture. A Physician that reads a lecture in the Schools, touching the curing of an ague, his reading will never doe it . . . the medicine must be applyed. So in Preaching . . . every one must spread the Plaster on his own heart.'[60] The art of hearing was intended to make sermons a pivotal part of the godly

---

[57]  Rogers, *Seven Treatises*, A6r.
[58]  Thomas Gataker, *Certaine Sermons* (1637), K5v, K6v; William Sclater, *A Briefe, and Plain Commentary . . . upon Malachy* (1650), E4r.
[59]  William Whately, *Gods Husbandry* (1619), K3r.
[60]  *A Method for Meditation, or a Manuall of Divine Duties, Fit for Every Christians Practice* (1651), C4r, D6r. This work is attributed on the title page to Archbishop Ussher, but Nicholas Bernard claimed that 'though some-what of the matter might have been collected from some Sermons of his in Ireland' it was not an authorised text: Bernard, *Penitent Death of a Woefull Sinner* (3rd edn., 1651), p. 337.

life, yet, in doing so, it created the conditions for a more private and internalised form of spirituality in which sermons played less part. Modern Protestantism is still living with the consequences.

MANAGING THE EMOTIONS

The art of hearing was a process of continual self-application, in which the hearers turned every point of doctrine into a practical 'use' by applying it to the heart and emotions. As such it was a highly affective activity. The hearers were urged to 'put on the preachers mind and affections, and by a certaine kind of spiritual alteration and change, be transformed into them'. They were to follow the preacher's discourse step by step, and 'in every point that is delivered . . . put upon themselves the like affection and feeling that is in their godly Teacher'.[61] The sermon was thus far more than the mere recital of doctrinal points that might appear on the printed page or in a hearer's notebook; in the hands of a skilled exponent it could become an almost theatrical event in which the preacher led his audience through various stages of penitence or consolation before bringing them to a kind of emotional resolution or catharsis. Yet many historians have asserted otherwise – for there is a long-standing scholarly tradition which regards early modern Protestant preaching as highly intellectual, rigorously logical and utterly averse to any display of emotion.

This tradition goes back a very long way – back, in fact, to Weber, who argued in *The Protestant Ethic and the Spirit of Capitalism* that Puritanism took an 'absolutely negative position' towards the sensuous and emotional aspects of religion, as being 'useless for salvation'.[62] This line of argument was further developed in Perry Miller's classic study, *The New England Mind*, first published in 1939, which associated Puritanism with an 'unremitting insistence that all conduct be rational' and argued that puritan psychology 'underlined this moral by describing the mechanism of behaviour so that the rule of reason became an inescapable factor in all actions'. Miller's Exhibit A was the puritan minister William Ames, author of one of the standard university textbooks on psychology, who 'founded the whole ethical system' upon the belief that the human will must necessarily follow the judgement of the intellect, and 'wrote this doctrine deep into the New England tradition'.[63] And Miller's interpretation was followed by

---

[61] Zepper, *Art or Skil*, G6r; Egerton, *Boring of the Eare*, E2r.
[62] Max Weber, *The Protestant Ethic and the Spirit of Capitalism*, trans. Stephen Kalberg (Los Angeles, 2002), p. 60.
[63] Perry Miller, *The New England Mind: The Seventeenth Century* (Boston, 1961), pp. 248–9, 265.

other scholars, notably David Leverenz, who asserted in *The Language of Puritan Feeling* (1980) that the chief characteristics of puritan preaching were 'intellectual control of feelings' and 'lengthy logical rigour', as opposed to 'emotional display or sprawl'. Leverenz's view of puritan preaching was a notably cheerless one. 'Congregations sat for up to two hours listening to God's familiar instructions repeated in the familiar format. Quite unabashedly, sermons were meant to be repressive.'[64]

The influence of Perry Miller is not as strong in England as in America, but even among historians of English Puritanism there has been a strong tendency to regard puritan preaching as austerely logical and unemotional. Many of the older literary studies of preaching, such as W. Fraser Mitchell's *English Pulpit Oratory* (1932), drew a distinction between two main styles of sermon – the Anglican 'metaphysical' style and the puritan 'plain' style – derived from Quintilian's distinction between two main styles of oratory, the grand and the plain. The difference between these two styles, according to Quintilian, was that the grand style was designed to appeal to the emotions, whereas the plain style was designed to teach and instruct.[65] This led literary scholars such as Mitchell to characterise puritan preaching as ferociously intellectual, concerned above all with imparting information, and opposed to the use of rhetorical techniques to move and persuade an audience. And this was borne out – or so it seemed – not only by the puritan preachers' constant invocation of 'plainness', and their attack on flashy rhetorical ornaments as having no purpose except to tickle the ear, but also by the sermons themselves, which, with their doctrines, reasons and uses, their logical structure and their lists of numbered points, seemed far more reminiscent of a school textbook than a piece of persuasive oratory.

Debora Shuger offered a powerful challenge to this tradition in *Sacred Rhetoric* (1988), in which she traced the origins and development of the 'Christian grand style' of oratory, 'an aesthetic of vividness, drama and expressivity' in which the preacher was expected to speak with passionate eloquence in order to stir the emotions of his hearers. As she showed, it was this grand style, not the plain style, that provided the template for most early modern preaching, Protestant and Catholic alike. Even Shuger, however, could not entirely shake off the assumption that puritan preaching was logical and unemotional; for example, she argued that some English preachers, such as Samuel Hieron, rejected the grand style in favour of 'a rigidly

[64] David Leverenz, *The Language of Puritan Feeling* (Rutgers, NJ, 1980), p. 142.
[65] Quintilian, *Institutio Oratoria*, 12.10, in *The Orator's Education*, Books 11–12, ed. and trans. Donald A. Russell (Cambridge, MA, 2001), p. 313.

plain teaching style, designed more to instruct than to move'.[66] And where scholars have encountered sermons that make a direct appeal to the emotions, they have tended to assume that this must represent an alternative to the mainstream puritan tradition. Historians of the Great Awakening, for example, have argued that emotional preaching was a product of the evangelical revival. Michael Crawford wrote in 1987 that 'the role of emotional appeal in eighteenth-century revivalist preaching was new'. Earlier preachers, he argued, had subordinated the emotions to the intellect, and 'appealed to the emotions only as a means of arousing the hearer to implement that which he had been convinced was the good and the true'; but 'as the understanding of psychology changed in the eighteenth century, rhetorical strategies changed as well'.[67] Emotional preaching, in other words, could not have existed before the eighteenth century, because the psychological theory that validated it had not yet been formulated.

In this section, I want to explore the affective aspects of the art of hearing and, in doing so, to challenge the common view of puritan preaching as addressed to the intellect rather than to the emotions. I wish to argue that Weber was fundamentally mistaken in regarding Puritanism as unsympathetic to religious emotion – just as Perry Miller was mistaken in regarding Ames's ethical system as governed primarily by the 'rule of reason'. As Norman Fiering has shown, Miller's theory rests on a misreading of the primary sources, which attributes to Ames the doctrine that he was actually attacking.[68] Ames was, in fact, drawing on a prominent school of thought within the scholastic tradition, which regarded theology as an 'affective science' chiefly concerned with goodness rather than knowledge. He argued that the scriptures did not resemble a list of 'universall and scientificall rules' so much as a collection of 'narrations, examples, precepts, exhortations, admonitions, and promises: because that manner doth make most for the common use of all kindes of men, and also most to affect the will, and stirre up godly motions, which is the chiefe scope of Divinity'.[69] That emphasis on the 'stirring up of godly motions' was central to the puritan understanding of preaching, which was not simply concerned with the imparting

[66] Debora K. Shuger, *Sacred Rhetoric: The Christian Grand Style in the English Renaissance* (Princeton, 1988), p. 93.
[67] Michael J. Crawford, 'Origins of the eighteenth-century evangelical revival: England and New England compared', *Journal of British Studies*, 26 (1987), pp. 361–97 (quotation p. 382). See also G. J. Barker-Benfield, *The Culture of Sensibility: Sex and Society in Eighteenth-Century Britain* (Chicago and London, 1992), p. 72.
[68] Norman Fiering, *Moral Philosophy at Seventeenth-Century Harvard: A Discipline in Transition* (Chapel Hill, NC, 1981), p. 121.
[69] William Ames, *The Marrow of Sacred Divinity* (1642), B1v, N3r.

of information but with the wider task of bringing the will of man into conformity with the will of God.

In accordance with this theory of affective identification, puritan ministers constantly reiterated the classical maxim that a preacher must stir up emotion in his own heart in order to communicate it to others.[70] William Perkins gave definitive expression to this view in his treatise on preaching, *The Arte of Prophecying*, where he insisted that a preacher must possess an 'inward feeling' of the doctrine to be delivered. 'Wood, that is capable of fire, doth not burne, unles fire be put to it: and he must first be godly affected himself, who would stirre up godly affections in other men. Therefore what motions a sermon doth require, such the Preacher shall stirre up privately in his owne mind, that he may kindle up the same in his hearers.'[71] The effects of this on pulpit rhetoric have been well summarised by Susan James as 'an emphasis on sincerity and expressiveness, and on the use of a felt, if irregular rhetoric, as opposed to a polished and carefully contrived style'.[72] There was also an emphasis on non-verbal forms of communication, such as voice and gesture, which – precisely because they were not so susceptible to rhetorical analysis – were deemed to be especially effective means of conveying the inward affections. Perkins recommended that the arms, hands, face and eyes should all 'have such motions, as may express and (as it were) utter the godly affections of the heart', though he did not specify exactly what these gestures might be, apart from advising preachers to follow 'the ensample of the gravest Ministers in this kind'. This was in line with most of the sixteenth-century rhetorical handbooks that Perkins would have known, which argued that gesture was better learnt by imitation than by rules and general principles, as it varied so much from country to country.[73]

The consensus of these handbooks was that preachers should cultivate a dignified moderation in their delivery, avoiding histrionic gestures such as waving the arms, stamping the feet or rolling the eyes, which Protestants tended to associate with the more theatrical preaching style of the Jesuits and monastic orders.[74] Richard Bernard, in his treatise on preaching,

---

[70] Quintilian, *Institutio Oratoria*, 6.2, in *The Orator's Education*, Books 6–8, ed. Russell, p. 59: 'we should ourselves be moved before we try to move others'.

[71] William Perkins, *The Arte of Prophecying*, in *Works*, vol. II (Cambridge, 1609), 3V4v.

[72] Susan James, *Passion and Action: The Emotions in Seventeenth-Century Philosophy* (Oxford, 1997), p. 231.

[73] Dilwyn Knox, 'Ideas on gesture and universal languages *c.* 1500–1650', in J. Henry and S. Hutton, eds., *New Perspectives on Renaissance Thought* (London, 1990), p. 101–36.

[74] See, for example, Wilhelm Bucanus, *Ecclesiastes, Seu de Formandis Sacris Concionibus* (Berne, 1604), E8v: condemnation of '*histrionica gesticulatio, et levitas*'; Amandus Polanus, *De Concionum Sacrarum Methodo* (Basle, 1604), Z2v: condemnation of histrionic gestures ('*quorum imitatores Jesuitae aliique monachi sunt*') such as '*agitatio et gesticulatis*' of the hands and feet.

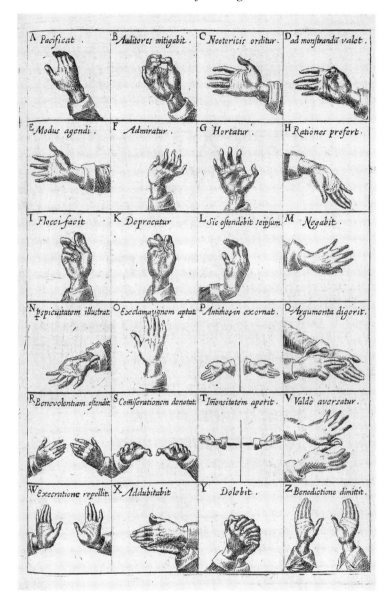

Figure 5 Hand gestures, from John Bulwer, *Chirologia, or the Naturall Language of the Hand* (1644). Reproduced by permission of Cambridge University Library.

stressed the need for 'seemly gesture' and criticised preachers who with 'rash boldnesse', 'inconsiderate zeale' or 'heat of affection', indulged in 'violent motions, as casting abroad of their armes, smiting on the Pulpit, lifting themselves up, and againe suddenly stamping downe very unadvisedly'. John Bulwer's treatise on hand gestures, *Chironomia, or the Art of Manuall Rhetorique* (1644), also took a fairly conservative approach, expressing reservations about some of the more dramatic forms of gesture. Bulwer noted, for example, that the gesture of striking the chest with the hand to signify grief or sorrow was employed by the Jesuits to such powerful effect that 'while they beat their Breasts, they raise oftentimes great motions in the minds of their Auditors, and religious teares are drawne from the eyes of many'. But this 'loud contact of the hand', he argued, was not perfectly 'fitted to the rule of Art', and preachers would be better advised to strike their chest with a 'peaceable meeknesse', without making any audible noise. In the same spirit of moderation, he urged preachers to strike their hand on a book instead of 'smiting upon the thigh', and to strike their fist on the pulpit instead of seizing and shaking the pulpit rail – the latter being, in Bulwer's words, a gesture of 'inconsiderate rashnesse' arising from 'a turbulent and furious motion of a vaine minde'.[75]

Not all preachers, though, were convinced of the need for moderation. In his *Treatise of the Affections* (1642), the Essex minister William Fenner attempted to justify the dramatic and emotional style of preaching that Bernard, Bulwer and others found so objectionable. Fenner's crucial move was to locate the seat of the affections in the will, rather than (with 'Aristotle and most of our Divines') in the sensual or irrational part of the soul. This enabled him to argue that the preacher's aim should not be to moderate the affections, but to stir them up through the uninhibited use of voice, gesture and emotion. 'O that wee would sigh, and *sob, and grone in our pulpits*, O that we could even wet our cushions with tears, and yearn over your soules as we preach … When the Minister is affected aright, and his affections direct the carriage of the voyce along, the voyce it selfe does more significantly expresse the matter: and this no question is very moving.' And Fenner argued that this would have a strongly physical effect, since the affections would work on 'the humours and parts of the body' in order to bring about the desired object. Thus the affection of joy would act upon the spleen, anger upon the gall bladder, fear upon the heart; 'yea the affections make humours, bloud, spirits, members, even bones and all the body for to

---

[75] John Bulwer, *Chirologia: or the Natural Language of the Hand [with] Chironomia: or the Art of Manual Rhetoric*, ed. James W. Cleary (Carbondale, IL, 1974), pp. 183, 186.

suffer. Hence it is, when a man sets his affections upon God, *his feare*, the feare of God makes him *tremble*; his *Love*, the love of God makes him to *weepe for his sinnes*.'[76]

By great good fortune we have an eyewitness account of Fenner in the pulpit, and can therefore get a sense of what this 'affectionate' style of preaching might mean in practice. John Rogers, at the age of ten, heard a sermon by Fenner and found it an unforgettable experience:

Hearing Mr *William Fenner* full of *zeal*, stirring about, and *thundring* and beating the Pulpit; I was *amazed*, and *thought* he was *mad*; I *wondred* what he meant, and whilest I was *gazing* upon him, I was *struck*, and saw it was we that were mad which made him so; O sayes he! you *knotty! rugged! proud piece of flesh!* You *stony, rocky, flinty, hard heart!* What *wilt thou doe when thou art roaring in Hell amongst the damned!* &c.[77]

In his writings, Fenner modestly disclaimed any special skill in the use of gesture ('for my part, I have little reason to name it'), but argued that it was a great asset to the preacher, 'a blessing of Christ to them that have it, for they have a great advantage over the affections of their hearers'. He justified the use of dramatic and symbolic gestures by pointing out that they were 'much employed in the Preaching of the Prophets and the holy men of God':

*Ezechiel* was commanded to *stamp with the feet. Isaiah* commanded to goe naked. *Ieremy* commanded to put a yoke on his neck. *Iohn Baptist* was *totus vox*. He was all-voyce; the voyce of a cryer in the wildernesse . . . his eyes spake, and his face spake, his hands spake, and his body spake, yea, his life, and dyet, and all spake, he was all-voyce.[78]

Fenner argued that the skilful preacher would achieve his effects through a series of vivid mental images: 'when hee preaches of hell, he preaches to the life, as if hell were before mens eyes; when he preaches of heaven, as if the people did see it with their eyes as it were'. He stressed that this was not to be taken literally – there was, for example, no justification for bringing a skull into the pulpit, 'as some that I have read of, have done' – but in other respects he seems to have felt that the preacher could hardly go too far in stimulating the imagination of his audience, maintaining that as long as the affections were 'fixed on their proper object, there is no danger in the excesse'.

---

[76] William Fenner, *A Treatise of the Affections: or, the Soules Pulse* (1642), B3r.
[77] John Rogers, *Ohel or Beth-shemesh, A Tabernacle for the Sun* (1653), 3H4r (p. 419).
[78] Fenner, *Treatise of the Affections*, I8v–K1r.

The best-known exponent of this type of preaching was another Essex minister, John Rogers of Dedham. There are accounts of Rogers imitating a hunting cry, 'Soho! Soho!' as he compared impenitent sinners to huntsmen following the hounds; Rogers 'taking hold with both hands at one time of the supporters of the Canopy over the Pulpit, and roaring hideously, to represent the torments of the damned'; Rogers lifting the Bible from the pulpit cushion as if to take it away, then falling to his knees and crying out 'Lord, whatsoever thou dost to us, take not thy Bible from us; kill our children, burn our houses, destroy our goods; only spare us thy Bible, only take not away thy Bible.' This led to extraordinary scenes: there are stories of Rogers reducing entire congregations to tears, and Thomas Goodwin described how he came out of one of Rogers's sermons so overcome that he was 'fain to hang a quarter of an hour upon the neck of his horse weeping, before he had power to mount'.[79] Nothing quite like this was to be found elsewhere in England; the closest equivalent was the revivalist preaching pioneered by Scottish preachers in Ulster in the 1620s. James Glendinning, the instigator of the Ulster revival, was celebrated for his 'great voice and vehement delivery', and for his 'thundering way of preaching' which 'exceedingly terrified his hearers'. One admiring eyewitness described Glendinning's hearers 'stricken into a swoon with the word; yea, a dozen in one day carried out of doors as dead; so marvellous was the power of God, smiting their hearts for sin'.[80]

Yet this type of preaching was not at all common. The situation in Ulster was highly unusual, in that the Irish bishops seem to have turned a blind eye to what was going on, leaving the Scottish ministers free to develop their own distinctive style of preaching with relatively little interference. Even some of the ministers themselves had reservations about the effects of their preaching on the hearers: John Livingstone was disturbed by the sight of 'some people who used in time of sermon to fall on a high breathing and panting, as those do who have run long', and doubted whether this could truly be the work of the Holy Spirit.[81] Fenner and Rogers were both Essex ministers, and their style of preaching could only have flourished as it did in a county such as Essex, with a highly developed puritan subculture. Rogers's

---

[79] Andrew Clark, 'Dr Plume's notebook', *Essex Review*, 13 (1904), p. 153; Oliver Heywood, *A Narrative of the Holy Life and Happy Death of . . . Mr John Angier* (1685), B2v (p. 6); Thomas Goodwin, *Works*, ed. J. C. Miller and R. Halley (Edinburgh, 1861–6), vol. II, p. xviii.

[80] *The Life of Mr Robert Blair*, ed. Thomas McCrie (Edinburgh, 1848), pp. 70–1; *A Brief Historical Relation of the Life of Mr John Livingstone*, ed. Thomas Houston (Edinburgh, 1848), p. 263. On the Ulster revival, see Marilyn J. Westerkamp, *Triumph of the Laity: Scots-Irish Piety and the Great Awakening, 1625–1760* (Oxford, 1988), pp. 23–30, and Leigh Eric Schmidt, *Holy Fairs: Scotland and the Making of American Revivalism* (Princeton, 1989; 2nd edn. Grand Rapids, 2001), pp. 29–32.

[81] Houston, *Life of Mr John Livingstone*, p. 82.

Tuesday lecture was a major public event, a magnet for godly hearers from all over the county who came for the sermon and then 'staid, discoursed, dispatched business' – putting it in a very different category from the ordinary Sunday parish sermon – and most contemporary observers seem to have regarded his style of preaching as highly exceptional. Ralph Brownrigg was said to have contrasted Rogers's 'wild Note' with the 'set Musick' of other preachers. 'Those that knew his manner of preaching, and actings in preaching', commented Giles Firmin, 'well knew what the Bishop meant by the *wild Note*', adding that only Rogers would have been able to carry off 'such actions and speeches' without appearing ridiculous. When Oliver Heywood described Rogers's sermons in 1685 he felt compelled to add that 'some expressions and gestures he used, would now seem indecent', an interesting reflection of the development of preaching style and the general distrust of 'enthusiastic' preaching in the later seventeenth century.[82]

Moreover, the psychological theory that legitimised this style of preaching does not appear to have been generally shared. Fenner, as we have seen, located the affections in the will, and argued that it was the preacher's duty to inflame them in order to draw the will more ardently towards God. Other writers, by contrast, located the affections both in the intellectual and sensual parts of the soul, and argued that it was the preacher's duty to moderate them in order to prevent the will being led astray by the sensual appetite. The Staffordshire minister John Ball revealingly expressed this in terms of a political metaphor. 'When the will, ruled by prudence, over-ruleth, moderateth and governeth passions', the soul is at peace, but 'when passions arise up and oppose themselves against the rule of Government', the soul is troubled. The passions must therefore be 'well guided, and discreetly moderated' to prevent them running riotously out of control and overthrowing the rational government of the will.[83] This was an implicit rebuke to the 'affectionate' style of preaching favoured by Fenner and Rogers – a rebuke echoed in plainer terms by other writers, who complained of 'some men in our daies' who were 'alwaies moving and perswading, but never teaching', or who sought 'to gaine an interest in our affections before they offer to informe our judgement'.[84]

---

[82] Giles Firmin, *The Real Christian, or a Treatise of Effectual Calling* (1670), R1v (p. 76); Heywood, *Life of Angier*, B2r (p. 5).

[83] John Ball, *The Power of Godlines, Both Doctrinally, and Practically Handled* (1657), Z2v. Ball died in 1640, though his treatise remained unpublished until 1657.

[84] Griffith Williams, *The Best Religion* (1636), 2M4r; Lake, *Sermons*, 4I3r (iii.101).

But while Fenner and Rogers were certainly unusual, even exceptional in their unabashed appeal to the emotions, they were not outside the religious mainstream. It was generally agreed that preaching should be addressed to the emotions; the only disagreement was over how, and to what extent, this should be done. Both Fenner and Ball saw it as the preacher's task to move and persuade; the difference between them was that Fenner saw the will as naturally hard and stubborn, needing to be 'wrought on', like iron, to make it responsive to God, whereas Ball saw it as naturally indolent and lazy, like an 'uncarefull Magistrate', inclined to submit to the emotions rather than keeping them in check, and therefore needing to be properly directed. Despite this difference, both were committed to an affective form of preaching in which the preacher sought to move others by being moved himself. And within this broad consensus on the need for affective preaching, the existence of Fenner's and Rogers's highly affective style of preaching is significant because it calls into question Eamon Duffy's argument that Protestant preachers were disadvantaged by their hostility to ritual and drama and their failure to use the 'emotional and emotive devotional practices' of their Catholic counterparts.[85] For all the conventional stress on moderation it is clear that Protestant preaching could, on occasion, be as dramatic and flamboyant as anything in the Counter-Reformation repertoire.

In trying to 'hear', in our minds, what an early modern sermon might have sounded like, we should therefore think of it as a dramatic, almost theatrical performance in which the preacher would have used expressive gestures and varied the pitch and tone of his voice in order to convey emotion. Richard Bernard noted that there was 'one voice and speech for doctrine, another for exhortation, threats, and dehortations', implying that the preacher would raise his voice as he moved towards the emotional climax of the sermon. Fenner typically took this to extremes by requiring the preacher to move through a whole range of different voices in the course of the sermon, 'compassionately in points of pity . . . rejoycingly in points of comfort . . . most terrible in points of terror'. These could have served as a series of auditory cues to mark the transition from one part of the sermon to another, and to alert the audience to the appropriate response. The ability to vary the tone of voice was clearly regarded as a major part of the art of preaching; Richard Baxter noted rather sadly in 1656 that he had once had 'as naturally persuading and moving a voice as most men had', but that the

---

[85] Eamon Duffy, 'The Long Reformation: Catholicism, Protestantism and the multitude', in Nicholas Tyacke, ed., *England's Long Reformation, 1500–1800* (1998), pp. 33–70 (quotation p. 64).

effort of preaching in a large church had overstrained his voice and it had subsequently become 'fixed in an ineffectual reading tone, which I never since could overcome'. And these different tones of voice may have been quite far removed from a natural speaking voice. Cotton Mather famously overcame his stammer by preaching in 'a Drawling ... little short of Singing', and this very deliberate way of speaking (possibly resembling the nasal tone or 'nose-twang' for which puritan preachers were sometimes mocked) does not seem to have been regarded as particularly eccentric.[86]

This highly affective style of preaching was intended to draw an equally affective response from the audience. The mass outbreaks of weeping which greeted some of John Rogers's sermons may have been rare events, but weeping at a sermon was widely encouraged in the art-of-hearing manuals and does not seem to have been at all uncommon. 'The tears of the people are the Ministers praise', declared William Jenkyn in his funeral sermon for the London puritan minister William Gouge, in which he praised Gouge for having succeeded so often in reducing his auditors to tears. Robert Hill described the 'good Sermon' as one which 'speakes especially to my heart, woundeth my conscience' and 'moveth me to teares'.[87] The Essex minister John Smith believed that hardly anyone could fail to weep for his sins 'at one time or other ... if God have a purpose to save him'. He was prepared to make an exception for 'those men whom their naturall hard and drie temper of their eyes disableth perpetually from all teares', but emphasised that this was 'a rare case, no ordinarie thing, it is that which seldome falls out one of a thousand'. Not only was it necessary to weep, it was necessary to do so frequently and copiously. John Mayer cautioned those who were 'most easily moved to weeping' that they 'cannot be godly sorrowful enough without shedding of many teares. It is not a little weeping upon some sudden motion, that is enough, but the most abundant weeping and gushing out of teares from their eyes.'[88]

This emphasis on weeping as the ultimate validation of a sincere repentance is encapsulated in Nicholas Bernard's account of the disgraced Irish prelate John Atherton, executed for sodomy in 1640. Bernard sanitises and

---

[86] Baxter to Henry Newcomb, 28 Nov. 1656: N.H. Keeble and G.F. Nuttall, *Calendar of the Correspondence of Richard Baxter*, vol. 1, *1638–1660* (Oxford, 1991), letter 338; Cotton Mather, *The Angel of Bethesda: An Essay upon the Common Maladies of Mankind*, ed. Gordon W. Jones (American Antiquarian Society, 1972), p. 231; Helen Wilcox, 'Puritans, George Herbert and "nose-twange"', *Notes & Queries*, April 1979, pp. 152–3.

[87] William Jenkyn, *A Shock of Corn* (1654), B2r; Hill, *Path-way*, T4v. For a typical example of an affective response to a sermon, see *Winthrop Papers*, vol. 1, ed. Worthington C. Ford (Massachusetts Historical Society, 1929), p. 199.

[88] Smith, *Essex Dove*, Z1r et seq; Mayer, *Praxis Theologica*, 3D2r.

spiritualises Atherton's humiliating death by turning it into a model conversion narrative and suffuses it with tears to an extent that would not seem
out of place in an eighteenth-century novel of sensibility. Atherton unbur-
dens his conscience with 'a flood of *teares*, casting himselfe downe to the
ground, taking me by the hand, and desiring me to kneele downe by him, and
pray for him'. He finds 'such sweetnesse in teares for sinne' that he wants
them to 'streame downe his Cheeks continually'. 'Naturally he was not apt for
teares, but now he was a man of teares . . . His very countenance was altered.'
On the morning of his execution he falls into 'abundance of teares, adding,
whereas *before I wept for sorrow, now I weepe for joy*', and looks forward to the
happiness of heaven, 'in the thought of which he was much ravished, and fell
into a *long continued weeping, from this ground*, that he should have offended
one that had prepared such inestimable things for him'. On the scaffold, he
makes a final prayer. 'We all kneeled down with him, but such a moving
prayer did I never heare, never was I compassed about so with tears, and sobs
in my life, not bare weeping, but gushing out of teares, which flowed from all
that heard him.' Finally he takes leave of his friends, telling them that he has
no fear of death, at which 'the whole company wept abundantly'.[89]

It is clear that many laypeople were strongly attracted to this culture of
affectivity. The spiritual testimonies collected by Vavasour Powell from
members of his gathered congregation in the 1650s frequently emphasise the
cathartic effect of tears. 'The most comfort to my spirit', wrote one woman,
'is when I am weeping for my infirmities . . . me thinks I find such joy in
them, that I could dwel there, having no comfort in the world like that'.[90]
And there are signs that some preachers were starting to get alarmed by the
power of the emotions released in this way. Paul Baynes, who succeeded
William Perkins in the pulpit of St Andrew's, Cambridge, advised the godly
to weep in private rather than in public, and warned them not to cultivate
'such a fluent and melting temper' that they wept on every occasion. Other
ministers pointed out that the expression of emotion varied greatly from
person to person, with some people being 'so dry and unapt to shed teares'
that they could hardly weep at all, while others were 'most easily moved to
weeping, when any passion commeth upon the minde', so that the capacity
to shed tears was not necessarily an indicator of a more powerful spiritual
experience.[91] The painful psychological contortions that some individuals

---

[89] Nicholas Bernard, *The Penitent Death of a Woefull Sinner* (Dublin, 1641).
[90] Vavasour Powell, *Spirituall Experiences, of Sundry Beleevers* (1653), E2r (p. 75).
[91] Paul Baynes, *A Helpe to True Happinesse: or, A Briefe and Learned Exposition of the Maine and
   Fundamentall Points of Christian Religion* (3rd edn., 1635), D11r; Mayer, *Praxis Theologica*, 3D2r; Arthur
   Hildersham, *The Doctrine of Fasting and Prayer* (1633), N1v; Thomas Taylor, *Works* (1653), (K)2r.

went through in trying to strike the right balance between too many tears and too few can be seen in the testimony of 'E.C.', another member of Powell's gathered congregation, who stated that 'through griefe that I could not sorrow enough, I have fallen into a great measure of weeping'.[92] Anna Trapnel recalled how, in her youth, she 'ran from Minister to Minister, from Sermon to Sermon . . . and if I had not shed some tears in a Sermon, I then went home full of horror, concluding my self to be that stony ground Christ spake of in the parable of the sower'. Her account of how she 'delighted in the thunderings of the Law', and in those preachers who 'preached most upon the Law', is highly revealing of the way that the powerful, hellfire preaching of a Fenner or a Rogers could be both alluring and terrifying, making the more consolatory sermons of other preachers appear 'cold, lean, poor' by comparison.[93]

Emotional preaching, and emotional responses to preaching, fell out of favour in the later seventeenth century, partly because of accusations of 'enthusiasm' and fears of religious melancholy. Firmin was very anxious to refute the accusation that 'when once men begin to be Puritans, they must loose all their mirth and cheerfulnes' and that 'nothing but mopishness, sadness, and sour faces' would suffice.[94] But it was also the result of a gradual relocation of religious emotion from the public to the private domain. Even in the early seventeenth century, there were hints of this in the art-of-hearing literature. 'An earnest exhortation, and the power of a good Sermon, may draw an hypocrite to teares', declared William Whately in 1619, 'but a godly man without any of these things, will set himselfe to mourne, and lament, and most willingly (out of the love hee beares to God, whom his sinnes have offended) wil even turne his joy into sorrow, and his laughter into teares.' Outward appearances, Whately was suggesting, might deceive both oneself and others; only private actions could provide a reliable guide to one's inner condition. As the term 'hypocrisy' became restricted to its modern meaning, of a deliberate attempt to deceive others rather than (as Whately understood it) an unconscious self-deception, so the emphasis on private behaviour as the only true test of sincerity became even more marked. Religious emotion should not be displayed in public, one eighteenth-century manual of etiquette advised its female readers, for 'nothing is more hidden than true Devotion, it being lodged entirely in

[92] Powell, *Spirituall Experiences*, E3v (p. 78).
[93] Anna Trapnel, *A Legacy for Saints* (1654), B1v, B2v (pp. 2, 4). Trapnel's testimony is perceptively analysed by David Como in *Blown by the Spirit: Puritanism and the Emergence of an Antinomian Underground in Pre-Civil-War England* (Stanford, 2004), pp. 435–6.
[94] Firmin, *Real Christian*, O3v (p. 56).

the Heart, whilst the false and affected is quite the Reverse, studying nothing but Exteriors in order to appear what it is not'. 'During the Time of Sermon' one should therefore behave 'with Gravity and Attention' rather than with any show of emotion.[95]

This was not, of course, the only way to hear sermons in the eighteenth century. The public display of emotion was still socially acceptable, both for women and men, to a quite surprising extent; and the preaching of the early Methodists shows that there was ample scope for emotional responses to sermons.[96] In eighteenth-century physiology, however, the eye was regarded as the sense organ most intimately connected with the emotions, and it was believed that sentiment could most easily be excited by physically beholding or mentally visualising an emotive spectacle. In the words of Henry Home, Lord Kames, 'writers of genius, sensible that the eye is the best avenue to the heart, represent everything as passing in our sight, and, from readers or hearers, transform us as it were into spectators'.[97] Given the demise of the reading/preaching distinction, as shown in the last chapter, this led to a strong emphasis on reading (books) or viewing (plays) rather than hearing (sermons). The emotions that would once have been felt on hearing a sermon were now more likely to be experienced in private prayer or meditation, or in the intimacy of personal engagement with a printed book.

NOTE-TAKING AND THE WRITTEN TRACES OF HEARING

Henry Smith, writing in the 1590s, was conscious of living in an era of rapid educational progress, when new technologies of reading and writing (short-hand being one example) were becoming much more widely used. 'This age', he remarked, 'hath devised divers methods to learne many things in shorter time than they were learned of old. A man may spend seven yeares in learning to write, and hee may meete with a Scribe which will teach him as much in a moneth.' And so it was with the art of hearing, which, in Smith's view, had the potential to transform the effectiveness of the preaching ministry in England. It might be unfamiliar to most of his hearers, but if they were willing to give it a try, they would find that they could 'learne

---

[95]  Whately, *Gods Husbandry*, H3v. *The Lady's Preceptor, or a Letter to a Young Lady of Distinction upon Politeness . . . By a Gentleman of Cambridge* (4th edn., 1752), pp. 6–7.

[96]  Anne Vincent-Buffault, *The History of Tears: Sensibility and Sentimentality in France* (London, 1991); Barker-Benfield, *Culture of Sensibility*, p. 72.

[97]  Quoted by Ann Jessie Van Sant, *Eighteenth-Century Sensibility and the Novel: The Senses in Social Context* (Cambridge, 1993), p. 29.

more in a moneth, than they have gathered in twentie yeares'.[98] His call did
not go unheeded. Sermon repetition – which Smith presented as a relatively
novel technique, little practised outside the universities – quickly became an
established part of the godly lifestyle; and by the 1620s there was a substantial body of literature devoted to the art of hearing, teaching the laity
how to engage, intellectually and emotionally, with the preacher's message
and reinforce it through repetition and prayer. But how successful was it?
Did it really have the transformative effect that Smith had hoped for? To
answer these questions, we need to move beyond the clerical advice literature and try to reconstruct, if we can, the personal experience of individual
hearers.

One crucial source that can help us reconstruct the audience response to
sermons is the large body of sermon notes surviving from the early modern
period. These were, of course, heavily influenced by clerical expectations,
and it would be quite wrong to think of them as providing a 'view from the
pew' that was wholly independent of the view from the pulpit. Yet it would
be equally wrong to think of them as derivative exercises written to the
preacher's dictation. Charles Lloyd Cohen, in his fine study of New
England Puritanism, *God's Caress* (1986), makes the point that sermons
had an afterlife beyond the pulpit and outside the preacher's control. As he
remarks, the appearance of a sermon fragment in a notebook or spiritual
autobiography 'testifies to a personal act of choice, for every selection
represents a talk plucked out of oblivion and accorded peculiar importance.
Once a sermon left a preacher's mouth it belonged to the congregation and
was subject to their interpretations.'[99] What we can occasionally glimpse, in
surviving sermon notes, is a gap between the preacher's intentions and the
hearer's response – and it is this gap that can help us measure the effectiveness of the art of hearing.

Note-taking not only assisted the memory but also helped the hearer to
grasp the overall structure of the sermon. By the early seventeenth century
most university-educated clergy framed their sermons according to a
doctrine-and-use structure, in which they began with a general observation
(or 'doctrine'), supported it with scriptural arguments (or 'reasons') and
then drew out a practical application (or 'use'). This was closely related to
the Ramist theory of dialectic, which – with the characteristically Ramist
emphasis on putting theory into practice – divided dialectic into three parts:

---

[98] Smith, 'Art of hearing', in *Sermons*, V6v (p. 316).
[99] Charles Lloyd Cohen, *God's Caress: The Psychology of Puritan Religious Experience* (Oxford, 1986),
   p. 188.

a natural origin (*natura*), a theory of discourse (*doctrina*) and a practical application (*usus*). One of its great attractions, in the eyes of its practitioners, was that it appeared so transparently logical. Nehemiah Rogers argued in 1631 that every sermon preached according to this method was capable of being resolved into a syllogism, with the doctrine as premise and the uses as conclusion – and one of the great advantages of this method, Rogers believed, was that it made it easier for the audience to follow the preacher's train of argument. 'A Burden well wrapped, and pack't up together, wee carry with greater ease: both *Minister* and *Hearer* is much help'd by *Method*.'[100] It was for this reason that note-taking was encouraged. Some ministers feared that it would dull the emotional force of the sermon, but most saw it as a useful aid to memory which, by helping the hearers to follow the preacher's argument, would also help them to appreciate its logical structure and its deduction from scripture.

The doctrine-and-use method was extremely popular in England, so much so that the Catholic convert Richard Sheldon, writing to Thomas James in 1612, went so far as to dub it the 'English method'.[101] It has sometimes been seen as a distinctively puritan style of preaching, but its popularity is indicative of a general respect for logical order and discipline in preaching, which was not exclusively puritan any more than it was exclusively Ramist. Nehemiah Rogers's sermon of 1631, quoted above, is a particularly instructive example of the way that the doctrine-and-use method could appeal to more than one style of churchmanship. Rogers was an alumnus of that most puritan of colleges, Emmanuel in Cambridge, and his sermon bears many of the hallmarks of puritan divinity – as, for example, when he encourages able ministers to preach twice on the sabbath-day, or advises young divines to study Calvin's *Institutes* as well as the Articles and Homilies of the Church of England. Yet it was preached before none other than William Laud, in the course of his episcopal visitation of the diocese of London, and many passages give the impression of having been written to Laud's dictation – as when Rogers attacks 'schismatics' and 'conventicles', and urges preachers to concentrate on the basic principles of Christianity rather than exercising their wits on 'the question of Predestination'.[102] In this context, Rogers's endorsement of the doctrine-and-use method can be seen as a way of bridging the gap

[100]  Nehemiah Rogers, *A Sermon Preached at the Second Triennial Visitation of . . . William Lord Bishop of London* (1632), C2v (p. 12).
[101]  Richard Sheldon to James, 3 April 1612, in G. W. Wheeler, ed., *Letters Addressed to Thomas James* (Oxford, 1933), p. 54.
[102]  Rogers, *Sermon*, D3v (p. 22).

between Laud and the puritan clergy of London. This was a preaching style with impeccable puritan credentials, yet it also answered Laud's desire for a sober and orthodox method of preaching that was solidly grounded on scripture, as opposed, in Rogers's words, to the 'raw and undigested meditations' of young preachers carried away by their own zeal.

Note-taking was also an established part of the grammar-school curriculum. The 1604 Canons required schoolmasters to take their pupils to the local parish church whenever a sermon was to be preached there, and then to examine them on the contents of the sermon after their return. The main purpose, of course, was to get children into the habit of regular church attendance and give them a diet of wholesome religious doctrine, but enterprising schoolmasters quickly realised that by requiring their pupils to take notes on the sermon, they could practise a variety of other transferable skills such as reading, writing and the art of memory. Note-taking also served the thoroughly practical purpose of keeping the boys quiet and well behaved; as the schoolmaster John Brinsley remarked, it would not only improve their religious knowledge but also 'keepe them from playing, talking, sleeping, and all other disorders in the Church'.[103] The custom quickly caught on; and our mental picture of an early modern sermon would be incomplete without the image of a crowd of schoolboys furiously scribbling notes under the watchful eye of their teacher. Ephraim Udall has left us a vivid description of the scene in many London churches, where the shortage of space meant that schoolboys commonly leant on the Communion table to write their notes, shoving aside the bread and wine 'to make roome for their writing' while 'fouling and spotting the linnen and table at the same time with inke'.[104]

Brinsley proposed a graduated series of note-taking exercises for boys at different levels of the school. The youngest pupils were to write down a few simple notes such as 'Without God we can do nothing', or 'All good gifts are from God', and learn these by heart. (With the wisdom of experience, Brinsley warned that 'there must be great care by the Monitours, that they trouble not their fellows, nor the congregation, in asking notes, or stirring out of their places to seeke of one another, or any other disorder; but to aske them after they are come forth of the Church, and get them written then.') 'Those who have been longer practised herein' were to write down the text, and then 'to marke as neere as they can, and set downe every doctrine, and what proofes they can, the reasons and the uses of them.' Those in the highest forms were to note down the whole substance of the sermon,

---

[103] John Brinsley, *Ludus Literarius: or, the Grammar Schoole* (1627), T1r.
[104] Udall, *Communion Comlinesse*, C2v.

'as Text, division, exposition, or meaning, doctrines, and how the severall doctrines were gathered, all the proofes, reasons, uses, applications'. On returning from church, one of the older boys should then 'make a repetition of the whole Sermon without book . . . rehearsing the severall parts so distinctly and briefly, as the rest attending may the better conceive of the whole, and not exceed the space of a quarter of an houre'.[105] Brinsley's recommendations are further testimony to the popularity of the doctrine-and-use method of preaching. And it is easy to see why this method was so pedagogically attractive, as it provided a clear and orderly structure which could be easily noted down, memorised and repeated without the need to copy down the whole sermon word for word.

As will be obvious, these techniques of hearing were heavily dependent on literacy skills, presupposing as they did a listener who could handle a pen and take notes on the sermon as an aid to memory and subsequent repetition. The methods of note-taking were highly regulated, even down to the physical layout of the sermon notebook. Brinsley directed his pupils to 'leave spaces betweene every part' of the sermon and 'divide them with lines' to distinguish clearly between them. They were to note the different parts of the sermon ('as Text, Division, Summe, First Observation, or first Doctrine, Proofes, Reasons 1.2.3, Uses 1.2.3.') in the margin, to help their memory. 'Direct them to leave good Margents for these purposes: and as soone as ever the Preacher quotes any Scripture, as he nameth it, to set it in the Margent against the place.' Afterwards, they should review their notes and set down 'the summe of every chiefe head, faire and distinctly in the Margent over against the place' to fix the structure of the sermon firmly in their minds. In repeating the sermon, weaker pupils were allowed to 'have their notes lying open before them, to cast their eye upon them here or there where they stick', but older pupils were expected to rely wholly on their memory, using the structure of the sermon as an *aide-mémoire*.[106] Many surviving sermon notebooks bear the unmistakable stamp of these peda-gogical practices. The notebook of Christopher Trevelyan, for example, divides sermons into their doctrines, reasons and uses, with the different parts separated by lines and spaces, and the scriptural citations noted in the margin, just as Brinsley had recommended.[107]

---

[105] Brinsley, *Ludus Literarius*, S8r–T1r. See the similar instructions for note-taking in Charles Hoole, *A New Discovery of the Old Art of Teaching Schoole* (1660), M4r.
[106] Brinsley, *Ludus Literarius*, S8v, T1v.
[107] Sermon notes of Christopher Trevelyan: Somerset Record Office, Taunton, DD/WO/61/5/5. The manuscript is briefly mentioned in *The Trevelyan Letters to 1840*, ed. Mary Siraut (Somerset Record Society, 1990), p. viii.

What was being inculcated here was not just the art of note-taking but the ability to grasp the structure of a sermon by visualising it on the page. John Downame revealingly described the art of hearing in visual terms: we must 'heare the Word with diligent attention, observing the method of the Teacher, and how he proceedeth from poynt to poynt, fastening the former poynt in our mindes, by casting our eye backe unto it, when as hee is leaving of it, and proceeding to another'.[108] This is a good example of what Walter Ong, in his classic account of the cultural effects of Ramism, describes as 'the spatial model as key to the mental world', and it led ultimately to the creation of a kind of mental filing system in which any doctrine heard in a sermon could be arranged, as in a commonplace book, under an appropriate subject heading for the purposes of storage and retrieval.[109] One of the benefits of catechising, Downame believed, was that it organised the whole body of Christian religion into a set of general divisions or subject headings, so that 'being grounded in the principles and maine parts of divinity, wee shall bee able to referre all things wee heare to their heads'. Robert Bolton wrote in similar terms of the need to 'digest' sermons by a process of mental rearrangement, 'sorting the particulars of the Sermon, unto our owne necessities', much as the notes taken at a sermon might be subjected to a process of physical rearrangement and transcription into a commonplace book.[110]

The doctrine-and-use method was ideal for these purposes, as it made it much easier for the hearer to visualise the sermon structure in diagrammatic form. And preachers often simplified things still further by announcing the doctrines and uses by name in their sermons, so that listeners knew exactly what to write down. Richard Bernard, in his influential handbook for preachers, *The Faithfull Shepheard*, expressed some misgivings about this practice, declaring that it made the sermon 'too disjointed, and lesse patheticall'.[111] How, he wondered, could preachers appeal to the emotions of their hearers if they had to keep calling out 'this is the doctrine, this is the proofe, this is the use: now to the reasons, now we will make application'? Even Bernard, however, admitted that this was 'a plaine way . . . easie to bee conceived and written of such as attend and will take the paines', and it is clear from surviving sermons that it was widely practised. Here, for example, is the London minister Henry Roborough in a sermon of 1626:

---

[108]  Downame, *Guide to Godlynesse*, 2T6r.
[109]  Walter J. Ong, *Ramus, Method and the Decay of Dialogue* (Cambridge, MA, 1958), pp. 314–18.
[110]  Downame, *Guide to Godlynesse*, 2G1v; Robert Bolton, *A Three-fold Treatise* (1634), R6r.
[111]  Richard Bernard, *The Faithfull Shepheard* (1607), L4r.

> Let us put this proposition to use. And first, it serveth for reproofe of many in
> these times, who answer not Gods call . . .
> [The hearer would write down 'Use 1. for reproof.']

> The use I will put this proposition to, shall be examination, and so conviction of
> many not to bee Gods people; and exhortation to all by this, to make that
> priviledge unto them sure.
> [The hearer would write down 'Use 1. for conviction, 2. for exhortation.']112

And it would be easy to multiply examples. 'Thus much of the Doctrine,
and this question. The Use followeth.'113 'Well we have heard of the partes
doctrines and uses of this text, nowe followeth the application . . .'114
Remarks such as these were designed for the benefit of hearers who were
taking notes on the sermon and looking out for the keywords, such as 'use'
or 'application', that signalled the transition from one part of the sermon to
another.

Once again this was heavily influenced by Ramist method. Ramus
divided the exercise of dialectic into two parts, analysis and genesis, each
the mirror image of the other. Analysis consisted of the breaking down of
discourse into its component parts, genesis the reassembling of those
component parts into a fully articulated discourse. Once the teacher had
shown his pupils how to analyse a text, by breaking it down into a set
of logical propositions (logical analysis) or rhetorical tropes and figures
(rhetorical analysis) – a process which Ramus described in terms of the
'unweaving' of the thread of discourse – the pupils could begin to generate
their own discourses, by taking the logical and rhetorical units revealed by
the process of analysis and building them up into new combinations.115
A grammar-school pupil who was well versed in this method would have
had no difficulty in analysing sermons in the same way – for preachers and
hearers, too, could be seen as participating in equal but opposite activities
based on the Ramist pairing of analysis and genesis. The preacher began the
process of composition by drawing up a skeleton structure of doctrines and
uses, and then proceeded to construct the sermon around it, enlarging and
amplifying particular points as he saw fit. The hearer promptly decon-
structed it again, turning the sermon back into a skeleton structure of
doctrines and uses, which could easily be memorised and repeated. The
attraction of this method was that it appeared to offer a perfectly transparent

112   Henry Roborough, *Balme from Gilead* (1626), Y2r, 2E3r.
113   Thomas Taylor, *Three Treatises* (1633), F4v.
114   Sermon by a Mr Hutton, 1602: Bodleian Library, Oxford, MS Rawl. C.79, f. 148r.
115   Ong, *Ramus, Method and the Decay of Dialogue*, pp. 193, 263.

form of communication, in which the sermon could be passed directly from preacher to hearer with no loss of sense or meaning along the way.

Whatever we may think of this as a theory of rhetoric, there can be no doubt of its extraordinary practical efficiency as an aid to memory. The Independent minister John Rogers – son of the Nehemiah Rogers whose sermon in praise of 'method' in preaching we have already encountered – left a remarkable spiritual autobiography in which he described his custom of memorising and repeating sermons, beginning as a schoolboy after his conversion at the age of ten. It is clear from his account that the doctrine-and-use method was crucial in enabling him to commit sermons to memory:

> I resolved to *write down* (as well as I could) *every Sermon* I heard, and to get them by *heart*, and to say every *night* one *Sermon* . . . So I began to write down the *Sermons*, (which for a time was very *little*, having no skill to *write fast* nor *orderly*) but I ever *observed* the *Doctrine*, and would write down the *Reasons* and the heads of the *Uses* . . . and this *course* which I took made me more ready (at night when my *Father* repeated the Sermons, or the *Landlord* where I boarded, for they both did it, being very *godly*) this made me *readier* to *answer* when we were *asked* what we *could remember*, or what the *Doctrine*, or *Reason*, or *Use* was, than any *other* . . .

Rogers eventually settled into a habit of repeating a sermon to himself every night before going to bed. On Sunday and Friday nights he repeated the sermon he had heard the previous Sunday morning; on Monday and Saturday nights he repeated the sermon he had heard the previous Sunday afternoon; while on Tuesday, Wednesday and Thursday nights he repeated older sermons, some of which he had carried in his memory for as long as five or ten years. 'I would *usually* get up the *oldest*, and of *longest* standing; and such as I had almost *forgot*, or not lately *recovered* my *memory* with, so that by this *means* I could *remember* many *Sermons*, and such as were *long* agone *preached*, perfectly.'[116]

The results of these teaching methods are beautifully illustrated in an anecdote told by Thomas Manton about the puritan gentleman Ignatius Jurdain. Both men had been to hear a sermon on the subject of heaven, which Manton found 'for the most part *frothy*, and beneath the dignity and worth of such an argument'. Meeting Jurdain later that day, 'he asked me, *if I had been at the Sermon that morning?* I told him, yea; and *did you* (saith he) *hear those wonderful things which God hath provided for them that love him?* and so readily picked out all those passages which were any way subservient to use and profit'.[117] At first glance, this might appear to be merely a story about Jurdain's exemplary piety, but it can also be read as an example of the

---

[116] Rogers, *Ohel or Beth-shemesh*, 3I1r (p. 421).
[117] Ferdinando Nicolls, *The Life and Death of Mr Ignatius Jurdain* (1654), a2v.

mental dexterity that resulted from the constant practice of note-taking and repetition. For an experienced hearer such as Jurdain, it was a relatively simple matter to pick out a few valuable points from an otherwise indifferent sermon, store them in a mental filing system (or physically, in a commonplace book) under an appropriate subject heading, and retrieve them later in order to apply them in a new context. At this level of attainment, sermon repetition was anything but a passive exercise. As Manton commented admiringly: 'twas wonderful to me, to see how an holy heart can draw comfort out of any thing: the Sermon as Mr *Jurdain* repeated it to me, was another kind of Sermon, and seemed to be very savoury and spiritual: I remember with what warmth and vigour he spake of it, even to this day, and hope that I shall never forget it'.

But to reach this degree of mental and verbal dexterity was by no means easy. Even grammar-school pupils often had initial difficulty in mastering the art of hearing: 'when I could not take notes of the sermon', wrote Thomas Shepard in his autobiography, recalling his schooldays, 'I remember I was troubled at it and prayed the Lord earnestly that he would help me to note sermons'.[118] For those without a grammar-school education, the problems were redoubled. Henry Mason observed some people who complained 'that their memories are fraile, and they cannot call to minde that which they have heard: when they bethink themselves of the Sermon, they can remember nothing, or nothing to any purpose, that the Preacher did say'. Another London minister, John Wall, recorded the laments of some of his hearers that 'before I get out of the Church, all the Sermon is lost, whereas I know some can repeat a whole Sermon *verbatim*'. One such was Nehemiah Wallington, who, despite his strong commitment to the preaching ministry, had great difficulty in understanding and remembering sermons. 'I did thinke to graspe and inclose abundance in my heart', he wrote unhappily after hearing a sermon in May 1642, 'but (to my sorrow and shame I speake it) my weake and shallow cappassity did understand but littel or nothing which grieved me very much. Nay although others did hiely commend it for sweet and excellent matter yet could I not remember nor prophet [i.e. profit] one jot by itt (the Lord of his mercy forgive mee) and there is a great contention in my poore soule about it why it should be so and yet cannot find out the reason of it.'[119]

[118] Michael McGiffert, ed., *God's Plot: The Paradoxes of Puritan Piety, Being the Autobiography and Journal of Thomas Shepard* (Amherst, MA, 1972), p. 39.

[119] Mason, *Hearing and Doing*, 2I1v; John Wall, *None But Christ, or a Plain and Familiar Treatise of the Knowledge of Christ* (2nd edn., 1650), Z6v (p. 348); Nehemiah Wallington, 'The growth of a

This might suggest that the art of hearing was so closely associated with the pedagogical practices of the early modern classroom that it would have been virtually incomprehensible to anyone who had not received at least a basic minimum of formal education. As we shall see, there is some truth in this view, but it needs to be heavily qualified. There were, after all, many ways in which the formal techniques of note-taking and commonplacing could have been passed on outside the classroom. As a schoolboy in Wakefield, the future puritan minister Jeremy Wakefield attended sermons at his local parish church followed by private repetition among 'those who were most religiously disposed', where, according to his biographer, 'being able to take Sermon Notes, both understandingly, and largely, he was very helpful to those private Christians in repeating what they had publickly heard'. At Beverley Minster in 1615, the schoolmaster and his pupils gathered in the chancel after Sunday morning prayer to repeat the sermon before a large crowd of local people.[120] The art of hearing could also have been taught within the household, and Samuel Clarke's life of Lady Elizabeth Langham reminds us that it was by no means an exclusively masculine skill: she is said to have required her stepdaughter, 'who was then about eleven years old', to repeat the sermons she heard, and 'by her instructions so logically methodised the memory of this young Child, that she was able to *Analise* a Sermon containing thirty or forty particular Heads, with the most remarkable inlargements upon them'.[121]

Nor should we assume that uneducated or illiterate hearers were unable to remember what they heard from the pulpit. On the contrary, some were capable of the most remarkable feats of memory. The future archbishop James Ussher was brought up by two aunts who 'by reason of their blindnesse from their Cradles, never saw letters' but could repeat any part of the Bible from memory, and even managed to teach their nephew to read.[122] John Favour, vicar of Halifax, described one of his parishioners as 'a very religiouse, zealouse honest old man, not able to read, yet very ready in the scripturs, with prompt use and application as I have heard any without learninge'.[123] Such memory skills are a well-known feature of oral culture,

---

Christian', BL Add. MS 40883, f. 97r. The passage from John Wall is copied out in another of Wallington's notebooks, 'An extract of the passages of my life', Folger Shakespeare Library, Washington, DC, V.a.436, f. 130r.

[120] Clarke, *A Collection of the Lives of Ten Eminent Divines*, X4v; Ronald A. Marchant, *The Puritans and the Church Courts in the Diocese of York 1560–1642* (London, 1960), p. 37.

[121] Samuel Clarke, *Lives of Sundry Eminent Persons in this Later Age* (1683), 2P2r.

[122] Nicholas Bernard, *The Life and Death of the Most Reverend and Learned Father of our Church, Dr James Usher* (1656), C3v.

[123] W. J. Walker, *Chapters on the Early Registers of Halifax Parish Church* (1885), p. 90.

and may not have been particularly uncommon in early modern England, even though they were plainly unusual enough, by the early seventeenth century, to excite special comment from literate observers. John Norden observed in 1610 that 'many unlearned men have better and more retentive memories than have some schollers', because 'such as have not the use of the pen, must use the memory only'.[124] This may help to explain Marjorie McIntosh's startling finding, in her study of the Essex village of Havering, of a negative correlation between strong Protestantism and literacy. There are a number of possible explanations for this (McIntosh herself attributes it to the fact that Puritanism was spreading down the social scale and becoming more popular among the middling and poorer sorts who were less likely to be literate), but whatever the explanation, it argues a basic compatibility between preaching and oral culture.[125]

One of the most fascinating accounts of an oral memory system occurs in William Hinde's life of John Bruen. According to Hinde, one of Bruen's servants was a man named Robert Pasfield, 'better knowne by the name of *old Robert*', who was 'utterly unlearned, being unable to read a sentence, or write a syllable' but 'so well acquainted with the history of the Bible, and the summe and substance of every Book and Chapter, that hardly could any ask him, where such a saying or sentence were, but he would with very little adoe, tell them in what Book and Chapter they might finde it'. To help his memory, he had a leather girdle which he marked off into sections 'as a Carpenter doth his Rule', each section representing a book of the Bible and threaded with a long string on which he 'made knots . . . to distinguish the chapters of that book'.

This instrument of his owne invention, hee framed and used (as others do their pen and writing) for the better helpe of his understanding, and reliefe of his memory in his hearing of the Word preached; which he did with so good effect and fruit, in observing all the points and Scriptures alleadged in a Sermon, and binding them upon the points, and partitions of his Girdle, as he heard them, that in repeating of the Sermon afterwards, he himselfe had great benefit, and many other professors, much comfort and helpe, by his handling of his girdle and fingering the points, and divisions of it.[126]

This example shows that it was possible for illiterate hearers to participate effectively in the art of hearing, yet it also reveals some of the limitations of

---

[124] For this and other examples, see Adam Fox, *Oral and Literate Culture in England 1500–1700* (Oxford, 2000), p. 22.
[125] Marjorie McIntosh, *A Community Transformed: The Manor and Liberty of Havering 1500–1620* (Cambridge, 1991).
[126] Hinde, *Faithfull Remonstrance*, E5r.

an oral memory system. Pasfield's system evidently worked well in helping him to remember a series of scriptural texts, but would not necessarily have worked so well in helping him to remember the division and sub-division of the sermon. (As Walter Ong aptly points out: '*Aides-mémoire* such as notched sticks or a series of carefully arranged objects will not of themselves retrieve a complicated series of assertions.'[127]) It was also a closed system, relying on a fixed sequence of markers as a guide to a fixed sequence of scriptural texts, as opposed to the open system of place headings capable of accommodating an ever-expanding body of knowledge.

Some writers recognised the problem, and recommended simplified memory systems for the use of the less educated, along the lines of the simple exercises that Brinsley had prescribed for schoolboys in the lowest forms. Lewis Bayly, in *The Practice of Pietie*, offered two alternative methods of note-taking, one more complex than the other. Ideally, he declared, the hearer should observe 'the coherence and application of the Text', 'the chiefe summe or scope of the Holy Ghost in that Text', 'the division or parts of the Text', 'the doctrines; and in every doctrine, the proofes, the reasons, and uses thereof'. This was 'a method of all others, easiest for the people (being accustomed thereto) to help them to remember the Sermon'. For less experienced hearers, however, Bayly offered a simpler system consisting of only three parts:

1. How many things be taught which thou knewest not before, and be thankefull.
2. What sinnes bee reproved, whereof thy conscience tells thee that thou art guilty, and therefore must be amended.
3. What vertues hee exhorteth unto, which are not so perfect in thee, and therefore endeavour to practise them with more zeale and diligence.

This still set the standard fairly high, but would have enabled hearers to carry away something from the sermon without having to grasp the whole structure of the preacher's argument. Similarly, Henry Mason suggested that a hearer who 'cannot make any orderly repetition' might still be able to 'remember the matter, and speak of it in a ruder phrase of his owne' or to 'tell, that such a sin was condemned, and such a duty enjoyned'.[128] The emphasis here was less on doctrine or theology than on the practical moral duties of the Christian life.

---

[127] Walter J. Ong, *Orality and Literacy: The Technologizing of the Word* (London, 1982), p. 34. For an actual example of a notched stick used as a memory aid, designed by the Welsh antiquarian Edward Williams (Iolo Morganwg) and presented to Joseph Banks, see BL Add. 11038, f. 39.
[128] Bayly, *Practice of Pietie*, X7r; Mason, *Hearing and Doing*, 2I1v, 2I4v.

Even so, there were still pitfalls to trip up the unwary. As Stephen Egerton remarked, those who could not understand the preacher's method were liable to 'take things by halves, or by snatches' and so carry away a simile without its proper application, or interpret 'things spoken comparatively . . . as if they were spoken simply', which could lead them to mistake the preacher's meaning in potentially disastrous ways.[129] One case from rural Dorset shows how easily this sort of confusion could arise. In 1627 Nicholas Day, rector of Hooke, near Beaminster, was accused by three of his parishioners of having preached a seditious sermon. None of them could remember what text Day had preached on, but all three remembered him saying that 'the land was not governed by justice but by bribery and extortion'. He had then launched into what sounded to his astonished hearers like an attack on the English naval expedition to La Rochelle, declaring that 'kings could not contain themselves within the limits of their own kingdoms but seeke to invade other kingdoms and to sack them of their goods, to ravish their wives and deflower their daughters . . . which bred such a scandal on our Religion, as it is said, Are these Christians? Is this the fruit of their Religion?' Two of the three parishioners were relying on their own memories of the sermon, but the third, Henry Minterne, the son of a local gentleman, had taken some written notes. On seeing him scribbling in his notebook, Day had snapped at him: 'Write on, Minterne, write on, I feare thee not, but would speake soe much though the Kinge were in presence'.[130]

The testimony of the three witnesses tallied closely and, at first sight, appeared to present an utterly damning case. But while Day admitted that he had spoken most of the words attributed to him, he denied that they carried any seditious meaning. The remark about bribery and extortion, he claimed, had been spoken 'in exposition of the 5th [chapter] of Esay speakinge in the wordes of the prophett of the land of Judah and Israell'. The remark about kings invading other kingdoms he denied having uttered at all. As for the remarks on the ravishing of wives and deflowering of daughters, these had been spoken in a totally different sermon, about a year earlier, 'expressinge the enormous crueltys the Spanyardes used towards the Indians and that thereby came a scandale to the Christian Relligion'. The case was deemed sufficiently serious to be referred to the assizes, but Day's version of events seems to have been accepted, as no further action was taken against him and he remained at Hooke until his death fourteen

[129] Egerton, *Boring of the Eare*, D6v.
[130] Depositions before Sir Francis Ashley: BL, Harl. MS 6715, f. 74.

years later.[131] Without other evidence, it is impossible to know precisely what Day said in his sermon or what meaning he intended his words to carry, but the case illustrates the difficulty of reconstructing the oral sermon (a point to which we shall return in the next chapter) and the wide scope for disagreement that this created, especially when a single remark was lifted out of context. How far can we ever know what was said in the pulpits of early modern England, even when, as here, we have first-hand reports of a sermon from multiple witnesses? At the very least this case should teach us to be wary.

Roger Fenton's sermons on usury, preached at St Stephen's Walbrook in London, provide an even more extraordinary example of how a preacher's intentions might be misunderstood. The sermons attracted a large and inquisitive audience, but when Fenton published a printed edition in 1612, he complained that a 'solemne hearing' had all too quickly turned into a 'solemne forgetting'. In particular, he claimed that some of his hearers had understood him to be preaching in defence of usury, whereas in fact he had been attacking it. This was no exaggeration: one set of notes on Fenton's sermons survives in the library of Trinity College, Dublin, and shows that the note-taker made precisely this mistake.[132] The notes begin by listing the evils of usury – it is against nature, against equity and against charity – but then move on to a qualified defence of the practice:

Old men, widdows, & children have mony but they want skill to use it. Younger men & traides men have skill but want mony, therefore usurie may ioyne theis two kindes, & seeing the commonwealth gaine by it, it is reason it should pay for both. Skill without mony is like hands without tools, & mony without skill is like a body without a head. As far forth as necessitie may lawfully dispense with it, & it be not against nature, & the commonwealth receive no harme by it, soe far forth usurie may be lawfull. Finis.

It is, of course, possible that Fenton changed his mind between preaching and publication, though he himself attributed the mistake to the ephemeral nature of preaching, 'for part of that which is only spoken, must needs vanish in the aire, before it can bee fullie fastned in the minde, and fitted to the whole frame and current of speech'.[133] And this brings us back to the question with which we began. How successful was the art of hearing? If

[131] F. J. Pope, 'A political sermon at Hooke in 1626', *Notes and Queries for Somerset and Devon*, 15 (1917), p. 156. (My thanks to David Crankshaw for this reference.)
[132] 'Mr Fenton uppon userie': Trinity College, Dublin, MS 1210, ff. 196–8.
[133] Roger Fenton, *A Treatise of Usurie* (1612), B1v.

even experienced hearers were capable of misunderstanding the preacher's meaning so profoundly, what hope was there for the less experienced?

The majority of surviving sermon notebooks were written by university-educated hearers who summarised what they heard with an accuracy born of long familiarity with the skills of note-taking and commonplacing. While they testify to the dedication with which the art of hearing was practised, they tell us little about the experience of less educated sermongoers. However, there are a few surviving examples of sermon notes written by hearers whose literacy skills were more limited and who plainly had more difficulty in making an accurate record of what they heard. It would be wrong to treat these as representative of the 'average' sermongoer, as the ability to handle a pen and make a written record of the sermon – no matter how imperfectly – automatically places them in the ranks, if not of the literate then at least of the semi-literate, and sets them apart from the many illiterate hearers whose response to preaching is largely irrecoverable. Yet they do take us some way beyond the experience of an educated godly élite, and bring us closer to members of the middling sort, such as Nehemiah Wallington, who may have valued the preaching ministry but still struggled to understand and remember sermons. As we shall see in a later chapter, sermon notes can often be of interest for what they reveal about the sermon as preached, bringing us closer to the preacher's voice than a printed text can do; but what is of interest about these particular sermon notes is what may have been lost in transmission, and what that might reveal about the effectiveness of the art of hearing.

A manuscript in the British Library (Sloane MS 2172) contains a collection of sermon notes taken by one William Platte in various London churches, including 'sant Laurans' (probably St Lawrence Jewry), 'Tatunnie' (possibly St Antholin's) and 'Stepneth' (Stepney), between 1604 and 1606. Platte was probably the son of the agricultural writer Sir Hugh Plat (1552–1608), among whose papers these notes are preserved.[134] If so, then the notes must have been a schoolboy exercise, written by Platte at the age of about twelve or thirteen, perhaps for presentation to his father. Platte seems to have been familiar with printed sermons, as the notes are prefaced by an epistle 'to all the trewe louers of the glorie of god and salvation of their owne soole', modelled on the dedicatory epistle of a printed book, in which he declares that these '8 excellent sermentes wich my memorie could apprehend . . . doe teach us the hole rule of this fraile

---

[134] William Platte's monument survives in St Pancras Old Church: *Survey of London*, vol. XIX, *Old St Pancras and Kentish Town* (1938), pp. 77–8 and plates 36–7.

and wicked worlde which sperituall foode is of an easie price and of easie digestion . . . [and] may be so handled in preachinge and instructinge as that it may well serue for one of the last and most delecate dises [dishes] at the spirituall table'. Despite this attempt to emulate the dignity of print, Platte's notes are heavily worked over, with numerous spelling and grammatical errors, and are plainly the work of an inexperienced note-taker. What we appear to have here, therefore, is a collection of notes by a pupil halfway through a grammar-school education and halfway through acquiring the skills of accurate note-taking and repetition.

In each case Platte begins by copying out the preacher's text, and follows this with a single-paragraph summary of the sermon in about 500 words. His grasp of the doctrine-and-use structure is fairly rudimentary. In reporting a sermon by a Mr Johnson on 2 Corinthians 5: 10 ('For we must all appear before the judgement seat of Christ'), he begins by summarising the preacher's remarks on the Day of Judgement, and the uncertainty of its time and place, before concluding with a brief list of uses:

now conserninge the uses that wee gathered by this serment, and so i will commit you to god, first wee most iudge our selfe, that we be not iudgged, seconly wee most confes our sinnes to god, 3ly wee most condem our selfe, 4ly we most appele to the allmighti thron of grase, 5ly wee most not iudge our Nebors, furst because wee are apte to make a thinge of our nebors worsser then it is, 2 because if it be good wee will make it bade, 3 if it be indiferent we will mak it rather worsser then better. finem of Mr Johnsonne serment at S Laurans

In most cases he makes no attempt to list the doctrines and uses. In listening to a sermon by a Mr Cartwright on 1 Timothy 6: 17 ('Charge them that are rich in this world, that they be not high-minded'), it was the preacher's use of proverbs and homely similitudes that stuck in his memory:

now a days mony Ruls all things, he that has mony cane do any thinge, now a day as the world stands now, he is no body that has not mony, *pecuniae obediunt omnia*, that is mony ouercoms all things, now a priuet [private] man will bankkete [banquet] as if he were a magistrate, i pray to god that all you in this congrigation cold excuse your selfe of beinge high mindded, i wold be very glad of it, if you cold do so . . . mony now a days is as good as lerninge nay it is nowe better then lerninge, *aracnianum teles similes diuitiae*, mony is lik the cobwebs of spiders, euery thing has his worme, the apple has his worme, the peare his worme, the nute his worme, so prid is the worm of riches . . .

Later in the same sermon, his summary of the preacher's exhortation to charity comes perilously close to a doctrine of works righteousness. 'As god geue us riches so wee ought to giue our brothers parte of them, we most do good works that we may obtaine eternall life, we most giue our almes now while we haue time and wealth . . . if you wold enioy life eternall hereafter you most do good here before that you can go thether, if you wold be with Lasarus here after, in the world to come, you most haue Lasarus in your bosume here in the world present.'

Platte's notes can be compared with the sermon notebook of Robert Saxby, now in Cambridge University Library (Add. MS 3117).[135] In this case we know a good deal about the note-taker. Saxby was born in 1568, the eldest son of John Saxby, a prosperous clothier in the parish of Brenchley, Kent, and inherited the family's clothmaking workshop and equipment when his father died in 1611. In 1629 he moved to London, where he settled in the parish of St Bartholomew the Great, and began to keep a record of the sermons he heard on the blank pages of an old account book. Though not in the top echelon of London's mercantile élite, he was a wealthy man, with landed property in Kent and Berkshire, and his wife's will, drawn up in 1638, styles him 'Robert Saxby, gentleman'.[136] Nevertheless, his unformed handwriting and idiosyncratic phonetic spelling suggest that he possessed only basic literacy skills. His manuscript represents a relatively low level of literacy, certainly below that of Nehemiah Wallington, who, despite his comparatively humble social status, was far better able to handle a pen and to express himself fluently in writing.

One of the most striking features of Saxby's notebook is the sheer quantity of sermons recorded, by many different preachers in many different City churches – 'preched at St Mary Overies at the sise befor the Judges'; 'preched at St Mary Stayning by Mr Chewt befor the Company of golsmithes'; 'preched at Christ Church by Mr Centishe lecter ther upon the friday nightes'. There were some preachers whom Saxby clearly admired, and whose names turn up regularly in the notebook, such as Thomas Westfield at St Bartholomew's (his home parish), William Gouge and his son Thomas Gouge ('yong Mr gudg') at Blackfriars. But in many cases it appears that Saxby simply attended a sermon out of curiosity, often without even being aware of the preacher's name – 'preched by the exchang a yong

[135] I am very grateful to John Craig for sharing his own notes on Saxby's manuscript, and to Michael Zell for sharing the fruits of his research on Saxby's family background in the Weald of Kent. For a brief account of the manuscript, see Caroline Skeel, 'A puritan's commonplace book', *The History Teachers' Miscellany*, 4: 12 (1926), pp. 177–8; once again I am indebted to John Craig for this reference.

[136] Will of John Sexbey (dated 10 January 1609, proved 31 July 1611): National Archives, PROB 11/118/65. Will of Mary Saxby (dated 5 June 1638, proved 15 August 1642): Guildhall Library, London, MS 9052/11. Robert Saxby's own will has not been traced. On his Berkshire property, see J. M. Goulding, ed., *Diary of the Corporation of Reading*, vol. III (1896), p. 274.

man that lecters upon wensday morning'; 'preched at poles by him that lectert the last Thorsday of Caundlmas terme'; 'preched at the church besid blackwell hall by a stranger'. Occasionally the notebook gives us a momentary glimpse of Saxby himself, and reveals some of the physical hindrances to sermongoing in early modern London. In his notes on a sermon at Paul's Cross 'by one Mr Ambler living by the poltre', he writes: 'I came after the sermon was begon'. Of a sermon at St Bartholomew's 'by Mr Tapley the bakers sonne', he notes that 'I could not her very well by reson I sat not very nere'; and of another sermon by a stranger at St Bartholomew's he notes that the preacher spoke 'mor at larg in his Teaching than I could Remember, & that because his speache was som thing short & low, Therfor I do but poynt at the chefe hedes according to my Rembrance'.

Saxby's notebook makes it clear that the hearing of the Word was a central part of his religious life. He seems to have attended, on average, three or four sermons a week, and paid serious attention to what he heard. His notes include a record of a sermon by John Downame, lecturer at St Bartholomew Exchange, on Acts 17: 11–12 (the men of Berea), which, as we saw in the first section of this chapter, served as the main scriptural precedent for the practice of sermon repetition. The lesson that Saxby took away from this sermon was 'that the scripters should be meditated of & the herers ought to be abell to desern whether it were true doctren or no & not to receue them hand ouer hed without meditacion' (f. 21). Another entry in his notebook suggests that he may have regarded himself as a member of a godly minority. Attending a Whitsunday sermon by Thomas Westfield at St Bartholomew's, Saxby recorded with evident approval Westfield's exhortation to his hearers not to be disheartened by anti-puritan polemic. 'This Reverint docter, willeth none of the Children of god to be any way descoreged: Though som have falen that have mad some profesion of the gospell: And by ther fallinges, som have tacken ocasion by their fales & slipes, to say these be your puritanes & profesers, in a scofing maner; ther be none worse, then these puritanes, but let not this discoriag [i.e. discourage] the profesion of the gospell of Christ, for it is the power of god to bring you to salvacion' (f. 26).

Yet Saxby's note-taking abilities were clearly fairly limited. He does not seem to have taken written notes in church, and therefore had to rely on his memory to reconstruct the sermon after the event. One Sunday sermon was 'writen out the same day' (f. 35), while another was 'writen out according to my short Remembrance the Monday before ester term began 1632' (f. 56). He began by writing out the preacher's text in full, often with a comment such as 'the holl chapter is very remarkabell' (f. 19), which suggests that he had a printed Bible open in front of him. In many cases he fails to give any details of the sermon beyond the bare comment that the preacher spoke 'very well' (or 'most excelently') 'in every particular doctren'. Sometimes his summary takes the form of a few simple moral precepts or exhortations, as in the following report of a sermon on Acts 17: 31, 'preched besid the exchang' one Easter Tuesday:

Out of this text he raysed many good remarckabell profes for our enstracon [instruction] That we should be carfull to walk in the fere of our lord god in all true obedience, That we may atayn at the end of our lives a Joyfull Reserecion in thy glorious kingdom of heven: & to pray for thy grace of thy holy sprit to derect us & be our continiall gider & defender from all evell: Amen & Amen

Like Platte, he often fastened on homely comparisons and similitudes, probably finding them helpful as memory aids:

And forther he showeth a famillyer excampell if the king should giue a great tree out of on of his foristes or out of his manners or grownds: for some use desired of the party that did big it: he must be at the cost to fell it & mack it Redy for his use upon his owne charg: so lickwise Christ being the tru Corner ston, we must pray for grace of his holy spirit to be living stones in the bulding & be forward in the fitting of our selves unto this spritiall bulding in Jesus Christ.

Many of these comparisons are interestingly suggestive of Saxby's sense of social hierarchy. In a sermon on John 3: 29 ('He that hath the bride is the bridegroom') he noted that 'if a sitisiones [citizen's] wife or the like or a marchant wido should mary a nobell man ... she must frame hir Carig [carriage] acording to hir place, & ranke, & forgett hir former living'; just so, he went on, we must obey the Gospel of Christ and put aside our former sins (f. 8). In another sermon he noted that just as we 'would not take it in good part ... to be over reweled by our Enemey or by our felow or by our servant', so we should pray for grace not to be overruled by our chief enemy, the devil (f. 22).

   Certain themes appear over and over again in Saxby's notebook: in particular, the impossibility of overcoming sin by our own efforts, and the need for us to pray to God, through Jesus Christ, for grace to bring us to salvation. 'The renewing of our mindes is no esey thing to do, for of our selves we can not do it but if we pray unto our gracious god for the grace of his holy sprit he will not denie it if we ascke it in faith in his sonne Jesus Christ for those who com unto him he will not denie as he hath promessed in his word' (f. 12). 'If sinne do raigne in our mortall bodyes & dominer & ber greatest sway: we must pray for the lordes gracious Asistance for grace to be our mercifull god in Christ Jesus, to help & strenthen us in the Casting of

the workes of darknes & poting on the Armor of light' (f. 19). It is
clear that Saxby had grasped the basic Protestant principle of justification
by faith, and also that he had a sense of the opposition between
Protestantism and Popery. In his notes on a sermon by Thomas Taylor at
St Mary Aldermanbury, he recorded the preacher's final exhortation 'to
Abandon & deney All the wicked workes of papestrey' (f. 19). Elsewhere, he
noted that in the time of Popery, 'the true Church, I menne the gospell of
Christ was allmost hiden & the light put out by the papest, & the great
dragon the divell did bere great sway'. But now, he went on, 'the light of the
gospell' is shining among us, 'and we pray unto our most gracious god to
Continew thy gospell Amonst us', that we may 'buld our selves in thy
Church wherof Christ Jesus is the chefe Corner stone & the Rocke that will
never be Remoued' (f. 23).

Sometimes, however, Saxby's stress on prayer as the means to activate
God's grace comes close to semi-Pelagianism. The Gospel promise, as he
summarised it in 1634, was that 'if any man will pray and use the means, he
may attain':

So he sheweth very Learnedly the lord doth promise, Condicionaly, that if any man
will heare his voyce, & open the dore of his heart: he will sup with ous, or who so
hath the grace of god in his heart, he will be with ous in all our waies, by the poor
[power] of his holy sprit, so he farther sheweth for our enstrocion his promise is, if
Any man will pray & use the menes, he may Attayne . . .

Salvation, he went on, was available to anyone who was prepared to 'live
holelly & justly in this present world, so nere as they canne, & pray for the
grace of gods holy spirit, to derickt [direct] them, in all theire waies' (f. 25).
This suggests that Saxby had not fully grasped the concept of prevenient
grace as coming before the human response to God. Similarly, his references
to Christ as 'the savour of the holl world' (f. 17), and as having died 'for the
sinnes of the holl world or to so many of them as tak hold of him by a tru &
lily [lively] faight' (f. 18), suggest that the theological debates over the extent
of Christ's atonement had largely passed him by. How far he would have
been aware of the doctrinal points at issue in the debates between Calvinists
and Arminians, or understood what was at stake in those debates, is open
to question.

Saxby's notes, as the work of a relatively uneducated sermongoer, are a
rare survival among the sermon notes of this period. Yet Saxby himself may
not have been so unusual. Elite commentators occasionally referred, rather
contemptuously, to uneducated sermongoers who took notes in quasi-
phonetic spelling. In 1601 John Dove preached a sermon at Paul's Cross

in which he criticised Beza's teaching on divorce, and complained afterwards that his sermon had been 'mistaken by some which understood it not,
and unjustly traduced by others which heard it not'. Some of his hearers, he
claimed, were outraged that he had questioned Beza's authority, even
though they 'have onely heard of his name, but knowe not how to spell
it, (for they call him *Bezer*, as also *Bellarmine* they call *Bellamye*)'.[137]
Similarly, some sermon notes found in the possession of a suspected nonconformist in 1628 were said to reveal the writer's 'grosse ignorance in
literature' by their spelling, 'viz. he writeth prodistant for Protestant,
Pillagians for Pelagians, A bundance for abundance, Seazer for Cesar with
many other of this kinde'.[138] Anthony Milton takes the first of these
examples as showing that early modern audiences understood the polemical
nature of religious discourse even if they did not understand the theology
behind it; Dove's audience, he writes, 'might not have grasped the subtleties
of his exposition' but, like a football crowd, they knew enough to cheer for
'Bellamye' and boo for 'Bezer'.[139] This is a fair point; but we should not be
too quick to jump to conclusions about popular ignorance. Saxby's notes
suggest that a relatively unsophisticated grasp of Protestant theology could
coexist with a deep and genuine commitment to the preaching ministry.

CONCLUSION

The set of techniques that I have labelled the 'art of hearing' – techniques for
the purposeful and structured hearing of sermons, including note-taking,
memorisation, repetition and self-application – proved extremely powerful
and effective. It was still something of a novelty in the late sixteenth century,
yet by the mid-seventeenth century it was widely accepted as the standard
method for listening to sermons and deriving lasting benefit from them.
And it was highly impressive in its social reach and penetration. Lady
Elizabeth Langham teaching her stepdaughter how to analyse a sermon
point by point; Thomas Goodwin sobbing on the neck of his horse as he
came out of the Tuesday lecture at Dedham; Nehemiah Wallington sur-
reptitiously biting on a clove to keep himself awake as he struggled to bring
the preacher's words home to his own heart: these and hundreds of other
men and women were all, in very different ways, drawing on the same set of

---

[137] John Dove, *Of Divorcement. A Sermon Preached at Pauls Crosse* (1601), A4r.
[138] 'The noat of such things as wear found about John Heydon Clarke, at Norwich': National Archives,
SP 16/119/22 (calendared in *CSPD 1628–29*, p. 358).
[139] Anthony Milton, *Catholic and Reformed: The Roman and Protestant Churches in English Protestant
Thought, 1600–1640* (Cambridge, 1995), pp. 542–3.

techniques for interactive and responsive listening. At the beginning of this chapter I suggested that the art of hearing could be seen as an attempt to export the puritan concern with preaching into the wider community. Judged by this standard it was an almost unqualified success.

Understanding the success of the art of hearing also makes it possible to understand the Laudian objection to it. The image of ignorant and deluded hearers led astray by fanatical puritan preachers, as presented in many Laudian writings of the 1630s, was in many respects a polemical caricature, but one that contained more than a grain of truth. The art of hearing put the sermon at the centre of public worship and encouraged frequent, even obsessive sermon attendance, sometimes to the neglect of common prayer; it carried people to a high pitch of zeal and excitement that raised the dreaded spectre of religious enthusiasm, and drew them into a searching self-examination not far removed from melancholy and despair; it led to higher standards of religious knowledge among the unlearned that did, to some extent, represent a challenge to clerical authority, and involved forms of group conference and repetition that could easily spin off into private conventicles and lay preaching. In all these respects the Laudian caricature was somewhat closer to reality than the image of godly and orderly households under the benign authority of sober and painful preachers, as presented in the sermons and writings of many puritan divines, that went out of its way to deny any subversive dimension to the art of hearing.

However, we can identify at least three factors that limited the effectiveness of the art of hearing. First, it required a sustained effort of mental concentration, which even committed sermongoers such as Nehemiah Wallington often found extremely difficult. Secondly, it functioned best in godly parishes where the minister held regular sessions of sermon repetition and catechised his parishioners on what they could remember; and where these conditions were lacking it seems to have been much less effective. Thirdly, it was closely linked to the pedagogical techniques practised in the grammar schools and universities, which would not have been easy for less educated hearers to acquire. The consequences are apparent if we look ahead to the later seventeenth century. While there were certainly some Anglicans who regularly took notes on sermons and made this a central part of their personal piety, John Evelyn being the best-known and best-documented example, the great majority of surviving sermon notes from this period are by nonconformists – a surprising number of them associated with a relatively small number of clergy, such as Oliver Heywood, whose congregations kept up the old traditions of sermon repetition and the fair-copying and circulation of sermon notes.[140] This strongly suggests that the art of hearing had put down much deeper roots in puritan (and latterly nonconformist) circles than in the wider Church of England.

Yet at the very least, the art of hearing did succeed in persuading a great many people that preaching mattered. This was no small achievement. It was widely remarked after the Restoration that the English 'place their religion in the pulpit'.[141] Not everyone was happy about this; Meric Casaubon, for example, was one of many Anglican clergy who felt that preaching was over-valued, and that the 'ordinarie meanes of salvation' was to be found not in sermons but in public prayers and catechising. And yet Casaubon believed that 'as things stand in this kingdome . . . there is not any thing more necessary for the preservation of this Church . . . than frequent & powerful preaching'. For 'since the generallity of people are soe possest, that in preaching & hearing of sermons, pietie & religion doth chiefly consist . . . what hope is there, that by any other way they can ever be wrought out of it'? People had to be weaned away from preaching; but the only way to do this was, paradoxically, to preach them into a different way of thinking.[142] Casaubon's remarks are a striking testimony to the central place that sermons had come to occupy, and would continue to occupy, in the religious life and practice of many ordinary people. This was the legacy of the art of hearing, and it remained extremely powerful even when sermon repetition, note-taking and all the other customs associated with the puritan sermon culture of the early seventeenth century had largely fallen into disuse.

---

[140] On the sermon notes of John Evelyn and his family, see John Spurr, '"A sublime and noble service": John Evelyn and the Church of England', and Gillian Wright, 'Mary Evelyn and devotional practice', in Frances Harris and Michael Hunter, eds., *John Evelyn and His Milieu* (London, 2003), pp. 145–63 and 221–32.

[141] The words of the Marquis of Halifax, quoted in John Spurr, *The Restoration Church of England 1646–1689* (New Haven and London, 1991), p. 368.

[142] Meric Casaubon, *Generall Learning*, ed. Richard Serjeantson (Cambridge, 1999), p. 125.

# CHAPTER 3

# *From pulpit to print*

Early modern England was a society in which print was rapidly becoming ubiquitous. In the field of religious print alone – to say nothing of secular texts – the period covered by this book saw a huge increase in the volume and variety of publications, from academic theology at one end of the market to broadside ballads and chapbooks at the other. Printed sermons accounted for a large proportion of this material, but as Ian Green has shown in his recent survey of religious bestsellers, *Print and Protestantism in Early Modern England*, sermons were only part of a bewilderingly wide range of new publications – including biblical commentaries and concordances, catechisms, devotional books and a whole range of 'tractates', 'treatises' and 'discourses' – that almost defies categorisation.[1] The cultural penetration of print was increasing too. In his study of the interplay between oral and literate culture, Adam Fox asserts that 'no one lived beyond the reach of the written and printed word', and that while oral communication remained vitally important, it is impossible to identify an oral culture or tradition that was not, to some extent, infiltrated by written or printed texts. In short, 'the written word, in both manuscript and print, penetrated to a far deeper level in society and circulated in much greater quantities than was once imagined'.[2]

It is often assumed that there was a natural affinity between Protestantism and print, and that Protestant preachers must have been quick to grasp the possibilities of the new medium. Laurence A. Sasek, writing in 1961, was so firmly convinced of what he called the 'literary temper' of Puritanism that he found it hard to credit puritan writers when they expressed doubts about the efficacy of print. He admitted that 'for many puritans, writing had to be

---

[1] Ian Green, *Print and Protestantism in Early Modern England* (Oxford, 2000). See also Patrick Collinson, Arnold Hunt and Alexandra Walsham, 'Religious publishing in England 1557–1640', in John Barnard and D. F. McKenzie, eds., *The Cambridge History of the Book in Britain*, vol. IV, 1557–1695 (Cambridge, 2002), pp. 29–66.
[2] Adam Fox, *Oral and Literate Culture in England 1500–1700* (Oxford, 2000), pp. 19, 413.

excused', yet he found the excuses 'so eloquent or insistent that one suspects many puritans believed that writing was, in the long run, more efficacious, that a written sermon or treatise might more effectively promote the work of salvation than a sermon preached before a congregation'.[3] Traces of this assumption still linger. Even Ian Green, in his far more sophisticated analysis of Protestantism and the printed word, cannot quite free himself from the assumption that preachers must have designed their sermons for future publication. He comments that 'it is hard to imagine zealous and educated preachers not having in mind the possibility of transfer to another medium, rather as the author of a play or a thriller today might have in mind the possibility of its being turned into a screenplay. And how far might such a prospect have inhibited the operation of the Spirit and a preacher's ability to respond to the reactions of a live audience?'[4] Perhaps so. Yet if we neglect the tension between preaching and printing – the sense that these were two separate and not entirely compatible activities – then we may be missing something very important.

A more helpful model for understanding the relationship between preaching and print can be found in a brief but luminous essay by the late D. F. McKenzie, 'Speech–manuscript–print'. McKenzie makes two crucial points. First, he points out that oral, written and printed forms of communication were (and are) 'complementary, not competitive'. This is exemplified in the religious culture of early modern England, which, despite the emergence of print, was still in many respects highly oral in character. Religious ideas were passed on through public prayer and recitation of scripture, preaching and catechising, psalm-singing, conference and disputation; and throughout this period, there was constant interchange between orality and print. But McKenzie's second point is that we should not expect the transition between speech, manuscript and print to be smooth or seamless. Rather, we should expect to find it marked by 'moments of anxiety and hesitant adjustment', as speakers and writers faced up to the challenge of converting their words into printed form. As McKenzie shows, these moments of adjustment occur across a whole range of different literary genres. He quotes the playwright John Marston declaring that a printed playbook is intrinsically inferior to dramatic performance because it lacks 'the soule of lively action', and the lawyer Sir Matthew Hale arguing that oral testimony is preferable to written deposition because it offers more opportunities for sifting truth from falsehood. Many of his most striking

---

[3] Lawrence A. Sasek, *The Literary Temper of the English Puritans* (New York, 1961).
[4] Green, *Print and Protestantism*, p. 215.

examples, however, are drawn from printed sermons. As he notes: 'almost every printed sermon in the first half of the [seventeenth] century has something to say by way of apology for the loss of the preacher's presence'.[5]

This chapter examines the publication and use of printed sermons in the late sixteenth and early seventeenth centuries, with particular attention to those 'moments of adjustment' that McKenzie teaches us to look for. We shall see that the early seventeenth century saw a profound shift in attitudes to printed sermons among the English clergy. In the 1580s and 1590s, when printed sermons first began to be published in quantity, many preachers were highly suspicious of this new medium, but by the 1620s, as they began to appreciate the evangelical uses of print, they gradually – and sometimes grudgingly – came round to a more favourable view of it. With hindsight, it may seem surprising that they took so long to recognise the possibilities of sermon publication as a means of disseminating Protestant doctrine. Yet their concerns about the effects of print were not unfounded, for the medium did, ultimately, change the message. Printed sermons were not merely a way of giving wider currency to the spoken word; they actually undermined the primacy of the spoken word and, in doing so, effected a profound change in the style of preaching, as sermons lost their distinctively oral character and became indistinguishable from other forms of religious literature. Moreover, as we shall see, the expectations of the clergy who put their sermons into print did not always match the expectations of the laity who bought and read them.

## ATTITUDES TO PRINT

In the preface to his *Anatomy of Melancholy* (1621), Robert Burton drew attention to the extraordinary number of printed sermons on the market. To readers who objected that, as a clergyman, he should stick to religion instead of writing about medicine, he responded that the market for religious books was already glutted. What need was there for him to publish a work of divinity when so many of his brother-clergy had already done so?

For had I written positively, there be so many books in that kind, so many commentators, treatises, pamphlets, expositions, sermons, that whole teams of oxen cannot draw them; and had I been as forward and ambitious as some others, I might have haply printed a Sermon at Paul's Cross, a Sermon in St Mary's,

---

[5] D. F. McKenzie, 'Speech–manuscript–print', *Library Chronicle of the University of Texas at Austin*, 20: 1–2 (1990), pp. 86–109, reprinted in McKenzie, *Making Meaning: 'Printers of the Mind' and Other Essays*, ed. Peter D. McDonald and Michael F. Suarez (Amherst, 2002), pp. 237–58.

Oxford, a Sermon in Christ-Church, or a Sermon before the Right Honourable, Right Reverend, a Sermon before the Right Worshipful, a Sermon in Latin, in English, a Sermon with a name, a Sermon without, a Sermon, a Sermon, &c. But I have been ever as desirous to suppress my labours in this kind, as others have been to press and publish theirs.[6]

To anyone who has ever leafed through the Short-Title Catalogue or searched for sermons in Early English Books Online, the quantity of printed sermons may indeed seem endless. Every clergyman, it seems, nourished an ambition to see his sermons in print. Or did he? Some contemporaries took a different view, and pointed out that the clergy who published their sermons were in a very small minority. Thomas Rogers declared in 1590 that Suffolk contained more preaching ministers than virtually any other county in England, but that not more than half a dozen were 'approved writers'.[7] Even as late as 1641, by which time the printed sermon was a well-established genre, it was possible for Sir Edward Dering to declare that there were 'very few' clergy 'able and active both for Pulpit and Pen', since a minister who conscientiously devoted himself to preaching could not be expected to have the time to prepare his writings for print.[8]

It also comes as a surprise to realise how many of the most admired preachers of the early modern period deliberately withheld their sermons from the press. Archbishop Tobias Matthew's preaching diary records the delivery of nearly 2,000 sermons over a period of forty years, but not a single one of these sermons was published during his lifetime, and Matthew's labours in the pulpit would have gone entirely unrecorded were it not for the survival of some of his sermons in manuscript.[9] Only a handful of Richard Greenham's writings were published during his lifetime, and his reputation as a preacher and pastor rested almost entirely on the writings published posthumously by the editors of his collected *Works*.[10] Josias

---

[6] Robert Burton, *The Anatomy of Melancholy*, ed. Thomas C. Faulkner, Nicolas K. Kiessling and Rhonda L. Blair, vol. 1 (Oxford, 1989), pp. 20–1.

[7] Thomas Rogers, *Miles Christianus, or a Iust Apologie of All Necessarie Writings and Writers* (1590), C3r. Admittedly, Rogers was attempting to refute Miles Mosse's claim that 'many Ministers of the worde at this daie, are publique writers', so his estimate may be on the conservative side.

[8] Sir Edward Dering, *A Collection of Speeches* (1642), Q1r.

[9] Patrick Collinson, *The Religion of Protestants: The Church in English Society 1559–1625* (Oxford, 1982), pp. 48–51. The manuscript of Matthew's sermons published in the *Christian Observer* (1847) and noted by Collinson as untraced (p. 51 n.48) is now in York Minster Library. Other sermons by Matthew can be found in BL Sloane 2172, f. 3 and Add. 22180, ff. 67, 99, 141, 165, 171, 188; Bodleian Library, Oxford, MS Eng. th. e.177, ff. 36–8 and Rawl. D.273, ff. 75–7; St John's College, Oxford, MS 212.

[10] Kenneth L. Parker and Eric J. Carlson, eds, *'Practical Divinity': The Works and Life of Revd Richard Greenham* (Aldershot, 1998), p. 33. The one sermon published during Greenham's lifetime, *A Godly Exhortation* (1584; STC 11503), may be a pirated text.

Shute, rector of St Mary Woolnoth, preached regularly three times a week and was fêted by contemporaries as '*Generalis Praedicatorum*', the preacher-general of the City of London, but none of his sermons appeared in print until after his death.[11] In the light of these examples, we should not be too quick to assume that the early seventeenth century was the heyday of the printed sermon. Instead, we need to ask why so many preachers took so little interest in putting their sermons into print.

Even when preachers did publish their sermons, or allow them into print, they were often extremely apologetic about doing so. In the preface to a Paul's Cross sermon of 1578, Laurence Chaderton declared that in his opinion, there were too many books on the market. 'Vaine glory, and desire of popular fame in the writers, and desire of filthy lucre in the printers, have stuffed our English studies with many superfluous and unnecessary bookes … For my part, I wish with all my heart, that we had fewer books.' He had not wished to publish his sermon, but had finally agreed to do so in the hope that it might serve as a 'fruitfull remembrance' of the occasion in 'the mindes of those that heard me'. He ended by reiterating the standard reading/preaching distinction, and stressing that the printed sermon could not possibly be a substitute for hearing the word preached. 'Let no man thinke, that the reading of this can be half so effectuall and profitable to him, as the hearyng was, or might be. For it wanteth the zeale of the speaker, the attention of the hearer, the promise of God to the ordinary preaching of his word, the mighty and inwarde working of his holy spirite, and many other thinges which the Lord worketh most mercifully by the preaching of his glorious Gospel, which are not to be hoped for by reading the written Sermons of his ministers.'[12]

Other Elizabethan preachers took the same view. In the preface to *The Meane in Mourning* (1596), Thomas Playfere insisted that he had 'alwaies utterly refused' to print his sermons, despite being repeatedly urged to do so, while in the preface to another printed sermon, Stephen Egerton declared that as a rule 'I could never be induced, by the perswasion or intreaty of any man, to publish any of my sermons in print', and was only doing so now in order to drive an imperfect edition out of the market. Egerton's recommendation of his sermon to the reading public is notable more for its candour than for its enthusiasm: his purpose, he wrote frankly,

---

[11] The phrase is John Hacket's: see Hacket, *A Century of Sermons* (1675), (b)2v. Notes on Shute's sermons on Exodus, *c.* 1626–8, can be found in BL Add. 14900.

[12] Laurence Chaderton, *An Excellent and Godly Sermon, Most Needefull for this Time* (1580), preface to the reader (A3r–3v).

was 'rather . . . to qualifie an errour that cannot be recalled, than to publish a worke that may be any way greatly commodious to others'.[13] Even so prolific a writer as Samuel Hieron, introducing a collection of his sermons in 1608, still feared that some readers might think ill of him 'because of my diverse publishings'.[14] These writers were hardly unusual in their attitude to print publication: indeed, their remarks are typical of the Elizabethan 'stigma of print', a phrase originally coined by J. W. Saunders to describe the reluctance of many Tudor poets to put their writings into print (as opposed to manuscript circulation), but which applies equally well to the reluctance of many Tudor and Stuart preachers to put their sermons into print (as opposed to oral delivery).[15]

Egerton's distrust of print stemmed in part from the belief, not dissimilar to Burton's, that the market was becoming overcrowded. What need was there for printed sermons when, as he remarked in 1603, readers could already choose from an 'infinite number of learned and godly books . . . more in number than the leisure of any man of calling wil permitte him to reade, or the strength of any ordinarie memorie can be able to beare away'?[16] Indeed, there was a risk that preaching might become cheapened, and its impact blunted, by being forced to compete for attention in the market-place. In the preface to the sermons of another London minister, Egerton expressed concern at 'the varietie and multitude, I say not of ignorant and unlearned bookes . . . but even of Sermons and Catechismes, which (through the infirmitie of man) do hinder the judgement, confound the memorie, and distract the mindes of many people'. Nevertheless, he iden-tified several legitimate reasons for going into print: first, to refute 'those prophane and satirical pamphleters, who have opened their mouths against God'; secondly, to discourage unauthorised editions of sermons based on inaccurate shorthand notes; and thirdly, to enable the godly to be 'further built up in spirituall wisedome and conscience' by reading the sermons that they had already heard delivered from the pulpit.[17] While firmly asserting

---

[13] Stephen Egerton, *A Lecture Preached by Maister Egerton, at the Blacke-friers, 1589, Taken by Characterie, by a Yong Practitioner in that Facultie: and Now Againe Perused, Corrected and Amended by the Author* (1603), A3r, A4r.

[14] Samuel Hieron, *Six Sermons* (1608), A3r.

[15] J. W. Saunders, 'The stigma of print: a note on the social bases of Tudor poetry', *Essays in Criticism*, 1 (1951), pp. 139–64.

[16] Egerton, *Lecture*, A3v.

[17] William Cupper, *Certaine Sermons Concerning Gods Late Visitation* (1592), A5r, A7v. Egerton identifies himself as the author of this passage in his 'admonition touching reading' prefixed to Matthew Virel, *A Learned and Excellent Treatise Containing All the Principall Grounds of Christian Religion* (1594), where he states that he has said more about reading in the 'Preface to master Cuppers sermons' (A2v).

the primacy of preaching over reading, Egerton was at least prepared to allow reading a subsidiary function in reinforcing the message of the word preached.

Allied to this was a fear that readers, faced with such a wide variety of printed matter, would not exercise proper discrimination in making their choice, and would 'buy and reade for their pleasure' rather than for their 'spirituall good'. Richard Rogers warned his readers to choose books that were 'fit for the building of them up in godlines', rather than 'filthie, lewd and wanton bookes . . . much lesse superstitious pamphlets, and Machivels blasphemies (which is a shame should be suffered to come into mens hands)', but, short of drastic censorship, there was no way to ensure that sacred and profane literature were kept apart, and preachers were well aware which of the two was likely to be more popular.[18] As Egerton observed gloomily, many people preferred 'the weake and imperfect writings of men' to the Word of God. 'Are not those books most vendible, that are most vaine? and most gainfull to the Stationer, that are least profitable to the reader? Whence commeth this, but from want of true taste and iudgement in the professors of these dayes?' Even if readers could be persuaded to buy religious books, there was still a risk that they might choose the wrong sort of book, or read it in the wrong way. Egerton complained that many people were attracted to works of religious controversy, which bred 'rather a spirit of contention and contradiction, than any sound edification in true god-linesse', and that on the rare occasions when they did read the Bible, they read it 'by patches and pieces, and (as it were) by snatching and catching'.

Perhaps the strongest motive for this distrust of print, however, was the fear that printed sermons might supplant oral ones – the seventeenth-century equivalent, *mutatis mutandis*, of the modern fear that television and recorded music might take the place of live performance. If the laity had access to a plentiful supply of sermons to read at home, they might well feel that they had no need to come to church to hear the sermons of their own minister. This was clearly the concern in Richard Rogers's mind when, in the preface to his *Seven Treatises* (1603), he warned of over-zealous persons who 'have given themselves (as they say) to grow by their private reading, when they might have been taught also in the publike assemblie: which some of them refuse to doe', and in Robert Cleaver's mind when he introduced the first edition of John Dod's *Exposition of the Ten Commandments* (1604) with a cautionary reminder: 'Beware thou grow not conceited of a sufficiencie to be found in reading good bookes, and so

---

[18] Richard Rogers, *Seven Treatises* (1603), 2C6v.

begin to distaste the Ministerie: they are not ordayned to kill our appetites to the word, but to sharpen them.'[19] It also explains why many preachers felt the need to present their printed works as little more than an *aide-mémoire* for the benefit of those who had already heard the sermons delivered from the pulpit. Andrew Willet, writing in 1604, dedicated the printed edition of his sermons to his Hertfordshire parishioners and explained that his purpose was 'to write the same thing, which sometime I spake, and to commit that to writing, which not long since in our weekely exercise I commended to your hearing', even though the length and complexity of the printed text suggests that it had been enlarged with additional material.[20]

Most of these examples date from the last decade of the sixteenth century and the first decade of the seventeenth, and seem to indicate a gradual shift of opinion occurring around this time, as preachers became aware that more and more sermons were finding their way into print. While some preachers were extremely reluctant to publish their sermons, other writers were quick to appreciate the advantages of print publication. In the second book of his *Advancement of Learning*, probably written around 1605, Francis Bacon declared that of all forms of religious discourse, the 'most rich and precious' was 'positive divinity, collected upon particular texts of scriptures in brief observations . . . a thing abounding in sermons, which will vanish, but defective in books which will remain, and a thing wherein this age excelleth'. Bacon approved of sermons because they were relatively concise (unlike scriptural commentaries, 'which grow to be more vast than the original writings, whence the sum was at first extracted'), uncontroversial (unlike polemical divinity) and drawn directly from the scriptures (unlike scholastical divinity, in which the scriptures were mediated through an artificial method); and for all these reasons, he urged the publication of more printed sermons, believing that if the choicest sermons of the Elizabethan period had been collected together and 'set down in a continuance, it had been the best work in divinity which had been written since the Apostles' times'.[21]

---

[19] Rogers, *Seven Treatises*, N5v; John Dod and Robert Cleaver, *The Bright Star which Leadeth Wise Men to Our Lord Iesus Christ* (1603), A1v.

[20] Andrew Willet, *Thesaurus Ecclesiae, that is, the Treasure of the Church . . . Set Forth in the 17 Chapter of the Gospel by S. Iohn* (2nd edn., 1614), E1r.

[21] Francis Bacon, *The Advancement of Learning*, ed. Arthur Johnston (Oxford, 1974), p. 209. Surprisingly, no English author seems to have taken up Bacon's suggestion (which would certainly have appealed to the Hartlib circle), but eighty years later a Swiss divine, Melchior Mittelholzer, published a collection of extracts from English sermons in Latin translation, *Florilegium Anglicanum* (Geneva, 1686).

Bacon's call did not go unheeded. By the 1620s, many preachers had come round to a far more positive appreciation of the benefits of print. The Yorkshire minister Nathaniel Jackson, publishing a sermon by his brother John in 1628, quoted the now-familiar passage from Burton's *Anatomy of Melancholy*, and admitted that some preachers had put their sermons into print for purely self-interested reasons, but then went on to quote Bacon ('the Censure and Sentence of a Noble and learned Gentleman speaking definitively'), and suggested that his brother's sermon might well find a place in Bacon's notional collection of the best modern divinity. 'I doubt not but some things in this discourse may very worthily be cast into that volume.'[22] An even more ringing endorsement of print publication came in 1626 from the Oxfordshire minister Robert Harris, who urged his fellow clergy to publish their sermons in order to convey the light of the Gospel to future generations:

Art thou learned? . . . If God hath given thee sufficiency in this kinde, thou mayest speake thy minde to men yet unborne, and convey to them that light which God hath reached to thee . . . We are infinitly bound to God for the blessing of Printing, and to our fathers for their labours: and wee of England are much to blame, if we leave not Arts and Tongues more refined and perfected than we found them, and the Scriptures more fully opened; no people being better furnished with meanes, no writings extant better accepted abroad, or to better purpose at home.[23]

Thomas Jackson, prebendary of Canterbury, declared in the preface to a printed sermon in 1622 that 'Printing is a kinde of Preaching', with the advantages of being 'more memorable (affording greater leave to pause and consider) and also of longer continuance', and concluded: 'I would account it a double happinesse, if I could doe good both waies'.[24]

Although there are no reliable figures for the total number of sermons printed in this period, there have been several attempts to produce comprehensive listings of particular types of sermon, and all of these show a sharp upward trend in the seventeenth century. Admittedly, these figures have to be set in the context of a general increase in the output of all types of print publication – between the 1570s and the 1620s, the number of books published in London more than doubled, from 200 to 500 titles per year – but the increase in the number of printed sermons is unusually marked, and appears to be concentrated in the Jacobean period. Ralph Houlbrooke has estimated that there were about twenty funeral sermons printed during the

[22] John Jackson, *Ecclesiastes. The Worthy Church-Man, or the Faithful Minister of Jesus Christ* (1628), A1v.
[23] Robert Harris, *Hezekiah's Recovery* (1626), D4r.
[24] Thomas Jackson, *Judah Must into Captivitie, Six Sermons* (1622), A1r–v.

reign of Elizabeth, but 'by the end of the 1630s that total had risen to well over one hundred, and possibly to nearly two hundred'.[25] A rough count of Paul's Cross sermons suggests that there were about sixty published during the reign of Elizabeth, and about twice as many during the reign of James (or, to put it another way, more published in the first ten years of James's reign than during the whole of Elizabeth's); while Peter McCullough's list of court sermons shows an even more marked increase, from 28 Elizabethan to 141 Jacobean examples, not including the collected editions of Andrewes's and Donne's sermons published after 1625.[26] These figures are all the more remarkable when we recall the misgivings expressed by Egerton, and clearly shared by many other preachers, about the publication of printed sermons.

The first two decades of the seventeenth century can thus be pinpointed, with some precision, as the period when the English clergy came to terms with the idea of print publication. There were several reasons for this change. One was the stricter enforcement of ceremonial conformity after the Hampton Court Conference in 1604, which meant that ejected puritan preachers such as John Dod and Robert Cleaver were forced to resort to print as an alternative outlet for their evangelical talents. When the sermons of William Negus were published posthumously in 1619, the editors identified this as the principal reason for Negus's decision to go into print: 'he being restrained from benefiting the Church by the ordinarie course of his ministerie, hee was both willing and desirous to be serviceable and helpfull to the same, in what he might, by this way and meane'.[27] One of Negus's editors was Stephen Egerton, whose new-found support for print publication makes an interesting contrast with his earlier views. Even in 1619, he was still suspicious of the mixed motives of the reading public, grumbling that new books were customarily read 'rather for the noveltie of the edition, than for any newnesse of matter contained in them'. Yet he was now convinced of the need for a constant supply of new publications, like 'new Phenixes rising out of the ashes of the old', to ensure 'the spreading and continuing of the truth' from generation to generation. Preaching and

---

[25] Ralph Houlbrooke, *Death, Religion and the Family in England, 1480–1750* (Oxford, 1998), pp. 298, 386–7.

[26] The figures for Paul's Cross sermons are based on Millar MacLure, *Register of Sermons Preached at Paul's Cross 1534–1642*, revised by P. Pauls and J. C. Boswell (Ottawa, 1989), excluding those sermons which were published at a later date or which survive only in manuscript. The figures for court sermons can be found in Peter McCullough, *Sermons at Court: Politics and Religion in Elizabethan and Jacobean Preaching* (Cambridge, 1998), p. 8 n. 19.

[27] William Negus, *Mans Active Obedience, or the Power of Godlines* (1619), A8v. See also Alexandra Walsham, 'Preaching without speaking: script, print and religious dissent', in Julia Crick and Alexandra Walsham, eds., *The Uses of Script and Print, 1300–1700* (Cambridge, 2004), pp. 211–34.

printing were 'the two great lights' of the world, 'as the Sunne and Moone to direct and comfort us'.[28]

But by far the most compelling reason for the publication of printed sermons was, quite simply, the growing public demand for them. Preachers may not have relished the attentions of shorthand writers and piratical printers, but they can hardly have failed to realise that the publication of sermons from unauthorised shorthand transcripts was gratifying testimony to the existence of a genuine popular desire for religious literature, casting doubt on the gloomy prognostications of Egerton and Rogers that printed sermons would be neglected or ignored. Indeed, some of these unauthorised editions claim to be published in order to satisfy popular demand: the editor of Henry Smith's sermon *The Benefite of Contentation* (1590) admitted that the author had not given his consent to the publication, but argued that 'the profit and utility of many in publishing it' should come before 'the pleasure of the Author in concealing it'.[29] Behind the publisher's hyperbole it is perhaps possible to discern a belief that sermons, once uttered from the pulpit, entered the public domain and could be treated as common property. Several printed editions of sermons from the 1620s, apparently part of an organised publishing project, carry the motto 'Uprightness hath Boldness' on their title pages.[30] This can be interpreted as an apology for unauthorised publication, on the grounds that the 'uprightness' of the desire for godly literature should be held to excuse the 'boldness' of publishing these sermons without the authors' consent.

Admittedly, images of bashful preachers reluctantly forced into print at the insistence of their friends need to be treated with some scepticism. This was a conventional excuse for print publication which cannot necessarily be taken as genuine evidence of popular demand. In the preface to a Paul's Cross sermon of 1609, Robert Johnson commented that 'the earnest entreatie of friends' was a 'common, and over-worne' excuse, while Charles Herle referred sardonically in 1631 to 'that commonly pretended midwife of the presse, importunity of friends'.[31] Some writers, though, are more plausibly circumstantial in their references to public demand, and carry conviction when they suggest that the demand for printed sermons

---

[28]  Negus, *Mans Active Obedience*, (a)2v.
[29]  Henry Smith, *A Sermon of the Benefite of Contentation* (London, R. Ward for J. Proctor, 1590; STC 22693), A3r.
[30]  These include John Smith, *Essex Dove* (1629), Richard Sibbes *et al.*, *The Saints Cordials* (1629) and Bodleian Library, Oxford, MS Lyell empt. 27, and are associated with the mysterious figure of John Hart (possibly a pseudonym), on whom see Green, *Print and Protestantism*, p. 483.
[31]  Robert Johnson, *Davids Teacher* (1609), A2r; Charles Herle, *Contemplations and Devotions on the Several Passages of Our Blessed Saviours Death and Passion* (1631), A5r.

was increasing. William Fuller noted in the preface to his funeral sermon for Lady Frances Clifton, second wife of the much-married Sir Gervase Clifton, that whereas his funeral sermon for Gervase Clifton's first wife, in 1613, had been circulated in manuscript, the growing demand for copies forced the present sermon, in 1628, to appear in print. 'The first long since went out in written copies: this last (it seemeth) must not be restrained within so narrow bounds, nor the desire of so many satisfied without more ample notice.'[32] It is also interesting to note the existence of some manuscripts apparently copied from printed texts, which suggests that printed sermons were being widely circulated and that in some cases demand outstripped supply.[33]

By the 1620s, sermons, like other texts, were part of a thriving culture of manuscript circulation and print publication. With so many sermons being copied and printed – and often being read by people who had never heard them preached – it became increasingly difficult to insist on the priority of the oral sermon, or to maintain the pretence that the printed sermon was only a memory-aid for members of the preacher's own congregation. Slowly but steadily, the distinction between reading and preaching was breaking down. Yet this did not mark the end of a speech-dominated model of language – as can be seen in Phineas Fletcher's poem 'Upon Mr Perkins his printed sermons', which depicts the printed word itself as a form of speech:

> Perkins (our wonder) living, though long dead,
> In this white paper, as a winding-sheet,
> And in this velome lies enveloped:
> Yet still he lives, guiding the erring feet,
> Speaking now to our eyes, though buried.
> If once so well, much better now he teacheth.
> Who will not heare, when a live-dead man preacheth?[34]

Fletcher's poem is an eloquent justification of the benefits of printed sermons, even going so far as to suggest that Perkins teaches 'much better' in print than he ever did in the pulpit. But it does not assert that print has displaced the spoken word. Rather, it suggests that print *is* the spoken word, with the printed text 'speaking now to our eyes' as Perkins the preacher once

---

[32] William Fuller, *The Mourning of Mount Libanon* (1628), A3v. A manuscript copy of Fuller's earlier sermon for Lady Penelope Clifton survives in Nottingham University Library, Clifton of Clifton MSS, Cl LM 10.

[33] The papers of Lady Elizabeth Cornwallis contain copies of Joseph Hall's sermons apparently transcribed from a printed edition (Essex Record Office, Chelmsford, D/Dby C27), and a manuscript in the Folger Shakespeare Library, Washington, DC (V.a.265) contains copies of Henry Smith's sermons also probably transcribed from print.

[34] 'Upon Mr Perkins his printed sermons', in Phineas Fletcher, *The Purple Island* (1633), 2O2v.

did to our ears. This idea had a long history, going back to a well-known passage in Augustine's *De Trinitate* in which Augustine draws a parallel between speech and gesture ('for even to nod, what else is it but to speak, as it were, in a visible manner?') and goes on to extend the parallel to the written word as being, like gesture, a form of visible speech 'by which we can also speak to those who are absent'.[35]

The idea of writing as a form of speech was a commonplace in the Renaissance period, and is frequently invoked by preachers in the prefaces to their printed sermons. In the preface to *Davids Remembrancer* (1623), Thomas Gataker argues – with specific acknowledgement to Augustine – that the great advantage of the written word is its ability to 'speak' to people at all times, in all places; and that while the spoken word is ephemeral, the written word may endure for centuries after its author's death:

Albeit Speech have no small advantage of Writing; in that it hath a greater vivacitie accompanying it, than the other hath by much: the latter seeming to bee but as a dead shadow of the former . . . In regard whereof, [writing] is not wont to make so deep an impression, or to worke upon the affections so powerfully as [speech] doth; and it is accounted therefore but a second shift, and as sayling with a side-winde, where a direct fore-winde faileth. Yet herein hath writing the ods of Speech; in that by it wee may speake as well to the absent as to the present; by it men restrained by sicknesse, weaknesse, or otherwise from publike imployment, yet may notwith-standing much profit the publike, and sitting themselves still at home, benefit others abroad; yea by it, not the living onely may converse with the living, though never so far both by Sea and Land severed either from other, but the living also may have profitable commerce and dealing with the dead, as wee have by meanes of their writings still extant with those that died and departed this World, even thousands of yeeres since, to our exceeding great comfort and inestimable gaine.[36]

The fact that Gataker felt it necessary to include this lengthy apology for publication suggests that some readers were still expressing doubts about the propriety of putting sermons into print. His emphasis on writing as a form of speech was well calculated to settle such doubts. It enabled preachers to publish sermons, and readers to read them, without letting go of a speech-dominated model of language in which the spoken word was primary and the printed word only secondary. It also enabled them to conceal, perhaps even from themselves, how profoundly the relationship between speech and writing was being altered by the availability of printed sermons.

---

[35] Augustine, *The Trinity*, ed. and trans. Stephen McKenna (Washington, DC, 1963), pp. 475–7 (XV. 10–11); Martin Elsky, *Authorizing Words: Speech, Writing and Print in the English Renaissance* (Cornell, 1989), pp. 45–6 (and p. 71 on Augustine).

[36] Thomas Gataker, 'Davids Remembrancer', in *Certaine Sermons* (1623), 2C6v.

It is instructive to compare Gataker's remarks with those of Richard Baxter precisely fifty years later. Both are plainly drawn from the same stock of commonplaces. Both attempt to strike a balance between speech and writing; both associate the spoken word with the power to move the emotions, and the written word with the power to instruct the intellect:

The Writings of Divines are nothing else but a preaching the Gospel to the eye, as the *voice* preacheth it to the ear. Vocal preaching hath the preheminence in moving the affections . . . But Books have the advantage in many other respects: you may read an able Preacher when you have but a mean one to hear. Every *Congregation* cannot hear the most judicious or powerful Preachers: but every *single person* may read the Books of the most powerful and judicious; *Preachers* may be silenced or banished when *Books* may be at hand: *Books* may be kept at a smaller charge than Preachers: We may choose Books which treat of that very subject which we desire to hear of; but we cannot choose what subject the Preacher shall treat of. Books we may have at hand every day and hour: when we can have Sermons but seldom, and at set times. If Sermons be forgotten, they are gone. But a Book we may read over and over till we remember it: and if we forget it, may again peruse it at our pleasure, or at our leisure . . . Books are (if well chosen) domestick, present, constant, judicious, pertinent, yea, and powerfull Sermons: and always of very great use to your salvation: but especially when Vocal preaching faileth, and Preachers are ignorant, ungodly or dull, or when they are persecuted and forbid to preach.[37]

But Baxter goes well beyond Gataker in suggesting that reading can serve as a substitute for preaching. For Gataker, the reading of godly sermons might supplement live preaching but could never wholly replace it. For Baxter, on the other hand, the two were essentially one and the same. To say that books were 'nothing else but a preaching the Gospel to the eye, as the *voice* preacheth it to the ear' was, in effect, to reject the reading/preaching distinction that had been so important earlier in the century.

The idea that speech was more immediately moving, whereas print was more enduringly instructive, is one we shall encounter again in the following two sections, which look, respectively, at how sermons found their way into manuscript and how they were revised for print. Although preachers were increasingly willing to consider putting their sermons into print, they did not regard the spoken word and the printed word as performing identical functions. By looking more closely at the process of revision, and comparing, where we can, different texts of the same sermon, we can identify some of the perceived differences between preaching and print, and pinpoint some of McKenzie's 'moments of anxiety and hesitant adjustment' in the textual changes introduced between the pulpit and the press.

---

[37] Richard Baxter, *A Christian Directory* (1673), I3v.

## FROM MANUSCRIPT TO PRINT

Most early modern sermons were never written down at all, and even in the rare cases when they were committed to paper, they frequently show signs of extreme textual instability and indeterminacy. This should not surprise us. As we saw in Chapter 1, many preachers drew a sharp distinction between preaching and 'mere' reading, the one being regarded as a creative, charismatic activity, the other as merely the mechanical recitation of the words on the page. This made it very awkward for them to deliver their sermons from a written text. Laurence Chaderton, in the preface to his Paul's Cross sermon of 1578, was at pains to stress that he did not prepare the sermon in writing and had not kept a written copy. Even when he had finally been persuaded to prepare the sermon for publication, he had made no attempt to reproduce the words spoken from the pulpit – 'for the Lord knoweth I never writ it, and therefore could not'.[38]

The need for preachers to learn to manage without a written text is repeated over and over again in the preaching manuals. Wilhelm Zepper's treatise on the art of preaching, first published in 1598, declared that sermons should not be read in public from a prepared text (*ex charta in publico legendae*) as this caused the ministry to be held in scorn and contempt by the common people, although he was prepared to make an exception in the case of inexperienced preachers (*tyrones*).[39] William Perkins agreed, noting that 'it is the received custome for preachers to speak *by heart* before the people'.[40] All that Richard Bernard, in his influential handbook on preaching, was prepared to countenance were very brief notes, summarising the 'chiefe heads' of the sermon, 'a word or two for every severall thing', which could be discreetly concealed in the pulpit in the form of 'little paper books bound like Testaments, or the Bible with a paper fastened in it'.[41] While it was not unknown for preachers to read their sermons, references to the practice tend to be disparaging or apologetic. Richard James, for example, thanked his Oxford auditors for allowing him 'the libertie of reading my Sermons, which I have once entreated, and I hope still obtained from your courtesie', but evidently regarded this as a special privilege granted to him because of his weak memory.[42]

---

[38] Chaderton, *An Excellent and Godly Sermon*, A3v.
[39] Wilhelm Zepper, *Ars Habendi et Audiendi Conciones Sacras* (Sigenae Nassoviorum, 1598), D4v–5r.
[40] William Perkins, *The Arte of Prophecying*, in *Workes*, vol. II (Cambridge, 1609), 3V3v ('Of memorie in preaching').
[41] Richard Bernard, *The Faithfull Shepheard* (1607), M3r.
[42] Richard James, *A Sermon Delivered in Oxford, Concerning the Apostles Preaching and Ours* (1630), B1r.

This accorded not only with the reading/preaching distinction but also with the rules and conventions of classical rhetoric. In his *Institutio Oratoria*, Quintilian declared that a speech delivered without notes, as if impromptu, would be far more effective than one that had obviously been rehearsed in advance, 'for the judge admires more, and fears less, those speeches which he does not suspect of having been specially prepared beforehand to outwit him'. For this reason, 'we must take care, above all, to make it appear that our words are casually strung together, and to suggest that we are thinking out and hesitating over words which we have, in fact, carefully prepared in advance'. But how should the orator commit his speech to memory? Should he memorise it word for word, or merely concentrate on getting the main points in the right order? Quintilian's answer was that it depended on the circumstances. For those with a good memory and plenty of spare time, it would be better to learn the speech by heart, but 'if our memory be somewhat dull, or if time presses, it will be useless to tie ourselves down rigidly to every word, for if we forget any one of them, the result may be an awkward hesitation or even a tongue-tied silence'.[43] Following this advice, early modern preachers prepared their sermons in one of two ways: either by making a full draft which they then memorised and preached verbatim, or by writing out the 'heads of the sermon' in note form and then preaching partly extempore.

Some preachers are known to have written their sermons out in full before delivery. Joseph Hall, on his own testimony, 'never durst climb up into the Pulpit to preach any Sermon whereof he had not before penn'd every word in the same Order, wherein he hoped to deliver it', though he insisted that he made no use of his notes in the pulpit, and described himself as 'no slave to syllables', implying that he left some room for improvisation. William Whately 'usually did pen his Sermons at large; and if before he preached, hee had but so much time as to read over what he had written, and to gather it up into short heades, hee was able if hee thought it fit to deliver it in publicke well neare in the same words'.[44] Of the preachers who followed this method, the best known is Lancelot Andrewes, the majority of whose sermons 'passed his hand, and were thrice revised, before they were preached', according to John Buckeridge, who edited them for publication after Andrewes's death. The surviving manuscript of one of Andrewes's

[43] Quintilian, *The Orator's Education*, Books 11–12, ed. and trans. Donald A. Russell (Cambridge, MA, 2001), pp. 81–3 (11.2.49).
[44] John Whitefoote, *Deaths Alarum . . . Given in a Funeral Sermon for the Right Reverend Joseph Hall* (1656), F2v (p. 68); William Whately, *Prototypes, or, the Primarie Precedent Presidents out of the Booke of Genesis* (1640), A4r.

sermons, preached at court on Easter Day 1620, bears witness to this painstaking process of revision. It consists of a fair copy in the hand of Andrewes's amanuensis Samuel Wright, with extensive corrections in Andrewes's own hand; its modern editor, P. J. Klemp, describes it as a 'revised semifinal draft' and points out that it underwent at least one further stage of revision before appearing in print later that year.[45]

But not all preachers prepared their sermons with such minute attention to detail. Many of the contemporary handbooks on preaching expressed reservations, similar to Quintilian's, about the word-for-word memorisation of sermons. Perkins warned that it might cause the preacher to lose the thread of his argument and would, in any case, divert his attention from more important matters such as gesture, delivery and 'the holy motions of affections'. John Wilkins described it as a 'more exact and elaborate' method of preaching, suitable for 'young beginners' as a means of cultivating a 'good stile and expression' but not so suitable for older or more experienced clergymen. As an alternative to word-for-word memorisation, Perkins advised the preacher to commit to memory the basic structure of the sermon, 'the severall proofes and applications of the doctrines, the illustrations of the applications, and the order of them all', while leaving the exact words to the inspiration of the moment. Wilkins – writing over half a century later, when the doctrine-and-application method favoured by Perkins had begun to fall out of fashion – did not insist on such a formal structure, but his advice to preachers, though couched in more general terms, was much the same: 'When we have the matter and notion well digested, the expressions of it will easily follow.'[46] This was a method of sermon preparation which gave more weight to reading, prayer and meditation than to prose composition, and encouraged preachers to concentrate on the logical coherence of the argument rather than the finer points of style.

The popularity of this method is evident from the many contemporary references to sermons having been prepared in note form. In the preface to a sermon preached at Paul's Cross in 1609, William Loe explained that he had initially been reluctant to publish the sermon because he had 'no Copy transcribed, except only some few briefe notes for the help of my memorie'. Thomas Gataker's sermon manuscripts are variously described as

[45] P. J. Klemp, '"Betwixt the hammer and the anvill": Lancelot Andrewes's revision techniques in the manuscript of his 1620 Easter sermon', *Papers of the Bibliographical Society of America*, 89: 2 (1995), 149–82.

[46] Perkins, *The Arte of Prophecying*, 3V3v; John Wilkins, *Ecclesiastes, or, a Discourse Concerning the Gift of Preaching* (1646), K3v.

'broken notes', 'raw notes', 'imperfect notes' and 'some general heads and briefe notes scribled in a loose paper before'.[47] Sermons prepared in this way were textually unstable, and since they were not written out in full until after they had been preached, any form of words that later appeared in print might differ substantially from the sermon as previously delivered from the pulpit. Thomas Sparke, in the preface to a printed sermon, explained that it was 'impossible for me to call to remembrance the very wordes wherein I uttered it', because 'I had taken but short notes before', and it was not until afterwards that he had been persuaded to commit the sermon 'to writing, and so to the print'.[48] This occasionally caused difficulties when the ecclesiastical authorities wished to investigate precisely what a preacher had said in a particular sermon. In 1629 Robert Moore, one of the prebendaries of Winchester, was required to hand over 'the coppies or notes of certaine sermons he hade preached in our cathedrall church contrarie to the receaved customes of our Church'. His reply was that he was unable to do so, 'for coppies he had non'.[49]

Experienced preachers would have switched between these different methods of sermon preparation as they saw fit. John Donne is a case in point. On special occasions he seems to have written out his sermons in full before delivery (he describes one of his court sermons as having been 'put upon that very order, in which I delivered it, more than two months since'), but at other times he speaks of 'short notes' which were later 'reviewed' and 'written out'.[50] The letters of George Coke, future Bishop of Hereford, to his brother John, Secretary of State to Charles I, clearly indicate the different levels of preparation required for different types of sermon. John Coke had apparently been trying to secure an invitation for his brother to preach at court, and in May 1628 George sent him a couple of sermons, one preached at Easter in his parish and another 'which I have only begunne but not yet perfited . . . I pray you send me them both back againe so soone as you can, for I have no other coppies especially of the last, but those that are written in broken papers as I made them.' A few days later he sent the remainder of the second sermon, but warned his brother that 'this upon the psalme, is not my

---

[47] William Loe, *The Ioy of Ierusalem: and Woe of the Worldlings* (1609), dedication; Gataker, *Certaine Sermons*, P5r ('broken notes'), 3Q6r ('raw notes'), 3X2r ('imperfect notes'), 3C5r ('scattered notes').

[48] Thomas Sparke, *A Sermon Preached . . . at the Buriall of the Right Honorable the Earle of Bedforde* (Oxford, 1594), A4r. For another example, see the preface to Miles Mosse, *Iustifying and Saving Faith* (Cambridge, 1614): 'Writing nothing at large . . . I had no safer rule to walke by, than the *method* by which I had in short notes digested my meditations.'

[49] F. R. Goodman, ed., *The Diary of John Young S. T. P., Dean of Winchester* (London, 1928), p. 84.

[50] John Sparrow, 'John Donne and contemporary preachers', in *Essays & Studies*, vol. XVI, ed. H. J. C. Grierson (Oxford, 1931), pp. 144–78 (ref. pp. 165–6).

usual manner of preaching: and I cannot gett such a sermon by heart, but with as much or more time, than in which I made it: I could never doe it, and therfore I never strive for it. Therfore, I pray you if you like this latter better, as I suppose you may doe, draw me not too soone upon the stage, for the deliverie of it.'[51] This implies that a court sermon would need to be written in a more polished style than an ordinary parish sermon, and would therefore need to be prepared more carefully – 'cribrated, and re-cribrated, and post-cribrated', as Donne remarked ruefully on another occasion – and committed to memory almost word for word.[52]

Court sermons would sometimes be transcribed by the preacher for presentation to the monarch. The preface to an Elizabethan sermon by one 'H. B.', possibly the Hebrew scholar Hugh Broughton, describes it as having been 'preached at the court' in 1580, 'and afterward (upon speciall, or rather a generall approbation of it in that place) commaunded by some in authoritie, to be then set down in writing by the preacher himselfe'; similarly, after Lancelot Andrewes's sermon at court on Christmas Day 1609, it was reported that 'the King with much importunitie had the copie delivered him . . . and says he will lay yt still under his pillow'.[53] This was sometimes the prelude to publication. Donne wrote to Sir Thomas Roe in December 1622 apologising for not sending him a copy of his recent sermon at Paul's Cross, but explaining that the copy which 'by commandment I did write after the preaching, is yet in his Majesty's hand, and I know not whether he will . . . after his reading thereof, command it to be printed'.[54] If the monarch approved of the sermon, the manuscript would be returned to the preacher with the royal imprimatur, as in the case of Matthew Wren's sermon preached before Charles I in 1627, where the manuscript bears an inscription in the king's own hand, 'Lett this Sermon bee printed.'[55] Roger Maynwaring's two court sermons, also preached in 1627, received a verbal imprimatur from the king, followed by a written imprimatur from Bishop Montaigne of London, who endorsed the manuscript, 'Lett these Sermons be printed (according to his Majesties Speciall Command)'. A few days later Montaigne had second thoughts,

[51] George to John Coke, 4 May 1628: BL Add. MS 69868 (Coke papers, series 2, vol. 1), ff. 112–13; same to same, 8 May 1628: ibid., ff. 114–15.

[52] John Donne, *Letters to Severall Persons of Honour* (1651), 2R2v (p. 308).

[53] H. B., *Moriemini. A Verie Profitable Sermon Preached before Her Maiestie at the Court, about xiij. yeares since* (1593), A3r. John Chamberlain to Sir Ralph Winwood, 13 January 1610, in *Letters of John Chamberlain*, ed. N. E. McClure (Philadelphia, 1939), vol. 1, p. 295.

[54] Donne to Roe, 1 December 1622, printed in Edmund Gosse, *The Life and Letters of John Donne* (1899), vol. 11, p. 175.

[55] Sermon by Matthew Wren on Proverbs 24: 21: Trinity College, Cambridge, MS B.14.22 (James 307), later published as *A Sermon Preached before the Kings Majestie* (Cambridge, 1627).

recalled the manuscript and crossed out the words in brackets, but Maynwaring then appealed to Laud, who authorised him to reinstate the royal imprimatur. Maynwaring accordingly 'gave notice to the printer . . . and soe the Sermons were printed as they are'.[56]

Paul's Cross sermons, too, were often transcribed at the request of an influential auditor or patron. George Creswell, who preached at the Cross in 1607, explained that he had 'at the request of a religious Knight (an Alderman of the Cittie of London) gathered this my Sermon into writing, and delivered him the Copie', while John Pelling, who preached there a few weeks later, claimed that his patron, the Earl of Hertford, had persuaded the Bishop of London, Thomas Ravis, to request a copy of his sermon; Ravis then 'vouchsafed to peruse it, and by his authoritie hath allowed it' (i.e. licensed it for the press).[57] These examples suggest that Paul's Cross preachers did not submit their sermons to the ecclesiastical authorities unless specially asked to do so; but by 1633 the standard form of summons to preach at the Cross specifically required the preacher to bring a copy of his sermon with him.[58] This rule, probably introduced by Laud, not only enabled the authorities to vet sermons more carefully, but also meant that sermons could be licensed and published more quickly. Previously, it was not unusual for a month or more to elapse between preaching and publication: Creswell's sermon, for example, was preached on 9 August 1607, entered in the Stationers' Register on 23 September, and the dedicatory epistle is dated 8 October, two months after the date of delivery; similarly, Pelling's sermon was preached on 25 October 1607, entered in the Stationers' Register on 18 November, and the dedicatory epistle is dated 25 November, one month after the date of delivery. By contrast, William Watts, who preached at Paul's Cross on 21 May 1637, had his sermon licensed the following day; it was entered in the Stationers' Register on 5 June and the dedication is dated 8 June, only eighteen days after delivery.[59]

But while they were willing to transcribe their sermons for an important patron, preachers were understandably anxious to prevent the proliferation of unauthorised copies. When Lancelot Andrewes preached at court on Easter Day 1621, the newswriter John Chamberlain reported that the

---

[56] Statement by Roger Maynwaring: Lambeth Palace Library, London, MS 943, p. 567.

[57] George Creswell, *The Harmonie of the Lawe and the Gospel . . . Delivered in a Sermon at Pauls-crosse* (1607), A3r; John Pelling, *A Sermon of the Providence of God* (1607), A3r.

[58] For invitations to preach at Paul's Cross, see MacLure, *Register of Sermons Preached at Paul's Cross*, revised by P. Pauls and J. C. Boswell, p. 138, and Bodleian Library, Oxford, MS Rawl. D.399, f. 115.

[59] William Watts, *Mortification Apostolicall, Delivered in a Sermon in Saint Pauls Church, upon Summons Received for the Crosse* (1637).

sermon had been 'excellently commended', but that Andrewes 'will not be intreted to let yt come abroad, unles the King commaund him'.[60] In his letter to Sir Thomas Roe, quoted above, Donne explained that the only copy of his Paul's Cross sermon was in the king's hands, 'and while it is in that suspense, I know your Lordship would call it indiscretion to send out any copy thereof'. As with his poems, Donne evidently took some pains to control the manuscript circulation of his sermons. A letter to Sir Henry Goodyere gives the impression of a strictly limited number of copies, restricted to a small circle of readers: 'I send you a copy of that sermon, but it is not my copy, which I thought my Lord of Southampton would have sent me backe. This you must be pleased to let me have again, for I borrow it.'[61] Many of the surviving manuscripts of Donne's sermons can, in fact, be linked to someone in Donne's immediate circle: the Merton manuscript, for example, was copied by Henry Field, who appears to have been connected with Bishop Theophilus Field, one of Donne's colleagues on the Court of Delegates, while the Ellesmere manuscript probably belonged to Donne's patron the Earl of Bridgewater. Even John Chamberlain, well connected as he was, did not always succeed in obtaining copies: in 1617, when Dudley Carleton requested a copy of one of Donne's recent sermons, Chamberlain had to confess, 'I know not how to procure a copie of Dr Donnes sermon yf yt come not in print, but I will inquire after yt.'[62]

One might assume that sermons were a fairly specialised taste. John Sparrow stated categorically that 'the copying and circulation of sermons in manuscript . . . was not as frequent as that of poems', and it is true that poems tended to be shorter and easier to copy.[63] But the relatively small number of sermon manuscripts may, to some extent, be an accident of survival – whereas poems were preserved for their literary interest, and political tracts for their historical interest, sermons were much more likely to be discarded by later generations of readers – and there is no doubt that the manuscripts that have come down to us are only a small fraction of the total. A letter from the young Oxford don Gilbert Sheldon, alluding to a sermon by a slightly older Oxford contemporary, Richard Steward, offers a glimpse of what was clearly a vigorous scribal culture: 'I have sent you Mr Stewards sermon which if my

[60] Chamberlain to Carleton, 18 April 1621, in *Letters*, vol. II, pp. 362–3.
[61] Donne, *Letters to Severall Persons*, 2C4v (p. 200). In the 1651 edition this letter is addressed to Sir Thomas Lucy, but I. A. Shapiro argued persuasively that the recipient must have been Goodyere: Shapiro, 'The text of Donne's *Letters to Severall Persons*', *Review of English Studies*, 7 (1931), pp. 291–301 (ref. pp. 297–8).
[62] Chamberlain to Carleton, 10 May 1617, in *Letters*, vol. II, p. 74.
[63] Sparrow, 'John Donne and contemporary preachers', p. 160.

businesses would have permitted, I would have copied out for you my selfe, but now I must intreate you to send it backe as soone as with conveniency you can, for besides his owne I thinke there is not another perfect coppie in Oxford.' This probably refers to Steward's sermon on 1 Corinthians 10: 32 ('Give none offence'), which caused a stir because of its assertion that it was acceptable to follow Rome in matters of ceremony, though not in matters of doctrine; the sermon was never printed at the time, but survives in several contemporary manuscript copies.[64]

The demand for sermons is illustrated by the fact that where authorised copies were not put into circulation, unauthorised copies often appeared instead. In 1595, for example, the university authorities in Cambridge joined forces with the ecclesiastical authorities in London to prevent the unauthorised publication of a Latin sermon *ad clerum* by William Whitaker. On hearing that the sermon 'was lyke to be prynted here in secrete', the Heads interviewed the university printer, Thomas Thomas, and admonished him not to publish the sermon without permission; while the vice-chancellor, Roger Goad, wrote to Whitgift to warn him that 'some who have coppies of that Sermon' might 'attempt in secrete to have the same printed at London'.[65] A Paul's Cross preacher in 1609 claimed to have received over a hundred requests to put his sermon into print, and declared that although he had not originally intended to publish it, he had been forced to do so after 'some of my well affected friends in the Citie' threatened to print it 'in more indigested manner, out of some unperfect copies which they had taken by note'.[66] Another Paul's Cross preacher, some years later, offered a similar excuse for publication, declaring that he had been forced to publish his own copy of the sermon in order 'to suppresse certaine bastard and illegitimate Copies ... which wandred up and down the Town, like vagrants; and were taken Begging, here for a Crown; and there for an Angel': a rare allusion to the commercial production of sermon manuscripts, perhaps by professional scribes.[67]

---

[64] Gilbert Sheldon to John Newdigate, 6 February 1621/2: Warwickshire Record Office, Warwick, CR 136/B467. Steward's sermon is copied in National Library of Wales, Aberystwyth, MS 5310B, and Corpus Christi College, Oxford, MS 288, ff. 231–46; it was finally printed in Steward's *Three Sermons* (1658).

[65] Roger Goad to Whitgift, 22 December 1595, copied in Whitgift's letter-book: Trinity College, Cambridge, MS B.14.9, p. 126. For the immediate context, see Peter Lake, *Moderate Puritans and the Elizabethan Church* (Cambridge, 1982), pp. 227–30.

[66] George Webbe, *Gods Controversie with England* (1609), A3v, A4r.

[67] John Andrewes, *The Brazen Serpent: or, the Copie of a Sermon Preached at Pauls Crosse* (1621), A3v. Andrewes was vicar of St James's Clerkenwell, and should not be confused with the chapbook author of the same name: see Tessa Watt, *Cheap Print and Popular Piety, 1550–1640* (Cambridge, 1991), p. 307.

The copying of sermons was greatly assisted by the invention of shorthand in the late sixteenth century. Some form of shorthand was in use in Geneva as early as 1549, when a French Huguenot named Denis Raguenier was commissioned to take down notes of Calvin's sermons, using his own private system of speed-writing 'by number and cipher' (*par nombre et chiffre*), which he then dictated to an amanuensis who produced a fair copy for wider circulation. The surviving manuscripts suggest that Raguenier's system was remarkably accurate.[68] However, shorthand was not widely used in England until the last decade of the sixteenth century. The first English manual of shorthand, Timothy Bright's *Characterie*, appeared in 1588, and was swiftly followed by a number of printed sermons, including Stephen Egerton's *An Ordinary Lecture* (1589) and Henry Smith's *A Sermon of the Benefite of Contentation* (1590), claiming to have been 'taken by characterie'. 'A. S.', the anonymous copyist of Egerton's sermon, attempted to gloss over the awkward ethical questions raised by the unauthorised copying and publication of another man's sermon, and drew attention instead to the utility of shorthand in making sermons more widely available:

It hath beene (Christian Reader) till of late, much wished, that there were an ordinarie way of swift writing, whereby Sermons and Lectures of godly Preachers might be preserved for the use of the absent and posteritie hereafter ... This desire of many hath lately bene satisfied by an Art called Characterie: which I having learned, have put in practise, in writing sermons therby to preserve (as it were) the life of much memorable doctrine, that would otherwise be buried in forgetfulnesse, wherof I here give thee a fruit, (Christian Reader) in publishing this godly Sermon so taken.[69]

By the mid-seventeenth century, note-taking at sermons had become commonplace. When Lodewijck Huygens attended a sermon at the Chapel Royal in Whitehall in December 1651, he observed that the preacher was attended by 'two or three men who wrote down his sermon' – possibly an organised team of stenographers – and his comments on a visit to the

---

[68] Jean-François Gilmont, 'Les sermons de Calvin: de l'oral à l'imprimé', *Bulletin de la Société de l'Histoire du Protestantisme Français*, 141 (1995), 145–62 (pp. 150–1 on shorthand). See also T. H. L. Parker, *Calvin's Preaching* (Edinburgh, 1992), pp. 65–7. On medieval systems of shorthand, see M.B. Parkes, 'Tachygraphy in the Middle Ages: writing techniques employed for *reportationes* of lectures and sermons', in Parkes, *Scribes, Scripts and Readers: Studies in the Communication, Presentation and Dissemination of Medieval Texts* (1991), pp. 19–33.

[69] Stephen Egerton, *An Ordinary Lecture, Preached at the Blacke-Friers, by M. Egerton, and Taken as It Was Uttered by Characterie* (1589), A2r–3v. Other shorthand copies surviving from the 1590s include Nicholas Felton's 'Certaine sermons godly & learnedly preached ... and taken from his mouth' (University of London, Carlton collection, Box 17/8) and 'A sermon preached before the L. Maior, taken by charactery' (BL Lansd. 377, ff. 67–85).

new church in Covent Garden the following month bear witness to the popularity of the practice: 'In the box next to ours three or four ladies were writing down the entire sermon, and more than fifty other persons through-out the whole church were doing the same.'[70] Shorthand systems rapidly improved during the course of the seventeenth century, until by 1671 it was possible for the stenographer Jeremiah Rich to note down a sermon 'in less than half a quarter of a sheet of Paper' with such accuracy (or so he claimed) that when he read it back, the preacher declared 'that he did think there was not one word added or diminished, from what he then Preached'.[71]

In some cases, preachers were prepared to collaborate with shorthand writers in putting a sermon into print. In the preface to *A Fruitfull Sermon* (1589), Anthony Tyrrell declared that he had not originally intended to publish the sermon, but had changed his mind after learning of the existence of a shorthand copy. The copy, he explained, had been made without his knowledge or permission, and afterwards presented to him by the transcriber:

At the time I made my exhortation publicklie in Christ his Church in London, my wordes were no sooner out of my mouth but a yong youth had penned my Sermon verbatim by Characterie, an art newly invented. It was this youthes pleasure, for the manifesting of his skill in that swift kind of writing, to publish my Sermon in print, yet honestlie he came unto me, to enforme me first of the matter. Hee was to me a meere straunger, of whom, after I had understood his intent and purpose, I craved respite to pause of the matter before I would give my consent.

At first, fearing that the publication of the sermon might appear 'foolish and vainglorious', and observing that 'the youth did it but to shew his skill and cunning in the dexteritie of his owne handwriting . . . not simply for the health of soules or spirituall profite of any man', Tyrrell wanted to suppress the copy. After further reflection, however, he agreed to publish it, in the hope that 'the comming of it forth might yeelde perhaps some devout and penitent soule some comfort and profite'. He therefore revised the text, 'altering some words, but nothing of the matter', and sent it to the press.[72]

However, not all preachers were so tolerant of unauthorised note-taking. Stephen Egerton, writing in 1592, condemned 'the greedie covetousnesse,

---

[70] Lodewijck Huygens, *The English Journal 1651–1652*, ed. and trans. A. G. H. Bachrach and R. G. Collmer (Leiden, Sir Thomas Browne Institute, 1982), pp. 42, 55.

[71] William Leybourn, *Pleasure with Profit* (1694), 'Mechanical recreations', p. 28.

[72] Anthony Tyrrell, *A Fruitfull Sermon Preached in Christs-Church* (1589), A6r–8r. Other shorthand copies corrected by the preacher include Eusebius Paget's 'Six sermons . . . taken by charactary and after examyned' (Bodleian Library, Oxford, MS Rawl. D.320, ff. 67–103) and the second edition of Henry Smith's *Benefite of Contentation* (1590), 'taken by characterie, and examined after'.

and injurious boldnesse of certaine men', especially 'certaine hungrie
Schollers and preposterous noters of Sermons, who at the first pretending
pietie, are in processe, beguiled with hope of gaine and vainglorie'. Thomas
Playfere expressed similar annoyance at the unauthorised publication of his
1595 Spital sermon, describing it as 'one of the greatest injuries that ever was
offered mee'. He was particularly irritated by the printer's promotional
tactics 'in terming it very vainely and most fondly, *A most excellent
Sermon*', and when the work was reprinted in an authorised edition in
1596 it was given the more modest title *The Meane in Mourning*.[73] The
popularity of note-taking led to a lively debate in London puritan circles, as
is clear from Egerton's remarks in 1603 'touching noting at Sermons'.
Egerton was prepared to condone the practice, with certain qualifications,
but admitted that others were of a different opinion: 'For the thing it selfe, I
dare not (with some) condemne it as unlawful, but rather commend it as
expedient, if there be judgement, memory and dexteritie of hand in the
partie. Above all things (in mine opinion, as in other matters so in this) a
good conscience is most requisite, both for the present time, that his own
hart who writeth be not hindred, and defrauded of the fruite and power of
the word, by the exercise of his head, and the labour of his hand: neyther yet
the Minister wronged, nor filthy lucre or vaine-glory aymed at.'[74]

It is not surprising that preachers should have had mixed feelings about
the popularity of shorthand and the increasingly widespread copying of
sermons. Not only was the production and circulation of shorthand copies
largely outside the preacher's control, they also had a well-merited reputation for inaccuracy. Egerton complained that 'betweene the Printer and the
noter, we have in stead of sounde and profitable Treatises, diverse mangeled
and unperfect pieces, even according to the slow hand, slipperie memorie
and simple judgement of him that tooke them', and William Gouge,
writing nearly half a century later, echoed his complaint: 'Many have
beene much wronged ... by the *Short-writers* omissions, additions, mis-
placings, mistakings. If severall Workes of one and the same Author (but
some published by himselfe, and others by an *Exceptor*) be compared
together, they will easily be found in matter and manner as different, as
Works of different Authors.'[75] In the preface to the 1589 edition of Egerton's

---

[73] William Cupper, *Certaine Sermons Concerning Gods Late Visitation in the Citie of London* (1592), A7r;
see also Sidney Thomas, 'A note on the reporting of Elizabethan sermons', *The Library*, 5th ser.,
3 (1948–9), pp. 120–1, where this passage is cited; Thomas Playfere, *The Meane in Mourning*
(1607), A2v.

[74] Egerton, *Lecture*, A4r.

[75] Cupper, *Certaine Sermons*, A7r; William Gouge, *A Recovery from Apostacy* (1639), A3r.

sermon, the copyist 'A. S.' boasted that he had 'not missed one word', but Egerton himself was later to observe that 'the swiftest hand commeth often short of the slowest tongue: as I have perceived by diverse things which I have seene penned from mine owne mouth, who am constrained thorough the straightnes of my breast, and difficulty of breathing, to speake more laysurely than most men doe, or I my selfe willingly would'. A. S.'s preface was adjusted in the revised edition of 1603 to take account of Egerton's criticisms, resulting in the rather more modest claim that he had 'not *wittingly* missed one word'.[76]

Fortunately we do not need to rely solely on the claims and counter-claims of preachers and shorthand writers, since the accuracy of Elizabethan shorthand has been systematically analysed by a number of literary scholars seeking to test the hypothesis that the early quartos of Shakespeare's plays were based on shorthand reports. In 1922, H. T. Price published a parallel-text edition of Henry Smith's sermon *The True Trial of the Spirites*, which had been printed from shorthand in 1591 (STC 22664) and reprinted in a corrected version (STC 22706) later the same year. Price showed that the two texts were remarkably similar, and argued that this demonstrated the general accuracy of Elizabethan shorthand, though he admitted that it would have been easier to take down a sermon than a play. However, he made the mistake of assuming that Smith would have corrected the short-hand copy against his own manuscript. As we have already seen, most Elizabethan preachers did not copy out their sermons in full, and a compar-ison of the two texts makes it clear that Smith's corrected version was based on the shorthand copy, not on his own manuscript. Since the two editions are not textually independent, the corrected edition cannot be used as a check on the accuracy of the shorthand copy. As W. Matthews pointed out in 1932, minor errors which were 'wrong according to the sermon as it was preached' but 'adequate to express the meaning' would tend to be over-looked by 'a corrector who was not amending from his own notes of the sermon as it was first delivered'.[77]

Matthews went on to examine the shorthand systems themselves, argu-ing that it would have been virtually impossible to take down a sermon or a play with any degree of accuracy. Bright's system of 'charactery', for example, is based on a range of 536 characters, each corresponding to a

---

[76] Egerton, *Lecture*, A5v (emphasis mine).

[77] Henry Smith, *A Fruitfull Sermon upon Part of the 5. Chapter of the First Epistle of St Paul to the Thessalonians*, ed. H. T. Price (Halle, 1922); W. Matthews, 'Shorthand and the bad Shakespeare quartos', *Modern Language Review*, 27: 3 (July 1932), pp. 243–62 (quotation pp. 257–8).

particular word. Other words are denoted by the character nearest to them in meaning: thus 'tomb' is expressed by the letter 't' plus the symbol for 'grave', 'fury' by the letter 'f' plus the symbol for 'anger', and so on. G. I. Duthie, who published a detailed study of Elizabethan shorthand in 1949, described this system as 'primitive and cumbersome in the extreme', and drew attention to the contemporary testimony of another shorthand writer, Edmund Willis, who declared that Bright's method required 'such understanding and memory, as that few of the ordinary sort of men could attaine to the knowledge thereof'.[78] In Duthie's view, the first real step towards a modern system of shorthand was not taken until the early seventeenth century, when John Willis developed an alphabetic system in which each symbol represented a single letter or sound, thus greatly reducing the number of symbols that had to be learned. Duthie's critique of the Elizabethan systems of 'characterical' shorthand has been generally accepted: even Adele Davidson, the most recent proponent of the shorthand hypothesis, does not attempt to rehabilitate Bright's system, but argues that Willis's system might have been in use earlier than is generally supposed.[79]

However, this does not fully explain the group of late Elizabethan sermons, such as Egerton's *An Ordinary Lecture* (1589) and Playfere's *A Most Excellent and Heavenly Sermon* (1595), that were published from shorthand notes. These were probably copied with the help of Bright's system (indeed, Egerton's sermon advertises itself as having been 'taken as it was uttered, by characterie'), yet, despite some obvious mistakes, they appear to report the preacher's words fairly accurately – so accurately, in fact, that Matthews was reluctant to believe they could have been copied by shorthand at all.[80] How did the writers manage to overcome the limitations of Bright's system? One clue to the origin of the texts may lie in their curious pattern of errors, most of which were corrected in later editions:

(1589) not according to his profession, but according to his faith
(1603) not according to the flesh, Rom. 4.12. but according to his faith
(1595) as otherwise he would, if he had by a whoore or wife any such thing
(1607) as otherwise hee would if he had bin aware or wist any such thing

---

[78] G. I. Duthie, *Elizabethan Shorthand and the First Quarto of King Lear* (Oxford, 1949), p. 7.
[79] Adele Davidson, '"Some by stenography"? Stationers, shorthand, and the early Shakespearian quartos', *Papers of the Bibliographical Society of America*, 90: 4 (1996), pp. 417–49.
[80] Matthews, 'Shorthand and the bad Shakespeare quartos', p. 259: 'the conviction that it would be impossible to get anything approaching a reliable transcript from Characterie notes . . . [makes] me believe that the sermons were not taken down in Bright's shorthand at all'.

(1595) and withstanding: so then he would not throwe downe himselfe
(1607) and withstanding Sathan hee would not in any wise throw down himself

The most likely explanation of these errors is that they are misreadings of longhand notes (the 'wife'/'wist' error, for example, appears to be the result of a confusion between 'f' and long 's'). This strongly suggests that these are not 'pure' shorthand copies, but a mixture of shorthand and longhand. If so, then the shortcomings of Bright's system would not have been so damaging to the accuracy of the text, as the copyist would have relied not on shorthand alone, but on a combination of shorthand, longhand and his own memory.

The use of shorthand in combination with longhand was apparently fairly widespread. This was recognised by some shorthand teachers, who provided lists of common abbreviations to be used by note-takers who did not want to learn the full system. Edmund Willis's shorthand system, for example, included a list of about 200 symbols for particular words which he described as 'so necessarie to be learned, and so frequent in use, that a man shall hardly read a Chapter or Verse in any English Booke, but halfe the said Chapter or Verse consisteth of them'. To help his readers memorise these symbols, Willis arranged them into sentences – 'By faith in Christ Jesus and not by workes onely, elecete men have parte in the kingdome of heaven, as saith the apostle'; 'Never was there any one people, church or age, that enjoyed the peace of the gospell in that manner as we now doe' – with one symbol for each word or particle.[81] The diary of the Devonshire MP Walter Yonge includes a list of shorthand characters representing common words such as 'omnipotent', 'pray', 'promise', 'religion', 'salvation' and 'scripture', and another commonplace book now in the Inner Temple Library contains a similar list of abbreviations for commonly used words such as 'church' or 'faith', and even a few longer phrases ('but if a man', 'if we do but reflect'), evidently designed to assist a note-taker writing at speed.[82] The choice of these words is interesting as showing the very close connection between shorthand and sermon notes – a connection remarked on by Samuel Hartlib, who wrote in 1634 that shorthand had been invented at the time when powerful preaching began in England.[83]

---

[81] Edmund Willis, *An Abbreviation of Writing by Character* (2nd edn., 1627), B5r (p. 17) and facing plate.

[82] Yonge's diary, BL Add. MS 18778, f. 96; Inner Temple Library, London, Add. MS 214/5. See also Chicago University Library, MS 160, which includes a list of commonly used sigla to be used when taking notes, and also illustrates the use of shorthand characters in a longhand text. These rudimentary shorthand systems hark back to the 'Tironian notes' used in the classical and medieval periods.

[83] Cited from Hartlib's *Ephemerides*, 1634, by Vivian Salmon, *The Works of Francis Lodwick* (1972), p. 62.

It is also very likely that some shorthand reports of sermons are based on more than one set of notes. Playfere's sermon, for example, survives in two different shorthand texts, both published in 1595 by the same London stationer. The two are closely related, but there are places where they differ both from each other and from the author's corrected version – as in the following passage, an extended metaphor on the fear of death:

(1595; STC 20014) Before, death was much like a Bugbegger which they fray children with, who being masked, jettes it about up and downe, and makes all the people afraid of him, untill such time as some one lustie fellowe amongst the rest, steps to him and takes a good staffe and cudgelleth him well favouredly, and puls his vizarde from his face, and makes him knowne to the whole world: and then whereas before lustie and tawle men were afraide of him: now every childe mockes him and laugheth him to scorne, and stand pointing at him.

(1595; STC 20014.3) The Hobgoblins, those merrie companions, so long as they speake in a vault, and have vizards over their faces, are terrible unto some, otherwise of reasonable wisedome: but if a lustie fellowe come unto them, and cudgell them well favoredly, and take away their vizards, they become so ridiculous, that even the boyes laugh them to scorn.

(1607) Those which will needs play the hobgoblins or the nightwalking spirites (as we call them) al the while they speak under a hollow vault, or leape forth with an ugly vizard upon their faces, they are so terrible that he which thinkes himselfe no small man may perhaps be affrighted with them. But if some lusty fellowe chaunce to steppe into one of these and cudgle him well favoredly, and pull the vizarde from his face, then every boye laughes him to scorne.

This is a good illustration of the indeterminacy of sermon texts and the impossibility of ever establishing an 'authentic' version. It also suggests that the sermon may have been copied by two or perhaps even three different note-takers, who could have compared their copies in order to correct obvious mistakes. There are other cases where note-takers are known to have collaborated: for example, Ussher's *Eighteen Sermons* (1660) consists of sermon-notes by three ministers 'who wrote them from his mouth, and compared their copies together'.[84]

There is no doubt that Bright's charactery is greatly inferior to the shorthand systems that superseded it. Where Duthie and Matthews may have gone wrong, however, is in judging it by modern standards of textual purity. If we look at charactery in the context of the 'art of hearing' discussed in the previous chapter, a rather different picture emerges. Charactery could have been used to take down the gist of a sermon, rather than to reproduce it with word-perfect accuracy; to assist the memory, rather than to serve as a

---

[84] James Ussher, *Works*, ed. C. R. Elrington and J. H. Todd, vol. I (Dublin, 1847), p. 314.

substitute for it; and to enable the hearer to repeat the sermon orally, with the help of other members of the audience, rather than to write it down unaided. In these circumstances, the technical deficiencies of Bright's system would not have mattered so much. Used in conjunction with long-hand notes, memory and collaborative repetition, it would at least have served the purpose of producing a rough approximation of the sermon as preached, which is what we appear to have in these unauthorised editions. This also helps to explain why Egerton and Playfere could criticise the shorthand copies for their inaccuracy while, at the same time, using those copies to prepare their own revised versions. As Laurie Maguire has pointed out, the goal of modern textual scholarship – 'the reproduction of copy, noise-free' – was not widely shared in the early modern period, and Elizabethan preachers would not necessarily have seen any contradiction in the use of a 'bad' shorthand text as the basis of a 'good' edition.[85]

It follows that while the shorthand systems of the early seventeenth century were considerably less user-friendly than the systems used today, they served their purpose and were by no means as faulty as has sometimes been assumed. Frances Henderson has independently reached a similar conclusion with regard to William Clarke's manuscript of the Putney debates. The shorthand system used by Clarke was primitive and inadequate, yet his final report of the debates is 'surprisingly complete', probably, she suggests, because it was produced by two or three shorthand writers working as a team.[86] Much research still remains to be done on the use of shorthand, particularly with regard to parliamentary and law reporting, but the evidence so far suggests that when it was skilfully used, it lived up to its promise as the new high-fidelity recording technology of the early modern period.[87] This leaves us with an interesting paradox. The unauthorised shorthand editions so often condemned by preachers as inaccurate and untrustworthy may, in some cases, provide a relatively accurate account of the sermon as originally delivered. Conversely – as we shall see in the next section – the sermons that appear most unstudied and

[85] Laurie E. Maguire, *Shakespearian Suspect Texts: The 'Bad' Quartos and Their Contexts* (Cambridge, 1996), p. 147.
[86] Frances Henderson, 'Reading, and writing, the text of the Putney debates', in Michael Mendle, ed., *The Putney Debates of 1647* (Cambridge, 2001), pp. 36–50.
[87] On law reporting, see David Ibbetson, 'Law reporting in the 1590s', in Chantal Stebbings, ed., *Law Reporting in England* (1995), pp. 73–88. On parliamentary reporting, see John Morrill, 'Reconstructing the history of early Stuart parliaments', *Archives*, 21 (1994), pp. 67–72, and the ensuing debate between Morrill and Maija Jansson in *Parliamentary History*, 14 (1995), pp. 179–86, and 15 (1996), pp. 215–30.

spontaneous, and that appear to preserve traces of an authentic plain style, may be the very ones that have been most carefully rewritten for print.

## REVISING THE SERMON

In his study of the text and transmission of Calvin's sermons, Jean-François Gilmont poses one crucial question: 'were the same texts used for oral delivery and for visual reading?' The answer, as he shows, is almost certainly not. Calvin was relatively prolix in his preaching but much more concise in his written style, and while he never explicitly distinguished between the two, he appears to have been very conscious of the difference between them. Although the title pages of his printed sermons frequently claim that the sermons have been published without anything altered or omitted, a comparison of one printed edition with the manuscript copy on which it was based has found about 450 significant textual variants, mostly stylistic. His printer Conrad Badius explained that the sermons were preached in a simple and unadorned style suitable for an unlearned audience ('*simplement et nuement pour s'accommoder à la rudesse du peuple*') and had not been designed to appear in print. Gilmont sums up: 'The logic of the spoken discourse is not that of the text intended for reading.'[88]

English historians, too, are increasingly coming to realise that printed sermons are not always a reliable guide to what was spoken from the pulpit. In his study of the puritan clergy in early Stuart England, Tom Webster poses much the same question as Gilmont: 'How far is a sermon preached the same thing as a sermon published?' As he points out, the two may have been addressed to substantially different audiences: 'It takes a great deal more commitment to buy a substantial volume than to attend a parish church. Printed collections of sermons are for the committed, if not necessarily the converted.'[89] Peter Lake makes a similar point in his study of the London puritan minister Stephen Denison, where he observes that 'the transition from pulpit to print was an extremely charged moment for the aspiring divine', marking the point when the preacher moved beyond the confines of his own parish or congregation, and when he might feel the need for 'a certain care over matters of theological propriety',

---

[88] Gilmont, 'Les sermons de Calvin'. Lee Palmer Wandel makes the same point with regard to the surviving texts of Zwingli's sermons, which appear 'not to be verbatim records of what was preached' but 'later versions of a text that had been preached, revised, lengthened, expanded, altered in any number of ways'. Wandel, 'Switzerland', in Larissa Taylor, ed., *Preachers and People in the Reformations and Early Modern Period* (Leiden, 2001), pp. 221–47 (quotation p. 232).

[89] Tom Webster, *Godly Clergy in Early Stuart England* (Cambridge, 1997), p. 105.

as he submitted his sermons to the formal censure of the licensing process and to the critical scrutiny of his peers.[90] The sermon as printed may often have been more intellectually demanding than the sermon as preached, but at the same time it may have been more theologically cautious, with more checks and balances to protect the preacher from hostile criticism.

In the last section we saw how sermons found their way on to the written or printed page, either through an authorised text corrected by the preacher or through an unauthorised text made by a member of the audience. In this section we shall be looking in more detail at the way that preachers revised their sermons for publication. As we shall see, this often involved a stylistic revision as well as a theological one. What works in the classroom or lecture-hall does not necessarily work so well in cold print, as any teacher can testify; and the plain, colloquial style that might go down well with a rustic audience in a country parish on an ordinary Sunday would not necessarily be suitable for a printed sermon. As Stephen Egerton commented in 1603: 'It is one thing to speake profitably to the common people, and another thing to write commendably in this ripe and learned age; nether is evry one that can make a good sermon, able to write a good stile.' But we shall also see that there was pressure in both directions: preachers may have wanted to make their printed sermons more learned and dignified than their spoken sermons, but some of their readers wanted sermons that were more personal and colloquial in style, and closer to what they were accustomed to hearing from the pulpit.

In some cases we can be fairly confident that the sermon as originally preached was very close, if not identical, to the sermon as subsequently written or printed – as, for example, in the *cause célèbre* of the Lincolnshire minister John Burges, who rashly defended puritan nonconformity in a sermon preached before the king in 1604 and was imprisoned for his pains. While in prison, he sent a transcript of his sermon to the Privy Council, with a covering letter in which he declared that it was a faithful copy of the sermon as originally delivered. He admitted that there were likely to be some minor variations – for 'to say that there is no word added, abated or altered, were a speech not credible of a Sermon penned since, and not before the preaching of it' – but insisted that it was as close to the spoken version as he could reasonably make it.[91] The London preacher Richard Ball, sending

---

[90] Peter Lake, *The Boxmaker's Revenge: 'Orthodoxy', 'Heterodoxy' and the Politics of the Parish in Early Stuart London* (Manchester, 2001), p. 34.

[91] John Burges, *A Sermon Preached before the Late King James* (1642), C4r. See McCullough, *Sermons at Court*, pp. 142–4, for a discussion of Burges's sermon and a list of surviving manuscript copies.

a copy of one of his sermons to the Bishop of London in 1614, also claimed to have reproduced the spoken version almost verbatim, declaring that 'the wordes which I have written are the verie same which I have spoken word for word . . . without alteration or change', even though – as with Burges – the sermon had apparently not been written out in full before delivery.[92] Both these cases are somewhat out of the ordinary, as Burges and Ball had got into trouble for their sermons and were trying to establish their innocence by showing that they had nothing to conceal. Even so, their claims to have copied out their sermons approximately or (in Ball's case) precisely as delivered would not have been plausible had it not been possible for preachers to reconstruct their words from memory with considerable accuracy.

It is clear from other sources, however, that preachers generally revised their sermons for print. As mentioned above, Hugh Broughton's sermon on Psalm 82, preached before Queen Elizabeth in 1580, was later copied out by the preacher at the request of 'some in authoritie'. When the sermon was printed in 1593, the anonymous editor explained that it was being published without Broughton's knowledge, 'wherin perhaps I may seeme to do him the more wrong, especially if he minded to use herein any part of his *second cogitations*, as they cal them', implying that it was standard practice for preachers to revise their sermons before putting them into print.[93] Some fifty years later, it was possible for Cornelius Burges to refer casually to the process of authorial revision as 'that just liberty which all others have [taken] before us', though his remarks imply that the revision was not expected to be too drastic: 'we trust it shall not be imputed', he writes, 'so long as in the most materiall passages we have kept to the very words which at first were used, so farre as was necessary; and have not wittingly swerved an haires bredth from the sense and substance in the residue'.[94]

In a few cases it is possible to gauge the extent of this authorial revision. Thomas Bedford's sermon *The Sinne Unto Death*, preached at Paul's Cross on 21 August 1621, went through several stages of revision, as the author explained in the preface to the printed edition. On being summoned to preach at the Cross, Bedford took an old sermon which he had delivered some years earlier, and 'did . . . take it once againe in hand, and alter, change, correct, and enlarge it' to make it suitable for 'a more noble

[92] Richard Ball to Bishop John King, 29 August 1614: National Library of Scotland, Advocates MS 33.1.6, vol. xx, f. 68. Ball was rector of St Christopher-le-Stock, London.
[93] H. B., *Moriemini*, A3r. For a similar reference to 'second thoughts', see John Jackson, *Ecclesiastes. The Worthy Church-Man* (1628), A1r.
[94] Cornelius Burges, *The First Sermon, Preached to the Honourable House of Commons* (1641), A3r.

Audience', only to find that he had made it too long, so that 'I was constrained againe to Epitomize it'.[95] This shorter version survives in manuscript in Bedford's sermon notebook, and can be compared with the longer version which he later put into print. The two are virtually identical in structure, even though the sermon as printed is considerably longer and more developed in its argument than the sermon as preached. The most interesting difference between the two is a passage attacking Arminian divines who 'beguile unstable soules' with their doctrine of 'falling from saving grace once received'. This passage is cancelled in the manuscript but then reappears in the printed edition, suggesting that Bedford had second thoughts about including it in the sermon as delivered at Paul's Cross but then chose to reinstate it when preparing the sermon for publication.[96]

John Donne's 'Sermon of valediction', preached at Lincoln's Inn on 18 April 1619, survives in two versions, the first 'communicated to some friends in written copies' and the second published posthumously from Donne's revised manuscript. Most of the revisions are fairly minor, but Donne eliminated several topical remarks, including a passing reference to the religious controversies in the Netherlands ('those bitternesses amongst persons nearest us'). His Paul's Cross sermon of 5 November 1622 also survives in two states, an earlier version 'which . . . by commandement I did write after the preachinge', and a later revised version. The latter contains, in the words of its modern editor, 'innumerable stylistic alterations' and a few substantive changes which clarify or qualify the political argument of the sermon. The earlier version declares that princes are 'excusable' for their part in evil actions, whereas the later version points out that they may still be guilty of 'countenancing and authorising an evill instrument' even if they are not directly implicated in the action itself.[97] A sermon by Bishop John Williams, probably preached during the parliamentary sessions of 1628 or 1629, survives in a scribal copy marked up with authorial corrections, and reveals a similar pattern of minor but significant revision: where Williams had previously extolled the benefits of 'an After-noones Sermon on the Lords day', he now added the phrase 'upon some Catecheticall head' to bring the passage into line with the royal instructions of 1629.[98]

[95] Thomas Bedford, *The Sinne Unto Death . . . In a Sermon Preached at Pauls Crosse* (1621), preface to the reader.

[96] BL Add 47618, f. 117r; Bedford, *The Sinne Unto Death*, D4r (p. 23).

[97] E.M. Simpson, *A Study of the Prose Works of John Donne* (Oxford, 1948), pp. 261–8; Jeanne Shami, 'Donne's 1622 sermon on the Gunpowder Plot: his original presentation manuscript discovered', *English Manuscript Studies*, 5 (1995), pp. 63–86.

[98] Sermon notes by Bishop John Williams: Magdalene College, Cambridge, Pepysian Library, no. 1441, p. 221.

All these examples bear out Burges's suggestion that revision tended to be fairly sparing. However, they are not altogether typical, for, as we have already seen, sermons preached on major public occasions were more likely to be written out in full before delivery, leaving less scope for subsequent revision. Sermons composed in note form, on the other hand, were far more fluid and adaptable. Several of the sermons published in Thomas Taylor's *Works* (1653) are said to be 'taken out of Notes not perfected', and consist of a fragmentary text with considerable room for expansion – as in the following example, where the '&c' appears to denote a passage marked for enlargement in delivery:

And to move us to build up our selves, consider what a Season and Summer we enjoy; even such means, as no people under heaven have the like: especially in this City. And shall we stand at a stay, and not be built up? . . . Oh, what a curse of God appears in this barrennesse! &c.[99]

Similarly, Thomas Cooper's sermon *The Converts First Love* (1610), published from the preacher's own 'general and short notes', includes a reproof of men who fail to persevere in godliness, also ending with '&c' to indicate that there was room for enlargement:

3. And those likewise, that feare to abound in holinesse, zeale, &c. lest they bee accounted singular noted men, precise, vaine-glorious, &c.
4. And these especially, that have not onely slacked their zeale in religion, but doe justifie this decay, as being now more wise, sober, &c. in their profession, whereas before they were fierie, rash, indiscreet, &c.[100]

Did Cooper have particular individuals in mind here? Whatever the background to these particular remarks, it seems very likely that the version delivered from the pulpit would have been longer and more specific.

The famous puritan preacher William Gouge, minister of Blackfriars, provides a good illustration both of the practice of preaching from skeleton notes and also of the difficulties this can cause in trying to reconstruct what was actually said in the pulpit. Gouge followed the standard doctrine-and-use method in his preaching, 'first opening the true literall sense of the text, then giving the Logical Analysis thereof, and then gathering such proper observations as did thence arise, and profitably and pertinently applying the same'. His commentary on Hebrews, which was printed posthumously from his unrevised sermon notes, shows how little he normally wrote down before preaching. It moves systematically through the text, dividing

---

[99] Thomas Taylor, *Works* (1653), 4A4v (from 'The spiritual building', a sermon preached at St Magnus, London Bridge, in 1627). The 'notes' in question are probably the author's own, as the title page describes the collection as 'Published according to his own Manuscripts'.
[100] Thomas Cooper, *The Converts First Love* (1610), C2r.

and subdividing each verse in the standard Ramist fashion and then drawing out a series of doctrines. This would have given Gouge a basic sermon structure which he could then have enlarged as much or as little as he chose, depending on the occasion, the audience and the amount of time at his disposal. In the preface to another of his sermons he refers to 'many amplifications of sundry generall heads then in concise summes onely uttered': that is, passages that were abridged in preaching, for want of time, but later expanded for print. He goes on to explain that he had prepared a lengthy list of Protestant martyrs which he had intended to include in the sermon, but 'when he espied the time to slip away apace, he contracted the matter, and summarily delivered, especially in the latter part of his Sermon, the points that are now more fully set downe'.[101]

Some of Gouge's sermons survive in more than one version, making it possible to compare the sermon as preached with the sermon as printed. His famous series of sermons on Ephesians, for example, survives in two editions, one based on shorthand notes by a member of the congregation, and the other, *Of Domesticall Duties* (1622), prepared for the press by Gouge himself.[102] In the preface to the latter edition, Gouge admitted that when the sermons were first preached at Blackfriars, some of his remarks on 'the particular duties of wives' had caused him to be attacked as a 'hater of women'. He insisted that his critics had misunderstood him, but a comparison of the two versions shows that when he came to revise the sermons for the press, he made careful adjustments to some of the more controversial passages. In the original version he had argued very strongly that a wife had no right to give money to the poor without her husband's consent:

She may not, because her husbands goods are not hers to give away. Yes, but it is to a good end. Well, but a good end cannot justifie a bad action; and indeed children that are under the government of their parents, may as well doe it, steale away from them, and give it to the poore: and if good ends may serve the turne, then couzeners and fraudulent persons that get their goods by deceit, &c. may be excused, if they say they doe it to a good end, as to build an Hospitall, and such like. (2D2r)

In the revised version he restated this in much less inflammatory terms, omitting the offensive comparison of the wife's almsgiving to theft or fraud:

[101] William Gouge, *A Recovery from Apostacy* (1639), A3r.
[102] William Gouge, *Of Domesticall Duties, Eight Treatises* (1622); *An Exposition on the Whole Fifth Chapter of S. Iohns Gospell: also Notes on Other Choice Places of Scripture, Taken by a Reverend Divine, now with God, and Found in His Study after His Death* (1630; STC 12114). On Gouge's revisions for print, see also Patrick Collinson, *The Birthpangs of Protestant England* (1988), p. 71.

With reverend respect to better judgements, I thinke she may not (except [as] before excepted.) For it being before proved in generall, that she had no such liberty in disposing goods, I cannot see how this particular end of giving almes can dispence with her generall subiection in every thing, except there were some particular warrant for it in Gods word. (X1r)[103]

In general, the two versions agree closely in structure and argument, but differ considerably in wording and in the choice of illustrations and examples. This is very much what we would expect, given that Gouge prepared the structure of his sermons very carefully but did not write them out in full before preaching, and allowed himself considerable room for extemporisation. The doctrinal content of the sermons probably did not vary greatly between preaching and print, but the way that Gouge chose to flesh out that doctrinal content, and the particular examples that he chose to illustrate it, could make all the difference to the audience response – for, as he observed, 'many that can patiently enough heare their duties declared in generall termes, cannot endure to heare those generals exemplified in their particular branches'.

This can be seen in Gouge's commentary on Hebrews, where again we have the opportunity to compare two versions of the same sermon. In his notes on Hebrews 11: 7 ('By faith Noah being warned of God of things not seen'), Gouge draws out a series of thirty-two doctrines or 'observations', beginning as follows:

1. *Justifying Faith manifesteth it self in temporal matters.* This Faith here spoken of was a justifying Faith: yet it was exercised about a corporal preservation.
2. *A good name is to be made good.* That is, he that hath a good name, must answerably carry himself.
3. *God foretold the Deluge that came upon the old World.* This word, *warned*, intends as much.
4. *Gods warning is a sufficient ground for attempting any thing.* This was Noah's ground.
5. *Faith is exercised about things not seen.* In such things was Noah's faith exercised.[104]

This gives the impression of an extremely dry and technical exposition. However, we also have Robert Saxby's notes on the sermon that Gouge

---

[103] Gouge's reference to 'better judgements' may be an allusion to another London minister, John Downame, who took the contrary position in *The Plea of the Poore, or a Treatise of Beneficence and Almes-Deeds* (1616), maintaining that a wife could lawfully give alms without her husband's consent (M1v, p. 102). He based this argument on 'the common use which the wife hath in her husbands goods' and 'the custome of our countrey, which ordinarily authorizeth them to doe these workes' (O4v, p. 124)

[104] William Gouge, *A Learned and Very Useful Commentary on the Whole Epistle to the Hebrewes* (1655), vol. 11, 4D2v (p. 28).

preached on this text at Blackfriars in 1630. These show that he applied the text in a highly practical fashion, referring to the plague of 1625 and ending with an exhortation to short hair and sober attire:

So this Reverent docter sheweth, out of very many places of scriptur for our further enstrocion, And how it was very usfull & Remarkable for to Thinke of our last great sickness scant 5 yers past of our great deliverance by the lords most mercifull hand, in delivering us so Merecolusly [miraculously], in so short a space, the sicknes being so great & so contemciously desperst thorow the holl sity, Therfor we must aknowleg it to be the Lords mercy unto us in sparing us so merecolously & with so gret pitie to us misarabell sinners: And to macke good use of his great mercy to us: And seing the lord hath shaken his Rodd of Corocion [correction] agaynst us now, in giving warning of a new Coriting hand by the plage newely begon, so he most lovingly doth Admonishe us to upseseck [? beseech] the lord by true & harty prayer that he may torne away our deserved ponishments from us in being mercifull unto us & not laying our sinnes to our Charge as we have Justly deserved: And forther this Reverent man doth so lovingly Admonishe menn & wemen to be Carfull to live in all Thinges like obedient servantes of god in all holines of life & to abstayne from all profanacion in walking in the waies of the wicked world, in any excese [excess], of aney wicked way that ledeth to destrocion: And to be Carfull to walke in sober Atire as it becometh the servent of god: And that men should not forget to Cutt their hair, According to a comly fashion & not wering it in length Acording to the fashion of this wicked world & so gentellwemen that do exced in garish Apparell he Admonisheth for to goo in there Apparell & haire as it becometh True Christians in all lowliness & True homblnes, consithiring the lord shakes his Rod over us & will stricke if we torn not to him by true Repentance.[105]

If all we had to go on were Gouge's own notes, all this would be lost to us; it only survives because we are lucky enough to have Saxby's recollections of what was actually said from the pulpit. This is one of the (not infrequent) occasions when a report by a member of the congregation – however garbled and inaccurate – proves to be more informative than the preacher's own authorised version of the sermon.

These examples allow us to draw some general conclusions about the textual transmission of early modern sermons. As a rule, the doctrinal part of the sermon, in which the preacher expounded the sense and meaning of his text and drew out its theological and moral significance, was likely to be written down in the preacher's notes and carried over into any subsequent printed edition, whereas the more practical part of the sermon, in which the preacher drew out 'uses' or 'applications' suited to a particular occasion, or a particular audience, stood much less chance of being recorded in written or

[105] Cambridge University Library, Add MS 3117, f. 24r ('preched at black frires by docter gudg the .11. hebures .7. vers').

printed form. George Gifford's preface to his *Sermon on the Parable of the Sower*, first published in 1581, explains that 'particular applications and exhortations' have been omitted in print, while William Struthers, in a letter accompanying the gift of a manuscript sermon in 1620, claims to have 'sett downe the groundes only, leaving out large amplificatiounes and particular applicatiounes'.[106] Similarly, Francis Bacon's proposal for a collection of the best modern English sermons only envisaged the inclusion of the doctrinal passages, 'leaving out the largeness of exhortations and applications thereupon'.[107] This has important implications for the understanding of early modern preaching, as it means that printed sermons will tend to appear more intellectual, and less practical, than would actually have been the case in oral delivery. This is where shorthand reports can provide a valuable corrective, in bringing us closer to the sermon as originally preached.

John Dod's sermons on the Ten Commandments shed further light on the process of textual transmission, and on the revisions that a preacher might typically make when preparing his sermons for print publication. They were first published in an unauthorised edition of 1603, based on shorthand notes by a 'young man, sometime scholler in Cambridge', probably one of the young men whom Dod took into his household at Hanwell, Oxfordshire, to train them for the ministry. Some copies of this edition have a preface by Dod's colleague Robert Cleaver, betraying considerable ambivalence about the publication of sermons without the author's consent. He recommended the book to godly readers as containing the 'fruitefull doctrines' of a 'reverent faithfull Pastor', but stressed that the sermons were 'neither penned nor perused by himselfe, nor published with his consent or knowledge' and contained some inaccuracies. 'They were collected by a godly ingenious young man, whose diligent attention and painefulnes, deserve no small commendations: yet what hand or memorie can follow so fast the fluent speech of an eloquent Pastor, as to set downe all in the same forme and elegancie wherein it is delivered?'[108] The sermons were reprinted the following year in a new edition, based on the earlier shorthand text but with revisions by Dod and Cleaver, and in this form they

---

[106] George Gifford, *A Sermon on the Parable of the Sower* (1584), A2r; William Struthers, sermon on Matthew 1: 21: National Library of Scotland, Advocates MS 33.3.12, vol. XV, f. 111.

[107] Bacon, *The Advancement of Learning*, p. 209 (Book II, xxv. 18).

[108] Dod and Cleaver, *The Bright Star which Leadeth Wise Men to Our Lord Iesus Christ* (1603), preface 'To the Christian Reader'.

became one of the religious bestsellers of the early seventeenth century, reaching a nineteenth edition by 1635.[109]

In the preface to the 1604 edition, Dod and Cleaver claim to have 'set downe every thing, without addition or detraction, as it was first delivered in the publique ministery'. However, a comparison of the two editions suggests otherwise. Much of the vivid idiomatic language of the first edition – which seems very likely to be a faithful transcription from oral delivery – is edited out of the revised version:

(1603) prig a sheet from off the hedge
(1604) steale a sheet from off the hedge
(1603) earth, earth, straight to the rooting
(1604) earth and earthly things
(1603) proud, foolish, vaine, fantasticall, mad-headed youths
(1604) ungodly discoursers
(1603) they think, why alasse, youth must have a swing
(1604) they say, youth must have some libertie
(1603) to give you any helpe
(1604) to minister any succour unto you

Out come colloquial words and phrases, to be replaced by more dignified alternatives (thus 'vilde' is altered to 'wicked', 'moolters' to 'consumes', 'scamblinglie' to 'remissely, and by peeces'). Out come proverbial expressions ('I warrant you they be all alike, never a barrell better herring'); out come rhymes and jingles ('they shall toyle and moyle, and tumble and tosse, and carke and care, and struggle and strive'); out comes the reference to Christ as having 'seemed a poore base fellow of no reckoning or note', and out comes the reference to the Prodigal Son as one who 'must behang himselfe with such costly coates'. The cumulative effect of all these changes is to make the revised edition a much less lively and less colourful work.

These revisions suggest that Dod and Cleaver were uneasy at seeing the plain style of oral preaching reproduced in print. In the preface to the revised edition, they explained somewhat defensively that 'when these Sermons were first preached, it was never once intended that they should come to the presse . . . and therefore the whole discourse was so framed both for matter and manner, as might best fit the capacity and necessity of the present auditorie'. A poem prefixed to the revised edition unfavourably contrasts the 'rude' and 'homely' style of the earlier edition with the 'grave', 'sober' and 'modest' style of the revision:

---

[109] John Dod and Robert Cleaver, *A Plaine and Familiar Exposition of the Ten Commandments* (1604).

And what then, though 'gainst authors mind, it first appear'd in sight,
By noters hand, in ruder tyre compos'd, and homely dight?
Yet marke herein a worke of God, bringing, to publike view
Of many, what intended was for private good of few;
And now revis'd by authors eye, and faults of print correct,
In grave and sober modest weede, not garishly bedeckt.

The same uneasiness about the plain style is evident in the revised edition of Playfere's sermon *The Meane in Mourning*, where the word 'plain' is consistently edited out:

(1595) And Ierome yet more plainly
(1607) And Hierome yet more vehemently
(1595) touching repentance one sayth plainly
(1607) touching repentance one sayes truely

This may seem surprising, since puritan preachers such as Dod and Cleaver are often regarded as the great champions of the plain style. But attitudes to the plain style were more complex and ambivalent than is generally realised, and the puritan preference for plain and accessible language was very often qualified by concerns that plain preaching, particularly in a printed sermon, might be regarded as rustic and unpolished. Plainness was all very well in an oral sermon addressed to uneducated hearers, but was it an appropriate style for a printed sermon addressed to a more literate and sophisticated reader-ship? Another preacher, Samuel Wales, imagined a reader saying to him: 'Your matter is trite and ordinary, your stile homely, untrimmed, creeping on the ground, here is nothing which might satisfie, or please the learned and curious: me thinkes you should spare your pen, and paines, till you can bring something rare and singular.'[110]

It is possible, then, that a whole genre of plain preaching has remained virtually invisible to us because it rarely found its way into print. In John Day's comedy *The Ile of Gulles* (1606) the confidence trickster Manasses delivers a burlesque of pulpit rhetoric on the parable of the lost sheep (Luke 15: 4–7), guaranteed to 'make the auditors eyes runne a water like so many waterspouts':

Belou'd, you must imagine this Sheepe was a Sheepe, a lost Sheepe, a Sheepe out of the way: but my deare flocke and loving Sheepe, whom like a carefull Shepheard, I have gathered togeather with the whistle or pipe, as it were of mine eloquence, into this fold of peacefull Communitie; Doe not you stray, doe not you flie out, doe not you wander, doe not you loose your selves: but like kinde Sheepe, and valiant Rams; I speake to you the better part and head of my flocke. As I say, you shall

---

[110] Samuel Wales, *Totum Hominis: or the Whole Dutie of a Christian* (1627), A4v.

see the valiant Rammes turne all their hornes together, and oppose themselves against the Woolfe, the hungrie Woolfe, the gredie Woolfe, the Lams-devowring Woolfe, the Woolfe of all Woolfes, to defende their Eawes and young ones. Durst you lay all your heades together, and with the hornes of your Manhood defende your families, your owne wives, and your neighbours children . . .'[111]

This was taken up by Ben Jonson and turned into a much sharper piece of anti-puritan satire in a speech put into the mouth of the hypocrite Busy in *Bartholomew Fair* (1614):

Downe with *Dagon*, downe with *Dagon* . . . I wil remove *Dagon* there, I say, that Idoll, that heathenish *Idoll*, that remaines (as I may say) a beame, a very beame, not a beame of the *Sunne*, nor a beame of the *Moone*, nor a beame of a ballance, neither a house-beame, nor a Weavers beame, but a beame in the eye, in the eye of the beholder; a very great beame, an exceeding great beame . . .[112]

This is of course a parody, but for the parody to be successful, it must have corresponded to a certain sort of pulpit rhetoric – highly repetitive, with a few keywords reiterated over and over in an impassioned harangue – that the audience would instantly have recognised. Commenting on the passage from *Bartholomew Fair*, Peter Lake asks: 'Was this what ministers . . . sounded like when they really got going in the pulpit?' It seems very likely that it was – not in every sermon, and probably not at high-profile pulpits such as Paul's Cross, where audiences would have expected something considerably more sophisticated, but certainly in the fiery denunciations of sin and exhortations to repentance that formed the backbone of early modern preaching.[113]

What is striking, to a modern reader, is that there is very little in the printed sermons of the period that resembles the style of preaching being parodied here. It is only occasionally that we can catch an echo of what Lake calls the 'distinctive tone or timbre' of the London pulpit, with the steady rise and fall of the preacher's voice and its 'almost incantatory repetitions'. One of William Cupper's sermons, published from a shorthand report, contains a sustained barrage of similes on the misery of mortality: 'what is our time here but as the dead of winter, as a smoake, as vapors, as grasse, as a span, as a weavers shuttle, as a shadow, as a tale told, as a dreame, as a watch in the night, as a race, and as floing water: to all which things the scripture

---

[111] John Day, *The Ile of Guls* (1606), reproduced in facsimile with an introduction by G. B. Harrison (1936), F1v.
[112] Ben Jonson, *Bartholomew Fair*, 5.5, in *Works*, ed. C. H. Herford and P. and E. Simpson, vol. vi (Oxford, 1938), p. 133.
[113] Peter Lake and Michael Questier, *The Antichrist's Lewd Hat: Protestants, Papists and Players in Post-Reformation England* (New Haven and London, 2002), p. 605.

compareth this life of ours to set before us the shortnes, the vanitie, the frailtie, the uncertaintie, and the miserie of it.'[114] The commonplace book of John Moulton, vicar of St Bartholomew the Less, includes some sermon notes in the same highly repetitive, highly proverbial style: 'What more noysome weedes, more corrupt putrefaction, more infectious humours or more pernitious dangers can there be in us than our sinnes . . . Noe marveile then if [the Holy Ghost] useth a sharpe ploughshare to teare up these unsavory weedes, a cutting corrosive to take away this putrified corruption, a bitter pill to purge these contagious humours, and a severe precept to beate downe these rebellious enormities.'[115] This hammer-blow rhetoric was the essence of what contemporaries meant by 'plain' preaching. Yet it rarely survives in print, except in a few cases where a sermon is preserved in a shorthand report uncorrected by the preacher.

But there were other factors drawing the printed sermon closer towards the sermon as preached. In revising the sermons on the Commandments, Dod and Cleaver altered many of the pronouns, with third-person passages ('one') being adjusted to the first or second person ('thee' or 'us'), and first-person singular ('I') to first-person plural ('we'), as in the following examples:

(1603) This I am sure of, that if I cry to God, hee will deliver me from my sinne

(1604) This we are sure of, that if we cry to God, he will deliver us from our sin

(1603) But if Gods spirit reprove one, and if he have sinned it check him, and make him feare, blessed is he, for God is his God.

(1604) But if Gods spirit reprove thee, and checke thee for thy sin, and make thee feare: blessed art thou, for God is thy God.

(1603) Is he a master? hath God made him a governour? then for the time that one is a servant, he stands in the place of Christ in his family.

(1604) Is he thy maister? hath God made him thy governour? Then, for the time that thou art his servant, he stands in the place of Christ, unto thee, beeing of his family.

The direct address – 'blessed art *thou*'; '*thou* art his servant' – seems intended as a printed alternative to the preacher's pointing finger; a way of ensuring that the reader was included within the scope of the preacher's exhortations. In this respect, Dod and Cleaver's revisions actually enhance the plain style of the sermons, by making the text 'speak' to the reader bluntly and directly.

[114] Cupper, *Certaine Sermons*, Y4r.
[115] Commonplace book of John Moulton: Wellcome Library, London, MS 571.

Even this, however, is a plainness that has been deliberately written into the printed text, rather than carried straight over from oral preaching.

This is by no means unusual. Many printed sermons contain examples of what might be termed 'scripted extemporisation', that is, passages which appear to be spontaneous oral asides but which have, in fact, been specially written for print. Playfere's sermon, for example, includes a well-known passage commenting on the audience's response:

> Blessed bee God, I am yet very much revived (being otherwise almost quite spent with speaking so long) when I look about me and beholde every one that is present. For I see no place in this great auditory, where there are not very many readie to weepe, the water standing in their eyes, and some alreadie weeping right-out, in true remorse and sorrow for their sinnes.

At least one modern commentator has taken this literally. ('Thomas Playfere's 1595 sermon *The Meane in Mourning* brought his audience to tears. So moving was the performance that two pirated editions of the sermon appeared before Playfere could issue a carefully edited version.'[116]) However, the passage only appears in the 'carefully edited' version of 1596, not in the earlier editions, and was evidently inserted by Playfere when he revised the sermon for print. Whether or not his auditors actually did weep, Playfere evidently wanted to give his readers the impression that they had done so, in order to recreate the experience of participating in a 'live' event.

Many of the apparently 'oral' elements in printed sermons turn out, on closer inspection, to have been carefully scripted in the same way. Bunyan scholars are prone to suggest that Bunyan's writings, particularly early works such as *Some Gospel Truths Opened*, draw water from the wellsprings of an uncontaminated oral tradition. Roger Sharrock has argued that they embody 'a total unselfconsciousness in regard to the function of the writer ... because the book is treated simply as an extension of the oral sermon ... Bunyan's own words and phrases remain those of speech'.[117] However, Bunyan is known to have written out his sermons after preaching them, and it is likely that the texts as they have come down to us were designed for reading, not for hearing. No study of early modern sermons

---

[116] Bryan Crockett, '"Holy cozenage" and the Renaissance cult of the ear', *Sixteenth Century Journal*, 24 (1993), pp. 47–65 (quotation p. 47).

[117] Roger Sharrock, 'Bunyan and the book', in N. H. Keeble, ed., *John Bunyan, Conventicle and Parnassus: Tercentenary Essays* (Oxford, 1988), pp. 71–90 (quotation p. 75). On Bunyan's practice of writing his sermons after preaching them, see his *Works* (1692), A1v.

that relies on printed sources can afford to ignore this distinction. As P. M. Oliver has noted in his recent study of Donne's sermons: 'When Donne revised sermons for the press, he in effect set out to create new texts which give readers the illusion of being listeners. Most of the sermon-texts we possess contain addresses to a listening congregation which have been written into them.'[118] Donne was peculiarly sensitive to the differences between speech and print: the first edition of *Pseudo-Martyr*, for example, uses italic type to create 'deeper impressions' in the mind of the reader, a sort of typographical substitute for the emphases that a speaker might supply when reading the text aloud.[119]

Other preachers were much exercised by the distinction between a 'sermon' and a 'treatise'. Theophilus Higgons, in the preface to his anti-Catholic diatribe *Mystical Babylon*, was careful to explain that although the work had begun life as a pair of sermons, and 'in all the pages thereof, beareth the title of a *first*, and of a *second Sermon*', it had now been 'framed . . . more copiously into the body of a *Treatise*, which therefore I present unto thee, rather under this name; as exceeding the proportion, and, in some thing, differing (perhaps) from the qualitie of *Sermons*'.[120] Another writer presented the distinction more bluntly: 'that which I lately delivered in a Sermon in the voice of a living man . . . I have in this Treatise laid it open to scanning and censure, and buried it in a dead letter of lesse efficacie.'[121] The difference between a sermon and a treatise may seem simple enough: one is designed to be preached, the other to be read on the page. According to Ian Green, a sermon originates in oral delivery and is usually devoted to the unpackaging of a particular biblical text, whereas a treatise is a 'literary composition' offering 'a methodical treatment of a definite theme or topic'.[122] But on closer examination the two categories start to blend into one another. Taking the distinction between sermons and treatises as our starting point, we can identify two contrasting approaches to the use of printed texts. Some writers tried to pull their printed sermons away from oral delivery by making them more like treatises, whereas others tried to bring their printed treatises closer to oral delivery by making them more like sermons.

The first approach is exemplified by Dod and Cleaver, who, as we have seen, revised the plain style of Dod's sermons on the Commandments to

---

[118] P. M. Oliver, *Donne's Religious Writing* (1997), p. 238.
[119] John Donne, *Pseudo-Martyr*, ed. Anthony Raspa (Montreal and Kingston, 1993), p. 10.
[120] Theophilus Higgons, *Mystical Babylon, or Papall Rome* (1624), A3r.
[121] W. L., *The Incomparable Iewell* (1632), A3v.
[122] Green, *Print and Protestantism*, p. 194 (sermon), p. 217 (treatise).

purge them of the more obvious traces of oral delivery. It can also be seen in Gouge's *Domesticall Duties*, which, despite having originated as a course of sermons, is described on the title page as 'Eight Treatises'. But the alternative approach is exemplified in Thomas Stoughton's *Two Profitable Treatises* (1616), which, despite being 'much enlarged' for print, was written in the style of an oral sermon so that readers could imagine it 'rather . . . as presently by lively voice uttered, than as formerly by dead letter onely written'. Whereas Dod and Cleaver had removed colloquial expressions in order to achieve a more dignified style, Stoughton went to the other extreme, filling the text with proverbial and colloquial remarks ('soft fire maketh sweetest malt'; 'Sathan bestirreth his stumps to hurt and destroy') and repetitions ('labour, labour, I beseech you'; 'alas, alas'; 'take heed, take heed') in order to recreate the effect of hearing a live sermon.[123] It can also be seen in Anthony Wotton's sermons on John, which are deliberately written in a style of 'discourse for exhortation' (as opposed to 'commentary for instruction') and are conspic-uous for their oral phrasing ('Marke I pray you'; 'See I pray you'), even, on occasion, addressing an imaginary congregation ('Me thinks I discerne a certaine cheerefulnes in your countenances') or glancing at an imaginary hourglass ('But I find my self so much overtaken by the time').[124]

There were also two contrasting views on how far the 'uses' or 'applica-tions' of a sermon could be reproduced in print. Some writers felt that these parts of the sermon carried an emotional charge which could not be repeated on the printed page. In the preface to his *Doctrine of Faith* (1627), John Rogers explained that the work consisted of 'the summe of sundry Sermons . . . which I wrote brokenly and briefly for my owne memory, leaving out many things in the Uses and Applications of the Points delivered in Preaching, which should set an edge upon the Doctrines that were handled'. He admitted that this was a defect, but declared that it could not be remedied. 'Sundry of my friends, some by Letters, som by word of mouth have told me, that the Uses of the Points are very short and weak in comparison of that they were in Preaching. I easily confesse it, and know not how to mend it, unlesse I had Preacht them over againe, or had more leisure to enlarge them than I can attaine to. Neither finde I it possible to me, in cold blood, and so long after, to call to minde or write those stirring passages that God brought to hand in the heat of Preaching.'[125] Other writers, however, made a special effort to include the

---

[123] Thomas Stoughton, *Two Profitable Treatises* (1616), A5v.
[124] Anthony Wotton, *Sermons upon a part of the First Chapter of the Gospel of S. John* (1609).
[125] John Rogers, *The Doctrine of Faith* (5th edn., 1633), A5r–6r.

uses and applications in their printed sermons. In the preface to his edition of Josias Shute's sermons in 1649, Edward Sparke observed that while there were already many printed sermons on the market, Shute's sermons were particularly worth reading because they were exceptionally 'copious and insinuative in the Applications'.[126]

The printed sermons of this period are thus characterised by two alternative textual strategies. One strategy used the printed sermon solely and simply as a means of doctrinal instruction. The other tried to convey to the reader, or the listener being read to, something of the sensation of hearing a sermon preached – and there are strong indications that this proved extremely popular with readers. Sermons were sometimes marketed by their publishers as 'a plain sermon' or even, in one case, 'a very feeling and moving sermon', suggesting that there was a significant demand for printed sermons that mimicked the plain style and emotional effects of oral preaching.[127] In the final section of this chapter, we shall look in more detail at the way that printed sermons were bought, read and used. As we shall see, sermons found their way into the hands of a growing number of lay readers, who brought to them sophisticated textual strategies of their own.

OWNERSHIP AND USE OF PRINT

One small anecdote sums up the growing demand for printed sermons at the turn of the seventeenth century. In the autumn of 1607, the stationer Nathaniel Butter sent the manuscripts of two new books – one of them a sermon, the other a play – to the printer Nicholas Okes. The sermon, which had just been preached at Paul's Cross, was sent straight to the press, while the play was put aside to wait its turn in the queue. The author of the sermon, John Pelling, never published anything else, though his sermon evidently found appreciative readers, as one surviving copy is annotated: 'a very good Sermon you have a good judgment'. The play happened to be the first edition of *King Lear*.[128]

Who were the readers who bought Pelling's sermon and others like it? The core readership was probably drawn from the ranks of the better sort,

---

[126] Josias Shute, *Sarah and Hagar, or, Genesis the Sixteenth Chapter Opened, in XIX Sermons* (1649), preface.

[127] Robert Harris's *Davids Comfort at Ziklag* (1628) is described on the title page as 'a plaine sermon', while Anthony Cade's *Saint Paules Agonie* (1618) has a running title describing it as 'a very feeling and moving sermon'.

[128] Peter Blayney, *The Texts of 'King Lear' and Their Origins: Nicholas Okes and the First Quarto* (Cambridge, 1982), p. 81. The annotated copy of Pelling's *A Sermon of the Providence of God* is in St John's College, Cambridge (Ee.3.33).

members of the London mercantile and professional élite, who bought sermons by preachers they had heard and admired. In the library of Scipio le Squyer, Deputy Chamberlain of the Exchequer, printed editions of sermons by Lancelot Andrewes, John King and Thomas Taylor, among others, rubbed shoulders with two volumes of le Squyer's own sermon notes.[129] Robert Harley's library catalogue includes an entire section of 'sermons in quarto', including many sermons by preachers whom Harley knew personally, such as Thomas Gataker, who had preached at Harley's wedding.[130] Similarly, the accounts of John Buxton, a student at the Inns of Court in the 1620s, show that he was buying the sermons of several well-known London preachers, including Richard Sibbes and John Preston; and it seems likely, as the editor of his accounts has suggested, that Buxton had heard both men preach and bought their works accordingly.[131] Printed sermons were thus aimed at a public who were accustomed to hearing sermons as well as reading them. It is likely, too, that there was considerable overlap between the market for sermons and the market for plays. The diary of another student at the Inns of Court records an occasion when he bought sermons and a play on the same day: 'Pauls yard, emi sermons, Duck lane, game of chesse'.[132]

In many cases, printed sermons may have been even more precisely aimed at members of the preacher's own congregation. What little evidence we have about the financing of printed sermons suggests that preachers were often paid in kind, by being given a proportion of the edition to sell or give away to their friends and neighbours. Edward Fornis sold the copyright of his sermon to the printer in exchange for half the impression, which he then distributed among his parishioners in Wisbech: 'necessity (my counsel) saith print it, and the Printer again saith, let it be neither mine, nor thine, but divide it. So I have my number to give, which I aymed at, and he his to sell (if Sermons will sell) which he aymes at.'[133] The account book of the Devonshire minister Thomas Larkham shows that he made a

---

[129]  F. Taylor, 'The books and manuscripts of Scipio le Squyer, Deputy Chamberlain of the Exchequer (1620–59)', *Bulletin of the John Rylands Library*, 25 (1941), pp. 137–64.

[130]  'A catalogue of bookes taken the 12th day of July 1637': BL Add. 70001, f. 330.

[131]  David McKitterick, '"Ovid with a Littleton": the cost of English books in the early seventeenth century', *Transactions of the Cambridge Bibliographical Society*, 11: 2 (1997), pp. 184–234.

[132]  Commonplace book of Justinian Pagitt: BL Harl. MS 1026, entry for 3 Jan. 1633/4. Duck Lane was the location of several secondhand bookshops, and the reference to 'game of chesse' is almost certainly to Middleton's *A Game at Chess* (1625).

[133]  Edward Fornis, *Looke Not upon Me* (1648), A2r. Richard Baxter's practice was to take 'the fifteenth booke' (i.e. one copy in every fifteen) as his share: see N. H. Keeble and G. F. Nuttall, *Calendar of the Correspondence of Richard Baxter*, vol. 1 (Oxford, 1991), letters 410, 507.

down payment of £10 to the London stationer Francis Eglesfield to print his sermons, and received fifty-six copies which he then sold to local booksellers and members of his congregation. Larkham's total outlay, including the cost of transporting the books from London to Tavistock, came to £10 14s, while the total retail value of his copies (at 4s bound and 3s unbound) came to £10 16s, so that if he had sold all the copies he received, he would just have broken even.[134] The chance survival of a scrap of book-trade correspondence shows that a work by the Welsh puritan minister William Erbury was expected to sell 600 copies (at least half the total print run, if not more) in Erbury's home town of Cardiff, and it seems likely that other sermons were printed in anticipation of a strong local sale.[135]

But hearing and reading did not always go hand in hand. The reading of sermons or other printed books could sometimes be an alternative to hearing the word preached. The godly Mrs Elizabeth Wilkinson, whose conversion narrative was published in Samuel Clarke's *Collection of the Lives of Ten Eminent Divines . . . and of Some Other Eminent Christians* (1662) as a model spiritual autobiography, wrote that she had lived for several years in 'a place where I heard very little powerfull preaching' and had therefore come to rely heavily on printed books for spiritual sustenance. Her minister, Robert Harris, did not regard this as particularly exceptional, noting that troubled souls might derive comfort from either reading or hearing: 'Sometimes [God] directs them to some special Book or Treatise which fits their case . . . sometimes he sends an Interpreter, one of a thousand, that shall rip up their misery and shew them their remedy.'[136] Richard Baxter, too, believed that in certain circumstances printed books could serve as a substitute for sermons. His own father had been converted 'by the bare reading of the Scriptures in private, without either preaching or godly company, or any other books but the Bible', and he himself had been converted by reading godly books; as he later wrote, 'the reading of Mr *Ezekiel Culverwell*'s Treatise of Faith did me much good, and many other excellent Books were made my Teachers and Comforters: And the use that God made of Books, above Ministers, to the benefit of my Soul, made

---

[134] Diary of Thomas Larkham: BL Loan MS 9. On the publication of the sermons, see also William Lewis, ed., *Diary of the Rev. Thomas Larkham* (Bristol, 1888), pp. 35–9, and Susan Hardman Moore, '"Pure folkes" and the parish: Thomas Larkham in Cockermouth and Tavistock', in Diana Wood, ed., *Life and Thought in the Northern Church c.1100–c.1700: Essays in Honour of Claire Cross* (Woodbridge, 1999), pp. 489–509.

[135] Paul Morgan, 'Letters relating to the Oxford book trade', in R.W. Hunt, I.G. Philip and R.J. Roberts, eds., *Studies in the Book Trade in Honour of Graham Pollard* (Oxford, 1975), pp. 71–89 (quotation p. 82).

[136] Samuel Clarke, *A Collection of the Lives of Ten Eminent Divines* (1662), 3X4v (p. 526).

me somewhat excessively in love with good Books; so that I thought I had never enow.'[137]

Some suggestive evidence on the use of printed sermons in a godly household can be found in the recently discovered autobiography of the Northamptonshire gentlewoman Elizabeth Isham (1609–54).[138] When her mother Judith was troubled with doubts about predestination, it was not to a minister that she turned but to 'a Sermon booke which Mrs Nicolls sent her', John Randall's *The Saints Conjunction with God*, which 'fully resoulved' her difficulties. Elizabeth herself seems to have found it much easier to read sermons than to hear them. As a teenager 'I found no or litle benefit of those sermons which hetherto I heard, because I aplied not my hart so much unto them that I might have learnt', and in her twenties she continued to struggle with the difficulties of remembering and noting sermons. Her diary records that in 1631 'I purposed to take more heed to remember sermons', in 1632 'I writ out sermons what I could remember', and in 1633 'I purposed to give to good use in sted of writing sermons which I was not well able 5 sh[illings] a year'. Thereafter she appears to have turned to the reading of printed sermons as an alternative to writing out the sermons she heard, and by 1637 she had begun to read the sermons of Thomas Adams as a regular Sunday routine.[139]

In the English colonies overseas, preaching was sparse and printed books often had to serve as a substitute. Henry Herrick, writing from New England, lamented the lack of a regular preaching ministry – 'truly we are in a sad condition for we have not a preacher in neare twenty miles of us, the Lord helpe us I beseech him' – and asked his brother John to send him a 'sermon booke' to read.[140] Another English expatriate, Richard Norwood, living in Bermuda, had no access to a preaching ministry ('we had then no minister but Mr Lewes, who was constantly at the town with the Governor') and was forced to rely on private reading and prayer. Norwood's small personal library included a Latin Bible, an edition of Augustine's commentary on John, and 'some of Mr Perkins' books'. He later dated one of the decisive changes in his spiritual condition to his reading of a passage in Augustine on the ability of words to remain in the mind even after the

---

[137]  Richard Baxter, *Reliquiae Baxterianae* (1696), B2r, B3r. On reading and conversion, see also Baxter, *Against the Revolt to a Foreign Jurisdiction* (1691), Mm6r.
[138]  Autobiography of Elizabeth Isham: Princeton University Library, RTC01.62. I am very grateful to Elizabeth Clarke and Erica Longfellow for sharing their transcription of the manuscript and discussing it with me.
[139]  Diary of Elizabeth Isham: Northamptonshire Record Office, Northampton, I.L. 3365.
[140]  Henry Herrick to his brother John, 1653: Bodleian Library, Oxford, MS Eng. hist. c.481, f. 132.

sound of speech has died away – a passage which would surely have had particular significance for a solitary reader.[141] These examples suggest that by the early seventeenth century, many godly individuals had grown accustomed to a shifting relationship between preaching and print, where their religious activities would sometimes be organised around the hearing and repeating of sermons and at other times around the reading of books. They clearly cherished the preaching ministry, but the idea that preaching was primary and reading only secondary is not reflected in the records of their spiritual lives.

We can be fairly confident, then, that printed sermons were widely available and that they circulated well beyond the confines of a preacher's own congregation. But how far down the social scale did they penetrate? Evidence of the ownership of printed sermons is easiest to find at the upper levels of society. When Jean Verneuil published a bibliography of English printed sermons in 1642 – based on the holdings of the Bodleian Library, where he was under-librarian – he took it for granted that the book would be most useful to élite readers buying sermons for their own libraries. Not only were there 'many *Country* Ministers' with extensive collections of printed sermons, but many laypersons as well: 'yea of mine owne knowledge, there are some of the *Nobility*, and *Gentry* of this *Kingdome*, as well furnished, as most *Ministers of Gods Word*'.[142] That many of the nobility and gentry did indeed collect printed sermons is amply confirmed by contemporary library catalogues and booklists. The library of Sir Roger Townshend, scion of two prominent Norfolk gentry families, the Bacons and the Townshends, was particularly rich in sermons, not only the standard collected editions of Joseph Hall, Henry Smith and others but also a large number of more fugitive sermons by less celebrated preachers.[143] Another Norfolk gentleman, Henry Gurney (1589–1616), owned sermons by Henry Smith, John King, William Barlow, Thomas Playfere and Leonard Wright, some of which he lent to friends and relatives in the locality.[144] The Isham family library was also well supplied with printed sermons, ranging from '3 great Bookes of Mr Perkins' (i.e. William Perkins's three-volume collected works) down to sermon collections such as John

---

[141] Richard Norwood, *Journal*, ed. W. F. Craven and W. B. Hayward (New York, 1945), pp. 71, 84.

[142] Jean Verneuil, *A Nomenclator of Such Tracts and Sermons as Have Been Printed, or Translated into English upon any Place, or Booke of Holy Scripture* (2nd edn., Oxford, 1642), A3v.

[143] 'An inventory of books in the possession of Sir Roger Townshend, *c.* 1625', in R. J. Fehrenbach and E. S. Leedham-Green, eds., *Private Libraries in Renaissance England*, vol. 1 (Binghamton, NY, and Marlborough, UK, 1992), pp. 79–135.

[144] Steven W. May, 'Henry Gurney, a Norfolk farmer, reads Spenser and others', *Spenser Studies*, 20 (2005), pp. 183–223.

Fosbroke's *Six Sermons* (1633) and Richard Sibbes's *The Soules Conflict* (1635) and single sermons such as Thomas Adams's *The Souldiers Honour* (1617), Robert Harris's *Absaloms Funerall* (1610) and William Worship's *The Pattern of an Invincible Faith* (1616).[145]

But printed sermons found avid readers among the middling sort as well. Few readers, admittedly, can have been as avid as Nehemiah Wallington, who calculated in 1650 that he had read over two hundred books, and lamented his tendency to buy 'more than I need, having enough already'.[146] Nevertheless, a recent edition of Suffolk wills has revealed several small collections of sermon literature among the middling sort, and similar books would probably have been found in many other households elsewhere in the country. The library of Thomas Scott, an Ipswich yeoman who died in 1620, consisted of a Bible and three works of divinity: 'Mr Babington upon the Commandments', 'Mr Moore's Sermons' and 'a book called the Christian Righteousness'.[147] Margaret Barret of Cavendish owned copies of the New Testament, the Book of Common Prayer, Dent's *Plaine Mans Path-way to Heaven*, 'a book called the General Epistle of St Jude', the Essex minister Samuel Smith's *David's Blessed Man*, and 'my booke of sermons made by Mr Henry Smith', all of which were distributed among her grandchildren when she died in 1632.[148] However, these were relatively prosperous individuals – Mrs Barret's will, for example, lists a large quantity of linen, furniture and other household goods in addition to the books, as well as the contents of a dairy and a buttery adjoining the house – and the books in question were fairly substantial quartos and octavos, which would probably have been valued in shillings rather than in pence.

At the poorest levels of society, where the evidence of library catalogues and probate inventories is largely unavailable, it is more difficult to gauge the impact of print. There is certainly a case for arguing that printed sermons failed, on the whole, to penetrate beyond the middling sort.

---

[145] 'A note of my mothers bookes in the chest' (i.e. Judith Isham, 1607–25) and 'A note of my sisters Judiths bookes' (i.e. Judith Isham, 1610–36): two booklists in the hand of Sir Justinian Isham, Northamptonshire Record Office, Northampton, I.L. 4046.

[146] Paul Seaver, *Wallington's World: A Puritan Artisan in Seventeenth-Century London* (1985), p. 5.

[147] Marion E. Allen, ed., *Wills of the Archdeaconry of Suffolk 1620–1624* (Suffolk Records Society, vol. XXXI, Woodbridge, 1989), pp. 108–9. 'Mr Babington upon the Commandments' was Gervase Babington's *A Very Fruitfull Exposition of the Commaundements*, first published in 1583; 'Mr Moore's Sermons' was probably John More's *Three Godly and Fruitfull Sermons* (1594); 'the Christian Righteousness' has not been identified.

[148] Nesta Evans, ed., *Wills of the Archdeaconry of Sudbury 1630–1635* (Suffolk Records Society, vol. XXIX, Woodbridge, 1987), pp. 159–60. All of these works are readily identifiable except for 'the General Epistle of St Jude', possibly Martin Luther's *A Commentarie or Exposition upon the Two Epistles Generall of Saint Peter and Saint Jude* (1581).

Most sermons were printed in quarto, rather than in the smaller octavo and duodecimo formats which could have fitted easily into a pedlar's pack, and even those that were printed in smaller formats were often aimed at the middle rather than the lower end of the market. The earliest posthumous editions of Henry Smith's sermons, for example, were collections of *Seven Godly and Learned Sermons* (1591) and *Thirteene Sermons* (1592), which must reflect an assumption on the part of the publisher that collected editions would be more marketable than single sermons.[149] Many writers seem to have been unaware of the financial constraints inhibiting the purchase of books at the lower end of the market, and while claiming to address their works to the poor, were in fact restricting their readership to the middling sort. The preface to Richard Preston's *The Doctrine of the Sacrament of the Lords Supper* (1621) is addressed to a reader who may be 'not over willing to part with thy silver' but who can, if necessary, 'bestow two or three groates upon a booke' (i.e. eightpence or a shilling). Even a book such as Henry Scudder's *The Christians Daily Walke*, which claimed to be 'digested . . . with such brevitie and perspicuitie, as was necessary to make the Booke a *vade mecum*, easily portable, and profitable to the poore and illiterate', ran to 800 pages in duodecimo and would probably have cost about 1s 6d.[150]

The best-known example of this sort is Richard Rogers's *Seven Treatises* (1603), based on the sermons preached in his parish of Wethersfield, in Essex, and intended, in Rogers's own words, 'to aide my poore neighbours and brethren' by making Christianity 'more easie and pleasant unto them, than many finde it'. Despite Rogers's good intentions, the size of the book (over 600 pages in folio) effectively kept it out of reach of the poor; and although it evidently found a market, as it had reached a fourth edition by 1616, it is unlikely to have penetrated to the middling sort until the publication of Stephen Egerton's abridgement *The Practice of Christianitie* in 1618.[151] In his commendatory preface to the first edition, Ezekiel Culverwell acknowledged that some readers might be 'offended with the largenes of the work (as too deare for the poore, and too much to be read over in long time)', and Rogers himself made the revealing admission that

---

[149] Similarly, Henry Greenwood's sermons appear to have sold best in collected editions: see Green, *Print and Protestantism*, p. 220.

[150] Richard Preston, *The Doctrine of the Sacrament of the Lords Supper* (1621), A4v (preface by Ezekiel Charke); Henry Scudder, *The Christians Daily Walke* (7th edn., 1637), A11v (preface by John Davenport).

[151] Rogers, *Seven Treatises*, A5r. Stephen Egerton, *The Practice of Christianitie* (1618), is described on the title page as 'published for the benefit of such, as either want leisure to reade, or meanes to provide larger Volumes'. See also Green, *Print and Protestantism*, pp. 316–17.

'in the wealthy estate' there were many more opportunities for reading, meditation and other godly activities 'than are to be found in the needie and poore'. The poor man 'is through meere necessitie constrained to his great griefe, to cut off many times of reading'; while, according to Rogers, some masters even refused to employ servants who were religious, 'who (they say) when their minds should be upon their worke, are found oftentimes at their booke and at prayer'.[152]

Tessa Watt, in her influential study, *Cheap Print and Popular Piety, 1550–1640* (1991), lays stress on the emergence of the 'penny godly' in the 1620s as being the crucial innovation that enabled the publishers of cheap religious print to market their wares to a genuinely popular readership. Only with the development of the single-sheet penny chapbook, she suggests, did printed material become affordable to the mass of husbandmen and agricultural labourers whose disposable income may have been as little as 14d to 18d a week.[153] Watt's emphasis on the penny godly may be misleading, however, if it suggests that publishers were breaking into hitherto untapped markets. The stock of the stationer Roger Ward in 1585 included '45 Dentes sermones' (probably Arthur Dent's *Sermon of Repentance*, first printed in 1582 and pirated by Ward the following year), together with substantial stocks of sermons priced at two and a half- or threepence each. The stock of the York stationer John Foster in 1616 included a wide variety of sermons and other godly chapbooks, including four copies of Dent's *Sermon of Repentance* (valued at 2d each), four copies of Dent's *Pastime for Parents* (3d each), and seven copies of Gabriel Price's newly published Paul's Cross sermon *The Laver of the Heart* (3d each).[154] The penny godly, therefore, was not a radical innovation but the culmination of a gradual trend towards smaller and cheaper sermons which was already well underway by the late sixteenth century.

The practice of reading sermons aloud would also have made their contents available to many who perhaps could not have afforded to buy them. Lady Margaret Hoby's diary records several occasions when sermons and other religious books were read aloud by various members of the household. Richard Rhodes, her domestic chaplain, read 'Latimers sarmons', 'Gyffard upon the songe of Sallemon' and 'a sarmon of the Revelation', while at other times 'one of the men', presumably a servant, 'read of the book of Marters', and 'one of my wemen' read from the works of

---

[152] Rogers, *Seven Treatises*, A4r, 2S3r, 2K2r.    [153] Watt, *Cheap Print*, pp. 306–15.

[154] Alexander Rodger, 'Roger Ward's Shrewsbury stock: an inventory of 1585', *The Library*, 5th ser., 13 (1958), pp. 247–68 (esp. pp. 259, 267); Robert Davies, *A Memoir of the York Press* (1868; repr. York, 1988), p. 363; see also John Barnard and Maureen Bell, *The Early Seventeenth-Century York Book Trade and John Foster's Inventory of 1616* (Leeds, 1994).

William Perkins.[155] Similar examples survive from humbler households.
Mary Pennington, the future Quaker, recalled that in her childhood, in
the mid-1620s, 'a maid-servant that waited on me and the rest of the
children … used to read Smith's and Preston's sermons on [Sundays]
between the sermon times'. Cicely Johnson of Colchester – who, like
Mary Pennington, would later gravitate towards radical Protestantism –
also recalled that, as a child, 'when I would have my parentes heare mee read
I would read in the Scripturs and good Sermon bookes, such as my father
had and some I would borrow'.[156] The members of an Oxfordshire conventicle in the 1630s regularly came together on Sunday evenings 'to make
tryall what they could remember that Sunday of the sermons they had
hearde', and then to read aloud from a selection of printed books, including
the Book of Homilies and the sermons of John Preston and Richard
Sibbes.[157]

This may explain why some printed sermons are strongly oral in their
phraseology, as if designed to be read aloud. Tessa Watt has drawn attention
to a group of penny godlies in which references to patristic authors are
introduced by the formula, 'heare his words which he saith'. 'The orality of
this phrasing is conspicuous', she points out, 'since the texts were almost
certainly composed as written works, not as sermons.'[158] In a few cases it
may even be possible to detect traces of oral delivery carried over into the
printed text, as in the following passage from a sermon by the Wiltshire
preacher and 'penny godly' writer John Andrewes:

Fourthly, of the infinite and unspeakable mercy of God towards us most miserable
sinners. The quantity of mercy is not strange, it droppeth as the gentle dew from
heaven upon the place beneath, it is twise blest, it blesseth him that gives, & him
that takes, it is mightiest in the mightiest, it becomes the *throne of Monarchie* better
than his crowne; his Scepter shewes the force of temporall power, the attribute to
awe & maiestie, wherein doth sit the dread & feare of kings, but mercy is above the
Scepters sway, it is inthroned in the hearts of kings, it is an attribute to God

[155] Dorothy M. Meads, ed., *Diary of Lady Margaret Hoby 1599–1605* (1930), pp. 68, 74, 75, 94, 129. The
'sarmon of the Revelation' was most probably taken from George Gifford's *Sermons upon the Whole
Booke of the Revelation* (1596). On Hoby's reading practises, see Andrew Cambers, 'Readers' marks
and religious practice: Margaret Hoby's marginalia', in John N. King, ed., *Tudor Books and Readers:
Materiality and the Construction of Meaning* (Cambridge, 2010), pp. 211–31.
[156] Naomi Baker, ed., *Scripture Women: Rose Thurgood, 'A Lecture of Repentance' & Cicely Johnson,
'Fanatical Reveries'* (Nottingham, 2005), p. 30.
[157] E. R. Brinkworth, 'The study and use of Archdeacons' court records: illustrated from the Oxford
records (1566–1759)', *Transactions of the Royal Historical Society*, 4th ser., 25 (1943), pp. 93–119
(quotation p. 114).
[158] Watt, *Cheap Print*, pp. 311–12. For similar examples, see William King, *The Strait Gate to Heaven*
(1616) and Robert Wakeman, *The Poore-mans Preacher* (1607).

himselfe, and earthly powers do then shew most like to Gods, when mercy teacheth
iustice.[159]

Though printed as prose, this is immediately recognisable as an extract from
Portia's famous 'mercy' speech in *The Merchant of Venice*. There could
hardly be a better illustration of the complex reciprocal relationship between
speech and print. Here we have a passage written for oral delivery in the
theatre, later published in a printed playbook, borrowed by Andrewes and
perhaps repeated by him in a sermon to his Wiltshire parishioners, and then
reproduced in a printed sermon, which may in turn have been read aloud by
its earliest readers.[160]

The practice of reading aloud would, of course, have served as a means of
extending print culture to the illiterate. William Tye, writing in 1608, instructed
'simple, rude and unlearned people who cannot reade themselves' to 'lend their
eares to such as can reade good bookes'; he added that printed books were now
so plentiful, and 'in such abundance brought home almost to their owne
doores, wheresoever in any place within the Realme of England they have
their dwelling', that there could be no possible excuse for ignorance.[161] It may
also help to explain the perplexing inability of social historians to establish a
firm connection between literacy and Protestantism. In her study of the Essex
village of Havering, Marjorie McIntosh has gone so far as to suggest that there
was actually a negative correlation between literacy (as measured by will
signatures) and Protestant commitment (as measured by will preambles).
David Cressy has also drawn attention to several Essex parishes where puritan
activity was coupled with exceptionally low levels of literacy.[162] These findings
are highly problematic, but it is at least arguable that religious ideas could be
transmitted more effectively in communities where literacy was limited and
books therefore had to be read aloud. As Mark Byford has pointed out, literacy

---

[159] John Andrewes, *Christ His Crosse, or the Most Comfortable Doctrine of Christ Crucified* (Oxford, 1614),
F1v. Tessa Watt discusses this tract at some length (see *Cheap Print*, pp. 306–11), though without
noting this passage; she points out that Andrewes was closely involved in the marketing of his
publications, and speculates that he may have 'sold his little books from a box after a rousing session
of preaching'. Andrewes's own description of *Christ His Crosse* as 'rawly comprised in a few scattered
leaves, and as rudely composed in a sort of scribled and unlettered lines' (A2v) supports the
hypothesis that it may originally have been written for oral delivery rather than print publication.
[160] Andrewes must have taken the passage from the 1600 Quarto of *The Merchant of Venice*, which
would have been the only printed edition available in 1613. The variations from the 1600 Quarto (e.g.
strange/strained; throne of Monarchie/throned monarch; teacheth/seasons) are strongly suggestive
of some form of oral transmission, but the passage as a whole is so close to the Quarto that it can
hardly have been derived from any other source.
[161] William Tye, *A Matter of Moment, or a Case of Waight* (1608), C3v.
[162] Marjorie McIntosh, *A Community Transformed: Havering 1500–1620* (Cambridge, 1992), chapter 4;
David Cressy, *Literacy and the Social Order* (1980), p. 84.

was by no means an essential prerequisite for the spread of Protestantism. 'Reading the Bible often meant reading it out aloud. Sermons, catechisms, prophesyings, combination lectures, all were primarily oral activities, yet all aspired to communicate ideas culled from literate culture.'[163]

Those with literacy skills, however, were not limited to reading aloud, or hearing others read, but could engage with the printed text in other ways. How they did so can be deduced from the marginal notes and directions to the reader which occur in many printed sermons and other religious books. One of the religious bestsellers of the period, *A Garden of Spirituall Flowers*, contains extensive marginal notes drawing attention to passages of particular importance, including 'Note', 'Note it well', 'A good observation', 'Note for thy comfort', 'A speciall note', and 'An especiall note whereby we may be assured our sinnes are pardoned'.[164] Similarly, many readers personalised the texts they read by adding handwritten notes of their own. In one surviving copy of Henry Smith's sermons on the Lord's Supper, an early reader was inspired by the printed sidenotes, such as 'Note' and 'Similitude', to add further notes in a straggling, semi-literate hand. Smith's claim that the Papists were incapable of explaining their own doctrine of transubstantiation prompted the marginal comment, 'Note this'. His observation that Christ was not a rich man – 'the Lorde of all had least of all' – drew the remark, 'A note for a rich man', while his exhortation to the clergy to examine their parishioners before admitting them to the sacrament is annotated, 'A verie good note for minesters'. His exhortation to all people to examine their own consciences is annotated, 'A good note for every man', and his set form of self-examination before receiving the sacrament, 'Here is a good note for a man to exsamen hemselfe'.[165]

Another popular black-letter sermon, Henry Greenwood's *Tormenting Tophet* (1615), identifies doctrines ('Obser.') and uses ('Use.') in the margin, and contains a whole battery of other marginal notes, including 'Simile', '*Adagium*' and '*Exemplum*'.[166] These were evidently intended as aids for inexperienced readers, transforming the sermon from a solid block of text

---

[163] Mark Byford, 'The price of Protestantism: assessing the impact of religious change in Elizabethan Essex' (unpublished DPhil thesis, University of Oxford, 1988), chapter 5. Byford is responding here to Christopher Haigh's argument that 'in Elizabethan conditions, with low levels of literacy . . . the English people could not be made Protestants'.

[164] Richard Rogers *et al.*, *A Garden of Spirituall Flowers* (1625; earliest known edition 1609), F4r, B6r, B7r, D3v, B6v.

[165] Copy of Henry Smith, *A Treatise of the Lordes Supper, in Two Sermons* (1591) in Cambridge University Library, Syn. 8.59.83. A copy of Dod and Cleaver's *Plaine and Familiar Exposition of the Ten Commandements* (1604), also in Cambridge University Library, Syn. 7.60.190, is annotated 'note' (against a condemnation of uncharitable persons, 2A7r) and 'note this' (against a warning about the 'immoderate use of the marriage bed', 2A2r).

[166] Henry Greenwood, *Tormenting Tophet: or a Terrible Description of Hel . . . Preached at Paules Crosse* (1615).

into a series of assorted doctrines, comparisons, proverbs and examples which could easily be picked out and read separately. Special emphasis was given to similes, as being particularly suitable for unlearned readers. 'Many times', declared Robert Cawdrey in his *Treasurie or Store-House of Similies* (1600), 'that thing which cannot bee perceived or understood of Readers of Bookes, and hearers of Sermons, by a simple precept, may yet by a Similitude or plaine example, bee attained unto.' Thus, although similes were 'apt and profitable for all men . . . meete for Magistrates, lawdable for Lawyers, a Iewell for Gentlemen', they were especially useful as a way of making matters plain to 'even the very simplest and ignorantest Reader'. Cawdrey advised his readers to refer to the book when they returned home after hearing a sermon, in order to drive home the doctrines they had heard with the help of a memorable comparison. 'The industrious and carefull Reader may receive great benefit and comfort by this worke, if, (after his returne home from the hearing of any godly Lecture or Sermon, where he hath either heard any principle of God his Religion, handled and spoken of: or else any vertue commended, or vice condemned) he shall turne to that point, and first search it out in the Table, and so then to Read all such Similies in the Booke, as he shall there find, touching the same point and matter.'[167]

The same reasoning can be seen at work in many printed sermons and other religious treatises, where similes are highlighted in the margin: the sidenotes in Ezekiel Culverwell's *Treatise of Faith*, for example, include 'A fit comparison', 'Simile' (where the text refers to 'a plaine comparison for the weaker sort'), 'O consider this', 'Observe', and 'A speech too true'.[168] And, once again, the evidence of surviving copies suggests that readers enthusiastically participated in this textual strategy. In one copy of Robert Wolcomb's sermon, *The State of the Godly*, an early reader has marked several passages, including the following, with the marginal note 'compa.' (i.e. 'comparison'):

For as the Urchin or Hedghog folded up round together in his prickly skin, seems not possible to bee opened without killing and flaying it of: and yet if hot water be sprinkled on it, it opens it selfe immediately: so some that are so hardned and wrapped up in the custome of sinning, as it seemes, that death only may end their ungodlines, yet when the hot water of tribulation is powred upon them, they are softned and dissolved, and made open to repentance.[169]

[167] Robert Cawdrey, *A Treasurie or Store-House of Similies* (1600), A2v.
[168] Ezekiel Culverwell, *A Treatise of Faith* (7th edn., 1633), C4r, D1v, F9v, G2v, H12r.
[169] Robert Wolcomb, *The State of the Godly Both in this Life, and in the Life to Come: Delivered in a Sermon at Chudleigh in Devon* (1606), copy in British Library (1418.i.5), B7v.

The message of Wolcomb's sermon may thus have been communicated not so much through formal doctrine as through a series of memorable and colourful similitudes. The gathering of such flowers of wisdom, and the copying of them into collections of *florilegia*, was of course part and parcel of the commonplace-book tradition, but the works we have been discussing were not aimed solely at the educated compilers of commonplace books. Cawdrey's anthology of similes, with its subject classification, can be seen as a ready-made commonplace book for those who were unable to compile their own, while Culverwell's treatise was specifically addressed to those who could read but not write.[170]

It is clear that similes and comparisons were regarded as detachable features of a printed text, capable of being lifted out of their initial context and transplanted into new surroundings, or (to use a modern idiom) cut-and-pasted by individual readers as they saw fit. Several surviving manuscripts give us a glimpse of this process in operation. One, entitled 'Certaine collections taken out of Dr Sibbs his sermons preached by him att Grayes Inne in London and elsewhere', consists of a series of short extracts, some in the form of proverbs ('The bitterest things in Religion are sweete'; 'Christianitie is a busie trade'; 'Sinceritie is the perfection of a Christian') and others just two or three sentences long, the following being a typical example:

That man hath made a good progresse in Religion that hath a high esteeme of the ordinances of God. And though perhapps hee finde himselfe dead and dull, yet the best things have left such a taste, and relish in his soule that hee cannot bee long without them. This is a sign of a good temper.[171]

A similar assortment can be found in another manuscript, 'A godly profit-able collection of divers sentences out of Holy Scripture and variety of matter out of severall divine authors', compiled by the puritan gentleman John Bruen of Chester. Bruen was an obsessive transcriber of sermons: according to his biographer William Hinde, he took notes on all the sermons he heard, 'and when he came home, did write over againe in a

---

[170] Culverwell advises his readers to compile their own personal anthologies of scriptural quotations, 'if they can write', but provides a ready-made collection of such passages 'for such as be not able': *Treatise of Faith*, E3r.

[171] 'Certaine collections taken out of Dr Sibbs his sermons': Folger Shakespeare Library, Washington, DC, V.a.4. The manuscript has the ownership inscription 'Joseph Hunton his Booke Anno Domini 1634', apparently in the same hand as the body of the manuscript. It is not clear whether the extracts have been copied from another manuscript or from a printed collection of Sibbes's sermons, though they may be related to the manuscript tradition that produced Bodleian Library, Oxford, MS Lyell empt. 27, which does not appear to be dependent on a printed source.

more legible hand, all that hee had gathered . . . Insomuch that hee hath left unto the heires of his family, so many volumes of Manuscripts, under his owne hand, set up in a comely order in his owne Study, as is scarce credible to report, being yet there to be seene, as so many worthy Monuments of his conscionable diligence and faithfulnesse in the Lords service.'

The manuscripts specifically mentioned by Hinde, including a collection of notes on Christian practice drawn out of the Bible and other authors ('to justifie his course, and stop the mouthes of all such as without any just cause did open them so wide against it') and a commonplace book with extracts from 'the workes of divers learned and godly men' such as Joseph Hall, Richard Greenham and Richard Rogers, appear to have been lost, but this one surviving example gives us a taste of Bruen's reading and note-taking habits. Again, the transcribed passages are very brief, rarely more than a few sentences long:

All outward ceremonies and rites that are not grounded on the word of god, are misbegotten geare. Mr Calvin on Psal. 50. 5.

B. Babbington on Exod. pag. 303. A cleargie mans cheife enimies, are those of his owne cote: Jer. 20. 2.

Humility is the lowest scholler in Christs schoole but yet it is the best scholler.

A rich man which is not attyred with holy vertues is but an Asse trimmed for the devill to ride upon. Yet riches and religion may go together. 1. riches are gods blessings, 2. they bee meanes to come by good things, 3. they be promised to the godly as rewards of obedience.[172]

These passages, according to the title page, were 'commonly by him called his Cardes being 52 in Number', and it is possible that Bruen designed them to be used in his household as a godly alternative to playing cards, with the individual slips of paper being dealt out or selected at random and then read aloud. If so, they provide an extreme example of the way that extracts from printed texts were cut up and reassembled with almost total disregard for their original context.

Another remarkable example of textual bricolage, illustrating the way that sermons could become part of the stock of proverbial wisdom, is *Old Mr Dod's Sayings*, a collection of moral sayings attributed to the puritan divine John Dod, printed in broadsheet format to be pinned up on the walls of houses.[173] The origin of these sayings is unclear: some were probably

---

[172] 'A godly profitable collection . . . by that deare and faithfull servant of God, John Bruen', BL Harl. MS 6607. Other printed sources cited in the manuscript include 'Topsell on Ruth' (f. 50), 'Josiah Hall' (f. 80) and 'A bride bush 1619 William Wheatley' (f. 106).
[173] *Old Mr Dod's Sayings* (1667), copy in Bodleian Library, Oxford, Wood 276 a (286). This was the best known of a group of broadsheets containing moral sayings by godly ministers, e.g. *Old Mr Edward*

drawn directly from Dod's printed sermons, or from the collection of his table talk widely circulated in manuscript under the picturesque title *Dod's Droppings*; some probably came at second hand, via Samuel Clarke's biography of Dod; one or two may preserve a genuine oral tradition passed down from those who had heard Dod preach; but others may simply have been free-floating sayings that happened to attach themselves to Dod's name. Some of the longer sayings certainly bear an unmistakable resemblance to sermon notes:

There be five tyes by which the God of Heaven hath bound himself to be the Saints Life-Guard against the Powers of Darkness. 1. His relation to them as Father. 2. His Love to them, in respect as they being the Birth of his Everlasting Council, as partakers of his own likeness. 3. The price of his Sons Blood, and his Covenant with them. 4. Their Dependance upon him, and expectation from him, in all their straits. *Now the expectations of the Poor shall not perish*, Psal. 9.18. 5. Christs present Employment in Heaven, is to see all things carried fairly between God and them.

However, the majority of the sayings are short, pithy and proverbial, evidently designed for easy memorisation:

So much Sin, so much sorrow; so much Holiness, so much Happiness.

A man that hath the Spirit of Prayer, hath more than if he had all the World.

To perswade us not to return railing for railing, he would say, That if a Dog barked at a Sheep, a Sheep will not bark at a Dog.

The Sinner is the Devil's Miller, always grinding; and the Devil is always filling the Hopper, that the Mill may not stand still.

Brown-bread with the Gospel, is good Fare.

In view of Dod's concern to purge the more colloquial and proverbial expressions from his printed sermons in order to achieve a more dignified style, it is ironic that he should have gone down to posterity as the author of such sayings as 'Brown-bread with the Gospel is good Fare'. But *Old Mr Dod's Sayings* was immensely popular and lastingly influential: first printed in 1667, twenty years after Dod's death, it was still being reprinted in the mid-eighteenth century, when many copies were 'still to be seen pasted on the walls of cottages'.[174] Incongruous as the combination of

*Calamy's Former and Latter Sayings upon Several Occasions* (1674), *Most Holy and Profitable Sayings of that Reverend Doctor, Dr Thomas Goodwin* (1680). Many of these are collected in one volume in BL 816.m.21.

[174] Fox, *Oral and Literate Culture*, p. 149; Green, *Print and Protestantism*, pp. 407–8. Green draws attention to the existence of another, later version in which the sayings were turned into crude doggerel 'for the better help of memory', e.g. 'Though we have things below very rare, Yet brown bread with the Gospel is good fare.'

puritan covenant theology and proverbial wisdom may seem to modern eyes, it does not seem to have troubled contemporary readers.

This cut-and-paste approach was not at all the sort of reading favoured by the preachers themselves. The godly preachers of the early seventeenth century tended to assume that the activity of reading a sermon on the printed page was much the same as hearing a sermon preached, involving the same techniques of repetition and memorisation with the same purpose of internalising the preacher's message. 'When thou hast begun a good booke', Egerton admonished his readers, 'give not over till thou have ended it, and when thou hast read it over once, let it not be tedious unto thee to read it over again and again, for thou shalt finde the second reading more fruitfull than the first, and the third more fruitfull than the second, and so the oftener the better.'[175] They also tended to assume that it would proceed in the same linear fashion, with readers following the preacher's argument through the same sequence of doctrines and uses in order to put themselves through the same process of self-examination and self-application. William Whately's advice to 'those that read bookes, specially Sermons', was that they should read with the intention of 'reflecting their thoughts upon themselves'. He urged them to study his sermons 'with none other intention, but that one of trying thy selfe, whether thou beest an hypocrite, yea or no' and assumed that this would lead to the same sort of division between the godly and the unregenerate as might result from a sermon preached before a mixed congregation: 'either (in finding out thine hypocrisie) thou shalt perceive thine unhappinesse, and bee capable of helpe; or else (in meeting with uprightnesse) thou shalt enjoy thy good estate, and be encouraged to proceede'.[176]

The reality was very different, as the preachers quickly recognised. Egerton complained of 'a great vanitie and an evill sicknesse among men, that if they have once seene the title of a booke, and the authors name, and read two or three leaves, it is cast at their heeles for ever after'. Richard Rogers lamented that 'idle readers' did not limit themselves to a few well-chosen books, but tended to read 'a leafe of one and a chapter of another . . . for novelties sake'. What was taking place here – and creating these tensions between lay and clerical expectations – was, in effect, the mass-marketing of Puritanism through print culture. Just as in the early sixteenth century, the distinctive forms of private devotion used at Syon Abbey and other religious houses had been made available to a lay readership through the publications of Catholic writers such as Richard Whitford, so in the early seventeenth century, some of the distinctive forms of puritan devotion

---

[175] Virel, *Learned and Excellent Treatise*, A3r.     [176] William Whately, *Gods Husbandry* (1619), A3r.

and self-examination were being disseminated to a wider public through the publication of printed sermons.[177] It was now possible for the casual reader to get a taste of the comforts and consolations of puritan spirituality without the commitment of regular sermon attendance, or, indeed, the strenuous mental discipline of the art of hearing. We should not underestimate the appeal of this, nor the novelty of the hundreds of printed sermons suddenly appearing on the market in the early seventeenth century, which for many people may have been their first encounter with puritan divinity.

Printed sermons were part of the complex give-and-take relationship between Protestantism and cheap print – 'Grub Street and the godly' – that Peter Lake has described so well in relation to the murder pamphlets of Elizabethan and early Stuart England. Godly preachers, as Lake shows, were well aware of the potential advantages to be gained from harnessing cheap print to their own purposes. The publication of their sermons gave them the opportunity to 'speak' to an audience much larger even than the hundreds who gathered at Paul's Cross each Sunday, and as we have seen in this chapter, printed sermons succeeded remarkably well in extending the cultural influence of godly Protestantism to the point where 'brown bread with the Gospel' became part of the common stock of proverbial wisdom. But if there was great potential for popularisation, there was also great scope for simplification and misunderstanding. It is hardly surprising that godly preachers were so often ambivalent in their attitude to print publication; hence the extraordinary spectacle of preachers trying to discourage potential readers of their books – Rogers, for example, warning that only faithful hearers of the word could expect to benefit from reading his *Seven Treatises*, as 'for the most part, they profit not by our writing, who doe not before regarde and take good by our preaching'.[178] But once they entered the marketplace, there was no going back. In putting their sermons on the market they were exposing them to a wider readership and surrendering control over the way they were read.

CONCLUSION

Most of this chapter has been devoted to the process by which sermons passed from speech to print. In conclusion, however, I want to look at the other side of this relationship, and explore the process by which printed

---

[177] J.T. Rhodes, 'Syon Abbey and its religious publications in the sixteenth century', *Journal of Ecclesiastical History*, 44: 1 (1993), pp. 11–25.

[178] Whately, *Gods Husbandry*, L2r, V4v; Rogers, *Seven Treatises*, A5v.

sermons fed back into oral delivery. It is widely accepted that the spread of print can often lend additional vitality to oral culture. The circulation of printed ballads, for example, may have killed off the pure oral tradition but certainly did not kill off ballad-singing; indeed, Adam Fox suggests that it may actually have strengthened it, quoting the Elizabethan preacher Nicholas Bownde, who observed in the 1590s that 'the singing of ballades is very lately renewed, and commeth on a fresh againe'.[179] In the same way, the availability of printed sermons certainly did not displace live preaching and may even have reinforced the belief that preaching was the most important of the clergy's responsibilities. But it also meant that the differences between oral and printed sermons gradually disappeared, as printed sermons increasingly came to set the standards to which live preaching was expected to conform.

The practice of reading printed sermons from the pulpit goes back almost as far as the invention of printing itself. Printed editions of ready-made sermons were in wide circulation before the Reformation and went on being used long after it. In one astonishing case preserved in the records of the Court of High Commission at York, a lay reader in the parish of East Drayton, in Nottinghamshire, was still delivering sermons from John Mirk's *Festial*, a fifteenth-century collection of homilies for the major feast-days of the Church year, as late as the 1580s.[180] It was to drive out such relics of medieval preaching, and to provide an approved course of readings for ministers who could not compose their own sermons, that the Book of Homilies was issued at the beginning of Edward VI's reign and reissued under Elizabeth.[181] By the late sixteenth century, however, many Reformed clergy had set their face firmly against the use of homilies, regarding them as a crutch for idle or unlearned ministers. The contempt for ready-made homilies is exemplified in Wilhelm Zepper's treatise on preaching, which complains that homilies remove the need for study and meditation, and that they enable the clergy to repeat the same sermon many times, or to deliver a sermon that was written many years before. Zepper illustrates his point with an anecdote about a preacher who announced in a sermon that 'God has permitted the plague to rage among us', causing

---

[179] Fox, *Oral and Literate Culture*, p. 9, quoting Nicholas Bownde, *The Doctrine of the Sabbath* (1595).

[180] Veronica M. O'Mara, 'A Middle English sermon preached by a sixteenth-century "athiest": a preliminary account', *Notes & Queries*, 232 (June 1987), pp. 183–5; David Cressy, 'The atheist's sermon: belief, unbelief and traditionalism in the Elizabethan North', in *Travesties and Transgressions in Tudor and Stuart England* (Oxford, 2000), pp. 162–70.

[181] On the English Homilies, see Susan Wabuda, 'Bishops and the provision of homilies', *Sixteenth Century Journal*, 25 (1994), pp. 551–66.

consternation among his audience. After the sermon he was asked which households had been affected by the plague, and had to admit that there was no plague; he had simply been reading an old homily written for a different occasion.[182]

Yet the early seventeenth century also saw the publication of a number of sermon collections that may have been specifically intended for use in the pulpit. Richard Bernard and Richard Alleine's *Davids Musick* (1616) consists of expositions of Psalms 1–3 in outline doctrine-and-use format, 'briefly set downe without any further enlargement, more than the quotations of proofes out of the holy Scriptures', and serving as a basis on which readers could 'set on worke their own invention'. This may have been intended as a set of ready-made sermon notes for godly readers to use in the context of repetition and private conference, but could equally well have served as a collection of skeleton sermons for young clergymen to take into the pulpit and flesh out in their own preaching.[183] Bernard had formerly tried to discourage the clergy from using printed sermons as a guide to composition: 'surely, he that understands his text well, and knowes how to draw a doctrine, needs no printed or written Sermons, to helpe for to inlarge it'.[184] But since it was virtually inevitable that some clergy would use printed sermons in this way, he may have concluded that it would be as well to provide some godly and orthodox models for them to borrow.

From the mid-seventeenth century, English preachers also had access to a range of advice manuals and bibliographies that could direct them to printed sermons on particular texts or subjects. One of the best known, John Wilkins's *Ecclesiastes* (1646), contained a bibliography of sermons and commentaries on particular books of the Bible, together with a list of some of the 'most eminent' English preachers (including most of the leading puritan divines, such as John Dod, Richard Greenham, Samuel Hieron, William Perkins and Richard Rogers, alongside Lancelot Andrewes and Richard Hooker) and a further list of 'postillers' (i.e. writers of homilies or paraphrases on the texts prescribed in the liturgical calendar), with John Boys singled out as one of the most reliable.[185] Later editions of *Ecclesiastes* contained even more extensive reading lists (indeed, many surviving copies are interleaved with blank pages for readers to insert their own references), while the growth and specialisation of the London book trade made it

---

[182] Zepper, *Ars Habendi*, D1r.
[183] R. B. and R. A. (i.e. Richard Bernard and Richard Alleine?), *Davids Musick: or Psalmes of that Royal Prophet . . . Unfolded Logically* (1616), A4r.
[184] Bernard, *The Faithfull Shepheard*, F4r.
[185] John Wilkins, *Ecclesiastes, or a Discourse Concerning the Gift of Preaching* (4th edn., 1653), E4v.

increasingly easy for the clergy to get hold of sermons on particular texts or designed to be preached on particular occasions. The London stationer Benjamin Tooke informed a customer in 1688 that there were 'two or three Booksellers who keepe Catalogues of all Sermons whatsoever whether in volumes or single, under the names of the Authors and by the Text they were preached on'.[186]

All this evidence leaves no doubt that printed sermons had a profound influence on oral preaching, not only directly, in supplying preachers with model sermons to use in the pulpit, but also more subtly and indirectly, in conditioning clerical expectations of what a sermon should be. This is vividly illustrated in a number of surviving sermon manuscripts, in which preachers have fair-copied their sermons in the style and format of printed sermons. When Christopher Hudson, lecturer at Preston, copied out a selection of his sermons in 1640 as a present to his godson, he gave them the sort of elaborate titles that had by that time become customary in printed sermons: 'The Best Arte of Thriveing', 'The Pursuit of Peace and Holines', 'The Blessed Flood of Justice', 'The Feareles Feare'.[187] Similarly, when Richard Hunt, preacher at Warwick, made a fair copy of his sermons in 1617, he drew up an eye-catching title page – 'The Sinfull Soules sweete solace, Contayned in the fyftenth Chapter of the Gospell according to St Luke, And in 13 sermons briefly explaned, & with doctrines & uses aptly applyed, to the edification & comfort of all true penitent sinners' – followed by an epistle dedicatory, preface to the reader and list of contents, all modelled on the format of a printed edition. The manuscript preface, somewhat prematurely, invites the reader 'to emend all faultes escaped in the printyng', but if Hunt hoped that his work would eventually appear in print, he was to be disappointed; a mock-imprimatur in another hand, appended to the manuscript, declares unkindly that the author 'neither writes well nor speaks to the point'.[188]

While it is more difficult to gauge the effect of print on lay expectations of preaching, it is clear that laypeople drew extensively on printed sermons when they debated religious matters among themselves. A fascinating case preserved in the State Papers Domestic records an occasion when a Protestant, disputing with a Catholic, made use of a printed sermon by William Crashaw. Christopher Newkirk, examined in July 1615, stated that

---

[186]  Benjamin Tooke to Sir Robert Southwell, 22 September 1688: Derbyshire Record Office, Matlock, D364 Z/B1–45.
[187]  Lancashire Record Office, Preston, DP 353; see R. C. Richardson, *Puritanism in North-West England* (Manchester, 1972), pp. 52, 120, 146, for references to this manuscript.
[188]  Bodleian Library, Oxford, MS Rawl. C.766, ff. 3–5 (preface), 9 (mock-imprimatur, signed 'Ita censeo M. Day, Feb. 18 1619', and heavily crossed out, presumably by the enraged author).

'he mett at Chester in the streete … with one Humfrey Clesbye, who abideth, or dwelleth (as he said) about Morpeth, who talking with him, and a Plaisterer, upon occasion that the Enformer did read in Craweshawes sermon preached at Pauls Cross of the twentie woundes founde in the present Romish Religion: the said Humfrey Clesbie said, they who wrote those were but novesies, who had no grounde, but their owne pregnant wittes, and that they scandalized the Catholickes, and that he hoped, that ere longe were, that there should be an alteration, or redress of their oppression'.[189] This shows how printed sermons could be used, precisely as clergy such as Crashaw hoped they would be used, as a convenient source of anti-Catholic arguments and talking points. It also suggests that the increasingly strident tone of anti-Catholic polemic to be found in printed sermons may have contributed to a general ramping-up of anti-Catholic rhetoric in sermons and private disputations all over the kingdom.

The power of print to procure uniformity was readily apparent to contemporaries. There were some who believed that, just as the printed Book of Common Prayer had been used to bring about uniformity of worship, so printed sermons should be used to bring about uniformity of doctrine. The most far-reaching proposal of this sort was put forward by William Cavendish, Earl of Newcastle, in a treatise of advice addressed to Charles II. Believing, like his old tutor Thomas Hobbes, that unrestricted liberty of prophesying had contributed in large part to the outbreak of the Civil War, Cavendish called for the introduction of a new set of printed homilies dealing with the essential doctrines of the Christian faith – 'Jesus christe our salvation, Godlye life, to avoyde Sin, and exercise charetye, and perpetualye to instructe the people of their obedience to their superiors and Governors' – to be preached in all parishes throughout the kingdom. 'I shoulde wishe no man to preach his own sermons butt such as our Reverende Bishops shoulde aprove off, that is as so many Homiles for the proper Sundayes and Holadayes for the Compas off a yeare to be made and printed, and so sente to Everye Parson off Each parishe to bee prechte, and to preach no other.' Bishops and deans were to be allowed to compose their own sermons, 'butt otherwise all to preach nothinge butt the Printed Sermons'.[190] This proposal never stood much chance of being adopted, but Cavendish had put his finger on a crucial point: that printed

---

[189] Examination of Christopher Newkirk, July 1615: PRO, SP 14/81/54 (calendared in *CSPD 1611–18*, p. 301). William Crashaw's *Sermon Preached at the Crosse* had been printed in 1608 and reprinted in 1609.
[190] S. Arthur Strong, ed., *A Catalogue of Letters and Other Historical Documents Exhibited in the Library at Welbeck* (1903), p. 186.

sermons could have the effect of setting the standards for oral preaching and discouraging deviation from the norm. Thanks to 'a multitude of English books', one commentator remarked in 1663, most people were now well able to 'look through the ignorance of a Clergyman . . . yea, and to chastise his very method and phrase, if he speaks loosely or impertinently'.[191]

By the eighteenth century, printed sermons were so firmly established as the model for oral preaching that there no longer appeared to be any substantial difference between preaching one's own sermon and reading someone else's. This is well illustrated in a celebrated episode of 1712 involving Susanna Wesley, mother of the future Methodist leader, John Wesley. While her husband, Samuel, was absent in London, Susanna took charge of the household prayers and began inviting her neighbours to join her while she read a sermon on Sunday afternoons. Soon these gatherings were attracting several hundred people. 'I chose the best and most awakening sermons we had', she wrote to her husband, and as a result 'those people which used to be playing in the streets, come now to hear a good sermon read, which surely is more acceptable to Almighty God'. When Samuel suggested that someone else should be invited to read the sermons, she firmly refused: 'Alas! you do not consider what a people these are. I do not think one man among them could read a sermon without spelling a good part of it; and how would that edify the rest?'[192] In Methodist historiography this episode is often seen as foreshadowing the later history of the movement, with Susanna's family prayers being the unconscious prototype for her son John's society meetings. But it is also significant in showing how reading and preaching had merged together so closely that a woman reading printed sermons aloud seemed to some hardly distinguishable from her preaching original sermons of her own composition. Indeed, Susanna informed her husband that one local clergyman had objected to the gatherings because 'he thinks the sermons I read better than his own'.

This can also be seen in eighteenth-century handbooks of rhetoric. In William Cockin's treatise of 1775 on *The Art of Delivering Written Language*, preaching is treated in two senses, either as a 'display of oratorical powers' or as the reading aloud of a written discourse:

SERMONS or other ORATIONS . . . may be conceived intended for a double purpose. First as matter for the display of oratorical powers, and secondly, as

---

[191] *Ichabod: or, Five Groans of the Church* (Cambridge, 1663), E3v (p. 36). This tract is sometimes attributed to Thomas Ken, but the *Oxford DNB* rejects the attribution.

[192] Susanna Wesley, *The Complete Writings*, ed. Charles Wallace, Jr (Oxford and New York, 1997), pp. 78–83.

persuasive discourses, &c. which may be read like any other book. Therefore it appears . . . that according as clergymen are possessed of the talents of elocution, they may consistently either rehearse their sermons, in the manner of an extemporary harangue, or deliver them in the more humble capacity of one, who is content to entertain and instruct his hearers with reading to them his own or some other person's written discourse.[193]

Cockin regarded both forms of preaching as equally acceptable: indeed, a preacher might move from one to the other in the course of a single sermon, and 'we are so far from thinking such transitions wrong, that, without a particular attention that way, we scarce ever perceive them at all'. Nothing more was required for effective preaching than the ability to read aloud from a written or printed text – a theory of preaching which naturally reduced its oral dimension to a bare minimum.

By the late eighteenth century, some writers were expressing anxiety about the very dry style of preaching that resulted from over-reliance on a written text. James Burgh, in *The Art of Speaking* (1761), tackled the perennial problem of why preaching was not more popular, and why it seemed to produce so little effect on the hearers. His answer was that, as long as 'reading is thought to be preaching', matters could not improve. Most preachers, he complained, thought that it was enough to read out their sermons from a prepared text, without practising any of the arts of oratory, and the results were predictably dreary. 'If the Greek and Roman orators had *read* their sermons, the effect would have been, I suppose, pretty much the same as that which sermons produce among us. The hearers might have, many of them, *dropped asleep*.'[194] Yet Burgh did not suggest that preachers should abandon the use of a prepared text. Instead, he suggested that they should 'bestow a little pains in committing to memory the substance of their discourses' so that they could deliver their sermons more naturally, without having to glance down at their written notes. And rather than suggesting, as early modern preaching handbooks had done, that preachers should work on their own affections in order to move their hearers, he advised them to follow the example of 'the *actors*, or even of the *actresses*, who, by study and practice . . . attain an elegant and correct utterance'. If preachers could only learn to deliver their lines correctly, and 'labour to acquire a masterly *delivery*', then sermons would begin to rival the popularity of stage plays. 'Places of public *instruction* would be crowded, as places of public *diversion* are now. Rakes and

[193] William Cockin, *The Art of Delivering Written Language; or, an Essay on Reading* (1775), p. 134.
[194] James Burgh, *The Art of Speaking* (1761), p. 32.

infidels, merely to shew their taste, would frequent them. Could *all* frequent them, and *none* profit?'[195]

This did not spell the end of orality in preaching – how could it, when preaching was by definition an oral mode of communication? – and it is certainly not my intention here to portray orality and print as fundamentally opposed, or to suggest that the one was superseded by the other. As Robert Ellison has shown in his excellent study of nineteenth-century preaching, there were still many Victorian preachers who argued for the superior merits of extempore preaching as having 'more life and vigour and power' than the reading of a sermon from a prepared script. But what does seem to have disappeared by the nineteenth century is the idea of a pure oral component to preaching that resisted translation to written or printed form. As Ellison points out, even the great Baptist preacher Charles Haddon Spurgeon, whose sermons were in many ways a self-conscious throwback to the classic puritan tradition of plain preaching and orthodox Calvinist divinity, still 'used the written word throughout the preaching process, writing outlines of his sermons, referring to his outlines as he preached, and revising transcripts for publication', as well as attaching great importance to the circulation of his printed sermons in cheap editions.[196] We began this chapter with D. F. McKenzie's theory of a 'hesitant adjustment' between speech, manuscript and print. Much of this chapter has been devoted to showing that McKenzie was right – and that many seventeenth-century preachers were extremely uncomfortable at the prospect that the words that left their lips might be captured in written or printed form and thereby take on a new life outside their control. By the nineteenth century these hesitations had largely been forgotten, and the ditch between orality and print, which an earlier generation of preachers had been so reluctant to jump over, had become a faint, almost invisible line in the grass.

---

[195] Burgh, *Art of Speaking*, p. 33. For some suggestive remarks on the parallels between eighteenth-century preaching and the theatre, see Harry S. Stout, *The Divine Dramatist: George Whitefield and the Rise of Modern Evangelicalism* (Grand Rapids, MI, 1991), pp. 241–4.

[196] Robert H. Ellison, *The Victorian Pulpit: Spoken and Written Sermons in Nineteenth-Century Britain* (Selinsgrove, PA, and London, 1998), p. 76.

# CHAPTER 4

# *Reconstructing the audience*

One of the frustrations of working on early modern preaching is that we know so little about the audiences who heard the sermons delivered. In some cases, of course, the sermons themselves give us the information we need. Assize sermons, for example, usually end with a series of exhortations addressed to judges, justices of the peace, lawyers, constables, witnesses and jurymen, suggesting that the members of the audience were placed in strict hierarchical order, and that the preacher would have gestured towards each group in turn. But most sermons do not contain this sort of information, leaving us to wonder who might have been included in the preacher's 'dearly beloved'. Was the audience composed of single individuals, or family and household units? Did it include members of all social groups, or were the poorest members of society frequently absent? Were men and women equally represented – and what about children and young people? Without the answers to these questions it is hard to answer the larger questions about the effectiveness of preaching as a means of religious instruction and the social penetration of Protestant ideas.

This is not just a problem for historians of the early modern period. A recent collection of essays entitled *Preacher, Sermon and Audience in the Middle Ages* acknowledges that the difficulty of establishing the intended or actual audience of a given sermon is 'an ongoing problem in the field of sermon studies . . . Identifying the audience is elusive because the sermon text often does not indicate this significant morsel of information.'[1] A further problem is that internal evidence can be deceptive. Medieval collections of *sermones ad status*, addressed to particular persons – soldiers, merchants, farmers, labourers, servants and others – may appear to tell us a great deal about the preachers' relationship with their audience. In fact, as recent scholarship has shown, they have more to do with contemporary perceptions of the social order than with the actual behaviour of particular

---

[1] Carolyn Muessig, ed., *Preacher, Sermon and Audience in the Middle Ages* (Leiden, 2002), p. 6.

social groups.[2] Similarly, the fact that Paul's Cross sermons often contain exhortations to the different estates of the realm does not necessarily mean that members of all these estates were present to hear the sermons preached, but simply that preachers were accustomed to treat the audience at the Cross as a microcosm of the social order.

There is a parallel debate among historians of early modern drama, beginning with Alfred Harbage's *Shakespeare's Audience* (1941), about the social composition of the audience in the playhouses. Some of the most important work in reconstructing the playhouse audience has been done by Andrew Gurr, who makes the crucial point that we should not think of the audience as a single homogeneous mass. There were distinctions between the audiences at different types of playhouse, with the indoor or hall theatres such as Blackfriars serving a more gentlemanly clientele, while the open amphitheatres such as the Red Bull and the Fortune served a more plebeian one. There were further distinctions within the audience at particular theatres, with a sliding scale of admission charges to enable the gentry to sit apart from their social inferiors and closer to the stage. And there is every reason to suppose that authors had these distinctions constantly in mind when writing their plays. As Martin Butler has argued, the social composition of the audience 'comprehensively and continually affected the type of play which was being produced, the way that the audience was addressed, the confidences that were made or withheld, the expectations that were indulged or denied, the range of possibilities that was available or not to the dramatist to attempt and to exploit.'[3]

The late sixteenth and early seventeenth centuries saw major changes in the pattern of sermon attendance, particularly in large cities such as London, where the increasing provision of preaching made it possible to attend sermons more frequently and in a variety of different venues. When the young John Wallington came to London as an apprentice in 1572, there was no preaching ministry in the parish where he lodged, St Andrew Hubbard, and he did not hear a single sermon in the eight years he lived there. Eighty years later, the establishment of a new lectureship in the parish caused his son, Nehemiah Wallington, to reflect on how profoundly things had changed: 'I now have heard neere unto thirty Sarmons in one month at that very Church (besids other places) which

[2]  Muessig, 'Audience and preacher: *ad status* sermons and social classification', in Muessig, ed., *Preacher, Sermon and Audience*, pp. 255–76.
[3]  Andrew Gurr, *Playgoing in Shakespeare's London* (Cambridge, 3rd edn., 2004), pp. 14–15, 26–27, 90; Martin Butler, *Theatre and Crisis 1632–1642* (Cambridge, 1984), p. 305.

my Father could not heare one Sarmon in eight years.'[4] This increase in the supply of preaching, which to Wallington and others was a miraculous sign of God's favour to England, had two contradictory effects. On the one hand, it meant that more people now had access to a regular preaching ministry in their own parish churches. On the other, it offered them a greater freedom of choice, and encouraged the custom of sermon-gadding – crossing parish boundaries to attend sermons in other churches – thus making individual habits of sermon attendance much more difficult to reconstruct.

This chapter uses sermon-gadding as a means to explore the physical and social geography of sermon attendance in early modern England. The first section discusses the contemporary debate on sermon-gadding, while the second section looks at the practice of sermon-gadding in London, where the patterns of sermon attendance were exceptionally intricate and complex. In an earlier chapter I set myself the challenge of trying to 'hear' what an early modern sermon might have sounded like; I now want to propose a similar challenge in trying to 'see', in the mind's eye, what the audience at an early modern sermon might have looked like, in the hope that a clearer mental image of the audience may lead to a richer understanding of the sermons themselves. In doing so I also want to draw out some of the parallels between preaching and the theatre. These have recently attracted the attention of a number of scholars who have argued that the apparent antithesis between sermons and plays – assiduously propagated by the preachers, who portrayed the stage as the ungodly antitype of the pulpit – actually conceals the close similarities between the two.[5] Gurr has shown how evidence from sermon notebooks can be used to reconstruct the mental range of educated playgoers, giving us an insight into how far they might have been able to remember passages from a play or recognise the playwright's literary allusions.[6] Following these leads, I want to explore some of the ways in which, through a close attention to the audience, the culture of sermongoing and the culture of playgoing can be used to shed light on each other.

---

[4] Nehemiah Wallington, 'An extract of the passages of my life', Folger Shakespeare Library, Washington, V.a.436, p. 203, printed in David Booy, ed., *The Notebooks of Nehemiah Wallington, 1618–1654: A Selection* (Aldershot, 2007), p. 299.

[5] I have in mind Jeffrey Knapp, *Shakespeare's Tribe: Church, Nation and Theater in Renaissance England* (Chicago, 2002), esp. pp. 115–20, and Peter Lake and Michael Questier, *The Antichrist's Lewd Hat: Protestants, Papists and Players in Post-Reformation England* (New Haven and London, 2002), esp. pp. 483–504.

[6] Gurr, *Playgoing in Shakespeare's London*, p. 98.

## THE DEBATE ON SERMON-GADDING

Sermon-gadding is generally regarded as one of the issues that divided puritans from their opponents, following the lines of the reading/preaching debate which we encountered in Chapter 1. Those who accepted the reading/preaching distinction, and saw preaching as the ordinary means of salvation, could not be content with a mere reading ministry. Viewed in this light, sermon-gadding was a sign of godly zeal, indeed a positive necessity for anyone lacking a regular supply of preaching in their own parish. By contrast, those who did not accept the reading/preaching distinction saw no reason why laypeople should abandon the ministry of their own pastor in order to hear sermons elsewhere. Viewed in this light, sermon-gadding was a worrying sign that some people were becoming dangerously addicted to sermons and were ready to break away from the lawful ministry of the Church of England in order to satisfy their craving. The situation was further complicated by the fact that sermon-gadding occupied a legal grey area. The 1552 Act of Uniformity required the laity to come to their parish church every Sunday, 'or upon reasonable let thereof to some usual place where common prayer and such service of God shall be used in such time of let . . . and then and there to abide orderly and soberly during the time of the common prayer, preachings or other service of God there to be used and ministered'.[7] This could be interpreted as requiring them to attend preaching as well as common prayer, thus making it possible for Sir Henry Marten, dean of the Arches, to argue in 1628 that there was no law forbidding a man to go to hear sermons in other parishes if he had none in his own.[8] Alternatively, it could be interpreted as tying them to their own parish churches, thus placing sermon-gadding outside the law.

It thus comes as no surprise to find that the most outspoken attacks on sermon-gadding come from the pens of anti-puritan polemicists. They included Thomas Willis, minister of Preston in Suffolk, who seized the opportunity offered by a sermon on Jude verse 19 ('these be they who separate themselves') to deliver an impassioned attack on those of his parishioners who gadded to sermons in Norwich or Bury. 'As sheep troubled with an itch in their hyde, runn frisking and scrapping continually from bush to bush, from feild to feild, from pasture to pasture . . . So this

---

[7] G.R. Elton, ed., *The Tudor Constitution: Documents and Commentary* (Cambridge, 2nd edn., 1982), p. 406.

[8] Patrick Collinson, *The Religion of Protestants: The Church in English Society 1559–1625* (Oxford, 1982), p. 249.

itch, in the eare of the giddye and unstayed hearers, makes them run and ryde, from church to church, from parish to parish, from towne to towne, in such a fyerie and feirce agony of unquenchable lust, to heare the new preacher and the new sermon, that they cannot brooke nor digeast the wholsome doctryne, that they have dayly, at home.' Willis offered various proof-texts against sermon-gadding, including Hebrews 13: 17 ('Obey them that have the oversight of you') and John 10: 27 ('My sheep hear my voice'),'which wordes', he argued, 'though they properly signifie the inseperable combination and association betwixt christe and the elect, yet in a generallitye they contayne a very lively simillitude betwixt a pastor and a parisshioner'.[9]

The sermon was first delivered in 1613, but acquired new relevance fourteen years later, in 1627, when – to Willis's delight – Bishop Samuel Harsnett's visitation articles for the diocese of Norwich inquired whether there were any parishioners 'having a preacher to their minister, that doe absent themselves from his sermons, and resort to other places to hear other preachers'.[10] This official crackdown on sermon-gadding encouraged Willis to revise his sermon (which, he noted, had angered some of his hearers so much that they remained unreconciled 'to this very day') and put it into private circulation. The surviving copy of his sermon includes some of the enthusiastic responses that he received from his friends, including 'I. N.' (unidentified, but probably one of Willis's neighbour ministers in Suffolk) who even broke into verse to express his approval:

> Unfeynedly, without all flatterye,
> I like this Purytano-Batterye.

Indeed, Willis's sermon includes many of the stock themes of anti-puritan polemic, such as the allegation that puritan preachers were swollen with pride by the acclamations of their hearers: 'When they have ended their sermons, they descend out of their Pulpitts . . . They shall have a multitude crowding to see their persons . . . some thronging to speake to them, to salute them, to shake hands with them, to thanke them, to bowe more knees to them than ever they did to the name of Jesus, to invite them to all dayntye feastes . . .' Willis also pointed out – very shrewdly, as we shall see – that sermon-gadding was a highly divisive issue among the clergy, one which 'hath allready caused more variance, dislike and hatred among the

[9] Thomas Willis, Bodleian Library, Oxford, MS Rawl. E.21, ff. 74r, 77v.
[10] Kenneth Fincham, ed., *Visitation Articles and Injunctions of the Early Stuart Church*, (Church of England Record Society, 1994–8), vol. 1, p. 166. This inquiry had first appeared in Bishop John Overall's visitation articles of 1619, though Willis seems to have been unaware of this.

sheppards themselves . . . [than] all our fyerie puritans will be able soundly to quench perhapps while they live'.

It would be easy to conclude that opinion on sermon-gadding divided cleanly along puritan and anti-puritan lines; and some recent scholarship has indeed presented sermon-gadding as one of the distinctive features of puritan culture. Martin Ingram, for example, describes it as 'the most characteristic offence of puritan laypeople'.[11] Patrick Collinson has suggested that it could be an ostentatious display of religious difference, 'an organized, demonstrative thing' which, by undermining the institution of the parish, might have accentuated a tendency towards semi-separatism.[12] Yet the puritan attitude to sermon-gadding was considerably more ambivalent than this might suggest. In the case of parishes with no resident preaching minister, there was general agreement among puritan divines that parishioners ought to be free, for the good of their souls, to attend sermons elsewhere. But what of parishioners who did have a preaching minister, but deliberately absented themselves from his sermons in order to hear another preacher whose sermons they preferred? This was far more problematic: and while most puritan divines were willing to defend the general principle of sermon-gadding, there were far fewer who were prepared to grant the laity the unrestricted right to choose between different preachers, as if the parochial system were nothing more than an administrative convenience.

Sermon-gadding began to emerge as a potential problem for the puritan clergy in the late Elizabethan period, as the number of preaching ministers started to increase and, for the first time, preachers found themselves competing with each other for an audience. It became a long-running and intractable problem for the members of the Dedham conference in the 1580s, as they struggled to mediate between two rival Colchester ministers, Robert Lewis and George Northey.[13] Lewis and Northey were of comparable age and seniority, Lewis having been appointed vicar of St Peter's, Colchester, in 1579, and Northey the town's 'common preacher' in 1580,

---

[11] Martin Ingram, 'Puritans and the Church courts', in C. Durston and J. Eales, eds., *The Culture of English Puritanism 1560–1700* (New York, 1996), pp. 58–91 (ref. p. 87); see also Durston and Eales's introduction to the same volume, p. 20, where sermon-gadding is treated as part of a distinctive 'puritan ethos'.

[12] Patrick Collinson, *The Elizabethan Puritan Movement* (London, 1967), pp. 373–4, reiterated in 'The politics of religion and the religion of politics in Elizabethan England', *Historical Research*, 82 (2009), pp. 74–92 (quotation p. 90).

[13] The following account is based on the records of the Dedham conference (John Rylands Library, Manchester, MS 874) as edited by Patrick Collinson, John Craig and Brett Usher in *Conferences and Combination Lectures in the Elizabethan Church: Dedham and Bury St Edmunds 1582–1590* (Church of England Record Society: Woodbridge, Suffolk, and Rochester, NY, 2003).

when they were both around the age of thirty, so Lewis was understandably annoyed when he found some of his parishioners starting to drift away from St Peter's in order to attend Northey's sermons. In February 1583 Lewis asked the Dedham conference to determine 'whether the people ought to leave their pastor when he teacheth to goe to heare others ordenarely'. The conference ruled in his favour, agreeing that it was 'meete that the people of every congregation shuld joigne with their owne pastors in the use of the word and Sacramentes', but attempted to heal the rift between the two men by ordering Lewis to give up his course of sermons on Genesis, 'the same texte beinge publikely at the same tyme enterpreted by Mr Northey' – perhaps a tacit recognition that Northey was the better preacher of the two.

The conflict between Lewis and Northey dragged on for another six years. In April 1585, Lewis requested advice on 'what course he shuld take with some, that refused to heare him on the lordes daie when Mr [Northey] did preache, and told of one woman that professed a desire to come to the Communion with him, and yet thought she shuld not overcome herself to be present at the Sacrament bicause she shuld lose thexercise of the worde'. The conference put off a decision for several months before finally appointing three of its members to speak to Northey and the Colchester bailiffs in an attempt to reach a settlement. In March 1587, Lewis 'moved the brethren to have their hande set to a writinge for confirmation of that which they had alreadie set downe, that a Pastor shuld have his owne people'. This led to 'much debating', with some of the clergy suggesting that it should be delivered as a point of doctrine in their sermons, and others objecting that this would be 'daungerous', but it was finally agreed 'that if two or three of the brethren did againe talke with Mr Northie and the people of it, and could not prevaile', then they should put it in writing. Further discussions with Northey proved fruitless, but the promised agreement in writing was not forthcoming. In February 1588 Lewis asked the conference, in evident frustration, 'what he might doe for his matter soe often propounded to them'. Again the conference put off a firm decision, but a year later Lewis took matters into his own hands by leaving Colchester to take up a new post at Bury St Edmunds.

Reading between the lines of the Dedham conference minutes, it seems clear that the Essex puritan clergy were torn on the issue of sermon-gadding, with most of them feeling that Lewis had right on his side but reluctant to issue a firm ruling in his favour. Part of the explanation may lie in the fact that, on other occasions, sermon-gadding could work very much to their advantage. In the town of Maldon, only a few years later, it provided a way for the godly to express their preference for the town preacher, George

Gifford, over the vicar, Robert Palmer. According to one disgruntled parishioner, writing in 1596, Gifford's lectures had drawn large crowds from the surrounding area, so much so that when they were discontinued, the shopkeepers of Maldon protested that they were 'greatly decayed and become poore for wante of the concourse of people on those dayes'. Meanwhile, Palmer found himself preaching to empty pews: 'If Mr Gyffard preach, the church is full, but if the other, not half so.' On the days when Palmer was preaching, 'the phantasticall sort run by flockes, two or three myles off, to one Ralph Hawden, another Gifford (so knowen to be this two seaven yeares) or rather the very same, as well in consent for his part as conceipte for theirs'.[14] Both Gifford and Hawden were members of the Dedham conference, whereas Palmer, who had succeeded Gifford as vicar of Maldon after the latter's deprivation for nonconformity, was despised by the godly for allegedly spending his days in the bowling alley and his nights in the alehouse.[15]

The private debates which had taken place behind closed doors in the Dedham conference, and no doubt elsewhere, finally emerged into the public domain in an anonymous pamphlet entitled *Sophronistes* (1589), which takes the form of a dialogue between two London sermongoers, Arizelus and Sophronistes, on the morality of sermon-gadding. Arizelus explains that he is dissatisfied with the sermons of his own minister: 'Our Pastor M. Timotheus I have always esteemed and knowne to be a right honest and godly man, and one that walketh blamelesse with his people. I also acknowledge his learning and understanding in holy things to be sufficient for mine instruction. Hee wanteth not also a plaine and easy kind of utterance, neere unto the meane and weake capacitie of the multitude.' But 'I never delighted in his Ministerie, nor tooke my selfe anything edified thereby', finding his sermons 'always dead and without spirit in mine eares' – and for this reason, Arizelus explains, he has taken to attending the sermons of another London preacher, 'master Eulalus, who of late began to preach beyond the River'. He admits that the sermons of Master Eulalus are no different in doctrine from those of Master Timotheus, 'but the handling is all, wherein this man passeth all that I have heard'.[16] In reply,

---

[14]  William Arthur to Gabriel Goodman, dean of Westminster, 25 March 1596: Westminster Abbey muniments, no. 8125. Goodman was involved in the town's affairs because the parish of St Mary's, Maldon, was a peculiar of the dean and chapter of Westminster: see Collinson, Craig and Usher, *Conferences and Combination Lectures*, p. 211.

[15]  On Palmer, see Collinson, *Elizabethan Puritan Movement*, p. 377, and Collinson, Craig and Usher, *Conferences and Combination Lectures*, pp. 92–3, 212.

[16]  *Sophronistes. A Dialogue, Perswading the People to Reverence and Attend the Ordinance of God, in the Ministerie of Their Owne Pastors* (1589), C2v–3v.

his friend Sophronistes tries to persuade him that this is not a sufficient reason to forsake the sermons of his own minister.

Sophronistes' first argument is based on the principle underlying the parochial system, that 'everie congregation or parish shoulde consist of so manie Christians, as are meete for one assemblie, and are nearest seated unto the place of the exercises of Religion for their better and more easier accesse thereunto'. This, he argues, is not merely a matter of custom or tradition, but a God-given ordinance dating back to the very beginning of the Christian Church, when the apostles separated new converts into distinct congregations, each with its own elders (Acts 14: 23). Thus 'it is of God, and not of man, that severall Pastors are imposed upon severall congregations, and several congregations allotted unto several Pastors'. Arizelus willingly concedes the point. 'I will make no further question of this matter, for I plainelie see, that as the commonwelth is devided into Cities, Townes, and families: so it must needs be also in the Church. And you have sufficientlie prooved unto me, that the distinction of perticuler Churches or assemblies, is not of humaine but divine ordination.'

Sophronistes' second argument – following from the first – is that clergy and congregations are joined together in a reciprocal relationship: just as ministers are bound to preach to their people, so the people are bound to be faithful to their ministers. 'If the Pastor must feed his owne flocke, and that because the Lord hath appointed unto him to break unto them the bread of life: tell mee (I pray you) how are not the people likewise bound to submit themselves unto his ministerie: and to receive their foode at his hand, whom God hath commaunded to feede them?' 'That I cannot grant', protests Arizelus. 'Why so?' asks Sophronistes. 'Because', Arizelus replies, 'I think it not unlawful to use the better and more fruitefull gifts of other Pastors, if may be, unto my farther edifying and comfort.' There follows a quick-fire exchange of New Testament proof-texts, in which Sophronistes tries to convince his friend that God does not speak 'by every pastor unto all churches', but 'to every church principally by her owne Pastor'. Arizelus is finally persuaded – but only reluctantly. 'My judgement yeeldeth to that you say; but my heart and affection dooth yet strive against it.'[17]

It must be stressed that this is not a debate between a puritan sympathiser and an anti-puritan opponent. Despite their differences, Arizelus and Sophronistes share a lot of common ground: they take it for granted that the purpose of the parish system is to provide a regular supply of preaching; they agree that 'the pastor is strictlie tied unto his flocke'; and they both

---

[17] *Sophronistes*, B3r–C2r.

employ the same method of scripture-based argumentation. In short, this is a debate *within* Puritanism; and although the dialogue is constructed so as to give Sophronistes an easy victory, there is no reason to doubt its overall accuracy as a reflection of real-life debates in puritan circles, in London and elsewhere, about the legitimacy of sermon-gadding.[18] It would thus be a mistake to regard sermon-gadding as a standard feature of puritan culture, or as a logical consequence of the puritan emphasis on preaching. Some of the strongest opposition to sermon-gadding came, in fact, from moderate puritan clergy, who regarded it as a dangerous step in the direction of separatism. *Sophronistes* ends with a stern warning: 'Some have gon from their own [minister] to others, and from them to none at all, or to such as have carried them into most strange and dangerous opinions', even into the heresies of 'the Brownists, Anabaptists, or the Familie of Love'.[19]

The deeply ambivalent attitude of puritan clergy towards sermon-gadding emerges again in the sermons of Arthur Hildersham, lecturer at Ashby de la Zouch in Leicestershire. In a sermon preached on 19 June 1610, Hildersham came out strongly in favour of the practice of sermon-gadding: 'I dare not condemne such Christians, as having Pastours in the places where they live, of meaner gifts, do desire . . . to enjoy the Ministry of such as have better gifts; and sometimes do leave their owne, to heare the other.' The only conditions he laid down were that sermon-gadders should not show 'contempt of their own Pastours' or be a cause of 'scandall and offence to them and their people'.[20] Four weeks later, however, Hildersham returned to the subject, declaring that his previous remarks were 'not well understood by some', and that he therefore wished 'to deliver my minde more fully and plainely for the resolving of this doubt'. His attitude to sermon-gadding had now changed completely. 'No Christian may usually and ordinarily leave his owne Pastour . . . to heare another of better gifts.' He warned his hearers that they had no right to gad to sermons without the permission of their own minister, for 'thou owest a duty to him, as to thy superiour, in the things that belong to thy soule'. Even though their minister's sermons might be 'farre inferiour to some others', they were still obliged to attend them as long as he was 'consciable in his place, and of unblameable life'.[21]

---

[18] It may even refer to particular individuals: Master Eulalus, 'who of late began to preach beyond the River', may be Edward Philips, who had taken up his lectureship at St Saviour's, Southwark, in 1588.

[19] *Sophronistes*, D2r.

[20] Arthur Hildersham, *CVIII Lectures upon the Fourth of Iohn* (2nd edn., 1632), Y6r (p. 253).

[21] Hildersham, *CVIII Lectures*, 2A1v (p. 268).

Hildersham's efforts to save face by presenting this as merely a clarification of his earlier teaching cannot disguise the fact that it was an almost complete retraction. Something, or someone, had caused Hildersham to withdraw his support for sermon-gadding. The most likely explanation is that, as in Essex, some kind of presbyterian organisation was in operation among the puritan clergy in Leicestershire, and that Hildersham had been called to order by his fellow ministers, who may have complained that they were losing a large proportion of their audience to him. If so, then Hildersham's sermons give us another valuable insight into the internal debates among the puritan clergy. In defence of sermon-gadding, Hildersham claimed that some ministers were preaching sermons that were too simple for their audience: it was, he declared, 'a great shame for a Teacher, to have nothing but milke to set before his people, that are able to beare, and stand in neede of strong meate'. He advised such ministers to 'teach diligently, teach zealously, teach profitably, using not onely doctrine, but application, grounding thy exhortations and reproofes substantially upon sound doctrine', implying that some ministers were losing their audience because they did not employ the preferred doctrine-and-use method in their sermons. He also hinted that much of the clerical opposition to sermon-gadding was purely self-serving, since the ministers who were 'most vehement and bitter in complaining of their people for going from them' were, for the most part, the very ones who were least able to 'teach profitably'.[22]

However, Hildersham also admitted that some people were rejecting their ministers, and gadding to sermons elsewhere, on insufficient grounds. Some 'admire and follow another, rather than their owne Pastour, because hee can make more ostentation of eloquence, and learning, and such like humane gifts', while others 'leave their owne Pastour, and goe to others, onely for varieties sake'. A third group 'preferre others before their owne Pastours, onely because they shew more zeale in their voice, and gesture, and phrase of speech, and manner of delivery; though (haply) the Doctrine it selfe be nothing so wholesome, or powerfull, or fit to edifie their conscience, as the Doctrine of their owne Pastour is. These, though they be the best of the three sorts, and pretend much love and zeale, yet we may wish to them more knowledge and judgement.' Even more worryingly, some people were reported to avoid the sermons of their own minister because 'hee knowes them better than a stranger' and could therefore be more specific in reproving their sins. Hildersham conceded that these were

---

[22] Hildersham, *CVIII Lectures*, 2A3v (p. 272).

unacceptable reasons for semon-gadding, and exhorted all sermon-gadders to examine their own consciences to ensure that they 'seeke nothing in it but sound edification only'.[23]

These were all fairly pragmatic arguments against sermon-gadding, based on personal and pastoral considerations. But there was another reason why many of the puritan clergy were reluctant to endorse sermon-gadding, which was that it appeared to contradict their own presbyterian principles. The point was not lost on their opponents. Bishop Aylmer argued for the removal of Thomas Barber from his lectureship at St Mary le Bow in 1583 not only because it was against the canons of the primitive church 'to have any stranger to intrude hym selfe into another mans flocke' but also because 'yt is against their own Cartwritian doctrine'.[24] This was also one of the arguments used by Thomas Willis, who, though no presbyterian himself, gleefully cited presbyterian writings – including 'Mr Travers, in his booke of Ecclesiasticall discipline', and the *Fruitful Sermon* on Romans 12: 3–6 generally attributed to Laurence Chaderton – to the effect that ministers had no authority to preach outside their own pastoral charge. As Willis pointed out, many divines believed that a minister and his flock were like 'a husband and his married wife, so that the one ought never to forsake the other till death part them . . . Hereupon some ministers have seemed upon meere conscience this way, never to goe from their chosen people, though other places that wanted a pastor have desired them, and offered more large maytenance than they had in their owne former charge.' He quoted with approval the 'order of the Election of Ministers in Scotland', which took the form of a mutual contract between minister and people, 'even moste like the solemnization of marriage in our English churches'.

Willis was, of course, citing these examples for polemical purposes, in order to embarrass his opponents. However, many puritans did indeed view the relationship between pastor and people as a form of spiritual wedlock, analogous to the relationship between husband and wife. In 1585 the Dedham classis debated whether Bartimaeus Andrewes, vicar of Wenham, could lawfully resign his cure to take up a new post as town preacher at Yarmouth, and, more generally, 'whether a pastor called to a place may leave the people they being unwilling of his departure'. There was a strong feeling that he should not, one speaker remarking 'that ther was a neere coniunction betwene the Pastor and the people that thone should not

[23] Hildersham, *CVIII Lectures*, 2A2v (p. 270).
[24] Aylmer to Sir Francis Walsingham, 11 March 1583, BL Egerton MS 1693, f. 103.

forsake thother no more then man and wieff shuld'.[25] Similarly, during the plague epidemic of 1603 there was a dispute among the London clergy on whether it was lawful for a minister to flee into the country to escape the risk of infection. One participant in the debate, 'W. T.' (possibly Walter Travers), argued that ministers should not desert their people under any circumstances. 'A wife chooseth her husband for terme of life, as well in sicknes as in health . . . So you being, or at least ought to be as a husband to the Church, whom in love you are devoted to . . . will you in time of sicknes runne from it, and not comfort it? then you must either take her for a whore, and no wife, whom you cannot love; or prove an unkind, or no husband, to leave her in her most miserie.'[26]

Not all puritans were presbyterians, yet the distinctively presbyterian insistence on the indissoluble relationship between pastor and people helped to create the lofty ideal on which most puritan clergy tried to model themselves, of the minister as shepherd, guardian and watchman, exercising a wide-ranging spiritual authority over his flock. Moreover, the early modern fascination with correspondences made it perfectly natural to see the minister's relationship to his people as equivalent to that of the husband to his wife.[27] Preaching on Matthew 12: 25 ('Every city or house divided against itself, shall not stand'), Robert Jenison, lecturer at Newcastle upon Tyne, sought to demonstrate 'the benefit of union between pastor and people, and the danger of division' by analogy with 'all the other relations in the house, of husband and wife, father and child, master and servant, and in the city of Magistrate and people'. Such an analogy could be used to stress the duty of a minister towards his people, and the mutual love that should exist between them, as between husband and wife. But it could also serve to draw attention to the minister's authority over his flock: as Jenison argued, the people owed their pastor not only a personal tribute of 'affection and love' but also 'obedience' to his teaching.[28]

The obvious implication was that sermon-gadding was a form of spiritual adultery. Samuel Clarke's eulogy of Mrs Margaret Corbet shows how

[25] Collinson, Craig and Usher, *Conferences and Combination Lectures*, pp. 20–1.
[26] W. T., *A Casting Up of Accounts of Certain Errors* (1603), C3r, C4r. On this controversy, see Paul Slack, *The Impact of Plague in Tudor and Stuart England* (1985), pp. 228–35.
[27] For a typical example, see Richard Turnbull, *An Exposition upon the XV. Psalme* (1592), D3r, where the reciprocal duties of husband and wife are said to be 'derived' from those of pastor and people. In William Bradshaw's congregational model of Church government, the analogy is turned on its head, with the congregation compared to the husband and the minister to the wife. Bradshaw, *English Puritanisme* (1605), B4r.
[28] Letter from Robert Jenison to Samuel Ward, 2 April 1628: Bodleian Library, Oxford, MS Tanner 72, f. 269.

natural it seemed to associate the fidelity of a good wife towards a beloved
husband with that of a godly parishioner towards a beloved minister. 'She
kept close to the public Ministry where she lived . . . She neither was of their
opinion, nor practice, who out of I know not what kinde of singularity,
separate from the Ministry of a godly Pastor and Husband.' And this sort of
patriarchal rhetoric, as used by puritan clergy to discourage sermon-gadding,
spilled over into anti-puritan invective as well. There was a lively tradition of
scandalous stories about women who went to sermons on their own: in 1587 a
Colchester innkeeper told two country yeomen that 'there be a sort of women
of thys towne that goe to the Sermons with the bookes under their
armes . . . & when they come there the whores must be pued & there they
set & slepe & what they doe we cannot see & then they come home to there
husbandes & saye he made a good & godlye Sermon, & yet they playe the
Whores before they com home'. A witness in a London consistory court case
in 1629 told a similar tale about a woman who 'did make shewe of going to a
sermon unto St Antholins Church', whose husband, fearing 'that she goinge
without a man went to play the whore, followed after her, and observed her to
goe into a bawdy house in St Swithins Lane'.[29] These stories show how easily
sermon-gadding could be associated with marital infidelity. Similar stories
were told about women going to the theatre, which tells us something about
the way that sermons and plays, as forms of leisure activity in which women
could participate without their husbands, occupied the same cultural space
and inspired some of the same anxieties.[30]

The husband-and-wife analogy also served as an argument against pluralism, which could be seen as another form of spiritual adultery. 'Can it be
honesty for any mans wife, to love another womans husband?' demanded
Thomas Myriell in a Paul's Cross sermon of 1623. He was referring not to
sermon-gadding, but to clergy who held both a country living and a city
lectureship, and to the laity who supported them. 'You have here in this
City, many that feede upon your bounty, who have Livings, yea, charge of
soules of their owne abroad in the Countrey. Do you thinke you doe well,
to give entertainment to these men?'[31] The same charge was levelled, even

[29] Mark Byford, 'The price of Protestantism: assessing the impact of religious change on Elizabethan
    Essex' (unpublished DPhil thesis, University of Oxford, 1988), p. 413; Laura Gowing, *Domestic
    Dangers: Women, Words and Sex in Early Modern London* (Oxford, 1996), p. 68.
[30] On women at the theatre, see Gurr, *Playgoing in Shakespeare's London*, pp. 7–9. See also Laura
    Gowing, '"The freedom of the streets": women and social space, 1560–1640', in Paul Griffiths and
    Mark Jenner, eds., *Londinopolis: Essays in the Cultural and Social History of Early Modern London*
    (Manchester, 2000), pp. 130–51, and J.F. Merritt, *The Social World of Early Modern Westminster*
    (Manchester, 2005), pp. 171–2.
[31] Thomas Myriell, *The Christians Comfort* (1623), H4r.

more bluntly in a contemporary anti-puritan epigram, '*In Ecclesias Puritanicas, ac Pastores duplo beneficiatos*':

> The pastor husband is, the church his wife;
> Each should be knit to other during life.
> Many pure-whorish churches have we then,
> Who love their husbands less than other men,
> And whoremongers to one who should be tied,
> And yet with two wives scarce are satisfied.[32]

It was thus very difficult for puritan divines to condone sermon-gadding, which not only contravened their presbyterian principles but also laid them open to charges of hypocrisy if they criticised other clergy for pluralism and absenteeism.

The fullest development of the husband-and-wife analogy is to be found, appropriately enough, in a letter from a husband to his wife. Writing from London in July 1606, Sir John Coke copied out an 'accompt of a sermon preched here this last saboth by a zealous minister of verie good note' which he thought would interest his wife, Mary. (He added that he had not been present at the sermon, and was relying on someone else's notes – an interesting example of the way that sermon notes circulated among the laity.) The sermon put forward a wide-ranging doctrine of social, political and religious obedience, arguing that as subjects were not entitled to disobey a wicked monarch, nor husbands to divorce an unfaithful wife, so parishioners were not entitled to forsake an unworthy minister:

Wee doe not sett them as pastors over our sowls by yeelding to heare them, more than wee place the Magistrates over us by yeilding to obey them. But as the king and the state placeth Magistrates and officers over us whom we must obey, bee they good or bad: so it is the church that appoincteth Ministers unto us whom wee must heare bee they never so unworthie ... Neither are wee bownd to change our dwellings, or to seperate our selves from that congregation or parish wher god hath geven us our portion, in regard of the insufficiencie or mislyke of our minister, more than subjects are bownd to change their contrie, if they doe live under a wicked king: or husbands to forsake their wives if they bee unfaithfull: or children to leave their parents if they bee ungodlie: or servants to forsake their masters if they bee not devout.

It followed that even though ministers might be 'insufficient and contemptible ... yet wee must not refuse to joyne with them and to

---

[32] W. C. Hazlitt, ed., *Inedited Poetical Miscellanies* (1870), from a manuscript of 'Verses translated and epigrammes satyricall composed upon sundry offered occasions', written in the 1620s.

heare them in the publique service of the church'. If God places unworthy
ministers over us, our duty is not 'to seperate our selves from the congregation' but rather 'to humble our selves under gods hand: and to strive by
our diligence and zeale to supplie the wants of our ordinarie means'. We are
to worship God not 'in private conventicles ... nor in scandalous and
disordered pilgrimages, but everie one in his vocation and place of his
charge'.[33]

Coke's letter is an excellent illustration of what Patrick Collinson calls
the 'conservative, presbyterian puritan conscience' wedded to 'the principle
of a settled parish ministry'.[34] Yet it also resembles certain forms of anti-
puritan polemic – as, for example, when Coke comments, with regard to the
danger of 'private conventicles', that 'good men here begin to take knowledg
of this factious doctrine which the unseasoned zeale of some as it seemeth
hath lately brought hither [from abroad] to make our rent greater, and
instead of reforming to ruin our church'. Here, as elsewhere, the puritan
and anti-puritan positions on sermon-gadding seem to blend into one
another. This is not simply an instance of the polemical appropriation of
puritan arguments by anti-puritan writers; rather, it reflects the fact that the
godly and their opponents held similar assumptions about order and
hierarchy, which made it natural for them to use similar arguments against
the perceived disorder of sermon-gadding. Indeed, as far as the debate
on sermon-gadding is concerned, the difference between puritan and
anti-puritan writers seems far less significant than the difference between
moderate puritans whose theory of Church discipline was essentially presbyterian, and radical puritans whose theory of Church discipline was closer
to the congregational idea of the gathered Church – this being the faultline
that would eventually develop, in the 1640s, into the division between
Presbyterians and Independents.

Christopher Hill and others have argued that there was an inherent
congregational tendency within Puritanism, leading to the disintegration
of the traditional parish community and to a new form of religious
organisation in which the parish, 'a geographical unit which brings the
members of a community together for cultural, social and ceremonial
purposes', was replaced by the sect, 'a voluntary unit to which men
belong in order to hear the preacher of their choice'. Hill regarded

---

[33] John Coke to his wife Mary, 1 July 1606: BL Add. MS 64874, ff. 78–9 (calendared in *HMC
Cowper* I: 62).
[34] Collinson, *Religion of Protestants*, p. 245.

sermon-gadding as a prime example of this trend. 'In the early seventeenth century men broke the law by straying from their own parish to hear a favourite preacher; or they hired a lecturer to preach their chosen theology. Looking back we can see each of these as a half-way stage on the way towards congregational independency.'[35] This argument has been carried further by David Zaret, again with specific reference to sermon-gadding. Zaret sees sermon-gadding as an expression of 'lay intellectual initiative', one which was discouraged by the ecclesiastical authorities, and indeed by many of the puritan clergy, but 'emerged more fully and openly' during the Civil War 'in the form of congregationalism and free lay choice of ministers'.[36]

It would be quite wrong to suggest that there was an inbuilt logic within Puritanism leading naturally and inevitably to congregationalism and separatism. As the work of Patrick Collinson, Peter Lake and others has made abundantly clear, Puritanism was in many respects a highly conservative movement, very far from the seedbed of social revolution that Hill suggests in *Society and Puritanism in Pre-Revolutionary England*. And as we have seen, it was not easy for puritans to make the case for sermon-gadding, as it challenged the received view of the pastor as the 'husband' of his people, and also undermined their arguments against clerical pluralism. However, Zaret's view of sermon-gadding as an expression of 'lay intellectual initiative' opens up a more promising line of inquiry. Sermon-gadding enabled the laity to compare the sermons of different preachers and – in the words of Arizelus to Sophronistes – 'to heare those by whom I am most edified'. It did not lead automatically to separatism, but, in Collinson's words, it helped to create the sort of 'fluid and unstable religious environment' that was one of the preconditions for the growth of separatist congregations.[37] In the next section, we will look at this 'fluid and unstable religious environment' as it existed in early modern London, and consider whether it was necessarily destructive of the parish system, or whether it was possible for parochial and congregational patterns of church attendance to coexist.

---

[35] Christopher Hill, *Society and Puritanism in Pre-Revolutionary England* (New York, 1964), pp. 492–3. Susan Brigden makes a similar argument in *London and the Reformation* (Oxford, 1991), p. 635, where she suggests that the long-term effect of sermon-gadding was to 'undermine the solidarity of the Christian community of the territorial parish'.

[36] David Zaret, *The Heavenly Contract: Ideology and Organization in Pre-Revolutionary Puritanism* (Chicago and London, 1985), pp. 116–22.

[37] Collinson, *Religion of Protestants*, p. 276.

PATTERNS OF SERMON ATTENDANCE

Early modern London was widely regarded by contemporaries as the great success story of the English Reformation.[38] In 1571 a visiting preacher at Paul's Cross declared that to come from the country to the City was to 'come into another world, even out of darkness into light. For here the word of God is plentifully preached'.[39] Anthony Maxey, preaching at court in 1606, gave a graphic description of London on a Sunday morning, with its crowded churches and empty streets:

How generally is [the sabbath] observed, how religiously sanctified, even in this great and busie Citie, wherein the streetes may often be seene in a manner desolate, and few stirring upon the Saboth, in the time of divine prayer and preaching: The painfull preaching frequented with infinite congregations, and mightie assemblies in this famous Citie; the diligent and daylie prayers, the devotion and thanksegiving, the readinesse and attention in hearing the word of God both preached and reade even in this place where I stand, doth witnesse what I say.[40]

For many visitors to London – such as the godly Lady Margaret Hoby, or the Hampshire MP Sir Richard Paulet – the abundance of preaching was one of the capital's main attractions. Indeed, one preacher even suggested that the generous supply of 'Lectures and Exercises ... every day, and almost every hour of the day' was the reason why so many country gentry had chosen to move to London with their families.[41]

The large number of churches within easy walking distance of each other made it a simple matter for Londoners to cross parish boundaries, and led to some heroic feats of sermon attendance. Stephen Denison's funeral sermon for Mrs Elizabeth Juxon records that 'when she was in the Citie, she heard for the most part, nine or ten Sermons every weeke; whereof foure of them constantly upon the Sabbath day, besides catechizing' – and even this record was surpassed by the indefatigable Nehemiah Wallington, who once

---

[38] Important general studies of religion in early modern London include H.G. Owen, 'The London parish clergy in the reign of Elizabeth I' (London, PhD thesis, 1957); Paul Seaver, *The Puritan Lectureships: The Politics of Religious Dissent 1560–1662* (Stanford, 1970); Brigden, *London and the Reformation* (Oxford, 1991); Peter Lake, *The Boxmaker's Revenge: 'Orthodoxy', 'Heterodoxy' and the Politics of the Parish in Early Stuart London* (Manchester, 2001); and Merritt, *The Social World of Early Modern Westminster* (esp. ch. 9, 'Religious life and religious politics c. 1558–1640', pp. 308–51).

[39] E. B., *A Sermon Preached at Pauls Crosse on Trinity Sunday, 1571* (1576), F2r.

[40] Anthony Maxey, *The Churches Sleepe, Expressed in a Sermon Preached at the Court* (1606), C4v.

[41] John Hacket, *A Century of Sermons* (1675), 2Q2r. On Hoby and Paulet, see Pauline Croft, 'Capital life: members of parliament outside the House', in Thomas Cogswell, Richard Cust and Peter Lake, eds., *Politics, Religion and Popularity in Early Stuart Britain: Essays in Honour of Conrad Russell* (Cambridge, 2002), pp. 65–83.

attended nineteen sermons in a single week.[42] It was examples like this that Nicholas Byfield, minister of Isleworth, Middlesex, had in mind when he complained of the misguided zeal of 'some that live in great Cities' who 'thinke it Religion to heare all sorts of men, and all the Sermons that can bee come unto'.[43] Indeed, there seems to have been a substantial 'floating' congregation of sermon attenders who migrated from church to church, flocking to the newest or most popular preachers. Daniel Featley claimed that when a minister began to preach in the City, people would 'throng and croud at the Church doores, and not onely fill all the seates, but climbe into the windowes, and hang upon iron barres' to hear him. After a few years, however, the same preachers would find themselves 'forsaken of the better part of their auditory, who runne a gadding after some new schismaticall Lecturer, whose *name is up*'.[44]

Nor was it only the godly who attended sermons. One Paul's Cross preacher described the typical Londoner as one who 'goeth to the Church upon the Sabbath both to morning and evening prayer, and when hee can have leisure on the weekday if there be any exercise, and when hee can attend' – and this was not a description of a godly puritan, but of a 'meere civill honest man'.[45] In London, it was impossible to avoid exposure to the Protestant preaching ministry, even if, for some, it was merely part of the background hum of urban life. As the Elizabethan preacher Henry Smith pointed out, in a famous passage on 'accidental hearers', people attended sermons for a great variety of reasons. 'Some come with a fame, they have heard great speech of the man, and therefore they will spend one hower to heare him once . . . Some come because they be idle, to passe the time they go to a Sermon . . . Some heare the sound of a voyce, as they passe by the church, and step in before they be aware.'[46] This was no exaggeration: William Kiffin tells us in his spiritual autobiography that his interest in hearing sermons was first kindled early one morning, when 'wandering up and down the streets, and passing by St Antholin's church, I saw people going in, which made me return and go in also'. Another London preacher observed that attendance at sermons tended to be highest on winter

[42] Stephen Denison, *The Monument or Tombe-stone: or, a Sermon Preached at Laurence Pountnies Church . . . at the Funerall of Mrs Elizabeth Iuxon* (1620), F8r; Paul Seaver, *Wallington's World: A Puritan Artisan in Seventeenth-Century London* (1985), pp. 37–8.

[43] Nicholas Byfield, *The Marrow of the Oracles of God* (6th edn., 1628), M4r.

[44] Daniel Featley, *Clavis Mystica* (1636), S1r, from a sermon 'at the Archbishops visitation in Saint Dunstans', probably Laud's metropolitical visitation in 1635.

[45] William Holbrooke, *Loves Complaint, for Want of Entertainment, A Sermon Preached at Paules Crosse* (1610), C1r.

[46] Henry Smith, *Thirteene Sermons upon Severall Textes of Scripture* (1592), C1r.

evenings, which may suggest that many people who could not afford fuel in their own houses went to church in order to keep warm.[47]

It was not uncommon, therefore, for Londoners to attend services and sermons outside their own parish churches. The ecclesiastical authorities tolerated this and occasionally found it useful. After the crackdown on nonconformist clergy in London in 1566, Matthew Parker wrote to Cecil that it was 'no great inconvenience' if some people in London had no ministers in their own parishes: 'London is no grange. They may go elsewhere.'[48] Thirty-five years later there was a revealing exchange between Bishop Bancroft and Stephen Egerton, the preacher at Blackfriars. Bancroft noted that at the time of his last visitation, in 1598, 'the ministers of London did greatly complayne of the disorder of many of theire parishioners, leavinge theire owne pastors and flocking after Mr Egerton and some others to the apparent contynuance of a schisme amongst us'. Egerton retorted that sermon-gadding was an unavoidable fact of life in London and, moreover, that Bancroft knew this and was prepared to tolerate sermon-gadding when it worked to the benefit of other, more conformable preachers: 'Touching the concourse of people it is a thing that in soe populous a Citye can hardlie be avoided, and is endured att worser exercises, and is farre greater after some whome my Lord of London seemeth to like and love.'[49] Even in the 1630s the authorities seem to have turned a blind eye to Londoners from other parishes who came to Blackfriars to receive Communion without kneeling; Laud may have reasoned that it would be easier to enforce conformity elsewhere if Blackfriars was allowed to remain a nonconformist enclave.[50] Peter Lake sums up the situation very well when he observes that in London, 'activities like sermon gadding, which elsewhere might remain somewhat deviant and even risqué, were almost entirely

---

[47] William Orme, *Remarkable Passages in the Life of William Kiffin* (1823), p. 3; James Balmford, *A Short Dialogue Concerning the Plagues Infection* (1603), A4r.

[48] Parker to Cecil, Good Friday (12 April) 1566: *Correspondence of Matthew Parker*, ed. John Bruce and Thomas Perowne (Parker Society, Cambridge, 1853), p. 279.

[49] Stephen Egerton to Robert Cecil, 4 April 1601: Cecil Papers (Hatfield House), vol. CIV no. 125.

[50] William Gouge, minister at Blackfriars, was said to have been willing to administer Communion to outsiders 'who could not either at all, or at least purely (in regard of superstitious gestures, genuflexions, &c) enjoy that ordinance' in their home parishes: William Jenkyn, *A Shock of Corn . . . A Sermon Preached at the Funeral of that Ancient and Eminent Servant of Christ William Gouge* (1654), G1v. Daniel Featley may well have had Blackfriars in mind when he declared that in certain London parishes it was possible to see 'scores, nay hundreds receiving the Communion standing, or sitting at their best ease': Featley, *Clavis Mystica*, S1r. A letter from Gouge to Laud, acknowledging Laud's courtesy on a previous occasion 'when complaintes were made . . . about my manner of celebrating the holy communion', suggests that Blackfriars received especially lenient treatment from the authorities: Gouge to Laud, 19 Oct. 1631, National Archives SP 16/202/3.

normal', and, consequently, that 'the religious lives of the godly cannot be studied solely through the unit of the parish and its records'.[51]

Yet this stands in striking contrast to other recent research on early modern London, which has stressed the importance of the parish in defining the local community. As Ian Archer has pointed out, 'it was by reference to their parish, and only very rarely to a ward, that Londoners defined where they lived'.[52] The sermons of London preachers are suffused with parochial rhetoric: John Downame argued that 'our common friends and neerest neighbors, who dwell in the same place and parish' had first claim on our charity, while Edward Elton declared that quarrels among neighbours were particularly grievous because they were 'of the same parish, and of the same particular congregation' and therefore 'ought the more to love and regard' each other.[53] And it is interesting to compare Stephen Egerton's apparent tolerance of sermon-gadding with his successor William Gouge's description of his parish as 'our little state in the Blackfryers'. This makes it sound like a self-governed and self-contained community, an impression reinforced when we learn that the precinct of Blackfriars was 'enclosed about with walls and gates' and could be sealed off from the outside world at times of danger or public disorder.[54] While Lake is quite right to insist that we must look beyond the parochial unit, we also need to consider the possibility that the custom of sermon-gadding might have coexisted with a strong sense of attachment to a particular parish.

What we know of individual patterns of sermon attendance points strongly towards the same conclusion. In London, one characteristic pattern was to attend one's own parish church on Sunday morning, dine at home or with friends, and then go to the church of one's choice in the afternoon. This is reflected in *Sophronistes*, which, as mentioned above, takes the form of a dialogue between two Londoners returning home after Sunday morning service and sermon: one invites the other to come with him to 'the

---

[51] Lake, *The Boxmaker's Revenge*, p. 395.
[52] Ian Archer, *The Pursuit of Stability: Social Relations in Elizabethan London* (Cambridge, 1991), pp. 82–92 (quotation p. 83). Other important studies of parochial identity include Jeremy Boulton, *Neighbourhood and Society: A London Suburb in the Seventeenth Century* (Cambridge, 1987), on the Southwark parishes, and Merritt, *The Social World of Early Modern Westminster*, on the parishes of St Margaret's Westminster and St Martin in the Fields. See also Vanessa Harding, 'City, capital and metropolis: the changing shape of seventeenth-century London', in Merritt, ed., *Imagining Early Modern London: Perceptions and Portrayals of the City from Stow to Strype* (Cambridge, 2001), pp. 117–43 (esp. pp. 138–40).
[53] John Downame, *The Plea of the Poore, or a Treatise of Beneficence and Almes-Deeds* (1616), Q2v; Edward Elton, *An Exposition of the Epistle of Saint Paul to the Colossians* (1620), 3L1r.
[54] William Gouge to Sir Robert Harley, 24 June 1613: BL Add MS 70001, f. 134; Gouge, *Gods Three Arrowes* (1631), 2E5r.

Sermon of master Eulalus, who of late began to preach beyond the River',
but his friend replies that he was 'so well satisfied' with the preacher at his
parish church 'as I meane not to leave him in the afternoone for any other'.[55]
When James Gregory, of the parish of St Margaret Pattens, was presented in
1620 for absence from evening prayer, he explained that on Sundays he was
frequently 'at dynner with his brothers or other frends and went with them
in thafternoones to the churches of the parishes they dwelt in'.[56] The young
Simonds D'Ewes, as a student at the Middle Temple, adopted a similar
pattern, regularly attending the morning sermon by Mr Masters, the
preacher at the Temple, then going to another church in the vicinity,
often St Paul's or Lincoln's Inn, to hear a sermon by another preacher in
the afternoon:

[27 April 1623:] In the morning I heard Mr Master; in the afternone, Mr Squire a
verye good preacher in Mercers Chappel . . . after I heard a parte of a sermon in
Paules Church and supped in the towne.

[16 Nov 1623:] Our reverend minister M. Master preached in the forenoone, after
dinner I studied divinitye till I went to Lincolnes Inn to have heard Doctor Preston,
though I mist him.

[23 Nov 1623:] In the morning wee had an excellent sermon, how a man ought to
eradicate and kill the very seedes of sinne. After dinner I heard Mr Iefferayes, my
olde freind, and after him Docter Dunn in Paules church, and at night supped at
my kinsmans howse with Mr Iefferay.[57]

D'Ewes's Sabbatarianism led him to expect that the table talk at dinner,
between morning and evening prayer, would be of the sermon or other
matters of religion, so that the whole day could be applied to the service of
God.[58] Not all his fellow Inns of Court men were so punctilious. One Paul's
Cross preacher reproved 'you that are of the Temples and Innes, in and
about the Citie' for conducting secular business on the sabbath: 'Are not
your Staires troad, and your Chambers frequented, as much upon the
Sabboth as upon other dayes? This cannot be denied.' Even so, the preacher's remarks suggest that most wealthy Londoners would at least have
attended morning service even if they did not return to church in the

---

[55] *Sophronistes*, A3r.    [56] London Metropolitan Archives, DL/C/621 (office act book, 1619–20), p. 317.
[57] *The Diary of Sir Simonds D'Ewes (1622–1624)*, ed. Elisabeth Bourcier (Paris, 1974), pp. 132, 170–1.
[58] In August 1630 D'Ewes went with Lady Coventry to hear 'a very learned sermon', but halfway
through the sermon they were unexpectedly joined by Lord and Lady North, who, as D'Ewes
reported disapprovingly to his father, 'did soe fill upp all the dinner time with the needless and vaine
discourse of a dogg they had died a little before, as shewed them to bee ill catechized in the principles
of religion': BL, Harl. 379, f. 47.

afternoon. 'If they come to the Sermon it is well', but 'if once of the day, they thinke that sufficient, if twise, they thinke that more than needeth'.[59]

It seems likely, therefore, that the congregation at a Sunday morning sermon would have consisted largely of parishioners, many of them in a family or household group, whereas a Sunday afternoon or weekday lecture would have attracted a higher proportion of outsiders. And there is a good deal of evidence to suggest that women were particularly well represented in the audience on Sunday afternoons and weekdays. When the diarist John Manningham visited Blackfriars to hear Egerton preach on a Sunday afternoon in December 1602 he observed 'a great congregacion, specially of women'.[60] As we shall see later, Egerton's Wednesday and Friday morning lectures contain many doctrines specifically applied to the female sex, suggesting that he was deliberately slanting his sermons to take account of the presence of a large number of women in the audience. William Gouge's celebrated treatise on household government, *Of Domesticall Duties*, also originated as a series of weekday lectures at Blackfriars, again with particular reference to women – some of whom famously objected to Gouge's doctrine of female subjection as being too strict. Another London preacher addressed a sermon 'to women, who (for the most part) are the chiefest in this assembly, at this time'.[61]

Early morning and evening sermons, by contrast, would have had a special appeal to servants and apprentices, who could not usually attend sermons during normal working hours. The author of *The Prentises Practice in Godlinesse* (1608) noted the common complaint of servants that 'all the weeke wee are kept so straight that we cannot so much as get out to speake with any friend' and even on Sundays 'never go into the fields or to any merriment until evening prayer be done'. Most servants, not surprisingly, regarded Sunday evenings as their sole opportunity for recreation. However, the author proposed an alternative sabbath-day routine, beginning with family prayers, after which 'we may if we will directly goe where there shall bee a Sermon until eight, so comming home we are to goe to our owne Parish Church, both in the forenoone and in the afternoone; and after that to some Lecture as there be divers (blessed bee God) in divers parts of the City', before returning home about six o'clock in the evening. In other

---

[59] Holbrooke, *Loves Complaint*, E1v, E4v.

[60] *The Diary of John Manningham, 1602–1603*, ed. R.P. Sorlien (Hanover, NH, 1976), p. 151. Several months earlier Manningham had heard John Dove, in a sermon at Paul's Cross, reprove 'Mr Egerton, and such an other popular preacher, that their auditory, being most of women, abounded in that superfluous vanity of apparaile' (p. 115).

[61] Peter Lily, *Two Sermons* (1619), E4v. On the objections to Gouge's sermons, see above, p. 152.

words, servants should try to attend two additional sermons every Sunday, one before morning prayer and the other after evening prayer. Any servant who quailed before this demanding regime was sternly informed by the author – supposedly an apprentice himself – that 'you ought not to prophane or misspend one houre of the Sabbath'.[62]

We might be tempted to dismiss this as wholly unrealistic, were it not for the evidence of spiritual autobiographies and conversion narratives, which reveal the existence of a number of godly servants and apprentices eagerly seizing opportunities to hear sermons in their spare time. 'I. H.', a member of Vavasour Powell's Independent congregation in the 1650s, recalled that 'about twenty years agoe I dwelt in Black Friers' and used 'to heare the Word opened by Doctor *Gouge*, though it was but seldome, by reason that I was a servant'.[63] At about the same time, the London apprentice William Kiffin joined a group of godly young men who made it their 'constant practice to attend the morning Lecture, which began at six o'clock, both at Cornhill and Christ Church'. The conversion narrative of another London artisan, the printer Anthony Wildgoose – later to acquire a small niche in literary history as one of the journeymen responsible for printing the first edition of *Paradise Lost* – gives us another precious scrap of information about patterns of sermon attendance among the middling sort. 'Being at my work' one day in November 1643, 'my fellow workman, and I falling into discourse of good ministers, he told me that that evening I might heare a good sermon at Bartholmew Lane, neere the Exchange, so we having no great hast of work, we concluded to go together to hear it.'[64]

Weekday lectures, on the other hand, were for those who could devote a good deal of time to regular sermon attendance. Writing in the 1630s, the anti-puritan polemicist Christopher Dow noted that Wednesday was the most popular day for midweek lectures, and claimed that some of the godly spent the entire day moving from one sermon to another – in effect, holding a private exercise or fast-day, with the tacit support of sympathetic clergy:

The course they take is this: Some good *Christians* (that is, *Professors*) intimate their necessities to some *Minister* of note among them, and obteine of them the promise

---

[62] B.P., *The Prentises Practise in Godlinesse* (1608), G8r, L1r.

[63] Vavasour Powell, *Spirituall Experiences, of Sundry Beleevers* (1653), R11v (p. 382).

[64] Orme, *Remarkable Passages in the Life of William Kiffin*, p. 11. Anthony Wildgoose, *The Young-Mans Second Warning-peece* (1643), A4r. On Wildgoose, see D.F. McKenzie, ed., *Stationers' Company Apprentices 1605–1640* (Charlottesville, 1961), p. 21, and 'Printing and publishing 1557–1700: constraints on the London book trades', in John Barnard and D.F. McKenzie, eds, *The Cambridge History of the Book in Britain*, vol. IV (Cambridge, 2002), pp. 553–67 (ref. p. 563).

of their paines to preach upon that occasion, pitching upon such dayes and places, as where and when Sermons and Lectures are wont to bee; and having given *under-hand* notice to such as they judge *faithfull*, of the day to bee observed, and the places where they shall meet for that end, thither they resort, and mixing themselves with the crowd, unsuspected have the word they so much desire, with the *occasion covertly glanced at*, so as those that are not of *their counsell*, are never the wiser. Thus I have divers times known them to begin the day upon a *wednesday*, where they had a Sermon beginning at six in the morning, and holding them till after eight: that being done, they post (somtimes in troopes) to another Church, where the Sermon beginning at nine, holds them till past eleven, and from thence againe, they betake themselves to a third Church, and there place themselves against the afternoone Sermon begin, which holds them till night.[65]

Evidence of just such an arrangement comes from a case in 1597, when two London ministers, Edward Philips of St Saviour's Southwark and George Downame of St Margaret's Lothbury, were accused of having joined forces to organise an exercise. Philips denied allegations that he had led 'a great multitude through the Citty after my heeles to Mr Downams Sermon'. However, he admitted that he and Downame had arranged to preach in conjunction, Philips's sermon ending just before noon and Downame's sermon beginning about an hour and a half later, giving the congregation time to cross the river from one church to the other.[66]

Here, it seems, we have a situation where godly audiences moved freely around London's churches with no regard to parish boundaries. But even here, local loyalties still mattered. During the 1620s and 1630s, the most popular weekday lecture in the City was William Gouge's Wednesday lecture at Blackfriars, attended 'not only by his Parishioners, but by divers City Ministers, and by sundry pious and judicious Gentlemen of the *Innes of Court*, besides many other well-disposed Citizens'. But in 1622, when Gouge tried to organise a day-long exercise (probably a private fast) at Blackfriars, it seems to have been a comparative failure. 'Wee observed that wednesday wherof you wrote', he informed Sir Robert Harley, 'but it was the unfittest day of all the weeke for that purpose, and we are resolved never againe to set a wednesday.'[67] The reason why Gouge regarded Wednesday as 'the unfittest day of all the weeke' was, most probably, that it was the day when other London parishes, including St Antholin's, St Bartholomew Exchange and St Olave Jewry, held their own weekday lectures. It is a reasonable guess that the audience which Gouge had

---

[65] Christopher Dow, *Innovations Unjustly Charged upon the Present Church and State* (1637), 2E4v.
[66] Defence of Edward Philips to the articles objected against him: BL Lansd. MS 83, f. 98.
[67] Gouge to Harley, 11 May 1622: BL Add. MS 70001, f. 78.

hoped to attract to the fast-day at Blackfriars had been drawn away by sermons in other churches nearby. This suggests that patterns of sermon attendance were rather less fluid than we might suppose, and that even though people may have crossed parish boundaries, they often developed strong loyalties to particular preachers.

The Paul's Cross sermon was, of course, in a special category of its own, outside the normal parochial structure. In theory, Londoners should have attended the morning service in their own parish church (which was supposed to end by 9 a.m.) before coming on to the Paul's Cross sermon (which started at 10 a.m.), but by the early seventeenth century there were complaints that people 'resort to *Paules* Crosse and will not come at their own Church'.[68] The diary of Richard Stonley, one of the tellers of the Exchequer, shows that when in London he often absented himself from the morning service in his home parish of St Botolph's Aldersgate, and attended the Paul's Cross sermon instead, after which it was his custom to spend the afternoon 'at home reading the Scriptures with thankes to god at night'.[69] It was for this reason that many Paul's Cross sermons included lengthy exhortations to Londoners to be more regular in attending their own parish churches. George Benson, preaching at the Cross in 1609, pleaded with 'you of this honourable City . . . that you will not be willing to entertaine (you care not whom) so it be not your owne Minister, that you will not gad (you care not whither) so it be from your owne parish Church, but rather thinke that God in his wisdome hath placed your owne Ministers over your owne parishes'.[70] Attacks on the 'wanton levitie' of sermon-gadding also reinforced the common stereotype of the audience at Paul's Cross as a crowd of 'Athenians' more interested in news and novelty than in the Word of God.

The problem was by no means peculiar to London, but occurred in other towns where there was a 'common sermon' which all the inhabitants were encouraged or expected to attend.[71] One preacher in early seventeenth-century Reading expressed anxiety that the common sermon had begun to take precedence over the services in the three parish churches of St Mary's, St Laurence's and St Giles's. True, it was 'a goodly sight . . . to see all come to one Churche together to the sermon', but it would be better for the town

---

[68] Francis Marbury, *A Sermon Preached at Pauls Cross* (1602), E3r. On the timing of the Paul's Cross sermon, see Owen, 'The London parish clergy', p. 195.

[69] Diary of Richard Stonley: Folger Library, Washington, DC, V.a.459.

[70] George Benson, *A Sermon Preached at Paules Crosse* (1609), D1r, L4v. For another Paul's Cross sermon attacking sermon-gadding, see Thomas Adams, *The Temple* (1624), D1v.

[71] More research still needs to be done on 'common sermons' in English provincial towns, but in the meantime Mark Byford provides an exemplary account of the town sermon in Colchester in chapter 4 of 'The price of Protestantism'.

if 'every pastoure mighte have perfourmed something in his owne place for the discharge of his owne duetie, before the resorte had beene to the common sermon'. In part, his objection to the common sermon was the familiar one voiced by opponents of sermon-gadding, that the people ought to rest content with the sermons of their own pastors. 'I holde it would be more for the praise of Redinge, to have it said, behold a religious and wise people that duly attend the ministry of their owne pastours, than to have it said, a fantasticall and giddy headed people (especially of the chiefest) that are more devoted to strangers.' But he also seems to have feared that the emphasis on the common sermon was making it possible for some people to slip through the parochial net. It was, he argued, 'more fitt for every minister to attend his owne flocke', not only to discharge his duty but also to enforce church attendance by 'those that otherwise would goe to no churche'.[72]

This does not mean that city-wide sermons were bound to come into conflict with parish sermons. There was undoubtedly room for coexistence, especially in a city as large as London, where wealthy individuals such as the haberdasher Roger Jeston can be found leaving money both to the Paul's Cross sermon and to a parish lectureship.[73] But in London as in Reading, some preachers apparently felt that the existence of a 'common sermon' provided a handy excuse for people seeking to evade their religious obligations. When Thomas Gataker took up the Lincoln's Inn lectureship in 1602, the Sunday morning sermon began at 7 a.m. so that members of the Inn had time to go on to the Paul's Cross sermon afterwards. However, Gataker found that many members of his audience, rather than going to the Cross, 'spent a great, if not the greatest part of the day, the Afternoon especiallie, in entertaining of their Clients'. He therefore moved his Sunday morning sermon to a later time, and was gratified to find that although 'some few would now and then step to Pauls Cross', and 'one or two' to hear John King at St Andrew's Holborn, the majority of his congregation did not 'stray much abroad'.[74] We do not know if other London preachers followed Gataker's example; but by the early seventeenth century Paul's Cross sermons turn up surprisingly rarely in sermon notebooks, which suggests

---

[72] Cambridge University Library, MS Dd.14.16, p. 103. Useful information on religious affairs in Reading can be found in G. P. Crawfurd, ed., *The Registers of the Parish of St Mary, Reading, 1538–1812* (Reading, 1891), and J. M. Guilding, ed., *Diary of the Corporation of Reading*, vols. II and III (1895–6).

[73] Reginald R. Sharpe, ed., *Calendar of Wills Proved and Enrolled in the Court of Husting, London*, vol. II (1890), pp. 747–8.

[74] Thomas Gataker, *A Discours Apologetical* (1654), C4v, F2v, G2r.

that the Cross was increasingly regarded as a place to be visited occasionally rather than every week.

It also appears that patterns of sermon attendance, while not necessarily limited to a particular parish, were often limited to a particular locality or neighbourhood. The point is neatly made in Richard Andrews's satirical character of a London sermongoer, written in the mid-1620s:

> Let her goe oft to Church, to Paules the huge,
> Or to black Fryers, to heare Maister Gowge,
> Unto Saint Gregories, Saint Faithes, Saint Fosters . . .[75]

Andrews's sermongoer attends sermons in the parishes of St Ann Blackfriars, St Gregory by St Paul's, St Faith under St Paul's and St Vedast Foster Lane, all within a few minutes' walk of each other, in a cluster of wealthy parishes surrounding St Paul's Cathedral. This is a highly localised pattern of sermon attendance, and bears out a point that has often been made by historians of early modern London, that there was a sharp social and cultural divide between the east and west ends of town. As M. J. Power remarks: 'In distance Aldermanbury and Aldgate were not a mile apart; in character they were different worlds.'[76]

Surviving sermon notebooks, such as the diary of John Manningham, reveal similarly localised patterns of sermon attendance. On Sunday mornings Manningham usually went to the Temple church, to the neighbouring parish of St Clement Danes or to the sermon at Paul's Cross; on Sunday afternoons he went slightly further afield, patronising a select number of West End churches including St Ann Blackfriars, St Leonard Foster Lane and St Peter Paul's Wharf. Occasionally he went west of the City to hear a sermon at Westminster or at court, but he very rarely crossed the river and, as far as we can tell from the diary, never ventured east of Paul's.[77] Simonds D'Ewes, as a student at the Middle Temple, had a similar itinerary of West End churches. On one Sunday in May 1623, for example, he went in the

---

[75] Richard Andrews, 'Dirae': BL Harleian MS 4955, f. 157. Andrews's poems are discussed in W.H. Kelliher, 'Donne, Jonson, Richard Andrews and the Newcastle Manuscript', *English Manuscript Studies*, 4 (1993), pp. 134–73.

[76] M. J. Power, 'The east and west in early modern London', in E. W. Ives, R. J. Knecht and J. J. Scarisbrick, eds., *Wealth and Power in Tudor England: Essays Presented to S. T. Bindoff* (London, 1978), pp. 167–85. The same east/west divide can be seen in eighteenth-century patterns of sermon attendance. James Boswell, for example, attended West End churches, but never went south of the Thames or east of Bow: see James Caudle, 'James Boswell and the bi-confessional state', in William Gibson and Robert G. Ingram, eds., *Religious Identities in Britain 1660–1832* (Aldershot, 2005), pp. 119–46 (ref. p. 136).

[77] Manningham, *Diary*, ed. Sorlien, e.g. pp. 114–5 (Dr Dove at Paul's Cross, Mr Marbury at the Temple), 145 (Mr Layfield at St Clement's).

morning to Blackfriars, 'where Mr Gouge did well', then in the afternoon to a 'good sermon' at St Andrew's Holborn, and finally to the chapel at Lincoln's Inn, where he hoped to hear John Preston preach. The reputation of Josias Shute occasionally tempted him to St Mildred Poultry, a short walk along Cheapside to the east, but more often he was to be found at St Faith's, St Martin Ludgate or one of the other churches in close proximity to St Paul's.[78] The West End bias of these and other surviving sermon notebooks is not particularly surprising, as so many of them are products of the thriving textual culture centred on the Inns of Court. However, it means that our surviving sample is slanted very much towards what we might call the 'gentry Puritanism' of churches such as Blackfriars, which may not be representative of London churches in general, any more than the city comedies performed at the neighbouring playhouse in Blackfriars are representative of London theatres in general. The congregation at Blackfriars seems to have preferred a fairly moderate brand of Calvinism, and did not respond at all favourably to the appearance of more radical or controversial preachers in the pulpit there.[79]

One additional factor affecting sermon attendance – in some ways, the most important of all – still remains to be mentioned. This was population pressure. As one writer observed in 1609 ,'the people of diverse parishes in and about London' were 'so many, and their Churches, or places of meeting, so small, that it is not possible to assemble all together at any one time, though they should be crowded never so much'. The problem was most acute in large suburban parishes such as St Olave's and St Saviour's, Southwark, St Giles without Cripplegate or St Botolph without Aldgate, whose churches, according to Ephraim Udall in 1641, 'are not capable of the greater part of the Parishioners, some of them, not of the tenth part of them, and some, not of the tenth part of the Communicants'.[80] The parish church of Stepney was said to be so crowded that 'manie for their health or ease are compelled by reason of the great presse to come forth into the Churchyard and others to walke there and stand listning without the Church that cannot

---

[78] *Diary of Sir Simonds D'Ewes*, ed. Bourcier, pp. 103, 111, 138.
[79] For the hostile reception given to George Walker when he substituted for Gouge at a Wednesday lecture, see Peter Lake and David Como, '"Orthodoxy" and its discontents: dispute settlement and the production of "consensus" in the London (puritan) "underground"', *Journal of British Studies*, 39: 1 (2000), pp. 34–70 (ref. p. 42), and Lake, *The Boxmaker's Revenge*, p. 223.
[80] Ephraim Udall, *Good Workes, if They Be Well Handled* (1641). Udall's figure is probably an exaggeration; the parishioners of St Botolph Aldgate estimated more plausibly in 1635 that their church was too small to contain 'the halfe parte or number of the parishioners': LMA, DL/C/343 (vicar-general's book, 1627–37), f. 210v.

have roome in the said Church'.[81] Again there were fears that some people were using this as an excuse to avoid church attendance – Udall complained that 'those Parishes be harbours for all kinds of vicious and lewd People, that pretend they have no room in the Church' – though the suburban parishes do seem to have succeeded remarkably well in enforcing attendance at Easter Communion. One undoubted result, however, was that the residents of the London suburbs overflowed into less crowded churches in the city centre.

Some of this outflow from the suburbs can be reconstructed from the records of the London church courts. In 1619 a group of élite parishioners from St James's Clerkenwell were cited to the London consistory court for attending service and sermons at St Bartholomew the Great, St Martin Ludgate and St Ann Blackfriars instead of their own parish church. One of them, Sir Edward Blount, explained that 'the reason is because they can have no seates in the same churche', adding that he 'would frequent that Churche as by lawe he ought yf he might have a convenient pewe to sit in and so would the Lady his wife also yf she might have a convenient pewe assigned to her fit for her degree and calling she being a noble mans daughter'. He succeeded in obtaining a court order requiring the church-wardens of St James's to provide him and his wife with suitable seats.[82] Blount's social position was almost certainly the reason why this case came before the church court: his contribution to the parish finances would have been a significant one, which the churchwardens would naturally have wished to retain. But for every élite parishioner, able to use his social prestige to obtain a seat in his parish church, there may well have been a host of other individuals who simply migrated to other churches without any official action being taken.

However, the residents of inner-city parishes did not welcome this influx of sermongoers from the suburbs. Outsiders were resented because they made no contribution to parish expenses: in 1630 the churchwardens of St Bartholomew Exchange complained that when collections were taken after sermons, 'straungers (of which our Congregation upon lector dayes con-sisteth mostlye)' would 'withhould their charitie' if they thought the money was being used to pay the wages of the parish officials. Worse still, outsiders might drive the parishioners out of their seats. One reason why Bancroft ordered Egerton to discourage sermon-gadding on Sunday afternoons was so that 'the parishioners in the black fryers may have . . . the use of their seates and not be compelled (as many have been) to absent them selves from

---

[81]  LMA, DL/C/343, f. 206.     [82]  LMA, DL/C/620 (office act book, 1618–19), p. 169.

the Churche for want of roome'. The parishioners of St Botolph without Bishopsgate complained in 1617 that 'when sermons are preached', their church 'is filled with multitude of people a greate parte of them beinge rude and thronginge togeither and manie of them straingers of other parishes will give no waie to the better sorte of people to passe by them either to come into their seates or to goe owte from them'. Their solution was to put a door in the south wall of the church so that 'the better sorte of the parishioners' could reach their pews.[83]

Patrick Collinson has speculated that weekday lectures might have been characterised by 'indiscriminate seating arrangements, people taking their places on a first-come-first-served basis, as they did in the theatres'. This is certainly true of Paul's Cross – where there are reports of servants arriving early to reserve a place for their masters – but it is unlikely to have been the case in parish churches, where seats were valuable possessions, jealously guarded by their owners.[84] Seating arrangements were rarely indiscriminate, either in church or in the theatre. When Lodewijck Huygens visited the new church at Covent Garden in 1652, he described it as 'divided into boxes, just like a place where comedies are performed, except for a space in the middle where the common people stand'. Only in this central space was admission free of charge; and Huygens had to pay an entrance fee of two shillings in order to get a seat in one of the boxes closest to the pulpit. Similar arrangements were probably in force in other London churches. When Gouge preached at Blackfriars he was praised for 'his tender compassion toward the multitudes of his hearers', in that 'out of this Pulpit he was wont (before he began his Sermons) to observe what Pues were empty, and to command his Clark to open them, for the ease of those who thronged in the Isles'.[85] This makes it clear that the pews were not opened until the sermon began, and also suggests that Gouge was unusual in allowing them to be opened at all. John Donne observed in a sermon at Paul's Cross in 1629 that it was more difficult for the poor to benefit from preaching because 'they cannot have seats in Churches, whensoever they come;

---

[83] LMA, DL/C/341 (vicar-general's book, 1616–23), f. 23v.
[84] Collinson, *Religion of Protestants,* p. 259, quoting a letter from Sir Thomas Wroth to Sir Robert Harley: 'I pray let us go togeither to mr Damport's in the morning, where I will provide a seat for you' (BL Add. MS 70001, f. 248); but as Collinson acknowledges, Wroth 'was perhaps offering Harley accommodation in his family pew'. For an instance of a servant 'sitting at St Pauls Cross keeping a place for his master', see PRO, SP 16/142 (calendared in *CSPD 1628–29,* p. 552); and for a warning that latecomers at Paul's Cross 'shall have no place, for all the formes will be taken up', see William Stepney, *The Spanish Schoole-maister* (1619), F6v (quoted below, p. 321).
[85] Lodewijck Huygens, *The English Journal 1651–1652,* ed. and trans. A. G. H. Bachrach and R. G. Collmer (Leiden, 1982), p. 55; Jenkyn, *A Shock of Corn,* F1v.

They must *stay*, they must *stand*, they must *thrust*, they must overcome that difficulty, which St Augustine makes an impossibility, that is, for any man to receive benefit by that Sermon, that he hears with pain: They must take pains to hear.'[86]

Sermon-gadding was therefore held in check by a number of restraining factors: the determined efforts of the clergy to discourage the practice; the unsympathetic attitude of the laity towards strangers in their parish churches; and the personal ties binding individuals to their own parish or neighbourhood. One London preacher challenged sermon-gadders to say 'whether it be enough for a Minister to preach twice a day anywhere, at his owne church or anothers? I thinke they will cry noe. He is bound to his owne charge. I would know then why it should be lawful to heare twice a day anywhere &c? I say (for they will not) noe. For the obligation is mutuall ... We are confined to a place of preaching, you to a place of hearing.'[87] Even those preachers who were the beneficiaries of sermon-gadding had decidedly mixed feelings about it. Edward Philips – whose lectures at St Saviour's Southwark attracted many visitors from north of the river, and who may, as I suggested above, have been the model for the crowd-pulling Master Eulalus in *Sophronistes* – stressed that gadding could only be tolerated in those who 'come for conscience to heare, and not for contempt to their own Pastor at home'. During the plague outbreak of 1603, James Balmford, lecturer at St Olave's Southwark, noted with satisfaction that 'wheras before the Plague our Church was partly filled by strangers, both on Sondayes and Fridayes', his audience was now drawn largely from the parish.[88]

Even that inveterate sermongoer Nehemiah Wallington seems to have been deeply ambivalent in his attitude to sermon-gadding. In January 1641 he reproached some of his fellow parishioners at St Leonard Eastcheap – 'divers gidiheaded people', as he called them – for not attending the sermons of their own minister Henry Roborough, telling them 'that it could not be the motion of the Spirit of God to have them to goe forth in this manner, but it must needs be the tentation of the Divel. For the Divel is with Mr Robroh in his Study and can Read his writings and Books and knows what matter he is to preach on, And so the Divel knows what sin we are given

---

[86] Sermon at Paul's Cross, 22 Nov 1629: Donne, *Sermons*, ed. G.R. Potter and E.M. Simpson (Berkeley, 1953–62), vol. IX, pp. 123.

[87] Sermon notebook, 1628–9: University of London, Institute of Historical Research, MS 979 (sermon dated 12 July 1629).

[88] Edward Philips, *Certaine Godly and Learned Sermons, as They Were Delivered by Him in Saint Saviors in Southwarke* (1605), N2v (p. 178); Balmford, *Short Dialogue*, A4r.

unto and what matter will do us most good, And therfore he puts toys in our heads to drive us away from our Souls good.' In September 1642 Wallington himself crossed parish boundaries to hear a sermon by Joseph Caryll, but wondered as he did so whether he might not be better employed 'by hearing of Mr Roborough . . . he being a minister of God and teaching the truth as well as others'. Could it be, he asked himself uneasily, that he was suffering from 'an itch in the ear that I know not who to hear nor how to relish wholesome doctrine'? Wallington's writings show that there was a constant tension between the temptations of sermon-gadding and the gravitational pull of a home parish.[89]

Despite this tension, sermon-gadding did not necessarily represent a threat to the parochial system. As Nick Alldridge has shown in his study of Chester, an individual's primary loyalty to a home parish was perfectly compatible with secondary loyalties to other parishes where he had family connections, owned property or frequented the sermons of a particular preacher.[90] As long as the authorities tolerated sermon-gadding – and in London and other large towns they could hardly do otherwise – most people did not have to choose between these different loyalties. The first serious challenge to this *modus vivendi* came in the early 1640s from John Goodwin, vicar of St Stephen's Coleman Street, who attempted to limit Communion to members of his own gathered congregation – effectively detaching the parish from its territorial roots – and the opposition to this new model of church organisation, not least from Goodwin's own parishioners, shows what an innovative experiment it was. The result, as Adrian Johns has shown, was to make Coleman Street notorious for decades to come as a byword for anarchic radicalism.[91] Londoners valued the freedom to attend sermons where they wished, but they also valued their attachment to a home parish and were not prepared to relinquish it without a struggle.

CONCLUSION

I have argued in this chapter that different sermons might have attracted very different types of audience. It is temptingly easy to generalise about puritan preaching, but even among the sermons delivered by godly preachers in London there could have been a considerable difference between, say,

---

[89] Booy, ed., *Notebooks of Nehemiah Wallington*, pp. 245, 171.

[90] Nick Alldridge, 'Loyalty and identity in Chester parishes 1540–1640', in Susan Wright, ed., *Parish, Church and People: Local Studies in Lay Religion 1350–1750* (London, 1988), pp. 112–17.

[91] Adrian Johns, 'Coleman Street', *Huntington Library Quarterly*, 71: 1 (2008), pp. 33–54.

a weekday morning sermon at St Antholin's addressed to an audience of servants and apprentices, and a Sunday afternoon sermon at Blackfriars addressed to an audience of affluent gentry and their wives. In conclusion, I want to read this back into the sermons themselves, and consider how preachers might have varied the style and content of their sermons according to the audience.

One particularly helpful guide to the different types of preaching on offer in London is the commonplace book of Gilbert Frevile, a Durham gentleman who lived in the capital between about 1604 and 1611 and kept a detailed record of the sermons he attended.[92] His notes provide a good sample of the range of preaching available to a diligent London churchgoer in the first decade of the seventeenth century. Among the preachers he heard were Richard Stock, lecturer at All Hallows Bread Street, Francis Marbury, rector of St Pancras Soper Lane, John King, rector of St Andrew's Holborn, and Thomas Westfield, rector of St Bartholomew the Great, displaying the same bias towards West End churches that we have encountered in other sermon notebooks, though with less of an exclusive focus on the area around St Paul's. The centrepiece of Frevile's notebook, however, is a detailed set of notes on three concurrent courses of sermons preached by Stephen Egerton at Blackfriars, two 'upon the weeke daies (viz) on wednesdaie, and friday in the forenoone', on Ruth and 1 Samuel respectively, and the third 'upon the sabbath daies', on Acts. As these were never printed, Frevile's notes provide the best surviving record of Egerton's preaching, but they also make it possible to compare his Sunday and weekday sermons, revealing some interesting differences between the two.

The weekday sermons are chiefly concerned with questions of civil and social relationship, such as the reciprocal duties of husbands and wives, masters and servants, or parents and children. One of the sermons is applied to a twofold use, first 'to all magistrates, officers and judges' and secondly to all godly Christians, which suggests that the audience must have included some gentry and office-holders. However, the frequent applications to women and young people suggest that Egerton's core weekday audience consisted of gentlewomen accompanied by their children and servants. Preaching on 1 Samuel 1: 21 ('And Elkanah and all his household went up to offer unto the Lord the yearly sacrifice'), he drew the moral that we must not only come to church ourselves, but must bring our whole household

---

[92] Frevile's commonplace book is BL Egerton MS 2877. Frevile died in 1652; his will (National Archives, PROB 11/220) suggests that he owned a considerable library, as he left 'the best and choicest of my books' to his son-in-law Cuthbert Sisson, with the remainder to be divided among his friends.

with us. Other sermons prescribe rules for behaviour 'at gossiping, comforting and visiting our neighbours', or offer consolation to women who are unmarried, childless or mistreated by their husbands:

Hannah in this place [1 Sam. 1: 8] thoughe she wanted children, yet she forgott that she had a kind and godly husband, and so do many now-a-daies if they have no children though they have never so good and religious a husband, yet are they not content and comforted with that, but the want of th'other is great greife unto them. Now if any will saie that they want children and also good husbands, and all the ioyes and comforts of this life, yet lett this be their comfort and releife, if they be of the number of gods children, they are then ioyned unto him that shalbe better unto them than xM [ten thousand] husbands or as many children. [f. 23r]

The Wednesday sermons on Ruth are also addressed particularly to women and young people. The story of Ruth and Boaz, for example, is applied to a threefold use. First, as Boaz 'followed the rule of gods law' in taking Ruth as his wife, so we ought 'to subiect and submitt our selves in the matter of our marriage to the ordinance of god, and the good and godly advise of our frendes and parents'. Secondly, as Ruth and Boaz were 'carefull to keepe a good name and credytt before men' so 'the yonger sort are to learne from the example of Ruth . . . to direct their course circumspectly'. Lastly, as Ruth rendered her mother an account of the corn that Boaz gave her, so we should learn that we are accountable to men as well as to God. This led Egerton to a reproof of 'manie young men' who 'for lack of perfourmance of this example of Ruthes giving accompt, do bring their parents and masters into debt, and themselves into utter discredytt and ruine', and finally to the general conclusion that young people must be content to submit to the government of their elders. 'The reason why elders are the most fittest persons to rule and governe, is because they have experience . . . neither are the elder sort so prone and ready to be drawne away by the heate of affection as the yonger sort are.'

In contrast, Egerton's Sunday afternoon lectures on Acts are highly topical and controversial. While these sermons are addressed primarily to the parishioners of Blackfriars, it is clear that Egerton was also conscious of speaking to a city-wide audience, and used the presence of sermon-gadders as an excuse to appropriate some of the prophetic rhetoric of civic preaching:

This doctrine maie you of London, and particularly you of Blackfriers, applie to your selves, That if for all the instruction, teaching and painfull preaching, that hath so long continued amongst you, you do not repent and leave your sinnes, then the most wicked and prophane Cittyes in the world, either in Spaine, Turkie, Italy, or wheresoever, shall rise in iudgment against you. [f. 29v]

The high public profile of the Sunday afternoon lecture gave Egerton an opportunity to launch a set-piece attack on the sins of London, the most disgraceful of which, in his opinion, was the toleration of Popery. St Paul, he pointed out, had condemned the Athenians for their idolatry (Acts 17: 16), and rightly so, for idolatry is 'that great sinne . . . which maketh a stone wall of separation betwene god and us'. But in 'this Athens of ours, (this City of London)', our love of the gospel has diminished, and our zeal against idolatry has grown cold, for we are 'well content to suffer the masse (that great sinne of Idolatry) even under our noses every sabboth within this Citty and land', showing plainly that 'the zeale of the detesting of popery (that abhominable Idolatry) is departed from us, which formerly we have had'. Even though 'the faithfull pastors and ministers of gods word . . . speake and preache against it, yet they shall find oppositions, as Paule did at Athens, and by whome? Not by the meane, simple and ignorant people, but by some of those that be accounted the wise and learned of the land.' (f. 26v)

It is obvious from these sermons that Egerton was courting disciplinary action from the ecclesiastical authorities. One sermon discussed the nature of sedition, which he defined as a stirring of the mind and an expectation of some change, either for better or worse, among a multitude of people. But, Egerton went on, 'it is not the beleeving preachers that are the workers of sedition (as some saie), but the unbeleeving people which beare envious mindes against the good pastors of Jesus Christ.' Thus John the Baptist was 'presently clapt up and cutt off as a turbulent fellow' for teaching that it was unlawful for Herod to marry his brother's wife, 'whereas (indeed) it was Herods owne corruption that was the cause of trouble and sedition . . . If anie thing be commanded by the Prince that is not agreeable with the word of god, there is no disloyaltie in us, thoughe we do not obey, it being better to obey god than man.' Later sermons show him anticipating, even relishing, the possibility of suspension or deprivation. From St Paul's departure from Athens (Acts 18: 6) he derived the conclusion that God permits 'the flitting, removing, and depriving of the ministers of god from their places' as a just punishment for the people's sins, and it is 'an evident argument, and token . . . that in suche place, there be no more sheepe to gather unto the true fould, nor anie more to be converted by their labors, for if there were, god would never suffer them to be deprived'. (f. 29v)

The contrast, both stylistic and doctrinal, between Egerton's weekday and Sunday sermons suggests that they were intended for markedly different types of audience. The weekday sermons, focused as they are on practical moral instruction expressed in a plain proverbial style ('as we may saie verifying an ould proverb amongst us, that which is bred in the bone will cleave to the flesh'), seem to be addressed primarily to family and household groups, whereas the Sunday afternoon sermons are considerably more controversial and seem to be addressed to a more diverse audience drawn to Blackfriars from other parts of the City. Egerton's predestinarianism is far more muted in the weekday sermons, where it is chiefly directed towards personal self-examination; for example, he argues that while the faithful and the faithless may both have cause to rejoice, they differ in the manner of their rejoicing, 'for those maie saie, that god lifts up their harts, and th'other cannot saie so, and in suche reioycing as the latter there is greater cause of mourning because they do not reioyce in the salvation that cometh of the lord, but in themselves'. Only in his Sunday sermons does Egerton make it clear that preaching will have the effect of precipitating a separation between the godly and the wicked. 'The word of god, as it is to the elect and to them that profitt by hearing thereof, a savor of life unto life, so unto those that reiect the same, it is the savor of death unto death.' 'Unto all the elect and godly' the Gospel brings perfect peace, but 'unto the wicked and reprobate' it is a sword and a consuming fire. We will return to the subject of predestination in Chapter 7, where we will see further evidence of the care taken by preachers to shape the presentation of their doctrine to fit their audience.

Egerton's example shows that there could be great diversity even in the sermons preached by a single preacher from a single pulpit, and that, to a far greater extent than has generally been realised, early modern sermons were addressed to specific and distinct types of audience. This is true not only of London but of other large cities, where the variety of sermons on offer made it possible for preachers to be more specialised in the theological fare they offered to their congregations. This urban economy of preaching, though largely hidden from our view, emerges into the historical record from time to time, usually when something went wrong. In April 1612, for example, Thomas Thompson, town preacher of Bristol, preached a farewell sermon in St Thomas's church, Bristol, which he later published under the somewhat disingenuous title *A Friendly Farewell from a Faithfull Flocke*, ending with an extraordinary outburst in which he accused some of the town's leading citizens, 'whom yet in dutie I reverence', of having 'utterly neglected and shunned' his sermons, 'to their owne hurt, and no whit to my disparagement, as they in their stiffe pride did imagine'. Their main complaint, according to Thompson, was that his sermons were 'unprofitable, because their subiect was many times *philosophicall*, and the manner of discourse most commonly too high or deepe for a popular auditorie'. This, he declared, was utterly unjustified. He had preached regularly twice a week, once on Sundays 'handling the body of *Theologie* from point to point' and again on Tuesdays on the Book of Esther, and 'for manner of preaching, never spake I any word, which was not either expresse Scripture, or other good learning, borrowed and excerpted from other gardens, but always composed to the proportion of faith'. While conceding that his sermons had been pitched at a fairly high level, Thompson defended himself by claiming that the demand for more popular sermons was already supplied by other preachers in the city. Having observed his fellow ministers 'in their good discretion to stoope down to the lowest conceit', he had chosen to address his sermons to a more discriminating audience, learned in 'divers deepe points of divinitie' and taking pleasure in 'varietie'.[93]

Similar tales could probably be told of other English towns. In Canterbury there seems to have been an exceptionally wide variety of different types and styles of preaching, ranging from John Boys's solid and reliable sermons on calendrical texts, nicely characterised by Patrick Collinson as 'a thousand pages of middlebrow theology', to Richard Colfe's course of sermons on the mystery of iniquity (2 Thessalonians 2: 6–17) 'wherein he demonstratively and substantially proved the *Papacy* to be *Antichristianity*'.[94] One Canterbury preacher observed in 1626 that there were 'diversities of gifts' among the city's preachers, not just among the Dean and Chapter, or the Six Preachers attached to the cathedral, but also 'amongst us *ordinarie and rurall Ministers*, who come hither now and then ... *One* surpasseth in expounding the words; *another* is excellent at delivering the matter; *a third* happy for cases of conscience; *a fourth* exquisite in determining Schoole-doubts. In a word, *some* be iudicious to enforme the understanding, *others* powerfull to reforme the will and affections.'[95] If even a member of the clergy was prepared to admit that there were wide differences of ability among the city's preachers – some having 'bad utterance, but a good conceit; others an excellent utterance, but a meane wit; some neither; and some both' – it is reasonable to suppose that the laity, too, were willing and able to pass critical judgement on the sermons they heard.

---

[93] Thomas Thompson, *A Friendly Farewell from a Faithfull Flocke* (1616), H4r–I1r (pp. 57–9). For details of the Bristol town lectureship, see Mark Pilkinton's introduction to *Records of Early English Drama: Bristol* (Toronto, 1997), pp. xxiii–xxv.

[94] 'The Protestant Cathedral, 1541–1660', in Patrick Collinson, Nigel Ramsay and Margaret Sparks, eds., *A History of Canterbury Cathedral* (Oxford, 1995), pp. 154–203 (ref. p. 178). Two volumes of Boys's sermon manuscripts are in the library of Corpus Christi College, Cambridge, MSS 215–6. Thomas Wilson, *Christs Farewell to Jerusalem, A Sermon Preached in the Quier of the Cathedrall Church of Canterburie, at the Funerall of that Reverend and Worthy Man, Mr Doctor Colfe* (1614), A7v.

[95] James Cleland, *Iacobs Wel, and Abbots Conduit* (1626), D4v (p. 24).

It can hardly be a coincidence that the early decades of the seventeenth century also saw a growing number of preachers expressing concern about the itching ears of their congregations. Such complaints often took a fairly stereotypical form, based as they were on St. Paul's condemnation of hearers who 'will not endure sound doctrine' but 'heap to themselves teachers, having itching ears' (2 Timothy 4: 3), but they reflect a genuine anxiety about sermongoers who were perceived to be picking and choosing the sermons that suited them best. Robert Wilkinson, preaching at Paul's Cross in 1607 on the story of Lot's wife, complained that listeners craved novelty and would not pay attention to sermons on the familiar topics of faith and repentance:

Men come now adaies to a Sermon as to a play, *Aut novum dicas, aut nihil dicas*, either some new thing or nothing, either a new matter or none at all. Speake ye of *Lots* wife! and what of her! our pulpits are made for *Moses* that tels the tale while it is new; the bel-frey is good enough for him that remembreth it when it is old. Preaching is become like apparelling, we can fancie it no longer than the fashion is new: If wee come to a Sermon and heare no new thing, we think that time was lost, and bid Fie on such a man, as the Israelites did on Manna, because they had it every day; heere is Manna, and Manna, and Manna, and nothing but Manna; and so say we, we heard today the high-way points of faith and good workes, with the vulgar doctrine, and common place of repentance, and heard nothing but that we knew before, and men grow angrie if they heare of one thing twice, as if their patience was greatly abused.[96]

William Pulley, preacher at Lincoln's Inn, remarked that 'a partiall and schismaticall choise of ministers' was 'usuall in great townes and cities where is varietie of Preachers'. Like Wilkinson, he complained that sermongoers were drawn to novelty – 'nothing doth please them but what doth suit their fancie . . . nothing but that which exceeds the vulgar capacitie' – and also suggested that they were easily captivated by an eloquent show of rhetoric: 'So the ignorant multitude of this wanton age, affect their severall Teachers, some for plaine preaching, others for round rebuking, a third for smooth utterance, a fourth for fine eloquence, few or none that their consciences may be edified and their soules saved, yea, so itching are the eares of many hearers that so longe as the Preacher useth a sett composition of words, preceptes of art . . . he shall be heard and applauded.'[97] Thomas Sutton,

---

[96] Robert Wilkinson, *Lots Wife, A Sermon Preached at Paules Crosse* (1607), C1v–2r (pp. 10–11).

[97] William Pulley, 'The art of hearing', Trinity College, Cambridge, MS B.14.51, ff. 106r, 108r. Pulley was preacher at Lincoln's Inn from 1599 to *c.*1602, when he was succeeded by Thomas Gataker: see Wilfrid R. Prest, *The Inns of Court under Elizabeth I and the Early Stuarts 1590–1640* (London, 1972), p. 189. Three other volumes of his sermons and treatises survive at Trinity (MS B.15.6–8); Prest, who was apparently unaware of these manuscripts, states (p. 197) that Pulley's religious position is not known.

lecturer at St Saviour's Southwark, also noted that London sermongoers had very specific expectations of their preachers, both in doctrine and delivery, and would be quick to discard a preacher who failed to satisfy them. 'Some must bee pleased onely by length, some by lowdnesse, some by squeezing of zeale, some by pushing at a Father, some by declaiming against a Latine sentence, others by betraying their sillinesse in squibbing authoritie. If he doe none of these, hee shall finde the love of many burning Professors as cold as snow water.'[98]

Moreover, the establishment of parish lectureships meant that preachers sometimes depended, for their livelihood, on a favourable audience response to their sermons. The typical procedure for appointing parish lecturers is illustrated by a case in the London church court records concerning the lectureship at St Lawrence Pountney. The churchwardens testified that after the death of their lecturer Mr Lloyd, four other London clergy 'knowing that Mr Lloyd was dead and that the place was voyd were desyrous to obteyne the place, and came at severall tymes and offered to give them a sermon for a tryall of theyr giftes'. Accordingly, the churchwardens invited them to preach a series of trial sermons, 'two sabbath dayes together, forenoone and afternoone eache of them one sermon'. Shortly afterwards, the feoffees (the trustees of the lectureship) called a vestry meeting and announced that 'they had three persons in nomination who did stand to be chosen for theyr curate and preacher, and asked theyr opinions which of them they lyked and desyred every one of them to give theyr voice'. The churchwardens 'gave theyr voices by a marke with a penne to Mr Crabtrees name, and so did the greater number present and then the feoffees made aunswere that they had done well for they had given their voyces to him whome before they had chosen or agreed uppon'.[99] Two features of this case are particularly worth noting. The first is that the parishioners clearly knew what they wanted from their preacher, and seem to have participated very willingly in the process of comparing different sermons and voting for their preferred candidate. The second is that this system of selection seems to have been looked on by the ecclesiastical authorities as nothing out of the ordinary; the only reason the case got into court was because the church-wardens were accused of having allowed some of the candidates to preach without a licence.

---

[98] Thomas Sutton, *Lectures upon the Eleventh Chapter to the Romans* (1632), D3r (p. 37).
[99] Answers of George Watkins and William Cooke, churchwardens of St Lawrence Pountney, Nov. 1619: LMA, DL/C/192 (London consistory court, personal answer book 1617–21), f. 98.

The lectureship system was criticised by some contemporaries for enabling the laity 'to tye the tongues of their teachers to their purs-strings' and thereby compromising the preacher's independence.[100] This was at the root of the Laudian objection to schemes for the lay patronage of the preaching ministry, such as the Feoffees for Impropriations, which were interpreted as a covert attempt to set up a lay presbytery in the Church of England. In this as in other respects, the Laudian portrayal of Puritanism, though distorted and unfair, bore enough relation to reality to be polemically effective, for it was true that the lectureship system did encourage close and often cosy relations between the preachers and the parish oligarchies who selected them and paid their salaries. But this should not be pushed too far. 'If the history of the lectureships demonstrates anything', Paul Seaver has written, 'it is the existence of a powerful drive among the laity to control the Church, at least at the parochial level.'[101] Yet it is not at all clear that the lectureships did in fact do much to extend lay control over the preaching ministry, as they tended to be financed by a small group of the wealthier parishioners, not by the parish at large. The election at St Lawrence Pountney reveals the limits of popular participation: the parishioners were invited to vote for their favoured candidate, thereby preserving the semblance of a popular choice, but in fact the appointment had already been made by the feoffees, and the parishioners merely confirmed it. The great majority of Londoners had little or no leverage over the appointment of preachers and, as we have seen, might well go gadding to sermons in other parishes where they had no responsibility to pay for the upkeep of the preaching ministry. Indeed, it can even be argued that the lectureship system actually reduced the opportunities for lay control of the Church, since, as one London incumbent pointed out, the tithe system fell disproportionately heavily on the poorer sort of parishioners – 'the rich men, for the most part, paying very little . . . so that the Ministers maintenance ariseth, for the most part, from the meanest and poorest people' – whereas the financing of lectureships was weighted in the other direction.[102]

But perhaps it is misleading to focus on a struggle for 'control' as the key to understanding the preaching ministry in early modern London, when the

---

[100] Thomas Morton, *A Defence of the Innocencie of the Three Ceremonies* (1618), Z3r.
[101] Seaver, *The Puritan Lectureships*, p. 292.
[102] Udall, *Good Workes*. At St Bartholomew Exchange, for example, the lecturer's stipend was supposedly paid by a voluntary contribution from every householder in the parish, but actually depended heavily on the generosity of a few prominent individuals: in 1585 the seven largest contributions accounted for over half the total; Edwin Freshfield, ed., *The Vestry Minute Books of the Parish of St Bartholomew Exchange 1567–1676* (1890), p. 17.

patterns of sermon attendance explored in this chapter have far less to do with the control than with the consumption of sermons. They did not lead to the breakdown of the parish system, nor to a lay takeover of the Church, but they did allow the laity to compare different styles of preaching and to vote, if not with their purses then with their feet, by attending the sermons of the preachers they liked best. In this respect Seaver is absolutely right to draw attention to the presence of 'an educated and confident laity who followed the thought of the preacher critically' as one of the most significant aspects of the London lectureship system. The theologian Karl Rahner once suggested slightly mischievously that the quality of clerical ministry might be improved by giving the laity the freedom to cross parish boundaries: 'It is not at all a bad thing if a preacher knows that his listeners can go away to someone else if he preaches badly.'[103] The situation that Rahner was envisaging – in effect, a free market for sermons – is not so very far removed from the situation described in this chapter. And if we are looking for the origins of modern-day 'church consumerism' or 'consumer religion', it may not be entirely fanciful to find them in the throngs of sermongoers criss-crossing the streets and parish boundaries of early modern London.

---

[103] Karl Rahner, 'Peaceful reflections on the parochial principle', in Rahner, *Theological Reflections*, vol. ii (1963), p. 317.

# CHAPTER 5

# Preaching and the people

Nearly forty years after its publication, Keith Thomas's *Religion and the Decline of Magic* (1971) is still a current work of scholarship, an indispensable starting-point for anyone interested in the relationship between religious doctrine and popular culture. At one level, it can be read simply as a sourcebook, documenting the extraordinary variety of magical beliefs and superstitions that existed and flourished in sixteenth- and seventeenth-century England. But it also puts forward a compelling argument about the failure of the Protestant Reformation. The reason why these magical beliefs flourished as they did, Thomas suggests, was because 'the hold of any kind of orthodox religion upon the mass of the population was never more than partial', and because many people, particularly among the poor, 'remained throughout their lives utterly ignorant of the elementary tenets of Christian dogma'. And he lays the blame for this failure squarely at the door of the Protestant preaching ministry. 'The clergy often pitched their discourse far above the capacity of most of their listeners . . . In the process they tended to forget that the majority of their local congregation lacked the intellectual sophistication of an educated schoolboy.' As a result, many people – if they came to church at all – simply slept through the sermon, or interrupted the preacher with 'frivolous or insulting asides', and headed straight for the alehouse as soon as the service was over.

This bears a strong resemblance to the 'revisionist' interpretation of the English Reformation that began to emerge in the 1970s and 1980s in the work of historians such as Christopher Haigh and J. J. Scarisbrick. The resemblance is not so surprising, as the revisionists were drawing on the same sort of evidence, including presentments to the church courts and Protestant complaint literature such as George Gifford's *A Brief Discourse of Certaine Points of the Religion which is among the Common Sort of Christians* (1581). Haigh emphasised the unpopularity of Protestant preaching in very much the same terms as Thomas had done. 'If hostility to their preaching was a problem for godly ministers, sheer uncomprehending boredom in congregations was another. We should not suppose that Elizabethan churchgoers sat in attentive rows, listening patiently to their preachers: they chattered, scoffed, squabbled and fought, and if the tedium grew unbearable they walked out.' In addition, he argued that there was a basic opposition between the religion professed by most ordinary churchgoers – a religion of charity, good fellowship and salvation by works – and the religion taught by their ministers. Thus he concluded, with provocative overstatement, that the Protestant preachers were attempting the impossible. 'In Elizabethan conditions, with low levels of literacy and with the alehouse and the village green to distract the people from sermons and catechism, the English people *could not* be made Protestants – they could not be made to understand, accept and respond to the Protestant doctrines offered to them, justification by faith and predestination.'[1]

'It is well on the way to being an axiom', wrote Eamon Duffy in 1986, 'that the poor in early modern England were hostile, or resistant, or at best indifferent to protestant Christianity.'[2] By that time, however, the tide was beginning to turn. The following year, Martin Ingram borrowed one of Keith Thomas's chapter headings, 'Religion and the people', for an account of popular religion very different from Thomas's, in which he argued that most people occupied the middle ground of 'unspectacular orthodoxy' rather than the extremes of piety or indifference. Duffy himself put forward a very similar argument, stressing that it was seriously misleading to judge the religion of the people according to the high and demanding standards set by the puritan preachers. There were, he suggested, 'many who sincerely accepted the traditional forms of English protestantism' while rejecting Puritanism, an argument that has since been elaborated by Christopher Marsh and Judith Maltby, among others. Indeed, Duffy's study of chapbook literature led him to conclude that even the puritan tradition had succeeded remarkably well in penetrating popular culture. This positive assessment of the Protestant Reformation may surprise those who see Duffy as an arch-revisionist in the school of Haigh and Scarisbrick; but one of the distinctive features of Duffy's work, and one that sets him somewhat apart

---

[1] Christopher Haigh, 'The Church of England, the Catholics and the people', in *The Reign of Elizabeth I* (London, 1984), p. 213; Haigh has returned to this theme in two more recent articles, 'The taming of Reformation: preachers, pastors and parishioners in Elizabethan and early Stuart England', *History*, 85 (Oxford, 2000), pp. 572–88, and 'Success and failure in the English Reformation', *Past & Present*, 173 (2001), pp. 28–49.

[2] Eamon Duffy, 'The godly and the multitude in Stuart England', *The Seventeenth Century*, 1: 1 (January 1986), p. 31.

from the other revisionists, is his sensitivity to the threads of continuity between pre- and post-Reformation culture, and to the ways in which Catholicism and Protestantism can be regarded as expressions of a common religious impulse.

Any temptation to view this purely as a 'top-down' Reformation, with Protestant ideas trickling downwards from élite into popular culture, is dispelled by the work of other historians who have treated the relationship between Protestantism and popular culture in terms of a dynamic inter-action. (In passing, it may be noted that this is a useful corrective to earlier scholarship which tended to regard popular culture as a container waiting to be filled. In Keith Thomas's work, religious heterodoxy fills the vacuum created by the failure of Protestant evangelism; while Haigh can describe sixteenth-century churchgoers as 'de-catholicized but un-protestantized', empty vessels not yet filled by the new wine of Protestant ideas.[3]) Tessa Watt's study of religious ballads and chapbooks, *Cheap Print and Popular Piety* (1991), presents the encounter between Protestantism and popular culture as a 'gradual modification of traditional piety', as elements of Protestant doctrine were incorporated into the existing religious culture to create a 'patchwork of beliefs', distinctively 'post-Reformation' but not wholly 'Protestant' in character.[4] More recently, Alexandra Walsham has shown how providentialist language served as a point of contact between Protestantism and popular belief; an insight taken up and extended by Peter Lake, who shows how Protestant pamphleteers tried to appropriate the providentialist language of cheap print and use it as a kind of Trojan horse to smuggle Calvinist ideas into popular culture.

Thus, in the space of little more than a decade, the landscape has been completely transformed. The emerging consensus is summed up in Diarmaid MacCulloch's much-quoted remark that the English Reformation was a 'howling success' – and to judge by the response to Eamon Duffy's *The Voices of Morebath* (2002), this consensus appears to have carried all before it. One review praised Duffy for bringing out the 'intense personal and com-munal involvement which distinguished the religion of some rural parishes in the years before the Reformation', but complained that he 'underrates the extent to which Protestant worship ... could also give scope for personal involvement and express local identity'. And who was this reviewer who chastised Duffy, of all people, for placing insufficient emphasis on the success

---

[3] Christopher Haigh, *English Reformations* (Oxford, 1993), p. 290.
[4] Tessa Watt, *Cheap Print and Popular Piety, 1550–1640* (Cambridge, 1991), p. 327.

of the Protestant Reformation? None other than Keith Thomas.[5] With that, the historiographical revolution would appear to be complete. As often happens in revolutions, however, there is a certain amount of unfinished business – that is to say, some questions posed by the old consensus that are only partially answered by the new.

Some of the most interesting questions, for me, concern the contribution of preaching to the success story of the English Reformation. For if we are to believe the testimony of the preachers themselves – and as Haigh asks, 'if we cannot entirely trust the preachers, where can we look?' – it seems that popular resistance to the new religion was focused, above all, on the preaching ministry. In his dialogue *The Preachers Plea*, based on his pastoral experience in Devon, Samuel Hieron remarked that the question 'What need all this preaching?' was 'common in the mouthes of many, either ignorant or ill disposed persons' and had brought the ministry into general disrepute. 'In former times when there was lesse preaching . . . the world (they say) was much better, there was more love, more hospitalitie, more trueth, more mercie, more good dealing amongst men than is to be found at this day.' The objection was often expressed in proverbial fashion: 'the merry world is gone, since preaching came up'; 'the world was never merry, since there was so much preaching'.[6] Now, it is possible to argue that this is exaggerated: that godly preachers were conditioned to expect opposition to their ministry, that they took an over-pessimistic view of popular religion or that they were simply reporting the views of a diehard Catholic minority. But the evidence remains compelling – and it is worth examining the possibility that the Reformation may have succeeded in spite of the preaching ministry rather than because of it.

Moreover, preaching is conspicuously absent from many recent accounts of the success of the Reformation. Keith Thomas lists 'communion in both kinds, psalm-singing and Bible-reading' as the aspects of the new religion that offered most scope for popular participation; Haigh sees catechising as the 'one undoubted educational success' of the Elizabethan Church; David Cressy draws our attention to the bonfires and bells of the Protestant calendar; Watt, Walsham and Lake all stress the influence of cheap print. But what about preaching? Again, it seems as though the Reformation

---

[5] Keith Thomas, 'A vanished world', *New York Review of Books*, 7 November 2002, pp. 56–9.

[6] Samuel Hieron, *The Preachers Plea: or, a Treatise in Forme of a Plaine Dialogue, Making Known the Worth and Necessity of that which We Call Preaching* (1605), E7r. Thomas Turvell, *The Poore Mans Path-way to Heaven* (1616), B1v; William Sclater, *An Exposition with Notes upon the First and Second Epistles to the Thessalonians* (1627), 2F6r. A Northamptonshire woman was refused the sacrament in 1590 for declaring that 'it was a merry world before there was so much preaching': W. J. Sheils, *The Puritans in the Diocese of Peterborough 1558–1610* (Northampton, 1979), p. 45.

succeeded in spite of itself, or in spite of the efforts of its most committed ministers. The godly preachers of the Elizabethan Church believed that preaching was the spearhead of the Reformation: that if only the people could be exposed to the converting power of the Word – that is, the Word preached, not merely the Word read – all else would follow. 'Get you preachers into your parishes', the Elizabethan puritan John More urged the Norfolk gentry, and then 'we shall begin to be rich in the Lord Jesus'.[7] The implication of recent scholarship is that they were mistaken: that the Reformation captured the hearts and minds of the people not so much through preaching as through the ritual and liturgical apparatus of the new religion: bells, music and the Prayer Book. In Duffy's words: 'Cranmer's sombrely magnificent prose, read week by week, entered and possessed their minds, and became the fabric of their prayer, the utterance of their most solemn and their most vulnerable moments.'[8]

There is also considerable force in Haigh's argument that the new model of the minister as preacher conflicted with the traditional social role of the parson as pastor and peacemaker, just as it did with the traditional religious role of the priest as confessor and intercessor. Haigh suggests that in many people's eyes, the ideal clergyman was one 'who read services devoutly, reconciled quarrellers in his parish, and joined his people for "good fellowship" on the ale bench' – a stereotype far removed from that of the godly preacher rebuking his people for their sins. This is not to suggest that Protestant ministers simply withdrew from the business – or, to use John Bossy's term, the 'moral tradition' – of settling disputes among their parishioners: but it is undeniably true that their role as peacemakers now came a poor second to their role as preachers. 'Thousands of our times', remarked Jeremiah Dyke, 'will uphold it for a truth, that a minister may do God better service in taking up quarrels betweene neighbours, and composing differences betweene parishioners, than with all his paines in preaching . . . Ridiculous follie!'[9] Bossy has argued persuasively that in the world of post-Reformation Christianity, churches and clergy – Catholic and Protestant alike – 'secured or retained the loyalty of their populations by

[7] Quoted in Patrick Collinson, *Godly People: Essays on English Protestantism and Puritanism* (London, 1983), p. 297.

[8] Duffy, *The Stripping of the Altars: Traditional Religion in England 1400–1580* (New Haven & London), p. 593.

[9] Jeremiah Dyke, *A Counterpoison against Covetousnesse* (1619), B1r. See also William Perkins, *Exhortation to Repentance . . . Together with Two Treatises on the Duties and Dignitie of the Ministrie* (1605), F4v, where it is argued that even if a minister 'keepe good Hospitalitie, and make peace amongst his Neighbors' he will not discharge his duty unless he preaches, 'for if a Minister have not this vertue, hee hath none'. On the traditional ministry of reconciliation, see Peter Marshall, *The Catholic Priesthood and the English Reformation* (Oxford, 1994), chapter 7, 'The priest as neighbour'.

proving themselves fit vessels of the moral tradition'. If so, then it is hard to resist the conclusion that the Protestant clergy, brandishing the weapon of godly preaching, had shot themselves in the foot.

In this chapter, I want to suggest that there is a case to be made for the success of the Protestant preaching ministry. However, the case for pastoral failure has to be taken seriously, and I also want to revisit some of the material studied by Thomas and Haigh, particularly the Protestant complaint literature, which presents a vivid and richly detailed account of parish religion, much of it clearly based on firsthand experience. Alongside this, I want to set another class of material which has, until now, been relatively neglected – sermon manuscripts, which bring us as close as we are likely to come to what was actually preached in the parishes of late sixteenth- and early seventeenth-century England. With the help of this evidence, we can transcend the stark alternatives of 'success' and 'failure', and build up a rather more nuanced and ambiguous picture of the relationship between Protestant preachers and their audiences. The complaint literature, I will suggest, is by no means as unrelievedly pessimistic as Haigh's account of it might lead us to suppose. And the sermon manuscripts are not simply a record of preachers talking to a silent auditory; they also enable us to gauge something of the audience response, and remind us that in many respects the preaching ministry was not a monologue but a dialogue.

### POPULAR IGNORANCE

Seventeenth-century clergy liked to make their flesh creep by telling horror stories about the ignorance of the common people. One of the most famous of such stories first appeared in print in 1628, but had probably been in oral circulation long before that, as the narrator, William Pemble, claimed to have heard it 'from a reverend man out of the pulpit'. It evidently struck a nerve, as it was retold by a Devonshire preacher in 1640, by which time it had acquired semi-legendary status ('As historye sayth . . .') as a fable of Protestant failure:

As historye sayth a meere naturall man, haveinge noe more knowledge of god than he was borne in, and lyeinge on his death bed in his old age was demanded what god was, he answered a good old man; being asked what Christ was, he sayd a towardly younge man, a third question what his soule was, answered a great bone in his bodye, and being asked what should become of it when he was dead, answered if he had lived well att his departure it should reioyce in the pleasant greene meadowes, if not it should continue with his bodye. Here is an example of natureall knowledge, which exceeds not the heathen in theire ignorance; yett lived he where the gospel was preached constantly.[10]

The point of the story was that this man had not lived in one of the dark corners of the land, but under a settled preaching ministry. In Pemble's account, he had 'lived and dyed in a parish, where there had beene preaching almost all his time, and for the greatest part twice on the Lords day'. 'This man was a constant hearer as any might be, and seemed forward in the love of the word . . . a man of good understanding, and one that in his dayes, had heard by the least two or three thousand Sermons.' How was it possible for such a man to have remained so ignorant? For those who believed in the power of the preaching ministry as an invincible instrument of conversion, this was a deeply troubling story.

Given the wide oral circulation of this story, we might be tempted to dismiss it as an urban myth (or rural myth?), the early modern equivalent of the vanishing hitchhiker or the pet dog in the microwave. Yet it can be paralleled, in less vivid form, by many other clerical descriptions of parish religion. Robert Parker remarked in 1607 that 'as there be monsters in the sea, which the seafaring man doth meete, though the Ilander will not beleeve it', so 'the poore and vigilant Pastor meeteth in the countrey' with popular superstitions which his brethren in the universities could scarcely imagine.'[11] Other ministers agreed, and stressed that this was not due to any lack of preaching. As a Dorset preacher observed in 1613, sermons were 'heard and daily continued (Gods name for ever be blessed) in everie corner of this land', yet the multitude still remained in a state of 'grosse and sottish ignorance . . . through the whole body of our Churches'. The Derbyshire cleric Richard Kilby expressed similar astonishment that 'in some places even where learned preachers have killed themselves with sore labours the greater number of people are grossly ignorant'. Peter Ince, rector of Donhead St Mary, Wiltshire, told Richard Baxter in 1655 that the majority of his parishioners 'hate instruction and are as ignorant of Christianity I meane of the plainest principles (which they have heard of mee I believe an hundred times) as if they had never heard of them', adding: 'I did not think

---

[10] Sermon by John Moore, curate of Huxham, Devonshire: Beinecke Library, Yale, MS Osborn b.303. The story was first told in Pemble's *Five Godly and Profitable Sermons* (1628), reprinted in Pemble's *Workes* (1635), 3B4r (p. 559), and introduced to modern scholarship by Keith Thomas, *Religion and the Decline of Magic* (1971), p. 194. Writing in 1670, Giles Firmin assumed it would be familiar to his readers: 'The story which blessed Pemble gives us of that fine civil man, who had heard three thousand Sermons . . . is very famous.' Firmin, *The Real Christian* (1670), 2D4v. It appears again in Richard Steele's *The Husbandmans Calling* (1670), I1v: 'Who could have believed the sad story that Mr *Pemble* tells us in his Sermon about Ignorance, if it had not an Author of credit?'

[11] Robert Parker, *A Scholasticall Discourse, against Symbolizing with Antichrist in Ceremonies* (Middelburg, 1607), H1r.

rationall creatures subject to so grosse and affected ignorance: they seeme to be affraid of knowledge.'[12]

And how did the clergy respond to this dismal situation? Some, 'disheartened with lack of success', were reported to have given up preaching altogether, 'suffering their worthy gifts to rust'.[13] Others went in search of more fruitful pastures elsewhere. Samuel Gardiner gave up his Norfolk living in disgust, lamenting that there were 'few or none . . . that ever he could make to understand, but were as simple as the least child' – though some of the fault may have lain with Gardiner himself, as Lady Dorothy Bacon, reporting his departure to Sir Roger Townshend, added that his parishioners 'were I believe as glad he was gone' as he was to be rid of them.[14] Richard Greenham's biographer tells us that he left the parish of Dry Drayton, Cambridgeshire, because of the 'intractableness and unteachableness' of his parishioners, and settled in London, where he rapidly built up a reputation as a healer of wounded consciences: a striking instance, it would seem, of a godly minister turning his attention from 'mission' to 'maintenance', abandoning his efforts to convert the unconverted and settling instead for a more limited but more rewarding ministry of spiritual direction within the godly community. Christopher Haigh takes this as symptomatic of the general failure of Protestant evangelism. 'If Richard Greenham, of all men . . . could not make committed Protestants of more than a tiny handful of his parishioners, then nobody could and the task was impossible.'

So much for the prosecution case. The case for the defence has tended to focus on the distinctive features of particular parishes, with the aim of showing that while there may have been occasional cases of pastoral failure, these cannot be taken as representative of the fortunes of the Protestant preaching ministry as a whole. Eric Carlson, for example, has shown that Dry Drayton had a long tradition of self-government, with no resident lord of the manor, relatively few incomers from other parishes and local offices monopolised by a few leading families – a state of affairs which may have made it difficult for Greenham, as an outsider, to make much of an impression.[15] Similarly, one might observe that many of the complaints

---

[12]  Bodleian Library, Oxford, MS Rawl. C.764, f. 33; Peter Lake, 'Richard Kilby: a study in personal and professional failure', in W. J. Sheils and D. Wood, eds., *The Ministry: Clerical and Lay* (Oxford, 1989), p. 224; Peter Ince to Richard Baxter, 1 March 1655, in N. H. Keeble and G. F. Nuttall, *Calendar of the Correspondence of Richard Baxter*, vol. 1 (Oxford, 1991), p. 166.

[13]  Sclater, *Exposition*, 2N3v.

[14]  Lady Dorothy Bacon to Sir Roger Townshend, July 1622, printed in Jane Key, 'The letters and will of Lady Dorothy Bacon, 1597–1629', *A Miscellany* (Norfolk Record Society, vol. LVI, 1991), pp. 96–7.

[15]  Eric Josef Carlson, *Marriage and the English Reformation* (1994), pp. 157–63.

about popular resistance to Protestant preaching come from western coun-
ties such as Somerset, Wiltshire and Dorset, and seem to fit in with the
findings of David Underdown's study of the chalk downlands, where a
pattern of settlement based on arable farming led to small, nucleated villages
with a strong local identity and a conservative popular culture.[16] In the final
analysis, however, this is not really enough to shake Haigh's case for
Protestant failure, which rests not on the evidence of specific preachers in
specific parishes, but on the general sense of failure expressed in the
Protestant complaint literature, and the perceived gap between clerical
aims and parochial achievements. It is a strong case, and deserves to be
answered on its own terms – which is what I shall attempt to do here.

We might begin with a remark of Patrick Collinson's, that 'we should
only write off the effectiveness of the instructive ministry when we have
carefully considered the almost universal practice of the catechism and
found it wanting'. In the late sixteenth century, as they came to realise
that simply parachuting a preaching minister into a parish was not enough,
Protestant clergy began to move towards a greater emphasis on catechising
as a way to teach the basic principles of the Christian faith to unlearned
congregations who might have difficulty in understanding sermons. Indeed,
catechising soon came to be regarded as a necessary precondition for a
successful preaching ministry, not least because it was a more interactive
form of religious instruction, which made it easier for the clergy to monitor
the progress of their parishioners. William Crashaw declared that without
catechising 'all our labour in Preaching is utterly lost in many of our hearers,
as lamentable experience shewes in many Congregations of this Kingdome'.
Nehemiah Rogers maintained that a minister who 'preacheth twice or thrice a
weeke, and so hath continued for many yeares together, omitting Catechizing
of his People' would be less successful than one who preached and catechised
for a single year. Richard Bernard went so far as to criticise 'a proud conceit in
some Ministers, which may thinke that they onely are to be respected which
doe Preach', and even suggested that some ministers would do better if they
gave up preaching altogether and concentrated solely on catechising.[17]

We must be careful not to overstate the effects of catechising, especially
since the attendance records that survive for two London parishes, St Olave
Jewry and St Botolph Aldgate, suggest that there was a high rate of

---

[16] David Underdown, *Revel, Riot and Rebellion: Popular Politics and Culture in England 1603–1660* (Oxford, 1985).

[17] William Crashaw, *Milke for Babes: or, a North-Countrey Catechisme* (5th edn., 1628), A3r; Nehemiah Rogers, *A Sermon Preached at the Second Triennial Visitation of . . . Lord Bishop of London* (1632), E1v; Richard Bernard, *Two Twinnes: or Two Parts of One Portion of Scripture* (1613), A4r, C4v.

absenteeism. At St Olave's, all the young people of the parish were supposed to be catechised in rotation, three or four households at a time. Between January and October 1578, fifty-seven householders were ordered to send their families to be catechised, but only twenty-six obliged; and on five out of the nineteen recorded catechising sessions during that period, no catechumens appeared at all. At St Botolph's, catechising was conducted on a smaller scale, with three or four children being examined by the minister after Sunday evening prayer. Even so, the parish clerk's memorandum book records a fair number of defaulters: in the first few months of 1598, one catechumen 'fayned himselfe sick and did not answer the preacher', another 'said he had lost his part' so that someone else had to answer for him, another 'was negligent and also lost his part wherfore he did not com to be cattechysed', and another 'was gone into the countrie to his frends'.[18] While it would be unwise to extrapolate directly from urban to rural areas, these examples do suggest that attendance levels were generally low. According to Cornelius Burges, householders were reluctant to release their servants, complaining: 'wee must now let our people leave all their busines to goe to him to bee catechised every time they goe to the Communion, and so loose half a daies work for nothing . . . why, they have been with him often enough already, will not that serve the turne?'[19]

Some ministers, while granting the beneficial effects of catechising, doubted whether those effects were at all widespread. 'I am fully perswaded', declared one, 'if the people of this land were called to their Catechisme and required to give an account of their faith, not one of ten thousand would be able to do it.' William Chibald wrote in 1622 that 'ordinarily the yonger sort wil be afraid to be catechized, and the older sort ashamed'.[20] However, Ian Green's recent survey of the practice, *The Christian's ABC* (1996), arrives at a much more positive verdict. One of the most telling findings of Green's research is the sheer number of printed catechisms that appeared in England: at a rough count, about 400 published before 1640, and at least

---

[18] Guildhall Library, London, MS 4415/1 (St Olave Jewry, vestry minute book), ff. 60–6: lists of 'those that were warned to the catechism', 1576–8; and MS 9234/7 (St Botolph Aldgate, parish clerk's memorandum book).

[19] Cambridge University Library, Add. MS 6165, p. 29. For examples of non-attendance at catechising, see Hilda Johnstone, ed., *Churchwardens' Presentments: Part I. Archdeaconry of Chichester* (Sussex Record Society, vol. XLIX, 1947–8), pp. 8, 22, 30, 66; and Paul Griffiths, *Youth and Authority: Formative Experiences in England 1560–1640* (Oxford, 1996), pp. 81–96.

[20] Folger Library, Washington, DC, V.a.204: sermon on Hebrews 11: 6, dated 1618; William Chibald, *A Tryall of Faith* (1622), F8v. Chibald evidently did not intend to disparage the utility of catechising, as he added that he had attended catechising sessions 'where both yong and old . . . have answered readily and discreetly'.

as many again by 1700, in addition to the official Prayer Book catechism. It is clear that the parish clergy took catechising very seriously indeed, and that – rather than drilling their parishioners to recite the catechism in a purely mechanical way – many clergy were creatively adapting other people's catechisms, or even writing their own, in order to make their instruction more effective. The availability of printed catechisms must, in turn, have encouraged the introduction of catechising in other parishes. In his conclusion, Green strikes a note of modest optimism: 'in trying to ensure that the majority of its charges had grasped some of its basic tenets, the church had adopted an approach designed to meet the needs of the less well-educated, and . . . may have achieved a moderate degree of success.'[21]

In the light of Green's research, most scholars have now come round to a broadly positive assessment of the effectiveness of catechising. What is not so clear, however, is whether this was enough to turn early modern layfolk into Protestants. The Prayer Book catechism, as Eamon Duffy has pointed out, 'might have been written at any time since 1215 . . . it said nothing whatever about the distinctive Protestant *ordo salutis*, nothing about the Fall or original sin, it never discussed the nature of salvation, except in terms of duties towards God and neighbour, and it never once used the word faith' – which helps to explain why so many clergy felt the need to supplement the Prayer Book catechism with additional material of their own.[22] Haigh argues that while the Church of England had succeeded in imposing the Prayer Book catechism on its people as a basic minimum of religious knowledge, it never succeeded in raising the threshold any higher – to the dismay of clergy who felt that the catechism, on its own, was not enough: 'not Protestantism . . . not sufficient Christian knowledge, much less an adequate foundation for a saving faith'. Green makes the same point in a slightly different way when he suggests that, in their eagerness to simplify their message for the sake of simple folk, some clergy may have done 'relatively little . . . to undermine the existing popular trust in the value of works' and may thus, paradoxically, have made it harder for their flocks to grasp more complex doctrines such as justification by faith.[23]

It would be easy to conclude, then, that most early modern layfolk were Christians without being Protestants. But this is not the impression given

[21] Ian Green, *The Christian's ABC: Catechisms and Catechizing in England* c. *1530–1740* (Oxford, 1996), pp. 557–63.

[22] Eamon Duffy, 'The Long Reformation: Catholicism, Protestantism and the multitude', in Nicholas Tyacke, ed., *England's Long Reformation, 1500–1800* (1998), pp. 33–70, p. 43.

[23] Haigh, 'Success and failure', p. 47; Green, *The Christian's ABC*, p. 569; for another version of this argument, see Christopher Marsh, *Popular Religion in Sixteenth-Century England* (1998), p. 84.

by the writings of contemporary clerical commentators. While many ministers were extremely disparaging about the religious competence of their parishioners, they did not deny that there was a widespread low-level acceptance of Protestant doctrine. 'Christ died for us, is a principle in all mens mouths', observed William Sclater. 'That faith justifies, what Libertine amongst us professeth not to know?' Edward Elton claimed that most people were unable to give satisfactory answers 'if they be examined touching Originall sinne, justification in the sight of God, and the like points', but admitted that most of them had, or thought they had, some understanding of the doctrines of faith and repentance. 'There is never a one of us living under the preaching of the Gospell, but wee will seeme to have gotten thus much knowledge, that wee are to repent of our sinnes, and beleeve in Christ, that wee may be justified and saved: we will thinke there is great disgrace and indignitie offered the meanest of us, if we be told we know not these things: though few indeed know them as they ought.' According to Thomas Bedford, most people knew enough to be able to say 'that God made us, that we must be saved by faith in Christ and not by our owne workes'.[24]

This goes even for Arthur Dent's dialogue *The Plaine Mans Path-way to Heaven*, one of Haigh's principal exhibits in the case for Protestant failure. The character of Asunetus, the ignorant countryman in the dialogue, is generally associated with the semi-Pelagian belief that one could be saved by prayers and good works. In a much-quoted passage, he declares that if a man 'say his Lords praier, his ten Commandements, and his Beliefe, and keepe them, and say no bodie no harme, nor doe no bodie no harm, and doe as hee would be done to ... no doubt he shall be saved'. 'This', Haigh has commented, 'was the "works religion" which Luther and the Protestants had condemned, a gut conviction that salvation came from prayer and charity, whatever the preachers said.'[25] Later on in the book, however, Asunetus makes a general confession of his sins and affirms his reliance on Christ for salvation: 'I am a sinner. Wee are all sinners: there is no man but he sinneth'; 'I neede a Saviour: and it is my Lord Iesus that must save me: for he made me.' He is still chided by his pastor for his inability to itemise his sins in detail – 'such ignorant and sottish men as you are, will in generall say you are sinners: because your conscience telleth you so; but when it

---

[24] Sclater, *Exposition*, 2A5r; Edward Elton, *An Exposition of the Epistle of St Paul to the Colossians* (2nd edn., 1620), F4v; BL Add. MS 47618, f. 73.
[25] Haigh, 'The Church of England, the Catholics and the people', p. 213; Arthur Dent, *The Plaine Mans Path-way to Heaven* (14th impr., 1612), C5r; Haigh, *English Reformations*, p. 281.

commeth to particulars, you know not how you sinne, nor wherein' – but he does appear to have grasped, however imperfectly, the key Protestant belief that salvation came through faith in Christ and not through the merit of good works.[26]

Indeed, even to describe *The Plaine Mans Path-way to Heaven* as a piece of Protestant 'complaint literature' may be somewhat misleading; for while Dent is highly critical of the religious beliefs of many ordinary laypeople, he is far from pessimistic about the possibility of improvement. The dialogue ends with Asunetus telling the godly minister Theologus: 'I am greatly comforted and cheared up with your words . . . I can never be thankfull enough for all the good instructions and comforts which I have heard from you this day.' In the words of Dent's authorial gloss: 'The ignorant man, beeing afflicted in his conscience, is exceedingly comforted with the hearing of Gods abundant mercie preached unto him, and thereupon doth gather great inward peace, converteth unto God with all his heart, and doth exceedingly blesse God for the preachers counsell.'[27] We may reasonably doubt whether conversions took place quite as easily as this: *The Plaine Mans Path-way* is, after all, a didactic work rather than a piece of dramatic realism or factual reportage, and Asunetus should be seen not as a single individual but as a portmanteau character embodying a variety of popular attitudes to religion, a reminder that 'popular religion' is not a unitary phenomenon but a catch-all term for a multiplicity of beliefs operating at different levels of doctrinal sophistication. Nevertheless, the work reflects a widespread confidence that the laity would be receptive to Protestantism if it was presented to them in attractive and accessible terms; and it is, to say the least, curious to treat it as a damning indictment of Protestant failure.

Nor was this confidence wholly unjustified. On the whole, the clergy seem to have succeeded in teaching their flocks to regard themselves as Protestants: even William Pemble, in his harsh characterisation of 'customary' religion, admitted that most people were accustomed to say of themselves, 'I thanke God . . . I am a Christian, a Protestant, baptized and brought up in the true faith of Christ Jesus.' Along with this sense of Protestant identity came a widespread popular distrust of Catholicism. In 1604 Jeremy Corderoy remarked that 'untill within these fewe yeares' the principal evil affecting the Church had been doctrinal error. Now, however, this disease was 'almost cured', since the errors of the Church of Rome were plain for all to see, so that preachers could turn their attention to the reformation of manners instead, 'and not wholy in these daies spende our

---

[26] Dent, *Plaine Mans Path-way*, X5r.    [27] Dent, *Plaine Mans Path-way*, 2C4r.

studies and labours against errour in doctrine'. Edward Elton, too, remarked on the extent of popular anti-Popery: 'there is no doubt, but most of us, if not al of us, can discerne the grossenes of poperie, and cry shame on it'. Indeed, it appears that ministers had been almost too successful in convincing people that England, as a Protestant nation, was under the special protection of God. John Rogers complained that people were unimpressed by warnings that God might punish England for their sins, and would reply that 'God hath defended this Nation these sixtie yeares, as in Eightie-eight, and at the Kings comming in, and from the Powder-treason, and so he will still, we have no feare.'[28]

Admittedly, many of these clerical writers also complain of popular resistance to their preaching. But on closer examination, most of these complaints turn out to refer specifically to sermons on Sunday afternoons or weekdays, and do not appear to reflect a dislike of sermons in general. The 'right honest man', as characterised by Thomas Taylor, 'cares not for these runners to Sermons, hee is none of them', but nevertheless 'keeps his Church, and heares Service, and a Sermon, if there be any', on Sunday mornings. This pattern of sermon attendance is not hard to explain. Sunday afternoon sermons had to compete with other forms of popular sociability – sports, recreations and the alehouse – while weekday sermons were commonly regarded as time-wasting distractions in the middle of the working week. One preacher was forced to plead that 'it is but rising a little earlier, or sitting up a little later, or making a little shorter at meales, and such a little time might be easily gained'; moreover, 'those who come themselves and bring their servants to a Lecture, have their worke as well done, and their land as well tilled, and their harvest as well inned, and everything in as good order' as their neighbours.[29] This ingenious justification of weekday sermon attendance, on the grounds that it was not incompatible with social and neighbourly obligation, introduces us to a theme that we shall encounter again later.

Puritan preachers, believing that the whole of the sabbath day should be consecrated to God's service, naturally disapproved of hearers who came to church on Sunday mornings and then took the rest of the day off. 'Many wil heare a Sermon in the forenoone', wrote Dent, 'and they take that to be as much, as God can require at their hand . . . But as for the afternoones, they

---

[28] Jeremy Corderoy, *A Short Dialogue, wherein Is Proved, that No Man Can Bee Saved without Good Workes* (Oxford, 1604), A10v; Elton, *Exposition*, 2K2r; John Rogers, *The Doctrine of Faith* (5th edn., 1633), V2v.

[29] Thomas Taylor, *The Parable of the Sower and of the Seed* (1621), T1r; Corpus Christi College, Oxford, MS 409, f. 151v.

will heare none: then they will to Bowles or Tables. These men serve God in the forenoone, and the divel in the afternoone.'[30] Dent and his fellow ministers were pushing for higher standards of religious observance: it is not entirely fair to say that they 'thought they had failed', since as far as they were concerned the prize was yet to win; but there is no doubt that they were deeply dissatisfied with the present state of the English Church, and saw no reason to rest content with what the Reformation had already achieved. Nevertheless, we have come a long way from Haigh's challenging assertion that 'the English people *could not* be made Protestants'. By the early seventeenth century, most people seem to have been acquainted not just with the basic Christian vocabulary of sin and salvation, but also with basic Protestant concepts such as justification by faith; they had a sense of Protestant identity; and they were willing to attend Protestant sermons on Sunday mornings, if not at other times. This was no mean achievement. It was not enough to satisfy the hotter Protestant clergy, but it was a foundation on which they could build, and one that made their drive for higher standards seem capable of attainment.

### UNPOPULAR PREACHING

A Protestant preacher coming into a parish in 1600, towards the end of Elizabeth's reign, would thus have had a considerable advantage over the first generation of Elizabethan clergy. His task, for the most part, would not have been to convert his people to Protestantism, but to make them better and more committed Protestants. As yet, however, we have only answered half of the case for the failure of the Protestant preaching ministry. The other half asserts that godly preachers squandered their advantage, and alienated many of their parishioners, by adopting a deliberately confrontational form of preaching. A hostile observer claimed in 1584 that the puritan clergy liked to quote Christ's words, 'Think not that I am come to send peace on earth: I came not to send peace, but a sword' (Matt. 10: 34), and had even maintained that it was 'the note of a good precher' to stir up controversy. And the clergy of Kent, it was alleged, had put this maxim into practice with disastrous effect. 'Hath not [Joseph] Minge brought Ashford from being the quietest towne of Kent to be at deadly hatred and bitter division? . . . hath not [George] Eelie set Tenterden, his parish, together by the ears, which before was quiet? what broile and contention hath [Dudley]

---

[30] Dent, *Plaine Mans Path-way*, 16r.

Fenner made in Cranbrooke, and all the rest likewise in their severall Cures?'[31]

It is possible to dismiss this as mere polemic, but it seems to fit in with what we know of the changing priorities of the preaching ministry in the late Elizabethan period. Patrick Collinson has argued that as early as the 1570s, Protestant preachers found that they were contending 'not so much with Catholicism . . . as with a way of life and especially a pursuit of pastimes and pleasures which had lived happily alongside the old religion but found that it could not put up with the new'. In this second phase of the Elizabethan Reformation, 'it was' – as he felicitously puts it – 'minstrels more than mass-priests who proved to be the enemy'.[32] And not minstrels alone. When the Somerset minister Thomas Turvell denounced sabbath-breakers, he was not just thinking of those who worked at their ordinary employments on the sabbath day, or of those who indulged in 'wicked dancing and foolish May-gaming'. In his view, 'those that will neither worke at their ordinarie calling, nor go to those unlawfull games nor wicked pastimes, but will sit at their doores talking, and looking one upon another' were also in breach of the fourth commandment. 'Those sort of people, are something more charitably to be thought of, than the other, because they doe it out of ignorance: but that cannot excuse them from being prophaners of the Sabbath.'[33] This was an extraordinarily sweeping attack on popular culture – not just on popular revels and festivities, but on the common forms of sociability that held rural communities together.

It is hard not to see this as a recipe for conflict. A preacher who denounced popular culture in such comprehensive terms was almost bound to split his congregation into two unequal halves: a small group of godly parishioners who were willing to conform to a strict Sabbatarian regime, and a much larger group of those who were not prepared to give up their traditional customs and recreations. And this was precisely what godly preachers were conditioned to expect. One of the subject headings in Robert Cawdrey's collection of pulpit similitudes, *A Treasurie or Store-House of Similies* (1600), declares flatly: 'Preaching maketh a separation.' As a fan separates the wheat and the chaff, 'even so Christ by the Preaching of his word, doth dissever his elect and reprobate'. Preaching 'worketh in the godly and the wicked, a contrarie effect . . . it allureth some to repentance, but other some it causeth (through their perverse nature) to encrease in

---

[31] Albert Peel, ed., *The Seconde Parte of a Register* (Cambridge, 1915), vol. 1, pp. 233, 238; also quoted in Collinson, *Birthpangs of Protestant England*, p. 56.

[32] Collinson, *Birthpangs of Protestant England*, p. x.

[33] Thomas Turvell, *The Poore Mans Path-Way to Heaven* (1616), E2r (p. 51).

pride and contumacie.' Eusebius Paget, a fellow minister of Cawdrey's in late Elizabethan Northamptonshire, and a fellow sufferer for nonconformity, interpreted this separation in explicitly predestinarian terms. 'We come to heare the word to one Church . . . we sit together in one forme, in one seate, yea and two looke in one book', yet 'the one receiveth fruit and comfort, the other is the more hardened to goe on forwarde in wickednesse.' Why these opposing reactions? 'There is no reason, but onelie the fruite of the eternal predestination of God: for it is not in the teacher, hee teacheth the worde of God.'[34]

This does not mean that ministers went out of their way to precipitate a division in their congregations. In his handbook for preachers, William Perkins declared that the 'assemblies of our Churches' were a 'mixt' or 'mingled people', composed of both believers and unbelievers. Rather than speaking separately to these two groups, preachers should address both at once, by describing the doom prepared for the wicked while simultaneously promising deliverance to those who repented. They did not need to separate the godly from the ungodly, since the power of the Holy Spirit, working through their preaching, would do this unaided. As Perkins wrote elsewhere: 'the preaching of the word is one of Gods fans', and when the Gospel is preached to a mixed congregation 'it fannes them, and tries them, and purgeth them, and so severs them, that a man may see a manifest difference of the chaffe and the wheate, that is, of the godly man and the wicked man'.[35] But it is not surprising that some preachers took the logical next step, and began to single out individual members of their audience – as William Hieron, minister of Hemingby in Lincolnshire, was alleged to have done:

Item in his sermons he vanteth that he maye speake at his pleasure and no man dare to controwle him. And he likeneth his parishioners to the theves in geale saying that divers of them sit before him with worse countinances then such as are going to hanging this assise with such like phrases, and in the Pulpitt devideth his auditorie thus havinge one or twoe that he thinketh affect his novelties he pointeth unto them I speake to yow Regenerat and then turning his Bodie countenance and hand to the rest of the parisheners he sayeth I speake to yow also.[36]

This is a highly unusual case, and can hardly be taken as representative of the preaching ministry as a whole. Yet the potential for conflict and division

---

[34] Robert Cawdrey, *A Treasurie or Store-House of Similies* (1600), 4C2v; Eusebius Paget, *A Verie Fruitful Sermon . . . Concerning Gods Everlasting Predestination* (1583), B1v.
[35] William Perkins, *The Arte of Prophecying*, in *Works*, vol. II (Cambridge, 1609), 3V2v; *Exhortation to Repentance*, G2v. Richard Bernard similarly advised preachers to 'intermix' mercy and judgement in their sermons: *The Faithfull Shepheard* (1607), P4v.
[36] Lincolnshire Archives Office, Lincoln, Lincoln diocesan records, 58/1/5.

was always latent within godly preaching, as the preachers themselves understood very well. They may have disclaimed any intention of sowing discord
among their hearers, but they fully expected to encounter opposition from
some members of their congregations, and regarded such opposition as a
validation of their ministry. Perkins warned ministers living in 'very prophane, or very popish' parts of the country that they should be prepared to
face physical violence. Anthony Lapthorne's biographer saw nothing surprising in the fact that Lapthorne should have had to carry a sword under his
gown to protect himself against murderous attacks by aggrieved parishioners,
or that one man should have entertained his friends with the antics of a
puppet named 'Lapthorne' whom he hanged in effigy every Sunday. Yes, it
was true that his sermons 'procured him many Enemies', but this was an
occupational hazard of the preaching ministry: 'as long as there is a Devill in
the world, God's painfull faithfull ministers shall never want an Enemy'.[37]
Charles Richardson urged ministers not to be discouraged even 'though our
people become our enemies, and persecute us. As many times it commeth to
passe, especially, if we bee sincere in our Ministerie, and doe plainly rebuke
them, and not suffer them to sin. And there are but a few faithfull Ministers at
this day, but they have experience of it.'[38]

Richardson's point is neatly illustrated by the dispute between Thomas
Bankes, minister of Slaidburne in Yorkshire, and one of his parishioners,
John Whippe. In August or September 1595 Bankes preached a sermon on
Matthew 5: 22, 'and handling the worde (Racha) dyd then declare that not
onelie all iniuryous and opprobrious speaches and wordes . . . but also all
disdainfull gesture and actyon expressinge mans mallyce and enmytie were
thearby utterlie condemned and forbidden amongst christians'.[39] These
seemingly uncontroversial remarks were evidently taken by Whippe as a
personal challenge. A few weeks later Bankes travelled to York and was
waylaid on the return journey by Whippe and some of his companions, 'in
the highe streete between Yorke and Tadcaster'. According to Bankes,
Whippe shouted at him: 'Thou arte an Asse parson, I dyd never see suche
an Asse as thou arte . . . I am ordayned to do thee a mischeiffe, parson, I am
ordayned to plague thee, parson; Thou arte learned indeed, I confesse, but
thou wantest worldly wytt and discretyon.' He then attempted to pull
Bankes off his horse, and was only prevented from doing him further injury

---

[37] Life of Anthony Lapthorne: Dr Williams's Library, MS 38.34, pp. 388–91.
[38] Charles Richardson, *A Workeman, that Needeth Not to Be Ashamed: or the Faithfull Steward of Gods House* (1616), F3v.
[39] 'Whosoever shall say to his brother, Racha, shall be in danger of the council: but whosoever shall say, Thou fool, shall be in danger of hell fire' (Matt. 5: 22).

by one of his companions, who drew his rapier and kept the two men apart.[40] Again, no one seems to have been surprised that a sermon should have provoked threats of physical violence; it was simply taken for granted that this was a regrettable but inevitable side effect of the preacher's ministry of reproof and admonition.

Historians have not always found it easy to accept that the preaching ministry could have had this divisive effect – largely, perhaps, out of an understandable reluctance to believe that any sensible preacher could have adopted an approach which flew in the face of pastoral common sense. Christopher Marsh, for example, argues that 'ultras' such as Hieron or Lapthorne, who gloried in stirring up controversy, were not unknown in early modern England but were probably fairly thin on the ground. The majority of the parish clergy, he suggests, were 'gentle persuaders' rather than 'busy controllers', who avoided contentious or divisive preaching and accepted that the moral and spiritual reformation of their parishioners would be a gradual process. Tom Webster's study of the Essex clergy has led him to the same conclusions: that personal preaching was (in his words) 'not especially common', and that godly ministers did not neglect the ministry of reconciliation. Perhaps the most subtle and fruitful attempt to rescue the godly preachers from the consequences of their own divisive rhetoric has come from John Bossy, who argues that puritan divines made a determined effort to lay claim to the Christian virtues of 'peace, neighbourhood, and true friendship' (a quotation from Perkins) even though this went against the strict logic of their predestinarian position. He suggests that the mid-seventeenth-century retreat from predestinarian doctrine may have resulted in part from an awareness of its invidious social effects – which is to say that in the final analysis, charity took priority over theology.[41]

These are valid and valuable points. It is important not to airbrush the divisive elements out of one's portrait of the puritan ministry – as Samuel Clarke might be said to have done in his collections of godly biographies published in the 1660s and 1670s, and as Eric Carlson might be said to do in his characterisation of Richard Greenham as 'a gentle man, committed heart and soul to healing, and repelled by division and conflict'. It is worth remembering that even Greenham could speak of the preaching ministry

---

[40] Bankes v Whippe and Wallbanke: Borthwick Institute, York, High Commission cause papers, HC/CP 1597/12.
[41] Marsh; *Popular Religion*, p. 90. Tom Webster, *Godly Clergy in Early Stuart England: The Caroline Puritan Movement c. 1620–1643* (Cambridge, 1997), p. 100. John Bossy, *Peace in the Post-Reformation* (Cambridge, 1998).

in terms of its differing effects on 'the godly' and 'the wicked'.[42] Nevertheless, Marsh, Webster and Bossy are right to point out that the puritan clergy recognised the importance of social harmony and did their best to maintain it. One particularly suggestive aspect of Bossy's analysis concerns the way that puritan clergy employed concepts such as 'brotherly love'. Their understanding of 'brotherly love' was, potentially, highly divisive, for what they had in mind was not the common charity that ought to exist between neighbour and neighbour in the civil community of the parish, but the 'sanctified affection' that ought to prevail in the spiritual brotherhood of the elect. Yet the language of 'love' – or 'peace, neighbourhood, and true friendship', to use Perkins's phrase again – would have seemed reassuringly familiar to hearers who did not appreciate the predestinarian doctrine underpinning it, and would not necessarily have been divisive in practice unless a preacher went out of his way to make it so.

What is missing from these arguments, though, is a sense of the social implications of preaching – or rather, of an understanding of the clerical vocation in which preaching was the central and defining activity. The problem was not that ministers were indifferent to neighbourly love and charity, but that their role as preachers gave them a moral authority which distanced them from their parishioners: as Rosemary O'Day has commented, the godly preacher 'might be loved and respected, but he was certainly a man set apart'.[43] To put it bluntly: a good preacher could not afford to be too friendly with his neighbours, for fear that his authority to rebuke sin and to terrify sinners with the prospect of God's wrath – to 'pearce and wound the inward heart, make the haire to stand upright, the flesh to tremble' – might be compromised by over-familiarity.[44] Perkins warned ministers to be 'most carefull, that they doe not loosely and lavishly bestow themselves on all companies, as too many doe in our Church, to the great scandall therof, who care not with whom they converse'. 'It is a true saying', the Derbyshire curate Richard Kilby informed his fellow clergy, 'that too much familiaritie breedes contempt ... Therefore use to retire your selfe, and bee no common companie-keeper: for howsoever you may preserve your personall reputation, yet the power of your office which is

---

[42] Carlson, *Marriage and the English Reformation*, p. 163; Richard Greenham, *Two Learned and Godly Sermons* (1593), E5r: 'certaine it is, that both the godly and wicked are inlightned, but the inlyghtning of the godly is one, and the insght of the wicked is an other'.

[43] Rosemary O'Day, *The English Clergy: The Emergence and Consolidation of a Profession 1558–1642* (Leicester, 1979), p. 202.

[44] Thomas Walkington, *Salomons Sweete Harpe* (Cambridge, 1608), E4r.

much grounded upon a reverent estimation, will be by company-keeping manie wayes diminished.' Another preacher declared that 'I am content to undergoe the imputations of straungenes, and he will not come amonge us &c . . . because I see no good come of popular familiaritie, but contempt or scandale.'[45]

And the focus of this tension between preaching and neighbourliness was, of course, the alehouse. Contrary to what many godly Protestants believed, alehouses were not necessarily breeding grounds for Popery or irreligion. As Tessa Watt has shown, many displayed moralising ballads, wall paintings of biblical scenes or painted cloths with legends like 'Fear God' as part of their interior decoration; theologically conservative they may have been, but irreligious they were not.[46] Nor were they necessarily off limits to the parish clergy: Charles Richardson claimed that 'most men' preferred a minister who 'will sit neighbourly with them, and spend his penny, as they doe theirs in the Ale-house', and this is precisely what the more traditionalist clergy seem to have done. But for the reasons already stated, a godly preacher simply could not afford to compromise his authority by drinking with his neighbours in the alehouse. 'Is it fit for a man to undertake any Ministeriall charge, who is an haunter of Ale-houses?' demanded Robert Bolton in an assize sermon at Northampton. 'Is such a companion like to lift up his voyce like a Trumpet, against the sinnes of the time, and stand at sworde-point against the severall corruptions, all the sinfull prophanations of his Parish, himselfe being a notorious delinquent?'[47] Alehouses were thus transformed, at least in the minds of the puritan clergy (though one suspects that there was a self-fulfilling prophecy at work here as well), from relatively innocuous havens of religious traditionalism into symbols of everything that the godly most feared and detested.[48]

Ministers who stayed out of the alehouse had fewer opportunities to offer hospitality to their parishioners. Indeed, for many poorer clergy the alehouse may have represented their only opportunity to offer hospitality: when Thomas Bird, vicar of Somerby in Leicestershire, was charged in 1646 with frequenting alehouses, he admitted that he sometimes drank there with his neighbours but claimed that he did so 'havinge not

[45] Perkins, *Exhortation to Repentance*, G2v; Richard Kilby, *The Burthen of a Loaden Conscience* (10th edn., 1630), F3r; Cambridge University Library, MS Dd.14.16, pp. 24–5.
[46] Watt, *Cheap Print*, pp. 195–203, 331–2.
[47] Richardson, *Workeman*, G1r; Robert Bolton, *Two Sermons Preached at Northampton* (1635), I4v.
[48] For alehouses as centres of anti-clerical or anti-puritan feeling, see Samuel Hieron, *Aarons Bells A-sounding* (1623), G2v; Jeremiah Lewis, *The Doctrine of Thankfulnesse* (1619), G1r.

wherewithall to entertayne them at home'.[49] And the failure to offer
hospitality might do serious damage to a minister's reputation. In his
handbook of advice for the country parson, George Herbert suggested
that clerical hospitality could be used as an informal means of social
control, but also warned that people would be quick to take offence if
they felt that hospitality was being deliberately withheld: 'countrey people
are very observant of such things'.[50] Accusations of antisocial or inhospit-
able behaviour certainly caused problems for the clergy. Jeremiah Dyke
complained that the people 'crie us downe to be inhospitall, illiberall,
and covetous' simply because the poverty of the parish clergy forced
them to live humbly.[51] Robert Harris believed that the proliferation of
alehouses could be directly attributed to the decline in clerical hospitality:
in olden days, travellers could be sure of a welcome at the manor house
or the parsonage, but now that ministers had no maintenance and the
gentry were often absentee landlords, hospitality had to be sought elsewhere. 'Travellers must needs have drinke, therefore there must be
Alehouses; and what will follow next, who knowes not?'[52]

Since godly ministers could not seek out their parishioners in the alehouse, they hoped that their parishioners would take the initiative in
coming to them for private conference. William Pemble urged the laity to
come to 'the ministers house' and 'the learned mans study' for advice, but
confessed that few did so. 'How long shall a Minister sit in his study, before
any of his parish will trouble him about any such matters? . . . Ministers I am
sure complaine much of the backwardnes of people in this point.'[53]
In Robert Sherrard's dialogue *The Countryman with his Houshold* (1620),
the pastor complains that he is 'ignorant and uncertaine of the particular
persons estate in my flocke' and is therefore obliged to perform his office

[49] A. G. Matthews, *Walker Revised* (Oxford, 1948; repr. 1988), p. 232. On the socialising influence of
the alehouse, see also Peter Marshall, *The Face of the Pastoral Ministry in the East Riding 1525–95*
(York, 1993), pp. 10, 18, citing the case of a clergyman 'tabled at the alehouse' before his marriage, and
another who played at cards 'with honest company . . . for company's sake'.

[50] George Herbert, *A Priest to the Temple*, in *Works*, ed. F. E. Hutchinson (Oxford, 1941), p. 243. Felicity
Heal's discussion of clerical hospitality in *Hospitality in Early Modern England* (Oxford, 1990) is
chiefly concerned with episcopal hospitality, but also includes some valuable remarks on clerical
hospitality before the Reformation (pp. 253–6) and after (pp. 291–9).

[51] Dyke, *Counterpoison against Covetousnesse*, G4r. See also John Ward, *Diary*, ed. Charles Severne
(1839), p. 215: 'English ministers may preach of hospitality to their parishioners; but many of them are
not able to goe to the extent of practicing their doctrines.'

[52] Robert Harris, *The Drunkards Cup* (1619), A3v. This is doubtless an idealised picture of old-fashioned
rural hospitality, but bears an intriguing resemblance to Keith Wrightson's argument that alehouses
represented a new pattern of 'fragmented sociability' replacing older forms of social interaction.

[53] Pemble, *Workes*, 3B5r. Paul Bayne admitted that many people did not see the point of private conference
and 'thinke it curiosity in Ministers, if they looke into the manners more neerly of their people'. Bayne,
*A Commentarie upon the First Chapter of the Epistle of Saint Paul Written to the Ephesians* (1618), X5v.

'but by the halves, onely in preaching a Sermon or two out of the pulpit each weeke upon the Lords day, which yet I cannot so profitably performe in fitting my labour to their estate, as otherwise I might, if I and they had such private fellowship, as the Lord commendeth unto us in his holy word' – to which the householder humbly replies that he and his family 'have cause to greeve and be ashamed for our strangeness to you'.[54] In practice, much of the social life of the parish took place behind the minister's back. Richard Bernard instructed the minister 'to converse familiarly with his people, seeing and observing them' in order to find out 'what errours are amongst them, what practice of vertue, what vices generally, or in particular callings', but added that he would need to rely on informers to bring him news of matters which 'by himself alone he cannot come to understand'.

It is hardly surprising that ministers were so keen to encourage the practice of private conference, since it provided an invaluable opportunity for them to speak to their parishioners in confidence, and to admonish them for misbehaviour. Richard Kilby advised ministers that if they knew anyone in their parish who 'doth amisse', they should 'tell him his fault secretly, and very kindely, beseeching him in Christs behalfe to turne unto God'.[55] In effect, this was a Protestant substitute for the Catholic discipline of sacramental confession – the absence of which has often, and rightly, been regarded as the major pastoral weakness of the post-Reformation Church of England. But how could it be enforced? Kilby's advice was all very well, but if the sinner refused to amend his behaviour, what could the minister do? John Dod and Robert Cleaver suggested that he should enlist the help of 'two or three, or some more of the ancient men, that have some authoritie and sway, in the congregation' to support him.[56] This was admirably practical advice, yet it carried a sting in the tail, for Dod and Cleaver's point was that the 'private rebukes' of the parish worthies would serve to reinforce the minister's own 'publike reproofes' – and by 'publike reproofes' they meant sermons. In implying that a minister should name and shame his parishioners in his sermons – or, as was suggested by one minister in the diocese of Lincoln in 1614, 'that the preacher ought to particularize the faults of his parishioners in the pulpit' – they were treading on very dangerous ground indeed.[57]

[54] Robert Sherrard, *The Countryman with His Houshold, Being a Familiar Conference, Concerning Faith towards God, and Good Workes before Men* (1620), B3v.

[55] Kilby, *Burthen*, F4r. On parish visiting, see Richard Greenham, *Workes* (5th edn., 1612), 2G5v. On the use of private admonition and reproof, 'which though some stomack'd at, yet they durst not openly despise', see E. S. Shuckburgh, ed., *Two Biographies of William Bedell* (Cambridge, 1902), p. 30.

[56] John Dod and Robert Cleaver, *A Plaine and Familiar Exposition of the Ten Commandements* (1604), Q3r.

[57] 'A visitation of the diocese of Lyncolne, AD. 1614', in *Associated Architectural Societies' Reports and Papers*, vol. XVI, part i (1881), p. 48.

Ministers were very well aware of the dangers of 'particular preaching', as it was called, and most were reluctant to use it except as a last resort. Cornelius Burges, one of the few writers bold enough to discuss the practice in print, laid down strict conditions for its use. If a sin was known only to 'such as are privie to it as Actors, patients or abettors in it' then it would be unwise as well as uncharitable to reveal it in public. Only if it was already known 'by a common rumor and publique fame raised by persons of credit, either out of knowledge, or some strong presumptions', or if it had been prosecuted in court, could it lawfully be mentioned in a sermon. If it was a deliberate sin, then it should be rebuked sharply, but 'if it bee a sinne of infirmity, the party must bee handled with all compassion'. Most importantly, Burges argued that preachers should not refer to sinners by name from the pulpit. 'Publicke sinnes may bee publickly particularised by the names of the sins, but not by the name or any personall circumstances of the sinner.' No oblique allusion should be made 'to any mans person by his Complexion, cloathes, stature, gait in going' or 'speciall marks of his habitation', nor should the preacher make any attempt 'to let the Congregation see' that 'this man or this woman onely is now reproved'. Instead, the preacher should make his reproofs indirect – as, for example, by condemning the sin of slander, and addressing his remarks to 'any here . . . who are not ashamed thus to traduce their neighbours'.[58]

However, these caveats may be less important than they seem. Even if the preacher took care to speak indirectly, it was quite possible, as Burges admitted, that 'some Person in the Congregation' might be 'knowne to the rest to be more eminently guilty of this sinne, than any of the rest; so that as soone as ever such a speech is uttered, they begin to looke towards [him]'. According to Richard Bernard, it was not uncommon for a man to come up to his neighbour at the end of the service 'and strike him on the shoulder, and saie you have byn mett withall, or spoken of tooday'.[59] In any case, not all preachers observed the conditions stipulated by Burges. A Devon minister argued that if preachers wished to reprove sinners so plainly 'that they single them out by name', they were fully entitled to do so.[60] William Sclater even proposed that the public naming and shaming of incorrigible sinners should be used as a lesser form of excommunication, arguing that St Paul's command, 'if any man obey not our sayings . . . note that man'

[58] Cornelius Burges, *The Fire of the Sanctuarie Newly Uncovered, or, a Compleat Tract of Zeale* (1625), L2v, L12r, M4r. On personal preaching see also Juliet Ingram, 'The conscience of the community: The character and development of clerical complaint in early modern England' (PhD diss., Warwick University, 2004), pp. 31–3.

[59] Burges, *Fire of the Sanctuarie*, T10v; Somerset Record Office, Taunton, D/D/Ca 299, pp. 112–15.

[60] Radford Mavericke, *The Practice of Repentance* (1617), E3r.

(2 Thess. 3: 14–15), implied 'their publique noticing or pointing at by name in the Congregation . . . that they were such as from whose societie the people must abstaine'.[61] Anthony Lapthorne seems to have stopped short of naming names, but only just; he was accused of inveighing in his sermons 'at some one of his parishioners with whome he is offended in such manner as the more intelligent sort might easily perceive whome he meant thereby'.[62]

One of the commonest grievances against godly ministers, and obviously one of the most deeply felt, was that they abused their parishioners in their sermons. 'I pray you tell me', asks the parishioner in Edward Vaughan's dialogue *Ten Introductions* (1594), 'how are those ministers to be excused in this? If any of their parish offend them, they will preach it in the pulpit . . . This is a verie foule fault, and I assure you it is misliked of many.' Burges imagined a similar conversation among a group of neighbours:

Oh saith one, wee have a minister so fiery and cholerique that never a man though the best in the parish can say or do anything that he likes not, but, if he know it, they shall heare of it next day out of the pulpit, and he is so bitter and rayles so as you never heard the like. That is strange, saith another, that he should bee so indiscreet, so peevish, so rash; nay so madd, saith a third. Nay, and he will fall so upon the best freinds he hath too, quoth another. Why this is not well and I am sorry for it, say the rest: and it is rare to find any to give better censures of the faythfullest painfullest discreetest ministers if they endeavor to search the wounds of their hearers to the quick, than of hott, peevish, indiscreet, mad men that deserve to be punished with losse of livings, and ministry and all.[63]

A remark in one of Henry Roborough's sermons provides a vivid insight into the popular fear of 'plain dealing' preachers. Roborough noted that layfolk who heard their sins attacked from the pulpit would often respond with 'trouble or heavinesse, or discontent, if not a plaine opposition . . . and that to the face of that Minister; or at least, at home, and among companions', and might leave instructions that such a minister was not to preach at their funeral.[64]

[61] Sclater, *Exposition*, T6v (ii. 284). Sclater's own published sermons on Malachi include an exhortation against brawling coupled with a reference to an individual 'in our own congregation' who had been bound over to keep the peace. Sclater, *A Brief and Plain Commentary, with Notes . . . upon the Whole Prophecie of Malachy* (1650), I1v.

[62] PRO, SP 16/261 (High Commission act book), f. 83r. For similar examples of blatantly personal preaching, see C. W. Foster, ed., *The State of the Church in the Reigns of Elizabeth and James I* (Lincolnshire Record Society, 1926), p. cxxx; and Devonshire Record Office, Exeter, CC178/Hartland.

[63] Edward Vaughan, *Ten Introductions* (1594), M8r; Cambridge University Library, Add. MS 6165, p. 27. See also Hieron, *The Preachers Plea*, I2r.

[64] Henry Roborough, *Balme from Gilead* (1626), Y3r.

This is compelling evidence, and must, at the very least, place a serious question mark against the success of the Protestant preaching ministry. The problem, as will by now be apparent, was not that ministers deliberately tried to provoke confrontation with their parishioners. Rather, the problem lay deeper, in the self-image and self-definition of the godly preacher. Because ministers placed such a strong emphasis on preaching, they remained at a distance from their parishioners; because they remained at a distance, they were not asked to provide private counsel; because they did not provide private counsel, they had to rely on preaching as the principal means of moral coercion; and because they used preaching as a means of moral coercion, they were accused of making personal remarks in their sermons. It was not easy for even the best-intentioned minister to break out of this vicious circle. Even if he made his sermons as general and unspecific as possible – and even if he had no intention of striking at particular members of his congregation – he might still find himself criticised for being unneighbourly. Sclater admitted that 'our admonitions, instructions, exhortations, are many times censured as accusations of our people … But specially: if they bee sinnes we reprove, and they not apparent in the Congregation, that is presently interpreted, as a matter of slander, and no lesse than defamation laid upon the Parish. Shew the danger of Drunkennesse, Whoring, &c. He makes us, they say, a company of such Miscreants. There are none such amongst us.'[65]

So was there any alternative? The foregoing discussion has concentrated on the 'godly' (that is, puritan) clergy – partly because the majority of the printed sources are written from a godly perspective – but it should not be supposed that these pastoral problems were limited to a clearly defined and distinct minority of puritan preachers. As the scholarly literature of the last thirty years has made abundantly clear, it is impossible to draw a clear dividing line between 'Anglican' and 'Puritan' models of ministry, given that the puritan model of the godly preaching minister was, in Patrick Collinson's words, 'dominant and even normative … in the post-Reformation Church of England'.[66] It is true that the starkest and most uncompromising statements of the divisive potential of preaching are to be found in the writings of radical puritans such as John Traske, where the idea of preaching as 'making a separation' between the godly and the

---

[65] Sclater, *Exposition*, 2E8r (i. 461).
[66] Christopher Marsh, 'Piety and persuasion in Elizabethan England', in Tyacke, ed., *England's Long Reformation*, p. 158; Patrick Collinson, 'Shepherds, sheepdogs and hirelings: the pastoral ministry in post-reformation England', in Sheils and Wood, eds., *The Ministry: Clerical and Lay*, p. 186.

wicked began to shade into the separatist or sectarian ideal of the gathered Church. Traske predicted that preaching would cause some of its hearers to 'waxe worse and worse, and become more hard-hearted . . . Nor yet may wee wonder that they are filled with wrath, and rage at the Preachers of it: seeing they doe plainely see themselves sencibly bound, as it were hand and foote, and cast out amongst dogges, and swine: and also continually scorched, and vexed by the heate, and fervency of such powerfull preaching.'[67] But Traske was simply expressing, in a typically extreme form, a belief in the power of preaching that was as much a Protestant as a puritan commonplace.

By the early seventeenth century, however, a few writers had begun to express an alternative view of the pastoral ministry. One of the most interesting examples is to be found in an unpublished 'Treatise concerning the sabbath', composed by an anonymous author in 1608 and later revised and abridged by one James Cobbes from a manuscript 'remayning in the handes of my honoured freind Richard Peopys Esq. sometyme Recorder of Bury, who lent it me to transcribe for my owne use'.[68] The manuscript may well have originated in or around Bury St Edmunds, since it deals with the vexed question of parish wakes and dedication feasts, which we know from other sources to have been a particular cause of conflict between puritans and their opponents in East Anglia. John Munday, rector of Little Wilbraham in Cambridgeshire, wrote in the 1630s that 'in the countrie where I live there is scarse eyther Sunday or holyday between Easter and Holymass that hath not a feast (such as it is) in one town or other'; and this would have been a perpetual irritation to puritan ministers trying to enforce stricter standards of sabbath observance.[69] The 'Treatise' argues for the toleration of Sunday feasts and recreations, which alone is enough to make it interesting, as most contemporary works on the sabbath are written from the opposite point of view. But it is of special interest for our present purposes, as it portrays the debate on sabbath-day recreations in terms of a confrontation between two opposing views of preaching.

The work is written in the form of a dialogue between a 'countrye parson' and a 'precise preacher'. The preacher has come to visit the parson on the

---

[67] John Traske, *The Power of Preaching* (1623), C4v, D3r.
[68] 'The summe and substance of a treatise concerning the sabbath': Bodleian Library, Oxford, MS Rawl. D.1346. On Cobbes and his library, see Richard Beadle, 'The manuscripts of James Cobbes of Bury St Edmunds (*c.*1602–1685)', in T. Matsuda, R.A. Linenthal and J. Scahill, eds., *The Medieval Book and a Modern Collector: Essays in Honour of Toshiyuki Takamiya* (Cambridge and Tokyo, 2004), pp. 427–42.
[69] John Munday, 'Sabbatum Redivivum': St John's College, Cambridge, MS I.25, p. 50.

eve of the latter's parish feast-day, when he fears the sabbath will be 'much profaned by shooting, Bowling, Dancing, and other such ungodly sportes and delights'. 'I understand allso', he tells the parson, 'that it hath beene your Custome to preach only in the forenoone on this feaste daye; therfore my request is that I may preach in the afternoone, to keepe the people from the breach of the sabbath daye, and from their usuall ungodly sports, and delights, which no zealous godly man ought to suffer with patience.' The parson thanks him, but replies that an afternoon sermon will not be necessary, as he and his parishioners will be busy feasting and merrymaking with their friends:

> *PARSON.*   Preaching is good, and I like very well of it, for it is the power of God to salvation, the chiefe externall meanes to bring men to eternall life. But I had rather you had come at some other tyme: for it hath beene an ancient custome heere, and a good (as I thinke) once in the yeare to invite our kinsfolke and freindes to rejoyce, and be merry with us; and you may well imagine that in this feast we make our freinds more than usuall, and every dayes, fare: so that unto full stomacks a Sermon will not be so welcome; especially because we meete but seldome so many freinds and kinsmen together. They will be glad to have some tyme, betwene morning and evening prayer, for their solace and delight: and then especially to urge them to heare your sermon, when they are most unfitt and unwilling, will cause them to suspect, that you come rather to crosse, than to edifye them, so that in my opinion, your preaching will be very unseasonable. (f. 7r)

The preacher is horrified: 'Unseasonable? . . . Know you not the precept of the Apostle, to preach in season and out of season?'[70] But the parson replies that the exhortation to preach in season and out of season (2 Tim. 4: 2) does not mean that ministers should preach 'without respect of persons, tyme, place, and such like circumstances', for St Paul declares elsewhere that all things should be done 'decently and in order' (1 Cor. 14: 40).

With this rapid-fire exchange of proof-texts, the two speakers move on to discuss the best and most effective way of preaching. Should a minister seek to please his audience? The parson says yes, the preacher says no:

> *PREACHER.*   I doe not wonder now to heare the Common-people speake so well of you; contrarywise to see how for the moste parte, they are bente against us, for reproving the breach of the sabbath, sith, in plaine tearmes, you shew that you have more regarde to please Men than God.
> *PARSON.*   It seemeth then you take it for a noat of a flaterer, to be well spoken of; and to endeavour to please men, seemeth to you . . . to be a signe of no true

---

[70] Cf. Corpus Christi College, Oxford, MS 409, f. 151r, where the injunction to preach the Word in and out of season is cited in justification of weekday lectures.

Zeal of Gods honour; but of a preferring the love of men before the love of
God. And contrariwise to be hated and evil spoken of, a noat of a zealous
man. (f. 9r)

The parson goes on to maintain that 'if a Minister will profit his auditors,
he must be well thought of by them' (f. 9v). 'If you', he tells the preacher,
'by your bitter invectives against the weake, and by your austerity and
soure behaviour towarde them, doe alienate their mindes; and cause them
to be averse from you; then this blessing which you expect, pertayneth not
to you; for your doings are not only hatefull to men, but especially to God
himselfe' (f. 10v). He remarks that 'it is a rare thing [with you] to speake
familiarly with your parishioners, except such they bee, as sooth you in
your veyne; (to witte your rageing against the Crosse in Baptisme, the
surplisse, and church governement now established) or bring you tales of
their neighbours faultes: and these are with you the best Christians' (f. 11r).

Finally, the two speakers arrive at the heart of their disagreement. What
attitude should a good minister take towards his parishioners? Should he bear
with their infirmities for the sake of good pastoral relations – or should he
adopt a policy of zero tolerance? The preacher accuses the parson of negligence in failing to reprove his people's sins with sufficient severity, and argues
that the parson is dangerously naïve in his attitude to popular culture, treating
his parishioners as weak when they are, in fact, nothing less than evil:

PREACHER.    O sir with you all the common people are weake, and therefore must
be borne with, that is, in playne tearmes, must not be molested in their sinnes:
O we must beware of rebuking, least wee offende the weake, but whyle you
thus feare to offende, you lett them doe what they lyst, and wincke att their
faultes ... But doe you, as wee doe, and as becommeth a zealous preacher;
reprove them sharpely; and you shall see that many of your parishe (whome
you now take to be good, or weake Christians) will then discover themselves
not to be weake, but evill: yea they will not sticke to rayle att you. If I bee not
misinformed, I doe you no wronge to accuse you for wincking att your
parishioners faultes, and those no smaller ones neither, than the breach of
the firste table: for I am tolde that you commonly see them breake the sabbath
daye in Bowling, Shooting, Kettling, yea and in that insufferable abuse of
Dancing, and yett reprove them not. (f. 14r)

The parson denies the charge: 'you wrong me in saying that I account
all the common people weakelings and not to be reprooved ... whereas
I only affirme that in reproving sinne, regarde is to be had of the quality
both of the person and his offence' (f. 14v). Yet he implicitly accepts the
substance of the preacher's accusation, by acknowledging that he regards
his parishioners as weak rather than evil:

*PARSON.* To morow is our feaste daye, you knowe; a tyme that above all tymes in the yeare, they love to spende in mirthe: yett in the morning will they willingly heare the worde of God, readd and preached. Likewyse they will come to evening prayers: Only they desire to spend the tyme betwene in mirth with their freindes; that tyme especially you desire to preach, yett know their great desire to the contrary. Now Sir the worde of God requireth that a Minister should not be froward; and what is frowardenes, if this be not, to cross and offende a whole multitude? Come you att any other tyme, and you shall see them flock to your sermon; which is a manifest token that they are not evill Christians, though perhapps many of them weake, and full of infirmityes. (f. 16r)

In other words, they have no objection to the preaching ministry as such. They merely object to puritan ministers who adopt an inappropriately confrontational style of preaching, force them to attend church at inconvenient times and find fault with their leisure pursuits.

The parson's views may well have been shared by a good many Elizabethan and Jacobean clergy, but were not widely expressed until the 1620s and 1630s. The emergence of a more favourable view of popular religion during the reign of Charles I can be linked to a number of factors: chiefly, the republication of the Book of Sports in 1633; but also the new Laudian emphasis on the liturgical feasts of the Church calendar, and the sympathetic interest in popular festivities, which found its most famous literary expression in the poems of Robert Herrick. The immediate cause of the republication of the Book of Sports was the dispute over Church ales in Somerset, and for this reason the reissued version carried a new royal endorsement specially commending 'the feasts of the dedication of the churches, commonly called wakes' – much to the satisfaction of John Munday, writing in defence of the Book of Sports, who praised dedication feasts as being conducive to 'parochiall neighbourhood and neighbourly familiaritie'.[71] Another writer argued in 1637 that most country people were 'of good sound understanding' and well disposed towards the Church, even though they took relatively little interest in matters of religion. 'Alas the *summum bonum* which the common sort affect is a pudding or a pot of good drinke, and their thoughts seldome mount higher than an house or a Cart … yet many of these proove honest quiet men in the Common Wealth, and I hope through Gods grace, and my Ministers good paines at last finde the way to Heaven, by faith and repentance, and the choice of better objects.'[72]

---

[71] Kenneth Fincham, ed., *Visitation Articles and Injunctions of the Early Stuart Church*, vol. I (Church of England Record Society, 1994), p. 151. Munday, '*Sabbatum Redivivum*', p. 50.
[72] *Vox Ruris Reverberating Vox Civitatis* (1637), D2v.

It appears, then, that the puritan model of the godly preaching minister did not go uncontested. Some clergy seem to have favoured an alternative model of ministry, focused on pastoral activity rather than preaching, in which they sought to befriend their parishioners rather than stand over them in judgement. And if this alternative was at all widespread, then the implications are considerable. We may want to conclude, with Christopher Marsh, that the majority of the parish clergy were Protestant tortoises rather than Puritan hares, jogging along in the slow lane of a twin-track Reformation – or, with Judith Maltby, that these clergy were catering to a sizable constituency of 'Prayer Book Protestants' who were alienated by the more aggressive style of puritan preaching. We may even want to conclude, with Christopher Haigh, that such 'parish Anglicans' provided a bedrock of support for Laudian ceremonialism in the reign of Charles I. If we accept these arguments, then the puritan model of the godly preacher begins to seem a good deal more marginal, and less mainstream, than we might have supposed. Ultimately, we may find ourselves resurrecting the notion of Anglicanism as a moderate 'third way' between the polarised extremes of Puritanism and Popery.

However, we should not assume that puritan preachers were necessarily opposed to popular feasts and festivities, or to popular culture in general. Their objection was specifically to feasts and recreations on the sabbath: and as John Munday noted in the 1630s, many parishes which 'anciently had wakes, or feasts of Dedication, upon the Lords day' had chosen 'to put off the same to the day following', thus eliminating the main reason for puritan disapproval. Munday himself was unhappy with this change, on the grounds that it made it easier for neighbouring parishes to 'come pell mell together', so 'giving opportunity to vagrant people to pass and repass, up and down, to and fro, hither and thither, this way and that way, and every way at their pleasure'. This offended him because it seemed to threaten the integrity and identity of the parochial community; his ideal was that the parish should come together as a single, self-contained unit for worship on Sunday mornings and recreation on Sunday afternoons – a priority which clearly distinguishes him from puritan ministers, whose chief concern was that the sabbath should be strictly observed as a day wholly and solely dedicated to God's service. Yet, while puritan clergy differed from Laudians such as Munday in the importance they attached to sabbath observance, there were clear points of overlap between the two. Puritans were capable of extolling 'honest mirth' and 'lawful recreations' just as the Book of Sports had done; while Munday, for his part, was as firm in his condemnation of 'tippling and drunkenness' as any puritan minister.

Nor should we assume that puritan preachers were necessarily 'sons of thunder' who could not bring themselves to adopt an attitude of gentle forbearance towards their people's sins. 'Blessed agreement', exclaimed Robert Sanderson in a sermon preached at Heckington, Lincolnshire, in 1619, 'where [the] pastor goes before, and the people cherefully follow in Christian conversation.' In his notes for another sermon, he explained how this ideal state of affairs might be achieved. 'Domineering Pastor seldome profitable. People profit most, when persuaded of love . . . Ministers power persuasive, not coercive. Not with the sword to compell them, but with instance and prayers to incline them, worke upon by fayre meanes.' This led Sanderson to a 'reproofe of ministers having nothing but hell and condemnation and brimstone. Usefull indeede in tyme, but not only; not principall.' Rather, the pastor should practise the 'ministry of reconciliation . . . Cords of love draw, whom iron chaynes cannot hold.'[73] These remarks are particularly significant because Sanderson has been cited elsewhere as an example of the way that even moderate conformists could employ the harsh rhetoric of puritan preaching – this on the basis of a remark in a Paul's Cross sermon of 1627 that ministers 'should rather seek to profit our hearers, though perhaps with sharp and unwelcome reproofs, than to please them by flattering them in evil'.[74] Apparently Sanderson did not regard such 'sharp and unwelcome reproofs' as wholly incompatible with the ministry of reconciliation.

It would be rash, then, to conclude that the parishes of early modern England were populated by opposing groups of 'country parsons' and 'precise preachers' with opposing views of pastoral ministry. The parson and the preacher are fictional characters designed to serve a polemical purpose, with the preacher reinforcing the stereotype of puritan preaching as inherently factious and divisive, and the parson representing the 'moderate' anti-puritan alternative. The problem, for the historian, is to get behind these stereotypes, and to find out what was actually going on in particular parishes – something which is not at all easy to do if we confine our attention to the puritan complaint literature or its anti-puritan equivalent. In the next section, I want to look at some actual examples of sermons preached in country parishes. It will become clear that Sanderson's ideal of 'blessed agreement' between pastor and people was by no means the norm,

---

[73] Bodleian Library, Oxford, MS Eng. th. f.63, ff. 35v, 49v. Similarly, Richard Hunt of Warwick criticised 'such ministers as are too severe at the first, & soe drive away their auditors, & dismay them, losing their heartes, before they can imprint any knowledg of religion in their myndes': Bodleian Library, Oxford, MS Rawl. C.766, f. 50.

[74] Tom Webster, *Godly Clergy in Early Stuart England* (Cambridge, 1997), p. 100.

and that preaching was often a source of friction between ministers and their parishioners. To that extent, Haigh is quite right to stress the unpopularity of the Protestant preaching ministry. Yet, at the same time, I want to suggest that the sharply contrasting alternatives of the parson and the preacher are not a good guide to parochial reality. Many clergy seem to have combined elements of the parson and the preacher within a single ministry, recognising the power of preaching as an instrument of moral reform, but blending this with a conciliatory pastoral approach designed, in Sanderson's words, to 'persuade' rather than 'coerce'.

### THREE CASE STUDIES

It was generally recognised that country preachers would have to adapt their sermons to the needs of an uneducated audience. Andreas Hyperius, whose handbook on preaching was first published in English in 1577, distinguished between doctrines 'meete for the inhabitauntes of small townes and villages' and those 'to bee expounded in larger townes'. Sermons delivered to country congregations should handle simple doctrines such as 'the dilligente hearing of gods worde', while sermons preached in large towns could cover more difficult topics such as the doctrine of divine providence. A generation later, this advice was echoed by Richard Rogers, who warned preachers that instead of parading their own learning, they should try to pitch their sermons at a level their hearers could actually understand. 'There is nothing more like to hurt the people, than such a kinde of teaching, when they shall have a learned man to preach unto them . . . and yet they shall not be able thereby to receive light, edification in godlines, and sound comfort: that is not easie and plaine to them, which he himselfe understandeth . . . I know men of singular learning, and gifts, who have already much altered the manner of their teaching, framing themselves to the diligent hearers capacitie, and more and more desire to doe the same daily, rather than to be commended for learned men, of them which neither conceive or understand them.'[75] John Dod's famous complaint that 'most ministers in England usually shoot over the heads of their hearers' may suggest that this advice was not always followed, but it also shows that clerical commentators recognised the problem and were trying to correct it.[76]

But what sort of sermons would seventeenth-century preachers have regarded as suitable 'for the inhabitauntes of small townes and villages',

[75] Andreas Hyperius, *The Practice of Preaching* (1577), Lıv; Richard Rogers, *Seven Treatises* (1603), Eıv.
[76] Samuel Clarke, *The Lives of Thirty-two English Divines* (3rd edn., 1677), Z4v.

and how well did they succeed in making their sermons accessible to unlearned hearers? Printed sermons alone cannot help us to answer these questions: first, because, as we saw in earlier chapters, preachers often revised and enlarged their sermons for publication, so that printed sermons are not necessarily an accurate record of what was uttered from the pulpit; and secondly, because the printed record is heavily weighted towards sermons preached on special occasions, at court, assizes or Paul's Cross. For a reliable sample of ordinary parish preaching, we have to turn to manuscript sources. In this section, I shall be discussing three sets of parish sermons from different parts of the country – one from Cornwall, one from Oxfordshire and one from Derbyshire – all surviving in authorial manuscripts which, as far as we can tell, preserve the sermons in their 'raw' state, as delivered from the pulpit, without subsequent revisions. As will become clear, these sermons vary enormously in style and content, making it impossible to generalise about the 'typical' parish sermon. Yet, in their different ways, they are all focused on a common problem: how to communicate the Protestant message to an unlearned, indifferent or actively hostile audience – for, as will also become clear, the laity were anything but passive recipients of Protestant teaching.

A manuscript in the Bodleian Library contains a series of sermons preached in the parish church of St Minver, a small village close to the north coast of Cornwall, in 1609 and 1610.[77] Cornwall was very poorly supplied with preachers – according to a survey of 1586, there were 140 non-preaching ministers in the county and only 29 preachers, of whom 5 were non-resident – and the preacher of these sermons, John Wright, appears to have been a curate for the absentee vicar of St Minver, William Hele. Hele's predecessor, Giles Creed, was described in 1586 as 'no preacher', so Wright may have been one of the first to preach regularly in the parish.[78] Why he chose to keep a written record of his sermons is not entirely clear. He refers several times to 'my last booke' and 'my last years labours', implying that he had copied out some of his earlier sermons in another manuscript. However, he seems to have had particular reasons for compiling the present manuscript, as he includes a long self-justificatory preface explaining that he had copied out his sermons in order to refute some members of his congregation, by showing them 'that I am not so rude,

[77] Bodleian Library, Oxford, MS Rawl. D.319.
[78] Peel, ed., *Seconde Parte of a Register*, vol.II, p. 88, 105. A similar survey some twenty years later claimed that Cornwall had thirty-five preaching ministers of varying degrees of diligence: BL Add. MS 38492 (Lewkenor papers), f. 43. Joseph Polsue, *A Complete Parochial History of the County of Cornwall*, vol. III (1867–72; repr. 1974), p. 366.

ignorant and unlearned as they believe'.[79] As proof of his learning, Wright includes a running total of 'places of Scripture quoted hitherunto' and 'fathers Philosophers and Poetts sayinges', and uses a series of marginal symbols to highlight his use of quotations and similitudes. The intended readership is not made clear, but the manuscript was plainly intended not simply for private reference but for some kind of public circulation.

Wright's sermons are a remarkable survival, quite unparalleled in the printed sermons of the period. One of their most distinctive features is a heavy reliance on moral and allegorical interpretations of scripture, more reminiscent of pre-Reformation expositions of the 'fourfold sense' than of Protestant insistence on the literal meaning. The parable of the Samaritan, for example, is interpreted as an allegory of the human condition:

And yt was our great necessity for as yt was with the poore man in the ghospell . . . for as he descended from Jerusalem (which signifieth the vision of peace) unto Jericho (which signifieth the moone) Even so we descendinge downe from gods love unto the love of this changeable world (theryn well compared to the moone) went downe so farre and so longe untill we fell into the hands of theeves. The world the flesh and the devill, who having robbed us of all gods graces wounded us deadlye with the poysoned dart of sinne and lett us lye in the highe ways of the fashion of the world.

Similarly, the parable of the wise and foolish virgins is interpreted 'both in respect of the literall sense and Morall', in four ways. In that they are virgins, 'I liken them to the church visible and militant'; in that they are wise and foolish, 'I liken them to those that are good indeed and to those in the church that are hypocrites'; in that they slept, 'therein I see the naturall corruption of mans nature'; and in that some had oil and some had not, 'I consider the state of all men at domesday (as they call yt) or judgement' (f. 158).

Wright's sermons are very strongly oral in character, full of proverbs and colloquial expressions – 'stumble at a straw and leape over a blocke' (f. 162), 'as the markett goes (so they say) the market folkes wyll talke' (f. 183) – of the sort that rarely found their way into print. Wright has a special fondness for homely comparisons – or, in his own words, 'similitudes taken from Creatures better to express the meaninge of the matter in hand' – to illustrate his doctrinal points:

For as men preferre the Apple tree before the trees of the forrest, not onely because yt is fruitfull but also because of the profitt that the fruit therof ministreth unto

---

[79] Bodleian Library, Oxford, MS Rawl. D.319, f. 116. My thanks to Jane Stevenson for her advice on the translation of Wright's Latin preface.

men. Even so the Church because she fyndeth both many thinges in Christ and those most profitable therfore she preferres him in her love. (f. 117)

This sort of plain style was probably not unusual in early seventeenth-century preaching, even though it seldom survives in print. More unusual – and distinctly old-fashioned, by the standards of the early seventeenth century – is Wright's habit of quoting in Latin before translating into English. '*Acquiri potest aestimari non potest*, That which [Augustine] speaketh of the Kingdome of heaven, I may speake of gods love towardes us, we may tast of yt and receave yt but value yt we cannot' (f. 118). 'So sayth Seneca, *Inter bonos viros ac deum amicitia est Conciliante virtute*, Virtue is the meanes of freendshippe between god and good men, as though between god and evyll men ther could be no freendshippe' (f. 120).

This very traditional style of pulpit rhetoric is accompanied by an equally traditional stress on the virtues of neighbourliness. In one sermon, Wright takes the doctrine that 'love is the fulfilling of the law' (Rom. 13: 10) and uses it as the basis of a simple moral code, in which the love of God leads naturally and inevitably to the love of one's neighbour: 'for yf thou love god thou wilt not sin agaynst any of the commandments of the first table, And yf for gods sake thou love thy neighbour thou wilt not breake any of the praeceptes of the second table which concerne thy neighbour' (f. 146). He condemns 'malecontentes' who 'can not aford a cheerfull look unto their brother or neighbour, nor spare him a merry or friendly word', and conjures up a vision of *communitas* based on the reciprocal duties binding together rich and poor. The rich must relieve 'the needes and necessities of the distressed' and if the poor 'have not welth to gratify their neighbour at least let them have an heart to wish well unto their neighbour'. All men are equal: 'all the sonnes of Adam, all from the earth naked, and all to the earth naked agayne we shall goe', and therefore we must 'love all men indifferently, not some more because they are rich, and some lesse because they are poore'. And, at times, this emphasis on neighbourly duty seems to shade into a doctrine of justification by works. 'This is the doctrine of the ghospell, this ys yt that we are taught by the ghospell, viz to live godly', declares Wright in another sermon (f. 182), and goes on to define godliness in terms of its outward effects: good report, good appearance, good speech, good apparell, good companions.

On this evidence, categorising Wright would appear to present few problems. Here, we might suppose, is a conservative cleric, quite possibly a crypto-Catholic, whose sermons exhibit so many signs of continuity with the pre-Reformation past that they might as easily have been preached in 1509 as in 1609. But we would be wrong. In a sermon on Titus 2: 11–13 ('For the grace of God, that bringeth salvation to all men, hath appeared'), Wright lists the five effects of grace, which he calls a 'ladder of five roundes' – suggesting that he may have been familiar with Latimer's sermons, which use the same metaphor of 'the true ladder that bringeth a man to heaven'. The five rungs of the ladder are 'the grace of god', 'repentaunce', 'remission of sins', 'holines of lyffe' and finally 'everlasting lyffe' – and Wright makes it abundantly clear that the first stage in this process is divine grace, not human merit. 'So would I say to the prayse of the grace of god and confusion of all meritt mongers, That when salvation is not onely preached but brought unto us, Let us take heed that we attribute yt not to our righteouness.' It is 'more than evident, that all the whole worke of salvation is nothinge of us but of and from gods love in Christ' (f. 176). While maintaining that faith is always accompanied by good works, he stresses that works are merely a 'signe [and] marke of a justifying faith', not a cause of justification (f. 135). Wright clearly had no qualms about teaching Protestant doctrine – nor of including an attack on (Catholic) 'merit mongers' to underline his Protestant credentials and draw attention to the distinctive elements of the Protestant position.

Wright is equally Protestant in his emphasis on the importance of preaching as the ordinary means of grace, a doctrine which he illustrates with a characteristic piling-up of scriptural analogues: 'As Elisha followed Elijah and would not leave him, So the wyse men followed the starre which should lead them unto Christ. In lyke manner you have matter of joy and comfort, when ye heare the word preached. Which shall carry you to heaven, lyke the Chariottes which carryed Jaacob into Egipt.' In his view, the preacher should begin by preaching the law in order to bring his hearers to repentance, followed by the Gospel to assure them of God's mercy:

The meanes that the lord useth to bringe yt to passe is the preachinge of first the law to make a man see him selfe and his sinne . . . Uppon the sight of this sin comes a fearefull and tremblinge conscience, which will produce a detestation of a mans owne selfe, with desire to be delivered, then in good tyme lest he should despayre as not able to beare the burthen By the preachinge of the ghospell, comes the assurance of forgivenes uppon condition of true and harty repentaunce. (f. 174)

The preacher's reward lay in seeing his hearers ascend the ladder of heaven, from repentance to remission of sins, sanctification and everlasting life. Preaching on Ephesians 1: 15–17 ('I cease not to give God thanks for you'), Wright explained that the reason for St Paul's thankfulness was that the Ephesians had heard and believed the Word of God. 'This was the cause of

Pauls joy And I would yt might be myne, to see you of St Minfrey parrish receive and beleeve the word of god taught by the ghospell of his sonne' (f. 164).

However, Wright shows less awareness of later developments in the Reformed theology of grace. He is noticeably incautious in using conditional language, as in the quotation above, where he speaks of forgiveness as being granted 'upon condition' of repentance, and in his explanation of why all men are not saved, where he implies that divine grace is granted on condition that we ask for it. 'Christ excluded none, preached to all, healed all that were sicke and diseased … Why then may some aske are not all men saved? I answere Christ is a physitian, he heales none but those that come unto him. As he promiseth, Come unto me all ye that are weary and heavy loaden and I wyll refresh you. Yf we come not unto him he wyll neyther heale helpe releeve nor refresh us, therfor yf men be not saved, theim selves are in the fault that wyll not come to him' (f. 179). This is by no means incompatible with a Reformed interpretation, but could also be taken in a semi-Pelagian sense to mean that grace can be resisted. Wright certainly shows very little interest in expounding the doctrine of predestination, which he appears to dismiss as an unimportant speculation. 'It is not necessary to know that which God hath not revealed … Some would more gladly know what God dyd before he made the world, than to know what he wyll do with them when the world is ended' (f. 186).

On this basis, we might be tempted to offer an alternative categorisation of Wright. Here, it seems, we have a Protestant cleric of an old-fashioned variety, more in tune with the Lutheranism of the early Reformation than the Calvinism of the late Elizabethan Church. But again we would be wrong. One sign of this can be found in Wright's citations, where, alongside the references to mid-sixteenth-century divines such as Martin Bucer and Rodolf Gualter, there are references to 'Perkins de simbolo' and 'Perkins wrytinge on the creed' (ff. 106, 160) – that is, William Perkins's *Exposition of the Symbole or Creed of the Apostles* (1595) – showing that Wright was thoroughly up to date with his reading. And while some passages in the sermons evoke the familiar stereotype of the country parson reconciling his neighbours on the ale-bench, others are more redolent of a different stereotype, that of the hardline puritan minister using his sermons to 'make a separation' between the godly and the unregenerate members of his congregation. In the middle of Wright's exhortation to neighbourliness, for example, is a startling passage stressing, with the help of a quotation from Augustine, that membership of the visible Church is not a sufficient guarantee of godliness. In other words, it was possible to come to church each week, to join in public worship and still remain unregenerate:

*Dilectio sola discernit inter filios dei et filios diaboli*, love onely discerneth between the sonnes of god and the sonnes of the devill, for though all you come to the Church, all of you heare, all of you kneele, all of you pray all of you singe But yet these can not distinguish between you and the Children of Beliall. But as many as walke in love these are the Children of god, a marke that never deceiveth. (f. 147)

This sharp distinction between the 'Children of God' and the 'Children of Beliall' is carried over into other sermons. 'When a man comes into some of your houses', Wright told his parishioners, he 'fyndes some at cardes swearinge, some at drinke raylinge, some in talking of ribawdry ... What contrey may he thinke himselfe in, thinke you? had he not need to do as the prophett sayth, Aryse and depart?' But 'yf the same man should come into some other of your houses (wherof ther be too fewe)' he would find 'some readinge, some prayinge, some conferringe of scriptures, all ready as Cornelius and his [household] were to heare all thinges that are commanded of god. Would not he thinke this an heavenly place?' (f. 184). Needless to say, this is precisely the sort of divisive social rhetoric that is generally associated with Puritanism, in which an unregenerate multitude is set against an ostentatiously godly minority.

This was potentially explosive stuff, and it is clear from Wright's own testimony that his sermons provoked considerable hostility from some members of his audience, though not necessarily for the reasons we might expect. Some of the hostility seems to have been directed at preaching in general, from persons whom Wright describes as 'the scorners of these tymes ... the scorners of preachinge, preachers, and desirers to goe unto sermons'. But most of it, by Wright's account, was directed at particular aspects of his preaching, such as the fact that his sermons were entirely in English. In his preface, he explained that he had previously refrained from using Latin or Greek quotations in order to keep his sermons as plain and purely scriptural as possible:

My sole effort was to render clearly and eloquently what I could, without the affected eloquence of any tongue other than English. Moreover, I took pains to incorporate quotations from the Scriptures in such a way that my sermons would preach nothing else. However, some ignorant people, muttering among themselves, did not blush to condemn this method of preaching. With unceasing slander they took every opportunity to sow among the common people the notion that I abstained from using Latin and Greek because I did not know these languages. (f. 116)

To refute these accusations, Wright – in his own words – 'adopted a different method of preaching, and quoted Latin and Greek writers and theologians among my English citations'. However, this was not enough to satisfy his critics, who also complained that he had been preaching too much law and too little Gospel:

Some people complained, even to my face, that my previous year's sermons dealt only with the Old Testament – as if to imply that I had preached on the Law because I was unable to preach on the Gospel. For this reason, I made these sermons almost entirely on the New Testament, so that they might recognise their folly and finally desist from their slanderous accusations.

Wright also feared that he would be accused of personal preaching – 'I am afrayd that when I shall grow to particular pointes some wyll thinke that I point at them' (f. 183) – not without reason, since he went on to admonish 'many of you who are marked for ordinary drunkardes uppon every foolish occasion and company', with particular reference to 'those that are most notorious out of the rest' (f. 189).

This case study provides an interesting test of Christopher Haigh's 'parish Anglicanism' thesis, which holds that there was an inbuilt conflict between the high expectations of the Protestant preachers and the conservatism of their parishioners. What we have here, it seems, is a tension between two alternative views of preaching. Wright saw preaching as a powerful instrument of conversion, and sought to use his sermons to bring about a moral and social reformation among his parishioners. What many of his parishioners wanted – if we may draw a few deductions from Wright's account – were sermons of a rather different sort, salted with learned quotations but limited to relatively simple paraphrases of the familiar Gospel stories, without stirring up controversy or making any stringent moral demands. This is very much what the Haigh thesis would lead us to expect. And yet Wright does not fit very comfortably into Haigh's stereotype of the godly preacher. This is a preacher who has read the works of Perkins, but who can also treat his audience to an anecdote from *Scoggin's Jests* (f. 142); who denounces many forms of popular sociability, but who can also be eloquent in his praise of neighbourly virtue, and is clearly as firm a believer in 'the harmony and vitality of the village unit' as any of Haigh's parish Anglicans.[80] The conclusion must be that Haigh's distinction

---

[80] *Scoggin's Jests* was a popular jestbook of the period: see STC 21850.3. Its use in the pulpit caused controversy elsewhere: the churchwardens of Hempnet in Somerset complained in 1603 that although their curate William Hawkins preached regularly, 'his doctrine is prophaned with Scoggins jestes' (Somerset Record Office, Taunton, D/D/Ca 134). Compare the case cited by Patrick Collinson, 'Shepherds, sheepdogs and hirelings', pp. 206–7, where the parishioners of Egerton in Kent complain about the 'fryvolous tales' in the sermons of an itinerant preacher.

between old and new models of parish ministry – conciliatory pastor on the one hand, divisive godly preacher on the other – is overdrawn. Wright's preaching combines elements of both.

There is an illuminating parallel to be drawn here with William Sheppard, the Elizabethan rector of Heydon in Essex, who copied an autobiographical 'Epitome' into his parish register along with one of his sermons. Several recent studies of the popular reception of Protestant ideas have focused on Sheppard as a test case, and have come to strikingly different conclusions. For Patrick Collinson, Sheppard exemplifies 'old rather than new pastoral values'. He believed in a religion of good works, and 'his one surviving sermon suggests that he confined himself to short homilies of a traditional kind, punctuated with many "now good neybors" and "'therefore good neybors"'.[81] For Mark Byford, on the other hand, Sheppard was able to instil 'distinctively Protestant attitudes and priorities' into many of his parishioners without losing sight of the traditional values of charity and hospitality. His sermon is a model of unremarkable Protestant orthodoxy: the elect are predestined to salvation; good works proceed from faith; we must rely on the merits of Christ in order to be saved. In a sense, this difference of opinion is not surprising, since Sheppard served the cure of Heydon for over forty years, from 1541 to 1586, and is very much a transitional figure between the old world of pre-Reformation Catholicism and the new world of the Elizabethan Church. But the difficulty of distinguishing between 'old' and 'new' religion is significant, since it suggests that there was a considerable overlap between the two. The distinctive concerns of godly preaching were not necessarily incompatible with an old-fashioned appeal to neighbourliness and hospitality.

Indeed, it is possible to go a step further. Wright's sermons may be read as an attempt to advance the cause of the new religion, and new pastoral values, by appropriating certain aspects of the old. By his own account, he was prepared to adopt a more old-fashioned style of preaching, replete with Latin quotations, as a concession to the sensibilities of his listeners. And a careful reading of the sermons reveals that the invocations of neighbourly values are part of a carefully thought-out strategy of persuasion, designed to

---

[81] Mark Byford, 'The price of Protestantism: assessing the impact of religious change in Elizabethan Essex' (unpublished DPhil thesis, University of Oxford, 1988), chapter 1; Collinson, 'Shepherds, sheepdogs and hirelings', p. 212. Sheppard's sermon was copied by him into the Heydon parish register (Essex Record Office, Chelmsford, D/P 135/1/1) and is transcribed in full in Byford, 'Price of Protestantism', pp. 440–1. See also Marsh, *Popular Religion in Sixteenth-Century England*, p. 90, where it is pointed out that Sheppard's will includes a preamble from Thomas Becon's *Sick Man's Salve* (1561), but with the key Protestant clause deliberately omitted.

discredit popular pastimes such as drinking and cardplaying by associating them with sins against neighbourhood. Thus the ungodly house where the casual visitor finds 'some at cardes swearinge, some at drinke raylinge' also contains other persons 'talking . . . of newes, which indeed is tales of neighboures'. What Wright was trying to do, it seems, was to turn the accepted stereotype of good neighbourhood upside-down, by coupling drinking and cardplaying with the antisocial sins of 'raylinge' and tale-bearing, while presenting the godly as the true defenders of neighbourly love and charity. This sort of Protestant appropriation of popular culture would not be so surprising in, say, the murder pamphlets analysed by Peter Lake – very public; very polemical; very London-centred; very much a product of the market for cheap print – but it is considerably more unexpected to find it in the sermons of an obscure preacher in a remote West Country parish.[82] It warns us not to think of country preaching as rhetorically unsophisticated or naïve.

At about the same time as Wright was preaching these sermons to his Cornish parishioners, another preacher was embarking on his ministry in the small Oxfordshire parish of Alkerton, about five miles from Banbury. Thomas Lydiat (1572–1646), fellow of New College, Oxford, was presented to the rectory of Alkerton by his father, Christopher, in 1612. It was not an especially desirable piece of preferment, and several other clergy had rejected it before Lydiat agreed to accept it. As he later wrote: 'after some pausing, not without reluctancie of minde, I yeelded unto it with these words, Then it seemes it must be mine' – words that do not suggest any great enthusiasm for parish ministry; and indeed it seems that Lydiat only accepted the living because he had failed to gain any preferment from his patron Prince Henry, and because his scholarly publications had proved to be far less profitable than he had hoped.[83] Alkerton was a tiny parish, only a few hundred acres in size; in 1641 there were twenty-nine adult males in the parish, and about fifty communicants. Christopher Lydiat had acquired the manor in 1567, and Thomas had been born and brought up there, so would have known his parishioners well. Among his manuscripts in the Bodleian Library is a volume of sermons on the first three chapters of the Gospel of Luke (MS Rawl. E.168) which proves, on examination, to be the first course of

[82] Peter Lake and Michael Questier, *The Antichrist's Lewd Hat: Protestants, Papists and Players in Post-Reformation England* (New Haven and London, 2002), esp. chapters 1 and 5.

[83] Thomas Lydiat, 'The Christian scribe': Trinity College, Dublin, MS 388, f. 97r. On Lydiat's ministry at Alkerton, see *VCH Oxfordshire* IX (1969), pp. 44–53; on Lydiat's scientific interests and circle of correspondents, see Mordechai Feingold, *The Mathematicians' Apprenticeship: Science, Universities and Society in England 1560–1640* (Cambridge, 1984), pp. 148–52.

sermons preached by Lydiat at Alkerton, immediately after his induction on 19 August 1612. It is a fascinating collection, not only for what it reveals about Lydiat's expectations of parish ministry, but because it shows him gradually revising and adapting his preaching style to suit his audience.

In his very first sermon, on Luke 1: 1, Lydiat launched straight into a justification of the need for preaching and religious instruction. He emphasised the need to distinguish between true and false teachers, especially 'at this time, in regard of the swarming of those false Apostles the Popish Jesuits and Seminarie priests, which are in every corner buzzing and busying themselves to mingle the sincer milke of Gods word with the galle of their traditions'. The teachings of the Jesuits and seminary priests might seem superficially attractive; but if we examine them 'in the principal points of difference betweene us', we will find that 'howsoever they would seeme to professe the doctrine of Jesus Christ, they are thereby convinced to belong rather to the Synagogue of Antichrist'. Everyone, laity as well as clergy, must therefore be well versed in the scriptures in order to defend the truth against the common adversary. Obviously, this required a high standard of religious knowledge and commitment, and Lydiat anticipated some resistance from his audience:

But here peradventure some wil object, wee are laye men, who by reason of our callings and occupations and trades of life have smale skil in the Scriptures, and our knowledge is weake: and there are many places of Scripture that Papists and other heretikes and schismatikes alledge for them selves: Howe then possiblie can wee trye and examine them by the Scriptures, wherein are conteined so many harde and intricate points that so greate clerkes and doctors can not agree upon? (f. 35r)

However, Lydiat remained firm. 'To this objection I answere . . . that no man ought in regarde of his occupation or trade of life to thinke himself privileged from studying or exercising himself to get skil and knowledge in the Scriptures.' Moses, he pointed out, did not preach 'to the Priests and Levits, or to the Prelates of Israel onelye . . . but to the whole congregation from the highest to the lowest, as wel to poore as riche, of what state and condition of life soever'. Christian ministers, too, should preach to all, including simple and uneducated folk; and every member of their audience ought to be able to test their doctrines in order to ascertain their truth.

Lydiat was clearly aware of the need to make his sermons accessible to ordinary people. But how well had he succeeded? He had certainly set the doctrinal level of his sermon fairly low: there is no complex theology here, and the emphasis is on practical divinity, with exhortations to trust in God's providence, be guided by the Word of God and seek God's blessing in prayer. The anti-Catholic polemic is also expressed quite simply, in terms of an opposition between Protestant scripture and Catholic tradition, and would not necessarily have been beyond the grasp of his audience. However, Lydiat made little effort to simplify the structure of the sermon, and employed the standard doctrine-and-use format, which, as we saw in Chapter 2, was chiefly designed to assist note-taking and subsequent repetition: 'Of this doctrine I gather a threefold use. The first is consolation for poore Christians . . . The second use is for instruction . . . The third use is for terror to the persecutors and enemies of the Church of Christ.' Many of the separate doctrines and uses are further divided and sub-divided; and it seems unlikely that Lydiat's audience would have been able to follow the argument unless they were already well practised in the art of hearing. Moreover, the sermon is relatively long, and would have taken at least an hour and a half to deliver. Even if we assume that it was delivered in two parts, at morning and evening prayer, this still represents an extremely demanding Sunday routine; and it is hard not to feel that Lydiat was being over-ambitious.

Some of his hearers seem to have felt the same. In his sermons over the following weeks, Lydiat sought to explain and vindicate St Luke's manner of writing in terms that were clearly intended to be applied to his own style of preaching. He argued that when a man 'undertakes a peece of worke after another' – as St Luke had done in undertaking to tell a story that had previously been told by others – he should 'performe and effect the same more carefully and more thoroughly than the former . . . for otherwise hee shoulde do no more than what was done before'. The implication is that Lydiat had been criticised for the detail and complexity of his sermons; to which he was replying, in effect, that as he was not the first preaching minister at Alkerton, it was his duty to go further than his predecessors, and to preach more thoroughly, 'to adde what is wanting . . . to confirme what is doubtful, to cleare what is obscure' (f. 54r). In the same sermon, he emphasised that 'in hearing the word of God taught' one should not 'ascribe . . . too much to the persons of the teachers, in regard of their outward giftes of learning, eloquence, and auctoritie'. Moses himself declared that he was not eloquent, and we should not 'despise or neglect or think scorne of our ordinarie ministers of the Gospel' if they preach without eloquence, as long as they speak 'truly and sincerely' (f. 53v). Again, there is an unmistakably defensive note here, as though Lydiat felt the need to apologise for his own lack of eloquence.

Lydiat's failure to win over his audience is made even more obvious in the sermons that follow. By the time he reached Luke 1: 8, he felt obliged to reprove 'those who nowe adays, in some of our Churches, either trifle out the time, and are whispering amongst themselves, or else making toyes and games at the minister: or if they bee helde any longer than themselves thinke it fitte, bewraye their impatience by some unseemlie gestures: or else at leastwise sleepe out the most part of the time' (f. 68r). He returned to the same point in a sermon on Luke 1: 21, where he observed wistfully that Zechariah's congregation 'patientlie taryed and waited for him, staying longer in the Temple than the wonted time', without 'blaming of him, or murmuring against him, or making any tumultuous noyse, much lesse departing from the temple with indignation to their homes'. How different the situation 'now adayes in our Churches', where 'many are impatient of tarying to the ende of Gods publike service' and 'trifle out the time either whispering among themselves, or taking a nappe, or suffering their mindes to wander in vaine and idle and impure thoughts', because they do not realise the importance of the Word of God. But make no mistake, he warned his audience: God will punish those who neglect his Word, or who 'preferre most vaine and idle sportes and pastimes, such as have beene too usuall and common at wakes and revels, and suchlike riotous meetings . . . before all Gods publick service' (f. 84r).

It would be hard to imagine a better illustration of the Haigh thesis. Here we have a clear case of Protestant 'culture shock', with a university-trained preacher unprepared for the reality of parish ministry, and his parishioners in their turn unwilling to sit through his long and tedious sermons. But this is not the end of the story, for Lydiat's remaining sermons show that within a matter of months he had radically altered his style of preaching. As well as cutting the length of his sermons by about a third, he abandoned the rigid doctrine-and-use arrangement and adopted a much simpler structure, with a greater stress on practical moral behaviour. Preaching on the childhood of Christ (Luke 2: 40–52), he drew a few simple conclusions about the reciprocal duties of parents and children, summarised briefly at the end of the sermon for the benefit of inattentive listeners:

And so much bee spoken touching our Lord Jesus Christ his childhoode and education. But it is not enough to have spoken and hearde somuch, unlesse wee applye our selves to the imitating and folowing of his example and doctrine. And sith hee is both the doctor or teacher and Saviour of al degrees and estates of men, each one ought seriouslie to thinke that these thinges appertaine unto themselves. Especiallie and principallie parentes ought to remember that al the cares and labors wherewith they trouble and wearie themselves in providing for their families, are in vaine, unlesse they bring their children unto God, and institute them in his feare and service. Also children and youth of either sexe ought to acknowledge and yeelde that they have verie greate neede of discipline and instruction, and therefore quietlie and thankfullie to receive it and patientlie to endure it. (f. 191r)

In a retrospective account of his ministry written in 1638, Lydiat wrote that he had preached weekly sermons in a style 'suitable to my small Country Auditory', consisting of paraphrases on the four Gospels: 'translations not word for word but more free', with 'some things omitted, added and alter'd, as I thought fitting the time and place: holding it my duty to be carefull for the soundnes of the doctrine and profitablenes of it for my little flocke'. Despite his early difficulties, it appears that Lydiat had managed to come up with a more accessible style of preaching – and one that, by his own account, he put to good use by delivering 'above six hundred sermons' at Alkerton in the space of 'lesse than a dozen yeares'.[84]

But the story has a further twist. In the autumn of 1622, James I issued his *Directions to Preachers*, accompanied by a new edition of the Book of Homilies; and Lydiat chose to mark the occasion by preaching a special sermon commending the Homilies to his parishioners. His sermon reiterated many of the themes that we have already encountered in his preaching, with a strong line of anti-Catholic polemic expressed in terms of a distinction between scripture and tradition. The Homilies, he declared, were 'almost all of them directly intended and bent against severall poynts of Papistrie; and therefore at this time, wherein we feele to our griefe Popery beginne to make strong head againe, so much the more needfull and behovefull to be regarded'. For example, the first Homily, entitled 'A fruitful exhortation to the reading of Holy Scripture', taught that scripture 'is most profitable to be read of all people, as well Layty as Clergy, for the obtaining of true saving knowledge', that it 'containes all poynts necessary to be knowen for Salvation', and that 'it is plaine and easy to be understood, as well of the unlearned as learned'; all of which 'the Papists deny, thereupon obtruding their unwritten Traditions'. And Lydiat ended by returning to another of his favourite themes, the need for the laity to take an active part in the process of religious instruction. 'As it is our part to bring you good doctrine, so it is your part to bring us good attention: or else our doctrine be it never so good, can have no better successe amongst you than good seed cast away by the highwayside.'[85]

From Lydiat's account, it appears that this sermon did not go down well with his audience. Like Wright's parishioners, they evidently knew what they wanted from their minister, and did not hesitate to object if his

---

[84] Lydiat, 'The Christian scribe', f. 97r.  [85] Lydiat, 'The Christian scribe', ff. 97v–98r.

sermons did not match their expectations – but, as with Wright's parishioners, the nature of their objections was not quite what we might suppose:

In the publishing whereof to my Parishioners, I found two things especially distasted. The one was that they were not made upon any set Text of Scripture, and therefore some would hardly be perswaded, that Homilies were Sermons. As if they were not explications and applications of severall Texts of Gods word, pertinently alleadged and rightly expounded and applyed to the proofe and Confirmation of the poynts handled in them. But the maine distast was, as of my whole Ministry, that they were read and not uttered by memory. Here I leave it to any reasonable man to thinke, whether it were not a greife unto me, that in a dozen yeares exercise of my Ministery; be my Sermons what they might be, mine owne or others, in whole or in part, though the matter of them were never so good or pertinent: yet they were distasted only because they were not delivered without booke.[86]

This is in some ways the reverse of what the Haigh thesis would lead us to expect. Rather than demanding simple homilies and objecting to more elaborately prepared sermons, it appears that the inhabitants of Alkerton wanted elaborately prepared sermons and felt short-changed when they were given homilies read out of a book. Perhaps they shared William Prynne's view, that preaching from memory was part of the implicit bargain between preacher and audience: 'how can . . . Ministers exhort the people to remember what they heare; when as themselves commit not that to memory, which they Preach?'[87] They may have felt that it was part of the minister's duty to memorise his sermons, and that a preacher who read from a prepared script (with no guarantee that he had even composed the sermon himself) was not fulfilling his side of the bargain.

It is fascinating to see some of the themes of the reading/preaching debate recurring here at a parochial level. What Lydiat was attempting to do, in effect, was to persuade his parishioners that reading was a form of preaching, and therefore that homilies were a form of sermons. 'As therfore they are in very deed Homilies, what soever at any time you have heard or shall heare uttered by any godly Minister and preacher out of the Pulpit: so these are as truely Sermons which I intend now to utter unto you out of this booke, and out of this Pue: Wherefore be not vaine in your owne Conceits, but reverently and diligently hearken to what is uttered.'[88] His

---

[86] Lydiat, 'The Christian scribe', ff. 98v–99r.
[87] William Prynne, *A Briefe Survay and Censure of Mr Cozens His Couzening Devotions* (1628), L3r. See also Ian Green, 'The persecution of "scandalous" and "malignant" parish clergy during the English Civil War', *English Historical Review*, 94 (1979), p. 520: 'especial scorn was reserved for sermons that lasted less than an hour, or were read from books or notes'.
[88] The implication is that Lydiat normally delivered his sermons from the pulpit, but was proposing to read the Homilies from the reading pew (or the lower lectern of a two-decker pulpit).

audience, however, seem to have taken the view that sermons were only sermons if they were delivered 'without booke'. There is much more that we would like to know about the audience response to Lydiat's sermons – sadly, our knowledge is limited by the fact that (as so often) the voices of the laity only reach us at one remove, through a narrative written by a clergy-man – but several conclusions can be drawn. First, it is clear that the laity were not passive in their response to sermons – and what they wanted, it seems, were sermons based on particular texts of scripture, preferably the Gospels, with a display of learning and private study. Secondly, it is clear that the Haigh thesis which measures the effectiveness of sermons according to a single doctrinal criterion – how well they communicated certain key Protestant ideas – may conceal as much as it reveals about the relationship between preachers and their audiences.

With our third case study we move from the tiny hamlet of Alkerton to the market town of Ashbourne, Derbyshire. The vicarage of Ashbourne was too poorly endowed to attract a learned minister, but a lectureship was founded in the early seventeenth century to provide a regular preaching ministry in the town; and for twenty-five years – from 1601 until his death in 1626 – the lectureship was held by William Hull, a graduate of Christ's College, Cambridge, who also served as headmaster of the local grammar school from 1616 to 1626.[89] Hull's sermons survive in massive profusion: seven large folio volumes in Trinity College, Dublin, and an eighth volume in the British Library, all in the author's own hand, making his preaching ministry better documented than that of any other seventeenth-century English clergyman.[90] In these sermons we hear the unmistakable voice of godly preaching, fiercely intolerant of swearing and sabbath-breaking, and with a far more aggressive tone than anything we find in the sermons of Wright or Lydiat. Hull modelled his preaching on that of John the Baptist, whose example, he declared in a sermon of 1603, 'serves to enforme us, the ministers, how to deale with our people, to frame our sermons to the audience, and having to doe with barren professors . . . to urge them to repentance and reformation, by exhorting them and terrifying them with the vengence of god'.[91] The survival of his sermons in such quantity, and over such a long period of time, offers a rare opportunity to gauge the effectiveness of this confrontational style of preaching.

[89] On the Ashbourne lectureship, see Richard Clark, 'Lists of Derbyshire clergymen 1558–1662', *Derbyshire Archaeological Journal*, 104 (1984), pp. 31–3.

[90] BL Harl. MS 663; Trinity College, Dublin, MS 709. The TCD volumes are not foliated, and I have therefore indicated the texts from which Hull is preaching, as the best means of locating the passages referred to.

[91] Trinity College, Dublin, MS 709, vol. v, on Matthew 3: 8.

Confrontational it certainly was, from the very beginning. In March 1602, at the start of a course of weekday lectures on Amos, Hull stood up to announce: 'I have enterprised this day a labor neither by my selfe nor others heretofore performed in this place, the reading of a publique lecture' – and promptly launched into a fierce attack on the sins of Ashbourne and its inhabitants. 'I see sin swarming in it, religion dispised, the religious disdained; swearing, quarrelling, stealing, whoring, swilling, slandering, &c. dayly committed, so that we are almost for theise things grown into a Proverbe amongst other people and our neighboring Towns adjacent.' He complained of widespread contempt of the Word of God, 'some not at all coming to heare, others openly departing when the sermon begins, without noting or punishing', with 'too much negligence of the best sort, which heare not soe ordinarily and conscionably as I wish'.[92] It was this situation which Hull set himself to reform, though he had no illusions about the magnitude of the task. In a sermon of October 1603 he remarked that in these 'evill tymes' it was the fate of most ministers to have 'such hearers as will heare a lyttle, and at their leasure', but who were incapable of 'doing, or yealding any obedience to that we teach, either for the leaving any synne at all or doing any good at all'.[93] Even the most conscientious minister would have to resign himself to a measure of pastoral failure.

Looking around Ashbourne, Hull found many things in need of reformation. His sermons are a fascinating, and historically valuable, record of popular customs and superstitions in early seventeenth-century Derbyshire, with references to folktales of 'haunted places' and 'phaery ground'; the songs of 'jesters, rymers, and baudy singers', including 'many Christmas carrols' which Hull described as 'beastly'; sabbath-day feasts and other popular entertainments, 'common wakes as they call them', and night-time gatherings known as 'leech-watchings'; 'interludes and stage plays', including 'scripture plays' and 'pageants of Christ and his life and death', which in Hull's opinion were 'the very worst kinde of play ... for God hath appointed his word to be preached not played'.[94] Many of these popular customs clearly had their roots in pre-Reformation culture. In a sermon preached around Michaelmas 1603, Hull called his congregation to account for 'your heathenish customes and blinde consciences ... in coming in and going out at such a dore, in going processionwise about

---

[92] Trinity College, Dublin, MS 709, vol. III, on Amos 1: 1 (a stray from the series of sermons on Amos in vol. VII).

[93] Trinity College, Dublin, MS 709, vol. V, on Matthew 3: 6–12.

[94] BL Harl. MS 663, ff. 58v (leech-watchings), 66v (haunted places); Trinity College, Dublin, MS 709, vol. III, on Exodus 20: 8–11 (wakes; interludes and stage plays), vol. V, on Matt. 1: 25 (Christmas carrols).

church etc.' In a sermon of August 1617, he turned his attention to white witchcraft, 'when men or women only doe good, and bless cattle or people, and use good prayers', and characterised it in terms which suggest that it was a blend of Catholic survivalism and popular folklore. 'Those we call white witches' were 'poor ignorant superstitious men or women usually . . . they come not at church at all for the most parte. For their prayers they use, they are prescribed them such set words, so many tymes with such crossinges and ceremonyes (indeed a very charme, not a prayer) no more or fewer.'[95]

But Hull's chief concern was with the sins of drunkenness and swearing. In June 1605, in his course of sermons on the Book of Genesis, he reached the story of Lot's drunkenness (Gen. 19: 31–8) and drew the familiar contrast between the church and the alehouse. 'Its no marvell in this and other places so few come to church and love Gods house so lyttle that love the ale-house and the black pott so wel.'[96] Thirteen years later, in his sermons on Exodus, he was still harping on the same theme. Drunkenness was 'the (now) syn of our nation, a syn detestable to God and to good men, always evil, always to be abhorred, always accursed', and 'a most fearful profanation of the Lords holy day'. He was equally appalled by the ubiquity of swearing. 'As for swearing, who can say his heart is cleane? where is the man, the woman, the child, that doth not accustomably dishonor the Lord in it? . . . Are not oathes for most part as ordinary as words? Doe we buye or sell without them? Doe we eat or drink, doe we discourse or confer together but enter-lace our speech with oathes? . . . Surely it is so evident it cannot be denyed, that this synne (though not alone this) is fearfully encreased, so as the land grones under it, the righteous are greeved at it, and the Lord is pressed under it as a cart under the load.'[97]

This sort of moral rigorism – defining the limits of lawful behaviour very narrowly, and so placing a lot of popular customs, such as social drinking and swearing, beyond the pale – was what unsympathetic contemporaries described as 'preciseness' or 'Puritanism'. It is sometimes argued that the polemical connotations of the term 'puritan' render it unsuitable for use as a descriptive label. But Hull himself was perfectly willing to employ the term, and happy to associate himself with 'puritan' values. 'It's strange to see', he remarks in one sermon, 'how profanenes hath justled out all religion under

---

[95]  Trinity College, Dublin, MS 709, vol. II, on Exodus 20: 4–6 (witchcraft), vol. v, on Matthew 3: 6–12 (processions).
[96]  BL Harl. MS 663, f. 9v.
[97]  Trinity College, Dublin, MS 709, vol. II, on Exodus 20: 4–6 (swearing), vol. III, on Exodus 20: 8–11 (drunkenness).

the nick-name of puritanisme. If a man will not eat but with thanksgiving, he is a puritane, if he will not ride or journey but first commend himself to God by prayer, that is puritanisme.' If these are the defining features of Puritanism, he concludes, 'then Christ was a puritan'. Elsewhere, he treats the avoidance of swearing as a distinctively puritan practice, noting that some swear 'for fashion' or 'for that we would not be held puritans for forbearing of it'.[98] And Hull also seems to have carried his Puritanism to the point of nonconformity. In May 1605, not long after the Hampton Court Conference, he maintained that a good intention could not justify an evil action, which 'answers for those that dare not yeald to the ceremonyes, and subscription urged under pretence of doing good by preaching, seeing synne may not be comytted under any color of good intent or otherwise'.[99]

This does not mean, however, that Hull's preaching ministry was nothing more than a sustained diatribe against popular culture. The majority of his sermons were much less controversial in tone, and much more conventional in their moral teaching. This is most pronounced in his Sunday morning sermons, which moved steadily through the books of Genesis and Exodus, drawing out a series of simple doctrines and practical moral applications. The death of Sarah (Gen. 23) gave rise to a series of sermons on death and mourning; the marriage of Isaac (Gen. 24) to a series of sermons on the reciprocal duties of parents, children, husbands and wives; the death of Abraham (Gen. 25) to a series of sermons on wills and inheritances. There are few surprises here. Husbands, Hull told his congregation, must love their wives as Christ loved his Church, 'with a particular and speciall love ... bearing with their weaknesses wisely, providing for their wantes honestly'; while the wife, for her part, must be 'a helper in the government of the family ... a comforter in the tyme of misery ... a companion both in prosperity and adversity'. The story of Abraham is handled with relentless literal-mindedness. From Abraham's example, we learn 'prudency in this case to prevent enmyty and expence to have alway (as it wer in our bosome) a devise of a will touching the disposeing of our temporall estate'; and as Abraham left legacies to all his children but made Isaac his heir and executor, so 'we must accompt of all our children and give them portions, but cheefly the best to the best'.[100]

---

[98] BL Harl. MS 663, f. 68r; Trinity College, Dublin, MS 709, vol. II, sermon on Exodus 20: 4–6.

[99] BL Harl. MS 663, f. 3v. On the doctrine that a good end cannot justify an evil means, as applied by Stephen Egerton to the Essex Revolt, see also Arnold Hunt, 'Tuning the pulpits: the religious context of the Essex Revolt', in Lori Anne Ferrell and Peter McCullough, eds., *The English Sermon Revised: Religion, Literature and History 1600–1750* (Manchester, 2000), p. 99.

[100] BL Harl. MS 663, ff. 37v (husbands and wives), 38v (will-making).

This very practical reading of the Bible, with every chapter and verse applied to some form of moral improvement, is entirely in keeping with the moral rigorism that we have already identified in Hull's preaching. To regard the more obviously controversial or 'puritan' aspects of his sermons as an added ingredient, an optional extra which can be considered in isolation from the rest of his moral teaching, would be to ignore the way that his Puritanism runs like an insistent ground-bass through the whole of his ministry. At the same time, most of his moral teaching clearly belongs to what Martin Ingram has described as the 'moral consensus' common to all shades of Protestant opinion and shared by respectable layfolk in the parishes, including agreement on 'the need for responsible, stable marriage' and on 'the heinousness of blatant sexual immorality'.[101] In other words. Hull's Puritanism did not necessarily compromise the popular appeal or acceptability of his preaching. And although his sermons followed the standard doctrine-reason-use format, their structure was relatively simple, with no complex subdivision, and would have been readily accessible to ordinary hearers, particularly because of the way that individual doctrines or applications could have been lifted out of the sermon and turned into free-standing moral maxims. Preaching on the story of Isaac (Gen. 24: 62–7), Hull drew the moral 'that yonge men, unmarryed men, may be godly men, devout, zealous, pyous'.[102] His hearers would not have needed to be literate, or to participate in sermon repetition, in order to have extracted this single sentence from the sermon and committed it to memory as 'a note for young men'.

But if Puritanism was not wholly opposed to popular social mores, neither was it passively supportive of them. Reading Hull's sermons, the picture that emerges is that of a preacher working from within the moral consensus, trying to exploit these shared moral values in order to persuade his hearers towards a stricter definition of godliness and virtue – not, in fact, so very unlike Ingram's description of the Church courts as adopting a 'broadly consensual' approach, 'marching slightly in advance of popular attitudes'.[103] Thus Hull took it for granted that his hearers would accept the need for sexual temperance, but argued that they needed to revise their definition of it. 'Some suppose if they be no adulterers etc. they are temperate. But temperance is a right moderation of lawfull delightes, and not absteyning only from unlawfull.' Similarly, he could take it for granted that his hearers would accept the need for restrictions on sexual licence,

---

[101]  Martin Ingram, *Church Courts, Sex and Marriage in England, 1570-1640.* (Cambridge, 1987), p. 167.
[102]  BL Harl. MS 663, f. 36v.    [103]  Ingram, *Church Courts, Sex and Marriage*, p. 124.

but argued that the restrictions which applied to adults should also be applied to young men. 'Many excuse outragious actes thus, oh he is a yonge man', but those who 'think that their youth is a charter to them to doe evill by authoryty' were mistaken.[104] It is evident from these examples that Hull was trying to work with rather than against the grain of popular culture, and, like Wright at St Minver, was seeking to appropriate certain aspects of popular culture for his own didactic purposes.

This is especially noticeable in his repeated appeal to neighbourly values. Preaching on Genesis 19: 7, he observed that Lot addressed his neighbours as brethren, 'whence we have to note that neighbours are brethren of one and the same flesh and bloud'. Therefore, 'if neighbors be brethen, let them love as brethren. If they will not love as brethren, let them not be neighbors'. A few months later, preaching on Genesis 21: 6–8, he observed that Sarah's neighbours rejoiced with her at the birth of her son. 'Here note that neighbors are to rejoyce together, and to be glad in the good of one another. They and we are one body.'[105] Hull was capable of using this rhetoric of neighbourliness in an unashamedly conservative fashion, as in one sermon where he extolled 'that auncient vertue, that english honour of good hous-keeping, of true hospytalyty', and lamented the passing of a bygone age when men were 'full of charyty and abundant in good works . . . neighbourly love was fervent and self love was sett by' – a striking passage which would not be out of place in the sermons of a traditionalist cleric looking back nostalgically to pre-Reformation days. 'How unlike are the present to former tymes? Wher is that aunceint and commendable vertue of hospytalyty? Surely pride and private gaine and ryott have held a counsaile and banished hospytalyty beyond the seas.'[106] Here was the preacher in his traditional role as reconciler, striving to unite his people in the bond of charity.

Hull's strong emphasis on neighbourly unity and social cohesion is all the more remarkable because it coexists with an equally strong, and potentially divisive, doctrine of predestination. In January 1606, still work-ing his way through Genesis, he reached the story of Jacob and Esau, one of the key predestinarian proof-texts. From God's choice of Jacob over Esau (Gen. 25: 23), he drew the lesson that 'Gods election is a free election. He chuseth wher he pleaseth, he preferreth whom he listeth', referring his hearers to St Paul's interpretation of the passage (Rom. 9: 11, another key predestinarian proof-text) to emphasise his point that Jacob was chosen,

---

[104] BL Harl. MS 663, f. 36v (young men); Trinity College, Dublin, MS 709, vol. v, on Matthew 1: 25 (temperance).
[105] BL Harl. MS 663, ff. 3r, 16r.   [106] BL Harl. MS 663, f. 32r.

and Esau rejected, regardless of their own actions, 'being not yet born, neither having done any good or evil, that the purpose of God according to election might stand, not of works, but of him that calleth'. From Esau's hatred of Jacob (Gen. 27: 41) he drew the lesson that God's children would always be hated by the wicked.[107] Meanwhile, in his Sunday afternoon sermons on Matthew, he was expounding the doctrine of predestination in an even more uncompromising fashion. 'The number of the elect is smale', he declared in March 1605, 'and fewe, very fewe, hardly any. and those hardly, shalbe saved ... Grosse is their conceipt therfore that think all shalbe saved ... We cannot define of any mans damnation, though we for the present see him in the broad way, and very wicked. But this we may say, few shalbe saved, many shall goe to hel.'[108]

What, then, did Hull's hearers make of his preaching, with its blend of old and new pastoral values? In 1618, preaching on the commandment 'Remember the sabbath day, to keep it holy', Hull listed eight common faults he had observed in his people's observance of the sabbath. It is a detailed and informative list, and deserves quotation at length:

1. Some can be found 'preparing horses for their journeyes to ride to marketes or fayres and feastes, some preparing themselves to the bake-house, mille, shambles, some preparing themselves to sett open their shops and to make sale of their comodytyes as freely on the Sabbath as on any other day, never thinking of any such matter as to pray, meditate etc. before-hand'.

2. 'Some are so careles of preparing themselves for Gods public service, as they are fast on sleep when the bell summons them to the public assembly, and after 3 or 4 warninges by the bell, scarse 6 at church.'

3. 'Some are so farre from preparing themselves for the church by prayer etc. afore-hand as they come not at all to church. Nor those only popish recusantes but such as profess no other religion than our owne yet know not the way to the church, but haunt the ale-house and leave Gods house.'

4. 'Some come but unpreparedly, unwillingly, if in the morning they come, in the afternoone they will not: pretending its too much to heare 2 sermons a day, it is precisenes and plain puritanisme.'

5. 'Others come formally ... without preparation or almost any premeditation whither or wherabout they goe ... So they are forced to doe that at churche viz. to make their private prayer there, which should have bin don at home.'

6. 'Some use a kinde of preparation for the publique service of God and to come to church, but its only civil or rather sinfull for they prepare to come in their best

---

[107] BL Harl. MS 663, ff. 41v, 62v.   [108] Trinity College, Dublin, MS 709, vol. v, on Matthew 7: 13–14.

clothes and in their nicest and most curious dresses, decking themselves in their new and new-fangled habytes and attires to make ostentation, and to make admiration of their so gorgeous and glorious attire as Herod did Act 12: 21.'

7. 'Some prepare to come to church but doe not prepare to come to heare Gods word, to learne instruction, to better themselves, but to carpe, to censure, to judge, to take advantage, to complain, to tangle the minister . . . to heare what they may except at, laugh at, raile at.'

8. 'Some prepare to come, but its so late that half or more Gods service is don before. Some in my knowledge never yet come to the begynning of service.'

Hull saw this as a dismal catalogue of failure. 'We come unprepared, we heare negligently, we departe unedifyed, we goe away uncomfortably . . . We syt before the minister as dead men without heartes, as the seates we syt on without sense, having eares to heare but not hearing with any understanding, having memorye but like sieves that will hold no water.'[109] Yet the list does not suggest that the inhabitants of Ashbourne were wholly unprotestantised. To be sure, there were some who failed to come to church at all, but the majority would appear to fall somewhere within Martin Ingram's category of 'unspectacular orthodoxy'. Some arrived late, or said their private prayers in church rather than at home; some attended the sermon in the morning but not the afternoon; others would 'speak of the sermon' over dinner, but only to 'blame what [they] think amiss' rather than to 'obey what is good'. Some made time for household prayers in the morning, but not at night; others would occasionally 'sequester themselves from company' to pray in private, but failed to 'make it their dayly exercise' as Hull would have wished.

This has strong similarities to Richard Baxter's twelve-part taxonomy of the inhabitants of Kidderminster, which, as Eamon Duffy has commented, 'forces us to broaden our conception of the spectrum of religious opinion and commitment in Stuart England' by charting a whole series of subtle gradations of religious belief and practice in the intermediate zone between irreligion and 'precise' Protestantism. Some of his parishioners, according to Baxter, 'learn the words of the Catechism' and 'confess that we must mend our lives and serve God', but were otherwise ignorant of Christian doctrine and would not submit to teaching. Some appeared to be ignorant, but were merely 'weak in the Faith' and responded well to pastoral guidance and instruction. Some had 'tollerable knowledge' but were guilty of 'some notorious scandalous sins' such as drunkenness or

---

[109]  Trinity College, Dublin, MS 709, vol. III, on Exodus 20: 8–11.

neglect of the sabbath, while others were 'of tollerable knowledge, and no Drunkards or Whoremongers', but 'live in idle or tipling company, or spend their lives in vanity' and would not accept Baxter's strict policy of sacramental discipline.[110] Thus, in Duffy's words, 'the majority of those Baxter describes had some discernible contact with and affiliations to orthodox christianity, if only that of informed lip-service', and the same could be said of Hull's parishioners at Ashbourne. Much of Hull's preaching was directed towards these unspectacularly orthodox members of his flock, urging them towards a greater measure of religious commitment – that is, towards the typical puritan regime of two sermons on Sundays, preceded by private prayer and followed by 'meditation in and conference of the word'.

One should not underestimate the opposition that Hull's preaching undoubtedly provoked. He himself acknowledged, in a sermon of January 1617, that some of his hearers found his sermons 'tedious and troublesome'. But the question that his opponents put to him was not (as might have been the case fifty years earlier) 'what needs all this preaching?' but 'what needs such repetition?' They were not objecting to the existence of a Protestant preaching ministry, but to the particular type of preaching that Hull was giving them, and to his constant harping on the same well-worn themes:

Say some, what should we doe at church today, he is ever in one book and one point, nothing but against such as come not to church or against drunkenness? etc. Yes somwhat els but why not allwayes on these pointes so long as men love those syns?

For my self I am resolved so long as these syns are so rife, as long as I live I will not cease dayly to reprove them and to cry out of them. Leave of these faultes and I will leave to speake of them.

Els, if I hold my peace the stones will cry. So then its not barrennes of the preacher but zeale to God, conformyty to his will, that causes him to repeate the same thinges, to reprove the same syns, and thy blockish beastlynes that urges him to it.[111]

These do not sound like the complaints of ignorant or indifferent layfolk resolutely impervious to Protestant doctrine. Hull's opponents do not appear to have felt that his sermons were too theologically demanding, or too difficult to understand. What they seem to have found objectionable,

---

110   Duffy, 'The godly and the multitude', pp. 38–40.
111   Trinity College, Dublin, MS 709, vol. II, on Exodus 19: 25.

or perhaps just incomprehensible, was his obsession with apparently peripheral matters such as drunkenness and sabbath observance. They also objected to the fact that he was 'ever in one book' – not an unreasonable complaint, one may feel, given that Hull had spent the last fifteen years working relentlessly through Genesis and Exodus, and was now proposing to preach his way through the Ten Commandments for the second time.

There is no extant funeral sermon or other biographical account of Hull, and hence no contemporary verdict on his ministry from outside the echo chamber of his own sermons. However, we do have a biography of one of his successors in the Ashbourne lectureship, John Hieron (another Christ's graduate), who took up the post in 1633, about ten years after Hull's death. It includes a detailed description of Hieron's activities as preacher and catechist; and there is every reason to suppose that this may have been a direct continuation of a routine established by Hull. 'The younger he catechised in the Congregation, the elder at home ... The Sermons preached at Church were repeated in his house, all his willing Neighbours were welcome, and for some time considerable numbers did frequent those repetitions.'[112] The most revealing passage in Hieron's biography, however, concerns the reissue of the Book of Sports in 1633. As well as providing a glimpse of the working partnership between the clerical and lay leaders of the town, and their common concern with social control, it also helps us towards an assessment of the long-term impact of the preaching ministry in Ashbourne:

Unbridled youth presently took the liberty granted; and Tidings being brought to Mr *Hieron*, he got to Mr *Pegge*, a Man of Authority in *Ashborne*, to accompany him, and coming to them, they found Boys and Youths shooting at the Butts, and only one man with them; and being demanded why they did so? The man answered that the Bishop gave them leave. How doth that appear said Mr *Hieron*? The man answered, on such a Sabbath day I came through *Eccleshall* (where then the Bishops seat was) and saw there a Bear-baiting.[113]

It would be hard to find a better illustration of the sense of betrayal felt by the godly clergy in the 1630s. For decades, they and their predecessors had been preaching against sabbath-day games, and trying to enforce higher standards of sabbath observance. Now it seemed their work was being undone by the very authority that should have supported it. In discussing the religious background to the Civil War, John Morrill has drawn attention to what he describes as the 'coiled spring effect', the sense of mounting

---

[112] John Porter, *The Life of Mr John Hieron* (1691), C3v.    [113] Porter, *Life of Hieron*, C2v.

frustration building up during the Personal Rule, suddenly and explosively released in 1641. It was the preaching of men such as Hull that had helped to coil the spring.


CONCLUSION

Three preachers, three parishes: have they anything in common? Keith Wrightson has suggested that the impact of Protestant evangelism depended on a whole range of local variables, such as geographical location, rates of population turnover, patterns of land ownership, 'the personal aspirations and influence of individual landlords, patrons, magistrates and zealous ministers' – a suggestion which, taken to its logical conclusion, would imply that the success or failure of the Protestant preaching ministry can be evaluated only by a series of individual local studies, and that we should not necessarily expect any clear or consistent pattern to emerge.[114] Nevertheless, the three case studies we have been considering – Wright of St Minver; Lydiat of Alkerton; Hull of Ashbourne – bear some striking and revealing similarities. In particular, it is clear that all three ministers encountered a significant measure of resistance to their preaching, not merely from recusants or Church Papists but from within that usefully capacious category of 'unspectacular orthodoxy', from parishioners who attended church regularly, received Communion at least once a year and had no particular scruples about conformity to the reformed religion. This was no threat to the stability of the ecclesiastical settlement, but for conscientious preachers, who wished to transform their parishioners from nominal into committed Protestants, it was both a troubling problem and a serious hindrance to their ministry.

But what was the nature of this resistance? For Keith Thomas, it was simple indifference – as parishioners slumbered quietly through the sermon, or talked among themselves, then dashed for the alehouse as soon as the service was over. For Christopher Haigh, it had a theological dimension as well – as layfolk clung tenaciously to their semi-Pelagian religion of good works and neighbourly charity, refusing to accept the key Protestant doctrines of justification and predestination. However, neither of these factors is particularly prominent in our case studies. Instead, lay resistance seems to have been expressed in other ways – ways which are acknowledged in the Protestant complaint literature, but which historians have tended to

---

[114] Keith Wrightson and David Levine, *Poverty and Piety in an English Village: Terling, 1525–1700* (Oxford, 1995), p. 216.

overlook, largely, one suspects, because they cannot easily be fitted into the standard explanatory framework of progressive Protestant clergy versus conservative crypto-Catholic laity.

One unexpected form of lay resistance was the demand for learned sermons with a parade of Latin quotations – particularly marked in Wright's case, but also indirectly apparent in Lydiat's case, where opposition focused on the fact that he read his sermons from manuscript rather than delivering them from memory. The desire for Latin could be interpreted as a nostalgic folk-memory of pre-Reformation sermons, where the preacher would have quoted scripture passages from the Latin Vulgate before rendering them into English. This certainly seems to be the explanation implied by George Gifford, whose ignorant countryman Atheos complacently declares that he likes to hear a 'learned sermon', meaning one where the preacher 'is able to speake much Latine . . . I will not give a button for these English Doctors, which can alleage no more but out of Paule and Peter.'[115] Yet the desire for learned sermons may have been prompted by other considerations as well. In a dialogue by the Lincolnshire minister Thomas Granger, the 'common carnall Protestant' Mataeologus praises 'a fine man not farre off (you cannot but heare of him) a very good scholler, he is as perfect in his Greeke and Latine as in his English, it will doe one good to heare him'. According to Granger, many hearers demanded 'schollerlike sermons' and would criticise a minister for being 'no scholler' or 'no linguist' even if they could not understand these languages themselves.[116]

Something more than conservative nostalgia seems to be implied here; and we should not ignore the possibility that the presence of an educated preaching minister – amounting to a public declaration that a parish was in the forefront of the reformed religion – may have been a potent source of local pride. Protestant clergy were well aware of the power of local identity, and could sometimes be found exploiting it in their sermons as a means of moral persuasion. We have already encountered Hull trying to shame the inhabitants of Ashbourne into an admission that their disorderly behaviour had 'grown into a Proverbe amongst other people and our neighboring Towns adjacent'. We can see the same technique at work in one of Matthew Newcomen's sermons to the parishioners of Dedham, in Essex, where – extolling Dedham as a model of godly reformation, peculiarly privileged above other towns and villages – he declares that it would be particularly

---

[115] George Gifford, *Countrie Divinitie* (London, 1597), F4r.
[116] Thomas Granger, *Pauls Crowne of Reioycing, or the Manner How to Heare the Word with Profit* (1616), E1v, G2v, H2r.

shameful for a Dedham man to be damned. 'And when you com to hell, o how the divell will stand on his tiptooes and reioyce to see you come thither, what some come to hell from Dedham? how will this glad him …'[117] Skilfully used, local pride and parochial identity could have been powerful weapons of Protestant persuasion.

Another form of lay resistance – again, easily overlooked – was a dislike of sermons on the Old Testament, and a demand for sermons on the Gospels. 'Every man saith now, we live in the time of the Gospel, what have we to do with the judgements of the Law?' complained one minister in 1607, 'and therefore he that will set us a song, must set it to the tune of the Gospell: as if the Law (like an old almanacke) were cleane out of date'.[118] Again, there seems to have been an element of local pride involved here. Under the two-stage system of preaching advocated by Perkins and others (based on a distinction between the covenant of law and the covenant of grace), it was necessary for a preacher to threaten his hearers with the punishments of the Law, 'that being pricked in heart and terrified, they may become teachable', before comforting them with the promises of the Gospel.[119] Parishioners may have interpreted the choice of Old Testament texts, quite correctly, as a sign that in the eyes of their minister they had not yet been brought to repentance – in effect, were not yet Christians – and it would hardly be surprising if they found this insulting. Each of our three preachers was aware of the demand for more evangelical sermons, and each responded in his own way: Wright, by switching from Old to New Testament texts; Lydiat, by restricting himself to Gospel paraphrases; Hull, more cunningly, by preaching on the Old Testament on Sunday mornings and the New Testament on Sunday afternoons, so that layfolk who wanted Gospel preaching would be obliged to sit through the afternoon sermon as well.

But there was, of course, another reason for the objection to Old Testament texts. Layfolk were reacting against the perceived legalism of ministers who were constantly preaching against sin. William Sclater satirised the common response to godly preaching: 'Let him expound to us the Scriptures, deliver us instructions; but what hath hee to doe to be dealing with our sinnes?' Another clerical commentator remarked that 'if the Minister be good and faithfull in reprovinge of sinne and denouncing of Gods iudgments due for the same … then will they perswade him not to be soe precise, nor to preach soe often of judgment, but rather of mercy,

---

[117] Houghton Library, Harvard, MS Eng 1049, f. 29.
[118] Robert Wilkinson, *Lots Wife, a Sermon Preached at Paules Crosse* (1607), C4r.
[119] Perkins, *The Arte of Prophecying*, in *Workes*, vol. II, 3T6v.

and soe he shold have the more love of his neyghbours: and the like.'[120] The crucial word here is 'neighbour': for, as we have already seen, one of the commonest and most damaging objections to puritan preaching was that it was un-neighbourly. William Addister, minister of Gosberton in Lincolnshire, was presented in 1594 for failing to wear the surplice or use the sign of the Cross, and for being 'one that sekes the dishquytnes of his nighbours in meskaling and rewilinge and calling his nighbours Brason face and Liers within the Churche'. The combination of puritan non-conformity with antisocial behaviour is suggestive; so too is the implication that the minister was regarded as the 'neighbour' of his parishioners and expected to behave accordingly.[121]

Much more research still needs to be done into the concept of neighbour-liness in early modern England, the obligations that attached to it and the values of courtesy and charity that clustered around it. But there can be no doubt that the virtue of neighbourliness was held in universally high esteem, and that it could often operate as a powerful form of peer pressure, discouraging layfolk from adopting any ostentatiously 'godly' religious practices that set them apart from their neighbours. John Rogers remarked that anyone who displayed an unusual degree of religious observance would be 'called Puritane' and told: 'Oh you bee so precise, and shall no body be saved but you, and a few more? . . . You will bee wiser than all your neighbours.' This was, as he admitted, 'no smal thing to beare and resist'. As Thomas Turvell put it, worldlings 'doe shoot that bullet, Puritane' at the godly, 'to affright them, and to make them retire'.[122] Perhaps the best that could be hoped for was the sort of grudging toleration described by Thomas Taylor: 'aske any man almost of the state of one of his neighbours, who is diligent in good duties, frequents Sermons, &c. you shall heare him say, Oh he is a reasonable honest man, but that he is so forward to heare Sermons, and so precise, &c.'[123]

Given such sentiments, it is not surprising that many clergy expressed frustration with their parishioners' stubborn attachment to the idea of 'good neighbourhood', which they regarded as little more than an excuse for spiritual idleness. But some puritan ministers can be found trying to

---

[120] Sclater, *Exposition*, IIr (i. 113). *Sermon* by Richard Hunt: Bodleian Library, MS Rawl. C. 766, f. 23.
[121] Foster, *State of the Church*, p. xli.
[122] John Rogers, *The Doctrine of Faith*, S7v; Turvell, *Poore Mans Path-way*, D4r. See also Edward Willis, *The Blinde Mans Staffe* (1615), B1v. One early anti-puritan treatise, from 1582, complained of young preachers who failed to uphold the values of 'liberalitie, hospitalitie . . . trew dealing and neyghborly amity, and such-lyke' when preaching to the common people. 'Of absurdities in preaching the gospell', from Stephen Batman's commonplace book, Houghton Library, Harvard, MS Eng 1015, f. 55r.
[123] Taylor, *Parable of the Sower*, S8v. 'Sermons' in this context should be taken to refer specifically to Sunday afternoon and weekday sermons, not to Protestant preaching in general.

appropriate neighbourly values for their own purposes. The opening scene of *The Plaine Mans Path-way to Heaven*, for example, is more than merely a trivial piece of scene-setting. The godly minister, Master Theologus, greets the other participants in the dialogue – 'Welcome neighbours, welcome' – and enters with gusto into a discussion of local affairs:

*THEOLOGUS.* Hath my neighbour a Cow to sell?
*ANTILEGON.* We are told he hath a very good one to sell; but I am afraid, at this time of the yeere, we shall finde deare ware of her.
*THEOL.* How deare? What doe you thinke a very good Cow may be woorth?
*ANTIL.* A good Cow indeed, at this time of the yeere, is woorth very neere foure pound, which is a great price.
*THEOL.* It is a very great price indeed.

At this point Philagathus, the 'honest man' in the dialogue, interrupts: 'I pray you, M. Theologus, leave off this talking of Kine, and worldly matters, and let us enter into some speech of matters of religion' – and the parties repair to a 'goodly Arbour' with 'handsome seats' under a nearby oak tree, where they settle down to some serious conversation.[124] But Dent has made his point: that godliness and good neighbourhood should not be regarded as incompatible. The godly minister, it is implied, should be the 'neighbour' of his parishioners, conversant with their day-to-day activities and fully capable of sustaining a conversation with them about the price of livestock.

To a considerable extent, the popular acceptance and long-term effectiveness of the Protestant preaching ministry depended on its compatibility with the concept of neighbourliness. Here the sermons of Wright and Hull are of great significance, for we have seen them using a thoroughly traditional rhetoric of neighbourliness, but using it in a carefully calculated way – arguing, in effect, that neighbourliness needed to be redefined to include the true Christian charity practised by the godly, while excluding false forms of sociability such as drunkenness. John Bossy is quite right to point out that any inclusive understanding of neighbourliness was severely compromised, for puritan ministers, by their belief in the doctrine of predestination and 'the empirical division of the godly and the ungodly'. But while preachers never quite lost sight of the distinction between the community of neighbours and the fellowship of the elect, they could sometimes bring the two surprisingly close together: as Hull declared in one of his sermons, 'albeit ther be a speciall brotherhood, in a spirituall sense among those that are of the same profession in the true

---

[124] Dent, *Plaine Mans Path-way*, B2r.

religion, yet are all men in a generall sense brethren'.[125] This was to imply that godliness was the highest form of neighbourliness; that the godly were the best neighbours, and the true upholders of neighbourly values. The work of Margaret Spufford and her students on post-Restoration dissent – showing, in the words of Bill Stevenson, that 'religious differences did not always bring social alienation' – suggests that we need to take this neighbourly rhetoric seriously.[126]

It would be naïve to suppose that the use of neighbourly rhetoric in sermons was, of itself, enough to guarantee peace and harmony in a parish. We have seen that the appeal to neighbourly values could coexist with the vehement condemnation of many aspects of popular culture; and it could be argued that its role in pulpit rhetoric was a rather superficial one – a way of sugaring the pill, or disguising the full implications of a puritan ethic which the preachers knew to be dangerously divisive. Yet it was also a reflection of a much deeper ambiguity. As Peter Lake has argued, the puritan preaching ministry embodied a strong commitment to social order and harmony combined with a highly polarised vision of the world as divided between the godly and the profane; 'which aspect of this complex social and ideological mixture predominated, which tendency came out on top, depended on a whole series of social, political and doctrinal, local, national and intellectual forces'.[127] It is here, I would suggest, that the study of early modern sermons really comes into its own: for it is by studying sermons – and recognising them for the complex and ambiguous texts that they are – that we can begin to see how these tensions worked themselves out in practice in the pulpits and parishes of early modern England.

---

[125] John Bossy, *Peace in the Post-Reformation* (Cambridge, 1998), p. 96; Hull, sermon on Genesis 19: 6–15: BL Harl. MS 663, f. 3r.

[126] Bill Stevenson, 'The social integration of post-Restoration dissenters, 1660–1725', in Margaret Spufford, ed., *The World of Rural Dissenters 1520–1725* (Cambridge, 1995), pp. 360–87, p. 378.

[127] Peter Lake, '"A charitable Christian hatred": the godly and their enemies in the 1630s', in Christopher Durston and Jacqueline Eales, eds., *The Culture of English Puritanism 1560–1700* (1996), p. 183.

# CHAPTER 6

# Reading sermons politically

## Criticism and controversy

One of the most striking findings of recent scholarship on early modern preaching has been the importance of place and circumstance in determining meaning. Sermons were not preached in a vacuum, and to treat them simply as literary artefacts, without considering the time and place of delivery and the persons to whom they were addressed, is to miss much of their significance. As I have argued elsewhere, the 'meaning' of a sermon is not something that can simply be read off from the written text, but resulted from an act of interpretative collaboration between preacher and audience.[1] Recovering that meaning involves reading the written text back into the spoken event, with attention to such variables as the physical setting, the topical context and the rhetorical conventions appropriate to the occasion – a method which, needless to say, can be applied not just to sermons but also to plays, parliamentary speeches and all forms of live performance.

The best example of this methodology in action, as applied to a particular genre of sermons, is Peter McCullough's recent study of Elizabethan and Jacobean court preaching.[2] McCullough shows that court sermons characteristically display an acute awareness of the royal presence, an awareness which often turned the sermon into an exercise in the art of persuasion, and the other members of the audience into privileged eavesdroppers on a discourse addressed to a single person. The 'thou' of John Donne's sermon before Anne of Denmark in December 1617, for example, is apparently the queen in particular rather than the congregation at large, and the sermon can thus be read as a lightly veiled critique of Anne's crypto-Catholic

---

[1] Hunt, 'Tuning the pulpits: the religious context of the Essex Revolt', in Lori Anne Ferrell and Peter McCullough, eds., *The English Sermon Revised* (Manchester, 2000), p. 107. Mary Morrissey has also stressed the need to 'read rhetorically' with attention to both the sermon-as-text and the sermon-as-event: 'Interdisciplinarity and the study of early modern sermons', *Historical Journal*, 42: 4 (1999), pp. 1111–23.

[2] Peter E. McCullough, *Sermons at Court: Politics and Religion in Elizabethan and Jacobean Preaching* (Cambridge, 1998).

sympathies. McCullough is also attentive to the physical setting of court sermons, and shows that preachers had more liberty to exhort or admonish the monarch in the relative privacy of the royal chapels than in the more public arena of the outdoor pulpit at Whitehall, where the congregation included ordinary Londoners as well as courtiers, and where the monarch was visible to the audience throughout the sermon. Above all, he shows that court sermons were highly court-specific in their application. Lancelot Andrewes's attacks on 'the common error, that Sermon-hearing is the *Consummatum est* of all Christianitie' have often been taken as evidence of a deep-seated conflict between sermon-centred and sacrament-centred styles of piety. In the light of McCullough's research, however, it is clear that Andrewes's criticisms were precisely and specifically targeted at the neglect of the liturgy in the Jacobean chapel royal; how far they were intended to apply to the world outside the court remains a moot point.[3]

Some aspects of the spoken event are obviously impossible to recover. We can only guess at the ways in which preachers may have conveyed their meaning through a look, a gesture or an inflection of speech; although we know that Donne was widely admired by his contemporaries for his use of gesture, and it is not difficult to imagine how he might have indicated the identity of 'thou' by a movement of his hand or eye in the direction of the queen.[4] Then there is the familiar problem of textual instability, discussed in an earlier chapter, in that the written or printed texts that have come down to us may differ from the sermon as originally delivered. Again, Donne provides a good illustration. The revised version of his sermon on the Gunpowder Plot, preached at Paul's Cross in November 1622, includes several passages that are not present in a contemporary manuscript copy of the sermon and were, presumably, not included in the sermon as preached.[5] One of the textual differences is especially significant: where Donne had originally stated that kings 'are excusable' for the actions of evil counsellors, he now qualified this statement by declaring that they 'may bee excusable; at least, for any cooperation in the evill of the action, though not for countenancing and authorising an evill instrument'. It seems that Donne felt able to be more politically outspoken in the revised version of his sermon,

---

[3] McCullough, *Sermons at Court*, pp. 155–63. See also my review article, 'A Jacobean consensus? The religious policy of James VI and I', *The Seventeenth Century*, 17 (2002), pp. 131–40.

[4] Donne was praised in 1644 as having been 'most eminent' in his use of hand gestures: see John Bulwer, *Chirologia, or the Naturall Language of the Hand* (1644), part 2, C2v.

[5] Jeanne Shami, 'Donne's 1622 sermon on the Gunpowder Plot: his original presentation manuscript discovered', *English Manuscript Studies*, 5 (1994), pp. 63–86, and *John Donne's 1622 Gunpowder Plot Sermon: A Parallel-Text Edition* (Pittsburgh, 1996).

written for private manuscript circulation, than in the original version written for public delivery. If this example is at all representative, it suggests that we need to exercise considerable caution in reading politically controversial passages from the sermon-as-text back into the sermon-as-event.

Over and above these problems of insufficient or incomplete evidence, there is a more general problem of interpretation. Recent scholarship on the commonplace-book tradition has made it clear that seventeenth-century preachers drew heavily on a common stock of classical and biblical allusions, rhetorical figures and moral observations that passed freely from one text to another, often with little alteration. It is not easy for modern scholars, unfamiliar with this tradition, to reconstruct the way that topical and controversial ideas were filtered through this mass of commonplace material. In the older generation of Whiggish scholarship, preaching was depicted as an inherently revolutionary activity, in which every religious allusion could carry a political application, and even a seemingly innocuous exhortation to dedicate oneself to God's service could be interpreted as a call to arms against a political enemy. In later revisionist scholarship, by contrast, preaching is depicted as part of a 'commonwealth of meanings' in which political tensions and disagreements, while hardly unknown, were embedded within a framework of consensus, a set of shared assumptions which served to muffle the impact of radical and revolutionary ideas.[6] The reason why sermons have attracted such divergent readings – politically oppositional on the one hand, politically consensual on the other – is that in sermons, perhaps more than in any other literary genre, political criticism was mediated through the reassuringly familiar conventions of the commonplace-book tradition.

Turning away from what Peter Lake rightly calls 'the false polarity between conflict and consensus', scholars have now begun to look more closely at the way that the languages of conflict and consensus coexisted with each other.[7] Some of the most promising attempts to resolve this paradox have taken as their starting point the idea that early modern England contained a number of discrete 'linguistic communities'. Glenn Burgess, for example, has argued that the 'language of theology' needs to be distinguished from the languages of civil and common law. Few people in early Stuart England objected to the use of theological language to assert the divine origin of monarchical authority;

---

[6] Christopher Hill, 'The political sermons of John Preston', in *Puritanism and Revolution* (London, 1958), pp. 239–74; Kevin Sharpe, 'A commonwealth of meanings: languages, analogues, ideas and politics', in *Remapping Early Modern England: The Culture of Seventeenth-Century Politics* (Cambridge, 2000), pp. 38–123.

[7] Peter Lake, 'Wentworth's political world in revisionist and post-revisionist perspective', in J. F. Merritt, ed., *The Political World of Thomas Wentworth* (Cambridge, 1996), p. 275.

but when clerics such as Roger Manwaring and Robert Sibthorpe confused the languages of theology and law, and used general theological premises to draw specific legal conclusions about the royal prerogative, there was an immediate outcry. In rather similar fashion, Lori Anne Ferrell has drawn a distinction between the languages of 'theology' and 'polemic', arguing that the broad theological consensus that existed in Jacobean England did not preclude a number of sharp polemical exchanges between conformist divines and their puritan opponents. This did not matter too much as long as theology and polemic were kept apart; but in the reign of Charles I the polarised language of polemic began to invade the previously consensual language of theology, with disastrous consequences for the stability of the English Church.[8]

But these theories are not altogether satisfactory, largely because they fail to admit the possibility that theological language could have had a critical or controversial dimension. Burgess sees theological language as confined to platitudes about order and obedience, 'the commonplaces of early Stuart political thought', and argues that it functioned properly 'only at a high level of generality', when it limited itself to 'vague statements about the essence of kingship'. Ferrell's distinction between the 'taut logic' of theology and the 'politic flexibility' of polemic leads her to a similar conclusion: that theological language was extremely limited in its scope, and that while it may have had an intellectual contribution to make to the development of a broad-based doctrinal consensus, it was inherently unsuited to the subtleties of polemical dispute.[9] Yet the idea that theological language was vague or inflexible is hard to sustain when one considers the wide range of rhetorical techniques at the disposal of early modern preachers; nor is it really credible to suggest that preachers such as Donne or Andrewes suddenly modulated from 'theology' to 'polemic' whenever they had politically controversial ideas to express. Rather than dividing conflict and consensus into two separate discursive fields, what is needed is a more sophisticated analysis of the way that political and religious conflicts were expressed through the standard conventions and commonplaces of early modern preaching.

## REPROVING THE MAGISTRATE

On 19 June 1604, John Burges stood in the pulpit at Greenwich and, in an act of astonishing bravado, proceeded to deliver one of the most tactless sermons ever preached before an English monarch. In its formal structure,

---

[8] Glenn Burgess, *The Politics of the Ancient Constitution* (London, 1992), esp. pp. 115–38; Lori Anne Ferrell, *Government by Polemic* (Stanford, 1998).

[9] Burgess, *Ancient Constitution*, p. 136; Ferrell, *Government by Polemic*, p. 17. I develop this point further in 'A Jacobean consensus?', p. 139.

the sermon was entirely conventional, based on a text from Psalm 122, 'For my brethren and my neighbours' sake, I will now speak peace to thee; because of the house of the Lord our God, I will procure thy wealth', from which Burges drew the unsurprising doctrine that it was the duty of kings to 'speak peace unto their people', to promote 'the good of their subjects' and to provide for 'the true worship of God'. But the devil, as always, was in the detail. From these uncontroversial premises, Burges launched into a defence of puritan nonconformity, urging the king not to deprive puritan ministers merely for the sake of a few disputed ceremonies. Even more indiscreetly, he took the opportunity to complain of a monopoly of royal favour by a few influential courtiers, and to warn the king of his unpopularity. As he later explained in a letter to James, he felt himself bound in conscience to take notice of 'the generall murmurings and complaints (which every man heares sooner than your Majesty, or your nearest servants) as that you grace not your people, you speake not to them, you looke not at them, you blesse them not; and therefore (say they) you love them not'.[10]

It would be easy to depict Burges as a political innocent who overstepped the mark simply because he did not understand the rules of court preaching and the limits of acceptable criticism. But Burges did at least make some attempt to wrap up his criticisms, using the appropriate rhetorical techniques. The politically sensitive parts of his sermon were concealed behind similitudes or quotations from other authors; and the all-important plea for religious toleration was presented indirectly, in the form of an anecdote:

I will not direct, but pray leave to tell a story; It is reported of Augustus the Emperour, that supping with one Pollio, he was informed that a servant of Pollios had broken a christall glasse of his Masters; a foule fault if he had done it willingly, if negligently a fault: but for this the poore servant was adjudged to be cut in peeces, and cast to the fishes: a marvailous sore sentence for such a fault. The Emperour reversed the sentence, and thought it punishment enough to the servant, to have bin in feare of such a punishment; and after breakes all the glasses, that they might not be occasion of like rigorous sentence afterwards. I will not apply it, but do humbly beseech your Majesty to use your owne most godly wisdome, now to make peace in the Church, when so small a thing will doe it: that so the Bishops may love the poore Ministers, as brethren, and Ministers reverence the Bishops as fathers in the Lord, as Hierom adviseth, and every honest man wisheth they should doe.[11]

---

[10] On Burges's sermon, see McCullough, *Sermons at Court*, pp. 141–7 (and p. 142 n.167 for a list of surviving manuscript copies of the sermon). Quotations are from the first printed edition, *A Sermon Preached before the Late King James* (1642).

[11] Burges, *Sermon*, C3r.

Burges's refusal to draw any moral from this story – 'I will not direct . . . I will not apply it' – was a feeble attempt to ensure that he could not be held responsible for any construction his listeners chose to place on his words. The trouble was that the intended meaning was so transparent: as he later admitted, 'by Pollios glasses I did intend to notifie the Ceremonies for which this Church of God hath bin in vexation above fifty yeeres', with the obvious implication that the existing penalties for ceremonial nonconformity were monstrously unjust. Where Burges had gone wrong was not in ignoring the accepted conventions of pulpit criticism, but in employing them with such a lack of finesse.

And it was precisely the fact that Burges declined to 'apply' his examples that laid his sermon open to misapplication by members of the audience. In one passage, he exhorted the king to 'hunt away two beasts, the tame beast and the wilde, the flatterer and the false informer, which shall attempt to set off your sweet affections from any of your loving Subjects'. In context, this appears to be nothing more than a generalised attack on the sins of flattery and falsehood, but some listeners evidently interpreted it as a personal attack on two individuals, prompting Burges to an anguished disclaimer: 'I protest upon my knees unto your Majesty, I meant not any two particular persons, but kindes of such evill instruments.'[12] Burges's case serves as a warning against accepting too readily Annabel Patterson's view that court sermons, like plays and masques, followed 'a highly sophisticated system of oblique communication, of unwritten rules whereby writers could communicate with readers or audiences . . . without producing a direct confrontation'.[13] Such rules certainly did exist, but not all preachers could handle them with the subtlety and sophistication of an Andrewes or a Donne, and whereas Patterson's account of the hermeneutics of censorship stresses 'the importance of authorial intention in controlling meaning', Burges's case shows that preachers were not fully in control of the process of interpretation. Court preachers had to tread a fine line between plain-speaking (and the risk of causing offence) and tactful ambiguity (and the risk of being misunderstood).

Burges was no Donne: yet his sermon may have helped to create the conditions for Donne's style of preaching, by forcing Jacobean court preachers to come up with more subtle ways of advising or admonishing the monarch. As Peter McCullough has noted, the harsh reaction to Burges's sermon 'left a perceptible mark on future court preachers and the contents of their sermons'

---

[12] Burges, *Sermon*, B2r, D2v.
[13] Annabel Patterson, *Censorship and Interpretation* (Madison, WI., 1984), p. 45.

and served to define the limits of acceptable criticism. The sermon certainly achieved considerable notoriety: to judge from the number of surviving manuscripts, it must have circulated very widely, and although it was not printed during Burges's lifetime, it found its way into print soon after the collapse of ecclesiastical censorship in 1642. James himself never forgot it, and firmly squashed an attempt in 1613 to have Burges restored to royal favour; according to the newswriter John Chamberlain, the king 'was so moved that he shold dogmatise (as he called yt) in his court, that he commanded the archbishop to looke to yt who sending for him used him somwhat roughly'.[14] And Burges's sermon may well have been in the minds of two later writers, Cornelius Burges (apparently no relation) and John Dury, when they tried to codify the unwritten rules for pulpit criticism, for the guidance of preachers who wished to criticise the civil authorities without getting into trouble. Their advice provides a rare glimpse backstage, as it were, behind the scenes of pulpit rhetoric – and what it demonstrates is that preachers had considerable freedom to criticise the magistrate, as long as they took certain precautions.

Cornelius Burges's treatise *The Fire of the Sanctuarie* was published in 1625, in the wake of the crisis over the Spanish Match, a crisis which had witnessed the emergence of a thriving news culture to meet the demand for political information, and a growing anxiety about the way that matters of state were being laid open to popular discussion. Sermons had played a crucial part in this process, as one of the principal channels through which news and rumour were transmitted to a popular audience. Burges shared the general anxiety about the demand for news, criticising 'common Newse-mongers and seditious spirits, who cannot make a meale, spend a fire, drinke a pinte, or drive away one houre, without some pragmaticall discourse and censure of Princes and their State affaires', but he did not believe that preachers were wholly unjustified in alluding to current affairs in their sermons. Instead, he advised preachers to observe a distinction between public and private sins. 'The reproving or revealing of a sinne, to, or before more than such as are privie to it as Actors, patients, or abettors in it, is not onely uncharitable, but unsafe.' But a sin might be said to be public if it was known 'by a common rumor and publique fame raised by persons of credit, either out of knowledge, or some strong presumptions', and in this case a preacher was entitled to administer a public rebuke from the pulpit.[15] In

---

[14] Chamberlain to Sir Dudley Carleton, 1 August 1613, in N. E. McClure, ed., *The Letters of John Chamberlain* (Philadelphia, 1939), vol. I, p. 470.
[15] Cornelius Burges, *The Fire of the Sanctuarie Newly Uncovered, or, a Compleat Tract of Zeale* (1625), N1or (p. 283), L2v (p. 220), L12r (p. 239). On the relationship between sermons and news, with

effect, Burges was permitting preachers to exercise their own discretion in making use of news and rumour; and having established the general principle that preachers were entitled, indeed obliged, to 'thunder out reproofes freely when need requireth', he then proceeded to offer some more specific rules for sermons before particular audiences.

Burges laid down three rules for preachers wishing to admonish or rebuke the monarch. First, 'hee who undertaketh this office must bee sure of a *lawfull calling*, to deale with persons of that Qualitie, in the generall.' Ministers could claim to possess such a calling, but private persons could not. Secondly, 'this service requires a *speciall calling and Commission* to treate with this or that Prince in speciall. Every one that is a Minister may not flie upon his Soveraignes face, or back, when his supposed zeale would egge him to it.' Ministers could claim to possess this special calling when 'such as are in authoritie' appointed them 'to waite at Court'. Finally, and most importantly, 'great wisedome and moderation is required in the manner of doing such a service', and the preacher should, if possible, convey the reproof so delicately that 'no creature may be able to discerne it, but he to whom it was intended'. As for lesser magistrates, 'discretion teacheth all due respect to these also, in their places: and although so much be not due to them, as to him they serve . . . yet they must be honoured as much, in their proportion, for their Soveraignes sake: nor may any man take liberty to take them downe in the way of contempt and scorne.' In reproving magistrates, a preacher may 'fall upon the reproofe of particular sinnes sometimes committed by some men in that Calling, and call it the Magistrates sin, not naming any Person, or applying it to any present'. Thus the prophet reproved Jeroboam for setting up the altar at Bethel (1 Kgs. 13: 2–3) without naming him, though everyone in the congregation knew who was meant.[16]

It may seem surprising to find Burges endorsing this indirect approach when it was frowned on by most of the art-of-preaching manuals. Richard Bernard declared that it was not enough for a preacher to state a general doctrine; he must also apply it to the consciences of his hearers, not simply by way of 'instruction and comfort' but also, if necessary, by way of 'reprehension and correction'.[17] As an example, he cited Nathan's exhortation to King David (2 Sam. 12: 1–7). Nathan tells David a parable of a rich man who steals a poor man's ewe lamb, to which David responds with righteous indignation: 'the man that hath done this thing shall surely die'. 'Thou art the man', replies

---

particular reference to Thomas Lushington's sermon on Matthew 28:13 (which famously began 'What's the best News abroad?'), see Joad Raymond, *Pamphlets and Pamphleteering in Early Modern Britain* (Cambridge, 2003), pp. 146–8.

[16] Burges, *Fire of the Sanctuarie*, M12v (p. 264), N3v (p. 270), N4v (p. 272), O1r (p. 289), O3r (p. 293).

[17] Richard Bernard, *The Faithfull Shepherd . . . Made Anew, and Very Much Inlarged* (1621), P11r.

Nathan sternly; and David is forced to admit that he has 'sinned against the Lord' in taking the wife of Uriah the Hittite. The point of the story, for Bernard, was that hearers could not be trusted to apply the doctrines they heard. David was capable of perceiving the moral of Nathan's parable, but without Nathan's help he would not have realised that it applied to himself. Application was therefore 'the Ministers dutie', and preachers who fondly believed that their hearers were 'so wise, as they hearing the Doctrine and Use, can make application therof themselves' were grievously mistaken.[18] And Burges himself echoed Bernard's warning when he criticised preachers who failed to apply their doctrines for fear of offending their hearers. 'It is rather for a Parasite upon the Stage than a Divine in the Pulpit to flatter thus: *I need not to apply, I know your wisdome and discretion, I leave it to your godly care to make the application, I need not to exhort,* &c. when many times he knowes too well his hearers are too farre from such a care.'[19]

Such remarks were fully in the spirit of Elizabethan divines such as John Jewel, who saw the godly preacher as exercising authority in spiritual matters just as the magistrate exercised it in secular matters, and who took Nathan's exhortation to David as one of the exemplary models of the fearless preacher speaking truth to power. 'We flatter our princes as Nathan flattered King David', Jewel proudly informed his Catholic opponent Thomas Harding in 1567, 'as John Baptist flattered Herod; as St Ambrose flattered Theodosius; and as salt flattereth the green sore.' But as Patrick Collinson and others have pointed out, it was not at all easy for Elizabethan preachers to play Nathan to the queen's David, partly because of the monarch's role as supreme governor of the Church, and partly because of Elizabeth's intolerance of preachers who trespassed on affairs of state.[20] The situation was further complicated in the Jacobean period by the emergence of *jure divino* theories of episcopacy, which forced preachers of more moderate episcopalian views to be considerably more guarded in their assertions of spiritual authority and freedom from secular interference. This may explain why Burges's guidance to preachers was so ambiguous, not to say contradictory. His proposal that they should state their doctrine in general terms, 'not naming any person, or applying it to any present', is hardly consistent with his instructions to 'thunder out reproofes freely when need requireth' and apply their doctrine unsparingly, without fear or favour.

---

[18] Bernard, *Faithfull Shepherd*, P1or, P12r.
[19] Burges, *A Chain of Graces* (1622), B5v (p. 10). Burges also discusses the need for 'particular application' in a series of sermons preached at St Magnus in 1626: Cambridge University Library, Add. 6165, p. 26.
[20] Patrick Collinson, 'If Constantine, then also Theodosius: St Ambrose and the integrity of the Elizabethan *Ecclesia Anglicana*', in *Godly People: Essays on English Protestantism and Puritanism* (London, 1983), pp. 109–33.

Burges was not the only writer who sought to temper pulpit rhetoric to political reality. In 1649 John Dury published a short tract 'concerning Ministers medling with State-matters in their Sermons', in which he argued that it was unlawful for ministers to preach on matters of state (defined in the broadest possible terms, as all matters 'relating to the outward Possessions, Rights, Freedomes, Priviledges, Prerogatives, and Persons of men, as they are Members of an outward Common-wealth').[21] He offered a variety of reasons in support of this remarkable conclusion: among them, that preaching on such matters was inconsistent with the nature of the Gospel, since Christ's kingdom was not of this world, and Christ himself refused to act as a judge in temporal matters (Luke 12: 14); and that it violated the preacher's impartiality, since those who preached on state matters did so either to please the people by reproving the magistrates or 'to please the magistrates by commending them to the people'. Dury's tract was a response to the crisis of political allegiance brought about by the execution of the king; and, as Quentin Skinner has shown, it was the first of several attempts (culminating in the most famous of them all, Hobbes's *Leviathan*) to justify allegiance to the Commonwealth in terms of a *de facto* obligation to obey the powers that be. To illustrate his case, however, Dury cited examples of controversial preaching from the 1630s; and, whatever its immediate political context, his tract is clearly founded on pre-war discussions among puritan divines about the legitimacy of preaching against the ecclesiastical government.

Dury, like Burges, was interested in exploring the limits of acceptable speech, and in devising ways for preachers to reprove the magistrate, or to tackle politically controversial issues, within the boundaries set by the general principle of passive obedience. Preachers, he suggested, 'may decline an open Contradiction, and by asserting strongly that matter of Religion or Worship, which is opposite in its nature to that matter of State, which authority would settle, quit their conscience fully; and without naming the thing, which may not be professedly condemn'd, yet overthrow it in all mens minds'. In other words, they should proceed positively rather than negatively, by confirming a truth rather than condemning a falsehood. 'By this Method . . . a faithful Minister may prudently decline a snare laid to entrap him.' For example, 'he that did assert strongly from the Word of God, that the Lords Day is to be kept holy to God in spirituall duties . . .

---

[21] John Dury, *A Case of Conscience Resolved: Concerning Ministers Medling with State-matters in Their Sermons* (1649). On the political context, see Quentin Skinner, 'Conquest and consent: Thomas Hobbes and the engagement controversy', in G. E. Aylmer, ed., *The Interregnum* (1972; repr. 1974), p. 81.

he (I say) that did strongly make out this to be a truth which cannot be
controuled, did fully condemn and refute the Book of Sports on the Lords
day, which was set up by Authority, although he never did once name
it.' Alternatively, 'the Thesis of a matter may be so fully handled, that the
Hypothesis need not to be once named, but all men will be able to make
the application thereof by themselves.' By stating a general doctrine with
sufficient force and emphasis, a skilful preacher could ensure that his
audience would apply it to the particular example he had in mind. 'The
defensive postures in Fencing', Dury concluded, 'are easier and safer than
the offensive.'[22]

By a lucky accident of survival, we can identify the particular case to
which Dury was referring, from a manuscript apparently belonging to Dury
himself or to a member of his circle.[23] In 1634 the London minister Henry
Roborough was hauled up before the High Commission on charges of
seditious preaching, having allegedly said in a sermon 'that whosoever putt
forth or had any hand in his Majesties declarations for Recreations after
Eveninge prayer on Sundayes was a cursed man from the highest to the
lowest'. Roborough denied the charge, but admitted that he had preached
a sermon on the love of Christ to the Church, in which he had concluded
'that therefore wee ought to love Christ againe, and expresse that love in
all thinges required by Jesus Christ, particularly in our obedience to his
Commaundementes', including the commandment to 'observe the Daye
that the Lord hath made, meaninge the Lordes daye'; and that any man
who did the contrary 'shewed himself to be one that did not love Christ'.
Roborough was also alleged to have said, in the same sermon, that faithful
Christians were being persecuted both at home and abroad. Again, he
denied the charge, but admitted having said 'that Christs love was a grounde
not only of Doeing, but of sufferinge', ending with the following exhortation: 'You have not as yet suffered for Christ. It may be you shall never, it
may be you shall. God alone knoweth to what tymes wee are reserved by
his providence. Howsoever, the resolution and purpose to suffer for Christ
is requisite.'

Roborough's meaning was transparently obvious, but by limiting himself
to a set of generalised observations on the love of Christ, the divine
institution of the sabbath and the need for Christian fortitude, he ensured

---

[22] Dury, *Case of Conscience*, C4r, C4v.
[23] 'Articles obiected . . . against Henry Roborough': Trinity College, Dublin, MS 293, ff. 387–401. The
bulk of the volume consists of a collection of theological tracts relating to Dury's schemes for
ecclesiastical union.

that it was virtually impossible for the authorities to prove any seditious intention. He was dismissed on bail in June 1634, and seems to have continued preaching throughout the 1630s without official interference. What this case makes clear is that there was considerable scope for political criticism in sermons. It was extremely rare for preachers to be imprisoned for seditious preaching, and where this did occur it was usually because the preacher had not employed the customary rhetorical safeguards with sufficient care (as in John Burges's case) or had deliberately chosen to disregard them. It is also clear that audiences must have been well used to reading between the lines. The crucial role of the audience in helping to construe the preacher's meaning was acknowledged by the High Commission in its articles against Roborough, which alleged that 'the more intelligent sort' of his hearers would have interpreted Roborough's remarks on 'these base corrupt tymes, wherein heresie and superstition doth abound' as a reflection on the present ecclesiastical government. Controversial preaching was thus a collaborative process, requiring not only a preacher capable of encoding his political criticisms in the appropriate manner, but also an audience capable of decoding them.

The limits of the government's ability to regulate preaching were starkly revealed by the 1622 Directions Concerning Preachers, which attempted, among other things, to prohibit 'bitter invectives and indecent railing speeches' against Roman Catholics.[24] In his study of the Spanish Match crisis, Thomas Cogswell justly observes that the pulpits had been the source of 'the most troubling and persistent criticism' of James's pacific foreign policy, so it was hardly surprising that James should have wished to curb anti-Catholic preaching while the Spanish Match negotiations were in progress. But Cogswell greatly overestimates the effect of the Directions when he argues that they were a 'tactical success': by the end of 1622, he writes, 'few could deny . . . that James had reasserted control and had ridden out a particularly alarming storm of popular criticism'.[25] The task confronting the authorities was not simply one of 'control', but of the very definition of seditious preaching at a time when familiar and conventional forms of anti-Catholic polemic had suddenly acquired overtones of political opposition. In Cogswell's own words, 'the commonplace became inflammatory', and it would thus have been impossible to suppress all expressions of dissent

---

[24] The text of the Directions is most readily available in J. P. Kenyon, ed., *The Stuart Constitution* (Cambridge, 1966), pp. 145–6.

[25] Thomas Cogswell, *The Blessed Revolution: English Politics and the Coming of War, 1621–24* (Cambridge, 1989), pp. 27, 33–4.

without drastically redefining the limits of acceptable pulpit discourse. That the government of James I did not have the will to do this is shown by the let-out clauses in the 1622 Directions, permitting anti-Catholic preaching when 'occasioned . . . by the text of Scripture' or when the preacher had reason to suspect that there were Papists in the audience.

The result was that the Directions, while not wholly ineffective, had only limited success in deterring controversial preaching. The anonymous author of *Tom Tell-Troth* observed that 'our godliest preachers' had been praying earnestly against religious toleration, 'and though there be order given they shall preach nothing but Court Divinity, yet a man may easily perceive by the very choyce of their Texts and the Teares in their eyes, that if they durst they would speake their Consciences'.[26] What is most striking about this quotation is not that preachers were inhibited from speaking freely, but that they still managed to find ways of communicating their views indirectly: often by using the method recommended by Burges and Dury, of stating a general doctrine and leaving the audience to apply it. One London minister preached against apostasy, then concluded his sermon by remarking that although his listeners 'might expect some application', he did not wish to be thrown into prison.[27] Scarcely less blatantly, Archbishop Abbot preached at court in April 1623 on a text from Psalm 148, 'Old men and children praise the name of the Lord', and observed that old men often tended to 'growe uncertayne and unresolved in theyr relligion, and to leave theyr posteritye after them, in doubtes and waveringes which were the best'. Bishop John Williams, reporting the sermon to the Duke of Buckingham, commented that 'some men have applied' this passage, but that the king 'is most wiselye resolved to take noe notice at all of the same': and indeed it is hard to see how James could have taken any action without admitting that he had recognised himself in the preacher's remarks.[28]

In these circumstances, the most effective official response was not to suppress established forms of pulpit rhetoric, but to appropriate them. This was the strategy adopted in the aftermath of the Essex Revolt in 1601, when the government borrowed some of the arguments used by the earl's supporters – most notably, that Essex's crime had been to use evil means to accomplish a good end – in order to conciliate public opinion.[29]

---

[26] *The Honest Informer, or Tom Tell-Troths Observations* (1642), A2v.

[27] Joseph Mede to Sir Martin Stuteville, 28 September 1622, in T. Birch, ed., *The Court and Times of James I* (1849), vol. II, pp. 334–5. For other examples of indirect application, see John M. Wallace, '"Examples are best precepts": readers and meanings in seventeenth-century poetry', *Critical Inquiry*, I (1974), pp. 273–90.

[28] John Williams to the Duke of Buckingham, 11 April 1623: BL Stowe MS 743, ff. 52–3.

[29] Hunt, 'The religious context of the Essex Revolt', pp. 101–2.

Similarly in 1622–3, several of the propagandists writing in support of the Spanish Match borrowed the anti-Catholic rhetoric of their opponents: thus Edmund Garrard, a supporter of the marriage project, argued that it was the very abundance of anti-Catholic preaching 'by an Army of reverend Bishops, Doctors, and many famous learned Preachers in that kinde, the whole forces of our Kingdomes' that made it safe for the marriage to take place, since there was no risk of Popery gaining any converts.[30] Donne's sermon at Paul's Cross on 5 November 1622 uses anti-Catholic rhetoric in precisely this way, ending with an argument similar to Garrard's, that even if the king were to extend greater toleration to Catholics, this poses no threat to his Protestant subjects, who will simply exercise greater vigilance to prevent the spread of Catholicism within their own families. His anti-Catholic language in this sermon is uncharacteristically harsh (verging on the apocalyptic when he describes Catholics as 'men drunke with the Babylonian Cup'): perhaps too harsh for the king, who requested a copy of the sermon but did not order it to be printed.[31]

Donne's sermon can also be read as a warning about the dangers of 'application', addressed to a London audience that would have been only too ready to apply his general observations to contemporary political events. Noting that his text (Lam. 4: 20) refers to some unnamed King of Israel, Donne plays with his audience's expectations by hesitating over its potential application to James: 'Let it bee *Josiah* . . . Let it bee our *Josiah*, and will it hold in that application?' His answer is that the text can indeed be applied to James, but only in the disordered imaginations of 'those of the Romane persuasion', the point being that applications to specific persons or events can often be dangerously misguided.[32] As often in Jacobean polemic, the anti-Catholic critique doubles as an anti-puritan one. We have already encountered Cornelius Burges citing 1 Kings 13 (the story of Jeroboam offering incense before the altar of the golden calf at Bethel), a text routinely applied by Protestant divines to the idolatrous worship of the Papists, and thus having a potential application to James's toleration of Popery in 1622–3. When Donne cited this very text, and criticised Catholic writers who claimed 'that the Religion of our present King is no better than the Religion of Jeroboam', he may have intended an implicit rebuke to puritan

[30] Edmund Garrard, *The Countrie Gentleman Moderator* (1624), K1r.
[31] John Donne, *Sermons*, ed. G. R. Potter and E. M. Simpson (Berkeley, 1953–62), vol. IV, pp. 235–63.
[32] Donne, *Sermons*, vol. IV, p. 259; Shami, *Donne's 1622 Gunpowder Plot Sermon*, p. 161. For a valuable analysis of the political context of Donne's 1622 sermons, see Shami, '"The stars in their order fought against Sisera": John Donne and the pulpit crisis of 1622', *John Donne Journal*, 14 (1995), pp. 1–58.

preachers who were, in his view, guilty of the same sort of misapplication of the text as their Catholic opponents.

My purpose here is not to attempt a detailed political analysis of the pulpit rhetoric of the Spanish Match crisis, but merely to show that it was possible for preachers to express political opposition indirectly, by setting a generalised or uncontentious doctrine against a more specific and controversial application. The remainder of this chapter will examine this in more detail, through a discussion of two genres of preaching: assize sermons, and Paul's Cross sermons. In both cases the preacher spoke in the presence of authority and, to some extent, as the voice of authority, reiterating the familiar commonplaces of political obedience and social obligation; and as a result the sermons became highly stereotyped, confining themselves to a limited selection of scriptural texts, which they expounded in increasingly predictable ways. The sermon notebook of Robert Sanderson contains lists of 'Texts for Paules Crosse' and 'Texts before Judges', showing how narrowly genre-bound both occasions had become by the early seventeenth century; and an assize preacher in 1615 who chose an unusual text (Eccl. 5: 12, on the sin of covetousness) amused himself by imagining the puzzled reaction of his audience: 'Is this a fitte Text for the Assises? I might have kept this Sermon for the Citie, among Tradesmen and Usurers.'[33] Yet in both cases, as I shall show, the conventional nature of the occasion did not necessarily preclude the articulation of conflicts and tensions, using the rhetorical methods described above.

### ASSIZE SERMONS

Assizes, in early modern England, were a crucial point of contact between the centre and the localities. As well as enabling the government to publicise its policies and current preoccupations in the charges delivered by the circuit judges to the grand juries, they also enabled the judges, in the words of Sir Francis Bacon, to 'feel the pulse of the subject', by listening to the concerns of the local gentry and, if necessary, passing information back to the Crown or the Privy Council. The sermon, strategically positioned at the opening of the assizes, served two very important functions: first, to set the moral and religious tone of the whole proceedings, and secondly, to bring together the Crown's representatives and the county élite in an elaborate public show of amity and unity. In a ceremony that survived largely unaltered until modern times, the circuit judges were formally

---

[33] BL Add. MS 20066, ff. 3r, 6v; Thomas Pestell, *Morbus Epidemicus, or the Charles Sicknesse* (1615), A3v.

welcomed by the knights and gentlemen of the county and escorted to their lodgings, accompanied by trumpeters and liverymen; then, dressed in their robes, they attended church to hear prayers and a sermon, before proceeding to the crown court. The sermon, as one preacher told the judges in 1607, was thus 'your first entertainment' at the assizes, and 'a piece of your state and your solemnity'. It was also, as Glenn Burgess has pointed out, one of the relatively few occasions on which ordinary Englishmen were treated to a disquisition on political philosophy.[34]

As befitted its importance, the assize sermon was often delivered by the bishop or one of the senior clergy of the diocese. Bishop Heton of Ely and Bishop Cotton of Salisbury were among the preachers on the Oxford circuit in 1604; Bishop Tobias Matthew preached at the Durham assizes in 1605; and Bishop Miles Smith was a regular preacher at the Gloucester assizes. As a rule, the preacher was selected by the sheriff of the county (to whom printed assize sermons are often dedicated), though in certain cases the sheriff delegated this task to some other authority: at the Cambridge assizes, for example, the preacher was customarily chosen by the vice-chancellor; and elsewhere the bishop probably had a say in the appointment.[35] The Privy Council's order of May 1632 that assize preachers were to be chosen by the diocesan bishops, 'or (at least) with their knowledge and approbation', has been interpreted, probably rightly, as an attempt to guarantee the selection of suitably conformist clergy, but may also have been designed to place on a regular footing what had, until then, been an informal arrangement.[36] With due allowance for local variation, it is clear that assize preachers were generally selected by the civil or ecclesiastical authorities, often with some care; and it therefore comes as no surprise to find their sermons reflecting the values and assumptions of the governing élite.

Around fifty assize sermons survive in print from the period 1580–1640, with many more in manuscript; taken together, they provide an excellent

---

[34] J. S. Cockburn, *A History of English Assizes 1558–1714* (Cambridge, 1972), pp. 65–7; Cynthia Herrup, *The Common Peace: Participation and the Criminal Law in Seventeenth-Century England* (Cambridge, 1987), pp. 51–3; John Tuer, sermon on Psalm 2: 10: Lambeth Palace Library, London, MS 447, pp. 384–5; Burgess, *Politics of the Ancient Constitution*, p. 131.

[35] C. H. Karraker, *The Seventeenth-Century Sheriff* (Chapel Hill, 1930), p. 27. Samuel Garey, assize preacher at Thetford and Norwich in 1619, dedicated his sermons to Sir Thomas Holland, 'the very worthy high Sherife of Norfolke', at whose appointment they had been delivered: Garey, *Ientaculum Iudicum* (1623), A4v. On the appointment of assize preachers at Cambridge, see St John's College, Cambridge, Muniments 94/489 (letter from Miles Sandys to Owen Gwyn, 6 July 1616). The selection of Immanuel Bourne to preach at the Derby assizes in 1623 probably owed something to episcopal influence, as Bourne was chaplain to Bishop John Williams: Bourne, *The Anatomy of Conscience* (1623), A2v.

[36] Cockburn, *English Assizes*, p. 66.

illustration of the set of commonplaces, already familiar to historians of
early modern England, in which magistracy and ministry are seen as
natural allies in the promotion of public order and godly virtue. In one
of the earliest assize sermons to be printed, Edward Hutchins declared
that the magistrate and minister must deal with Papists in different but
complementary ways, 'the Minister by the woord, the Magistrate by the
sword: the one by love, the other by feare: the one by softnes, the other
by sharpnes: the one by perswading, the other by punishing, if that
persuasion may not prevaile'. Nearly half a century later, the preacher at
Lancaster assizes was still faithfully repeating the same well-worn commonplaces: 'The Magistracy and Ministry as the Elme and the Vine, the
garden and the bees, flourish pleasantly and plentifully together, or els
decay and wither together.' And it was in another assize sermon that, in
Patrick Collinson's words, 'the doctrine of the mutuality of magistracy
and ministry and its authoritarian, even repressive implications received its
most eloquent expression'. Magistracy and ministry, declared Nathaniel
Ward in the preface to his brother Samuel's sermon *Iethro's Iustice of Peace*
(1618), were 'the principal lights' of the body politic, 'which being as
Guardians and Tutors of the rest, should either prevent or reforme their
aberrations'.[37]

A contemporary account of the opening of the Sussex assizes in 1579
shows how this union of magistracy and ministry might work in practice,
with the preacher's words immediately echoed by the judges in their charge
to the grand jury:

For thys I sawe, and hearde my selfe the same tyme, when the Iudges were come
from the Church to the Hall, and were nowe sette downe, and the Countrey before
them, they did not onely imparte to the multitude what great fruite and comforte
they had receyved themselves by hearing that Sermon (giving it a singular commendation in the eares of all men, even from the benche where they sate) but also
then tooke occasion thereby, to gyve a verye quicke, and vehemente charge to the
graunde Iurie, yea, and to the Iustices themselves, and to all others that had anye
office or authoritie in the Sheere, to looke more narrowly to matters of Religion,
than heeretofore they had done, and to endeavoure themselves by all meanes
possible, to conserve the peace and unitie of Christes Church, and to search out,
and see punished all that were offenders to the contrary. And to tell you the truth, it

---

[37] Edward Hutchins, *A Sermon Preached in Westchester* (Oxford, 1586), B3v; Christopher Hudson, 'The
happines of governement' (Lancaster assizes, 20 August 1632), Lancashire Record Office, Preston, DP
353, f. 47v; Patrick Collinson, *The Religion of Protestants: The Church in English Society, 1559–1625*
(Oxford, 1982), p. 153; Samuel Ward, *Iethro's Iustice of Peace* (1618), A3r.

did my heart good to see so grave and wise a man (Judge Gaudie by name) to give so earnest and godly a charge, in God and the Gospels behalfe.[38]

Nor was the relationship between sermons and charges limited to a polite exchange of compliments between pulpit and bench. The scriptural and moral commonplaces that formed the staple fare of assize sermons were often repeated by judges and justices, with very little alteration, in their own speeches. The quarter-sessions charges of the Kentish JP and anti-quary William Lambarde contain many passages that could have come straight from assize sermons, while the charges of the Somerset JP John Harington are modelled even more closely on pulpit rhetoric, to the extent of taking a scriptural text and expounding it in the style of a sermon.[39] (Significantly, Harington drafted his charges in the same note-book he used for recording the sermons he heard.) Perhaps the most striking example of the overlap between magisterial and ministerial rhet-oric comes from Sir John Dodderidge's treatise on judicial duties, which illustrates the five qualities of the ideal judge (religion, courage, integrity, wisdom and learning) with reference to the Old Testament texts com-monly used in assize sermons.[40] What this example suggests is that judges conceptualised their role in precisely the way that assize preachers encou-raged them to do; or, to put it another way, that assize preachers drew on a set of commonplaces that their audience would have found familiar, acceptable and thoroughly congenial.

What, then, were these commonplaces? Assize sermons almost invar-iably began by comparing the body politic to a natural body, or to some artificial body such as the mechanism of a clock, in which each part was essential to the well-being of the whole. Lancelot Dawes, preaching at Carlisle assizes in 1614, declared that the three 'chiefe pillars to support a Christian commonwealth' were the physician, the divine and the magis-trate. 'These three are in the body politicke; as the three principall parts, the liver, the heart and the braine are in the body of man.' The physician was the liver, which dispersed the humours through the veins, and 'purgeth the body of man, from such noxious humours' as might endanger

---

[38] William Overton, *A Godlye, and Pithie Exhortation, Made to the Iudges and Iustices of Sussex, and the Whole Countie* (1579), A3r (prefatory epistle signed 'M. M.'). In this case the alliance between magistracy and ministry was embodied in the person of the preacher, who was not only a canon of Chichester (and future Bishop of Coventry and Lichfield) but also one of the justices of the peace.

[39] *William Lambarde and Local Government*, ed. Conyers Read (New York, 1962), e.g. p. 147 (on magistracy and ministry); BL Egerton MS 2711. Margaret F. Stieg, ed., *The Diary of John Harington, M. P., 1646–53* (Somerset Record Soc., 1977), prints Harington's charges (pp.87–108) but not his sermon notes.

[40] Sir John Dodderidge, *The English Lawyer* (1631), A4r. Dodderidge's discussion of judicial duties (the third part of his treatise) was never completed but survives here in outline.

it; the divine was the heart, which dispersed the vital spirits through the arteries to give life to the whole body; and the magistrate was the brain, 'the chiefe commander of the whole', which sat 'in the highest roome, as in a stately palace', and sent orders through the nerves to the other members of the body.[41] The inclusion of the physician in this list may seem somewhat incongruous, but assize preachers drew little or no distinction between the physical health of the individual and the moral health of the commonwealth. Robert Sanderson, preaching at Lincoln assizes in 1630, denounced the sin of 'riot' as both a physical and a moral sickness, giving rise to 'disorders in the Church, distempers in the State, distractions in our judgments, diseases in our bodies'.[42]

This familiar simile could be employed in various ways: most obviously, to spell out the need for hierarchy and authority among the members of the body politic. 'What the head is unto the body naturall', declared Theophilus Taylor in a sermon at Reading assizes, 'that is a ruler to the body politicall: a body without a head is neare corruption and fit onely for the grave, and the common wealth without a Governour is as neare unto ruine and destruction'.[43] Other examples – the hierarchy of the sun, moon and stars; the hierarchy of the angels in heaven; the hierarchy of notes in music; the hierarchy of bees in a hive – were invoked to show that authority and obedience were an integral part of the natural order of things. 'Government', declared Robert Bolton at Northampton assizes in 1621, 'is the prop and pillar of all States and Kingdomes, the cement and soule of humane affaires, the life of society and order, the very vitall spirit whereby so many millions of men, doe breath the life of comfort and peace; and the whole nature of things subsist.' If a man's heart were to stop beating, 'the whole body would presently grow pale, bloudles and livelesse'. If the sun were to grow dim, 'this goodly frame of the world would dissolve, and fall into confusion and darknesse. Proportionably, take Soveraignety from the face of the earth, and you turne it into a Cockpit. Men would become cut-throats and Canibals one unto another . . . We should have a very hell upon earth, and the face of it covered with blood, as it was once with water.'[44]

The same simile could also be used to stress the need for the members of the body politic to come to each other's aid. Michael Wigmore, preaching

---

[41] Lancelot Dawes, *Two Sermons Preached at the Assises Holden at Carlile* (Oxford, 1614), E7r. For other examples of the same analogy, see Thomas Sutton, *Iethroes Counsell to Moses* (1631), B1r, and Hudson, 'The happines of governement', f. 51v.

[42] Robert Sanderson, *Twenty Sermons* (1656), 2Y3r (p. 349).

[43] Theophilus Taylor, *The Mappe of Moses: or, a Guide for Governours* (1629), B2r.

[44] Robert Bolton, *Two Sermons Preached at Northampton at Two Severall Assises There* (1635), B4v.

at Lincoln assizes in 1640, declared that in the commonwealth, as in the human body, the disorder of any part affected the whole. 'And if the least finger were but out of joynt, the Eye would be ready to shed a teare, the Heart would ake, the Head be sorrie, the Tongue to complaine, the Legs and Feet to runne for help.'[45] In similar fashion, Robert Sanderson declared that all men were 'linked together, and concorporated one into another' as members of the same body, 'so that if any man stand in need of thy help, and it be in the power of thy hand to do him good: whether he be knowen to thee, or a stranger, whether thy friend, or thy foe; he is a limbe of thee, and thou a limbe of him'. This applied particularly to judges and magistrates, whose duty it was to support the weaker members of the body politic, to protect them from oppression, and to care for them in distress. A good magistrate should be like Job, 'eyes to the blinde, feet to the lame, a husband to the widow, a father to the orphane, a brother to the stranger'. Yet, as Immanuel Bourne pointed out in a sermon at Derby assizes in 1623, the magistrate, like the physician, might sometimes have to take drastic action in order to prevent the spread of disease. 'It were farre better that one rotten member should be cut off from the body, than the whole body perish.'[46]

Judges were therefore exhorted to strike a balance between mercy and severity: to be lenient wherever possible, but not to shrink from harsh measures when necessity demanded it. Again, preachers frequently drew an analogy between the magistrate and the physician, who would not willingly choose to inflict pain, but who might be forced to amputate a limb to save the patient's life. A good judge, declared Lancelot Dawes, should 'imitate a good Surgeon, who cuts the wound, though his patient weepe never so sore . . . Where there is hope of cure without searing, or cutting, use there a ladies hand; in this case a plaster is better than a knife. But where the member is incurable, and incorrigible, and like to endanger the whole, cut it off.' Nevertheless, 'all gentle meanes must be first tried: and even in this act of justice, you must not altogither exclude mercy . . . For justice without mercy is bloudy cruelty, mercy without justice is foolish pity; but justice with mercy is perfect Christianity.'[47] This pairing of justice and mercy was a staple theme of assize sermons, repeated over and over again with minor variations. Samuel Garey described justice as walking 'in a golden meane, betwixt acerbitie of Severitie, and communitie of Mercy'. Theophilus Taylor advised magistrates

---

[45] Michael Wigmore, *A Dissection of the Braine* (1641), A4r.
[46] Sanderson, *Twenty Sermons*, 2V4r (p. 335), 2X3r (p. 341). Immanuel Bourne, *The Anatomie of Conscience* (1623), F4r.
[47] Dawes, *Two Sermons*, E4r–5r. For a similar coupling of justice and mercy, see Sanderson, *Twenty Sermons*, 2X3v.

to follow the example of God, who 'alwaies steepes the sword of his severity, in the oyle of his mercy'. 'I may not presume', Taylor told the judges, 'to give directions to your wisedomes how to proportion your severity to the severall crimes you shall meet with', though he went on to call for special severity in the case of Catholic priests and Jesuits, 'the Popes bloud-hounds'.[48]

As this last example suggests, it was customary for assize preachers to single out particular sins for special condemnation. Elizabethan assize sermons were often directed against recusant Catholics, whose refusal to attend church placed them outside the symbolic community of the body politic; but by the early seventeenth century the focus had begun to shift from religious to social disorder, with drunkards, swearers and sabbath-breakers as the offenders most likely to be singled out as parasites on the social body, 'the most pestilent and cursed canker-wormes, that gnaw at the very heart and sinew of the glory and strength of the State'. Alexander Strange's attack on 'sturdie and stoute incorrigible common rogues and vagabondes', in a sermon at Hertford assizes in 1608, was typical in its range of social prescriptions, concluding with an exhortation to the judges, 'that the lawes for the punishment of rogues and vagabondes may be better executed'; to the justices of the peace, to 'looke to the suppression of needelesse and godlesse Alehowses, the seminaryes of Idlenes'; and finally to 'the countrye', meaning the county élite, to assist in 'the suppressing and abolishing of this idle and wicked generation' by denying them charitable relief.[49] Alehouses were again singled out by Christopher Hudson, in a sermon at Lancaster assizes in 1632, as being the seedbeds for other forms of social disorder. 'You often complaine of bastards, sheepstealers, quarrellers, &c. and would you cure these? Surely these assemble together in the foresaid houses as humors in the stomack before the fit of an Ague; Expell them hence, and in that one worke you shall heale infinite distempers.'[50]

The attack on these sins should not be taken as evidence of a narrowly puritan agenda, but as part of a wider campaign for the reformation of manners which, as recent scholarship has amply demonstrated, enjoyed the support of many lawmakers and magistrates.[51] In this, as in other respects, assize preachers were faithfully reflecting the social and moral values of their audience. The preachers' remarks on the legal system itself,

---

[48] Garey, *Ientaculum Iudicum*, G3v; Taylor, *Mappe of Moses*, F2r.
[49] Alexander Strange, 'Three sermons made upon severall occasions': Inner Temple Library, MS Petyt 530B, f. 43r. On Strange, see Heather Falvey and Steve Hindle, eds., *"This Little Commonwealth": Layston Parish Memorandum Book, 1607– c. 1650 & 1704– c. 1747* (Hertfordshire Record Soc., 2003), where this sermon is printed (pp. 163–84).
[50] Hudson, 'The happines of governement', f. 53r.
[51] For the best recent account, see Steve Hindle, *The State and Social Change in Early Modern England, c.1550–1640* (Basingstoke, 2000), chapter 7, 'The reformation of manners'.

however, were potentially more controversial. Some preachers argued that the prevalence of social disorder resulted from a failure in the legal system, for which the magistrates were chiefly to blame. William Yonger, preaching at Thetford assizes in 1617, echoed the complaint of Anacharsis, in Plutarch's life of Solon, that the laws 'are but as Spiders webbs . . . the little flies are caught, and hang by the heeles, but great ones burst through'. He attributed this to the negligence of magistrates who had failed to punish offenders with sufficient severity. 'When we see these sinnes of Adulterie, Fornication, Incest, flye about as fierie Serpents . . . wee must lay the fault upon the Magistrate . . . Doe yee punish sinne as yee ought, and execute Law with an upright heart? How then comes it to passe, that these sinnes are bolstred out, and that men are not afraid to commit such wickednesse?' He also criticised the ecclesiastical courts for their lenient treatment of adultery, claiming that the penance for adultery was generally commuted to a fine ('somewhat given in the nature of an Almes to redeeme the sinne') which went 'to fill the purses of corrupt men' rather than being applied to pious uses.[52]

Underlying such remarks, it is possible to discern a deeper ambivalence about the legal process, made all the more problematic by the growing number of lawsuits. Was the recourse to law a sign of a well-ordered and well-regulated society; or was it, on the contrary, a sign that social harmony was in decline? William Westerman, preaching at Hertford assizes, was in no doubt. 'It is a signe of badde and wicked education, and ill maners in any countrie, when the Common-wealth hath neede of manie Judges, manie Lawyers, manie Courtes. The multitude of these Physitians of our estate, telleth us with shame that wee are a sight of wrangling Christians, for the most part, without justice, without patience, without love and wisdome.' John Mayo urged justices of the peace to make every effort to settle disputes 'at home among your neighbours' rather than allowing them to come to court, while Samuel Ward complained that the assizes were clogged up with 'such petty causes, trifling actions and complaints . . . which a meane Yeoman were Judge fit enough to end in a chaire at home'. Thus 'the whole Shire must be troubled to heare and judge of a curtesie made out of the path, or a blow given upon the shoulder upon occasion of a wager, or such like bawble-trespasses which I shame to mention.'[53] These preachers looked back nostalgically to a time when, in Mayo's words, 'poore mens suits' had

---

[52] W. Yonger, *The Nurses Bosome* (1617), H1v–2r.
[53] William Westerman, *Two Sermons of Assise* (1600), E7v–8r; John Mayo, *The Universal Principle* (1630), C2r; Ward, *Iethro's Iustice of Peace*, E5r.

been 'quietly ended at home' with the help of neighbours, parish clergy or local gentry, and – in common with some modern historians – saw the rise in litigation as a sign that these informal methods of reconciliation and out-of-court settlement had broken down.[54]

Yet, at the same time, preachers could draw on the conventional stock of 'commonwealth' imagery to argue that the legal system was an essential part of the social order, and that it was not the legal process itself, but abuses of it such as bribery and perjury, that were 'the disjoynting of the body of the common-wealthe'. They found natural and divine analogies for the legal system in the conscience (traditionally seen as a court, with reason as the judge) and in the Day of Judgement (again, seen as a court, with Christ as the judge), which, as John Squire declared, could serve as a pattern for the judicial system, and 'will compell the Preacher to instruct bouldly, the Judge to determine justly, the Servant to informe honestly, the Plaintife to accuse uprightly, the Councellour to advise wisely, the Advocate to pleade warily, the under-Officers to execute law impartially, the Jurye to give their Verdite sincerely, the witnesse to sweare fearefully, and give evidence truely: and all of us to live conscionably'.[55] Seen in this light, the legal system was not a symptom of disorder, but a microcosm of the well-ordered commonwealth; and the lawyer was not merely a promoter of unnecessary litigation, but a servant of the community whose role was 'to helpe every man to his right, to cut away strife and contention, and to restore peace and unitie in the common-wealth, that all the members of the body politicke may be of one heart, and one soule'.[56]

Most of these examples are taken from printed assize sermons, but these can be supplemented by an important manuscript source, Sir Christopher Yelverton's notebook of assize sermons delivered on the Northern and Oxford circuits, which offers a valuable cross-section of assize preaching at the turn of the seventeenth century.[57] Yelverton makes little effort to record the thread of the preacher's argument; he is more interested in compiling an anthology of pithy and elegant moral sayings suitable for transcription into a commonplace book, and his notes provide further evidence of the extent to which assize sermons were drawn from a stock of familiar commonplaces, such as the following:

[54] On the increase in litigation, see C. W. Brooks, *Pettyfoggers and Vipers of the Commonwealth: The 'Lower Branch' of the Legal Profession in Early Modern England* (1986), pp. 132–4.

[55] John Squire, *A Sermon Preached at Hartford Assises* (1617), D2r.    [56] Dawes, *Two Sermons*, I8v.

[57] BL Add. MS 48106. The BL catalogue attributes this manuscript to Henry Yelverton, but the dates and places of preaching correspond to Christopher Yelverton's circuit ridings: see Cockburn, *English Assizes*, pp. 267–8.

The eyes of Judges ought to be on the cause, like the sunne that shineth alike to all, like the circle that reacheth alike to all, like the rule proportionable to all.

When money in the church is the patriarke, and in the common wealth the monarke, both of them perishe.

Too vigorous iustice may be termed synn, but temperate iustice is a vertue.

Clemency and mercy is most to be respected of great men and magistrates.

When sins are not punished, they be multiplied ... *Est quaedam misericordia puniens, et quaedam crudelitas parcens.* [It is sometimes merciful to punish, and cruel to pardon.]

The glory and felicity of all States & commonwealthes stande upon 4 principall pillars: mercy & truthe, Justice and peace.

The sayings collected in Yelverton's notebook reflect the themes we have already encountered: the divine institution of government; the alliance of magistracy and ministry; the need to strike a balance between justice and mercy; the need for equity and impartiality in executing the law. These ideas were hardly controversial, and, on this evidence, it is easy to see why some scholars have regarded assize sermons as merely a collection of 'well-worn platitudes and inoffensive generalizations'.[58] Certainly there is nothing to suggest that the sermons heard and noted by Yelverton offered any challenge to his assumptions about the legal system and his place within it. Yet it would be a mistake to read assize sermons purely in terms of consensus, for, as we shall see, the same commonplaces could also be used to articulate tensions and conflicts in the administration of justice.

For an alternative perspective on assize preaching, it may be helpful to consider the sermon preached by George Close at the opening of the assizes in Exeter in August 1603. Close was a turbulent priest whom we shall encounter again later in this chapter; his career was overshadowed by accusations of bribery and simony, and he was eventually deprived and degraded for scandalous conduct by the High Commission in 1615.[59] Preaching before the assize judges, Sir Edward Fenner and Sir Peter Warburton, and a 'great congregation' in Exeter Cathedral, he launched into a fierce tirade against the legal profession, in the following words:

I well knowe that two Reverente Judges of this Land, at two severall tymes to that effecte tould a Preacher that he might know divinitye, but he knewe not the lawe: The common lawe will dispatch a matter well enough with a single wittnes though hee be not very singuler: I must therefore intreate you to lett us have noe more objections against the lawe it selfe: lett it be soe obscure that noe man can knowe it,

---

[58] Cockburn, *English Assizes*, p. 66.
[59] On Close's deprivation, see Kenneth Fincham, *Prelate as Pastor: The Episcopate of James I* (Oxford, 1990), p. 317.

soe uncertaine that noe man can defyne it, perhaps in parte soe absurd, that noe scripture reason or learning can approve it: yett this you maye safelye beleeve which an auncient Barrester at the lawe answeared a preacher making theise obiections against it, whye sayth he, I can tell you what the lawe is, the preacher being desirous to be satisfyed prayed his opynion therein. It is (said he) a prittye tricke to catch mony withall . . .[60]

Incensed by this attack on the common law, Sir Edward Coke submitted a bill of complaint to the king, alleging *inter alia* that Close was motivated by a personal grudge, having been convicted of simony by an assize jury the previous year. In his reply, Close declared that he had not spoken against the law itself, but only against some 'supposed abuses' in the law, intending 'to applye his doctrine to the auditorye, according to his text, persons, place and occasion'. He had not directed his criticisms against any particular individuals, but 'onlye against offences and offenders in generall, according to the approved rules of Sacred Theologie'. He defended his right to do so by citing the example of Latimer, who 'uppon the like occasion, affirmeth, that a preacher must accommodate his matter to his auditory . . . and being accused that he reproved upon reporte and hearesaye, he maynteyneth it to be lawfull for a preacher soe to doe, according to the example of St Paule, reproving the factious Corinthians for tollerating incestuous offenders amongst them'.

This is clearly an exceptional case; no other Elizabethan or Jacobean assize preacher is known to have criticised the legal profession in such forthright terms. But Close's sermon also offers a fresh perspective on assize preaching because it expresses, in an extreme form, some common clerical grievances against the common law, and helps us to recognise the same grievances simmering quietly under other assize sermons of the period. Only a few years after Close's sermon, the Essex minister John Tuer preached a sermon before the judges (probably at Paul's Cross at the beginning of the law term in October 1607) in which he drew attention to 'the daily manifolde complaints of almost the whole Ministry rounde about mee' that the common law did not give adequate protection to the clergy.[61] He singled out two aspects of the legal system for particular criticism: first, the use of writs of prohibition to remove cases from the jurisdiction of the ecclesiastical courts, and secondly,

---

[60] Close's sermon and Coke's bill of complaint are copied in Bodleian Library, Oxford, MS Eng. th. c.71, ff. 7–28.

[61] Sermon by John Tuer on Psalm 2: 10 ('Be learned, ye that are judges of the earth'): Lambeth Palace Library, London, MS 447, p. 324. The sermon is dedicated to Archbishop Bancroft, who had represented the clergy's position against the common law before the Privy Council in 1605: see J. P. Sommerville, *Politics and Ideology in England 1603–1640* (Cambridge, 1986), p. 211.

the anticlerical bias of juries, whom he accused of a deep-seated prejudice against the clergy, especially in tithe and copyhold cases. Over and above these specific complaints, Tuer expressed bitter resentment at the reluctance of lawyers and judges to accept advice from the clergy. 'This is the thinge, which of all other things, you cannot, you will not abide to heare of, that wee shoulde take upon us to teach you … What doe you then here? and wherfore come wee hither?' What, he demanded, was the purpose of assize sermons, 'when you ride the Circuits in the Country', if not 'that we should preach to you, and put you in minde, at least of some parte of your duties'?[62]

Tuer's sermon demonstrates the fallacy of the argument that assize sermons were merely occasions for generalised statements about authority and obedience. No doubt many common lawyers might have preferred sermons of this sort, but at least some members of the clergy were determined to assert their right to admonish the legal profession and, in doing so, to engage in precise and detailed terms with particular aspects of legal practice. The sermon also illustrates the way that criticisms of the judiciary could be encoded in apparently uncontentious remarks about law and religion. Many of the statements in Tuer's sermon, such as his declaration that scripture and divinity are 'the only prescript line and level, whereby to order all our actions', or his exhortation to the judges to be guided by the Word of God – with a reminder to them 'that you are all but Gods Commissioners on these your Benches and Seates of Judgment', 'deputed under him, till himselfe come and judge us all' – do not sound particularly controversial; and encountering them in other assize sermons, one might easily dismiss them as unremarkable. In Tuer's sermon, however, it is clear that these commonplaces were being used to stake a claim to clerical authority, which many lawyers were intensely reluctant to accept. They serve to alert us to similar remarks in other assize sermons: in 1630, for example, the Suffolk minister John Rous attended a sermon at Thetford assizes, which opened with a deceptively bland apologia to the effect that 'judges and all must learne at the lips of the priest', followed by 'many touches upon the corruptions of judges and councellors'.[63]

This is not to suggest that all assize sermons should be read as coded attacks on the judiciary. Indeed, many assize preachers went out of their way to deny any controversial intention. Bishop Miles Smith, preaching at Gloucester assizes, made the usual attack on bribery and corruption but declared that he was certain the judges present to 'heare me this day' were not guilty of these

---

[62] Lambeth Palace Library, London, MS 447, pp. 384–5. For a similar complaint about the anticlerical bias of assize juries, also by an Essex minister, see Stephen Gosson, *The Trumpet of Warre* (1598), E7r.
[63] *Diary of John Rous*, ed. Mary Anne Everett Green (Camden Society, 1856), p. 50.

sins, 'for I heare well, yea, very well of them'. Preachers were also careful to stress that they were not instructing the judges but merely reminding them of their duties: thus Lancelot Dawes told the judges at Carlisle assizes that while it would be presumptuous of him 'to speake unto you, and offer to instruct you in the particular duties of a judge', he hoped they would allow him 'to move you to that, which yee both know, and are ready, I am sure, to put in practise'.[64] But even when assize preachers declined to apply their doctrines to particular individuals, it is clear that some members of their audience were only too eager to read between the lines. John Rous was probably not unusual among the hearers of assize sermons in being alert for any signs of tension between the clergy and the judiciary. In 1631 he noted that Thomas Scott, the assize preacher at Bury, had 'made a sore sermon in discovery of corruptions of judges and others', while Judge Harvey had felt so personally affronted by the sermon at Norwich assizes that he had burst out in frustration: 'It seemes by the sermon that we are corrupt, but know that we can use conscience in our places, as well as the best clergie man of all.'[65]

Historians have perhaps been too inclined to take the rhetoric of magistracy and ministry at face value, as a simple statement of fact rather than a means of negotiating a tense and delicate relationship. Samuel Ward's sermon *Iethro's Iustice of Peace* (1618), preached at Bury assizes, is a particularly instructive example: often regarded as the quintessential expression of the alliance between magistracy and ministry, this sermon is in fact a remarkably outspoken assertion of the preacher's right to admonish his social superiors. Admittedly, Ward does not extend his strictures to the circuit judges themselves, of whom, he says, 'fame … hath spoken all good' (though he still asserts his right to reprove them if necessary). But he is highly critical of the bench of justices – 'a worthy Bench' yet 'mingled with some drosse', containing some 'whose skill and ability the Countrey doubts of' and others 'whose religion they call into question' – and also urges his audience to 'stand fast in your lawfull libertie of election' by resisting the attempts of 'some of the Gentry of the Shires' to prejudice the free election of MPs. What makes this sermon particularly interesting is that it was revised for print by the author's brother Nathaniel Ward, who states in a postscript that he has taken the liberty of adding several passages of his own against 'the corruption of our times', which suggests that the more controversial passages may not have

---

[64]  Miles Smith, *Sermons* (1632), S3r; Dawes, *Two Sermons*, E4r.
[65]  *Diary of John Rous*, p. 62. 'When the preacher lacketh matter, then have at the lawyers' was a common proverb as early as the 1560s: see Lambeth Palace Library, Ms 739, f. 8v (sermon by John Bullingham at Paul's Cross, c. 1565).

appeared in the sermon as originally preached.[66] Its significance, in other words, lies in the fact that it says openly what other assize preachers may only have said indirectly and implicitly, and thus invites us to look for similar criticisms expressed in other assize sermons in more subtle ways.

In many cases, such criticisms were expressed through the familiar metaphor of the social body, which could be employed with a wide range of different inflections and shades of meaning. For Christopher Hudson, preaching at Lancaster assizes, the comparison of the physician, the divine and the magistrate to the liver, heart and brain of the body served to illustrate the point that, just as there were mysteries of religion with which the physician was not concerned, so there were mysteries of state which lay outside the province of the theologian: 'when the office of these three orderly is performed and succeeds one another, the Divine beginning where the Phisition ends, and the Magistrate where the Divine ends, all things in the body Politike are in excellent health'.[67] But Dawes, preaching at Carlisle, used the same comparison to draw a subtly different conclusion, that it was the magistrate's duty to take counsel from the divine. Just as the brain is 'continually busied in tempering the spirits received from the hart: which it sendeth by the nerves, through the whole body, thereby giving sense and motion to every part', so the magistrate must temper the body politic by 'using those spirituall admonitions, and instructions, which he shall receive from the minister of the Gospell, for the good, and benefit of all those that are under him'. He added pointedly that as the brain was prone to more diseases than the other parts of the body, so the magistrate was in more danger of falling into sin, 'because . . . he is not so freely reproved for his offences, as others are'.[68]

This metaphor, or cluster of metaphors, could be used either to affirm or to question the established political order. William Dickinson's unusually extreme theory of divine-right monarchy, expressed in a sermon at Reading assizes in 1619, compared the king's position in the state to that of the soul in the body: 'For as in the body of man the soule is said to be at once in the whole and every part . . . Even so it is in the Republike, the King is not limited, his power is diffused through the whole and every particular, and according to the instruments hee works by, so is his power denominated. In the Chancery hee is called Lord Chaunceler, in other courts Judge, Justice, and so of the rest.'[69]

---

[66] Ward, *Iethro's Iustice of Peace*, E2r, E2v, E8v.

[67] Hudson, 'The happines of governement', f. 51v.      [68] Dawes, *Two Sermons*, E8r, E8v.

[69] William Dickinson, *The Kings Right, Briefely Set Downe in a Sermon* (1619), C4v. Glenn Burgess describes this as an unusually powerful expression of divine-right monarchism (*Politics of the Ancient Constitution* (University Park, PA, 1993), p. 188) while arguing that it does not amount to absolutism (*Absolute Monarchy and the Stuart Constitution* (New Haven, 1996), p. 112).

This appears to undermine any claim for the independence of the common law, and raises the intriguing possibility that some clergy may have been attracted to divine-right theory as a way of resisting the anticlerical pretensions of common lawyers. Yet, at the other extreme, the preacher at Thetford assizes in 1630 used the same metaphor to offer a veiled criticism of royal authority, by way of 'a similitude . . . of the head receiving all the nourishment, and causing the other members to faile and the whole man to die, which he applied to the commonwealth, where all is sucked upwards and the commons left without nourishment'.[70] As Kevin Sharpe has pointed out, the metaphor of the king as the head and the people as the body, while 'traditional and conservative . . . was by no means a justification of absolute authority . . . In order to rule the body too, the head itself needed to be free of corruption.'[71]

Such commonplaces were useful precisely because they were commonplace: that is to say, they served as a reassurance that the speaker did not propose to depart from the accepted framework of ideas on order, authority, mutuality and commonalty. As Sharpe argues, they functioned as a common language of politics, ensuring that political disagreements would be limited and contained within a set of shared assumptions. Yet, as we have seen, preachers often used these commonplaces in a highly calculated manner, not simply to invoke consensus but to express criticism. In this sense, they bear less resemblance to a language than to a code, a rhetorical stratagem enabling preachers to register dissent in terms that were suitably veiled but that would, nevertheless, have been easily recognised and decoded by the experienced listener. If we now turn to the sermons preached at Paul's Cross, we shall see that these were characterised by a similar set of commonplaces, distinct from those found in assize sermons but performing a complementary function.

### PAUL'S CROSS SERMONS

The most vivid contemporary description of the sermons preached at Paul's Cross, in the churchyard of St Paul's Cathedral, comes from a most unexpected source: not a sermon or religious treatise, nor even a letter or diary, but an English–Spanish phrasebook. William Stepney's *The Spanish Schoole-maister*, first published in 1591, contains a dialogue between two London churchgoers on their way to Paul's Cross, showing 'what talke is most convenient to be used at our going to the Church':

Good morrow to you Maister *Antonie*, and to al your company.
And to you likewise Maister *Robert*, God give you good morrow.

---

[70] *Diary of John Rous*, p. 50.    [71] Sharpe, 'A commonwealth of meanings', p. 112.

How do you fare of your health?
I am well, at your service and commandement.
I thanke you a thousand times, I am bound to requite it.
Whither go you so early in the morning?
I go to the Church to heare a Sermon.
To what Church I pray you? I will beare you company.
Let us go together, and I will go to *S. Pauls* Crosse, for there preacheth a great Doctor this day, which is come now lately from *Oxford*.
Indeede it would do me good to heare such a learned man, for there preacheth none but such as be well learned and chosen men; and the cause is, for that there is alwayes an honourable audience, to wit, the Lord Maior, the right Worshipfull Shirifes, and the Worshipfull Maisters the Aldermen of London.
It is even so, and therfore we shal heare a good sermon.
Let us go, for it is time, or else we shall have no place, for all the formes wil be taken up.
What is it a clocke?
It is almost ten, and always at ten the people will be all assembled.[72]

Much of this information – such as the fact that the sermons started at ten o'clock, and that seats were not reserved, so that one had to arrive early to be sure of a good place – would be hard to glean from any other source. For our present purposes, however, the chief interest of this exchange lies in the remark about the 'honourable audience' – the Lord Mayor, sheriffs and aldermen of London – whose presence, in the writer's opinion, is enough to ensure that the sermon will be of a high standard.

The Paul's Cross sermons, preached every Sunday before an audience of several thousand people, were the Lord Mayor's most regular, and arguably most important, public appearances during his year of office.[73] In Thomas Middleton's pageant *The Triumphs of Truth*, written for the Lord Mayor's show in 1613, the figure of Time ('attired agreeable to his condition, with his hour-glass, wings, and scythe') greeted the Lord Mayor as he passed through Paul's Churchyard on his way to the Guildhall, and gestured to the pulpit:

---

[72] William Stepney, *The Spanish Schoole-maister* (1619), F6v.
[73] The standard history of Paul's Cross preaching is Millar MacLure, *The Paul's Cross Sermons 1534–1642* (Toronto, 1958), now somewhat dated but still useful. MacLure's census of recorded sermons has been updated by Jackson Campbell Boswell and Peter Pauls, *Register of Sermons Preached at Paul's Cross 1534–1642* (Ottawa, 1989), though there are still many omissions. Other recent studies include Mary Morrissey, 'Rhetoric, religion and politics in the St. Paul's Cross sermons, 1603–1625' (Cambridge, PhD diss., 1997), and David Crankshaw, 'Community, city and nation, 1540–1714', in Derek Keene, Arthur Burns and Andrew Saint, eds., *St. Paul's: The Cathedral Church of London* (New Haven and London, 2004), pp. 45–70. On the well-known painting of a sermon at Paul's Cross, now in the Society of Antiquaries, see Pamela Tudor Craig, *'Old St. Paul's: The Society of Antiquaries' Diptych, 1616* (London Topographical Soc., 2004).

Figure 6  A sermon at Paul's Cross: from Henry Farley, *St Paules-Church her Bill for the Parliament* (1621). Reproduced by permission of the Houghton Library, Harvard University.

> See'st thou yon place? thither I'll weekly bring thee,
> Where Truth's celestial harmony thou shalt hear;
> To which, I charge thee, bend a serious ear.[74]

Fourteen years earlier, when the German traveller Thomas Platter paid a visit to Paul's Cross, he had been greatly struck by the imposing appearance of the Mayor and his attendants: 'The sermon ended, the herald preceded the Lord Mayor, carrying a red sword with yellow stripes, bared and vertical, wearing a white hat, an ashen grey coat with black borders, trunks and tunic, and brown and yellow stockings. And after him the mayor, clad in black with velvet hat, wearing a red coat lined with fur, followed on foot to his residence, where the preacher and other fine gentlemen have lunch with him, for he must keep open house.'[75]

Trivial as they may seem to a modern eye, these details of costume clearly mattered a great deal to the civic authorities, as the clothes worn by the aldermen on formal occasions such as the Paul's Cross and Spital sermons – including, in the course of the year, virtually every possible combination of scarlet, violet or black gowns, with or without cloaks, tippets and chains of office – were prescribed in minute detail in the City's official calendar of ceremonies. One preacher in 1595 even paid a neat compliment to the mayor and aldermen by moralising the colours of their robes: 'As there bee two

---

[74] Thomas Middleton, *The Triumphs of Truth* (1613) in *Collected Works*, ed. Gary Taylor and John Lavagnino (Oxford, 2007) p. 973.
[75] *Thomas Platter's Travels in England*, ed. and trans. Clare Williams (1937), p. 177.

colours, red and blue in one raine-bowe: so there must be two affections, ioye and sorrowe in one heart. This the wisedome of our auncestors seemeth to insinuate, even in the apparell which they have appointed to be worn at this solemnitie. For the chief magistrates of the Citie this day weare scarlet gownes which is a kind of red like fire, but tomorrowe they weare violet gownes which is a kind of blew like water.'[76] No visitor to the Cross, and certainly no preacher there, could possibly have been unaware of the presence of the civic authorities, or of their role in lending additional dignity and authority to the proceedings. The result was that by the end of the sixteenth century, Paul's Cross sermons had become distinctively 'London' occasions, in which preachers addressed their exhortations to the mayor and aldermen in partic-ular, offering them moral guidance on the government of the City and drawing their attention to sins and divisions within the civic community.

To this end, Paul's Cross preachers drew on the same 'commonwealth' rhetoric that we have already encountered in assize sermons. This type of rhetoric had its roots in medieval preaching, and became established as the standard pattern for Paul's Cross preaching thanks, in large part, to the 'no less fruitfull than famous' sermon preached by Thomas Wimbledon at Paul's Cross on Quinquagesima Sunday 1388, first printed soon after the Reformation and remaining continuously in print down to 1640. Wimbledon divided his audience into the traditional three estates – clergy, magistracy and commons – and exhorted each man to 'see to what state God has called him, and live therein by labour, according to his degree'. In the same way, post-Reformation preach-ers treated the audience at Paul's Cross as consisting of 'divers degrees, con-ditions, and estates of men', each with their own duties and responsibilities, joined together in a single body. In most contexts, it was natural to apply this to the commonwealth in general – with the whole realm of England as the body, and the monarch as the head – but in Paul's Cross sermons, London was represented as a body in its own right, a microcosm of the whole nation. 'As the case stands with a man and the parts of his body', declared Edward Dalton, 'so it may fall out with a Citie and the members of it.'[77] Paul's Cross sermons thus belonged to a specifically civic genre of preaching which took the city, rather than the household, the parish or the nation, as its principal unit of reference, and served to encourage a strong sense of civic identity in its audience.

---

[76] Thomas Playfere, *The Meane in Mourning* (1607), C4r. This appears to be one of the passages added by Playfere when revising the sermon for publication, and may not actually have occurred in the sermon as preached; but it is, nevertheless, accurate in its reference to the details of civic ceremonial: see *The Order of My Lord Mayor, the Aldermen and the Sheriffs, for Their Meetings* (1604).

[77] R. Wimbledon, *A Sermon, No Lesse Fruitefull then Famous, Preached at Pauls Crosse . . . in the Yeare of Our Lord God 1388* (1617); Edward Dalton, *Londons Laurell: or a Branch of Gratitude* (1623).

At times, the metaphor of the social body could be used to reinforce a sense of civic pride, underlining the need to defend the City's political independence. 'If the body be in daunger', declared Stephen Gosson at Paul's Cross in 1598, 'the arme is presentlie lifted up to receive the blowes comming upon it selfe . . . This Honorable Citty is a body pollitike, everie good cittizen which is a member of it, when he spies the Charters, privileges, and immunities thereof granted by the grace and favour of our Princes, to be in danger, will with the hazzard of his own substance seeke to defend and keep it.'[78] One of the ceremonies most closely associated with the Paul's Cross sermons, though one to which historians have paid surprisingly little attention, was the candlelit procession of the mayor and aldermen to the tomb of Bishop William in St Paul's Cathedral, which took place four times a year, on All Saints Day, Christmas Day, Twelfth Night and Candlemas. Bishop William, the first post-Conquest Bishop of London, was revered as a defender of the City's liberties: an inscription placed on his tomb by the Lord Mayor in 1622 described him as one 'by whom this Citie hath assum'd large priviledges', and a Paul's Cross preacher in 1637 exhorted the citizens to honour 'the memorie of that good Bishop of this See which for iust Reasons is still pretious with you, and by you this night to be solemnizd'.[79] The procession to Bishop William's tomb, like the Paul's Cross sermons themselves, was an opportunity for the mayor and aldermen to affirm their political independence, while simultaneously paying a judicious compliment to the Bishop of London.

But the same metaphor of the social body could also be used to reprove, chasten and correct. In Wimbledon's sermon of 1388, the preacher repeatedly draws a contrast between rich men and poor men, denouncing the covetousness of the rich and lamenting the sufferings of the poor. 'Prelates . . . with divers paintings colour their chambers, and with divers silkes and cloathings of colours, make their Images gay: but the poore man for want of cloathes beggeth, and with an empty belly doeth cry at the doore.' 'Covetousnesse is cause that rich men eate poore men, even as Beasts eate grasse, keeping it under: this is daily seene.' Sin was thus depicted as a breakdown of the proper relationship between the members of the social body, in which the three estates failed to recognise their dependence on each other, and the rich failed to make proper provision for their social inferiors. The same vision of social breakdown, presented in the same proverbial terms, with the same stark contrast between rich and poor, can be found in the Paul's Cross sermons of

[78] Stephen Gosson, *The Trumpet of Warre* (1598), F4v.
[79] Stow, *Survey of London* (1633), 2H6r; Sermon by unidentified preacher, 2 February 1637: Folger Library, Washington, DC, V.a.1, f. 65r.

the sixteenth and seventeenth centuries. 'The rich afflict the poore, the poore lay wait for the riche mens substance', lamented Richard Turnbull, 'the creditor pincheth the borower, and the debtor defraudeth the lender.' These were sins which could only be averted by a corporate act of repentance, and which thus provided an affirmation of the unity of the civic community even as they threatened to bring about its dissolution.[80]

It was in this context of collective exhortation and repentance that the Paul's Cross sermons assumed their standard form, the so-called 'Hosead' or 'Jeremiad' based on Old Testament prophetic texts, drawing an extended comparison between England and Israel, London and Jerusalem, and thundering out the grim message: 'unless ye repent, ye shall likewise perish'.[81] Michael McGiffert has argued that by the early seventeenth century, Paul's Cross sermons were becoming more restricted in their scope, as preachers turned their attention away from the covenant of works (between God and the whole city or nation) towards the covenant of grace (between God and the elect). More recent scholarship on Paul's Cross preaching, however, has made it clear that McGiffert was mistaken. Sermons at the Cross were not addressed to a select group of visible saints, but to the entire city: thus Henoch Clapham, applying Ezekiel's description of Jerusalem to the City of London, noted that the 'city' in his text could be understood in two senses, either as the elect alone or as the whole visible Church, and opted to take it in the second, wider sense in order to address his exhortations to the City as a whole. It was of the essence of this type of civic preaching that the preacher should address his listeners as a corporate body to be judged, and punished, not as individuals but as a community. Sin, declared Richard Stock in 1606, was to be found 'thorow the Citie, in every place, in every familie, in every man, and woman, in every Church and assemblie', and Londoners should therefore expect a general visitation, for 'where sinne is general, there Gods iudgements shall be generall'.[82]

---

[80] Richard Turnbull, *An Exposition upon the XV. Psalme* (1592), D3v.

[81] There is now a substantial literature on the Paul's Cross jeremiad, beginning with Michael McGiffert, 'God's controversy with Jacobean England', *American Historical Review*, 88 (1983), pp. 1151–76; and continued by Patrick Collinson, 'Biblical rhetoric: the English nation and national sentiment in the prophetic mode', in Claire McEachern and Debora Shuger, eds., *Religion and Culture in Renaissance England* (Cambridge, 1997), pp. 15–45; Alexandra Walsham, '"Englands warning by Israel": Paul's Cross prophecy', in *Providence in Early Modern England* (Oxford, 1999), pp. 281–325; Mary Morrissey, 'Elect nations and prophetic preaching: types and examples in the Paul's Cross jeremiad', in Ferrell and McCullough, eds., *The English Sermon Revised*, pp. 43–58; and Peter Lake and Michael Questier, *The Antichrist's Lewd Hat: Protestants, Papists and Players in Post-Reformation England* (New Haven and London, 2002), pp. 335–76.

[82] McGiffert, 'God's controversy', p. 1151; see *American Historical Review*, 89 (1984), pp. 1217–18 for McGiffert's partial retraction of this claim. Henoch Clapham. *A description of new Jerusalem* (1601), G3r. Richard Stock, *A Sermon Preached at Paules Crosse* (1609), A6v, B7v.

But while preachers at the Cross addressed their sermons to 'London' as a single entity, they often turned to the mayor and aldermen to provide a clearer focus for their exhortations. This was made easier by the fact that many of the images and metaphors conventionally applied to London as the head of the body (to which, in the words of one sermon, 'all other places are but members') could also be applied to the Lord Mayor as head of the body politic.[83] For example, the exemplary status of London as the capital of England, giving 'instruction and light' to 'all the towns and villages about . . . like a becon which standeth upon a hill, and is seen over all the country', could easily be transferred to the Lord Mayor, who was, in the words of Anthony Munday's pageant for the Lord Mayor's show in 1618, 'mounted like a *Beacon* on an Hill, to flame forth brightly, and not to burne dimly'.[84] Similarly, exhortations to 'London' to repent and reform could easily be turned into exhortations to the Lord Mayor to initiate a campaign of moral reformation on London's behalf, on the grounds that the mayor was 'charged with the whole city' and had a duty 'to reforme them that will not reforme themselves'.[85] Roger Ley voiced the unspoken assumption behind many Paul's Cross sermons when he declared in 1622 that 'sermons delivered in that audience, are principally for the governours of this Honourable Citie'.[86] Preachers may have called for a collective act of repentance and reformation by the whole city, but what they expected was a magisterial reformation imposed from above.

Paul's Cross preachers prided themselves on their independence, and on their power to speak plainly and fearlessly 'as haply when there is great cause to reprove the Magistrate and Governors of some remissenesse in their duties, that they suffer sinne and sinners, as Idolaters, Adulterers, Drunkards, Swearers, Prophaners of the Sabbaths, and the like, to goe unpunished'.[87] As we shall see later, this was not an empty boast; yet in practice, such criticism was limited by the fact that ministers and magistrates were in broad agreement on the social problems of the City and the measures necessary to alleviate them. Unusually, Christopher Hooke's

---

[83] John Lawrence, *A Golden Trumpet* (1624), F3v.
[84] Henry Smith, quoted by Lawrence Manley, *Literature and Culture in Early Modern London* (Cambridge, 1995), p. 309; Anthony Munday, *Pageants and Entertainments*, ed. David M. Bergeron (New York, 1985), p. 129.
[85] William Holbrooke, *Loves Complaint, for Want of Entertainment* (1610), G4v; Christopher Hooke, *A Sermon Preached in Paules Church in London* (1603), C2v.
[86] Roger Ley, *The Bruising of the Serpents Head* (1622), A2v. A Paul's Cross sermon of 1616 was 'chiefly applyed to the Magistrates of this city, before whom it was preached': Charles Richardson, *A Sermon Concerning the Punishing of Malefactors* (1616), A2r.
[87] Radford Mavericke, *The Practice of Repentance, or a Sermon Preached at Pauls Crosse* (1617), E3r.

sermon of 1603 recognised the existence of able-bodied poor who were unable to find employment, 'none or litle worke, as they say, stirring', and made the enlightened proposal that a relief fund ('a banke for the poore') should be established to cover the shortfall in poor relief, with the wealthiest citizens voluntarily contributing a proportion of their disposable capital. Most City preachers, however, simply accepted the conventional distinction between the impotent and the able-bodied poor – a distinction which, as Ian Archer has shown, also governed the allocation of poor relief – and assumed that the latter were too idle to work. 'Althoughe we can not pitty them too muche that are impotent, and truly poore and needy indeed', explained Peter Lily, rector of St Nicholas Olave, 'so can we not speake too muche against idle, and vagabond rogues that deserve rather to be punished then relieved, wherof this kingdome, and particulerly this parte therof, (to witt) about this Citty of London, doth swarme, and is full.'[88]

Underlying these harsh social prescriptions was a growing sense of alarm at the threat to social stability represented by 'the infinite number of Poore, swarming in the streets', and by the 'rude, heathenish and ignorant' population of 'the suburbs of London and the adjacent places thereabouts'.[89] Paul's Cross sermons reveal a longing for a London that was enclosed, self-contained and, like the Psalmist's vision of Jerusalem, a city at unity in itself rather than an uncontrollable urban sprawl. John Dove suggested that the City authorities should keep a register of all strangers entering London, while William Holbrooke advised the Lord Mayor to follow the example of Nehemiah: 'Set a man at every Gate of the Citie, and let the Gates be shut before the Sabbath, and not opened untill the Sabbath bee ended.' Francis Marbury feared that in London – as in other towns 'where it is more easier to take a true survey than in this' – there were enough 'penurious and idle male-contents everie night couching, to expell all the substantiall inhabitants of the towne out of their houses before morning. For the well and civilly disposed in a common wealth are but an handfull to those that are stray-goods and of ill behaviour.'[90] Again, this chimed in perfectly with the concerns of the

---

[88] Christopher Hooke, *A Sermon Preached in Paules Church* (1603); Peter Lily, sermon on John 9: 2–7: BL Egerton MS 2877, f. 59; John Dove, 'A sermon preached at St Paules Crosse': Folger Library, Washington, DC, V.a.251. On the distinction between the impotent and idle poor, as applied to the distribution of poor relief, see Ian Archer, *The Pursuit of Stability: Social Relations in Elizabethan London* (Cambridge, 1991), p. 183.

[89] Thomas Myriell, *The Christians Comfort. In a Sermon Appointed for the Crosse, but Preached in S. Pauls Church on Candlemas day* (1623), H4v; Walter Bridges, *Division Divided* (1646), H1v.

[90] Dove, 'A sermon preached at St Paules Crosse'; Holbrooke, *Loves Complaint*, G4v; Francis Marbury, *A Sermon Preached at Pauls Crosse* (1602), F1r.

aldermen, who, in the words of Peter Clark and Paul Slack, were 'terrified lest by enlarging civic jurisdiction they weaken an oligarchy erected on the tight circle of City gild and ward elections' and therefore resisted all pressure to extend their authority to the suburban out-parishes beyond the medieval city limits.[91]

William Pemberton's sermon on 1 Timothy 6: 6 ('But godliness with contentment is great gain') is a particularly telling example of the way that Paul's Cross preachers tended to copy the attitudes and aspirations of the mercantile élite. It consists of an extended analogy between the merchant's calling and the Christian's duty, in which the church militant is compared to 'a great Citie, and a place of great *Trafique* and *Merchandize*: all the *Citizens* whereof having received, from the Lord, their number of *talents*, are become *Merchants*, or traders, in one kinde or other'.[92] Pemberton was at pains to stress that, in one sense, Christian merchandise was an inversion of civil merchandise, in that it attached little importance to worldly gain and taught its followers 'to content themselves with the least increase in their outward condition'. Yet he also perceived a connection between the two, in that both types of merchandise rewarded those who were 'busie at their worke' while penalising the idle, and were both based on an underlying profit motive. 'Desire new profits, seeke for better gaines', Pemberton exhorted his hearers, 'and give all diligence hereunto. For ... this gaine comes not in without good indeavour.' There could hardly be a better illustration of the way that many Paul's Cross preachers had internalised the values of the ruling élite, to the point where their ability to speak meaningfully to the poorer members of their audience, or to integrate rich and poor into a single social body, was severely compromised.

Should we conclude, then, that Paul's Cross sermons simply flattered the mayor and aldermen by telling them what they wanted to hear? This is certainly the conclusion reached by several distinguished scholars of early modern London. Michael Berlin, for example, has argued that civic ceremony in London emphasised 'civic honour and pecuniary worth' to the detriment of social integration – largely, he suggests, because of 'the early dominance of the mercantile élite in London', which 'mitigated the need felt in other towns to perform ceremonies which publicly integrated the various parts of the whole'. Similarly, Laurence Manley finds that 'the tonal

---

[91] Peter Clark and Paul Slack, eds., *Crisis and Order in English Towns 1500–1700* (London, 1972), p. 37. On London as Jerusalem, with particular reference to the image of the 'city at unity in itself', see Patrick Collinson, *The Birthpangs of Protestant England* (1988), pp. 28–30.
[92] William Pemberton, *The Godly Merchant, or the Great Gaine. A Sermon Preached at Paules-Crosse* (1613).

register of city preaching was typically high and narrow, seldom including the sort of derisory or sceptical tones that would question or deconstruct the social frame within which preaching was conducted', so that preachers were better able to criticise deviants from the social norm – dishonest tradesmen, rack-renting landlords and the like – than to challenge the social norm itself in the way that secular moralists such as Lodge, Greene and Nashe were able to do through the medium of the prose pamphlet.[93] Perhaps so: but while the public ritual of the Paul's Cross sermons was carefully designed to present a façade of seamless unity and concord between magistracy and ministry, the full picture is considerably more complex.

The Paul's Cross sermons of the early seventeenth century were in fact a classic example of invented tradition. The rhetorical continuity with pre-Reformation sermons such as Thomas Wimbledon's may have given the impression of an institution that had existed, in the words of Stow's *Survey of London*, 'time out of mind', but the ostentatious patronage of the sermons by the Lord Mayor and aldermen, which so impressed foreign visitors like Thomas Platter, was something new. Until the 1590s the sermons were severely underfunded; and when Bishop Aylmer tried to establish a fund to cover the expenses of visiting preachers, he was comprehensively snubbed by the City authorities. Aylmer complained that of those invited to preach at the Cross, scarcely 'twoe amongst tenne' agreed to come, a refusal rate which his chaplain William Fisher attributed to the 'greate coste and charge' of board and lodging in the City, 'which cannot stand with their poore and small abilitye'.[94] A succession of Paul's Cross preachers, recruited by Aylmer to support his appeal, put the blame on the tightfisted attitude of the City fathers. 'Your benevolence and liberality is much decreased', Andrew Willet told his audience bluntly; and John Jegon declared that 'after 20 publique motions in this place made to procure a small pension for yonge preachers charges that are called hither', nothing had been done.[95] Fisher claimed that as little as a pound a week would be sufficient to place the Paul's Cross sermons on a secure financial footing, adding sarcastically: 'I am not the first that hathe moved this sute, but you may be the first that ever tendered it, or provided for it.'

[93] Michael Berlin, 'Civic ceremony in early modern London', *Urban History Yearbook* (Cambridge, 1986), p. 20; Manley, *Literature and Culture*, p. 310.

[94] H. G. Owen, 'The London parish clergy in the reign of Elizabeth I' (unpublished PhD thesis, University of London, 1957), pp. 193–201.

[95] Andrew Willet, *A Fruitfull and Godly Sermon, Preached at Paules Crosse before the Honourable Audience and Assemblie There* (1592), C3r; Sermon by 'Dr Gygin' (John Jegon?) on 1 Timothy 5: 17–20: Lambeth Palace Library, London, MS 113, f. 38r.

Why were the City authorities so reluctant to support the Paul's Cross sermons? The answer is not hard to find. Fresh in the memories of the mayor and aldermen were several recent occasions when the Paul's Cross sermon had become a focus for opposition to the City élite. In September 1580, one Thomas Millington was imprisoned for having presented 'a libell to the preacher at Paules Crosse againste the magistrates of the Cyttye'; and this may not have been an isolated incident, since the Paul's Cross preacher seems to have been popularly regarded as 'the poor man's lawyer', that is, an advocate on behalf of the poorer inhabitants of London, and a spokesman for the redress of grievances.[96] The following year, Aylmer's own chaplain Laurence Deios was alleged to have 'publicly defamed [the aldermen] to their faces' and declared that 'if the appointing of preachers were committed to them, they would appoint such as would defend usury, the family of love, and puritanism', a galling reminder to the aldermen that they had no control over the appointment of preachers at the Cross. Relations between Aylmer and the City authorities hit a new low in 1582, when Aylmer delivered a stinging rebuke to the Lord Mayor, Sir James Harvey, warning him that if he did not show proper respect to the London clergy, 'I must then tell you your duty out of my chair, which is the pulpit at Paul's Cross, where you must sit, not as a judge to control, but as a scholar to learn'.[97] Four years later, in March 1586, the London minister George Close – the same George Close whom we encountered earlier as the preacher of an inflammatory sermon at Exeter assizes – delivered a sermon at Paul's Cross in which he accused the Lord Mayor, Sir Wolstan Dixie, of fraud and partiality in the administration of justice. Ordered to preach a recantation sermon, Close seized the opportunity to attack the Lord Mayor again, repeating his earlier charges.[98]

How far these sermons presented a genuine threat to the authority of the mayor and aldermen is more debatable. Writing in 1972, Peter Clark and Paul Slack argued that early modern London was a dangerously unstable society, 'notorious for popular unrest' and further weakened by the closed and unrepresentative nature of the ruling oligarchy. More recently, how-ever, other historians have argued persuasively that London was essentially a stable society, ruled by an open élite receptive to upward social mobility

---

[96] Corporation of London Record Office, Rep. 20, f. 104 (6 September 1580). A similar incident occurred in 1629, when a libel addressed to the king, 'wrapped up in another paper', was deposited at the Cross before the Sunday morning sermon: PRO, SP 16/142/102 (calendared in *CSPD 1628–29*, p. 552).

[97] Aylmer to Harvey, 1 March 1581–2: *Memoirs of the Life and Times of Sir Christopher Hatton*, ed. Sir Harris Nicholas (1847), pp. 236–8.

[98] W. H. and H. C. Overall, *Analytical Index to the Remembrancia* (1878), p. 366; MacLure, *Register of Sermons Preached at Paul's Cross*, pp. 61, 64.

and responsive to social and economic problems, so that even the inflationary pressures of the 1590s did not seriously threaten the aldermen's authority.[99] The failure of the Essex rebellion in 1601 is a case in point: Essex seems to have planned to use the Paul's Cross sermon as an opportunity to muster his supporters, yet, in the event, relatively few Londoners rallied to his cause. What is undeniable, however, is that – whether or not their anxieties were well founded – the governors of Elizabethan London, like other urban élites in the same period, were deeply preoccupied with the threat of social disorder. This is apparent in the conflicting priorities of the diocesan and civic authorities on the Sunday after the Essex rebellion: Bancroft, as Bishop of London, had immediately grasped the value of the Paul's Cross sermon as a means of disseminating the official version of events, but the automatic response of the mayor and aldermen was to impose a curfew on all adult males (thus limiting the audience at Paul's Cross to women) and to station armed guards 'all the day in St Paules churche yarde where the preaching place is' to prevent any disturbance.[100]

In the course of the next few years, however, the attitude of the City fathers underwent a remarkable change. By 1609 'a very fit and convenient chamber, with lodging' had been provided for visiting preachers 'at the cost of the Citie', and the sermons had come to be regarded as primarily civic occasions, even though the City authorities still played no part in the appointment of preachers.[101] Over the next two decades, the Paul's Cross sermons became steadily more prestigious and important (reflected in the increasing number of sermons that found their way into print), and, on several occasions, provided the setting for a public display of amity between the City and the government. In April 1619, when Bishop John King preached at Paul's Cross, the newswriter John Chamberlain noted that 'the audience was the greatest that I remember to have seene there, for besides the Lord Maior and Aldermen, with all the rest of the citie-companies in theyre best aray, there were almost all the counsaile and great men about this towne'.[102] In March

---

[99] Clark and Slack, eds., *Crisis and Order*, pp. 35–40; compare, e.g., Steve Rappaport, *Worlds within Worlds: Structures of Life in Sixteenth-Century London* (Cambridge, 1989), pp. 1–20, and Archer, *Pursuit of Stability*, pp. 13–14.

[100] Hunt, 'Tuning the pulpits', pp. 97–8.

[101] The lodgings seem to have been provided between 1607 and 1609: see Robert Wilkinson, *The Poore-mans Preacher* (1607), B6v, and George Webbe, *Gods Controversie with England* (1609), D1r. On provision for preachers at the Cross, see also Susan Wabuda, 'Shunamites and nurses of the English Reformation: the activities of Mary Glover, niece of Hugh Latimer', in W. J. Sheils and D. Wood, eds., *Women in the Church* (Studies in Church History, vol. xxvii, 1990), p. 338 n.10.

[102] John Chamberlain to Dudley Carleton, 17 April 1619, in Chamberlain, *Letters*, vol. ii, pp. 229–30.

1620 King James himself came to Paul's Cross to hear Bishop King inaugurate a public appeal for the restoration of St Paul's Cathedral, the first time that the monarch had attended a sermon at the Cross since Queen Elizabeth's visit in 1588 to mark the defeat of the Spanish Armada.[103] Somewhat belatedly, the City authorities had woken up to the enormous propaganda value of the Paul's Cross sermons, both as a public statement of their religious credentials and as a way of cementing good relations with the other agencies of government.

Benefiting as they did from the patronage of the mayor and aldermen, it became increasingly difficult for preachers at the Cross to maintain their independence. To be sure, there were occasional exceptions, demonstrating the power of the pulpit as a focal point for criticism of the City government. In March 1603, Richard Stock, lecturer at St Augustine's Watling Street, mounted an extraordinary attack on the aldermen and common councillors for increasing the burden of taxation on the poor. Modern research has confirmed that in relative if not in absolute terms, the tax burden on the poorer sections of society was increasing, partly because, in Ian Archer's words, 'a higher proportion of taxation was being levied in the form of fifteenths, which were much wider in their incidence than the subsidy'.[104] One London minister, Thomas Sorocold, rector of St Michael in the Poultry, had already advised his parishioners not to pay the fifteenth until the assessment had been revised; and Stock voiced the general resentment when he accused the aldermen of injustice in the assessment of fifteenths:

I have lived here some few yeares amongst you, and every yeare, I had almost said every Quarter, I have heard an exceeding outcry and pittifull complaining of the poorer sort, that they are much oppressed of the rich of this citty, that is in plaine termes, of the Common Counsell. For no chardges almost happen in the Citty, but they say the burthen of them is upon their backs. The rich and men in place, are like the scribes and Pharisees who did binde heavy burthens for other mens backs, but hardly touche it themselves with their little finger. All or most chardges are raysed by your fifteenes, wherein the burthen is more heavy upon a mechanicall and handicraft poore man than upon an Alderman: Understand me proportion for proportion: they of their poverty and these of their plenty. I perswade my selfe there is hardly a man of the Bench or of the Common Counsell, which hath not heard by their collectors at one tyme or other of the lamentable complaintes, the teares and the sighs of the poore in most parishes: many of them living of or by the Almes of

---

[103] John King, *A Sermon at Paules Crosse, on Behalfe of Paules Church* (1620); Sir Robert Somerville, 'St Paul's Cathedral repairs: the propaganda of Henry Farley', *London Topographical Record*, 25 (1985), pp. 163–75; Chamberlain to Carleton, 1 April 1620, in Chamberlain, *Letters*, vol. II, p. 299.
[104] Archer, *Pursuit of Stability*, p. 13.

the parish, that pay to a fifteenth, I say in their proportion more then an Alderman or rich Commoner.[105]

However, such inflammatory rhetoric became increasingly rare, as the City authorities gradually extended their control of the Paul's Cross sermons so as to discourage any public criticism of their policies. When John Everard criticised the Court of Orphans in a sermon at the Cross in 1618, he was forced to apologise to the Lord Mayor, declaring not only that his accusations were false, but that even if they had been true 'yet both in respect of the tyme, place, and persons, ther had wanted discretion and Modestye in me, in soe violent, bitter and precipitate a Manner to laye open the obliqueties of Maiestrates before a popular Auditorye'.[106] The result was that criticism of the magistrates became less overt and, as with assize preaching, tended to be expressed not through the naming and shaming of particular individuals but through the generic themes and conventions of the sermon. The most familiar theme of Paul's Cross preaching was, of course, the recital of London's sins – described by one preacher as 'the usual subject of Sermons made in this place' – followed by an exhortation to repentance and reformation.[107] Thomas Jackson's sermon at the Cross in January 1609 may serve as a representative sample of the genre. 'Alas, alas', he lamented, 'the sinnes of Atheisme, Idolatry, Blasphemy, Contempt of Gods Worship, Prophanation of Gods Sabbaths, Murther, Whoredom, Drunkennesse, Pryde, Covetousnesse, Perjurie, &c. did never more abound … If these things be not taken away, by Word, or Sword, or both; he that hath exalted London to heaven, will bring her downe to hell.'[108] These attacks on sin were such a familiar aspect of Paul's Cross sermons that scholars have often taken them for granted. One historian has described them, rather sneeringly, as 'highly stylised passages of denunciatory rant', while another has suggested that early modern audiences may actually have taken pleasure in hearing their sins anatomised in this way, 'much as their modern counterparts might relish a horror film or read an enthralling cliffhanger or thriller'.[109] This emphasis on the clichéd and

---

[105] 'A true coppy of a speeche uttered at Paules crosse the 13 of March 1602 [=1602/3] by Richard Stock minister, whereat the right honorable the Lord Maior, and some of the Aldermen of the city are offended', Salisbury (Cecil) papers, vol. XCII no. 24 (calendared in *HMC Salisbury*, vol. XII, p. 672), consulted on microfilm, BL M485/18. For Sorocold's opposition to the fifteenth, see PRO, STAC 5/A44/10.

[106] PRO, SP 14/95/61(calendared in *CSPD 1611–18*, p. 519).

[107] William Proctor, *The Watchman Warning* (1625), C4r.

[108] Thomas Jackson, *Londons New-Yeeres Gift.. A godly sermon preached at Pauls-Crosse (1609)*, E3v (p. 15). Thomas Jackson, *Londons New-Yeeres Gift.. A godly sermon preached at Pauls-Crosse* (1609), E3v (p. 15).

[109] Peter Lake, in Lake and Questier, *The Antichrist's Lewd Hat*, p. 376; Walsham, *Providence*, p. 324.

stereotypical nature of the Paul's Cross sermons, while not entirely misplaced, fails to appreciate that they can also be read as a coded critique of the mayor and aldermen for turning a blind eye to the moral failings of the City.

The sensitivity of the City authorities to such language is shown in their response to Thomas Nashe's *Christs Teares over Ierusalem* (1593), a moralising pamphlet which borrowed many of the tropes of the Paul's Cross jeremiad. Nashe attacked the sins of London in no uncertain terms – describing the City as 'the seeded Garden of sinne, the Sea that sucks in all the scummy chanels of the Realme' – and hinted darkly that many of the 'chiefest' inhabitants were making illicit profits by lending out orphans' money at interest and by accepting bribes from the recipients of charitable relief. Such 'deceite', Nashe warned, would call down divine punishment on the whole City: 'The Lord thinketh it were as good for him to kill with the Plague, as to let them kill with oppression.' These reflections (which were apparently drawn to the attention of the Lord Mayor by Nashe's old enemy Gabriel Harvey) were enough to earn Nashe a brief spell in prison; and the pamphlet was reissued the following year with a revised text, considerably less confrontational in tone, in which Nashe exhorted London to set a good example to the rest of England – 'London, thou art the welhead of the land, and therefore it behoveth thee to send foorth wholsome springs' – while taking care to exempt the City authorities from his criticisms. 'Many good men, many good magistrats are there in this City, diverse godly and wise counsellers hath she to provide for her peace, them no part of any reproofe of mine concerneth, how ever it may be otherwise thought.'[110]

Many of Nashe's criticisms were echoed, in more muted language, in the sermons preached at the Cross over the following decades. In August 1606, Dudley Carleton attended a sermon at Paul's Cross 'where the preacher fell very foul upon the mayor and aldermen, noting some of them in particular by way of rebuke of the sins of the city'.[111] The sermon that Carleton heard does not survive, but may have resembled the sermon preached three months later, in November 1606, by that scourge of the City magistracy, Richard Stock. On this occasion, Stock was careful not to criticise the aldermen in such direct terms as he had done in 1603, but he still took the opportunity to uphold the right – indeed, the duty – of preachers to admonish their social superiors, arguing that one of the causes of Israel's corruption, as shown in

[110] Thomas Nashe, *Workes*, ed. R. B. McKerrow (Oxford, 1958), vol. II, pp. 158–9. See also K. Duncan-Jones, '*Christs Teares*, Nashe's "Forsaken extremities"', *Review of English Studies*, n.s. 49 (1998), pp. 167–80.
[111] Dudley Carleton to John Chamberlain, 20 August 1606, in *Dudley Carleton to John Chamberlain 1603–1624: Jacobean Letters*, ed. Maurice Lee (New Brunswick, 1972), p. 91.

his text (Isa 9: 15), was the rise of false prophets whose only aim was to win 'the applause and liking of the people' and 'favour and countenance with the magistrate' by flattering them rather than denouncing their sins. He then went on to list some of London's principal sins, including pride, idleness, luxury, lack of charity towards the poor and insufficient zeal in executing the penal laws against Catholics, and made it clear that he held the mayor and aldermen personally responsible for these failings. 'God hath put the sword into your hands, to reforme things amisse, and withstand corruptions', he reminded them. 'If you doe it, well and good . . . But if you doe it not, you shall returne with dishonour to your long homes.'[112]

This is not to suggest that Paul's Cross preachers were invariably antagonistic to the magistracy, or that Londoners came to the Cross each week expecting to hear their social superiors taken to task. Some aldermen were undoubtedly sympathetic to the demands for moral reformation, and preachers were perfectly willing to give credit where credit was due. Charles Richardson, preaching at the Cross in 1616, congratulated the mayor and aldermen for their 'great paines' in cracking down on taverns and alehouses that remained open on the sabbath, while William Proctor, a few years later, applauded their piety in enforcing the laws against 'common swearing'.[113] Even when moral regulation was not effective, preachers recognised that the mayor and aldermen were not always to blame. John White, preaching at the Cross in 1615, attacked the sins of drunkenness and swearing but acknowledged that they 'could not so easily be reformed'.[114] Yet the preachers' ability to embarrass the magistracy, especially when they turned their attention to the negligent enforcement of the law, should not be underestimated. 'Have we no law against rash swearing?' demanded John Jones. 'God bee thanked, we have: but where's the execution? Have we no law against Sabbath breaking? Yes, against that too. Yet is it openly prophaned.' Jones had no doubt where the fault lay. 'Mistake me not, I aime at no particular person . . . Nor do I lay the fault upon Magistrats in generall, that all sorts of sinnes are so rife amongst us. Yet (to speake truth) when I consider how powerfully the Ministers of this land, especially they of this City, do labour to beate downe sinne, I begin to thinke there is some want of courage or diligence in the Magistrate.'[115]

[112] Stock, *Sermon Preached at Paules Crosse*. B4v (p. 24).
[113] Charles Richardson, *A Sermon Concerning the Punishing of Malefactors* (1616), C3v (p. 14). Proctor, *The Watchman Warning*, C4r. On the measures taken by the City government to control theatres, alehouses and brothels, see Robert Ashton, 'Popular entertainment and social control in late Elizabethan and early Stuart London', *London Journal*, 9: 1 (1983), pp. 3–19.
[114] John White, *Two Sermons* (1615), D4v.
[115] John Jones, *London Looking Back to Ierusalem* (1633), F2r–2v (pp. 43–4).

This type of criticism became particularly insistent at moments of crisis, when the providentialism of the Paul's Cross jeremiad came into its own. The plague epidemic of 1625–6, in particular, unleashed a flood of accusatory sermons, not just at the Cross but from other London pulpits, identifying the plague as God's long-expected judgement on the negligence of the City magistrates. Henry Roborough, lecturer at St Leonard's Eastcheap, declared that when the magistrate 'is not a terrour unto the wicked' or 'shall connive and winke at impiety', then it was time for God 'to send some extraordinary Judge or Executioner' such as the plague. Josias Shute, rector of St Mary Woolnoth, lamented that the alliance of magistracy and ministry had broken down: the preachers had done their part in drawing attention to the sins of London, but the magistrates had not taken action. 'Wee Ministers can goe no further than the sword of the Word gives us leave; but if when we have started the prey, the Magistrate will not pursue it, judge whose fault it is if sinne abounds: we the Ministers of God complaine of blasphemers, of uncleane persons, and places where they haunt: we complaine of unlawfull gaming, and recreations: if the Magistrate followed this by his sword, it could not be that men should be so wicked as they are.' These were not merely empty gestures: during the Elizabethan period, the embarrassing spectacle of 'the preachers dayly cryeing against the Lord Maior and his bretheren' had been extremely effective in forcing the aldermen to take emergency measures such as closing the playhouses.[116]

But it was when preachers got on to the subject of usury that their critique of the City élite became most pointed. This was an issue where the aldermen were acutely sensitive to criticism: it was, after all, the accusation of usury, in connection with the administration of the Court of Orphans, that had got Nashe into trouble in 1593 and was to get Everard into trouble in 1618. But while the aldermen were able to take action against personal allegations of financial impropriety, they had no redress against the more general and unspecific complaints that formed the stock-in-trade of the Paul's Cross preachers. Richard Turnbull declared that 'many of our chiefest citizens, and some of the guides and governours of this famous Citie of London' were guilty of the sin of usury, which he feared would bring ruin on the whole land. 'Doe not you put your money to Usurie?', demanded William Holbrooke, addressing the aldermen at Paul's Cross. 'Yes, let that epethite (though commonly spoken, yet peculiar appropriated to you) Usurie the

---

[116] Henry Roborough, *Balme from Gilead, to cure all Diseases* (1626), B5v (p. 10). Josias Shute, *Divine Cordials: Delivered in Ten Sermons* (1644), R3r (p. 125). Archer, *Pursuit of Stability*, p. 53 (corrected against the original in BL, Lansdowne MS 20).

Aldermans Trade, witnesse this.'[117] These remarks were entirely consistent with Cornelius Burges's advice to preachers to 'fall upon the reproofe of particular sinnes sometimes committed by some men in that Calling, and call it the Magistrates sin, not naming any person, or applying it to any present', rather than engaging in risky personal abuse. But it seems likely that Turnbull, Holbrooke and other preachers expected at least some members of their audience to read between the lines of these generalised attacks on usury, and to infer more specific criticisms which could not be stated openly.

From one perspective, the clerical condemnation of usury appears hopelessly impractical, stemming from an idealised and deeply conservative view of the social order that bore little resemblance to reality.[118] Preachers might have chosen to follow the example of other contemporary economic theorists in drawing a distinction between 'biting' and acceptable forms of usury, and use this to justify moneylending at moderate rates of interest. Instead, they persisted in condemning all forms of moneylending as wholly unacceptable, regardless of the rate of interest: 'all usurie signifieth byting', declared Henry Smith, 'to shewe that all usurie is unlawfull'.[119] Moreover, their attack on usury was based on some very traditional assumptions about the social order, and on the belief that money was somehow 'unnatural': in the words of Roger Fenton, 'the Gentleman liveth upon his rents; the poore labourer upon the sweate of his browes; the Merchant and Tradesman upon their adventures, skill, and industrie; the Husbandman and Grasier upon the increase of the earth, and breed of cattell', but the usurer lived on nothing except money, 'a thing of it selfe meerely artificiall' and of no intrinsic use.[120] Such arguments took no account of the way that borrowing and lending helped to promote economic activity (and also, remarkably, ignored the fact that many parish lectureships were themselves funded by interest payments). In this sense, Peter Lake is quite right to regard the attack on usury as largely symbolic in nature, with the usurer – alongside other stock figures such as the whore, the Papist and the drunkard – as a scapegoat, or negative exemplar, in whom the natural moral and social order had been inverted.

Yet the attack on usury was not just symbolic: as we have seen, it also served a very practical purpose, in enabling preachers to criticise the City magistrates in a suitably indirect manner. And it was effective precisely

[117] Turnbull, *Exposition upon the* XV. *Psalme*, G7v. Holbrooke, *Loves Complaint*, E2r.
[118] See, e.g., MacLure, *Paul's Cross Sermons*, p. 122.
[119] Henry Smith, *The Examination of Usurie, in Two Sermons* (1591; STC 22660), A6v. For an example of more progressive theories justifying money lending at moderate interest rates, see Michael MacDonald, 'An early seventeenth-century defence of usury', *Historical Research*, 60 (1987), pp. 353–60.
[120] Roger Fenton, *A Treatise of Usurie* (1612), C3r, O3r.

because it relied on accepted commonplaces which could not easily be called into question. London was depicted as a tight-knit community in which rich and poor were mutually dependent, the rich contributing their charity and the poor their labour. 'You are magistrates for the good of them that are under you', Richard Stock reminded the mayor and aldermen in 1603. 'Wherefore hath God made you rich and them poore, but that they should beare the service and you the charges?'[121] Usury had no place in this scheme because it was felt to undermine charity. Fenton maintained that the only acceptable form of money-lending was an interest-free loan, for 'it is the nature of loane to be free ... lending is a worke of mercie to the poore, of kindnesse to they neighbour; and therefore is ever free', and lending money at interest perverted this act of charity by 'turning it into an act of selfelove'.[122] That these commonplaces were not entirely accurate – that the rich might contribute to economic growth as much by lending money as by bestowing charity; just as the poor might be unem-ployed through a shortage of work rather than through their own idleness – did not alter the fact that they were a powerful means of influencing the policies and behaviour of the magistrates, not least because the magistrates themselves used the same paternalistic rhetoric to justify their actions.[123]

   It is clear that usury was, so to speak, a synecdoche for a variety of other issues and concerns: but there is still room for disagreement over precisely what preachers meant by it, and what they hoped to achieve by attacking it. Peter Lake would have us believe that the attack on usury was a symptom of a deep-seated cultural anxiety. Preachers offered their audi-ences an idealised vision of London in which deviants were relegated to the margins of civic society, but were uncomfortably aware that usury, far from being marginal, was actually central to the economic life and pros-perity of the city, and thus denounced it with increasing fervour and indignation. The reason why preachers were so disturbed by usury, in other words, was because it cut across the comfortable binary opposition between godly respectability and sinful disorder.[124] Yet the attack on usury was considerably more purposeful and self-conscious than this account

---

[121] Stock, 'A true coppy of a speeche'.

[122] Fenton, *Treatise of Usurie*, P2r, Q1v. For a similar passage in the sermons of another City preacher, see Edward Elton, *Gods Holy Mind* (1625), X3v.

[123] Archer, *Pursuit of Stability*, pp. 54–7. Archer draws attention to the fact that élite paternalism was 'most often mobilised in the support of widows and orphans' (p. 56), which shows why the aldermen were so sensitive to attacks on the administration of the Court of Orphans.

[124] This argument is elaborated in Lake and Questier, *The Antichrist's Lewd Hat*, esp. pp. 462–79, but is perhaps most clearly set out in Peter Lake, 'From Troynouvant to Heliogabulus's Rome and back: "order" and its others in the London of John Stow', in J. F. Merritt, ed., *Imagining Early Modern London: Perceptions Portrayals of the City from Stow to Strype* (Cambridge, 2001), pp. 217–49.

would imply. It operated, I would suggest, as a kind of code or shorthand for the perceived failure of the mayor and aldermen to live up to their public image as godly magistrates – their failure to punish drunkenness, swearing and the other vices of the City with sufficient severity; their failure to execute the penal laws against Catholics; their failure to perform their charitable obligations towards the poor – enabling preachers to register dissatisfaction with the magistracy, but ensuring that this dissatisfaction was mediated through a set of familiar and uncontroversial commonplaces, thus avoiding the risk of scandal or sedition.

It is also arguable that these commonplaces served to bridge the gap between puritan preachers and a more religiously conservative élite. There is no doubt that the City magistrates were sympathetic to some aspects of the puritan worldview: as Ian Archer has shown, many of the Elizabethan élite were willing to employ 'characteristically puritan rhetoric' in arguing that any decrease in preaching would lead to the breakdown of the social order, to the point where (in the words of a petition of 1584) the magistrate would no longer be obeyed by the people, 'neither the husband rightlie reverenced of his wife, the parents of their children, the maisters of their servaunts, nor charitie rightlie kepte amongst neighbours'.[125] Similarly, Lake has shown that the City authorities could, on occasion, employ the same language of 'starkly binary opposition' between virtue and vice, and the same providentialist view of plague and sudden death as divine punishments for sin, that loomed so large in the Paul's Cross sermons.[126] Yet, on the whole, the sermons at the Cross present the not-expected picture of a godly clergy trying to goad a reluctant magistracy into action; and the glaring ambiguity to which so many commentators have drawn attention – London praised as the archetype of godly cities, while simultaneously denounced as a cesspool of iniquity – should not be taken as a sign of confusion, but as an accurate reflection of their aspirations and frustrations. It was an ambiguity which preachers were able to exploit, with a skilful blend of criticism and compliment, in order to make their sermons an effective instrument of persuasion.

## CONCLUSION

It should by now be clear that preachers addressing those in authority – whether the judges at assizes, or the mayor and aldermen at Paul's Cross – had

---

[125] Albert Peel, ed., *The Seconde Parte of a Register* (Cambridge, 1915), vol. II, pp. 219–20. Archer has found that 'most of the common councillors of the wards in which the petition was circulated' were prepared to subscribe, suggesting a high level of élite support (*The Pursuit of Stability*, p. 46).

[126] Lake and Questier, *The Antichrist's Lewd Hat*, pp. 495–8.

a number of rhetorical strategies for expressing criticism: yet, with a few notable exceptions, scholars have failed to recognise the fact. Just as Nashe's first modern editor treated the controversial passages in *Christs Teares over Ierusalem* as consisting of little more than 'those familiar denunciations which have been the common stock of preachers and moralists from time imme-morial', so historians have described the Paul's Cross sermons as 'intellectually impoverished and almost unbearably repetitious', as a set of rhetorical varia-tions on a single theme ('a hundred new ways to say old things'), or as providing little more than 'a new ideological framework for an immemorial formulaic refrain'.[127] Assize sermons have come in for similar treatment, as 'well-worn platitudes and inoffensive generalisations', or as homilies 'usually of a stereotyped nature, consisting of general and conventional observations on law and order in normal times, and more specific comments on the duty of obedience in times of crisis'.[128] It needs to be asked why these writers have not been more alert to the presence of pulpit criticism, and, in particular, whether – to return to the historiographical issue with which we began – scholars working with a revisionist agenda have failed to go looking for criticism because they have assumed there is none to be found.

There is no doubt that sermons have often been read with an eye to signs of political breakdown that can be slotted into a broader narrative about the origins of the Civil War. Nor can it be doubted that, read in this way, they yield a disappointing harvest. The political theory expressed in most assize sermons, for example, was of a thoroughly conventional kind, perhaps best summed up by the preacher at Newcastle assizes in 1635 who began by remarking that there was no need for him 'to prove the lawfulnes of Kings and Judges' or to show 'that there ought to be a Superiority amongst the Sons of Men' since his audience could be assumed to take these obvious truths for granted.[129] Such evidence of political opposition as does exist has generally been read proleptically, against the background of the approaching Civil War, but with the exact point of departure varying according to the preconceptions of the writer. Indeed, it is remarkable how different writers have managed to draw utterly divergent conclusions from the same body of evidence. According to J. S. Cockburn, assize preaching became more controversial in the decade after 1615, as 'the more radical local clergy reminded the judges of their oath and their mortality, and condemned partiality in the judicial office';

[127] R. B. McKerrow, quoted in Duncan-Jones, '*Christs Teares*', p. 168; Collinson, 'Biblical rhetoric', p. 28; Walsham, *Providence*, p. 284.
[128] Cockburn, *History of English Assizes*, p. 66; J. A. Sharpe, *Crime in Seventeenth-Century England: A County Study* (Cambridge, 1983), p. 22.
[129] Francis Gray, *The Iudges Scripture, or, Gods Charge to Charge-Givers* (1636), A4v.

yet Ann Hughes reaches precisely the opposite conclusion, arguing that assize sermons became more conformist in the 1620s and 1630s, as Puritanism began to lose ground; whereas Kevin Sharpe sees no significant difference between the assize sermons of the 1630s and their Jacobean predecessors.[130]

The problem with these theories, as will readily be apparent, is not so much a problem with revisionism, or with any single school of thought, as with the use and interpretation of sermon evidence in general. These sermons are not barometers of public opinion from which it is possible to detect changes in political pressure.[131] They were preached on particular occasions, and reflect the particular concerns that preachers felt it appropriate to bring to the attention of their listeners. Assize sermons were an opportunity for preachers to express concern about tithe disputes and other threats to the clerical estate (which, *pace* Cockburn, may have led some clergy to cling to the royal prerogative for protection against the common law), while Paul's Cross sermons were an opportunity for preachers to take the mayor and aldermen to task for their failure to institute a moral reformation in London – and it is only when the sermons are placed in these particular contexts that their critical and controversial aspects can be fully perceived. Stephen Gosson, preaching at the Cross in 1598, described sermons as 'haileshot', fired indiscriminately into the congregation in the hope of striking certain targets, 'here a Judge, and there a Magistrate, heere a Nobleman, there a Gentleman, heere a Courtier, there a Countrieman, heere a Lawyer, there a Client'.[132] It was an apt metaphor for the way that preachers spoke generally but expected their doctrines to be applied more specifically, perhaps in ways that would not be apparent to all the members of their audience.

There is a further problem with the way that scholars have tended to use sermon evidence. It can perhaps be most clearly seen in the heavy-handed irony with which Paul's Cross sermons have been described by more than one historian: these preachers do not merely teach or exhort, they 'wail', they 'bellow', they 'thunder'.[133] Inasmuch as Paul's Cross sermons

---

[130] Cockburn, *English Assizes*, p. 231; Ann Hughes, *Politics, Society and Civil War in Warwickshire* (Cambridge, 1987), pp. 68–9; Kevin Sharpe, *The Personal Rule of Charles I* (New Haven and London, 1992), p. 425. For further variations, see Burgess, *Politics of the Ancient Constitution*, p. 188 (assize sermons less political in the 1630s), and Walsham, *Providence*, pp. 292–3 (Paul's Cross sermons more political in the 1620s and 1630s).

[131] Cf. Walsham, *Providence*, p. 293: Paul's Cross 'evolved into an increasingly accurate barometer of the current doctrinal climate and of prevailing ideological trends'.

[132] Gosson, *The Trumpet of Warre*, G6r. This was not entirely disinterested, as Gosson was stressing the random nature of such 'haile-shot' in order to clear himself of the charge of having 'stricken at some great person' in a previous Paul's Cross sermon.

[133] See, e.g., Walsham, *Providence*, p. 291; Lake and Questier, *The Antichrist's Lewd Hat*, p. 341 (and p. 361 for the 'mental world' image).

were highly dramatic oratorical performances, this is fair enough; but it also conveys the impression that the sermons were crude and unsophisticated pieces of rhetoric that can be taken at face value as a transparent window on the 'mental world' of the preachers. Allied to this is the disparaging tone in which historians have discussed the use of pulpit commonplaces. No modern scholar would go quite as far as Millar MacLure, writing of the Paul's Cross sermons in 1958 that 'to call these commonplaces "ideas" is to dignify them out of all conscience', but there is still a tendency to use the term 'commonplace' as synonymous with 'cliché', and even so careful a scholar as Patrick Collinson can speak of the 'familiar commonplace' of the godless multitude, as articulated from the pulpit at Paul's Cross, as merely a figure of speech, 'no doubt valued not at all for its intellectual originality but as we appreciate a virtuoso performance of a familiar piece of music', and bearing only a dubious resemblance to pastoral reality.[134]

It is no longer possible to sustain this view, in the light of a growing body of scholarship showing that commonplaces operated not merely as a collection of familiar quotations but as part of the structure of intellectual discourse, and that the recycling of *loci* and *exempla* did not merely amount to variations on a given theme but was, in the words of one recent commentator, 'an inherently active, discriminating and selective exercise' which left considerable scope for creative development and disagreement.[135] Commonplaces were an indispensable part of early modern preaching, serving both as a means of persuasion (illustrating the preacher's message in a familiar and consensual way that would compel ready assent) and as a means of protection (defending the preacher against any suggestion of teaching new or strange doctrine, and, to borrow a useful phrase first employed by Anthony Milton, providing 'plausible deniability' when a preacher strayed into dangerous territory). That preachers did not need and should not seek to please the 'itching ears' of their auditors by including anything novel or original in their sermons was itself an often-repeated commonplace of early modern preaching. It should not mislead us into supposing that they could not be critical or controversial when they chose.

---

[134] MacLure, *Paul's Cross Sermons*, p. 173; Collinson, 'Biblical rhetoric', p. 31.
[135] Pre-eminently, Ann Moss, *Printed Commonplace-Books and the Structuring of Renaissance Thought* (Oxford, 1996); most recently, Earle Havens, *Commonplace Books* (New Haven, 2001), quotation from p. 8.

CHAPTER 7

# *Reading sermons theologically*

## *Predestination and the pulpit*

The doctrine of predestination was an insistent presence in sixteenth- and seventeenth-century Protestantism. In the words of Richard Muller, it was one of the 'focal points' of Reformed theology.[1] It was the starting point for any discussion of divine providence and causality, and came to be regarded by many Protestant divines as a crucial part of Christian orthodoxy. It was the subject of some of the most intense and heated theological debates of the early modern period, as theologians struggled to explain how divine sovereignty could coexist with human free will, or how a belief in a loving and merciful God could be held together with a belief in a God who predestined men to damnation. And in England, it had extra importance as a way of defining the doctrinal identity of the established Church and its relationship to other forms of Protestantism. In an effort to align the Church of England more closely with the Protestant Reformed Churches, some English divines tried to introduce a stricter definition of predestinarian orthodoxy – most famously in the Lambeth Articles of 1595 – while, conversely, others sought to distance the Church of England from the Calvinist Churches of Holland and Germany by discouraging the preaching and teaching of predestination.[2]

But while accepting that predestination played a leading role in early modern theological debate, historians have found it much harder to accept

[1] Richard A. Muller, *Christ and the Decree: Christology and Predestination in Reformed Theology from Calvin to Perkins* (Durham, NC, 1986).

[2] Out of an extensive literature on these topics, the following are particularly important: Peter Lake, *Moderate Puritans and the Elizabethan Church* (Cambridge, 1982); Nicholas Tyacke, *Anti-Calvinists: The Rise of English Arminianism, c.1590–1640* (Oxford, 1987); Anthony Milton, *Catholic and Reformed: The Roman and Protestant Churches in English Protestant Thought, 1600–1640* (Cambridge, 1995), esp. pp. 412–26; Seán F. Hughes, 'The problem of "Calvinism": English theologies of predestination *c.1580–1630*', in Susan Wabuda and Caroline Litzenberger, eds., *Belief and Practice in Reformation England* (Aldershot, 1998), pp. 229–49; David Como, 'Puritans, predestination and the construction of orthodoxy in early seventeenth-century England', in Peter Lake and Michael Questier, eds., *Conformity and Orthodoxy in the English Church c.1560–1660* (Woodbridge, 2000), pp. 64–87; Tyacke, *Aspects of English Protestantism c.1530–1700* (Manchester, 2001); and Milton, ed., *The British Delegation and the Synod of Dort (1618–1619)* (Church of England Record Society, 2005).

that it might have been a subject of concern to ordinary laypeople, or that it might have played a part in the everyday practice of Christian religion. Some, indeed, have begun to question whether, for all the heat it generated in works of controversial theology, it actually had much impact outside the rarefied academic environment of the universities. Ian Green, for example, argues that the parish clergy were too preoccupied with 'the day-to-day matters of pastoral work among a largely illiterate population' to pay much attention to the finer points of predestinarian doctrine. Their sermons, he suggests, were characterised by a 'loud silence' on the doctrine of predestination, together with an emphasis on more practical matters such as faith and repentance, prayer and the sacraments, 'all of which represented common ground between Calvinists and non-Calvinists'.[3] George Bernard has reached a similar verdict, arguing that predestination had 'little practical relevance' outside 'the world of the universities', least of all in the country parishes of early modern England where 'scholastic predestinarian Calvinism was quite alien to parish life'.[4] And Alexandra Walsham, in her masterly study of providentialism in early modern England, has virtually nothing to say about predestination except for a passing comment that 'at the pastoral level' most Protestant clergy 'seem to have studiously avoided discussing the more arcane aspects of predestinarian theology'. Calvinist teaching on providence, she suggests, reinforced traditional beliefs about God's intervention in human affairs but did little to popularise the doctrine of predestination.[5]

Other historians have argued that predestination was incompatible with preaching and, in the final analysis, pastorally unsustainable. In Kevin Sharpe's words, 'the logic of strict predestination did not square easily with the vocation of a preaching ministry', for if men were predestined to salvation or damnation, what was the point of sermons exhorting them to repentance? John Spurr agrees that 'the clergy always faced a difficult problem in preaching predestination' and that in practice, seeking to overcome 'the blank incomprehension of their flocks', they were forced to dilute the doctrine with a strong dose of semi-Pelagianism.[6] This is supported by a chorus of other

---

[3] Ian Green, *The Christian's ABC: Catechisms and Catechizing in England c. 1530–1740* (Oxford, 1996), p. 356; Green, 'Career prospects and clerical conformity in the early Stuart Church', *Past & Present*, 90 (1981), p. 111.

[4] G. W. Bernard, 'The Church of England *c.*1529–*c.*1642', *History*, 75 (1990), pp. 183–206 (quotation p. 196).

[5] Alexandra Walsham, *Providence in Early Modern England* (Oxford, 1999), p. 104.

[6] Kevin Sharpe, *The Personal Rule of Charles I* (New Haven and London, 1992), pp. 298–9; John Spurr, *English Puritanism 1603–1689* (Basingstoke, 1998), pp. 169–70. Other scholars have argued that in order to square this theological circle, Protestant clergy had in effect to be Calvinist in their theology but Arminian in their preaching: see, e.g., David G. Mullan, *Scottish Puritanism 1590–1638* (Oxford, 2000), pp. 209, 242, and Richard L. Greaves, *Glimpses of Glory: John Bunyan and English Dissent* (Stanford, 2002), pp. 83, 110, 194.

historians who have looked at the matter from the laity's point of view and concluded that there simply was no demand for predestinarian preaching and teaching. Christopher Haigh has argued that when the parish clergy did try to preach the doctrine of predestination to their flocks, they were received with a mixture of fear and hostility: 'There was, it seems, a popular demand for non-Calvinistic religion, and some pressure on ministers to provide it.'[7] And Barbara Donegan has suggested that even laypeople who thought of themselves as Calvinists were content to leave the finer points of theology to be worried over by the clergy: 'Intelligent, conscientious and anxious lay attempts to live according to the precepts of pastoral Calvinism did not require comparable attention to the more recondite and intractable aspects of professional, theological Calvinism.'[8]

In this chapter I want to look in more detail at the preaching of predestination in early modern England, and, in doing so, to challenge the assumption that predestination was a subject of no interest or concern to most people outside the universities. As we shall see, sermons on this topic were not as uncommon as historians have tended to assume. As soon as the Articles of 1563 had made it part of the official doctrine of the Elizabethan Church, preachers began to assert their right to teach it, often in ways that went well beyond Article XVII's cautious and qualified endorsement of 'predestination to life'. John Bridges, preaching at Paul's Cross in 1571, scornfully dismissed the objections of 'the papists' (and, by implication, of some in the Church of England as well) that 'it is a perillous doctrine to be taught unto the people, ye ought not to preache it'. 'Why so?' demanded Bridges. 'Truthe never shames his mayster, Truthe wyll ever prevayle: and what shoulde we teache in matters of salvation but the Truthe, and all the truthe, and nothyng but the truth?'[9] Other preachers took the same line. Margo Todd's recent survey of sermon manuscripts from early modern Scotland has uncovered numerous examples of predestinarian preaching, much of it dealing with difficult and potentially divisive issues such as the differences between the elect and the reprobate, which, as Todd points out, are 'often thought by modern historians to have been too esoteric for popular preaching'.[10] A survey of English sermon manuscripts reveals much the same pattern, and warns us against drawing too sharp a contrast between academic theology and popular religion.

---

[7] Christopher Haigh, 'The taming of Reformation: preachers, pastors and parishioners in Elizabethan and early Stuart England', *History*, 85 (2000), pp. 572–88 (quotation p. 582).

[8] Barbara Donegan, 'The York House Conference revisited: laymen, Calvinism and Arminianism', *Bulletin of the Institute of Historical Research*, 64 (1991), pp. 312–30.

[9] John Bridges, *A Sermon Preached at Paules Crosse* (1571), F1r (p. 33).

[10] Margo Todd, *The Culture of Protestantism in Early Modern Scotland* (London, 2002), p. 51.

Understanding the preaching of predestination may also help us to understand the theological debate that lay behind it. This has generally been seen in highly polarised terms, with a body of 'Calvinist' (predestinarian) opinion on the one hand opposed to a body of 'anti-Calvinist' (anti-predestinarian) opinion on the other.[11] Some scholars have grown frustrated with this approach: Peter Lake, for example, in an influential article of 1993, wrote that 'the current debate is dominated by the single issue of predestination' and even went so far as to complain of a 'bizarre obsession with predestination' that, in his view, threatened to distract attention from 'the real issues at stake'.[12] But the way to get out of this impasse, I suggest, is not to turn away from predestination in pursuit of other issues, but to try to understand what made predestination important and why it was so often the focus for controversy. The best way to do this is to situate the theological disagreements in the context of popular preaching. Adding this extra dimension may help to bring some life back into what has increasingly come to be perceived as a rather sterile academic debate, and may also, as in the previous chapter, shed light on the way that conflict was mediated and articulated through the conventions of pulpit rhetoric. It may even help to make the obsession with predestination, both among early modern divines and their modern scholarly interpreters, seem slightly less bizarre. If the debate on predestination has come to seem intractably complex and far removed from the issues that really mattered in early modern England, that may be because so little attention has been paid to its reception history in the pulpit.

### PREACHING PREDESTINATION

'Whether Predestination, Election, &c. are to be preached unto Lay-men?' was a question posed by the Elizabethan preacher Henry Smith, lecturer at St Clement Danes in London, in a list of theological problems 'yet unanswered', compiled by Smith for private discussion and later published as an appendix to one of his sermon collections.[13] It was a question that all

---

[11] This is particularly the case with the debate between Nicholas Tyacke, in *Anti-Calvinists*, and Peter White, in *Predestination, Policy and Polemic: Conflict and Consensus in the English Church from the Reformation to the Civil War* (Cambridge, 1992). Peter Lake's review of White, 'Predestinarian propositions', *Journal of Ecclesiastical History*, 46:1 (1995), pp. 110–23, also draws attention to the debate's narrow focus on 'the single doctrinal crux of predestination' (p. 113).

[12] Peter Lake, 'The Laudian Style', in Kenneth Fincham, ed., *The Early Stuart Church, 1603–1642* (Stanford, 1993), pp. 161–85 (quotation p. 162).

[13] 'Questions gathered out of his owne confession', annexed to Henry Smith, *Three Sermons* (1599), G3r–4v. This list is said to have been compiled by Smith 'at the commandment of the Right

Calvinist ministers had to confront as they trod what Julia Merritt has termed the 'pastoral tightrope' between the predestinarian view of the world as divided between elect and reprobate, and the more inclusive view of the Christian community which they were required to adopt in their day-to-day dealings with their parishioners.[14] For the most part they preferred not to debate the question in public, but occasionally – most often as the result of a challenge from one of the anti-Calvinist divines who were starting to emerge as a distinct school of thought within the Church of England at the end of the sixteenth century – they found themselves put on the spot and forced to say whether, in their view, the doctrine of predestination could safely be handled in the pulpit before a popular audience. Their answer was a resounding yes.

One of the divines who tackled this question was Robert Hill, fellow of St John's College, Cambridge, and lecturer at St Martin in the Fields, whose career nicely straddles the worlds of academic theology and parish religion. In 1595, while still at Cambridge, Hill was involved in a dispute with John Overall, then vicar of Epping, over the teaching of predestination. Hill summed up his position in this dispute several years later in his treatise *Life Everlasting* (1601), in which he argued that 'the doctrine of Predestination is neither altogether to be suppressed, nor only to bee handled in schooles among the learned, but also to be preached publikely to the people, so it bee done soberly, wisely, and to edification'. He found his proof-text in Christ's commission to his disciples, 'Go ye, and preach the gospel to every creature' (Mark 16: 15). In Hill's view, it was impossible to preach the Gospel without preaching the doctrine of predestination, since 'the cheife part and foundation of the gospel is the doctrine of predestination . . . For by no other way is the grace of God, which is the substance of the Gospel, more manifested, than by this doctrine of Gods free and unchangeable predestination.'[15]

Hill's conviction that the doctrine of predestination was 'the chiefe part and foundation of the gospel' reflected the importance which he, and other Reformed ministers, attached to the quest for assurance. By preaching on the effects of true justifying faith, they hoped to enable their hearers to recognise those effects within themselves, and thus to reach a state of

Worshipfull his Uncle, Master Brian Cane, high Sheriffe of Leicestershire' and consists of an odd mixture of religious and secular questions, ranging from the proper use of religious images to the existence of fairies and hobgoblins and the genuineness of fairy gold.

[14] J.F. Merritt, 'The pastoral tightrope: a puritan pedagogue in Jacobean London', in Thomas Cogswell, Richard Cust and Peter Lake, eds., *Politics, Religion and Popularity in Early Stuart Britain: Essays Honour of Conrad Russell* (Cambridge, 2002), pp. 143–61.

[15] Robert Hill, *Life Everlasting: or, the True Knowledge of One Iehovah* (Cambridge, 1601), 4L4v (p. 640).

assurance as to their own election and justification. 'Woe is me if I preach
not the gospel' was a text frequently carved on Jacobean pulpits; and there
is no doubt that many Jacobean preachers interpreted this in specifically
predestinarian terms, as an admonition to teach the fundamental doctrines
of election, justification and assurance, which would, in Hill's words, be
'most profitable to the elect' and confirm them in the faith of the Gospel.[16]
What made Arminianism so threatening was that it appeared to break the
link between election and justification, thus, in the eyes of many Protestant
divines, taking away the possibility of assurance and leaving Christians in
a state of crippling uncertainty as to whether or not they were saved. This
enabled divines such as Hill to argue, against the common stereotype of
Calvinism as a religion of despair, that it was Calvinism alone that could
provide pastoral comfort, and Arminianism that left its adherents sunk in
the depths of spiritual anguish.

The extent to which predestination was regarded as a 'comfortable doctrine', confirming the elect in their faith, is made clear in John Davenant's
catalogue of its beneficial effects. Davenant had personal reasons for supporting predestinarian preaching, having been reprimanded by the Privy
Council in 1630 for handling the doctrine in a sermon at court; and his
response to Samuel Hoard's anti-Calvinist treatise *Gods Love to Mankind*
(1633) gave him an opportunity to justify himself, and strike back at his
opponents, by extolling the advantages of the doctrine of predestination.[17]
He began by observing that it illuminated many of God's attributes – his
'fore-knowledge of future events', his 'absolute dominion and soveraignty'
over his creatures, his 'omnipotent power of turning the hearts of men which
way he please', his 'unchangeable will' and his 'free and gracious mercy' –
whereas Arminianism called all these into question. Moreover, 'the doctrine
of Predestination doth serve to kindle in the hearts of the faithfull a most
ardent love towards God . . . because it doth teach that God did freely love
them from all eternity, and of his speciall favour loaded them with gracious
benefits', something which Arminianism was again unable to do because, in
attributing salvation to human freewill, it gave the elect no reason to be
grateful to God. And so Davenant went on, listing all the benefits that could
be derived from the doctrine of predestination: it encourages us to testify our
gratitude to God by our good works; it makes us truly humble, by showing us

---

[16] On pulpit texts, see J. C. Cox, *Pulpits, Lecterns and Organs in English Churches* (Oxford, 1915), chapter 6.
[17] Davenant describes the censure of his sermon in a letter to Samuel Ward, 16 March 1629–30: Bodleian
Library, MS Tanner 290, f. 86, printed in Morris Fuller, *The Life, Letters and Writings of John
Davenant* (1897), pp. 312–14.

that our salvation is from God and not from ourselves; it protects us from the temptation to despair; it stirs us up to constancy in prayer; it gives us patience in adversity. 'And thus you see how many excellent uses do flow from the Orthodox doctrine of Predestination.'[18]

However, Protestant preachers were not pastorally insensitive: and while they acknowledged the importance of predestination, they also regarded it as a potentially dangerous doctrine which had to be handled with extreme care. John Dod stressed that predestination was quite likely to lead to 'perplexity of mind' if it was presented to people without a proper doctrinal foundation:

Some meddle with predestination first of all, building the roof, before they have laied the foundation, striving to attaine to the highest rownd in the ladder att first stepp, and so not getting assurance, that they are predestinated to sallvation, grow into perplexity of minde . . . Such doe as itt wear take the sword by the point; so as to woond them seallues, in steed of taking itt by the handle: which if they did, itt might be forcible to fight with all.[19]

Hill's discussion of the pastoral effects of predestination is interestingly ambiguous. He pooh-poohed objections that the doctrine should not be preached because it was too difficult for ordinary people to comprehend, or because it might lead to despair; on the contrary, he declared, the doctrine was 'plaine' and easy to understand, and 'rather confirmeth us in hope, than throweth downe into despaire'. But he admitted that the doctrine might indeed cause people to despair if it was preached in the wrong way. 'Of this one thing are preachers to be admonished, that when they speake thereof, they goe not beyond Gods word, and never dispute of the same, but that they also shew the use therof: least that their hearers abuse the same either to licentiousnes or desperation, but use the same rather to the studie of good workes, and holines, and to the comfort of afflicted consciences.'[20]

Davenant provides the most extensive discussion of these potential risks and hazards, and lists three ways in which the doctrine of predestination may be 'abused' by careless or unskilled preachers. First, some preachers deliver it out of its 'due place', confronting their hearers with 'this great depth of Election and Reprobation' without having first called them 'to faith in Christ and to serious repentance', which is 'as if a man should purposely give to a sick and weak person strong and solid meat which his

[18] John Davenant, *Animadversions . . . upon a Treatise Intituled, Gods Love to Mankinde* (1641), 2C1r–7r (pp. 391–403).
[19] 'Dods droppings', Dr Williams's Library, London, MS 28.2, p. 174.
[20] Hill, *Life Everlasting*, 4M2v (p. 644).

stomach is not able to bear'. Secondly, some preachers 'wander into such
questions as through their too much subtilty do exceed the vulgar capacity':
and here Davenant reproves 'the folly and rashnesse of some (especially
young) Preachers, who as soon as they hear any new controversie concerning
Predestination started amongst Divines, be it never so intricate, never so
unfruitfull, yet presently they acquaint the people with it'. Thirdly, some
preachers 'separate the end from the means', by explaining that God has made
a double decree for 'the infallible salvation of the Elect, and the infallible
damnation of the Reprobate' without explaining how these decrees are
fulfilled, or what effects they have on the soul – thus giving their hearers the
impression that some people are saved, and others damned, irrespective of
their own actions. 'It is a dangerous matter to lay open before the eyes of
the vulgar the naked and bare doctrines of Predestination and Reprobation',
and may lead to antinomianism if it is not made clear that the elect are
predestinated not only to the end (salvation) but also to the means (faith and
holiness).[21]

  To avoid these 'abuses' of the doctrine of predestination, Davenant
advised preachers to follow the example of Christ, and 'contain themselves
within those bounds which the holy Scripture hath clearly chalked out unto
us'. Christ began his ministry by telling his hearers 'that God so loved the
world, that he gave his Sonne for the redemption of mankind' and that all
who believe in him will have everlasting life (John 3: 16). At this stage, Christ
spoke 'not one word concerning the mystery of Election and Reprobation';
only later, when he saw some of his hearers brought to repentance, did he
open to them 'the deep mystery of Election' to show them that their faith
'flowed from the decree of Predestination' and not from themselves. Thus,
Davenant concluded, when we preach to 'ignorant and carnall men . . . not
yet endued with true faith and holinesse, we are to move them to faith in
Christ and newnesse of life, and not to step into the doctrin of Election and
Reprobation untill we deal with those in whom we manifestly perceive the
effects of Election, that is faith and the fruits thereof'.[22] In other words,
predestination should not be preached indiscriminately to all, but select-
ively to those hearers who had the doctrinal equipment to be able to
interpret and apply it correctly.

  And even when speaking to this select audience, preachers still had to
be very careful in their presentation of the doctrine. Rather than stating
it in a coldly intellectual way, as a given fact about the nature of the
universe, they had to draw out the practical implications. In making this

[21] Davenant, *Animadversions*, 2A8v–2B2r (pp. 374–7).   [22] Davenant, *Animadversions*, 2B1r (p. 375).

distinction, Hill resorted to the doctrine-and-use terminology of the preaching manuals: a mere statement of the doctrine was not enough, it also had to be 'applied to the capacitie of the hearers . . . that is, to those uses for which it was delivered by the holy ghost'. Davenant offered a revealing illustration of this method of teaching:

A wise Minister . . . will never teach the people that some particular persons are absolutely predestinated unto life, but withall he will let them know that those persons are none other but such as by faith and holinesse do walk in the way to eternall life. He will never teach that some particular persons were passed-by in this infallible ordination unto life everlasting, but withall he will also shew that these are none other but they who by their own voluntary impeniency, infidelity and impiety did most deservedly pull upon themselves eternall destruction.

Davenant's conclusion was that ministers must not 'urge absolute Predestination' in such a way 'as in the mean time to forget the means', for while God's decree was absolute, the fulfilling of that decree depended on 'the conditionate use of the means'. In this way, it was possible to reconcile the doctrine of predestination with conditional expressions such as 'whosoever believeth shall be saved' or 'if thou believest and leadest a holy life, thou shalt be saved'.

How far, though, did preachers actually follow the advice of writers such as Hill and Davenant in handling the doctrine of predestination in their sermons? Printed sources do not necessarily take us very far in answering this question. As we saw in Chapter 3, many printed sermons are based on the preacher's own skeleton notes, which only give a bare outline of what was actually said in the pulpit. One of Thomas Taylor's sermons, for example – probably preached at St Mary Aldermanbury, London, in the 1620s, though not published until 1653 – appears to touch on predestination in only the very lightest detail:

QUEST.  How doth God fit men to be vessels of honour?
ANSW.   1. By eternal *Predestination*, Rom. 9. 11. Eph. 1. 4.[23]

However, Taylor would almost certainly have enlarged on this in the pulpit, and while we can only speculate on what he might have said, his choice of proof-texts, particularly Romans 9: 11 ('the children being not yet born, neither having done any good or evil'), is suggestive of a high Calvinist or Supralapsarian model of predestination. The same caution needs to be used in dealing with printed catechisms. In his study of the

---

[23]  Thomas Taylor, *Works* (1653), 3R2r; this particular sermon, on 2 Tim. 2: 20–1, is said in a marginal note to be 'taken out of Notes not perfected'.

catechetical tradition, Ian Green comments on 'the general dearth of predestinarian teaching' in the majority of catechisms, and argues that the discussion of predestination at an elementary level was 'limited in scale and often cautious or ambiguous in its wording'.[24] However, there are exceptions to this rule, such as the catechism used by William Hinton, vicar of St Michael's, Coventry, which is quite explicit in its assertion of election and final perseverance:

Q. Whom doth Christ save?
A. Onely his people, for ther hath been alwayes from the beginning of the world a certaine people seperated from the rest, whom god hath called and sanctified.
Q. Can any of gods elect perish?
A. Noe, for god will loose none of them, they are sealed for gods people, and the gates of hell shall not prevaile against them. John 10. Math. 16.[25]

Nor can we assume that the catechism gives us the sum total of what was being taught, as it may have served merely as an outline or *aide-mémoire* to be expounded in more detail in sermons accompanying the catechising sessions. The lack of overt predestinarian teaching in printed catechisms, therefore, does not necessarily mean that preachers regarded it as too difficult or dangerous to expound to their parishioners. With catechisms, as with sermons, the printed form may simply be summarising in brief what was actually being preached at length.

Manuscript sources, however, may bring us closer to what was being said from the pulpit. A manuscript in the Bodleian Library (MS Rawl. E. 204) contains notes for sermons by an unidentified preacher, with dates ranging from 1607 to 1614; the volume may have a London connection, and includes several sermons preached at 'St Olaus' (possibly St Olave Hart Street or St Olave Jewry, London). In a sermon on the parable of the unfruitful fig tree (Luke 13: 7), the writer argues that the reprobate are to be held responsible for their own damnation. God 'predestinates none to damnation, *quia voluit*, bycause he wold, no it is *qui noluisti*, bycause thou woldst not'. At first glance, this might seem to border on Arminianism in its emphasis on human free will, yet the preacher goes on to attack 'Pelagians' who teach that 'man hath free will of himself to fullfyll the Gospel'. His position – which marks him out as a moderate or Infralapsarian Calvinist – is that while election is entirely irrespective of human merit, reprobation is not irrespective of human sinfulness: in

---

[24] Green, *The Christian's ABC*, p. 384.
[25] 'Maister Doctor Hintons catachisme upon the ten comandements': Bodleian Library, MS Rawlinson C.79, f. 32v.

other words, we have no power to earn our own salvation, but we may bring ourselves to damnation by wilfully rejecting the means of grace offered to us. 'Man we confess hath not power of himself to fullfill the law, or to bringe forth frute . . . but this power he hath, to refuse the means which shold make him frutefull.'[26] Thus the fig tree is cut down, and justly so, for bearing no fruit.

The preacher then proceeds to draw out the practical implications of this doctrine. He warns his audience not to be 'too curious in searching into the doctrine of Gods predestination', still less 'to say, Sure ther are some to be damnd, and certainly must so be whatsoever they do'. Rather than prying into the mysteries of God's secret will, they should content themselves with his revealed will as made known in the scriptures, by which 'he wills all to be saved that bringe forth frute, and denyes not means to make thee frutefull, unless thou refuse'. This, he concludes, teaches us 'not to neglect the inward and outward callinge which [God] useth for mans salvation. Who is ther amonge us that at one tyme or other hath not heard the voyce of God, callinge him to repentance, tellinge him that such an action is a sinne, willinge to abstaine therfrom, and yet grievinge the spirit have neglected this voyce? Who hath not heard the outward callinge by preachinge of the word, wher we have bene instructed in matters of manners and faith? and yet we have cast it behind us.'[27] This could serve as a textbook illustration of the method recommended by Davenant, in which preachers were taught to stress, above all, that election and predestination did not take away the need for good works as a means to an end. We are not justified by our works, yet we must 'labour to shew our fayth by our workes', since it is the testimony of our faith that assures us of our election.

A further example of predestinarian preaching, twenty years later, can be found in the notebook of Robert Keayne, which contains notes on sermons heard in London in the years 1627–8.[28] On 11 July 1627 Keayne heard a sermon 'by a stranger at Cornhill' on Romans 5: 19 ('by the obedience of one man, many are made righteous'). Having discussed the means by which God's people were made righteous, the preacher moved on, in the last section of his sermon, to consider 'the parties that shalbe partakers of this benefit'. He noted that Christ was described elsewhere in the New

---

[26] Bodleian Library, Oxford, MS Rawl. E.204, f. 42v.

[27] MS Rawl. E. 204, f. 42v (punctuation added for clarity).

[28] Keayne's sermon notebook is in the library of the Massachusetts Historical Society, to whom I am indebted for kindly supplying me with a microfilm. See also 'Keayne's notes of sermons 1627–1628', *Proceedings of the Massachusetts Historical Society*, 2nd series, vol. 50 (1916–17), pp. 204–7.

Testament as 'the saviour of the world' (1 John 4: 14), but argued that this did not mean the whole world, 'but only such as god loved in the world', that is, the elect. 'Here we may see the intention of god in giving Christ to death . . . Christ died only for the elect, he suffered not for the sins of the reprobate; therfore was never intention in god that Christ his sonne should dye for wicked reprobate men.' Thus when St Paul declared that by Christ's death 'many were made righteous', he was referring solely to the elect.

Yet the preacher chose to wrap up this uncompromising doctrine of limited atonement in a message of pastoral comfort. 'Strive to make your election sure', he exhorted his audience, 'and you that find you are predestinated, make not soe litle reckninge of what it is to be a good christian: and though some dislike the doctrine of predestination, yet it is a most sweete and comfortable doctrine, not only to the elect but to the wicked alsoe, for no man can say of himselfe he is a reprobate.' His argument, baldly summarised in these brief notes, seems to have been that the offer of grace, and the possibility of repentance, were open to all, since no one, however wicked, could ever be certain that he was not among the elect. It was therefore possible to combine a stern reminder of eternal punishment with a concluding note of hope, addressed not merely to a select group of godly listeners but to the whole congregation in general. 'The more sin a reprobate lays on himself, the greater shall his torment in hell be: therfore strive to be one of this many [i.e. the 'many' of Rom. 5: 19] and you shall have peace.'

As we saw in Chapter 4, some preachers also targeted their message at particular sections of their audience by delivering parallel courses of sermons at different levels of doctrinal complexity. By a lucky accident of survival, we can compare the parallel courses of Sunday and weekday sermons preached by Edward Philips, lecturer at St Saviour's Southwark, as recorded in notes by a member of the audience, Henry Yelverton of Gray's Inn, who took them 'for his owne private use' but was later persuaded to publish them. Yelverton was a very skilful note-taker, helped, no doubt, by his legal training, and his report of Philips's sermons appears to be extremely accurate; the prefatory epistle by George Bard, another London minister, declares that Yelverton's notes are 'so carefully performed, that undoubtedly not a sentence, yea hardly will it appeare, that a word of moment escaped him, as those who were diligent hearers with him may remember and can witnesse'.

Yelverton's edition contains fifteen sermons on Matthew 1: 1 to 4: 25, preached on Sundays, and a further eleven sermons on Romans 8: 10–39, preached on weekdays, besides a handful of other weekday sermons on unrelated texts. These two courses of sermons both deal with the doctrine of predestination, but in strikingly different ways. Philips does not gloss over the potentially divisive effects of predestination, arguing, as other puritan preachers did, that 'when the Gospel is preached, then the Lord comes to make a separation between the elect and the reprobate, which could not before be discerned'. But in the sermons on Matthew he concentrates on the doctrine's practical implications, taking particular care to distance himself from any suspicion of antinomianism by stressing that the elect are not free to live as they please. Satan 'laboureth to bring men to destruction' by telling them that they were predestined to heaven or hell before they were even born, 'which he doth onely to make us rest in the providence of Gods predestination, without having any regard to our conversation'. But we must not 'make the decree of God a meanes of our securitie to live as we list', as if 'being elected we cannot perish, and being appointed to be damned, we cannot avoid it'. Rather, we must seek to make our election sure, by getting 'as many testimonies as we can to prove that this election pertaineth to us', and using all the means of grace that God has appointed for us, such as reading the scriptures and hearing the Word preached. 'We know there is a peremptory decree of election and reprobation: what of this? yet we must strive to obtaine the prize set before us, and work our salvation forth with feare and trembling: for there are none predestinate to life, but they are predestinate to the meanes.'[29]

The sermons on Romans, on the other hand, deal with the doctrine of predestination at a considerably higher level of theological complexity. Philips opens with the conventional warning against overmuch speculation, declaring that predestination is 'a mistery to be adored rather than to be scanned by reason . . . for we must not expostulate with the Potter, why he made this vessel to honor and that to dishonor; much lesse must we contend and plead with the Lord about it'. But he then launches into a detailed analysis of the process of reprobation: 'This learne thou, the Lord hardneth the reprobate, either by the substraction and drawing away of his mercy, or by giving it so and in such a maner as they do not profit by it, but only maketh them the more without excuse, because they have seen the light, and yet have loved darknes more than light. And if it be asked, why this mercy of the Lord hardneth them and not mollifieth them, and why the Lord doth not pull them out of the fire, it is because he found them corrupt in

---

29  Edward Philips, *Certaine Godly and Learned Sermons, as They Were Delivered by Him in Saint Saviors in Southwarke* (1605), I5r (p. 119), O1v–2v (pp. 192–4).

Adam.' Philips's doctrine of predestination is explicitly Supralapsarian: 'it was purposed in the Lords uncontrolable decree, that [the reprobate] should be damned before they ever sinned.' This is linked to a high Calvinist doctrine of limited atonement: 'Execrable is the opinion of *Andreas* a Lutheran, who holds that God delivered up his Son for an universal salvation, meaning thereby to save all, if all will be saved . . . But we say, the purpose of God was not that Christ should die effectually for all.'[30]

These examples are not particularly unusual or original in their handling of predestination. They are chance survivals from what must have been a large body of run-of-the-mill predestinarian preaching, which is precisely what makes them interesting. They show that predestination was a common topic of discussion in the pulpit, and also suggest that the stereotype of the hellfire Calvinist preacher was very far from accurate. Some hellfire preachers there certainly were, but the majority of Calvinist preachers were highly conscious of the potential risks of preaching predestination and highly sensitive to accusations that they were driving tender consciences to despair. The British divines at the Synod of Dort in 1618–19 declared that predestination, rightly handled, was 'a most sweet doctrine, and full of comfort', but also cautioned against preaching the doctrine to those 'who have not yet well learned the first foundations of religion', and warned that the doctrine of reprobation, in particular, had to be preached 'sparingly and prudently' in order to avoid 'those fearefull opinions . . . which tend rather unto desperation, than edification'.[31] This carefully qualified endorsement of predestinarian preaching looks back over decades of discussion among Calvinist divines about the best way to deal with the doctrine in the pulpit. It also, as we shall see, anticipates the official restrictions that were to be imposed on predestinarian preaching in the following decades.

### RESPONSES TO PREDESTINARIAN PREACHING: TWO CASE STUDIES

Intentions are one thing, results are another; and we need to consider the possibility that in spite of all the careful checks and balances introduced by preachers to mitigate the severity of predestinarian doctrine, the laity were left anxious and terrified, or perhaps simply puzzled and incredulous, by what they heard. As one preacher observed in 1583: 'When men do heare of this doctrine, they will either say that there is no predestination, or that

---

[30]  Philips, *Certaine Godly and Learned Sermons*, Z6r (p. 347), 2A1v (p. 354), 2A6r (p. 363).
[31]  Milton, ed., *The British Delegation and the Synod of Dort*, pp. 292–3.

God hath done injury in reprobating him whom he doth cast away: or that he is not righteous in choosing his.'[32] Reconstructing lay attitudes to the doctrine of predestination is not easy, but fortunately some evidence does survive which gives us a valuable insight into the popular reception of predestinarian ideas. Most remarkable of all, perhaps, is the case of the Lincolnshire minister William Williams, first brought to light by Helena Hajzyk in her study of the diocese of Lincoln, and subsequently discussed by a number of other scholars – notably Patrick Collinson and Christopher Haigh – but richly deserving further analysis. Haigh regards the Williams case as showing that 'the preaching of predestination was worrying and unpopular' and that although many clergy continued to uphold a hardline Calvinist position, they were coming under strong pressure from the laity to adopt a more moderate and inclusive doctrine of grace.[33] As we shall see, however, the evidence is more ambiguous; and while it is obvious from the Williams case that the doctrine of predestination was a flashpoint for religious controversy, it is not so obvious that it was being forced by over-zealous clergy on reluctant laity, or that it was wholly unacceptable to those who heard it expounded from the pulpit.

The trouble started with a visitation sermon at Sleaford in June 1598, in which Williams allegedly upheld a number of 'dangerous and suspicious doctrines and speeches tending to Popishe religion', maintaining, among other opinions, that God offered 'universalitie of grace to everie sinner' and that 'the will of man was subordinated and a working cause in his uprisinge'. This 'greatlie offended' a group of local clergy, who complained to Bishop Chaderton and also appear to have sent a copy of Williams's sermon to a group of Cambridge academics for comment and criticism. In January 1599 Williams appeared before the diocesan chancellor, John Belley, to be 'examined uppon certaine interrogatories drawne out of his sermon', and the ensuing court case rumbled on for over a year before finally disappearing into the Court of Arches in May 1600, never to re-emerge. In the process it generated a mass of documentation which still survives in the Lincoln diocesan archives. Williams himself escaped without censure and continued to preach unmolested for another forty years; but the case exposed deep

---

[32] *A Verie Fruitful Sermon, Necessary to Be Read of All Christians, Concerning Gods Everlasting Predestination, Election, and Reprobation* (1583); the sermon is attributed to an unnamed 'godly minister', possibly the Northamptonshire puritan Eusebius Paget.

[33] On the Williams case, see Helena Hajzyk, 'The Church in Lincolnshire *c.* 1595–*c.*1640' (unpublished PhD thesis, University of Cambridge, 1980), pp. 225–43; Patrick Collinson, 'Shepherds, sheepdogs and hirelings: the pastoral ministry in post-Reformation England', in W. J. Sheils and D. Wood, eds., *The Ministry: Clerical and Lay* (Oxford, 1989), pp. 204–5; Christopher Haigh, 'Taming of Reformation', p. 583.

theological divisions among the Lincolnshire clergy and created tensions and resentments that were not easily resolved.[34]

Even before the visitation sermon at Sleaford, Williams's theological views had clearly been causing a great deal of unease. A local gentleman, William Burton, remembered that in 1593 or 1594, he had heard Williams preach a funeral sermon in which 'he inveighed against predestination, and in the end his conclusion was this, or the like in effecte, viz. Though some greene heads at this day talke of predestination and reprobation and I knowe not what, yet this is the truth that I have delivered'.[35] A neighbour minister, Charles Wheldall, testified that in 1596 or 1597 he had had 'conference . . . about matters of religion' with Williams, who had declared that 'the difference betwene the Papistes and us was but wranglinge wordes'. On another occasion Williams had told Wheldall 'that in some thinges man hath free will, and then he being on horsbacke (for yt was at Michaellmas time laste as they came together from Lincoln) he turned his horse firste one way and then another, and said he had libertie and will to turne him which way he listed'.[36] Another minister, Richard Evatt, also recalled seeing Williams point to his horse with the words 'What, shall we say of this beaste that it was predestinate to goe?'[37] Williams was by all accounts a difficult and abrasive character, who gave offence not only by his theological views but by his outspoken manner of expressing them. Even in court, when questioned by the diocesan chancellor about his visitation sermon, he lost his temper and 'grewe into such irreverent and contemptuous behaviour . . . as he was bownd over by recognisance to appeare personallie'.

The anxiety caused by Williams's opinions is further shown by the fact that, a few weeks after the visitation sermon, he attended a meeting at the Angel Inn in Sleaford 'in the presence of manie persons' where he was asked to set down his views in writing. The persons present at the meeting included not only the vicar of Sleaford and several other local clergy, but also a number of laypeople drawn from the ranks of the gentry and middling sort.[38] William Barrow, an ironmonger, later testified that he had heard Williams declare 'that an elected man might fall away from grace totallie as David did: when he was in his adulterie and murder, the

[34] The cause papers relating to the Williams affair are in the Lincolnshire Archives Office, Lincoln diocesan records, box 80, with a summary of Williams's answers in Ci/12 (Court book 1598–1600), ff. 162–3.

[35] Deposition of William Burton of Haldingham, 7 May 1600.

[36] Deposition of Charles Wheldall, rector of Howell, 8 May 1600.

[37] Deposition of Richard Evatt, vicar of Burton Hussey.

[38] Deposition of Edmund Newton, vicar of Sleaford, 24 Jan. 1599–1600.

seed of Gods grace was extinguished altogether for the presente time, and after his repentance was renewed again'. Barrow was unconvinced, telling Williams 'that he thought there was no learned man in this land of his opinions in this'. His testimony was corroborated by another of the laypeople present at the meeting, the yeoman William Scochie, who also stated that on another occasion, some years earlier, he had heard Williams 'speake somewhat disdainefullie of Gods predestination'. When he had attempted to defend the doctrine of predestination, Williams had replied dismissively 'that they that taught him so, were ignorant and understood not what they said'.

This hardly suggests that the laity were flocking to Williams to free them from the burden of predestinarian doctrine. On the contrary, it suggests that they regarded him with considerable suspicion, all the more so because his ideas were felt to be dangerously Popish. Several witnesses had been present at another conference in the house of one John Taylor of Sleaford, in November 1599, where Williams had maintained 'that no man was either elected or rejected in the counsell of God, but accordinge to workes foreseene'. Edmund Newton, vicar of Sleaford, admonished Williams 'that herein he jumped with the papists', to which Williams replied 'that in his conscience yt was the truthe that he spake'. Newton then asked Williams if it was true that he had said 'that the papistes and wee might easilie be reconciled if both of us wold lay away our prowd stomackes'. Williams answered 'that he said so still and thought yt also, excepting the pointe aboute the sacramente. And when instance was given of the pointe of Justification, he did insinuate by his speeches that in that pointe he and they might easilye be reconciled.' John Newall, a local schoolmaster, had had several arguments with Williams 'aboute some pointes of papistrie', including the doctrine of 'meritt of workes'. Williams had maintained 'that we did not understand the meaning of the papists in that word *Meritum*', and on being shown 'a place in one of Mr Perkins bookes, allegeinge a place out of some papisticall author that did abuse the word *meritum*', replied 'that Mr Perkins did belye the author'.[39]

Judging by these reports, there seems to have been a widespread feeling that Williams, if not a secret Papist himself, was suspiciously sympathetic to Popery. Charles Wheldall's testimony is particularly significant in this regard. He claimed to have heard Williams declare that 'the Pope was a sillie old man wearie of the worlde, and that his predecessors had main-teined great errors, but yt may be that he leadeth a better life than a greate

---

[39]  Deposition of John Newall, schoolmaster, of Boston.

number of us doth'. Perceiving that Wheldall was scandalised by this remark, Williams had tried to brush it aside by adding hastily: 'it is no matter, the pope hath nothinge to doe with me nor I with him.' On another occasion, Williams had allegedly remarked to Wheldall, 'give me lawe and I will make anie religion nothinge', and on being asked what he meant by this, 'answered, because that religion in countries standeth good, which lawe doth mainteine, therefore give me lawe, and I will beate downe or sett upp anie religion in the face of the worlde'. Wheldall's evidence was not corroborated by other witnesses and should be treated with some caution, but whether or not we accept it as a true account of Williams's private opinions, the association of ideas is suggestive: anti-predestinarianism linked with Popery, and Popery in turn linked with a cynical, quasi-atheistical view of religion as merely an act of state.

This association of ideas goes a long way to explain why Williams's views caused such alarm. Many of Williams's listeners seem to have felt that in rejecting predestination, he was adopting a Popish doctrine of merit, which, in the words of one of his clerical opponents, 'was to make God subjecte unto man, and not man subjecte unto God'. His forthright insistence (as reported by another witness) 'that there was no necessitie that a man should receive grace, but he might refuse, yf he would', and that 'St Paule when he was stricken downe might have refused grace yf he would', was dangerous because it compromised the anti-Catholic line upheld by other ministers in the neighbourhood. This was why Williams's opponents were so anxious to have him censured. When William Scochie told the court 'that it is generallie thought and by some spoken that if Mr Williams be not punished for his doctrine, those which have heard him will not be perswaded but that his doctrine is righte and true', he was not suggesting that Williams's arguments might appeal to moderate Anglicans unhappy with the Calvinist doctrine of predestination, but that they might give comfort to recusants and Church Papists still hankering after the Catholic doctrine of justification by works. Like so much else in the religious culture of the period, the pressure to have Williams censured came from the perceived need to define the Protestant position in terms that were clearly distinct and separate from Popery.

Two other aspects of the Williams case are also worthy of attention. The first is that much of the evidence in the case concerned sermons delivered by Williams at christenings. Elizabeth Burton, the sole female witness, testified that she had heard Williams preach 'at two several Christeninges' where he had declared 'that the childe came thither in sinne, but being by him or anie other minister baptised and washed in that water should goe away a cleane and a sanctified creature till such time as yt committed actuall sinne'. Another witness had also been present at a christening where Williams had defended the doctrine of baptismal regeneration 'and did inveighe against those that taught the contrarie, whereby some that were there presente were much greeved, to heare that doctrine so spoken againste, which they held for an undoubted truth'.[40] In the light of this evidence, it is hard to sustain the argument that the debates on grace and predestination were of no concern to ordinary lay-people. Williams's opinions were not merely the stuff of visitation sermons and theological disputations; they also impinged on the Church's rites of passage. Nor did they necessarily have greater popular appeal than the opinions of Williams's Calvinist opponents, since one of the implications of Williams's robust defence of baptismal regeneration was that children dying without baptism were damned – a point that was not lost on Elizabeth Burton, who had heard Williams declare 'that all children dying unbaptised dyed as fleshe'.

But what is also clear from the Williams case is that even the academic debates on predestination were of interest to many people outside the universities. In particular, many of the inhabitants of Sleaford seem to have been remarkably well informed about the drawing up of the Lambeth Articles in 1595. At the debate at the Angel Inn, Williams was asked 'how yt came to passe that the article was agreed of in the convocation howse, wherein yt ys said that a true lively and justifieinge fayth doth never cease nor ys extin-guished neither finallie nor totallie'. He replied 'that neither that nor the rest of those articles were agreed of in the convocation but fownd in a learned mans studdy', and that 'my Lord his Grace of Canterbury was of his opinion concerninge totall fallinge away from grace'. This was a brief but highly pertinent exchange which succeeded in touching on many of the main issues surrounding the Lambeth Articles. Williams's opponents were plainly aware of the importance of the Articles as a statement of Reformed orthodoxy, and of the crucial significance of the terms 'totally' and 'finally'; while Williams knew that the Articles had never been officially adopted as part of the doctrine of the Church of England, and that Whitgift had been forced to distance himself from the Articles in the face of royal disapproval.

It is perhaps not so surprising to find an interest in predestination in this part of Lincolnshire; Nicholas Tyacke has pointed out that Sleaford was only thirteen miles from Boston, where the physician and alderman Peter Baro (son of the Peter Baro whose attack on the Lambeth Articles in

---

[40] Depositions of Elizabeth Burton and William Burton.

1596 had cost him his post as Lady Margaret Professor of Divinity at Cambridge) kept the flames of controversy alive by attacking Calvinist predestinarianism at every opportunity. In common with much of East Anglia, Lincolnshire also had close intellectual links with Cambridge University, strengthened by the presence of a large number of Cambridge graduates among the local clergy. A stray fragment of conversation between two of the witnesses in the Williams case reveals the extent to which Cambridge was regarded as the final court of appeal in matters of theological controversy. Returning home after Williams's visitation sermon, William Burton had fallen into conversation with the schoolmaster John Newall, and remarked to him, apparently with genuine puzzlement: 'I wonder that Mr Williams will thus publicklie speake againste predestination, consideringe that it is so approved by the writing of so manie learned men.' 'It is wonderfull indeed', Newall had replied, 'and if Mr Williams were at Cambridge, and should goe aboute to mainteine as much there as he hath now delivered, in twoe or three questions he would be so putt downe that he should not have a word to say.'

In many ways, Williams's situation is reminiscent of that of Thomas Rogers in Bury St Edmunds a few years earlier. Both Williams and Rogers were isolated figures who came into conflict with the powerful mafia of godly divines, mostly Cambridge graduates (the 'Cambridge boies', as the Oxford-educated Rogers sarcastically described them), who dominated the East Anglian clergy and whose style of divinity, heavily influenced by the teaching of William Perkins, was very much in the ascendant.[41] To that extent, the Williams case was atypical, indeed exceptional. It was the product of a particular time (the late 1590s), a particular place (East Anglia) and a particular combination of circumstances: a maverick clergyman whose unguarded behaviour made him vulnerable to censure; a network of godly clergy slightly on the defensive after the débâcle of the Lambeth Articles, and conscious of the need to reassert itself; a diocesan bishop who was himself a member of the Cambridge establishment, a graduate of Perkins's own college and a former Lady Margaret Professor of Divinity, and whose own sympathies in the matter could therefore be predicted with some confidence.

Yet it would be a mistake to interpret the Williams case purely in terms of clerical faction and ecclesiastical politics – for, as we have seen, one of the most interesting aspects of the case is the way it spread beyond the circle

---

[41] John Craig, 'The 'Cambridge boies': Thomas Rogers and the 'brethren' in Bury St Edmunds', in Wabuda and Litzenberger, eds., *Belief and Practice in Reformation England*, pp. 154–76.

of Williams and his clerical opponents, and into the ranks of the laity as well. What can it tell us about popular attitudes to predestination? First, it disproves the common assumption that academic theology was of no concern to ordinary people in the parishes. The disputes over the Lambeth Articles clearly had major repercussions at a local level, and, more generally, the cultural influence of Cambridge academic life was evidently diffused well beyond the confines of the university. Secondly, the Williams case suggests that the basic principle of predestination had found fairly wide-spread popular acceptance. The laypeople of Sleaford may not have under-stood or accepted all the details of the Reformed doctrine of predestination, but at the very least they seem to have felt, in common with many of their ministers, that predestination was a key element of the Protestant faith, and that to reject predestination was to relapse into Popery. Nowhere in the voluminous records of the case is there any sign of a groundswell of popular feeling in support of Williams's brand of anti-predestinarian teaching.

It is instructive to compare the Williams case with another controversy about predestinarian preaching which erupted in Dorchester less than a decade later. As David Underdown has shown in his history of the town, Dorchester in the early seventeenth century was sharply divided along religious lines. On the one hand, the puritan minister John White, rector of Holy Trinity, was attempting to turn the town into a model godly commu-nity; on the other, a group of citizens headed by the goldsmith Matthew Chubb were fighting a bitter campaign against White's brand of godly reformation. Such a division between puritan and anti-puritan factions was hardly unusual in English towns at this period, but the conflict in Dorchester seems to have been pursued with unusual ferocity, largely because Chubb's position as the richest man in the town made him a particularly formidable opponent. In 1607 Chubb used his influence to allow a company of travelling players to perform in the town on a Sunday, an action calculated to affront the godly; and the following year the conflict finally found its way into the courts, when a Dorchester tailor named John Conduit brought a Star Chamber suit against Chubb, accusing him of having written and published a series of libels against White and other inhabitants of the town. The libel suit has already been discussed by Underdown, but the recent publication of many of the relevant documents in the Dorset volume of *Records of Early English Drama* makes it possible to explore the case in more detail.[42]

---

[42] David Underdown, *Fire from Heaven: Life in an English Town in the Seventeenth Century* (New Haven and London, 1992), pp. 27–32, *Records of Early English Drama: Dorset and Cornwall*, ed. Rosalind Conklin Hays *et al.* (Toronto, 1999), pp. 173–98.

We may begin by looking at the libels themselves, which survive among the evidence presented in the Star Chamber case.[43] The second libel, beginning 'You Puritans all wheresoever you dwell', was said to have been 'found in the streete' and brought to Chubb, who had then read it aloud at the market cross 'with a lowde voyce in the presence and hearing of many persons'. For the most part, it consists of the familiar accusations of pride and hypocrisy which had become part of the stock-in-trade of anti-puritan polemic; but it also includes a more specific attack on one 'Parkyns' for presuming 'to judge the good and evill of every degree' and for claiming that many of his own friends and relatives were damned:

> But what a Clowne is this & Rascall Scismatike knave
> that will iudg his frends such uglie tormentes to have...
> yea this Scismaticke dogge and ympe of the dyvell
> doth maynteyne that god is the author of evill...[44]

Chubb claimed that he had no idea who 'Parkyns' was, but his opponents were in no doubt that the passage was intended as an attack on 'that reverend Preacher Mr William Perkins of Cambridge deceased, who in his liffe tyme was reverenced of all good men'. This provides an interesting parallel with the Williams case, where Williams was alleged to have said 'that all the printed bookes that Mr Perkins hath written ... are a lumpe of extreme follie'. The prominence given to Perkins suggests that he was regarded as the main English exponent of predestinarian doctrine, and that his name, like Calvin's, had become popularly associated with a particular school of theology, not just in academic circles but in the consciousness of many who had never read his writings.

But it is the third libel, a poem addressed 'To the Counterfeit Company & packe of Puritans', that most repays detailed scrutiny. It begins with an extended attack on a puritan minister, evidently John White, for having declared in a sermon that Christ died for the elect alone:

> Haueinge my self heard a Sermon now of late
> preached in Church by a puritan Prelate
> I could not well conteyne nor hold my penn still
> least I should participate in the same ill ...
> The Saviour of the world Christ Iesus in person
> of his sacred death was broughte in question
> How that he was not the Saviour of us all

---

[43] On libels and their place in popular culture, see Adam Fox, 'Ballads and libels', in *Oral and Literate Culture in England 1500–1700* (Oxford, 2000), pp. 299–334.
[44] *REED: Dorset and Cornwall*, p. 181.

> But of the elected which cann never fall
> And how he suffred & did dy for none
> but for his people and such as weare his owne. . .

The writer then proceeds to outline an alternative theory of the atonement in which Christ willed the salvation of all, even 'those that did him crucify', and could therefore be said to have died for all mankind:

> For Christ our redeemer without all exception
> for all mankind suffred his passion
> And when of his goodnes he dyed on the tree
> his bloud then extended to every degree
> Such was his Maiestie love, and Charitie
> as he would save those that did him Crucify
> yf soe he suffred to save and sett all free
> why the worlds savyour ought he not to be
> Though all be not saved defect is not his
> he performed his love to give us all blisse. . .

And the poem ends by associating Puritanism with a lack of charity. The puritans presumptuously declare that they are 'gods deere children, holy Saynctes', infallibly elected to salvation; yet they fail to extend this generosity to others. claiming that 'whosoever is not of their Sect a brother / is sure cast away'.[45]

The author of this poem was Robert Adyn, one of the defendants in the Star Chamber case. He freely admitted his authorship, explaining that he had written the poem in response to 'a Sermon preached as [he] was credibly enformed . . . by Mr John White' to the effect that 'Christ was not the Savyor of the whole world, nor did dye for the synnes of the whole world, but for his elected and chosen people only, and that our said Savyor Christ hath not his fatherly care over any more than his elected, shewinge the same by a familyar example that as every Shepherd taketh care and chardge over his own flock and no more, so hath Christ over his elected and chosen people and no more'. Adyn had found this so outrageous that he was moved to write a rejoinder 'in defence of the most meritorious passion of Christ . . . shewinge therby that Christ was the Savyor and Redeemer of all mankynde without all excepcion and that no defect of salvacion was in his said meritorious passyon'. He had then sent copies to three or four 'men of good callinge and reputacion' in Dorchester, of whom Matthew Chubb was one. Chubb, for his part, claimed that he had no hand in the composition of the poem and had known nothing

---

[45] *REED: Dorset and Cornwall*, pp. 182–3.

about it until a copy was left at his house 'folded up in the manner of a lettre sealed' and addressed to him.

Situating the poem in its proper theological context is not as straightforward as it may seem. The fact that Adyn was a recusant Catholic might suggest that the poem should be read as a Catholic apologia, attacking Protestantism in general rather than Puritanism in particular; and several passages in the poem do indeed appear to support this interpretation. One couplet, criticising puritans for neglecting the worship of the saints – 'as for all other Saynctes that are dead & paste / what have they to do with them or for them to faste' – is clearly intended as an indirect defence of Catholic devotional practices. Elsewhere in the poem, Adyn complains that the puritans seize on certain texts of scripture to prove that they are saved, but pay no heed to 'the conditions whereon those are grounded' – which seems to imply a Catholic understanding of justification as conditional upon good works. It was thus possible for Conduit and his fellow plaintiffs in the Star Chamber suit to depict the poem as a piece of Catholic propaganda, written by Adyn but aided and abetted by Chubb, who, it was alleged, had 'often mainteyned and defended publicklye the Popish doctrine of Salvacion by meritts and other poyntes of doctrine held and maynteyned by the Church of Rome contrary to the trueth professed in this Church of England'.

Not surprisingly, Adyn and Chubb saw things rather differently. Adyn insisted that he had never 'depraved the religion established in this Realme of England, or maintayned popishe doctryne and opinyons contrary to the said religion'; while Chubb declared that although he was friendly with Adyn he was not of his opinion 'in manie matters of religion' and had never upheld the Popish doctrine of merit. Both men firmly denied any seditious intention, and Chubb stressed that, far from being an opponent of the Protestant preaching ministry, he made a generous contribution to the town preacher's stipend and regularly entertained visiting preachers to dinner, as befitted his position as one of the town's leading men. Here, then – explicitly in Adyn's testimony, implicitly in Chubb's – was an alternative interpretation of the poem as an expression of mainstream religious orthodoxy, with no hidden Catholic agenda. In this view, it was Adyn and Chubb who were the true defenders of the established Church, and their opponents who were the seditious minority. Adyn argued that his poems were not libels, but 'rather Pamphlettes or Invectives against malefactors and reputed enemyes to the state such as are the Purytans or Brownistes'; they did not attack the Church of England, but 'maintained and defended' it against 'Purytans and Innovators of Religion'.

So how should the poem be read: as a Catholic polemic against Protestantism, or as a mainstream Protestant polemic against Puritanism? The answer, of course, is that it is capable of being read in both ways. The implicit moral of the poem is that only true Catholic doctrine can provide a secure refuge from the doctrinal excesses of Protestant extremists. To that extent, Adyn was clearly writing from a Catholic perspective – and it was very much in the interests of his opponents to draw attention to this fact, in order to smear the poem as a Popish libel. But his circulation of the poem to 'men of good callinge and reputacion' suggests that he was also trying to win the support of traditionalist-minded members of the Church of England for his campaign against White. This lends some credibility to Haigh's 'parish Anglican' thesis – for the obvious implication is that there existed a body of conservative 'Anglican' opinion which might be expected to be more sympathetic to the Catholic position on charity and good works than to the Calvinist position on election and predestination. In other words, Adyn was suggesting that Catholics and Anglicans should make common cause against the common enemy, Puritanism. Chubb – to judge from his friendship with Adyn, his alleged sympathy with Catholic doctrines and his well-attested hostility to White – may have found this message thoroughly congenial.

But this 'Anglican' position was not simply a state of latent discontent waiting to be mobilised into outright opposition to the Calvinist consensus. Rather, it had to be argued into existence by a strategy of persuasion which identified ministers like White as radical puritans and presented them as seditious and uncharitable. In short, it was a polemical construction, demonstrating the fluidity of religious categories rather than the presence of recognisable groups of 'Anglicans' in parishes across the country. And even if one does choose to regard Adyn's poem as an Anglican document, it would be misleading to see it as an expression of generalised hostility to the doctrine of predestination. The word 'predestination' does not occur either in the poem or in the records of the Star Chamber case; and Adyn's polemic is directed at certain particular aspects of predestinarian doctrine, such as the belief that Christ died solely for the elect, and the (alleged) implication that God was the author of evil. The very specific nature of this attack made it possible for his opponents, in turn, to deny that they had ever taught any such doctrine. White claimed that he had 'at no tyme preached taught or defended the poyntes of doctrine mentioned [in the poem] or any other sort than the same are held by the Church of England'. Neither Adyn nor his opponents, it seems, had any wish to treat this as a doctrinal conflict between Calvinists and anti-Calvinists over the fundamentals of predestination.

There is no doubt that Adyn's portrayal of 'puritan' predestinarian teaching was polemically slanted and unfair, but, like all effective caricatures, it bore a certain resemblance to reality. No Reformed minister would have taught that God was the author of evil, but it could be argued that this was a logical deduction from the high Calvinist or Supralapsarian doctrine in which God was seen as having created the reprobate expressly to be damned. As for the doctrine of limited atonement, this was well within the bounds of Reformed orthodoxy; and one has only to look, for example, at Arthur Dent's *Plaine Mans Path-way to Heaven* to find the doctrine stated in precisely the sort of blunt and uncompromising manner that Adyn found so objectionable. Dent's stereotypical rustic, Asunetus, declares confidently that 'Christ died for all: therefore all shall be saved'. No, replies the pastor Theologus, 'onely the Elect shall bee saved by his death'. Asunetus retorts that 'God is mercifull, and therefore I hope he will save the greatest part for his mercy sake.' No, replies Theologus, 'the greatest part shall perish'. Persuading the likes of Asunetus to accept this doctrine would have been a challenge even for the most dedicated pastor; it comes as little surprise to learn from John Rogers, minister of Dedham in Essex, that people were not receptive to the doctrine that 'few shall be saved and most perish', and that in 'all Parishes, even the rudest and most ignorant' there was a general belief that 'all shall be saved'.[46]

Yet White's claim that he had never taught the doctrines attributed to him was not an implausible one. As we saw in the last section, Protestant preachers were at pains to stress that the doctrine of predestination had to be expounded in a practical and pastorally sensitive fashion, in order to ensure that the hearers were not led into perplexity or tempted to despair. By the early seventeenth century, there was also a noticeable trend away from the high Calvinist position associated with William Perkins and his followers, towards a more inclusive pastoral theology which emphasised the general promises of salvation rather than their limitation to the elect. Andrew Willet's commentary on Romans, published in 1611, made cautious use of universalist language to argue that God 'offereth meanes of salvation to all' because 'he would have all to be saved'; and by the time of the Synod of Dort in 1618, a number of English divines had adopted a 'hypothetical universalist' position which held that Christ had died for all mankind, not just for the elect – precisely the point on which Adyn had laid such

---

[46] Arthur Dent, *The Plaine Mans Path-way to Heaven* (14th impr., 1612), S4v; John Rogers, *The Doctrine of Faith* (5th edn., 1633), V1v.

emphasis.[47] Adyn's poem, then, cannot be read as an attack on Reformed orthodoxy in general. Rather, it was an attack on one particular strand of Reformed orthodoxy – an attack which was all the more effective because it drew attention to some of the divisions within the ranks of its opponents, and expressed openly what many divines seem to have felt privately about the hardline Supralapsarian position.

Sadly, there is no surviving record of White's sermons to show how he presented the doctrine of predestination from the pulpit. However, a sermon preached in Dorchester a few years after the Star Chamber suit suggests that disagreements over predestination were continuing to fester. William Jones's sermon *The Mysterie of Christes Nativitie* (1614), preached in All Saints, Dorchester on Christmas Day 1613, was dedicated to a group of Dorsetshire gentlemen, including Matthew Chubb, 'my especiall kind and loving friends'. David Underdown describes it as 'unmistakably anti-Calvinist', and implies that it may even be a crypto-Catholic sermon, though this latter suggestion seems unlikely, as the dedicatory epistle goes out of its way to stress the importance of preaching, 'the greatest miracle that ever Christ wrought heere on earth, for our Conversion unto the faith', in a way that seems calculated to set at rest any doubts about Jones's Protestant credentials. However, the sermon has several unusual and distinctive features. Jones repeatedly declares that Christ died 'for the sinnes of all the world', and descants on the word 'fullness' in his text, citing John 1: 16, 'Of his fullness have all we received', and describing Christ's birth as 'the fulnesse of Gods Communication ... the fulnesse of mans Redemption ... the fulnesse of graces promotion'. For his Dorchester congregation, this could hardly have failed to recall Adyn's impassioned attack on the doctrine of limited atonement; and although Jones's sermon is not openly polemical, it is hard not to read it as an implicit critique of Supralapsarian predestination.

Jones's sermon is also stylistically unusual, with a piling-up of biblical metaphors in a manner reminiscent of late medieval preaching (or of John Wright's sermons at St Minver, discussed in Chapter 5) which would have looked decidedly old-fashioned by 1613:

Now a River flowed to water Paradise, when Christ was borne; with his bloud to wash away the sinnes of the world; Now the Mountaines did distil sweetnes, when Heaven did let God to descend on earth; Now Salamon made himselfe a Throne of

---

[47] On the shift from Supra- to Infralapsarianism among English divines, see Milton, *Catholic and Reformed*, pp. 414–6, and Jonathan D. Moore, *English Hypothetical Universalism: John Preston and the Softening of Reformed Theology* (Grand Rapids, MI, 2007), pp. 225–6.

Ivorie, when Christ made himselfe a bodie of flesh in the Virgins wombe; Now the Dove came from Noahs Arke, when the sonne of God came from the bosome of his Father: Now the bush burned and was not consumed, when a Virgine brought forth a Son, and was not corrupted; mercy and truth met together, when Christs Divinitie and Humanitie met in one person, to work our redemption.[48]

Particularly striking is the passage on the Virgin Mary, a subject which Protestant preachers tended to avoid because of its Catholic connotations. Jones plays with the paradoxes of Mary's virginity, and hovers on the verge of describing her as the Mother of God – as it were, flirting with Popish imagery, but remaining just within the boundaries of Protestant orthodoxy:

Wonders are in this mother . . . By bearing Christ, shee was the starre that gave light to the Sunne, the branch that bare the Vine, the River that yeelded the fountaine, the daughter that brought forth her Father, the creature that gave being to the Creatour: shee was I say the Mother of her Father, and the daughter of her Sonne, yonger than her birth, lesser than what shee contained . . . As the Sunne shines through glasse and corrupts it not: So God came made of a Virgine without breach of her chastitie.[49]

Nowhere in the sermon does Jones descend into theological controversy; but there is an intriguing passage in the dedicatory epistle, where Jones remarks that as the abuse of the grace of preaching is 'the greatest sinne that can be committed', he is at a loss to understand 'why Diotrephes with his Schollers will persist in resisting of this grace'.[50] This seems to suggest that Jones had encountered puritan opposition when he preached in Dorchester. It seems reasonable to conclude that Chubb and other religiously conservative gentlemen, whose position in the town gave them some control over the selection of visiting preachers, were inviting sympathetic clergy such as Jones to preach at All Saints as a deliberate snub to White and his puritan supporters at Holy Trinity.

What general conclusions can we draw from these two case studies? First, it seems that laypeople in the parishes were surprisingly well informed about theological debates in the universities. Both cases, as I have tried to show here, only yield up their full significance when they are subjected to detailed and precise theological analysis, with particular attention to the range of different opinions within the so-called 'Calvinist consensus'. Secondly, it is clear that the doctrine of predestination was a topic of intense fascination to

---

[48]  William Jones, *The Mysterie of Christes Nativitie. A Sermon Preached in the Parish Church of All-Saints in Dorchester* (1614), C1r.

[49]  Jones, *Mysterie of Christes Nativitie*, D3r.

[50]  'I wrote unto the church: but Diotrephes, who loveth to have the pre-eminence among them, receiveth us not' (John 3:9).

many people, and one which often served as a flashpoint for conflict between puritan preachers and their opponents. The claim that it was 'remote and irrelevant' simply cannot stand up to examination. Thirdly, there is relatively little sign of popular opposition to the doctrine of predestination as such. Williams's attack on the very notion of predestination seems to have caused considerable anxiety and puzzlement among his parishioners in Sleaford; and Adyn's attack on the preaching of John White was directed not at the doctrine of predestination but, more specifically, at the doctrine of limited atonement (i.e. that Christ died for the elect alone) – a doctrine which was associated with certain forms of predestinarian teaching, but not with the general principle of predestination, and was indeed rejected by many English Protestant divines who remained within the bounds of Reformed orthodoxy.[51]

It follows that, in acknowledging the existence of conflict over the doctrine of predestination, we must be very careful in the terms we choose to describe it. As we shall see in the following section, to present it as a conflict between proponents and opponents of the doctrine (or between 'Calvinists' and 'anti-Calvinists') does not really do justice to the complexity of the debate. A more fruitful approach is to look at the practical implications that flowed from the preaching of predestination in the parishes – and here the evidence of the Dorchester case is particularly useful. The difficulty facing Protestant preachers was not that their predestinarian teaching invariably alienated them from their parishioners. Rather, it was that their predestinarian teaching could be made to appear schismatic and uncharitable, limiting the number of the elect to a small group of godly brethren, while excluding their neighbours from the promises of salvation. The challenge for Protestant preachers was to vindicate the doctrine of predestination, and to present it in what they believed to be its true light, as a doctrine of comfort and reassurance to all true Christians, a safeguard against Popish error and an inducement to cast oneself wholly on the love of Christ rather than relying on one's own merits.

In conclusion, then, we may say of predestination what Peter Lake has said of Puritanism, that it had 'no stable ideological valence'. Puritanism, in Lake's words, 'could be moderate, hierarchical, repressive and orthodox, but it could also be divisive, extreme and heterodox', depending on the balance

---

[51] For another case where opposition to a predestinarian preacher focused on the doctrine of limited atonement, see Matthew Reynolds, 'Predestination and parochial dispute in the 1630s: the case of the Norwich lectureships', *Journal of Ecclesiastical History*, 59: 3 (2008), pp. 407–25 (esp. pp. 418–19).

of forces within a particular town or parish.[52] The doctrine of predestination, likewise, could be harsh, legalistic, threatening and exclusive, but it could also be evangelical, comforting and inclusive – and which of these two images of predestination ultimately prevailed would depend on the outcome of local conflicts such as we have seen played out in Sleaford and Dorchester. Certainly we should not underestimate the importance of predestination as a focus of religious conflict, nor its power to polarise opinion. But neither should we assume that the preaching of predestination was a lost cause, or that the dogmatic aspects of predestination inevitably prevailed over the pastoral. Moreover, it is important to realise that academic theology and parish religion were in continual dialogue with each other. News of university debates filtered down to the parishes, but the grass-roots reception of predestinarian preaching also fed back into academic debate and may have helped to propel English divines away from the high Calvinist position associated with William Perkins and his followers. In other words, this was not simply an exercise in rhetorical window-dressing. Efforts to portray the doctrine of predestination as moderate and inclusive were aided by the fact that English predestinarian theology was actually moving in a more moderate and inclusive direction.

## PREDESTINATION UNDER THE PERSONAL RULE

During most of the reign of James I, predestinarian preaching was tolerated with relatively little restraint. By the 1620s, however, there were signs of a shift in official policy, as restrictions on the preaching of predestination gradually began to be tightened. The 1622 Directions to Preachers forbade any minister below the rank of bishop or dean 'to preach in any popular auditorie, the deep poynts of predestination, election, reprobation, or of the universality, efficacity, resistibility or irresistibility of Gods grace', as such doctrines were 'fitter for the schooles and universities than for simple auditories'.[53] The effect of this prohibition was softened somewhat by the statement that predestination should be preached 'moderately and modestly by way of use and application, rather than by way of positive doctrine', which implied that there was nothing wrong with preaching predestination as long as it was done in a suitably practical manner. Archbishop Abbot, in his covering letter to his fellow

---

[52] Peter Lake, '"A charitable Christian hatred": the godly and their enemies in the 1630s', in C. Durston and J. Eales, eds., *The Culture of English Puritanism 1560–1700* (1996), pp. 145–83 (quotation pp. 182–3).

[53] The Directions are printed in Kenneth Fincham, ed., *Visitation Articles and Injunctions of the Early Stuart Church*, vol. 1 (Church of England Record Society, 1994), pp. 211–14.

bishops, insisted that the Directions were not intended to discourage 'discreet or religious preachers', but merely to restrain a few indiscreet ministers who handled difficult theological questions in a manner 'too deep for the capacitie of the people'. Nevertheless, the Directions were more ambiguous than Abbot was prepared to admit, and could certainly have been interpreted as a blanket prohibition of all predestinarian preaching. Bishop John Howson circulated copies to all parishes in the diocese of Oxford, with a covering letter warmly commending the Directions as conducive to 'a more religious and peaceable forme of preaching', without any of the qualifications that Abbot had been so careful to introduce.[54]

William Sclater's commentary on Thessalonians, first published in 1627, illustrates the suspicion with which many preachers regarded the Directions. Sclater was at least prepared to pay lip service to the new regulations, noting with only a touch of irony that 'in matter of Predestination wisedome of Superiors hath justly limited us Novices: wherefore I forbeare large handling'. Elsewhere in his commentary, however, he launched into a passionate defence of the preaching of predestination, declaring: 'me thinkes they are imprudently proudly cautionate, who by their good wils will have all mention thereof enclosed to the chaire in Schooles: not once to be whispered in our Homiles *ad Populum*: when yet Gods Spirit is plentifull in publishing this part of Gods counsell to the people . . . Prudence in publishing none but allowes; but they are over wise who wholly conceale it.' Not to preach on predestination, he insisted, was to deprive the Christian hearer of an 'incentive to faith and good workes' and a 'comfortable evidence of election'.[55] Such open criticism of the Directions suggests that they had relatively little effect in restricting controversial preaching, though even Sclater, while taking several pot shots at the doctrine of '*Arminius* and his Sectaries', seems to have felt inhibited by the Directions from refuting them as fully as he would have wished: 'my fingers itch at them', he wrote, slightly cryptically, 'but the backe akes'.[56]

The Directions were followed in 1628 by the royal Declaration for the Peace of the Church, accompanying a reissue of the Thirty-Nine Articles.[57]

---

[54] Fincham, *Visitation Articles*, vol. I, pp. 213–14 (Abbot's letter), p. 215 (Howson's letter).

[55] William Sclater, *An Exposition with Notes upon the First and Second Epistles to the Thessalonians* (1627), 2N1v (ii. 178). Sclater's commentary on 1 Thessalonians, first published in 1619 and reprinted here, contains a similar passage defending the preaching of predestination (2D4v, i. 438).

[56] Sclater, *Exposition*, 2N5r (ii. 185). Tyacke comments that the Directions 'seem to have been largely inoperative': *Anti-Calvinists*, p. 103. Jeanne Shami concurs that 'the practical impact of the Directions is difficult to document': *John Donne and Conformity in Crisis in the Late Jacobean Pulpit* (Woodbridge, 2003), p. 122.

[57] For the text of the Declaration, see Fincham, *Visitation Articles*, vol. II, pp. 33–4.

Like the Directions, this was an ambiguous document which left some room for interpretation. It made no specific mention of the doctrine of predestination, merely an oblique reference to the 'curious and unhappy differences, which have for so many hundred yeeres, in different times and places, exercised the Church of Christ'. It did not specifically forbid predestinarian preaching, but warned against 'unnecessary disputations, altercations or questions' and ordered the clergy to refrain from 'curious search' into matters of controversy. As with the Directions, it was possible to interpret this as referring only to a minority of sermons on particularly difficult or disputed points of doctrine, not to the broad mainstream of predestinarian preaching. Nor is it clear how much effect the new regulations actually had at a parish level: Robert Keayne's notebook, quoted earlier, shows that despite the 1622 Directions, sermons on predestination were still being preached from London pulpits in 1627–8, and it is unlikely that the publication of the Declaration did much to discourage this. More significant, perhaps, than the Declaration itself was the appointment of William Laud as Bishop of London in the same year, which has generally been seen as marking a new era of tighter repression in which the Declaration was used to curb predestinarian preaching in general.

Laud himself was reticent on the subject of predestination, and we know little for certain about his own views except that he particularly disliked the doctrine of Supralapsarianism. His answer to Lord Saye and Sele's speech on the liturgy, written in the Tower in the 1640s, lists the doctrinal errors of 'the Brownists or Separatists', including Supralapsarianism, which he rejects on the grounds that it makes God's decree of reprobation appear to be an act of arbitrary will rather than a just punishment for sin:

Almost all of them say that God from all eternity reprobates by far the greater part of mankind to eternal fire, without any eye at all to their sin. Which opinion my very soul abominates. For it makes God, the God of all mercies, to be the most fierce and unreasonable tyrant in the world. For the question is not here, what God may do by an absolute act of power, would He so use it upon the creature which He made of nothing, but what He hath done, and what stands with His wisdom, justice, and goodness to do.[58]

This has led Julian Davies to argue that Laud's policies were directed not at the doctrine of predestination in general but at double predestination in particular. Davies points out, reasonably enough, that as the doctrine of predestination was officially endorsed in the Thirty-Nine Articles, Laud

---

[58] William Laud, *Works*, ed. W. Scott and J. Bliss (Oxford, 1847–60), vol. VI, part 1 (Miscellaneous papers and letters), p. 133.

could hardly have expected or intended to prohibit all preaching on the subject. Instead, he suggests, Laud pursued a 'delicate policy of discriminating between single and double predestination', and only took discipliniary action against preachers who taught the doctrine of reprobation in such a way as to imply that God was the author of sin, that Christ had died only for the elect, or that those who fell from grace could never be saved.[59]

Official defences of Laudian policy certainly stressed that there was no intention to prohibit predestinarian preaching in general. In 1633 a group of London ministers headed by Henry Burton petitioned the king to complain that 'wee are not a litle discouraged and deterred from preaching those saving doctrines of gods free grace in election and predestination which greatlie confirme our faith of eternall salvation and fervently kindle our love to god'.[60] This provoked several responses from Laudian apologists attempting to explain and justify the new restrictions. Christopher Dow argued that the royal Declaration of 1628 was not intended to discourage 'sober' preaching on predestination, but to prevent 'disputes and clamorous invectives' and, more specifically, to restrain preachers from expounding the doctrine in such a way 'as to make God the author of sinne and obduration in sinne'.[61] Similarly, Thomas Jackson claimed that the Declaration was chiefly directed against the 'rigid doctrine of Absolute Reprobation' which held that 'God did from eternitie as truly hate the greater sort of men, as he did love the lesse, without all respect or reference to their works or qualifications', and that 'he did out of his eternal hatred, as peremptorily decree the endless torments of the One, as he did the everlasting happiness of the Other'.[62] The official line, therefore, was that ministers who taught the doctrine of predestination in a suitably moderate fashion had no need to worry; the Declaration was not aimed at them but at a small minority of extremists.

Other historians, however, have argued that Laud's agenda went much further. Nicholas Tyacke's analysis of the sermons preached at Paul's Cross

---

[59] Julian Davies, *The Caroline Captivity of the Church: Charles I and the Remoulding of Anglicanism* (Oxford, 1992), pp. 116–20.

[60] PRO, SP 16/408/170 (calendared in *CSPD 1638–9*, where dated [1638?]). Tyacke, *Anti-Calvinists*, pp. 181–2, assigns it to 1629, but it is clearly the 'petition directed to the King written in parchement and subscribed by 22. mynisters of the Cittie of London and liberties thereof' shown to Sir Thomas Jervoise by Henry Burton in February 1632/3 (Hampshire Record Office, Winchester, 44M69/G2/37; see also Sharpe, *Personal Rule*, p. 297).

[61] Christopher Dow, *Innovations Unjustly Charged upon the Present Church and State* (1637), S3v, Y4v.

[62] Thomas Jackson, 'A serious answer to Mr Burtons exception taken against a passage in his treatise of the divine essence and attributes', in Jackson, *An Exact Collection of the Works* (1654), 2B2v (p. 3188).

has shown that Laud's appointment as Bishop of London, which placed him in a position to control both the appointment of preachers and the subsequent publication of sermons, made it much more difficult for Calvinist preachers to get their views into print.[63] David Como has examined Laud's disciplinary action against puritan ministers in the diocese of London, and concluded that he was operating a blatant double standard in his enforcement of the 1628 Declaration. Ministers who continued to teach the Calvinist doctrine of predestination found themselves subjected to a campaign of sustained harassment and intimidation, whereas their anti-Calvinist opponents were quietly tolerated or, at most, gently dissuaded from expressing their opinions in too public a fashion. Como suggests that Laud saw the doctrine of predestination as a political as well as a religious threat, 'a danger to the harmony and unity of the political nation' as well as a departure from the received doctrine of the Church. Nor was Laud alone in this, for by the early 1630s, the king and his leading ministers had come to perceive 'a direct link between puritanism, predestination, and popular political disobedience', and the campaign against predestination can therefore be seen as part of a more general effort to quell sedition and disloyalty through the exercise of sovereign power.[64]

It is perfectly true, as Davies argues, that much of the official action, as well as the official rhetoric against predestinarian preaching was directed specifically at the doctrine of Supralapsarianism. But it would be unwise to take this at face value, as it seems likely that it was intended to have a broader application to other forms of predestinarian doctrine as well. An insight into the thinking behind Laudian policy is provided by a manuscript treatise from the mid-1630s which argues for much stricter limits on the preaching of predestination.[65] The writer begins in deceptively moderate fashion by declaring that the doctrine of predestination, if 'soberly handled', may have 'excellent uses': among others, 'it helpeth to fortify us against pride and carnall securitie', 'ingendreth love towardes our neighbours' and

---

[63] Tyacke, *Anti-Calvinists*, p. 263. See also Cyndia Clegg, *Press Censorship in Jacobean England* (Cambridge, 2001), p. 122, and S. Mutchow Towers, *Control of Religious Printing in Early Stuart England* (Woodbridge, 2003), pp. 209–72.

[64] David R. Como, 'Predestination and political conflict in Laud's London', *Historical Journal*, 46: 2 (June 2003), pp. 263–94.

[65] BL Harl. MS 5250, ff. 1–4, 'Whether we may lawfully dispute or preach of praedestination especially before the common people'. The manuscript is an incomplete copy of a treatise on the doctrine of the Church of England, which proceeds by setting out the respective positions of the English and Roman Churches and then arguing for a 'reconciliation' between the two. With regard to predestination, the author defends the Arminian doctrine of a 'conditional foreknowledge' (f. 30r) and attacks the opposing arguments of John Prideaux, 'our most learned Oxonian professor' (f. 41r).

'produceth in us a longing to doe good workes'. However, 'the more hidden and the now controverted pointes of predestination' are not to be handled 'in a popular auditorye', both 'in regard of their obscurity and difficulty' and also 'in regard of the peace of the Church, and of the scandall that may come thereby, especially in the preaching of the absolute decree of predestination'. The particular points singled out as unsuitable for popular preaching were precisely those in dispute between Calvinists and Arminians, such as 'whether predestination be of merits or workes foreseene' and 'whether the predestinate may be damned, or the reprobate saved'. Prohibiting discussion of these points would effectively have prevented Calvinist preachers from handling the doctrines of assurance and final perseverance, which they regarded as non-negotiable aspects of Reformed orthodoxy. Whether or not this was Laud's own intention, it is clear that some members of his circle would have liked to see predestinarian preaching cut back to the barest minimum.

It would, however, be misleading to suppose that Calvinism had simply been silenced and replaced by a new anti-Calvinist orthodoxy. The boundaries of orthodoxy were not so clear-cut: and instead of one dominant orthodoxy established by authority and disseminated through preaching, we find a more fluid and unstable situation in which different parties competed, through the pulpits, to present their opposing versions of orthodoxy to the public. As we have already seen, Laudian apologists sought to make their version of orthodoxy appear moderate and inclusive by arguing that it was only designed to exclude the more rigid and extreme forms of predestinarian preaching. Moreover, as Lake and Como have shown, Laudian and puritan versions of orthodoxy could sometimes coincide, as both parties were concerned about the dangers of antinomianism and could, on occasion, join forces to silence a troublesome radical preacher.[66] The rise of antinomianism in the late 1620s thus brought Laudians and puritans together in a temporary alliance of convenience, while at the same time serving to highlight the differences between them as they sought to exploit the perceived crisis and turn it to their advantage. It gave Laudians an opportunity to attack predestinarian preaching by associating it with antinomianism; it gave puritans an opportunity to demonstrate their moderation, and show that they were handling predestination soberly and responsibly, by distancing themselves from antinomianism; and it gave antinomians an opportunity to argue that there was no essential difference

---

[66] David Como and Peter Lake, 'Puritans, antinomians and Laudians in Caroline London: the strange case of Peter Shaw and its contexts', *Journal of Ecclesiastical History*, 59: 4 (1999), pp. 684–715.

between their opponents, whether Laudian or puritan, as they were all equally tainted with Arminianism. Which of these competing definitions of orthodoxy would stick depended on which could be presented most persuasively, and disseminated most widely, in the pulpit and the press.

We can see this in action in the disciplinary proceedings taken by Laud against preachers in the diocese of London. Some of the preachers targeted seem to have been genuine antinomians, but others were orthodox Calvinists whose doctrines were singled out because they could be plausibly linked with antinomianism. One such was Meredith Madey, lecturer at Christ Church Aldgate, who declared in a sermon in March 1631 'that election is not universall and common, but speciall and peculiar belonging to some'. He argued that since election was the work of the whole Trinity, it was expressed both in the will of the Father and in the death of the Son. 'God doth whatsoever he will, but God doth not save all, therefore he will not have all saved.' Likewise, 'none are elected but such for whom Christ died, but he died not for all', so not all are elected. Madey ended his sermon by promising 'the next day to deale upon reprobation and also to follow this very method in the prosecution thereof' – a promise that he was unable to fulfil, as Laud intervened to suspend him four days later.[67] Madey appears to have been teaching a fairly standard, if bluntly stated, doctrine of limited atonement, but the record of his sermon that landed on Laud's desk drew attention to certain passages in the sermon that seemed to verge on antinomianism. Starting from the premise that God's decree of election took no account of human merit, Madey argued that the elect were chosen 'before they had done good or evill, nay, before they had a being'. He went on to declare that the elect were 'by nature enemies, children of wrath, dead in sins', and 'therefore concluded there was no worthines in the elect to move God'. These incautious statements gave his opponents the excuse they needed to denounce him to the ecclesiastical authorities and, in doing so, to suggest that the preaching of predestination led inevitably to antinomianism.

The same pattern emerges in the High Commission case against the London preacher Henry Roborough in June 1634. The charge against Roborough was not simply that he had preached on the doctrine of predestination, but that he had told his congregation that Christ died for the elect alone. According to the indictment, he had declared

---

[67] Notes on Madey's sermon: PRO, SP 16/186/41 (calendared in *CSPD 1629–31*, p. 528), and his inhibition from preaching, SP 16/186/75 (calendared in *CSPD 1629–31*, p. 534). The case is discussed by Davies, *Caroline Captivity*, p. 119, and Como, 'Predestination and political conflict', p. 282–3.

that Christ maketh intercession for the elect and for the elect only, which confuted that false opinion (as you termed it) that Christ dyed for the Synnes of the whole world, and you further delivered in theis wordes, that it maketh against falling from grace, because (as you affirmed) Christ doth all for us; hee hath the Covenante whollie in his handes both to doe and execute all himselfe; and you further concluded and said that Christs intercession saves us from condemnation, soe as noe sinnes, be they never soe haynous, shalbe layed to the charge of the Elect, for that Christ had or hath allready acquitted them from the barr of Gods Justice. Soe then lett every Child of God saye there be tenn thousand sinnes that assault me yett I will never faint or doubt, or once stagger in the matter of salvation.[68]

Again, this was clearly designed to establish a link between limited atonement and antinomianism. However, Roborough's response to the charge is also very revealing. He admitted having taught that Christ 'dyed not for all', but took great care to dissociate himself from the suspicion of antinomianism. By his own account, he had told his congregation that 'there was noe cause for any of Gods elect and faithfull to faint or dispare of salvation whatsoever their synnes are', citing 1 John 2: 1 ('If any man sin, we have an advocate with the Father'). But he had then gone on to stress that assurance did not take away the need for repentance:

he willed them withall to remember what the same St John speaketh, if we confesse our Synnes he is faithfull and iust to forgive us Synnes, and the bloud of Jesus Christ Gods Sonn shall cleanse us from all our Synnes, which repentance for Synne must be practised by us as we looke for comfort from this Advocate.

In David Como's account of the case, Roborough is portrayed as a defiant opponent of the Laudian regime, crying out in frustration at the attempt to silence him.[69] Yet there was plainly some room for bargaining and negotiation here. Roborough's defence was cleverly designed to exploit the Laudian rhetoric of moderation by portraying himself as an orthodox preacher who had handled the doctrine of predestination in a sober and responsible manner. In this way ministers such as Roborough could fly under the Laudian radar, as it were, as long as they exercised some discretion in the way they preached predestination, and garnished their doctrine of assurance and perseverance with the necessary saving clauses about the need for repentance and good works.

Preachers who were prepared to compromise with the ecclesiastical authorities, and to package their sermons in suitably moderate language, had considerable room for manoeuvre: for while one aspect of the Laudian

---

[68] 'Articles obiected . . . against Henry Roborough', Trinity College, Dublin, MS 293, ff. 387–401.
[69] Como, 'Predestination and political conflict', p. 289.

programme was the suppression of preaching that was (or could be made to appear) rigid and extreme in its doctrine of predestination, another was the promotion of a moderate alternative that could be held up as a model for other preachers to follow. The Laudians therefore had every reason to encourage the development of less extreme varieties of Calvinism such as that represented by Arthur Lake, Laud's immediate predecessor as Bishop of Bath and Wells, whose sermons were published in a collected edition in 1629. Lake was no Arminian, as is clear from the anti-Arminian asides scattered throughout his writings, such as his attack on the 'Arminian dreame' that man has free will in the first act of conversion. At the same time, he was strongly opposed to the doctrine of limited atonement, and insisted that God willed the salvation of all men, not just the elect. Expounding 1 Timothy 2: 4 ('God will have all men saved and come to the knowledge of his truth'), he emphasised that 'all' really did mean all: 'not only the greater part, but every one, not only all sorts of men, but every one of every sort ... If any be excluded, hee excludeth himselfe.'[70] Lake's influence can be seen in the sermons of some of his clerical protégés, such as the London minister Nicholas Guy, who declared in 1625, in a funeral sermon for Elizabeth Gouge, wife of the celebrated puritan minister William Gouge, that God's offer of saving grace was 'without limitation of time or place or condition of men ... If we partake not of it, the fault is ours ... it is promised and proffered to all men living'.[71]

Lake's sermons are notable for their reluctance to deal with disputed points of divinity. 'Time and again', as Kenneth Fincham observes, 'he sidestepped points of academic debate or confessional controversy', particularly in his treatment of predestination, where he made it clear that, in his opinion, theological inquiry had got out of hand.[72] One of his sermons criticises ministers who 'over-studie themselves in the Booke of Gods providence, and would know more than is possible for man to conceive of Gods counsell in Predestination', while another sermon complains that sound and profitable preaching has all too often been supplanted by fruitless speculation: 'The world is much sicke of this disease, and you shall heare oftner of idle and curious questions, than of those that concerne the health of mens soules.' Again this is echoed in Guy's sermon, which warns against prying too closely into God's secret counsel, and urges his listeners to rest

---

[70] Arthur Lake, *Sermons* (1629), 2K4v (i. 420).
[71] Nicholas Guy, *Pieties Pillar: or, A Sermon Preached at the Funerall of Mistresse Elizabeth Gouge* (1626), B4v (p. 14).
[72] Kenneth Fincham, *Prelate as Pastor: The Episcopate of James I* (Oxford, 1990), pp. 261, 269–70.

content with the express words of scripture. Whether all men are allotted the same measure of saving grace, Guy declares, 'is a secret lockt up in the bosome of God . . . But laying that aside for the Schooles, this is that which is more fit to exhort and perswade withall in our Pulpits, and which our Church hath taught us, that we should content our selves with this, we must receive Gods promises in such wise as they be generally set forth unto us in holy Scripture; not restraining them or determining them in particular to this or that man.'[73]

In one sense, there is nothing particularly unusual about these remarks, which merely echo the 1622 Directions in drawing a distinction between the 'schools' and the 'pulpit' and reiterate what many Reformed divines had already said about the need to expound the doctrine of predestination in a suitably practical and pastoral fashion. But something more is going on here. In one of Lake's longest comments on predestination, he praises the doctrine of the Reformed Churches as 'sound and good' but frankly admits that it may have dangerous consequences:

We are not ignorant of the Romish calumnies, and of the distraction of our brethren in forraine parts about this doctrine; happily some occasion hereof may be because some deliver Theologie more Theoretically than practically. It were to be wished, that, at least, in so much as must come to the vulgar eye and eare, this method were changed: lest, as it hath, so it proove dangerous to many; though (I dare say) that, if the parts of the doctrine publikely authorized by the Reformed Churches be charitably laid together (and otherwise to construe the writing is against good manners by a rule in the Civill Law) wee shall find nothing but that which may passe for sound and good.[74]

This is a remarkably half-hearted defence of Reformed orthodoxy, all the more remarkable coming from a leading Calvinist bishop who had acted as a consultant to the British delegation at the Synod of Dort. Despite the measured and conciliatory rhetoric, it is clear that Lake was profoundly uncomfortable with certain aspects of Reformed teaching on predestination. True to his principle of avoiding controversy in the pulpit, he did not specify precisely what (or who) he had in mind; but it is likely that his reference to 'some' who handled the doctrine 'more Theoretically than practically' was a veiled criticism of the Supralapsarian position.

Lake's misgivings about Reformed orthodoxy also extended to the doctrine of assurance. He argued in one sermon that although faith was grounded in the covenant, it could only be judged by its outward effects. 'Wherefore the Covenant is not the first step where wee must begin our

---

[73] Guy, *Pieties Pillar*, B5v (p. 16).    [74] Lake, *Sermons*, 2S1r (i. 509).

triall, much lesse may wee begin at Predestination; we must by degrees of reason read the gifts of God in our Faith, Hope, and Charitie, to worke which, the Word and Sacraments were ordained; if wee find these, they argue Gods love to us, they proove we stand in good tearmes with him.' Again, there is nothing particularly unusual about this line of argument, but it seems to reflect a concern on Lake's part that some people were paying too much attention to the inward signs of election, and too little to the outward evidence of good works.[75] Remarkably, Lake was even prepared to treat the doctrine of final perseverance – one of the most important points of disagreement between the Arminians and their opponents – as an open question, at least in the context of pulpit exhortation. 'There is a question, *An iustus posset excidere a gratia?* [whether a justified man may fall from grace], but of this which is in my Text there is no question; Papists, Lutherans, Protestants, all are agreed that he that persevereth to the end shal be saved, shall be glorified; And I would to God the world did take more care to persevere, than to dispute of the certaintie of persevering.'[76]

This must have been music to Laud's ears. Here was a highly respected member of the Jacobean episcopate, the very model of the zealous 'preaching pastor', a staunch supporter of Reformed orthodoxy and an opponent of Popery and Arminianism, yet one who shared many of the Laudians' distinctive concerns. As a bishop, Lake took care to ensure that theological controversy did not get out of control, and warned his diocesan clergy that they should 'preach nothing but that which is profitable'. As a theologian, he was plainly uncomfortable with the divisive language of limited atonement and tried to promote a more inclusive alternative, declaring that 'in a Ministers Commission Grace is Universall' and that the clergy should therefore 'labour the conversion of all and every one' without attempting to distinguish between the elect and the reprobate. As a pastor, he feared that the quest for personal assurance might easily develop into an unhealthy obsession, and encouraged his listeners to ground their assurance not on minute self-examination, but on the public services of the church and the external evidence of their good works. All this brought him very close to Laud – so much so, indeed, that Lake's brand of moderate Calvinist churchmanship might even be regarded as a form of Laudianism *avant la lettre*.

A manuscript collection of sermons preached in the 1630s, now in the Folger Shakespeare Library in Washington, DC, shows how the doctrines of assurance and perseverance were expounded by the Laudians

[75] Lake, *Sermons*, 2R6v (i. 508).    [76] Lake, *Sermons*, 4K6v (iii. 120).

themselves.[77] A sermon on Romans 11: 20 ('Be not high-minded, but fear'), preached at St Mary's, Oxford, in April 1633, stresses the need for Christians to live in a state of pious fear. 'Feare, but what? Plainly this, lest [thou] who standest by faith shouldst fall . . . Whether the righteous at any time doth fall finally or totally, I cannot define . . . That which I desire to press in all Humility, is that yee take great heede lest ye fall.' The preacher went on to criticise Calvin (not mentioned by name, but merely described as 'a late man') for claiming that the text refers not to particular individuals but to the whole body of the visible Church. Such an interpretation would 'make all past feare', and encourage men to live in security; yet 'if any man presume he need not feare falling, it is a strong presumption against him that hee is not yet risen'. And the preacher concluded by outlining the proper doctrine of assurance. Our assurance should be 'a fullnes of hope, not of faithe' (Heb. 6: 11). Our fear should be 'not such a feare as might move us to distrust the Mercie of God (farr be that from any man) but a pious feare which makes us carefully to use all diligence in doing those things which St Peter tells us must be done to make our Election sure'.

Another sermon by the same preacher, also probably preached in Oxford, takes Genesis 13: 8 ('Let there be no strife, I pray thee, between thee and me') as the starting point for a discussion of religious controversy and schism.[78] It begins with a passage of fierce anti-papal polemic, arguing that the four major schisms in the Church – the Pope's usurpation of the title of universal bishop; his willingness to permit the idolatrous adoration of images; his pretended authority over princes; and his pretended authority over councils – are all the fault of the Papacy. But the preacher goes on to point out that there are schisms among the Protestant Churches too, caused by the arrogance of some men 'who presuming upon the familiar acquaintance they have with God, and insight into his Actions . . . will tell you the nature of his election'. This is followed by a highly significant passage on the doctrine of predestination. 'God hathe his Elect and his Election, and his Election shall stand firme, though perhaps it may bee in thine owne hand too to put thyselfe in or out of it. And though we cannot conceive how the predeterminate will of God may stand together with our loose free-will, yea free choice, yett since the Scripture is cleare bothe in the point of predestination and Mans free choice, for it was noe fain'd Ejaculation, Why will yee die O yee house of Israel? We ought to beleeve bothe, though wee cannot well spell them and put them bothe together.'

---

[77] Folger Library, Washington, DC, V.a.1, ff. 54, 57 ('St Maries Oxon Aprill 1633').
[78] Folger Library, Washington, DC, V.a.1, ff. 24–6.

These sermons neither accept nor reject the Calvinist doctrine of final perseverance. Instead, they treat it as an undecided question: 'Whether the righteous at any time doth fall finally or totally, I cannot define'; '[God's] election shall stand firme, though perhaps it may bee in thine owne hand too to put thyselfe in or out of it.' This seems to have been part of a concerted strategy on the part of Laud and his circle. When Laud's chaplain William Bray censored the text of Daniel Featley's sermon collection, *Clavis Mystica* (1636), he removed all the passages in which Featley upheld the doctrine of final perseverance, and replaced them with new passages leaving the doctrine unresolved:

Whatsoever may be alledged for the stability of evangelicall righteousnesse, and their permanency who are engraffed into the true Vine, Christ Jesus; daily experience sheweth that the most righteous on earth may and sometimes do remit of the strict observance of their duty.[79]

Not curiously to dispute the Scholasticall question concerning the absolute impossibilitie of the apostacy of any Saint, and the amissibility of justifying faith, which many learned Doctours of the Reformed Churches hold fitter to bee *extermined* than determined, or at least confined to the Schooles, than defined in the Pulpit: that wherein all parties agree is sufficient to *comfort the fainting spirits, and strengthen the feeble knees* of any relapsed Christian; That God will never bee wanting to raise him, if hee bee not wanting to himselfe.[80]

Here, then, we have the preferred Laudian model for the preaching of predestination. Calvinism was no longer to be endorsed as the received doctrine of the Church of England, but neither was it to be rejected outright. Rather, it was to be tolerated – at least in its more moderate, Infralapsarian form – as one of a range of alternatives within the fold of orthodoxy. The result, in terms of pulpit rhetoric, was a compromise, with the doctrines of assurance and perseverance expounded in a practical manner that would be suitable for unlearned audiences and that could be accepted by moderate Calvinists and Arminians alike.

There were, of course, significant theological differences between these different schools of thought. Lake's moderate Infralapsarianism (sometimes termed 'hypothetical universalism') would have been regarded by most Reformed divines as an acceptable variation of Reformed orthodoxy, whereas Arminianism would have been seen as an unacceptable deviation from it. Yet in terms of pulpit rhetoric, there was a genuine convergence

---

[79] Daniel Featley, *Clavis Mystica* (1636), 3V1r–1v (pp. 769–70), second state. I discuss the censorship of Featley's sermons in 'Licensing and religious censorship in early modern England', in Andrew Hadfield, ed., *Literature and Censorship in Renaissance England* (Basingstoke, 2001), pp. 127–46.
[80] Featley, *Clavis Mystica*, C2v (p. 16), second state.

between the two, even to the point where it can be difficult to tell the difference between them. In the case of John Donne, for example, it is by no means straightforward to tell whether the sermons preached at court in the late 1620s and early 1630s, with their warnings against unnecessary speculation into the 'secret purposes of God', and their encouragement of a 'holy certitude and a modest infallibility' rather than an absolute assurance of election, represent the views of a moderate Calvinist seeking to distance himself from the extreme Supralapsarian position, or of a convert to Laudianism seeking to align himself with the newly fashionable line of anti-Calvinist divinity.[81] Ultimately, of course, the similarities in pulpit rhetoric failed to disguise the doctrinal divisions underneath, and the alliance with moderate Calvinism that Laud had tried to broker was undone by political conflict and the widespread belief that it was merely the cover for an anti-Calvinist or even crypto-Catholic agenda. But for a short period in the 1630s it was not unreasonable for Laud to believe that the royal Declaration for the Peace of the Church had achieved its stated aim, and quietened the disputes over predestination, by setting a standard for predestinarian preaching that all parties could accept.

## CONCLUSION

I began this chapter with a roll-call of historians who have argued, in what amounts almost to consensus, that predestination was a subject of no great concern to most people in early modern England. These arguments have an important element of truth. They remind us that clergy and laity did not always see things in the same terms, and that works of controversial divinity do not necessarily have much to tell us about the way that religion was experienced and understood by ordinary laypeople. Lorna Jane Abray has suggested that for the laity in Lutheran Germany, doctrinal orthodoxy was of less moment than 'a simple Bible-based religion everyone could understand, good morals that everyone could appreciate and practise, [and] a church in which the clergy served the laity and did not dictate to them'. Mark Byford has put forward a similar argument in his important study of Elizabethan Essex, where he suggests that what Protestantism really boiled down to, as far as the laity were concerned, was an awareness of human

---

[81] The case for Donne as an Arminian is put by Achsah Guibbory in 'Donne's religion: Montagu, Arminianism and Donne's sermons, 1624–1630', *English Literary Renaissance*, 31 (2001), pp. 412–39. The case for Donne as a moderate Calvinist is put by me in 'The English nation in 1631', in Jeanne Shami, Thomas Hester and Dennis Flynn, eds., *The Oxford Handbook of Donne Studies* (Oxford, forthcoming 2010–11).

sinfulness and inability to merit salvation through works, coupled with access to the Word of God through bible-reading and sermon attendance.[82] It was thus possible to consider oneself a Protestant in early modern England, and for all practical purposes actually to *be* a Protestant, without an informed understanding of the doctrine of predestination.

But the idea that predestination was merely an academic speculation, confined to the universities and rarely expressed from the pulpit, is one that simply will not stand up to examination. I have argued in this chapter that there was widespread popular acceptance of predestination as a component of Protestant orthodoxy. This should not come as a surprise, given that, as Nicholas Tyacke has shown, the Elizabethan and early Stuart Church was in many respects doctrinally Calvinist, yet even Tyacke drew most of his evidence from élite sources, such as theological treatises and academic disputations, and did not have much to say about the extent to which predestinarian ideas might have trickled down into popular consciousness. In fact, as we have seen, the pulpit was a crucial point of interaction between élite and popular religion. Calvinist ministers defended the preaching of predestination by pointing to its pastoral benefits as a 'comfortable doctrine' establishing believers more securely in their faith. Many laypeople, even if they did not enter fully into the theological debates, were sufficiently aware of them to feel threatened by an attack on predestinarian doctrine, and to regard this as an attack on Protestant orthodoxy and a return to a Popish religion of free will and human merit.

At the same time, the theological conflict over predestination was mediated through pulpit discourse in ways that make it impossible to regard it simply as a confrontation between massed ranks of Calvinists and anti-Calvinists. In a remarkably candid and revealing passage from a sermon preached to an audience of London lawyers, Daniel Featley explained how theological disagreements could be expressed indirectly, using the familiar rhetorical technique of positioning oneself in the moderate centre while pushing one's opponents to the margins. Significantly, though, Featley chose to present this not as an observation about the preaching of sermons but about the way they were heard and interpreted. 'Such is the condition of most hearers,' he remarked, 'that the Minister of God, though upon good warrant from his text, can hardly rebuke the publike enemies of Church or

---

[82] Lorna Jane Abray, 'The laity's religion: Lutheranism in sixteenth-century Strasbourg', in R. Po-Chia Hsia, ed., *The German People and the Reformation* (Ithaca, NY, 1988), pp. 216–33 (quotation p. 232); Mark Byford, 'The price of Protestantism: assessing the impact of religious change on Elizabethan Essex' (unpublished DPhil thesis, University of Oxford, 1988).

State, but hee shall procure private enemies to himself.' Rightly or wrongly, every hearer tended to assume that the preacher's criticisms were directed at him:

If he stand for, or be inclinable unto the new, or newly taken up expressions of devotion, he suspects the Preacher glanceth at him under the name of a temporizer, or symbolizer with Papists. If hee bee averse from such customes and rites, hee conceiveth himselfe to bee taxed under the name of a refractory Non-conformitant. If hee make any great shew of religion, hee thinkes himselfe pointed at in the reproofe of an Hypocrite; if little or no shew, he feeles himselfe galled in the reprehension of the prophane worldling. If hee rellish the leaven of *Arminius*, he takes himselfe to bee wounded through the *Pelagians*; if of *Cartwright*, through the *Brownists*; if of *Cassander*, or the Catholike Moderatour, through the lukewarme *Laodicean* sides.[83]

These codes of pulpit discourse enabled preachers to signal disagreement without having to express it directly, knowing that the more attentive members of their audience would recognise an attack on 'Pelagians' as referring to Arminians, an attack on 'Brownists' as referring to puritans, or an attack on 'Laodiceans' as referring to Church Papists. In this way they could attack an opposing theological position that stood within the bounds of orthodoxy, by associating it with an extreme version of the same position that was clearly outside those boundaries. Crucially, however, these codes did not have a fixed meaning and could be applied in different ways. Coming from a moderate Calvinist preacher, a warning against excessive speculation on predestination might be used to indicate dissent from the high Calvinist position; coming from a Laudian preacher, it might be used to signal a rejection of Calvinism in all its forms. The same language, and the same set of uncontroversial commonplaces, could thus be used to express a range of very different religious opinions in ways that served not simply to disguise but actually to define, or redefine, the nature of the disagreement.

And what, finally, of the wider history of predestination, considered as an episode in the *longue durée* of the history of doctrine? 'We are all so much Arminians now', Christopher Hill wrote in 1972, 'that it requires a great imaginative effort to think ourselves back into the pre-revolutionary society which Calvinism dominated.' It was, he suggested, as though Calvinism had existed to serve its (predestined?) historical function as a carrier for the Protestant ethic, and having fulfilled this 'historic task' it then obediently

---

[83] Featley, *Clavis Mystica*, 2I5r (p. 369), from a sermon preached at Serjeants Inn, Fleet Street.

expired.[84] Yet the doctrine of predestination did not fade away overnight; indeed, it could be argued that it never faded away at all. The conflict between John Wesley's Arminianism and George Whitefield's Calvinism divided eighteenth-century Methodism and continued to be debated, though with less rancour, in nineteenth- and twentieth-century evangelicalism.[85] Peter Thuesen, in his recent book on predestination in America, points out that in the last few decades, the doctrine has been revived by several Protestant churches, notably the conservative Lutherans of the Missouri Synod and the biblical inerrantists of the Southern Baptist Convention.[86] To Hill's remark that the 'collapse of Calvinism' is 'one of the fascinating problems in the intellectual history of seventeenth-century England', Thuesen might well respond that the resurgence of Calvinism is one of the fascinating problems in the intellectual history of twenty-first-century America.

But Hill's argument about the decline of Calvinism, though over-schematic in the contrast it draws between an old (Reformation) religion founded on dogmatic theology and a new (Enlightenment) religion founded on moral self-improvement, should not be dismissed out of hand. Theusen ends his book with a visit to one of the mega-churches of suburban California, Pastor Rick Warren's Saddleback Church (affiliated, as he notes, to the Southern Baptist Convention), where he observes a curious paradox, that while there is much talk of God's purpose for creation, and his controlling influence over the lives of individuals, there is very little overt discussion of the doctrine of predestination, which emerges only as a 'ghostly presence ... like an erasure still visible on a manuscript page'. Writing of the early modern period, Alexandra Walsham has argued that providentialism put down deep roots in popular culture, but that predestination did not. Thuesen's observations suggest a similar conclusion: that while the providentialist vision of a 'purpose-driven life' still has widespread appeal, and the predestinarian vision of utter subjection to a sovereign God still exerts a powerful grip, the doctrine itself has largely ceased to matter.

---

[84] Christopher Hill, *The World Turned Upside Down* (1972; repr. 1975), pp. 342–3, repeated in *Some Intellectual Consequences of the English Revolution* (1980), pp. 71–2, and *Liberty Against the Law: Some Seventeenth-Century Controversies* (1996), p. 310.

[85] Boyd Hilton, *The Age of Atonement: The Influence of Evangelicalism on Social and Economic Thought 1785–1865* (Oxford, 1986), pp. 8–9. For a glimpse of the debate in mid-twentieth-century British evangelicalism, see D. Martyn Lloyd-Jones, *Letters 1919–1981*, ed. Iain H. Murray (Edinburgh, 1994), pp. 189–90.

[86] Peter J. Thuesen, *Predestination: The American Career of a Contentious Doctrine* (Oxford, 2009), pp. 167–8, 203–8. A poll of SBC pastors found that nearly half (47%) preached on the subject of Calvinism 'several times a year or more' (p. 208).

'Jesus commands my destiny', declares a popular evangelical hymn, written in 2001, which goes on to affirm the doctrine of final perseverance in language that might have come straight from the mouth of a seventeenth-century preacher: 'No power of hell, no scheme of man, can ever pluck me from his hand'. But it is doubtful how many of those who sing these words would interpret them in specifically predestinarian terms.

Perhaps, then, the final word should be given to Robert Darnton, who observes in *The Great Cat Massacre* that 'the best points of entry in an attempt to penetrate an alien culture can be those where it seems to be most opaque'. Darnton goes on: 'When you realise that you are not getting something – a joke, a proverb, a ceremony – that is particularly meaningful to the natives, you can see where to grasp a foreign system of meaning in order to unravel it.'[87] The current tendency among historians of early modern religion is to stand back from the close examination of doctrinal issues and to focus, instead, on the broader pattern of culture. But there may be something to be said for taking the opposite approach, and using the doctrine of predestination as a point of entry into the religious world of sixteenth- and seventeenth-century England. The fascination of predestination – and the reason why, for all its difficulty and complexity, it is a subject worth wrestling with – arises from the challenge of explaining how a doctrine that now matters so little could once have mattered so much.

---

[87]  Robert Darnton, *The Great Cat Massacre* (New York, 1984; repr. 1991), p. 82.

# Conclusion

My father always preached from notes, and I wrote my sermons out
word for word. There are boxes of them in the attic . . . His sermons
were remarkable, but he never wrote them out. He didn't even keep
his notes. So that is all gone. I remember a phrase here and there. I
think every day about going through those old sermons of mine to see
if there are one or two I might want you to read sometime, but there
are so many, and I'm afraid, first of all, that most of them might seem
foolish or dull to me. It might be best to burn them.

Marilynne Robinson, *Gilead* (2004)

This book has attempted to trace the outlines of a 'sermon culture' in the late
sixteenth- and early seventeenth-century Church of England; a religious
culture in which preaching was regarded as the principal duty of the minister,
the principal means of opening the scriptures and making them available to
the people, and in which the sermon – as speech act, as live performance and as
public event – therefore occupied a central place. This sermon culture was, to a
considerable extent, a puritan culture, achieving its most distinctive form in
godly parishes and households and in the set of practices that I have labelled
the 'art of hearing'. But its influence extended far beyond the godly community. It was a popular culture, which succeeded in establishing, among the
thousands who attended the open-air sermons at Paul's Cross or heard
sermons preached weekly in their parish church, an almost universal sense of
the importance of the word preached; and an élite culture, too, reaching its
finest literary expression in the great set-piece sermons preached by Lancelot
Andrewes and John Donne at the Jacobean court, which – more than any
other sermons of the period – have caused the early seventeenth century to be
regarded as a golden age of preaching.

This sermon culture was by no means static or unchanging. The
theory of confessionalisation, which currently dominates the field of Reformation history, holds that a period of creative anarchy in the early Reformation
gradually gave way, in the later sixteenth century, to a hardening of

confessional boundaries and, ultimately, a kind of trench warfare as opposing religious groups dug themselves in behind polemical lines. For evidence of this we need only look at the way that the great religious controversies of the Elizabethan period, such as Whitgift's debate with Cartwright, set the polemical agenda for decades afterwards. But recent studies of the 'long Reformation' in England have made it very clear that the period of creative fluidity lasted well into the seventeenth century; that Protestants and Papists, puritans and conformists, were often surprisingly close to each other, and that the polemical arguments that served to keep them apart are not always a good guide to religious reality on the ground. Sermon culture is no exception. It has been a major theme of this book, particularly the two final chapters, that preachers were not simply repeating the same tired old arguments over and over again. Sermon rhetoric had to be flexible in order to adapt to new political and theological challenges, and even the stock polemical figures of Puritanism or Popery could not simply be taken for granted but had to be constantly argued into existence by different preachers before different audiences. Now, in conclusion, I want to consider the afterlife of this sermon culture in the later seventeenth century and beyond. How long did it survive – or how far did it change? What were its long-term effects?

There is a case to be made that the sermon culture of the late Elizabethan and early Stuart period survived and flourished, largely unchanged, in the Restoration Church. It is not difficult to find examples of individuals whose religious life and practice revolved around the hearing of sermons: the diary of Mary Rich, Countess of Warwick (1624–78), for example, reveals a style of sermon-centred piety which would have been instantly familiar to an earlier generation of puritans. Lady Rich regularly attended two sermons on Sunday; her diary records the preacher and his text, often with a note that she found her 'affections much wrought upon' or her 'heart much melted'. On Sunday evenings she asked one of the other women in her household to repeat the sermon, and then, before going to bed, retired for a period of private prayer in which she meditated on the sermons she had heard that day and 'prayed them over'.[1] All the essentials of the puritan art of hearing are here: the fixed routine of sabbath observance organised around the sermon; the affective response to preaching; the repetition of the sermon, conducted both individually and collectively within the household; and the incorporation of the sermon into private prayer. If Lady Rich's diary had been written fifty years earlier, there

---

[1] Mary Rich's diaries are BL Add. 27351–5. Sara Mendelson provides a useful biographical account of Mary Rich in *The Mental World of Stuart Women* (Brighton, 1987), pp. 62–115, but is unsympathetic to her religiosity; for a more recent discussion, see Raymond Anselment, 'Mary Rich, Countess of Warwick, and the gift of tears', *The Seventeenth Century*, 22: 2 (2007), pp. 336–57.

would have been no difficulty about fitting her into the tradition of godly piety most famously represented by Lady Margaret Hoby; yet now, in the 1660s and 1670s, the same style of piety could be refashioned as an exemplary model of Anglican devotion – in the words of her funeral sermon, 'the most illustrious pattern of a sincere piety and solid goodness this age has produced'.

Another fascinating example of continuity can be found in *A Discourse of Profiting by Sermons* (1684) by the moderate Anglican bishop Simon Patrick, which drew heavily on a collection of puritan sermons published more than half a century earlier, Arthur Hildersham's *Lectures upon the Fourth of Iohn* (1629). The aim of Patrick's treatise was to dissuade London churchgoers from leaving their parish churches in order to hear sermons by nonconformist ministers, and Hildersham's arguments against sermon-gadding (which we encountered in Chapter 4) suited his purpose very well. His use of Hildersham's writings was partly tactical, in the knowledge that the nonconformist readers he was addressing would be more likely to respect the arguments of a famous puritan divine than those of an Anglican bishop. However, it also illustrates the remarkable continuity in habits and patterns of sermon attendance. Many people, it appeared, wanted sermons that would stir up their emotions, and therefore 'run from their own Minister to hear some other (though of the same way) meerly to have the affections more moved'. In attempting to persuade them otherwise, Patrick deployed some of the familiar commonplaces of the art of hearing, such as the need for reverent attention in public worship ('as if the whole congregation were but one man') and the benefits of private meditation in helping to reinforce the preacher's words and 'press them upon your hearts'.[2]

And preaching not only remained at the centre of personal piety, it also occupied a pivotal place in public discourse throughout the seventeenth and eighteenth centuries. The last few decades have seen a rising tide of new scholarship stressing the importance of religion in the 'long eighteenth century', which has made it increasingly difficult to maintain that preaching was pushed to the margins by a gradual process of secularisation. James Caudle's recent survey of political preaching in the first half of the eighteenth century challenges the view that sermons had ceased to matter or survived, at best, in 'a miserable sort of half-life, living off the memory of Tudor and early Stuart glory'.[3] Tony Claydon, too, has stressed the crucial

---

[2] Simon Patrick, *A Discourse of Profiting by Sermons, and of Going to Hear, where Men Think They Can Profit Most* (1684), C1v (p. 10), D1r–2v (pp. 17–20), E2r (p. 27).

[3] James Caudle, 'Preaching in Parliament: patronage, publicity and politics in Britain, 1701–60', in Lori Anne Ferrell and Peter McCullough, eds., *The English Sermon Revised: Religion, Literature and History 1600–1750* (Manchester, 2000), pp. 235–63 (quotation p. 235). On eighteenth-century preaching, see

role of preaching in promoting the emergence of a public sphere in the late seventeenth and eighteenth centuries. He draws particular attention to the Sacheverell affair of 1710, arguably 'the moment at which the Augustan political system came closest to rupture', when a sermon by the highest of high churchmen, Dr Henry Sacheverell, touched off a fierce party dispute which convulsed the political nation and carried the Tories into power, albeit temporarily, on a groundswell of popular support. 'No incident better illustrated the continuing importance of preaching at the heart of the late Stuart public sphere. Even after the settling of major religious disputes, and even after the rise of new cultural forms which allowed public discussion, the pulpit could still be the crucible of public debate.'[4]

The case for continuity is therefore a strong one. But the sermon culture of the early seventeenth century also changed in several significant ways. Perhaps the most important of these changes was the decline of the reading/preaching distinction (discussed in Chapter 1) by which live preaching was held to be inherently different from, and superior to, the reading of a written text. By the end of the century this distinction had been widely abandoned, even by low churchmen and nonconformists, as can be seen from Richard Baxter's well-known remark in his *Christian Directory* (1673) that 'the Writings of Divines are nothing else but a preaching the Gospel to the eye, as the *voice* preacheth it to the ear'. Baxter's father had been converted 'by the bare reading of the Scriptures in private, without either preaching or godly company, or any other books but the Bible', and Baxter himself had been converted by reading godly books, so it was natural for him to argue that reading could do the job of conversion every bit as effectively as preaching. The same shift in attitudes has been analysed from a slightly different angle by Mary Morrissey, in an important article on 'scripture, style and persuasion' in seventeenth-century sermons in which she argues that the classical Reformed theory of preaching, with its 'intimate relationship between the Word, the Spirit, the preacher and hearer', fell decisively out of fashion in the later seventeenth century. This is closely related to the decline of the reading/preaching distinction, for what was going on here, as Morrissey shows, was the disappearance of a 'charismatic' theory of preaching and its replacement by an altogether different idea of preaching as a rational form of eloquence which could

---

also the very helpful survey by Joris van Eijnatten, 'Reaching audiences: sermons and oratory in Europe', in Stewart J. Brown and Timothy Tackett, eds., *The Cambridge History of Christianity, Vol. VII: Enlightenment, Reawakening and Revolution 1660–1815* (Cambridge, 2006), pp. 128–46.

[4] Tony Claydon, 'The sermon, the "public sphere" and the political culture of late seventeenth-century England', in Ferrell and McCullough, eds., *The English Sermon Revised*, pp. 208–34 (quotation p. 224).

achieve its persuasive effect as well through the written as through the spoken word.[5]

One very noticeable result of this change was that preachers began to deliver their sermons from a written text. John Tillotson, arguably the most influential preacher of his day, began by copying his sermons out in full and committing them to memory, but found, as he told a friend, that the effort of memorisation 'heated his head so much, a day or two before and after he preached, that he was forced to leave it off'. By 1680 he had changed his practice and took a shorthand copy of his sermon into the pulpit with him, leading another contemporary preacher to declare 'that he was resolved to preach no longer without book, for everybody has now left it off, even Dr Tillotson'.[6] In his *Discourse of the Pastoral Care* (1692), Gilbert Burnet noted that the delivery of sermons from a written text was 'peculiar to this Nation, and is endured in no other'. Burnet approved of the practice on the grounds that it made sermons 'more exact' and also made it easier for preachers to put their sermons into print, thus giving English readers 'many Volumes of the best that are extant'. He admitted that not all preachers had mastered the art of reading aloud and tended to deliver their sermons 'with very little *Life* or *Affection*', but declared that others 'read so happily, pronounce so truly, and enter so entirely into those Affections which they recommend, that in them we see both the Correctness of *Reading*, and the Seriousness of *Speaking* Sermons'.[7] What Burnet meant by 'correctness' can be seen very clearly in Tillotson's mature prose style, which, with its long, flowing sentences, depends for its effect on a very precise choice of words and leaves little room for extemporisation. This was a highly polished literary style designed as much for the printed page as for the pulpit. Its increasing popularity led some writers to argue that the English genius for preaching was manifested in the written rather than the spoken word:

> In point of Sermons, 'tis confest,
> Our *English* Clergy make the best:
> But this appears, we must confess,
> Not from the *Pulpit*, but the *Press*.[8]

[5] Mary Morrissey, 'Scripture, style and persuasion in seventeenth-century English theories of preaching', *Journal of Ecclesiastical History*, 53: 4 (2002), pp. 686–706.

[6] David D. Brown, 'The text of John Tillotson's sermons', *The Library*, 5th ser., 13 (1958), pp. 18–36 (quotation p. 27).

[7] Gilbert Burnet, *A Discourse of the Pastoral Care* (1692), S2v–3r (pp. 114–15).

[8] 'Rules for preaching; wrote by Dr Byrom of Manchester to two young clergymen to whom he taught short-hand', in David Fordyce, *Theodorus* (3rd edn., 1755), p. xi; reprinted, as 'Advice to the Rev. Messrs H– and H– to preach slow', in John Byrom, *Miscellaneous Poems* (Manchester, 1773), vol. I, p. 123.

Increasingly, then, sermons achieved their effect not through the impact of live performance but through their subsequent print publication. Sacheverell's notorious sermon is a case in point. As Geoffrey Holmes comments in his study of the Sacheverell affair: 'if the offending sermon had remained unprinted it is highly unlikely the matter would have gone any further'. It was only when the sermon appeared in print that it began to attract widespread attention. Even Sacheverell's publisher Henry Clements failed to anticipate the level of public interest and printed only 500 copies of the first edition. Within days this was followed by a second edition of between 35,000 and 40,000 copies, and this in turn was followed by a series of pirated editions by other London publishers, who undercut Clements's sixpenny edition by selling copies of the sermon for as little as a penny. Holmes estimates that there may have been as many as 100,000 copies of the sermon in circulation before the end of Sacheverell's trial, making it probably the bestselling, and certainly the fastest selling, sermon of the century.[9] Claydon is therefore right, but only half-right, to argue that the Sacheverell affair illustrates the continuing importance of preaching at the heart of the public sphere; what it illustrates is not the power of preaching alone, but the power of preaching harnessed to print. To some extent this was simply the logical development of trends which had begun in the late sixteenth century with the emergence of the single printed sermon as a marketable commodity. But it was a long way away from the sermon culture described in this book, where the preacher's message was so often shaped and constrained by the occasion, the audience and the physical setting.

The second major change was brought about by the Civil War, which caused Anglicans in the second half of the century to turn sharply against the preaching styles they associated with pre-war Puritanism. This was most famously expressed by Thomas Hobbes in *Behemoth*, where he singled out puritan preaching as one of the principal causes of the war. The presbyterian ministers in Elizabeth's reign, he argued, had 'applied themselves wholly to the winning of the people to a liking of their doctrines and good opinion of their persons'. To this end, 'they so framed their countenance and gesture at their entrance into the pulpit, and their pronunciation both in their prayer and sermon . . . as that no tragedian in the world could have acted the part of a right godly man better than these did'. Hobbes emphasised the oral and performative aspects of puritan preaching – voice, gesture and expression – in

---

[9] Geoffrey Holmes, *The Trial of Doctor Sacheverell* (London, 1973), pp. 72–5. See also Jennifer Farooq, 'The politicising influence of print: the responses of hearers and listeners to the sermons of Gilbert Burnet and Henry Sacheverell', in Geoff Baker and Anne McGruer, eds., *Readers, Audiences and Coteries in Early Modern England* (Newcastle, 2006), pp. 28–41.

order to suggest that, for these men, preaching was a form of playacting rather than an exercise in rational persuasion. They had set out to charm their followers by 'the vehemence of their voice (for the same words with the usual pronunciation had been of little force) and forcedness of their gesture and looks . . . And by this art they came into such credit, that numbers of men used to go forth of their own parishes and towns on working-days, leaving their calling, and on Sundays leaving their own churches, to hear them preach in other places, and to despise their own and all other preachers that acted not so well as they.'[10] He also credited the puritan art of hearing, particularly the practice of sermon repetition ('an ability to repeat the sermons of these men at their coming home'), with a subsidiary role in causing the common people to fall under the spell of their preachers.

Looking back after 1660, many Anglicans seem to have felt that the sermons of the Civil War period were historically and stylistically distinctive. Samuel Pepys, for example, assembled a collection of printed sermons which he hoped would have permanent historical interest in 'transmitting to posterity a true notion of the Preaching so much in vogue with the Populace of England during the late Rebellion'. Anthony Wood compiled a bibliography of the fast sermons preached before Parliament in the 1640s, prefaced with a provocative motto from Isaiah, 'Behold, ye fast for strife and debate' (Isa. 58: 4).[11] What made them distinctive, however, was not so easy to identify. John Evelyn, in his 'Character of England', written in the persona of a foreign visitor to England, criticised the presbyterian style of preaching for 'consisting (like their prayers) of speculative and abstracted notions and things, which, nor the people nor themselves well understand'.[12] This was in many ways the diametrical opposite of Hobbes's critique, for whereas Hobbes argued that the oral and theatrical style of puritan preaching made it dangerously attractive to the common people, Evelyn argued that its abstract and speculative style made it virtually incomprehensible. He repeated the charge in his diary, in several entries added retrospectively after 1660, where he complained that during the 1650s 'people had no Principles, and grew very ignorant of even the common points of Christianity, all devotion being now plac'd in hearing Sermons and discourses of Speculative and notional things', and that 'there was now nothing practical preached, or that

[10]   Thomas Hobbes, *Behemoth or the Long Parliament*, ed. F. Tonnies (1889; repr. 1969), p. 24. For recent discussions of this passage, see Nigel Smith, *Literature and Revolution in England 1640–1660* (New Haven and London, 1994), p. 353, and Quentin Skinner, *Reason and Rhetoric in the Philosophy of Hobbes* (Cambridge, 1996), p. 434.
[11]   *Catalogue of the Pepys Library at Magdalene College, Cambridge*, vol. VII, part ii (Facsimile of Pepys's catalogue), ed. David McKitterick (Cambridge, 1991), p. 270. Bibliography of fast sermons begun by Henry Foulis and continued by Anthony Wood: Bodleian Library, Oxford, MS Wood F.17.
[12]   'A character of England' (1651), in John Evelyn, *Miscellaneous Writings*, ed. William Upcott (1825), p. 152.

pressed reformation of life, but high and speculative points and straines, that few understood, which left people very ignorant, and of no steady principles, the source of all our sects and divisions'.[13]

This made it possible for Anglicans to appropriate elements of the puritan art of hearing by arguing that they were the true exponents of 'plain' and 'practical' preaching. Evelyn's criticism of presbyterian preachers, that 'for the most part they read [their sermons] out of a book', is of particular interest in this context. It was taken up by Charles II in a letter to the universities in 1674 in which he complained that 'the practice of reading Sermons' had now become widespread, and gave orders that 'the said practice, which took beginning with the disorders of the late times, be wholly laid aside'. This fitted perfectly into the emerging Anglican commitment to a plain style, as opposed to what they saw as the tediously laboured and scholastic book-learning of their opponents. This was something of a polemical caricature – not least since, as we have just seen, the practice of reading sermons soon became widespread among Anglican preachers as respectable as Tillotson and Burnet. In private, Anglicans were sometimes prepared to admit that terms such as 'plain' and 'practical' had a long and distinguished puritan pedigree. John Wallis, writing to Archbishop Tenison in 1699, observed that the 'Plain, Familiar and Practical way of Preaching' which he associated with the 'Grave and Godly Divines' of the early seventeenth century had 'of late years . . . been much disused' and replaced by 'the more Elaborate Discourses which we dayly meet with'.[14] But the myth of an Anglican plain style was too valuable to discard lightly, as it enabled Anglicans, in effect, to steal their opponents' clothes – to claim 'plain preaching' and 'practical divinity' as their own, while purging them of their puritan connotations.

These various responses to the Church of England's puritan past were also very influential in shaping Anglican attitudes to Scottish presbyterian preaching. This is well brought out in *The Scotch Presbyterian Eloquence* (1692), a scurrilous attack by two Episcopalians writing under the pseudonym 'Jacob Curate', which ran through seven editions in forty years. Like Hobbes, the authors portrayed presbyterian preaching as having a highly oral and performative style that made it impressive to ignorant people but ridiculously uncouth to educated listeners. 'The most of their Sermons are Nonsensick Raptures, the abuse of Mystick Divinity, in canting and compounded Vocables, oft-times stuffed with impertinent and base Similes and always with homely, coarse, and ridiculous Expressions, very unsuitable to

---

[13] John Evelyn, *Diary*, ed. E. S. de Beer (Oxford, 1955), vol. III, pp. 160 (21 October 1655), 184 (2 November 1656).
[14] John Wallis to Archbishop Tenison, 22 May 1699: Lambeth Palace Library, London, MS 930/51.

the Gravity and Solemnity that becomes Divinity ... And yet such is the silliness of some deluded People, that they proclaim these for Soul-refreshing and powerful Preachers, and for Men that, as they Phrase it, have an inbearing Gift, speaking home to their Hearts.' Yet, at the same time, they also followed Evelyn's example in depicting presbyterian ministers as obsessed with high points of scholastic Calvinism, which prevented them from speaking plainly and practically to their congregations. The presbyterian idea of 'practical divinity', the authors observed scornfully, was drawn 'only from the study of some *Anti-Arminian* Metaphysicks' and from 'the Heads of Election and Reprobation, whereby they preach Men out of their Wits' by representing God as a harsh and unmerciful judge.[15]

By the early eighteenth century, these had become the commonplaces of English travellers north of the border. Edmund Burt, in his account of his travels in Scotland in the 1720s, wrote that he had heard so many pulpit oddities, and heard tell of so many others, 'that I really think there is nothing set down in the Book called *Scots Presbiterian Eloquence*, but what, at least, is probable'. He proceeded to follow the authors of *The Scotch Presbyterian Eloquence* in characterising presbyterian preaching as both flamboyantly theatrical and narrowly scholastic, without seeming to be aware of any contradiction between these two characteristics. The 'canting' style of preaching, he observed, was highly effective with ignorant listeners, 'into whom it instils a kind of Enthusiasm, in moving their Passions by sudden Starts of various Sounds', but the doctrinal content of the sermons was far above most people's heads. 'The Subjects of their Sermons are, for the most part, Grace, Free-Will, Predestination, and other Topicks hardly ever to be determined: They might as well talk Hebrew to the Common People, and I think to any Body else.' The one sermon which impressed him was by an Edinburgh minister, Mr Wishart, who had adopted a more polished, English style of preaching. 'Several of us went to hear him, and you would not have been better pleased in any Church in England ... This Gentleman, as I was afterwards informed, has set before him Archbishop *Tillotson* for his Model; and, indeed, I could discover several of that Prelate's Thoughts in the Sermon.'[16] Burt believed that this was typical of the younger generation of presbyterian ministers, who were gradually bringing a more 'decent and reasonable' manner of preaching into Scottish pulpits.

---

[15] Jacob Curate, *The Scotch Presbyterian Eloquence; or, the Foolishness of Their Teaching Discovered from Their Books, Sermons, and Prayers* (1692), D2r (p. 19), D3v (p. 22).
[16] Edmund Burt, *Letters from a Gentleman in the North of Scotland* (1754), vol. I, pp. 201, 209, 213.

The comments of another Scottish Episcopalian, David Fordyce, show how distant Elizabethan and early Stuart preaching appeared by the mid-eighteenth century. Fordyce, who taught at Marischal College in Aberdeen, began his *Theodorus: A Dialogue Concerning the Art of Preaching* (1752) with a potted history of pulpit rhetoric since the Reformation in which the two opposing views of puritan preaching (popular and enthusiastic on the one hand, dry and scholastic on the other) were ingeniously yoked together. The early Stuart period, he argued, had been the heyday of scholastic preaching:

Soon after the Reformation, when the two Nations fell under one Head, the first Appearance that Preaching made, was in the pompous, metaphorical Dress. Our learned King brought Learning into vogue; and to quote Greek and Latin Authors, even in common Conversation, was fashionable and courtly ... The whole Learning of the Age, was shaped after the royal Model, dark, scholastic, and controversial ... The style of Preaching was declamatory and figurative, pointed with Puns and Antitheses, and larded with Greek and Latin Quotations. The Preachers made a Parade of comparing different Versions, and tracing the Originals; distributed the Text into cold and dry Divisions, adorned their Compositions with Quibbles, and the silly Jingle of Words, becoming School-Boys rather than Men and Scholars; and often perverted them from their proper Design, to inculcate the Principles of Slavery and arbitrary Power, and to subserve their own sordid and ambitious Purposes.[17]

Then, during the Civil War, preaching had shifted to the other extreme, becoming highly passionate and affective in style:

As a perfect Freedom in Religion, succeeded to the Severity of ecclesiastic Tyranny, the religious Passions burst out with a Violence proportioned to the Restraints they had formerly lain under. Therefore the Genius of Preaching resembled that of the Age, and ran into a high, pathetic and enthusiastic Vein ... The Tone of Preaching was agitated and various, as were the Passions of the Hearers. It glowed with uncommon Fervours, sudden Lights, and supernatural Impulses, or strong Pretences to them, and with a mighty Zeal for Purity and Reformation, whether real or affected. No doubt, there was much Seriousness and undissembled Ardour, an higher Spirit of Devotion, a warmer Sense of divine Things, and stronger Affections to a public Interest, than have appeared before or since that Period ... But where they were wanting, the indiscreet Votaries endeavoured to supply their Room by affected Raptures, unmeaning Cant, wild Grimace, and all the Distortions of Enthusiasm, blended with Superstition.[18]

After the Restoration, preaching had become more refined in its language and risen 'to the highest Pitch of Beauty it had before, or has ever since attained'.

---

[17] David Fordyce, *Theodorus: A Dialogue Concerning the Art of Preaching* (1752), p. 54.
[18] Fordyce, *Theodorus*, pp. 57–8.

However, Fordyce felt that the reaction against the puritan style of preaching had now gone too far. Modern preachers, while displaying 'clear Reasoning', 'deep critical Skill' and 'Eloquence of Style', were too cool and dispassionate to stir up the passions of their hearers or inspire them with a sense of awe and wonder in contemplating the 'Sacredness and Sublimity of divine Things'.[19]

It is clear from Fordyce's remarks that seventeenth-century preaching had come to be regarded as something of an historical curiosity. This is not, of course, to suggest that preaching had ceased to be important. There is no shortage of evidence to demonstrate the continuing social and cultural importance of preaching in the eighteenth and nineteenth centuries. Robert Southey, in his *Letters from England* (1807) – in which, like Evelyn 150 years earlier, he adopted the persona of a foreign visitor commenting on the Church of England from the point of view of an outside observer – remarked that the sermon was generally regarded as 'the most important part' of the service; 'children are required to remember the text, and it is as regular a thing for the English to praise the discourse when they are going out of church, as it is to talk of their health immediately before, and the weather immediately after'.[20] Even in an essay entitled *The Decay of Modern Preaching* (1882), J. P. Mahaffy acknowledged the continuing popularity of preaching as a social institution: 'Most people, whether really religious or not, are conservative enough to go regularly to their church on Sunday, and would feel that they had been defrauded of part of their due exercise if the sermon were omitted. A great preacher, though perhaps no longer a great power, attracts crowds of hearers wherever he is to be heard.'[21]

But while the sermon still retained much of its cultural prestige, it was no longer perceived, as it had been in the sixteenth and seventeenth centuries, as defining and uniting the godly commonwealth. It was no longer the sermon that made the Church, it was the Church that made the sermon; or, to put it in Weberian terms, the preacher's charisma had been institutionalised and absorbed into the Church's routine. Preaching, according to Weber, 'unfolds its power most strongly in periods of prophetic excitation', but as religion becomes more routinised, preaching rapidly loses its importance, to the point where 'in the treadmill of daily living it declines sharply to an almost complete lack of influence upon the conduct of life'. Elsewhere, he suggestively relates this to questions of religious and political control, suggesting that charisma declines as other forms of power arise to supplant it. 'Charisma is a

[19] Fordyce, *Theodorus*, pp. 68–9.
[20] Robert Southey, *Letters from England*, ed. Jack Simmons (London, 1951), p. 104.
[21] J. P. Mahaffy, *The Decay of Modern Preaching* (1882), p. 2.

phenomenon typical of prophetic movements . . . in their early stages. But as soon as domination is well established, and above all as soon as control over large masses of people exists, it gives way to the forces of everyday routine.'[22] If we accept this analysis, then it is not surprising to find that as the Protestant Reformation became settled and established in England, so Protestant preaching gradually drifted away from its central emphasis on the prophetic power of the spoken word, to a point where the passionate, affective style of early modern preaching began to seem quaintly archaic.

There was, however, an alternative tradition of preaching which still relied heavily on the charisma of the preacher. This was typified in the religious revivals of the eighteenth and nineteenth centuries, particularly in Scotland, Ireland and America. It was highly emotional in style, with the preacher using all the resources in his power, including tears, exclamations and dramatic gestures, to elicit a corresponding reaction from the audience. Here, for example, is the Irish-American presbyterian minister James Waddell preaching in Virginia at the turn of the nineteenth century:

His enunciation was so deliberate, that his voice trembled on every syllable: and every heart trembled in unison. His peculiar phrases had that force of description, that the original scene appeared to be at that moment acting before our eyes . . . But when he came to touch on the patience, the forgiving meekness of our Saviour; when he drew, to the life, his blessed eyes streaming in tears to heaven; his voice breathing to God, a soft and gentle prayer of pardon on his enemies, 'Father, forgive them, for they know not what they do' – the voice of the preacher, which had all along faltered, grew fainter and fainter, until his utterance being entirely obstructed by the force of his feelings, he raised his handkerchief to his eyes, and burst into a loud and irrepressible flood of grief. The effect is inconceivable. The whole house resounded with the mingled groans, and sobs, and shrieks of the congregation.[23]

The revivalist style of preaching was much disliked, not just by Anglican clergy but by other dissenting ministers as well, who condemned it for its false theatricality and feared that it would draw away members of their own congregations. When George Whitefield began preaching in America in 1739, one hostile observer remarked that his sermons 'would equally have produced the same Effects, whether he had acted his Part in the Pulpit or on the Stage'.[24] The

---

[22] Max Weber, *Economy and Society: An Outline of Interpretive Sociology*, ed. Guenther Roth and Claus Wittich (New York, 1968), vol. I, pp. 252–3, vol. II, pp. 464–5.

[23] William Wirt, *The British Spy: or Letters Written during a Tour through the United States* (Richmond, 1803), pp. 52–3, quoted in part in Leigh Eric Schmidt, *Holy Fairs: Scotland and the Making of American Revivalism* (Princeton, 1989, repr. Grand Rapids, MI, 2001), p. 89.

[24] Harry S. Stout, *The Divine Dramatist: George Whitefield and the Rise of Modern Evangelicalism* (Grand Rapids, MI, 1991), p. 110; on Whitefield's theatrical preaching style, see also Frank Lambert, *Inventing the 'Great Awakening'* (Princeton, 1999), pp. 92–8.

same criticisms were still being made of revivalist preaching in the mid-
nineteenth century, but now given added force by new medical theories of
hysteria, as in this description of a sermon by an Ulster preacher in the 1850s:

> It was on the parable of Dives and Lazarus. There was nothing of the love of Christ,
> nor of the guilt of sin; there was nothing to awaken conscience – hell, h-e-ll, h – e –
> ll – was the one cry; and the sole object aimed at was to produce a sensation of
> intensified torture of physical self-feeling ... The skill shown in the wording was
> great; and the whole object of the study appeared to be the elimination of every idea
> or thought. It was evidently here the chief labour of preparation had been bestowed;
> and it was precisely here, where every idea had disappeared, that the preacher
> bestowed the whole force of voice, and tone, and gesture – a fact which I had
> observed in other sermons before ... Precisely as I expected, when all sense and
> meaning was gone, the preacher had his base and unmanly triumph in evoking a wild
> and long-continued scream of hysteric agony, which, as it rose more loud and thrilled
> more wild, did effectually silence the preacher, and left him standing in his pulpit
> with a most self-satisfied air, until her tardy removal enabled him to proceed.[25]

Leigh Eric Schmidt has observed that the modern history of hearing -
whether framed in terms of Weber's disenchantment of the world, Ong's
decay of dialogue or Adorno's atomised listening – has tended to be told as a
history of loss, 'a story of religious absence', as the living voice falls silent or
perceptions of it grow dim.[26] But as Schmidt eloquently argues, this is not
the only way of telling the story. The history of preaching in the British Isles
over the last four centuries is not simply a history of decline, as charisma is
swallowed up by routine, but a history of a continuously evolving relationship between charisma and routine, whose outcome is still uncertain.[27] It is
quite possible to imagine a future in which the forces of secularisation,
eating away at established religion, might actually contribute to a revival of
preaching. The established Churches gradually lose their institutional
power; the voice of the preacher re-emerges as a charismatic source of
authority; and the sermon culture described in this book awakens from its
long sleep.

---

[25] Edward A. Stopford, *The Work and the Counterwork; or, The Religious Revival in Belfast* (Dublin,
1859), pp. 41–2, quoted in part in J. N. Ian Dickson, *Beyond Religious Discourse: Sermons, Preaching
and Evangelical Protestants in Nineteenth-Century Irish Society* (Milton Keynes, 2007), p. 198.

[26] Leigh Eric Schmidt, *Hearing Things: Religion, Illusion, and the American Enlightenment* (Cambridge,
MA, 2007), pp. 28–9. On 'atomized listerning', see also Theord Adorno, *Essays on Music*, ed., Richard
Leppert (Berkeley & Los Angeles, 2002), p. 226.

[27] On the re-emergence of charisma, see also the perceptive observations of Steven Shapin in *The
Scientific Life: A Moral History of a Late Modern Vocation* (Chicago, 2008), p. 5, quoting the
social theorist Stephen Turner: 'Weber never imagined that what the future held was a new age of
charisma ... in which changes in values and attitudes led by the example and personal force of
publicly acclaimed personalities is a characteristic feature of the culture.'

# Select bibliography of manuscripts

## CAMBRIDGE, ST JOHN'S COLLEGE

I.25 (James 320)   John Munday, '*Sabbatum Redivivum*'
S.41 (James 431)   Notes on sermons preached at Cambridge, late 1620s

## CAMBRIDGE, TRINITY COLLEGE

MS B.14.51 William Pulley, 'The art of hearing'

## CAMBRIDGE, UNIVERSITY LIBRARY

Dd.5.31   Notes on sermons by Thomas Westfield
Dd.14.16   Sermons preached in Reading, early seventeenth century
Add. MS 3117   Sermon notebook of Robert Saxby
Add. MSS 6164–5   Sermons by Cornelius Burges, 1619–26
Add. MS 8469   Sermons by John Donne and others (the 'Ellesmere MS')

## DUBLIN, TRINITY COLLEGE

MS 293   Articles against Henry Roborough, 1634
MS 709   Sermons by William Hull of Ashbourne, 1601–24
MS 1210   Miscellaneous sermon notes

## LONDON, BRITISH LIBRARY

Add. 20066   Notes for sermons by Robert Sanderson
Add. 38492   Lewkenor family papers
Add. 40883   Spiritual journal of Nehemiah Wallington
Add. 47618   Sermons by Thomas Bedford, 1618–30
Add. 70001   Papers of Sir Robert Harley
Egerton 2711   Commonplace book of John Harington
Egerton 2877   Commonplace book of Gilbert Frevile
Harl. 663   Sermons by William Hull of Ashbourne, 1605–7
Harl. 1026   Commonplace book of Justinian Pagitt, 1633–4
Harl. 4955   Poems by Richard Andrews

Harl. 5068    Sermons by John Workman of Gloucester
Lansd. 83    Papers of Lord Burghley
Sloane 271    Letter-book of Robert Smart
Sloane 922    Letter-book of Nehemiah Wallington


## LONDON, DR WILLIAMS'S LIBRARY

MS 28.2    Collection of John Dod's casuistry
MS 38.34    John Quick, '*Icones Sacrae Anglicanae*'
MS 61.13    Diary of Richard Rogers


## LONDON, GUILDHALL LIBRARY

MS 204    Nehemiah Wallington, 'A record of the mercies of God', 1630
MS 1046/1    St Antholin, churchwardens' accounts 1574–1708
MS 4415/1    St Olave Jewry, vestry minute book
MS 9057/1    Archdeaconry court of London, deposition book
MS 9234/7    St Botolph Aldgate, parish clerk's memorandum book


## LONDON, INNER TEMPLE LIBRARY

Petyt MS 538/38    Miscellaneous theological papers


## LONDON, INSTITUTE OF HISTORICAL RESEARCH (ON DEPOSIT IN SENATE HOUSE LIBRARY)

MS 979    Sermons by unidentified preacher, 1628–9


## LONDON, LAMBETH PALACE LIBRARY

MS 113    Miscellaneous theological papers
MS 930    Papers of Archbishop Tenison
MS 3470    Selden (Fairhurst) papers


## LONDON, LONDON METROPOLITAN ARCHIVES (FORMERLY GREATER LONDON RECORD OFFICE)

DL/C/313    Consistory court of London, *ex officio* act book 1615–17
DL/C/314    Consistory court of London, *ex officio* act book 1617–18
DL/C/620    Consistory court of London, *ex officio* act book 1618–19
DL/C/621    Consistory court of London, *ex officio* act book 1619–20
P92/SAV/450    St Saviour, Southwark, vestry minute book 1581–1628

## LONDON, NATIONAL ARCHIVES (FORMERLY PUBLIC RECORD OFFICE)

SP 14    James I, State papers
SP 16    Charles I, State papers

## NORTHAMPTON, NORTHAMPTONSHIRE RECORD OFFICE

Isham 3365    Diary of Elizabeth Isham, 1609–48

## OXFORD, BODLEIAN LIBRARY

MS Eng. th. c.71    Sermons by John Donne and others (the 'Merton MS')
MS Eng. th. f.63    Sermons by Robert Sanderson
Rawl. C.79    Notes on sermons preached at Coventry, 1600–3
Rawl. C.764    Sermons preached in Dorset, 1613–37
Rawl. C.766    Sermons by Richard Hunt of Warwick, 1617
Rawl. D.319    Sermons by John Wright of St Minver, 1609–10
Rawl. E.21    Miscellaneous sermon manuscripts
Rawl. E.204    Sermons by unidentified preacher, early seventeenth century

## OXFORD, CORPUS CHRISTI COLLEGE

MS 288    Miscellaneous sermon manuscripts
MS 409    Sermons by unidentified preacher, 1618–24

## TAUNTON, SOMERSET RECORD OFFICE

D/D/Ca 299    Bath and Wells *ex officio* act book, 1634–9
DD/WO/61/5/5    Sermon notebook of Christopher Trevelyan, 1631

## WASHINGTON, DC, FOLGER SHAKESPEARE LIBRARY

V.a.1    Sermons by unidentified preacher, *c.* 1633–37
V.a.23    Notes by Henry Borlase on sermons preached at Oxford, *c.* 1604
V.a.204    Sermons by unidentified preacher, early seventeenth century
V.a.251    Sermon by John Dove at Paul's Cross, 1606

## YALE, BEINECKE LIBRARY

Osborn MS b.133    Sermons by unidentified preacher, *c.* 1633
Osborn MS b.303    Sermons by John Moore of Huxham, 1640

# Index of biblical passages

# Index